Advances in Fractional Differential Operators and Their Applications, 2nd Edition

Advances in Fractional Differential Operators and Their Applications, 2nd Edition

Guest Editors

Angelo B. Mingarelli
Leila Gholizadeh Zivlaei
Mohammad Dehghan

MDPI

Basel • Beijing • Wuhan • Barcelona • Belgrade • Novi Sad • Cluj • Manchester

Guest Editors
Angelo B. Mingarelli
School of Mathematics and Statistics
Carleton University
Ottawa, ON
Canada

Leila Gholizadeh Zivlaei
School of Mathematics and Statistics
Carleton University
Ottawa, ON
Canada

Mohammad Dehghan
School of Mathematics and Statistics
Carleton University
Ottawa, ON
Canada

Editorial Office
MDPI AG
Grosspeteranlage 5
4052 Basel, Switzerland

This is a reprint of the Special Issue, published open access by the journal *Fractal and Fractional* (ISSN 2504-3110), freely accessible at: https://www.mdpi.com/journal/fractalfract/special_issues/fract_diff_operator_ii.

For citation purposes, cite each article independently as indicated on the article page online and as indicated below:

Lastname, A.A.; Lastname, B.B. Article Title. *Journal Name* **Year**, *Volume Number*, Page Range.

ISBN 978-3-7258-5651-0 (Hbk)
ISBN 978-3-7258-5652-7 (PDF)
https://doi.org/10.3390/books978-3-7258-5652-7

Contents

About the Editors

Angelo B. Mingarelli

Angelo B. Mingarelli was a doctoral student of the late Prof. F. V. Atkinson (Toronto) who was in the Hardy-Littlewood school via E.C. Titchmarsh. He has published over 130 papers in various fields stemming from the history of art and mathematics to fuzzy cellular automata and finally differential equations. Starting at Pennsylvania State University (State College), he then went to the University of Ottawa in 1979 and finally Carleton University, where he has been and still is, Professor of Mathematics since 1990.

Leila Gholizadeh Zivlaei

Leila Gholizadeh Zivlaei is presently a Research Associate of Prof. Angelo B. Mingarelli (Ottawa) in the School of Mathematics and Statistics at Carleton University. She has published 14 papers (including editorial works) in the fields of fixed-point theory and fractional Sturm-Liouville differential equations. Starting her job as a tutor and researcher at various universities in her home country (Iran), she then went to Carleton University and obtained her PhD student in this university in 2024 under the supervision of Professor Mingarelli.

Mohammad Dehghan

Mohammad Dehghan graduated in 2024 as a doctoral student of Prof. Angelo Mingarelli in the School of Mathematics and Statistics at Carleton University. He has published 10 papers in the fields of linear programming and classical and fractional Sturm-Liouville differential equations. Starting his job at the Azad University of Sari branch in Iran, he then went to Carleton University as a visiting researcher and he is presently working as a Data Specialist in the Canadian Institute of Actuaries.

Preface

This reprint gathers recent advances in fractional differential equations and nonlocal modeling across discrete and continuous settings, united by a common theme: memory and long-range effects as first-class citizens in analysis, computation, and applications. The works here develop new objects (from fractional sequences to nonlocal Schrödinger dynamics), prove well-posedness under weak assumptions, and design numerics capable of honoring history dependence.

We begin at the discrete–analytic interface. One chapter introduces fractional Pell and Pell–Lucas numbers via Grünwald–Letnikov operators of various orders. Closed forms, characteristic equations, and a fractional silver ratio emerge, alongside numerical schemes, tiling interpretations, and a MATLAB implementation—illustrating how fractional "long memory" enriches classical integer sequences and their geometry.

From arithmetic to epidemiology, another chapter proposes a fractional SIR model with a power-Caputo fractional derivative and density-dependent recovery, unifying Caputo–Fabrizio and Atangana–Baleanu cases. The authors establish positivity, boundedness, and uniqueness (via a recursive sequence and Banach's fixed point theorem), derive the basic reproduction number, and conduct sensitivity and stability analyses. Calibrated to COVID-19 data, simulations show how the fractional order controls peak timing and severity, underscoring memory and healthcare capacity as key drivers of epidemic trajectories.

A medical modeling study develops a short-memory, interval-based framework for human liver disease, allowing model structure and derivative type to change across subintervals (classical vs. fractal–fractional order). Existence results follow from Banach and Krasnosel'skii fixed-point theorems; Hyers–Ulam stability is analyzed; and an extended Adams–Bashforth–Moulton scheme provides visual simulations across fractional orders.

On the discrete fractional side, a chapter treats nabla difference equations with two Riemann–Liouville-type orders. The authors build the related Green's function, split the theory into two regimes of orders, and—using Guo–Krasnosel'skii—prove conditions guaranteeing positive solutions. Worked examples highlight the novelty and suggest directions for further study.

Public-health dynamics returns in a chapter modeling smoking with five interacting classes (susceptible smokers, ingestion, unusual, regular, ex-smokers) and four optimal controls (education, gum, anti-nicotine drugs, public restrictions). Using Bernoulli-wavelet operational matrices and ABM time stepping, the work illustrates how fractional-order analysis exposes hidden couplings and guides strategy design for reducing smoking prevalence.

Signal processing and nonlinear dynamics meet in a study of a fractional-order multi-wing chaotic system for weak-signal detection. By scanning the fractional order, the authors chart transitions between double- and four-wing chaos (via phase/bifurcation/complexity diagrams), then exploit these regimes: a detection array leverages noise robustness to recover amplitudes (with deep-learning image classification of wing counts), while MUSIC with chaotic synchronization estimates frequencies—linking fractional calculus, chaos theory, and modern learning.

Spectral theory appears twice. One chapter analyzes nonlocal fractional Sturm–Liouville problems, identifying eigenvalue properties under varied boundary conditions, including geometric multiplicity for non-Dirichlet cases and continuous dependence on the potential for Dirichlet data. Another establishes existence and uniqueness for mixed Riemann–Liouville/Caputo differential equations with measurable coefficients and sign-indefinite leading terms, both for initial-value and two-point boundary problems; notably, solutions are square-integrable on finite intervals under transparent fractional-order conditions.

Another chapter looks at random walks on a lattice (a grid) and develops a family of "fractional" operators that blend the identity with the random-walk step in a graded way. The authors pin down exactly when these operators exist, can be inverted, and have square-summable kernels (so they behave well on the grid); work out their long-distance behavior using classical limit theorems for random walks; build and analyze random fields on the lattice that are driven by white noise and filtered by those fractional operators, including their large-scale limits; and illustrate the theory with concrete cases that act like fractional versions of the lattice Laplacian and the lattice heat operator.

Finally, quantum transport on constrained geometries is addressed through a generalized Schrödinger equation on a comb-like structure with nonlocal and fractional potentials in time and space. Using Green's functions, the authors solve four scenarios—time-nonlocal, space-nonlocal, space–time memory kernels, and fractional spatial derivatives—and uncover distinct spreading regimes shaped by the type of nonlocality and fractional operator, broadening the theory of quantum dynamics on backbone-like media.

Taken together, these contributions demonstrate how fractional operators, nonlocal interactions, and discrete analogs furnish a unified language for memory, heterogeneity, and scale interaction—and how careful analysis (fixed-point theory, Green's functions, spectral methods) can sit comfortably alongside efficient numerics (ABM schemes, wavelets) and data-facing applications (epidemics, physiology, control, detection). The result is a toolkit equal parts rigorous and practical, ready to inform the next wave of models where yesterday's state still shapes today.

Angelo B. Mingarelli, Leila Gholizadeh Zivlaei, and Mohammad Dehghan
Guest Editors

fractal and fractional

MDPI

Article

Existence and Uniqueness of Some Unconventional Fractional Sturm–Liouville Equation

Leila Gholizadeh Zivlaei and Angelo B. Mingarelli *

School of Mathematics and Statistics, Carleton University, Ottawa, ON K1S 5B6, Canada; leilagh@math.carleton.ca
* Correspondence: angelo@math.carleton.ca

Abstract: In this paper, we provide existence and uniqueness results for the initial value problems associated with mixed Riemann–Liouville/Caputo differential equations in the real domain. We show that, under appropriate conditions in a fractional order, solutions are always square-integrable on the finite interval under consideration. The results are valid for equations that have sign-indefinite leading terms and measurable coefficients. Existence and uniqueness theorem results are also provided for two-point boundary value problems in a closed interval.

Keywords: Riemann–Liouville; Caputo; Sturm–Liouville; fractional; existence; uniqueness

MSC: 34B24; 34A12; 26A33

1. Introduction

There has been keen interest of late in the area of fractional differential equations that are defined in terms of a combination of a left- and/or right-Riemann and/or Caputo differential operators. The reason for this is that it appears as if that, when the operators are defined appropriately, they may be a complete analog of the Sturm–Liouville theory, which is a fractional theory that generalizes equations of the form

$$(p(x)y')' - q(x)y = 0, \quad x \in [a,b], \tag{1}$$

as well as the eigenvalue problems associated with them such as

$$(p(x)y')' + (\lambda w(x) - q(x))y = 0, \quad x \in [a,b]$$

where, p, q, and w are real, or are complex-valued and continuous (although these conditions can be relaxed tremendously (see below and e.g., [1])).

In this paper, we consider the basic existence and uniqueness questions for equations of the form

$$\mathbf{D}_b^{\alpha}(pD_a^{\alpha}y)(x) + q(x)\,y(x) = 0, \tag{2}$$

where $0 < \alpha < 1$, $\mathbf{D}_b^{\alpha}$ is a right-Caputo differential operator and D_a^{α} is a left-Riemann–Liouville differential operator (see Section 2). The advantage of this formulation is that (2) includes (1) upon taking the limit as $\alpha \to 1$.

The recent results dealing with the existence and uniqueness of solutions of some fractional differential equations (but not including those considered here) can be found in [2]. Equations of the form (2) have been considered previously in recent papers such as [3–5] (and the references therein) under the assumption that these solutions actually exist and are unique in some suitable spaces. In [6], the question of the existence of eigenvalues and an expansion theorem was considered, whereas the variational characterization of the eigenvalues was given in the papers [7,8]. In [9], the new idea of Fuzzy-Graph-Kannan contractions were used to estimate the solutions of fractional equations.

Applications of fractional differential equations are now widespread. Among them, we cite some current ones such as [10–13] in a list that is far from exhaustive. We encourage the readers to look at these and the references therein for more insight.

To the best of our knowledge, the question of the actual existence and uniqueness of solutions to initial value problems associated with (2), let alone such problems where $p(x)$ is sign-indefinite, has not yet been considered. This is our main purpose herein.

Indeed, in this paper, we relax the continuity and sign conditions on p, q in (2) to a mere Lebesgue measurability over $[a, b]$, along with other integral conditions. In addition, we show that we retain the existence and uniqueness of continuous (specifically absolutely continuous) solutions over $[a, b]$. This is the main contribution of this paper, i.e., to address the fact that the existence and uniqueness of its solutions in appropriate spaces has been seemingly overlooked by authors who have considered equations of the form (2). In so doing this, we fill the gaps in regarding the presentations of such papers outlined in the references below where solutions are assumed to exist.

Our methods make use of the fixed-point theorem of Banach–Cacciopoli [14,15], (which is sometimes simply called the Banach fixed-point theorem). This latter result is a generalization of the classical sequence of Picard iterations in the study of solutions of differential equations. Its advantage lies in the fact that, in a normed space, the iterates, T^n, of the contraction map T itself must satisfy the relation $||T^n x - x_o|| < k^n||x - x_o||$, where x_o is the fixed point in question (i.e., $Tx_o = x_o$) and $k < 1$ is the contraction constant. As a result of this exponential decay in the error as the number of iterations increases, we can obtain excellent approximations to the solutions of (2) themselves. Insofar as there are numerical approximations to the solutions of fractional differential equations, we cite [16,17] among the current ones.

2. Preliminaries

For the sake of convenience, we adopt the following notation. In the sequel, Caputo (resp. Riemann–Liouville) derivatives will be denoted by boldface (i.e., upper case) letters, while the ordinary derivative has only superscript in the form of an integer. For the sake of brevity, we shall omit the obvious $\pm$ subscripts in expressions such $I_{a^+}^{1-\alpha}y(x)$, which will be written as $I_a^{1-\alpha}y(x)$, and $D_{b^-}^{\alpha}y(x)$ will be written as $D_b^{\alpha}y(x)$, etc. (this includes expressions involving Caputo derivatives). The following abbreviations will also be used from time to time: $(pD_a^{\alpha}y)(x)$ for $p(x)D_a^{\alpha}y(x)$ if p is continuous but otherwise it has a meaning of its own (as the quantity will still exist even if the coefficients are merely measurable); and $I_b^{\alpha}(qy)(x)$ for $I_b^{\alpha}(q(x)y(x))$. In addition, Caputo derivatives will be written with a bold face $\mathbf{D}$. Thus, $\mathbf{D}_a^{\alpha}$ and $\mathbf{D}_b^{\alpha}$ denote the left- and right-Caputo derivatives, respectively, while D_a^{α} and D_b^{α} will refer to the left- and right-Riemann–Liouville derivatives. Ordinary derivatives of order n and j will be denoted by D^n and D^j, respectively, etc.

We recall some of the definitions from fractional calculus and refer the reader to standard texts such as [18–20] for further details.

Definition 1. *The left- and the right- Riemann–Liouville fractional integrals I_a^{α} and I_b^{α} of the order $\alpha \in \mathbb{R}^+$ are defined by*

$$I_a^{\alpha} f(t) := \frac{1}{\Gamma(\alpha)} \int_a^t \frac{f(s)}{(t-s)^{1-\alpha}} ds, \quad t \in (a, b], \tag{3}$$

and

$$I_b^{\alpha} f(t) := \frac{1}{\Gamma(\alpha)} \int_t^b \frac{f(s)}{(s-t)^{1-\alpha}} ds, \quad t \in [a, b), \tag{4}$$

respectively, where $\Gamma(\alpha)$ is the usual Gamma function and $I_a^0(f) = f$, $I_a^{-n}(f) = f^{(n)}$ is the ordinary nth derivative of f [21]. The following properties may be found in any textbook on fractional calculus, see e.g., [18,20].

Definition 2. *The left- and the right-Caputo fractional derivatives $\mathbf{D}_a^\alpha$ and $\mathbf{D}_b^\alpha$ are defined by*

$$\mathbf{D}_a^\alpha f(t) := I_a^{1-\alpha} \circ Df(t) = \frac{1}{\Gamma(1-\alpha)} \int_a^t \frac{f'(s)}{(t-s)^\alpha} ds, \quad t > a, \tag{5}$$

and

$$\mathbf{D}_b^\alpha f(t) := -I_b^{1-\alpha} \circ Df(t) = -\frac{1}{\Gamma(1-\alpha)} \int_t^b \frac{f'(s)}{(s-t)^\alpha} ds, \quad t < b, \tag{6}$$

respectively, where f is assumed to be differentiable and that the integrals exist.

Definition 3. *Similarly, the left- and the right-Riemann–Liouville fractional derivatives D_a^α and D_b^α are defined by*

$$D_a^\alpha f(t) := D \circ I_a^{1-\alpha} f(t) = \frac{1}{\Gamma(1-\alpha)} \frac{d}{dt} \int_a^t \frac{f(s)}{(t-s)^\alpha} ds, \quad t > a, \tag{7}$$

and

$$D_b^\alpha f(t) := -D \circ I_b^{1-\alpha} f(t) = -\frac{1}{\Gamma(1-\alpha)} \frac{d}{dt} \int_t^b \frac{f(s)}{(s-t)^\alpha} ds, \quad t < b, \tag{8}$$

respectively, where f is assumed to be differentiable and that the integrals exist.

Property 1. *If $y(t) \in L^1[a,b]$ and $I_a^{1-\alpha} y, I_b^{1-\alpha} y \in AC[a,b]$, then*

$$I_a^\alpha D_a^\alpha y(t) = y(t) - \frac{(t-a)^{\alpha-1}}{\Gamma(\alpha)} I_a^{1-\alpha} y(a),$$
$$I_b^\alpha D_b^\alpha y(t) = y(t) - \frac{(b-t)^{\alpha-1}}{\Gamma(\alpha)} I_b^{1-\alpha} y(b).$$

Property 2 (See [18], p. 71).

$$D_a^\alpha\left((x-a)^\beta\right) = \begin{cases} 0, & \text{if } \alpha-\beta-1 \in \mathbf{N} = \{0,1,\ldots\}, \\ \frac{\Gamma(\beta+1)}{\Gamma(\beta-\alpha+1)} (x-a)^{\beta-\alpha}, & \text{otherwise.} \end{cases}$$

Property 3. *If $y(t) \in AC[a,b]$ and $0 < \alpha \le 1$, then*

$$I_a^\alpha \mathbf{D}_a^\alpha y(t) = y(t) - y(a),$$
$$I_b^\alpha \mathbf{D}_b^\alpha y(t) = y(t) - y(b).$$

Property 4 ([20], p. 44, [18], p. 77). *For $0 < \alpha < 1$ and $f \in L^1[a,b]$, we have*

$$D_a^\alpha I_a^\alpha f(t) = f(t), \text{ and, } D_b^\alpha I_b^\alpha f(t) = f(t).$$

Property 5. *The semi-group property holds, i.e., for any $\alpha > 0, \beta$, we have*

$$I_a^\alpha I_a^\beta f(t) = I_a^{\alpha+\beta} f(t), \qquad D(I^{\alpha+1} f)(t) = I^\alpha f(t),$$

are the case whenever all quantities are defined.

Property 6 ([18], p. 71, Property 2.1). *For $\alpha, \beta > 0$ there holds*

$$I_a^\alpha((t-a)^{\beta-1})(x) = \frac{\Gamma(\beta)}{\Gamma(\alpha+\beta)} (x-a)^{\alpha+\beta-1}.$$

3. Existence and Uniqueness

In this section, we derive an integral equation that will be used later to prove the existence and uniqueness of solutions to (9) and (10) as follows:

$$\mathbf{D}_b^{\alpha}(pD_a^{\alpha}y)(x) + q(x)\,y(x) = 0, \tag{9}$$

which is subject to a set of conditions of the form

$$I_a^{1-\alpha}y(a) = K_1 \text{ and given } (pD_a^{\alpha}y)(a) = K_2, \tag{10}$$

where the K_i are the constants, either real or complex. This is relevant to the case where $p(x) = 1, q(x) = 0$ on $[a,b]$ was considered, in part, in [3]. The analysis in the remaining pages will show that there are two types of solutions. Specifically, solutions that are continuous in $[a,b]$ if $I_a^{1-\alpha}y(a) = 0$, and are—in actuality—absolutely continuous and so are in $L^2[a,b]$, as well as those solutions that are in $L^2[a,b]$ and are continuous on $(a,b]$, if $I_a^{1-\alpha}y(a) \neq 0$. In either case, the solutions are always in $L^2[a,b]$, and so in $L^1[a,b]$, regardless of the value of the initial condition $I_a^{1-\alpha}y(a)$.

Proceeding formally from (9) and applying I_b^{α} to both sides (see Property 3), we find

$$(pD_a^{\alpha}y)(x) - (pD_a^{\alpha}y)(b) + I_b^{\alpha}(qy)(x) = 0, \tag{11}$$

i.e.,

$$D_a^{\alpha}y(x) - \frac{1}{p(x)}(pD_a^{\alpha}y)(b) + \frac{1}{p(x)}I_b^{\alpha}(qy)(x) = 0. \tag{12}$$

Now, by applying I_a^{α} to both sides of (12) and using Property 1 we obtain the general integral equation

$$\begin{aligned} y(x) = \frac{(x-a)^{\alpha-1}}{\Gamma(\alpha)}I_a^{1-\alpha}y(a) + I_a^{\alpha}\left(\frac{1}{p}\right)(x)(pD_a^{\alpha}y)(b) \\ -I_a^{\alpha}\left(\frac{1}{p}I_b^{\alpha}(qy)\right)(x). \end{aligned} \tag{13}$$

The relationship between $(pD_a^{\alpha}y)(a)$ and $(pD_a^{\alpha}y)(b)$ is given by (11), which is evaluated at $x = a$, i.e.,

$$K_2 = (pD_a^{\alpha}y)(b) - \frac{1}{\Gamma(\alpha)}\int_a^b \frac{q(s)\,y(s)}{(s-a)^{1-\alpha}}ds\,dt.$$

Thus, any solution of the initial value problem (9) and (10) must satisfy the equation

$$\begin{aligned} y(x) = K_1\frac{(x-a)^{\alpha-1}}{\Gamma(\alpha)} + K_2\,I_a^{\alpha}\left(\frac{1}{p}\right)(x) + I_b^{\alpha}(qy)(a)\,I_a^{\alpha}\left(\frac{1}{p}\right)(x) \\ -I_a^{\alpha}\left(\frac{1}{p}I_b^{\alpha}(qy)\right)(x). \end{aligned} \tag{14}$$

When dealing with (14), there will be two separate cases here, namely one where $K_1 = I_a^{1-\alpha}y(a) = 0$, i.e., a homogeneous Dirichlet type condition is set at $x = a$, and the other where $I_a^{1-\alpha}y(a) \neq 0$. Each case leads to different types of solutions (more on this in the following sections).

3.1. Solutions in $C[a,b]$

Let p, q be complex-valued Lebesgue measurable functions on $[a,b]$ and let $0 < \alpha < 1$. Here, we show that continuous solutions exist and are unique under various assumptions.

We will always assume that, for every α, $0 < \alpha < 1$, we have

$$c_1 \equiv \sup_{x\in[a,b]} I_a^{\alpha}\left(\frac{1}{|p|}\right)(x) < \infty, \tag{15}$$

and

$$c_2 \equiv \sup_{x\in[a,b]} I_b^\alpha(|q|)(x) < \infty. \tag{16}$$

Observe that there are *no sign restrictions* on the coefficients p, q other than Lebesgue measurability and the integrability conditions (15) and (16). As a result, we will obtain that solutions of (9) and (10), which are not only continuous, but are also absolutely continuous on $[a,b]$. The condition that $K_1 = 0$ is necessary in order that the solutions be continuous at $x = a$. In the next section, we will review the case where $K_1 \neq 0$.

Theorem 1. *Let p, q be complex-valued and satisfy* (15) *and* (16)*, as well as $|p(x)| < \infty$ a.e. on $[a,b]$. If*

$$2c_1c_2 < 1, \tag{17}$$

then the initial value problem (9) *and* (10) *with $K_1 = 0$ and K_2 is arbitrary, has a unique solution of $y \in AC[a,b]$.*

Proof. Consider the complete normed space $(X, ||\cdot||_\infty)$ of the real valued continuous functions that are defined on $[a,b]$. Note that $K_1 = I_a^{1-\alpha}y(a) = 0$ is in force in (14). We can define a map T on X by setting

$$Ty(x) = K_2\, I_a^\alpha\left(\frac{1}{p}\right)(x) + I_b^\alpha(qy)(a)\, I_a^\alpha\left(\frac{1}{p}\right)(x) - I_a^\alpha\left(\frac{1}{p} I_b^\alpha(qy)\right)(x). \tag{18}$$

By (15), the first term in (18) is the integral of an absolutely integrable function and so it is, itself, absolutely continuous. On the other hand, since $y \in X$ and q satisfies (16), the second term is also finite and absolutely continuous. Finally, since $y \in X$ and there holds (16), $|I_b^\alpha(qy)(x)| \le ||y||_\infty\, c_2$ over $[a,b]$ so that this, combined with (15), shows that the third term is also absolutely continuous in $[a,b]$ and is thus continuous. Therefore, $TX \subset X$.

Next, we show that T is a contraction. Observe that

$$\begin{aligned}|Ty(x) - Tz(x)| &\le I_b^\alpha(|q(y-z)|)(a)\, I_a^\alpha\left(\frac{1}{|p|}\right)(x) \\ &\quad + I_a^\alpha\left(\frac{1}{|p|} I_b^\alpha(|q||y-z|)\right)(x) \\ &\equiv A + B.\end{aligned} \tag{19}$$

The first term, A, in (19), is estimated using (15) and (16), i.e.,

$$A \le \sup_{x\in[a,b]} I_b^\alpha(|q|)(x)\, ||y-z||_\infty\, I_a^\alpha\left(\frac{1}{|p|}\right)(x) \le c_1\, c_2\, ||y-z||_\infty. \tag{20}$$

On the other hand, the second term, B, satisfies

$$B \le ||y-z||_\infty I_a^\alpha\left(\frac{1}{|p|} I_b^\alpha(|q|)\right)(x) \le c_1\, c_2\, ||y-z||_\infty. \tag{21}$$

Through combining (19) with (20) and (21), we obtain

$$||Ty - Tz||_\infty < 2\, c_1\, c_2\, ||y-z||_\infty, \tag{22}$$

such that T is a contraction on X provided there holds (17). The fixed-point theorem of Banach–Cacciopoli now implies the existence of a unique fixed-point $y \in X$ that satisfies

$$y(x) = K_2\, I_a^\alpha\left(\frac{1}{p}\right)(x) + I_b^\alpha(qy)(a)\, I_a^\alpha\left(\frac{1}{p}\right)(x) - I_a^\alpha\left(\frac{1}{p} I_b^\alpha(qy)\right)(x). \tag{23}$$

As inferred from above, since all integrands appearing in (23) are in $L^1(a,b)$, it follows that, in fact, $y \in AC[a,b]$. Finally, we can observe that both initial conditions in (10) are automatically satisfied (once the various properties in Section 2 are used). □

Remark 1. *The condition (17) is not sharp and can be readily verified in the case where $\alpha = 1$ (the theorem is clearly also true in that case). By setting $p \equiv 1$, $q \equiv 1$, and $[a,b] = [0,1]$, we can obtain $c_1 = c_2 = b - a$, such that (17) is violated, yet the classical problem $y'' + y = 0$, $y(a) = 0$, $y'(a) = K_2$ always has a solution that exists and is unique on $[0,1]$. In this example, our theorem only gives the existence and uniqueness of solutions on $[0,b]$, where $b < \sqrt{2}/2$. Closed-form solutions in the case where $\alpha < 1$ are generally difficult to find.*

Corollary 1. *Let $p, q \in C[a,b]$ and $p(x) > 0$ on $[a,b]$. If*

$$\frac{2\,(b-a)^{2\alpha}}{\Gamma(\alpha+1)^2}\,||1/p||_\infty\,||q||_\infty < 1, \tag{24}$$

then the initial value problem (9) and (10) with $K_1 = 0$ and K_2 is arbitrary, has a unique solution $y \in AC[a,b]$.

Proof. Note that

$$c_1 \le ||1/p||_\infty \sup_{x\in[a,b]} I_a^\alpha(1)(x) \le \frac{1}{\Gamma(\alpha)}||1/p||_\infty \sup_{x\in[a,b]} \frac{(x-a)^\alpha}{\alpha} \le ||1/p||_\infty \frac{(b-a)^\alpha}{\Gamma(\alpha+1)}.$$

Similarly,

$$c_2 \le ||q||_\infty \frac{(b-a)^\alpha}{\Gamma(\alpha+1)}.$$

Together, these two inequalities imply (17) on account of (24). The above result then follows. □

Corollary 2. *In addition to the conditions on p, q in Theorem 1, let f be measurable, complex-valued, and for every $0 < \alpha < 1$ satisfy*

$$\sup_{x\in[a,b]} I_b^\alpha(|f|)(x) < \infty. \tag{25}$$

Then, the initial value problem (9) and (10) (with $K_1 = 0$ and K_2 being arbitrary) for the forced equation

$$\mathbf{D}_b^\alpha(pD_a^\alpha y)(x) + q(x)\,y(x) = f(x) \tag{26}$$

has a unique solution in $AC[a,b]$.

Proof. The map T defined by

$$\begin{aligned} Ty(x) = {} & K_2\, I_a^\alpha\left(\frac{1}{p}\right)(x) + I_b^\alpha(qy)(a)\, I_a^\alpha\left(\frac{1}{p}\right)(x) \\ & - I_a^\alpha\left(\frac{1}{p} I_b^\alpha(qy)\right)(x) + I_a^\alpha\left(\frac{1}{p} I_b^\alpha(f)\right)(x) \end{aligned} \tag{27}$$

is a contraction on X as it is easily verified by the method of Theorem 1 and $TX \subset X$. The result follows by the contraction mapping principle. □

However, the next result, Theorem 2 below, is classical in the case of ordinary derivatives. It is unusual in the case we consider our differential operators as a composition of left-Riemann–Liouville and right-Caputo derivatives. Thus, initial conditions are normally at either the left- or right-endpoint of the interval under consideration, i.e., not in the interior as they are here. Still, we have a uniqueness result.

Theorem 2. *Let p, q satisfy the conditions in Theorem 1. In addition, let $x_0 \in (a, b]$ be*

$$I_a^\alpha\left(\frac{1}{p}\right)(x_0) \neq 0,$$

as well as assume that (17) *is satisfied. Then, the only solution of the initial value problem* (9) *satisfying*

$$I_a^{1-\alpha}y(x_0) = 0, \quad (pD_a^\alpha y)(x_0) = 0, \tag{28}$$

that is continuous on $[a, b]$ is the trivial solution.

Proof. From Theorem 1, a solution that is continuous on $[a, b]$ must satisfy $I_a^{1-\alpha}y(a) = 0$. As a result, there holds (18), where $K_2 = (pD_a^\alpha y)(a)$. By substituting the first of (28) and using the semi-group property, i.e., Property 5, we obtain the form

$$y(x) = c\, I_a^\alpha\left(\frac{1}{p}\right)(x) - I_a^\alpha\left(\frac{1}{p} I_b^\alpha(qy)\right)(x), \tag{29}$$

where

$$c = \frac{I_a^1\left(\frac{1}{p} I_b^\alpha(qy)\right)(x_0)}{I_a^\alpha\left(\frac{1}{p}\right)(x_0)}.$$

By applying Property 4 to (29), we obtain $(pD_a^\alpha y)(x) = c - I_b^\alpha(qy)(x)$, such that the second of (28) implies that $c = I_b^\alpha(qy)(x_0)$. Thus, the solution of (9) that satisfies both of (28) must look like the solution of the integral equation

$$y(x) = I_b^\alpha(qy)(x_0) I_a^\alpha\left(\frac{1}{p}\right)(x) - I_a^\alpha\left(\frac{1}{p} I_b^\alpha(qy)\right)(x). \tag{30}$$

We now show that (30) can only have the zero solution as a continuous solution. This, however, is similar to the proof of Theorem 1 above with minor revisions, which we now describe. On the space $(C[a, b], ||\cdot||_\infty)$, we define the map

$$Ty(x) = I_b^\alpha(qy)(x_0) I_a^\alpha\left(\frac{1}{p}\right)(x) - I_a^\alpha\left(\frac{1}{p} I_b^\alpha(qy)\right)(x).$$

As in the proof of Theorem 1, $TX \subset X$, and we also note that

$$Ty(x) - Tz(x) = I_b^\alpha(q(y-z))(x_0) I_a^\alpha\left(\frac{1}{p}\right)(x) - I_a^\alpha\left(\frac{1}{p} I_b^\alpha(q(y-z)\right)(x),$$

such that

$$\begin{aligned} |Ty(x) - Tz(x)| &\leq I_b^\alpha(|q(y-z)|)(x_0) I_a^\alpha\left(\frac{1}{|p|}\right)(x) + I_a^\alpha\left(\frac{1}{|p|} I_b^\alpha(|q(y-z)|\right)(x) \\ &\leq ||y-z||_\infty \left(I_b^\alpha(|q|)(x_0) | I_a^\alpha\left(\frac{1}{|p|}\right)(x) + I_a^\alpha\left(\frac{1}{|p|} I_b^\alpha(|q|)\right)(x)\right) \\ &\leq ||y-z||_\infty (c_2 c_1 + c_2 c_1) \\ &= 2 c_1 c_2 ||y-z||_\infty. \end{aligned} \tag{31}$$

Thus, T is a contraction on account of (17). The above result then follows. □

3.2. Solutions in $L^2[a, b]$

We now consider the initial value problem for (9) where $K_1 \neq 0$. Of course, in this case, there is a singularity at $x = a$, thus we can only expect continuity on $(a, b]$, but we will show that nevertheless solutions exist and are unique when considered in the Hilbert space, $L^2[a, b]$.

Theorem 3. *Let p, q be measurable complex-valued functions on $[a,b]$, $|p(x)| < \infty$ a.e., and let $\frac{1}{2} < \alpha < 1$. Assume further that, for every $\alpha \in (1/2, 1)$, we have*

$$c_4 \equiv \sup_{t\in[a,b]} \int_t^b \frac{q^2(s)}{(s-t)^{2-2\alpha}}\,ds < \infty, \tag{32}$$

$$c_5 \equiv \sup_{x\in[a,b]} I_a^\alpha\left(\frac{1}{|p|}\right)(x) < \infty, \tag{33}$$

and

$$\frac{2c_5\sqrt{c_4}\sqrt{b-a}}{\Gamma(\alpha)} < 1. \tag{34}$$

Then, the initial value problem (9) with

$$I_a^{1-\alpha}y(a) = K_1 \neq 0 \text{ and } (pD_a^\alpha y)(a) = K_2 \tag{35}$$

has a unique solution $y \in L^2[a,b]$. In addition, the solutions are locally absolutely continuous.

Proof. Note that since $\frac{1}{2} < \alpha < 1$, the Riemann–Liouville integrals I_a^α, I_b^α of L^2-functions exist by the Schwarz inequality; therefore, they are absolutely continuous functions of the variable in question.

On the complete normed vector space, $X = (L^2[a,b], ||\cdot||_2)$, for $K_1 \neq 0$, and where $||\cdot||_2$ is the usual norm, define a map T on X by (see (14))

$$\begin{aligned} Ty(x) = K_1\frac{(x-a)^{\alpha-1}}{\Gamma(\alpha)} + K_2\, I_a^\alpha\left(\frac{1}{p}\right)(x) + I_b^\alpha(qy)(a)\, I_a^\alpha\left(\frac{1}{p}\right)(x) \\ -I_a^\alpha\left(\frac{1}{p}I_b^\alpha(qy)\right)(x). \end{aligned} \tag{36}$$

Observe that the first term in (36) is $L^2[a,b]$ since $\alpha > 1/2$. The second term is square-integrable by hypothesis (33), while the third term in (36) is also square-integrable by a combination of (32) and (33). The square integrability of the last term in (36) is a consequence of the hypotheses and the Schwarz inequality. Specifically, for $y \in X$, we have

$$\begin{aligned} \left|I_a^\alpha\left(\frac{1}{p}I_b^\alpha(qy)\right)(x)\right| &\leq I_a^\alpha\left(\frac{1}{|p|}I_b^\alpha(|qy|)\right)(x) \\ &= \frac{1}{\Gamma^2(\alpha)}\int_a^x \frac{1/|p(t)|}{(x-t)^{1-\alpha}}\left(\int_t^b \frac{|q(s)|\,|y(s)|}{(s-t)^{1-\alpha}}\,ds\right)dt \\ &\leq \frac{1}{\Gamma^2(\alpha)}\int_a^x \frac{1/|p(t)|}{(x-t)^{1-\alpha}}\left(\int_t^b \frac{|q(s)|^2}{(s-t)^{2-2\alpha}}\,ds\right)^{1/2} \\ &\quad\times\left(\int_t^b |y(s)|^2\,ds\right)^{1/2} dt \\ &\leq \frac{1}{\Gamma(\alpha)}\sqrt{c_4}\,||y||_2\, I_a^\alpha\left(\frac{1}{|p|}\right)(x) \\ &\leq \frac{c_5}{\Gamma(\alpha)}\sqrt{c_4}\,||y||_2. \end{aligned} \tag{37}$$

Since the right side of (37) is independent of x and the interval $[a,b]$ is finite, we obtain that the fourth term in (36) is also in $L^2[a,b]$. There follows that $TX \subset X$.

We now show that T is a contraction on X. For $y, z \in X$, we have, as before (see (36))

$$\begin{aligned}|Ty(x) - Tz(x)| &\leq I_b^\alpha(|q(y-z)|)(a)\, I_a^\alpha\left(\frac{1}{|p|}\right)(x) + I_a^\alpha\left(\frac{1}{|p|} I_b^\alpha(|q(y-z)|)\right)(x) \\ &\equiv A + B. \end{aligned} \tag{38}$$

We estimated A and B separately. (Recall that the norm under consideration is the $L^2[a,b]$-norm.) Thus (see the calculation leading to (37)), we have

$$\begin{aligned} A &= I_a^\alpha\left(\frac{1}{|p|}\right)(x)\, I_b^\alpha(|q||y-z|)(a) \\ &= \left(\frac{1}{\Gamma(\alpha)} \int_a^x \frac{1/|p(s)|}{(x-s)^{1-\alpha}}\, ds\right) \left(\frac{1}{\Gamma(\alpha)} \int_a^b \frac{|q(s)|\,|y(s)-z(s)|}{(s-a)^{1-\alpha}}\, ds\right) \\ &\leq \frac{c_5}{\Gamma(\alpha)} \int_a^b \frac{|q(s)|\,|y(s)-z(s)|}{(s-a)^{1-\alpha}}\, ds, \\ &\leq \frac{c_5\sqrt{c_4}}{\Gamma(\alpha)}\, ||y-z||_2. \end{aligned} \tag{39}$$

The estimate for B was obtained exactly as in the details leading to (37) with y replaced by $y - z$. Hence,

$$B \leq \frac{c_5\sqrt{c_4}}{\Gamma(\alpha)}\, ||y-z||_2. \tag{40}$$

By combining (39) and (40), we obtain

$$|Ty(x) - Tz(x)| \leq \frac{2c_5\sqrt{c_4}}{\Gamma(\alpha)}\, ||y-z||_2$$

i.e.,

$$||Ty - Tz||_2 \leq \frac{2c_5\sqrt{c_4}\sqrt{b-a}}{\Gamma(\alpha)}\, ||y-z||_2. \tag{41}$$

As such, the result eventually follows from (34) as T is a contraction on X. □

Corollary 3. *Let $p, q \in C[a,b]$, $p(x) > 0$ for all $x \in [a,b]$, and let $1/2 < \alpha < 1$. If*

$$2\frac{||1/p||_\infty ||q||_\infty}{\Gamma(\alpha)\Gamma(\alpha+1)} \frac{(b-a)^{2\alpha}}{\sqrt{2\alpha-1}} < 1, \tag{42}$$

then the initial value problem (9) subject to

$$I_a^{1-\alpha}y(a) = K_1 \neq 0 \text{ and } (pD_a^\alpha y)(a) = K_2, \tag{43}$$

has a unique solution $y \in L^2[a,b]$. In addition, the solutions are at least absolutely continuous in $(a,b]$.

Proof. This is a straightforward consequence of Theorem 3 once the quantities (32) and (33) are estimated trivially and (34) is applied. □

Remark 2. *The constants appearing in both (24), (34), and (42) are not intended to be precise.*

Theorem 4. *Let p, q be complex-valued and measurable on $[a,b]$, $|p(x)| < \infty$ a.e. on $[a,b]$, and let $1/p \in L^1[a,b]$. Assume further that, for every $\alpha \in (1/2, 1)$, we have*

$$c_4 \equiv \sup_{t\in[a,b]} \int_t^b \frac{q^2(s)}{(s-t)^{2-2\alpha}}\, ds < \infty, \tag{44}$$

and, for every $\alpha \in (\frac{1}{2}, 1)$, there holds

$$c_5 \equiv \sup_{x\in[a,b]} I_a^\alpha\left(\frac{1}{|p|}\right)(x) < \infty, \tag{45}$$

as well as

$$\kappa < 1$$

where

$$\kappa = \frac{2}{\Gamma(\alpha)}\left(\frac{(b-a)^{2\alpha-1}}{2\alpha-1} + \frac{2}{\alpha}(b-a)^\alpha + b - a\right)^{1/2} c_5\sqrt{c_4}.$$

Then, for $\alpha \in (1/2, 1)$ and for $x_0 \in (a, b]$, the only solution of the initial value problem (9) *that satisfies*

$$I_a^{1-\alpha}y(x_0) = 0, \quad (pD_a^\alpha y)(x_0) = 0, \tag{46}$$

and that is in $L^2[a, b]$, is the (a.e.) trivial solution.

Proof. The case $x_0 = a$ is contained in Corollary 3; as such, we consider $x_0 \in (a, b]$. From (14), we know that every solution of (9) satisfies

$$\begin{aligned} y(x) = K_1\frac{(x-a)^{\alpha-1}}{\Gamma(\alpha)} + K_2\, I_a^\alpha\left(\frac{1}{p}\right)(x) + I_b^\alpha(qy)(a)\, I_a^\alpha\left(\frac{1}{p}\right)(x) \\ - I_a^\alpha\left(\frac{1}{p}I_b^\alpha(qy)\right)(x), \end{aligned} \tag{47}$$

where now K_1 and K_2 are to be determined such that (46) is satisfied for a given x_0. By applying the operator $I_a^{1-\alpha}$ to both sides of (47)—as well as by then using both Properties 5 and 6, and setting everything equal to zero for $x = x_0$—we can obtain the relation

$$\begin{aligned} &I_a^{1-\alpha}y(x_0) \\ &= K_1 + (K_2 + I_b^\alpha(qy)(a))\, I_a^1\left(\frac{1}{p}\right)(x_0) - I_a^1\left(\frac{1}{p}I_b^\alpha(qy)\right)(x_0) \\ &= 0. \end{aligned} \tag{48}$$

Next, by applying the operator D_a^α to both sides of (47) and using both Properties 2 and 4, we can obtain

$$pD_a^\alpha y(x) = K_2 + I_b^\alpha(qy)(a) - I_b^\alpha(qy)(x).$$

From this, the use of the second condition in (46) gives

$$K_2 = I_b^\alpha(qy)(x_0) - I_b^\alpha(qy)(a). \tag{49}$$

By substituting (48) and (49) back into (47) and simplifying it, we obtain

$$y(x) = K_1\frac{(x-a)^{\alpha-1}}{\Gamma(\alpha)} + I_b^\alpha(qy)(x_0)\, I_a^\alpha\left(\frac{1}{p}\right)(x) - I_a^\alpha\left(\frac{1}{p}I_b^\alpha(qy)\right)(x), \tag{50}$$

where

$$K_1 = I_a^1\left(\frac{1}{p}I_b^\alpha(qy)\right)(x_0) - I_b^\alpha(qy)(x_0)\, I_a^1\left(\frac{1}{p}\right)(x_0),$$

and K_1 is a constant. Thus, (50) represents the form of a solution of (47) that satisfies both conditions (46).

This now allows us to define a map T on $X = L^2[a,b]$ that is endowed with the usual, i.e, the L^2-norm by, when $y \in X$,

$$\begin{aligned} Ty(x) &= \frac{(x-a)^{\alpha-1}}{\Gamma(\alpha)}\left(I_a^1\left(\frac{1}{p}I_b^\alpha(qy)\right)(x_0) - I_b^\alpha(qy)(x_0)\, I_a^1\left(\frac{1}{p}\right)(x_0)\right) \\ &+ I_b^\alpha(qy)(x_0)\, I_a^\alpha\left(\frac{1}{p}\right)(x) - I_a^\alpha\left(\frac{1}{p}I_b^\alpha(qy)\right)(x). \end{aligned} \tag{51}$$

By construction, a fixed point of T will be a solution of (47) that satisfies conditions (46). To this end, we used the contraction mapping principle. For $y \in X$, $\alpha \in (\frac{1}{2}, 1)$—as well as p, q satisfying (44) and (45), and using the proof of Theorem 3—we can now verify that each integral appearing in (51) exists and is finite for all $x \in [a,b]$. As such, we have $TX \subset X$.

Next, we show that T is a contraction. For $y, z \in X$, $x \in [a,b]$, we have

$$\begin{aligned} &Ty(x) - Tz(x) = \\ &\frac{(x-a)^{\alpha-1}}{\Gamma(\alpha)}\left(I_a^1\left(\frac{1}{p}I_b^\alpha(q(y-z))\right)(x_0) - I_b^\alpha(q(y-z))(x_0)\, I_a^1\left(\frac{1}{p}\right)(x_0)\right) \\ &+ I_b^\alpha(q(y-z))(x_0)\, I_a^\alpha\left(\frac{1}{p}\right)(x) - I_a^\alpha\left(\frac{1}{p}I_b^\alpha(q(y-z))\right)(x), \end{aligned}$$

such that

$$\begin{aligned} &|Ty(x) - Tz(x)| \leq \\ &\frac{(x-a)^{\alpha-1}}{\Gamma(\alpha)}\left(I_a^1\left(\frac{1}{|p|}I_b^\alpha(|q(y-z)|)\right)(x_0) + I_b^\alpha(|q(y-z)|)(x_0)\, I_a^1\left(\frac{1}{|p|}\right)(x_0)\right) \\ &+ I_b^\alpha(|q(y-z)|)(x_0)\, I_a^\alpha\left(\frac{1}{|p|}\right)(x) + I_a^\alpha\left(\frac{1}{|p|}I_b^\alpha(|q(y-z|)|)\right)(x), \\ &\equiv A + B + C, \end{aligned} \tag{52}$$

where

$$A \equiv \frac{(x-a)^{\alpha-1}}{\Gamma(\alpha)}\left(I_a^1\left(\frac{1}{|p|}I_b^\alpha(|q(y-z)|)\right)(x_0) + I_b^\alpha(|q(y-z)|)(x_0)\, I_a^1\left(\frac{1}{|p|}\right)(x_0)\right), \tag{53}$$

$$B \equiv I_b^\alpha(|q(y-z)|)(x_0)\, I_a^\alpha\left(\frac{1}{|p|}\right)(x), \tag{54}$$

and

$$C \equiv I_a^\alpha\left(\frac{1}{|p|}I_b^\alpha(|q(y-z|)|)\right)(x). \tag{55}$$

Now, $A = A_1 + A_2$, where

$$A_1 \equiv \frac{(x-a)^{\alpha-1}}{\Gamma(\alpha)}\, I_a^1\left(\frac{1}{|p|}I_b^\alpha(|q(y-z)|)\right)(x_0)$$

and

$$A_2 \equiv \frac{(x-a)^{\alpha-1}}{\Gamma(\alpha)}\, I_b^\alpha(|q(y-z)|)(x_0)\, I_a^1\left(\frac{1}{|p|}\right)(x_0).$$

We estimate A_1 first using the calculations leading to (37). Thus,

$$\begin{aligned} A_1 &= \frac{(x-a)^{\alpha-1}}{\Gamma(\alpha)^2}\int_a^{x_0}\frac{1}{|p(s)|}\int_s^b\frac{|q(y-z)|(t)}{(t-s)^{1-\alpha}}\,dt\,ds \\ &\leq \frac{(x-a)^{\alpha-1}}{\Gamma(\alpha)}\, c_5\sqrt{c_4}||y-z||_2. \end{aligned} \tag{56}$$

Similarly,

$$A_2 \leq \frac{(x-a)^{\alpha-1}}{\Gamma(\alpha)} c_5\sqrt{c_4}||y-z||_2. \tag{57}$$

By combining (56) and (57), we obtain

$$A \leq \frac{2(x-a)^{\alpha-1}}{\Gamma(\alpha)} c_5\sqrt{c_4}||y-z||_2. \tag{58}$$

The estimate for B is similar to the estimate for A_2 but without all the terms involving α, i.e.,

$$B \leq \frac{c_5\sqrt{c_4}}{\Gamma(\alpha)}||y-z||_2. \tag{59}$$

Finally, C is estimated as in the B-term in (38), i.e.,

$$C \leq \frac{c_5\sqrt{c_4}}{\Gamma(\alpha)}||y-z||_2. \tag{60}$$

Therefore, (58)–(60) yield

$$|Ty(x) - Tz(x)| \leq k(x)\,||y-z||_2 \tag{61}$$

$$k(x) = 2\left(\frac{(x-a)^{\alpha-1}+1}{\Gamma(\alpha)}\right) c_5\sqrt{c_4}.$$

Then, it follows that

$$||Ty - Tz||_2 \leq \kappa\,||y-z||_2,$$

where $\kappa = ||k||_2$ is given by

$$\kappa = \frac{2}{\Gamma(\alpha)}\left(\frac{(b-a)^{2\alpha-1}}{2\alpha-1} + \frac{2}{\alpha}(b-a)^{\alpha} + b - a\right)^{1/2} c_5\sqrt{c_4}.$$

Thus, T is a contraction on X provided $\kappa < 1$. The conclusion then follows. □

In the case where p, q are (real-valued) continuous and $p(x) > 0$, a similar though more extensive argument gives a different bound for uniqueness. This is our next result.

Theorem 5. *Let $p, q \in C[a,b]$, $p(x) > 0$ for all $x \in [a,b]$, and let $\alpha > 1/2$. Thus, let*

$$c_1\left((b-a)c_2^2 + 2c_2c_3\frac{(b-a)^{\alpha}}{\alpha} + c_3^2\,\frac{(b-a)^{2\alpha-1}}{2\alpha-1}\right)^{1/2} < 1, \tag{62}$$

where

$$c_1 = 2\frac{||q||_\infty||1/p||_\infty}{\Gamma(\alpha)^2\sqrt{2\alpha-1}},$$

$$c_2 = \frac{(b-a)^{2\alpha-1/2}}{\alpha},$$

and

$$c_3 = (b-a)^{\alpha+1/2}.$$

Then, for $x_0 \in (a,b]$, the only solution of the initial value problem (9) that satisfies

$$I_a^{1-\alpha}y(x_0) = 0, \quad (pD_a^{\alpha}y)(x_0) = 0, \tag{63}$$

and which is in $L^2[a,b]$ is the (a.e.) trivial solution.

Proof. The case of $x_0 = a$ is contained in Theorem 3, such that we can consider $x_0 \in (a,b]$. From (14), we know that every solution of (9) satisfies

$$y(x) = K_1 \frac{(x-a)^{\alpha-1}}{\Gamma(\alpha)} + K_2 I_a^\alpha\left(\frac{1}{p}\right)(x) + I_b^\alpha(qy)(a)\, I_a^\alpha\left(\frac{1}{p}\right)(x) - I_a^\alpha\left(\frac{1}{p} I_b^\alpha(qy)\right)(x). \tag{64}$$

$$pD_a^\alpha y(x) = K_2 + I_b^\alpha(qy)(a) - I_b^\alpha(qy)(x).$$

By using the proof of Theorem 4, we have

$$Ty(x) = \frac{(x-a)^{\alpha-1}}{\Gamma(\alpha)}\left(I_a^1\left(\frac{1}{p}I_b^\alpha(qy)\right)(x_0) - I_b^\alpha(qy)(x_0)\, I_a^1\left(\frac{1}{p}\right)(x_0)\right) + I_b^\alpha(qy)(x_0)\, I_a^\alpha\left(\frac{1}{p}\right)(x) - I_a^\alpha\left(\frac{1}{p}I_b^\alpha(qy)\right)(x) \tag{65}$$

and

$$\begin{aligned}
&|Ty(x) - Tz(x)| \leq \\
&\frac{(x-a)^{\alpha-1}}{\Gamma(\alpha)}\left(I_a^1\left(\frac{1}{p}I_b^\alpha(|q(y-z)|)\right)(x_0) + I_b^\alpha(|q(y-z)|)(x_0)\, I_a^1\left(\frac{1}{p}\right)(x_0)\right) \\
&+ I_b^\alpha(|q(y-z)|)(x_0)\, I_a^\alpha\left(\frac{1}{p}\right)(x) + I_a^\alpha\left(\frac{1}{p}I_b^\alpha(|q(y-z|))\right)(x), \\
&\equiv A + B + C,
\end{aligned} \tag{66}$$

respectively. We estimated B using the same technique that was used in Theorem 3 and Corollary 3, except that a was replaced by x_0 in the latter, thus leading to minor changes in the estimate. This gives

$$\begin{aligned}
B &\leq \frac{||1/p||_\infty ||q||_\infty (b-a)^\alpha}{\alpha\Gamma(\alpha)^2} \int_{x_0}^b (s-x_0)^{\alpha-1}\, |y(s) - z(s)|\, ds \\
&\leq \frac{||1/p||_\infty ||q||_\infty (b-a)^\alpha}{\alpha\Gamma(\alpha)^2} \frac{(b-x_0)^{\alpha-1/2}}{\sqrt{2\alpha-1}}\, ||y-z||_2, \\
&\leq \frac{||1/p||_\infty ||q||_\infty (b-a)^{2\alpha-1/2}}{\alpha\Gamma(\alpha)^2\sqrt{2\alpha-1}}\, ||y-z||_2.
\end{aligned} \tag{67}$$

Now, C is estimated as in Theorem 3, i.e.,

$$C \leq \frac{||1/p||_\infty ||q||_\infty}{\alpha\,\Gamma(\alpha)^2} \frac{(b-a)^{2\alpha-1/2}}{\sqrt{2\alpha-1}} ||y-z||_2. \tag{68}$$

Finally, A in (66) consists of two terms, and we can write $A = A_1 + A_2$ as before, which is where the associations should be clear. Then, we have

$$\begin{aligned}
A_1 &= \frac{(x-a)^{\alpha-1}}{\Gamma(\alpha)} I_a^1\left(\frac{1}{p}I_b^\alpha(|q(y-z)|)\right)(x_0) \\
&= \frac{(x-a)^{\alpha-1}}{\Gamma(\alpha)^2} \int_a^{x_0} \frac{1}{p(s)} \int_s^b \frac{|q(y-z)|(t)}{(t-s)^{1-\alpha}}\, dt\, ds \\
&\leq \frac{(x-a)^{\alpha-1}}{\Gamma(\alpha)^2} ||q||_\infty \int_a^{x_0} \frac{1}{p(s)} \int_s^b (t-s)^{\alpha-1}\, |y(t) - z(t)|\, dt\, ds \\
&\leq \frac{||1/p||_\infty ||q||_\infty}{\Gamma(\alpha)^2} \frac{(b-a)^{\alpha-1/2}}{\sqrt{2\alpha-1}} (x-a)^{\alpha-1}(x_0-a)\, ||y-z||_2.
\end{aligned} \tag{69}$$

Of course, (69) may be strengthened by a bound that is independent of x_0, i.e., one such as

$$A_1 \leq \frac{||1/p||_\infty ||q||_\infty}{\Gamma(\alpha)^2} \frac{(x-a)^{\alpha-1}}{\sqrt{2\alpha-1}} (b-a)^{\alpha+1/2} ||y-z||_2. \tag{70}$$

Similarly,

$$A_2 \leq \frac{||1/p||_\infty ||q||_\infty}{\Gamma(\alpha)^2} \frac{(x-a)^{\alpha-1}}{\sqrt{2\alpha-1}} (b-a)^{\alpha+1/2} ||y-z||_2. \tag{71}$$

By combining (70) and (71), we obtain

$$A \leq 2\frac{||1/p||_\infty ||q||_\infty}{\Gamma(\alpha)^2} \frac{(x-a)^{\alpha-1}}{\sqrt{2\alpha-1}} (b-a)^{\alpha+1/2} \, ||y-z||_2. \tag{72}$$

Thus, through using (67), (68) and (72) together with (66), we obtained the bound

$$\begin{aligned} &|Ty(x) - Tz(x)| \leq \\ &\frac{2\,||1/p||_\infty ||q||_\infty}{\Gamma(\alpha)^2\sqrt{2\alpha-1}} \left\{ \frac{(b-a)^{2\alpha-1/2}}{\alpha} + (b-a)^{\alpha+1/2}(x-a)^{\alpha-1} \right\} ||y-z||_2, \\ &\equiv c_1 \left\{ c_2 + c_3\,(x-a)^{\alpha-1} \right\} ||y-z||_2, \end{aligned} \tag{73}$$

where the definitions of the various constants $c_1, c_2,$ and c_3 in (73) should be clear from the display. Using (73), we can now obtain

$$\begin{aligned} &\int_a^b |Ty(x) - Tz(x)|^2 dx \\ &\leq c_1^2 ||y-z||_2^2 \int_a^b \{c_2^2 + 2c_2c_3(x-a)^{\alpha-1} + c_3^2(x-a)^{2\alpha-2}\}\, dx \\ &\leq c_1^2 ||y-z||_2^2 \left((b-a)c_2^2 + 2c_2c_3 \frac{(b-a)^\alpha}{\alpha} + c_3^2\,\frac{(b-a)^{2\alpha-1}}{2\alpha-1} \right) \end{aligned} \tag{74}$$

or

$$||Ty - Tz|| \leq c_1 \left((b-a)c_2^2 + 2c_2c_3 \frac{(b-a)^\alpha}{\alpha} + c_3^2\,\frac{(b-a)^{2\alpha-1}}{2\alpha-1} \right)^{1/2} ||y-z||_2. \tag{75}$$

From (75), we find that T is a contraction on X provided that

$$c_1 \left((b-a)c_2^2 + 2c_2c_3 \frac{(b-a)^\alpha}{\alpha} + c_3^2\,\frac{(b-a)^{2\alpha-1}}{2\alpha-1} \right)^{1/2} < 1. \tag{76}$$

The fixed-point theorem guarantees the existence of a unique fixed point, which—of course—must be the (a.e.) zero solution. □

4. Two-Point Boundary Problems

We show that the analysis in the previous sections extends naturally to the study of the so-called *two-point boundary value problems* on an interval $[a,b]$. In other words, the initial conditions are placed at two points (usually the end points a and b of the interval under consideration), and then one seeks solutions to the problem at hand with those conditions imposed. As such, now we consider the problem

$$\mathbf{D}_b^\alpha (pD_a^\alpha y)(x) + q(x)\,y(x) = 0, \tag{77}$$

which is subject to a set of conditions of the form

$$I_a^{1-\alpha} y(a) = K_1 \text{ and given } (pD_a^\alpha y)(b) = K_2, \tag{78}$$

where the K_i are both the given constants, i.e., a Dirichlet-type condition at $x = a$ and a Neumann-type condition at $x = b$. Note that the quantity $(pD_a^\alpha y)(x)$ is now evaluated at $x = b$ in lieu of $x = a$. This change leads to a two-point boundary value problem where solutions of (77) are now sought that satisfy both conditions in (78). The techniques from the previous sections led us to formulate the existence and uniqueness results for the solutions of such two-point boundary value problems, i.e., (77) and (78). As will be noted, the problem in this section is actually a little easier to solve than the initial value problem (9) and (10) that were considered earlier.

As before, we proceed formally from (77), except that we now apply I_b^α to both sides (see Property 3) to find

$$(pD_a^\alpha y)(x) - (pD_a^\alpha y)(b) + I_b^\alpha(qy)(x) = 0, \tag{79}$$

i.e.,

$$D_a^\alpha y(x) - \frac{1}{p(x)}(pD_a^\alpha y)(b) + \frac{1}{p(x)} I_b^\alpha(qy)(x) = 0. \tag{80}$$

This time, by applying I_a^α to both sides of (80) and using Property 1, we can obtain (when compared with (13))

$$\begin{aligned} y(x) = \frac{(x-a)^{\alpha-1}}{\Gamma(\alpha)} I_a^{1-\alpha} y(a) + I_a^\alpha\left(\frac{1}{p}\right)(x)(pD_a^\alpha y)(b) \\ - I_a^\alpha\left(\frac{1}{p} I_b^\alpha(qy)\right)(x). \end{aligned} \tag{81}$$

As before, there are two different cases: the case where $I_a^{1-\alpha} y(a) = 0$, and the one where $I_a^{1-\alpha} y(a) \neq 0$. The conditions leading to the existence and uniqueness of solutions to the problems at hand are identical, however. Once again, we do not assume any sign restrictions on the leading coefficient p. The proofs are sketched as they lead to no new methods.

Theorem 6. *Let p, q be complex-valued measurable functions on $[a, b]$, $|p(x)| < \infty$ a.e. on $[a, b]$, which also satisfy* (15) *and* (16). *If $c_1\, c_2 < 1$, then the two-point boundary value problem* (77) *which is subject to* (78) *with $K_1 = 0$, and where K_2 is arbitrary has a unique solution $y \in AC[a, b]$.*

Proof. Once again, we considered the normed space $(X, ||\cdot||_\infty)$ of the real valued continuous functions defined on $[a, b]$. Note that $I_a^{1-\alpha} y(a) = 0$ is in force in (81). We can define a map T on X by setting

$$Ty(x) = I_a^\alpha\left(\frac{K_2}{p}\right)(x) - I_a^\alpha\left(\frac{1}{p} I_b^\alpha(qy)\right)(x). \tag{82}$$

Then, any fixed point of T will satisfy both the first and the second of (78). The proof of Theorem 1 shows that all quantities appearing in (82) are continuous such that $TX \subset X$. Next, let $y, z \in X$. Then, we obtain

$$|Ty(x) - Tz(x)| \leq I_a^\alpha\left(\frac{1}{|p|} I_b^\alpha(|q\,(y-z)|)\right)(x).$$

The term on the right above corresponds to the term denoted by B in Theorem 1. Hence, by that discussion, we have $|Ty(x) - Tz(x)| \leq c_1 c_2 ||y - z||_\infty$, from which we can obtain

$$||Ty - Tz||_\infty \leq c_1\, c_2 ||y - z||_\infty.$$

As such, T is a contraction on X if $c_1\, c_2 < 1$. The above result then follows. □

The case of continuous coefficients and $p(x) > 0$ are covered as a special case, as was expected.

Corollary 4. *Let $p, q \in C[a,b]$, $p(x) > 0$ for all $x \in [a,b]$. If*

$$\frac{(b-a)^{2\alpha}}{\Gamma(\alpha+1)^2}\,||1/p||_\infty\,||q||_\infty < 1, \tag{83}$$

then the two-point boundary value problem (77) *that is subject to* (78)*, with $K_1 = 0$ and K_2 being arbitrary, has a unique solution $y \in AC[a,b]$.*

Proof. Using the definitions, it is easy to show that

$$c_1 \leq \frac{(b-a)^{\alpha}}{\Gamma(\alpha+1)}\,||1/p||_\infty$$

and

$$c_2 \leq \frac{(b-a)^{\alpha}}{\Gamma(\alpha+1)}\,||q||_\infty.$$

Thus, (83) implies that $c_1 c_2 < 1$; thus, the theorem applies and gives the conclusion. □

We will now review the case where $K_1 \neq 0$. It is covered similarly but we also now seek solutions in $L^2[a,b]$.

Theorem 7. *Let p, q be complex-valued measurable functions on $[a,b]$, $|p(x)| < \infty$ a.e. on $[a,b]$, which also satisfy* (32) *and* (33)*. Let $1/2 < \alpha < 1$. If*

$$\frac{c_5\sqrt{c_4}\sqrt{b-a}}{\Gamma(\alpha)} < 1 \tag{84}$$

then the two-point boundary value problem (77) *that is subject to* (78)*, with $K_1 \neq 0$ and K_2 being arbitrary, has a unique solution $y \in L^2[a,b]$.*

Proof. Let $X = (L^2(a,b), ||\cdot||_2)$, and let us define a map T on X by (see (81)). We thus have

$$Ty(x) = \frac{(x-a)^{\alpha-1}}{\Gamma(\alpha)}K_1 + I_a^{\alpha}\left(\frac{K_2}{p}\right)(x) - I_a^{\alpha}\left(\frac{1}{p}I_b^{\alpha}(qy)\right)(x). \tag{85}$$

$TX \subset X$ is a consequence of the discussion in Theorem 3. Next, we have

$$|Ty(x) - Tz(x)| \leq I_a^{\alpha}\left(\frac{1}{|p|}I_b^{\alpha}(|q(y-z)|)\right)(x) \leq \frac{c_5\sqrt{c_4}}{\Gamma(\alpha)}||y-z||_2,$$

by the estimate (37). Hence, we have

$$||Ty - Tz||_2 \leq \frac{c_5\sqrt{c_4}\sqrt{b-a}}{\Gamma(\alpha)}||y-z||_2,$$

which shows that T is a contraction on X provided that

$$\frac{c_5\sqrt{c_4}\sqrt{b-a}}{\Gamma(\alpha)} < 1.$$

The result then follows as before. □

Corollary 5. *Let $p, q \in C[a,b]$, $p(x) > 0$ for all $x \in [a,b]$, and let $1/2 < \alpha < 1$. If*

$$\frac{k}{\alpha\,\Gamma^2(\alpha)}\frac{(b-a)^{2\alpha}}{\sqrt{2\alpha-1}} < 1, \tag{86}$$

where $k = ||1/p||_\infty ||q||_\infty > 0$, then the two-point boundary value problem (77) that is subject to

$$I_a^{1-\alpha}y(a) = K_1 \neq 0 \text{ and } (pD_a^\alpha y)(b) = K_2 \tag{87}$$

has a unique solution $y \in L^2[a,b]$.

Proof. In using the definitions and the continuity assumptions, we obtain

$$c_4 \le ||q||_\infty^2 \int_t^b (s-t)^{2\alpha-2}\,ds \le \frac{||q||_\infty^2 (b-a)^{2\alpha-1}}{2\alpha-1}$$

and (see the proof of Corollary 1)

$$c_5 \le \frac{||1/p||_\infty (b-a)^\alpha}{\Gamma(\alpha+1)}.$$

With these estimates, it is a simple matter to see that (86) implies (84), and that this completes the proof. □

Remark 3. *We have shown that, under some mild assumptions, the mixed Riemann–Liouville–Caputo fractional differential equation defined as in (77) and (78) always possesses two types of solutions. Either all the solutions are continuous in $[a,b]$ (if $I_a^{1-\alpha}y(a) = 0$ and $0 < \alpha < 1$), or they are continuous in $(a,b]$ but are still in $L^2(a,b)$ (if $I_a^{1-\alpha}y(a) \neq 0$ and $1/2 < \alpha < 1$).*

5. Conclusions

In this article, we have stated and proved the existence and uniqueness theorems for fractional differential equations of the form

$$\mathbf{D}_b^\alpha(pD_a^\alpha y)(x) + q(x)\,y(x) = 0,$$

where $0 < \alpha < 1$, $\mathbf{D}_b^\alpha$ is a right-Caputo differential operator and D_a^α is a left-Riemann–Liouville differential operator under very general conditions on the coefficients of p, q, which involve measurability and no sign conditions on either p or q. The advantage of this formulation is that our equation includes the classical Sturm–Liouville equation upon taking the limit as $\alpha \to 1$. We have shown that the initial value problem, when properly formulated and under suitable conditions on p, q, will always have its solutions in $L^2[a,b]$. We have also given conditions under which the two-point boundary problem

$$I_a^{1-\alpha}y(a) = K_1 \text{ and given } (pD_a^\alpha y)(b) = K_2$$

that is associated with the above equation has a unique solution in some suitable spaces depending on whether K_1 is or is not zero.

Author Contributions: Conceptualization, L.G.Z.; methodology, L.G.Z. and A.B.M.; validation, L.G.Z. and A.B.M.; formal analysis, L.G.Z. and A.B.M.; investigation, L.G.Z. and A.B.M.; writing—original draft preparation, L.G.Z. and A.B.M.; writing—review and editing, L.G.Z. and A.B.M.; supervision, A.B.M.; project administration, A.B.M. All authors have read and agreed to the published version of the manuscript.

Funding: This research received no external funding.

Data Availability Statement: No new data were created or analyzed in this study. Data sharing is not applicable to this article.

Acknowledgments: The authors should like to thank Tahereh Houlari (formerly of Carleton University) for their useful conversations and helpful remarks. The authors are grateful to the referees for their useful comments that have led to improvements in this paper.

Conflicts of Interest: The authors declare no conflicts of interest.

References

1. Atkinson, F.V. *Discrete and Continuous Boundary Problems*; Academic Press: New York, NY, USA, 1964.
2. Gambo, Y.Y.; Ameen, R.; Jared, F.; Abdeljawad, T. Existence and uniqueness of solutions to fractional differential equations in the frame of generalized Caputo fractional derivatives. *Adv. Differ. Equ.* **2018**, *2018*, 134. [CrossRef]
3. Dehghan, M.; Mingarelli, A.B. Fractional Sturm-Liouville eigenvalue problems, I. *Rev. Real Acad. Cienc. Exactas Fis. Nat. Ser. A Mat.* **2020**, *114*, 46. [CrossRef]
4. Dehghan, M.; Mingarelli, A.B. Fractional Sturm-Liouville eigenvalue problems, II. *Fractal Fract.* **2022**, *6*, 487. [CrossRef]
5. Klimek, M.; Ciesielski, M.; Blaszczyk, T. Exact and Numerical Solution of the Fractional Sturm-Liouville Problem with Neumann Boundary Conditions. *Entropy* **2022**, *24*, 143. [CrossRef] [PubMed]
6. Klimek, M.; Agrawal, O.P. Fractional Sturm Liouville problem. *Comput. Math. Appl.* **2013**, *66*, 795–812. [CrossRef]
7. Klimek, M.; Odzijewicz, T.; Malinowska, A.B. Variational methods for the fractional Sturm Liouville problem. *J. Math. Anal. App.* **2014**, *416*, 402–426. [CrossRef]
8. Pandey, P.K.; Pandey, R.K.; Agrawal, O.P. Variational Approximation for Fractional Sturm-Liouville Problem. *Fract. Calc. Appl. Anal.* **2020**, *23*, 861–874. [CrossRef]
9. Younis, M.; Abdou, A.A.N. Novel Fuzzy Contractions and Applications to Engineering Science. *Fractal Fract.* **2024**, *8*, 28. [CrossRef]
10. Mainardi, F. *Fractional Calculus and Waves in Linear Viscoelasticity: An Introduction to Mathematical Models*; World Scientific: Singapore, 2010; p. 368.
11. Metzler, R.; Nonnenmacher, T.F. Space- and time-fractional diffusion and wave equations, fractional Fokker-Planck equations and physical motivations. *Chem. Phys.* **2000**, *284*, 67–90. [CrossRef]
12. Metzler, R.; Klafter, J. The random walk's guide to anomalous diffusion: A fractional dynamics approach. *Phys. Rep.* **2002**, *339*, 67–90. [CrossRef]
13. Rossikhin, Y.A.; Shitikova, M.V. Application of fractional calculus for dynamic problems of solid mechanics: Novel trends and recent results. *Appl. Mech. Rev.* **2009**, *63*, 010801. [CrossRef]
14. Caccioppoli, R. Un teorema generale sull'esistenza di elementi uniti in una trasformazione funzionale. *Rend. Accad. Naz. Lincei* **1930**, *11*, 794–799.
15. Hale, J.K. *Ordinary Differential Equations*; John Wiley & Sons, Inc.: New York, NY, USA, 1969.
16. Singh, J.; Kumar, D.; Kilicman, A. Numerical Solutions of nonlinear fractional partial differential equations arising in spatial diffusion biological populations. *Abstr. Appl. Anal.* **2014**, *2014*, 535793. [CrossRef]
17. Zayernouri, M.; Karniadakis, G.E. Fractional Sturm-Liouville eigen-problems: Theory and numerical approximation. *J. Comput. Phys.* **2013**, *252*, 495–517. [CrossRef]
18. Kilbas, A.A.; Srivastava, H.M.; Trujillo, J.J. *Theory and Application of Fractional Differential Equations*; Elsevie: Amsterdam, The Netherlands, 2006.
19. Podlubny, I. *Fractional Differential Equations: An Introduction to Fractional Derivatives, Fractional Differential Equations, to Methods of Their Solution and Some of Their Applications*; Academic Press: New York, NY, USA, 1998; 340p.
20. Samko, S.G.; Kilbas, A.A.; Marichev, O.I. *Fractional Integrals and Derivatives*; Gordon and Breach: Amsterdam, The Netherlands, 1993.
21. Riesz, M. L'intégrale de Riemann-Liouville et le problème de Cauchy. *Acta Math.* **1949**, *81*, 1–222. [CrossRef]

fractal and fractional

Article

Existence of Positive Solutions for a Class of Nabla Fractional Boundary Value Problems

Nikolay D. Dimitrov [1,*,†] and Jagan Mohan Jonnalagadda [2,†]

1 Department of Mathematics, University of Ruse, 7017 Ruse, Bulgaria
2 Department of Mathematics, Birla Institute of Technology and Science Pilani, Hyderabad 500078, Telangana, India; j.jaganmohan@hotmail.com or jjaganmohan@hyderabad.bits-pilani.ac.in
* Correspondence: ndimitrov@uni-ruse.bg
† These authors contributed equally to this work.

Abstract: In this manuscript, we study a class of equations with two different Riemann–Liouville-type orders of nabla difference operators. We show some new and fundamental properties of the related Green's function. Depending on the values of the orders of the operators, we split our research into two main cases, and for each one of them, we obtain suitable conditions under which we prove that the considered problem possesses a positive solution. We consider the latter to be the main novelty in this work. Our main tool in both cases of our study is Guo–Krasnoselskii's fixed point theorem. In the end, we give particular examples in order to offer a concrete demonstration of our new theoretical findings, as well as some possible future work in this direction.

Keywords: nabla fractional difference equations; Green's function; positive solutions; fixed-point theorems

MSC: 26A33; 34A08; 39A27

1. Introduction

Lately, fractional differential and difference equations and their applications have generated much attention [1–4]. One of the main reasons for this is the fast development of the theories of fractional and discrete fractional calculus, since they are widely used in biology, chemistry, mechanics and medicine. More precisely, some examples of models in environmental science, uncertainty, approximation or control theory, stability analysis, quantum physics or astrophysics, signal and image processing and many others can be found in [5–8]. Moreover, various real-life models can be modeled by both fractional operators of the Riemann–Liouville type or the Liouville–Caputo type [9–13]. We also refer the reader to some important and some very recent results about both fractional delta difference operators [14–17] and fractional nabla difference equations [18–21].

In particular, nabla problems provide a powerful tool for describing the nonlocal memory of different viscoelastic materials. The clear physical background of these studies opens up a new directions of scientific research, including both theoretical analysis and numerical methods. And while in the last few years different solvers for systems of fractional boundary value problems with boundary or initial conditions have been developed, the analysis of the existence and uniqueness of solutions to the fractional difference equations concerning boundary value problems is still paramount in comprehending discrete fractional calculus. Thus, all being said, finding new positive solutions to fractional problems is an undoubtedly important task.

Recently, in [22], the author studied the two-point nabla fractional problem

$$\left(\nabla^{\alpha}_{d_1} u\right)(\varrho) + h(\varrho) = 0, \quad 1 < \alpha < 2, \quad \varrho \in \mathbb{N}^{d_2}_{d_1+2},$$
$$u(d_1) = \left(\nabla^{\beta}_{d_1} u\right)(d_2) = 0, \quad 0 \le \beta \le 1$$

and managed to obtain a Lyapunov-type inequality for it.

Inspired by this work, we continue this research as we consider

$$-\left(\nabla^{\nu}_{\rho(d_1)} u\right)(\varrho) = \lambda f(\varrho) g(u(\varrho)), \quad \varrho \in \mathbb{N}^{d_2}_{d_1+2}, \tag{1}$$
$$u(d_1) = \left(\nabla^{\mu}_{\rho(d_1)} u\right)(d_2) = 0, \tag{2}$$

where $f : \mathbb{N}^{d_2}_{d_1+2} \to (0, \infty)$ and $g : [0, \infty) \to [0, \infty)$ are continuous functions, while $0 \le \mu \le 1 < \nu < 2$, $\nabla^{\nu}_{\rho(d_1)}$ and $\nabla^{\mu}_{\rho(d_1)}$ are νth- and μth-order nabla difference operators of the Riemann–Liouville type, respectively. Here, we use the standard notation $\mathbb{N}^{f}_{e} = \{e, e+1, e+2, \ldots, f\}$ for any real numbers e and f such that $f - e \in \mathbb{N}$.

Our aim is to extend the findings given in [22]. We shall use some of the results from there and we shall deduce new fundamental properties of the related Green function. Then, using our new findings, we are going to obtain existence and nonexistence results for the considered problem (1) and (2). To the best of our knowledge, this has never been carried out so far in the existing literature, which we consider to be the main novelty of this manuscript.

The rest of this paper is structured as follows: In Section 2, we deduce the exact expression and we recall some of the properties of the Green function that is related to the linear problem. Then, we split our study into two main cases depending on the values of ν and μ. In each one of them, we impose some suitable conditions on the right-hand side of our problem, in order to obtain existence results, presented in Sections 3 and 4, respectively. To validate our theoretical results, some numerical examples are given in Section 5. Finally, in Section 6, we finish with a summary of our results and some possible future directions for expanding this research.

2. Preliminaries

In this section, we recall some previous results that we will extend in the next sections and a classical theorem, which will be our main tool for establishing our new results. Let us consider the following linear problem:

$$-\left(\nabla^{\nu}_{\rho(d_1)} u\right)(\varrho) = h(\varrho), \quad \varrho \in \mathbb{N}^{d_2}_{d_1+2}, \tag{3}$$
$$u(d_1) = \left(\nabla^{\mu}_{\rho(d_1)} u\right)(d_2) = 0. \tag{4}$$

Here, $0 \le \mu \le 1 < \nu < 2$ and $h : \mathbb{N}^{d_2}_{d_1+2} \to \mathbb{R}$ are continuous functions.

For any $\alpha, \beta \in \mathbb{R}$, we denote the generalized rising function as

$$\alpha^{\overline{\beta}} = \frac{\Gamma(\alpha + \beta)}{\Gamma(\alpha)}$$

and for $\nu \in \mathbb{R} \setminus \{\ldots, -2, -1\}$, the νth-order nabla fractional Taylor monomial is denoted as

$$H_{\nu}(\alpha, \beta) = \frac{(\alpha - \beta)^{\overline{\nu}}}{\Gamma(\nu + 1)}.$$

Recall the following theorem:

Theorem 1 (Theorem 3.9 in [22]). *The linear boundary value problem* (3) *and* (4) *has a unique solution given in the form*

$$u(\varrho) = \sum_{s=d_1+2}^{d_2} \mathfrak{W}(\varrho, s)h(s), \quad \varrho \in \mathbb{N}_{d_1}^{d_2},$$

where

$$\mathfrak{W}(\varrho, s) = \begin{cases} \mathfrak{W}_1(\varrho, s), & \varrho \in \mathbb{N}_{d_1}^{\rho(s)}, \\ \mathfrak{W}_2(\varrho, s), & \varrho \in \mathbb{N}_{s}^{d_2}, \end{cases} \tag{5}$$

with

$$\mathfrak{W}_1(\varrho, s) = \frac{H_{\nu-1}(\varrho, d_1)H_{\nu-\mu-1}(d_2, \rho(s))}{H_{\nu-\mu-1}(d_2, d_1)}$$

and

$$\mathfrak{W}_2(\varrho, s) = G_1(\varrho, s) - H_{\nu-1}(\varrho, \rho(s)).$$

Moreover, the maximum of the nonnegative Green function $\mathfrak{W}(\varrho, s)$ defined in (5) *is given by*

$$\max_{(\varrho,s)\in \mathbb{N}_{d_1}^{d_2}\times \mathbb{N}_{d_1+2}^{d_2}} \mathfrak{W}(\varrho, s) = \begin{cases} \max_{s\in \mathbb{N}_{d_1+2}^{d_2}} \mathfrak{W}(s-1, s), & 0 \le \mu \le \nu - 1, \\ \max_{s\in \mathbb{N}_{d_1+2}^{d_2}} \mathfrak{W}(s, s), & \nu - 1 < \mu < 1. \end{cases}$$

Based on the findings in the above theorem, we will split our study of the existence of positive solutions of (1) and (2) into two main cases. Our main tool for both will be the classical Guo–Krasnoselskii fixed point theorem in cones [23].

Theorem 2. *Let $B = (B, \|\cdot\|)$ be a Banach space, and let $K \subseteq B$ be a cone. Assume that Ω_1 and Ω_2 are bounded open subsets contained in B such that $0 \in \Omega_1$ and $\Omega_1 \subseteq \Omega_2$. Assume further that $T : K \cap (\overline{\Omega_2} \setminus \Omega_1) \to K$ is a completely continuous operator. Here, either*

(1) $\|Ty\| \le \|y\|$ for $y \in K \cap \partial\Omega_1$, and $\|Ty\| \ge \|y\|$ for $y \in K \cap \partial\Omega_2$; or

(2) $\|Ty\| \ge \|y\|$ for $y \in K \cap \partial\Omega_1$, and $\|Ty\| \le \|y\|$ for $y \in K \cap \partial\Omega_2$.

Then, T has at least one fixed point in $K \cap (\overline{\Omega_2} \setminus \Omega_1)$.

3. Case I: $0 \le \mu < \nu - 1$

First, let us study the case $0 \le \mu \le \nu - 1$. Following the idea given in [14], we have the next result.

Lemma 1. *There is $\gamma_1 \in (0, 1)$ such that $\mathfrak{W}(\varrho, s)$ given in* (5) *has the following property:*

$$\min_{d_1+2\le\varrho\le d_2} \mathfrak{W}(\varrho, s) \ge \gamma_1 \mathfrak{W}(s-1, s) \text{ for all } s \in \mathbb{N}_{d_1+2}^{d_2}.$$

Proof. In this case,

$$\frac{\mathfrak{W}(\varrho, s)}{\mathfrak{W}(s-1, s)} = \begin{cases} \dfrac{(\varrho - d_1)^{\overline{\nu-1}}}{(s - d_1 - 1)^{\overline{\nu-1}}}, & \varrho \in \mathbb{N}_{d_1}^{\rho(s)}, \\ \dfrac{(d_2 - s + 1)^{\overline{\nu-\mu-1}}(\varrho - d_1)^{\overline{\nu-1}} - (d_2 - d_1)^{\overline{\nu-\mu-1}}(t - s + 1)^{\overline{\nu-1}}}{(d_2 - s + 1)^{\overline{\nu-\mu-1}}(s - d_1 - 1)^{\overline{\nu-1}}}, & \varrho \in \mathbb{N}_{s}^{d_2}. \end{cases}$$

For $\varrho \in \mathbb{N}_{d_1+1}^{\rho(s)}$, we find that

$$\frac{\mathfrak{W}(\varrho, s)}{\mathfrak{W}(s-1, s)} = \frac{(\varrho - d_1)^{\overline{\nu-1}}}{(s - d_1 - 1)^{\overline{\nu-1}}} \ge \frac{2^{\overline{\nu-1}}}{(d_2 - d_1 - 1)^{\overline{\nu-1}}}. \tag{6}$$

For $\varrho \in \mathbb{N}_s^{d_2}$, we know that $\mathfrak{W}(\varrho, s)$ is decreasing with respect to ϱ, which implies that

$$\begin{aligned}\frac{\mathfrak{W}(\varrho,s)}{\mathfrak{W}(s-1,s)} &= \frac{(d_2-s+1)^{\overline{\nu-\mu-1}}(\varrho-d_1)^{\overline{\nu-1}}-(d_2-d_1)^{\overline{\nu-\mu-1}}(\varrho-s+1)^{\overline{\nu-1}}}{(d_2-s+1)^{\overline{\nu-\mu-1}}(s-d_1-1)^{\overline{\nu-1}}} \\ &\geq \frac{(d_2-s+1)^{\overline{\nu-\mu-1}}(d_2-d_1)^{\overline{\nu-1}}-(d_2-d_1)^{\overline{\nu-\mu-1}}(d_2-s+1)^{\overline{\nu-1}}}{(d_2-s+1)^{\overline{\nu-\mu-1}}(s-d_1-1)^{\overline{\nu-1}}}.\end{aligned}$$

Denote

$$\varphi(s) = \frac{1}{(s-d_1-1)^{\overline{\nu-1}}}\left[(d_2-d_1)^{\overline{\nu-1}} - \frac{(d_2-s+1)^{\overline{\nu-1}}(d_2-d_1)^{\overline{\nu-\mu-1}}}{(d_2-s+1)^{\overline{\nu-\mu-1}}}\right].$$

One can check that

$$\frac{(d_2-s+1)^{\overline{\nu-1}}(d_2-d_1)^{\overline{\nu-\mu-1}}}{(d_2-s+1)^{\overline{\nu-\mu-1}}}$$

is decreasing for $d_1+2 \leq s \leq d_2+1$. Then,

$$\begin{aligned}\varphi(s) &\geq \frac{1}{(s-d_1-1)^{\overline{\nu-1}}}\left[(d_2-d_1)^{\overline{\nu-1}} - \frac{(d_2-d_1-1)^{\overline{\nu-1}}(d_2-d_1)^{\overline{\nu-\mu-1}}}{(d_2-d_1-1)^{\overline{\nu-\mu-1}}}\right] \\ &\geq \frac{1}{(d_2-d_1)^{\overline{\nu-1}}}\left[(d_2-d_1)^{\overline{\nu-1}} - \frac{(d_2-d_1-1)^{\overline{\nu-1}}(d_2-d_1)^{\overline{\nu-\mu-1}}}{(d_2-d_1-1)^{\overline{\nu-\mu-1}}}\right].\end{aligned}$$

The last inequality, combined with (6), shows us that for each $s \in \mathbb{N}_{d_1+2}^{d_2}$,

$$\min_{d_1+2\leq\varrho\leq d_2} \mathfrak{W}(\varrho,s) \geq \gamma_1 \mathfrak{W}(s-1,s),$$

where

$$\gamma_1 = \min\left\{\frac{1}{(d_2-d_1)^{\overline{\nu-1}}}\left[(d_2-d_1)^{\overline{\nu-1}} - \frac{(d_2-d_1-1)^{\overline{\nu-1}}(d_2-d_1)^{\overline{\nu-\mu-1}}}{(d_2-d_1-1)^{\overline{\nu-\mu-1}}}\right], \frac{2^{\overline{\nu-1}}}{(d_2-d_1-1)^{\overline{\nu-1}}}\right\}.$$

Moreover, it is clear from the above expression that $\gamma_1 < 1$. □

Define the Banach space B by

$$B = \left\{y : \mathbb{N}_{d_1+2}^{d_2} \to \mathbb{R} : y(d_1) = \left(\nabla^{\mu}_{\rho(d_1)} y\right)(d_2) = 0\right\},$$

coupled with

$$\|y\| = \max_{\varrho\in\mathbb{N}_{d_1+2}^{d_2}} |y(\varrho)|.$$

Set the cone

$$K_1 = \left\{y \in B,\ y(\varrho) \geq 0,\ \min_{d_1+2\leq\varrho\leq d_2} y(\varrho) \geq \gamma_1\|y\|,\ \varrho \in \mathbb{N}_{d_1+2}^{d_2}\right\}$$

and the operator $T_\lambda : K_1 \to B$ by

$$(T_\lambda y)(\varrho) = \lambda \sum_{s=d_1+2}^{d_2} \mathfrak{W}(\varrho,s) f(s) g(y(s)).$$

By using Lemma 1, we have

$$\begin{aligned} \min_{d_1+2\le\varrho\le d_2}(T_\lambda y)(\varrho) &\ge \lambda\sum_{s=d_1+2}^{d_2}\min_{d_1+2\le\varrho\le d_2}\mathfrak{W}(\varrho,s)f(s)g(y(s)) \\ &\ge \lambda\gamma_1\sum_{s=d_1+2}^{d_2}\max_{d_1+2\le\varrho\le d_2}\mathfrak{W}(\varrho,s)f(s)g(y(s)) \\ &\ge \gamma_1\|T_\lambda y\|, \end{aligned}$$

which gives us $T_\lambda : K_1 \to K_1$.

3.1. Positive Solutions

Here, we will establish some suitable conditions that will allow us to confirm that (1) and (2) has a positive solution.

Let us assume the following conditions about function g:

(G1) $\lim_{y\to 0^+}\frac{g(y)}{y} = 0$ and $\lim_{y\to+\infty}\frac{g(y)}{y} = +\infty$;

(G2) $\lim_{y\to 0^+}\frac{g(y)}{y} = +\infty$ and $\lim_{y\to+\infty}\frac{g(y)}{y} = 0$.

Define

$$\mathfrak{W}^* = \max_{(\varrho,s)\in\mathbb{N}_{d_1}^{d_2}\times\mathbb{N}_{d_1+2}^{d_2}}\mathfrak{W}(\varrho,s) = \max_{s\in\mathbb{N}_{d_1+2}^{d_2}}\mathfrak{W}(s-1,s).$$

Then, for $0\le\mu<\nu-1$,

$$\mathfrak{W}^* = \mathfrak{W}(s^*-1,s^*), \tag{7}$$

where

$$s^* = \left\lfloor\frac{(d_2+1)(\nu-1)+(d_1+2)(\nu-\mu-1)}{2(\nu-1)-\mu}\right\rfloor.$$

For $\mu=\nu-1$,

$$\mathfrak{W}^* = \mathfrak{W}(d_2-1,d_2). \tag{8}$$

In particular,

$$\mathfrak{W}(s-1,s) = \frac{H_{\nu-1}(s-1,d_1)H_{\nu-\mu-1}(d_2,\rho(s))}{H_{\nu-\mu-1}(d_2,d_1)} = \frac{\Psi(s)\Gamma(d_2-d_1)}{\Gamma(\nu)\Gamma(d_2-d_1+\nu-\mu-1)},$$

with

$$\Psi(s) = \frac{\Gamma(s-d_1+\nu-2)\Gamma(d_2-s+\nu-\mu)}{\Gamma(d_2-s+1)\Gamma(s-d_1-1)}.$$

Consider, for $s\in\mathbb{N}_{d_1+3}^{d_2}$,

$$(\nabla\Psi)(s) = \frac{((1-\nu+\mu)(s-d_1-2)+(\nu-1)(d_2-s+1))\Gamma(s-d_1+\nu-3)\Gamma(d_2-s+\nu-\mu)}{\Gamma(d_2-s+2)\Gamma(s-d_1-1)}.$$

Then, the equation $(\nabla\Psi)(s)=0$ has a unique solution, and so we set s^* as the critical point of Ψ. If $s\le s^*$, the term

$$\frac{(d_2+1)(\nu-1)+(d_1+2)(\nu-\mu-1)}{2(\nu-1)-\mu}$$

is positive, and thus Ψ is increasing. On the other hand, if $s\ge s^*$, the same term is negative, and thus Ψ is decreasing. As a result, we obtain (7).

If $\mu=\nu-1, \Gamma(s-d_1+\nu-3)>0$, since $(1-\nu+\mu)(s-d_1-2)+(\nu-1)(d_2-s+1)>0$, then $(\nabla\Psi)(s)>0$ implies that Ψ is increasing. Thus, we obtain (8).

Also, take

$$\mathcal{F}_* = \min_{\varrho \in \mathbb{N}_{d_1+2}^{d_2}} f(\varrho) \text{ and } \mathcal{F}^* = \max_{\varrho \in \mathbb{N}_{d_1+2}^{d_2}} f(\varrho).$$

Our first main result in this section is as follows:

Theorem 3. *Let condition (G1) hold. Moreover, if there is a sufficiently small positive constant ϵ and a sufficiently large constant C_1, $\mathcal{F}^*\epsilon < C_1\mathcal{F}_*$ holds. Then, for each*

$$\lambda \in \left((C_1(d_2-d_1-1)\mathcal{F}_*\mathfrak{W}^*)^{-1}, ((d_2-d_1-1)\mathcal{F}^*\mathfrak{W}^*\epsilon)^{-1}\right),$$

the boundary value problem (1) *and* (2) *has at least one positive solution.*

Proof. From the first limit in (G1), there is $r_1 > 0$ and a sufficiently small constant $\epsilon > 0$ satisfying $g(y) \le \epsilon r_1$ for all $y \in (0, r_1]$. Thus, for any $y \in K_1$ with $\|y\| = r_1$,

$$(T_\lambda y)(\varrho) \le \lambda \mathfrak{W}^* \sum_{s=d_1+2}^{d_2} f(s)g(y(s)) \le \lambda(d_2-d_1-1)\mathfrak{W}^*\mathcal{F}^*\epsilon r_1 \le r_1 = \|y\|.$$

Therefore, if we set $\Omega_1 = \{y \in B : \|y\| < r_1\}$, the above inequality implies

$$\|T_\lambda y\| \le \|y\| \text{ for } y \in K_1 \cap \partial\Omega_1.$$

Moreover, from the second limit in condition (G1), one can show that there is $r_2 > r_1 > 0$ and a sufficiently large constant C_1 satisfying $g(y) \ge \frac{C_1 r_2}{\gamma_1^2}$ for every $y \ge r_2$. Set $r_2^* = \frac{r_2}{\gamma_1} > r_2$ and $\Omega_2 = \{y \in B : \|y\| < r_2^*\}$. Hence, for every $y \in K_1$ with $\|y\| = r_2^*$,

$$\min_{d_1+2 \le \varrho \le d_2} y(\varrho) \ge \gamma_1\|y\| = \gamma_1 r_2^* = r_2.$$

As a result, one can verify

$$(T_\lambda y)(\varrho) = \lambda \sum_{s=d_1+2}^{d_2} \mathfrak{W}(\varrho,s)f(s)g(y(s)) \ge \lambda(d_2-d_1-1)\gamma_1\mathfrak{W}^*\mathcal{F}_*\frac{C_1 r_2}{\gamma_1^2} \ge r_2^* = \|y\|.$$

This gives us

$$\|T_\lambda y\| \ge \|y\| \text{ for } y \in K_1 \cap \partial\Omega_2.$$

From Theorem 2, we find that the operator T_λ possesses a fixed point $y \in K_1 \cap (\overline{\Omega_2} \setminus \Omega_1)$ with $r_1 \le \|y\| \le r_2^*$. □

Our second main existence result states the following:

Theorem 4. *Let (G2) hold. Furthermore, if there is a sufficiently large constant C_2 such that $\mathcal{F}^* < C_2\mathcal{F}_*$ holds, yhen, for each*

$$\lambda \in \left((C_2(d_2-d_1-1)\mathcal{F}_*\mathfrak{W}^*)^{-1}, ((d_2-d_1-1)\mathcal{F}^*\mathfrak{W}^*)^{-1}\right),$$

problems (1) *and* (2) *possess at least one positive solution.*

Proof. From the first limit in (G2), there is $r_3 > 0$ and a sufficiently large constant $C_2 > 0$ satisfying $g(y) > \frac{C_2 r_3}{\gamma_1}$ for $y \in (0, r_3)$. If we choose $\Omega_1 = \{y \in B : \|y\| < r_3\}$, for each $y \in \Omega_1$,

$$(T_\lambda y)(\varrho) = \lambda \sum_{s=d_1+2}^{d_2} \mathfrak{W}(\varrho, s) f(s) g(y(s)) \geq \lambda (d_2 - d_1 - 1)\gamma_1 \mathfrak{W}^* \mathcal{F}_* \frac{C_2 r_3}{\gamma_1} \geq r_3 = \|y\|,$$

which gives us

$$\|T_\lambda y\| \geq \|y\| \text{ for } y \in K_1 \cap \partial\Omega_1.$$

Next, we consider two cases in order to set Ω_2.

Case 1. Let g be bounded. In other words, there is some $R_1 > r_3$ such that $g(y) \leq R_1$ for $y \in K_1$. Hence, for $y \in K_1$ with $\|y\| = R_1$,

$$(T_\lambda y)(\varrho) \leq \lambda \mathfrak{W}^* \sum_{s=d_1+2}^{d_2} f(s) g(y(s)) \leq \lambda \mathfrak{W}^* (d_2 - d_1 - 1) \mathcal{F}^* R_1 \leq R_1 = \|y\|.$$

Case 2. On the other hand, if g is unbounded, there is some R_2 and a sufficiently small ϵ_2 with $g(y) \leq \epsilon_2 y$ for $y \geq R_2$. Set $R = \max\{R_1, R_2\}$ and $\Omega_2 = \{y \in B : \|y\| < R\}$. Hence, $g(R) \leq \epsilon_2 R$ and $\lambda < \frac{1}{\epsilon_2 (d_2 - d_1 - 1) \mathcal{F}^* \mathfrak{W}^*}$. As a consequence,

$$(T_\lambda y)(\varrho) \leq \lambda \mathfrak{W}^* \sum_{s=d_1+2}^{d_2} f(s) g(y(s)) \leq \lambda \mathfrak{W}^* (d_2 - d_1 - 1) \mathcal{F}^* \epsilon_2 R \leq R = \|y\|,$$

which means that in both cases, we have

$$\|T_\lambda y\| \leq \|y\| \text{ for } y \in K_1 \cap \partial\Omega_2.$$

Thus, Theorem 2 ensures us that the operator T_λ has a fixed point $y \in K_1 \cap \left(\overline{\Omega_2} \setminus \Omega_1\right)$ with $r_3 \leq \|y\| \leq R$. □

3.2. Nonexistence

Now, we will establish some sufficient conditions that will allow us to show when problems (1) and (2) do not possess any positive solutions.

Suppose that the following conditions are satisfied:

(G3) $\lim\limits_{y \to 0^+} \sup \frac{g(y)}{y} = g_0$, $\lim\limits_{y \to +\infty} \sup \frac{g(y)}{y} = g_\infty$,

(G4) $\lim\limits_{y \to 0^+} \inf \frac{g(y)}{y} = g_0^*$, $\lim\limits_{y \to +\infty} \inf \frac{g(y)}{y} = g_\infty^*$.

Theorem 5. *Suppose that (G3) holds. Moreover, assuming that both $g_0 < +\infty$ and $g_\infty < +\infty$, then there is a λ_1 such that for each $\lambda \in (0, \lambda_1)$, problems* (1) *and* (2) *do not possess any positive solutions.*

Proof. From $g_0 < +\infty$ and $g_\infty < +\infty$, it follows that there are some positive m_1, m_2, r_4 and r_5 such that $r_4 < r_5$, $g(y) \leq m_1 y$ for $y \in [0, r_4]$ and $g(y) \leq m_2 y$ for $y \in [r_5, +\infty)$. Choose

$$m = \max\left\{m_1, m_2, \max_{r_4 \leq y \leq r_5} \frac{g(y)}{y}\right\}.$$

Hence, $g(y) \leq my$. Now, let y_1 be a positive solution of (1) and (2). In other words, $Ty_1(\varrho) = y_1(\varrho)$ for $\varrho \in \mathbb{N}_{d_1+2}^{d_2}$ and

$$\|y_1\| = \|Ty_1\| \leq \lambda \mathfrak{W}^* \mathcal{F}^* \sum_{s=d_1+2}^{d_2} g(y_1(s)) \leq \lambda \mathfrak{W}^* (d_2 - d_1 - 1) \mathcal{F}^* m y_1 < \|y_1\|,$$

which is a contradiction if we choose $\lambda_1 = \frac{1}{\mathfrak{W}^*(d_2-d_1-1)\mathcal{F}^* m}$. Therefore, (1) and (2) have no positive solutions for every $\lambda \in (0, \lambda_1)$. □

Theorem 6. *Let (G4) hold. Furthermore, if $g_0^* > 0$ and $g_\infty^* > 0$, then there is a λ_2 such that for all $\lambda > \lambda_2$, the boundary value problem* (1) *and* (2) *has no positive solution.*

Proof. From $g_0^* > 0$ and $g_\infty^* > 0$, it follows that there are positive numbers m_3, m_4, r_6, r_7 such that $r_6 < r_7$, $g(y) \geq m_3 y$, for $y \in [0, r_6]$, and $g(y) \geq m_4 y$, for $y \in [r_7, +\infty)$. This time, choose

$$m = \min\left\{ m_3, m_4, \max_{r_6 \leq y \leq r_7} \frac{g(y)}{y} \right\}.$$

We have $g(y) \geq my$ for all $y > 0$. Suppose y_2 is a positive solution of (1) and (2). Then, $Ty_2(\varrho) = y_2(\varrho)$ for $\varrho \in \mathbb{N}_{d_1+2}^{d_2}$ and

$$\|y_2\| = \|Ty_2\| \geq \lambda \sum_{s=d_1+2}^{d_2} \mathfrak{W}(\varrho, s) f(s) g(y_2(s)) \geq \lambda (d_2 - d_1 - 1) \gamma_1 \mathfrak{W}^* \mathcal{F}_* m y_2 > \|y_2\|,$$

which is a contradiction if we set $\lambda_2 = \frac{1}{\mathfrak{W}^*(d_2-d_1-1)\mathcal{F}_* m}$. Therefore, (1) and (2) have no positive solutions for every $\lambda > \lambda_2$. □

4. Case II: $\nu - 1 < \mu \leq 1$

In the considered case, we will prove the existence of positive solutions of the following more general equation:

$$-\left(\nabla_{\rho(d_1)}^{\nu} u\right)(\varrho) = \lambda f(\varrho, y(\varrho)), \quad \varrho \in \mathbb{N}_{d_1+2}^{d_2}, \tag{9}$$

coupled with boundary conditions (2), where $f : \mathbb{N}_{d_1+2}^{d_2} \times \mathbb{R} \to \mathbb{R}$ is continuous and $f(\varrho, y) \geq 0$ for all $\varrho \in \mathbb{N}_{d_1+2}^{d_2}$ and $y \geq 0$. We know that in this case

$$M = \max_{(\varrho,s) \in \mathbb{N}_{d_1}^{d_2} \times \mathbb{N}_{d_1+2}^{d_2}} \mathfrak{W}(\varrho, s) = \max_{s \in \mathbb{N}_{d_1+2}^{d_2}} \mathfrak{W}(s, s).$$

In particular,

$$\mathfrak{W}(s,s) = \frac{H_{\nu-1}(s, d_1) H_{\nu-\mu-1}(d_2, \rho(s))}{H_{\nu-\mu-1}(d_2, d_1)} - 1 = \frac{\psi(s)\Gamma(d_2 - d_1)}{\Gamma(\nu)\Gamma(d_2 - d_1 + \nu - \mu - 1)} - 1,$$

with

$$\psi(s) = \frac{\Gamma(s - d_1 + \nu - 1)\Gamma(d_2 - s + \nu - \mu)}{\Gamma(d_2 - s + 1)\Gamma(s - d_1)}.$$

Consider, for $s \in \mathbb{N}_{d_1+3}^{d_2}$,

$$(\nabla \psi)(s) = \frac{((1 - \nu + \mu)(s - d_1 - 1) + (\nu - 1)(d_2 - s + 1))\Gamma(s - d_1 + \nu - 2)\Gamma(d_2 - s + \nu - \mu)}{\Gamma(d_2 - s + 2)\Gamma(s - d_1)}.$$

Thus, $(\nabla\psi)(s) > 0$, implying that

$$\max_{s\in\mathbb{N}_{d_1+2}^{d_2}} \psi(s) = \psi(d_2).$$

Consequently,

$$M = \max_{s\in\mathbb{N}_{d_1+2}^{d_2}} \mathfrak{W}(s,s) = \mathfrak{W}(d_2,d_2) = \frac{\Gamma(d_2-d_1+\nu-1)\Gamma(\nu-\mu)}{\Gamma(\nu)\Gamma(d_2-d_1+\nu-\mu-1)} - 1.$$

Moreover, since $\mathfrak{W}(\varrho,s)$ is increasing for $\varrho \in [d_1+1,s-1]$ and decreasing for $\varrho \in [s+1,d_2]$, one proves that

$$m = \min_{(\varrho,s)\in\mathbb{N}_{d_1+1}^{d_2}\times\mathbb{N}_{d_1+2}^{d_2}} \mathfrak{W}(\varrho,s) = \min_{s\in\mathbb{N}_{d_1+2}^{d_2}} \{\mathfrak{W}(d_1+1,s),\mathfrak{W}(d_2,s)\}.$$

In particular,

$$\min_{s\in\mathbb{N}_{d_1+2}^{d_2}} \mathfrak{W}(d_1+1,s) = \frac{H_{\nu-\mu-1}(d_2,a\ +1)}{H_{\nu-\mu-1}(d_2,d_1)} = \frac{d_2-d_1-1}{d_2-d_1+\nu-\mu-1}$$

and

$$\min_{s\in\mathbb{N}_{d_1+2}^{d_2}} \mathfrak{W}(d_2,s) = \frac{\Gamma(d_2-d_1+\nu-1)\Gamma(\nu-\mu)}{\Gamma(d_2-d_1+\nu-\mu-1)\Gamma(\nu)} - \frac{\Gamma(d_2-d_1+\nu-2)}{\Gamma(d_2-d_1-1)\Gamma(\nu)}.$$

Therefore,

$$m = \min\left\{\frac{d_2-d_1-1}{d_2-d_1+\nu-\mu-1}, \frac{\Gamma(d_2-d_1+\nu-1)\Gamma(\nu-\mu)}{\Gamma(d_2-d_1+\nu-\mu-1)\Gamma(\nu)} - \frac{\Gamma(d_2-d_1+\nu-2)}{\Gamma(d_2-d_1-1)\Gamma(\nu)}\right\}.$$

Define a different cone than before, namely

$$K_2 = \left\{y \in B,\ y(\varrho) \geq 0,\ \min y(\varrho) \geq \frac{m}{M}\|y\|,\ \varrho \in \mathbb{N}_{d_1+2}^{d_2}\right\},$$

and an operator $A_\lambda : K_2 \to B$,

$$(A_\lambda y)(\varrho) = \lambda \sum_{s=d_1+2}^{d_2} \mathfrak{W}(\varrho,s)f(s,y(s)).$$

Lemma 2. *If $y \in K_2$, then $A_\lambda y \in K_2$.*

Proof. Indeed, let $y \in K_2$. From the definition of the operator and from (5), we deduce that $A_\lambda y \geq 0$ for all $\varrho \in \mathbb{N}_{d_1+2}^{d_2}$. Moreover,

$$\min_{\varrho\in\mathbb{N}_{d_1+2}^{d_2}} A_\lambda y(\varrho) \geq \lambda m \sum_{s=d_1+2}^{d_2} f(s,y(s)) \geq \lambda\frac{m}{M} \sum_{s=d_1+2}^{d_2} \max_{\varrho\in\mathbb{N}_{d_1+2}^{d_2}} \mathfrak{W}(\varrho,s)f(s,y(s)) = \frac{m}{M}\|A_\lambda y\|.$$

□

Now, our first existence result for this case is

Theorem 7. *Let $f_0(\varrho)$ and $f_\infty(\varrho)$ be nonnegative functions for all $\varrho \in \mathbb{N}_{d_1+2}^{d_2}$, and there is $0 < r < R$ such that for $\varrho \in \mathbb{N}_{d_1+2}^{d_2}$,*

$$f(\varrho, s) \leq s f_0(\varrho) \text{ for } s \in [0, r] \text{ and } f(\varrho, s) \geq s f_\infty(\varrho) \text{ for } s \geq R$$

and

$$M^2 \sum_{s=d_1+2}^{d_2} f_0(s) \leq m^2 \sum_{s=d_1+2}^{d_2} f_\infty(s).$$

Then, for each

$$\frac{M}{m^2 \sum_{s=d_1+2}^{d_2} f_\infty(s)} \leq \lambda \leq \frac{1}{M \sum_{s=d_1+2}^{d_2} f_0(s)}, \tag{10}$$

problem (9) *and* (2) *possess a positive solution* y. *Moreover, for all* $\varrho \in \mathbb{N}_{d_1+2}^{d_2}$,

$$\frac{mr}{M} \leq y(\varrho) \leq \frac{MR}{m}. \tag{11}$$

Proof. Let λ be such that (10) holds, and let $y \in K_2$ with $\|y\| = r$. For $s \in [0, r]$, one can deduce that

$$A_\lambda y(\varrho) \leq \lambda M \sum_{s=d_1+2}^{d_2} f(s, y(s)) \leq \lambda M \sum_{s=d_1+2}^{d_2} y(s) f_0(s) \leq \lambda M \|y\| \sum_{s=d_1+2}^{d_2} f_0(s) \leq \|y\|.$$

As a result, we prove that $\|A_\lambda y\| \leq \|y\|$ for $y \in K_2 \cap \partial\Omega_1$, with $\Omega_1 = \{y \in B, \|y\| < r\}$.

Next, set $R_1 = \frac{MR}{m}$ and $\Omega_2 = \{y \in B, \|y\| < R_1\}$. It is easy to verify that for $y \in K_2 \cap \partial\Omega_2$,

$$\min_{\varrho \in \mathbb{N}_{d_1+1}^{d_2}} y(\varrho) \geq \frac{m}{M}\|y\| = \frac{m}{M} R_1 = R.$$

Hence,

$$A_\lambda y(\varrho) \geq \lambda m \sum_{s=d_1+2}^{d_2} f(s, y(s)) \geq \lambda m \sum_{s=d_1+2}^{d_2} y(s) f_\infty(s) \geq \lambda \frac{m^2}{M} \|y\| \sum_{s=d_1+2}^{d_2} f_\infty(s) \geq \|y\|.$$

In other words, $\|A_\lambda y\| \geq \|y\|$ for $y \in K_2 \cap \partial\Omega_2$. Using Theorem 2, it follows that A has a fixed point in $y \in K_2 \cap (\overline{\Omega}_2 \backslash \Omega_1)$, which is a solution of (9) and (2) satisfying (11). □

Corollary 1. *Suppose that*

$$\lim_{s \to 0^+} \frac{f(\varrho, s)}{s} = f_0(\varrho) \text{ and } \lim_{s \to +\infty} \frac{f(\varrho, s)}{s} = f_\infty(\varrho) \text{ for } \varrho \in \mathbb{N}_{d_1+2}^{d_2},$$

and

$$M^2 \sum_{s=d_1+2}^{d_2} f_0(s) < m^2 \sum_{s=d_1+2}^{d_2} f_\infty(s).$$

Hence, for each

$$\frac{M}{m^2 \sum_{s=d_1+2}^{d_2} f_\infty(s)} < \lambda < \frac{1}{M \sum_{s=d_1+2}^{d_2} f_0(s)},$$

problem (9) *and* (2) *has at least one positive solution* y.

Proof. Suppose that λ is the interval stated above and set as $\epsilon > 0$ such that

$$\frac{M}{m^2 \sum_{s=d_1+2}^{d_2} (f_\infty(s) - \delta(s))} \leq \lambda \leq \frac{1}{M \sum_{s=d_1+2}^{d_2} (f_0(s) + \epsilon)},$$

with $\delta(s) = \min\{\epsilon, f_\infty(s)\}$. Hence, for this choice of δ, there is $0 < r < R$ such that

$$f(\varrho, s) \leq s(f_0(\varrho) + \epsilon) \text{ for } s \in [0, r], \text{ and } f(\varrho, s) \geq s(f_\infty(\varrho) - \delta(\varrho)) \text{ for } s \geq R.$$

Having these conditions, one can use Theorem 7 in order to verify that there is a positive solution y for (9) and (2). □

Our second main existence result states the following:

Theorem 8. *If $f_0(\varrho)$ and $f_\infty(\varrho)$ are nonnegative functions for all $\varrho \in \mathbb{N}_{d_1+2}^{d_2}$ and there is $0 < r < R$ such that for $\varrho \in \mathbb{N}_{d_1+2}^{d_2}$,*

$$f(\varrho, s) \geq s f_0(\varrho) \text{ for } s \in [0, r], \text{ and } f(\varrho, s) \leq s f_\infty(\varrho) \text{ for } s \geq R$$

and

$$M^2 \sum_{s=d_1+2}^{d_2} f_\infty(s) \leq m^2 \sum_{s=d_1+2}^{d_2} f_0(s).$$

Then, for each

$$\frac{M}{m^2 \sum_{s=d_1+2}^{d_2} f_0(s)} \leq \lambda \leq \frac{1}{M \sum_{s=d_1+2}^{d_2} f_\infty(s)},$$

problem (9) and (2) has at least one positive solution y such that for all $\varrho \in \mathbb{N}_{d_1+2}^{d_2}$, we have $\frac{mr}{M} \leq y(\varrho) \leq \frac{MR}{m}$.

Proof. One can easily verify this result using similar arguments as the ones given for the proof of Theorem 7. □

Corollary 2. *Suppose that*

$$\lim_{s \to 0^+} \frac{f(\varrho, s)}{s} = f_0(\varrho) \text{ and } \lim_{s \to +\infty} \frac{f(\varrho, s)}{s} = f_\infty(\varrho) \text{ for } \varrho \in \mathbb{N}_{d_1+2}^{d_2}$$

and

$$M^2 \sum_{s=d_1+2}^{d_2} f_\infty(s) \leq m^2 \sum_{s=d_1+2}^{d_2} f_0(s).$$

Then, for each

$$\frac{M}{m^2 \sum_{s=d_1+2}^{d_2} f_0(s)} < \lambda < \frac{1}{M \sum_{s=d_1+2}^{d_2} f_\infty(s)},$$

we find that (9) and (2) possesses a positive solution y.

Proof. We omit it, as it follows from Theorem 8. □

5. Examples

Now, we are going to establish three numerical examples to validate our theoretical findings.

Example 1. *Let us study (1) and (2) with $d_1 = 0$, $d_2 = 5$, $\nu = 1.5$, $\mu = 0.5$, $g(u) = u^2$ and $f(\varrho) = \varrho$. Clearly, g satisfies condition (G1). Then, $\mathcal{F}_* = 2$ and $\mathcal{F}^* = 5$, so*

$$\mathfrak{W}^* = \frac{(d_2 - d_1 - 1)\Gamma(d_2 - d_1 + \nu - 2)\Gamma(\nu - \mu)}{\Gamma(\nu)\Gamma(d_2 - d_1 + \nu - \mu - 1)} = \frac{2\Gamma(4.5)}{\Gamma(1.5)} = 26.25.$$

If we choose $\epsilon = \frac{1}{2}$ *and* $C_1 = 3$*, then* $\mathcal{F}^*\epsilon < C_1\mathcal{F}_*$ *is true. Thus, by Theorem 3, for each*

$$\lambda \in \left(\frac{1}{630}, \frac{1}{262.5}\right),$$

we deduce that (1) *and* (2) *possess a positive solution.*

Example 2. *Consider* (1) *and* (2) *with* $d_1 = 0$, $d_2 = 5$, $\nu = 1.5$, $\mu = 0.5$, $g(u) = ue^{-u}$ *and* $f(\varrho) = \varrho$*. Clearly,* g *satisfies condition (G3) with* $g_0 = 1 < +\infty$ *and* $g_\infty = 0 < +\infty$*. Then,* $m = 1$, $\mathcal{F}_* = 2$, $\mathcal{F}^* = 5$*, and* $\mathfrak{W}^* = 26.25$*, so*

$$\lambda_1 = \frac{1}{525}.$$

Therefore, by Theorem 5, for all $\lambda \in (0, \lambda_1)$*, problem* (1) *and* (2) *have no positive solutions.*

Example 3. *Consider* (9) *and* (2) *with* $d_1 = 0$, $d_2 = 5$, $\nu = 1.5$, $\mu = 0.75$*, and* $f = u(e^{-\varrho} + e^{-u})$*. Hence,*

$$f_0 = e^{-\varrho} + 1 \text{ and } f_\infty = e^{-\varrho}.$$

Also,

$$M = \frac{\Gamma(5.5)\Gamma(0.75)}{\Gamma(1.5)\Gamma(4.75)} - 1 = 3.3636$$

and

$$m = \min\left\{\frac{(4)}{(4.75)}, \frac{\Gamma(5.5)\Gamma(0.75)}{\Gamma(1.5)\Gamma(4.75)} - \frac{\Gamma(4.5)}{\Gamma(4)\Gamma(1.5)}\right\} = 0.8421.$$

Furthermore,

$$(3.3636)^2 \sum_{s=2}^{5} e^{-s} \leq (0.8421)^2 \sum_{s=2}^{5} (e^{-s} + 1).$$

Thus, by Corollary 2, for each

$$\frac{3.3636}{(0.8421)^2 \sum_{s=2}^{5} (e^{-s} + 1)} < \lambda < \frac{1}{(3.3636) \sum_{s=2}^{5} e^{-s}},$$

that is,

$$\lambda \in (1.1266, 1.4144),$$

problem (9) *and* (2) *has at least one positive solution.*

6. Conclusions

In this work we were able to deduce new important properties of the Green's function related to the considered problem (1) and (2). Depending on the values of ν and μ, we studied two cases, and for each one of them, we obtained suitable conditions, under which we have shown some existence results. In the end, we were able to show the applicability of these theoretical findings with some particular examples. As far as we know, this is the first research study where such results are established for this problem.

According to us, the above-mentioned results can be extended in some future works, where the authors may study both cases, and using different methods, they may obtain different existence results or multiplicity.

Author Contributions: Conceptualization, N.D.D. and J.M.J.; methodology, N.D.D. and J.M.J.; software, N.D.D. and J.M.J.; validation, N.D.D. and J.M.J.; formal analysis, N.D.D. and J.M.J.; investigation, N.D.D. and J.M.J.; resources, N.D.D. and J.M.J.; data curation, N.D.D. and J.M.J.; writing—original draft preparation, N.D.D. and J.M.J.; writing—review and editing, N.D.D. and

J.M.J.; visualization, N.D.D. and J.M.J.; supervision, N.D.D. and J.M.J.; project administration, N.D.D. and J.M.J.; funding acquisition, N.D.D. All authors have read and agreed to the published version of the manuscript.

Funding: This research was financed by the European Union-NextGenerationEU through the National Recovery and Resilience Plan of the Republic of Bulgaria, project BG-RRP-2.013-0001-C01.

Data Availability Statement: Data are contained within this article.

Acknowledgments: The authors thank the anonymous referees for their useful comments that have contributed to improving this paper.

Conflicts of Interest: The authors declare no conflicts of interest.

References

1. Ferreira, R.A.C. *Discrete Fractional Calculus and Fractional Difference Equations*; Springer Briefs in Mathematics; Springer: Cham, Switzerland, 2022.
2. Goodrich, C.; Peterson, A.C. *Discrete Fractional Calculus*; Springer: Cham, Switzerland, 2015.
3. Kilbas, A.; Srivastava, H.; Trujillo, J. *Theory and Applications of Fractional Differential Equations*; North-Holland Mathematics Studies; Elsevier Science B.V.: Amsterdam, The Netherlands, 2006.
4. Kostic, M. *Almost Periodic Type Solutions to Integro-Differential-Difference Equations*; Walter de Gruyter: Berlin, Germany, 2025.
5. Atici, F.M.; Atici, M.; Nguyen, N.; Zhoroev, T.; Koch, G. A study on discrete and discrete fractional pharmacokinetics-pharmacodynamics models for tumor growth and anti-cancer effects. *Comput. Math. Biophys.* **2019**, *7*, 10–24. [CrossRef]
6. Podlubny, I. *Fractional Differential Equations. An Introduction to Fractional Derivatives, Fractional Differential Equations, to Methods of Their Solution and Some of Their Applications. Mathematics in Science and Engineering*; Academic Press, Inc.: San Diego, CA, USA, 1999.
7. Ostalczyk, P. *Discrete Fractional Calculus. Applications in Control and Image Processing*; Series in Computer Vision; World Scientific Publishing Co. Pte. Ltd.: Hackensack, NJ, USA, 2016.
8. Gil, M.I. *Difference Equations in Normed Spaces: Stability and Oscillation*; North HolandMathematics Studies; Elsevier : Amsterdam, The Netherlands, 2007; Volume 206.
9. Ahrendt, K.; Kissler, C. Green's function for higher-order boundary value problems involving a nabla Caputo fractional operator. *J. Differ. Equ. Appl.* **2019**, *25*, 788–800. [CrossRef]
10. Gholami, Y.; Ghanbari, K. Coupled systems of fractional ∇-difference boundary value problems. *Differ. Equ. Appl.* **2016**, *8*, 459–470. [CrossRef]
11. Ikram, A. Lyapunov inequalities for nabla Caputo boundary value problems. *J. Differ. Equ. Appl.* **2019**, *25*, 757–775. [CrossRef]
12. Liu, X.; Jia, B.; Gensler, S.; Erbe, L.; Peterson, A. Convergence of approximate solutions to nonlinear Caputo nabla fractional difference equations with boundary conditions. *Electron. J. Differ. Equ.* **2020**, *2020*, 1–19. [CrossRef]
13. Peterson, A.; Hu, W. Caputo nabla fractional boundary value problems. In *Progress on Difference Equations and Discrete Dynamical Systems: 25th ICDEA, London, UK, 24–28 June 2019*; Springer Proceedings in Mathematics & Statistics; Springer: Cham, Switzerland, 2020; Volume 341.
14. Atici, F.M.; Eloe, P.W. Two-point boundary value problems for finite fractional difference equations. *J. Differ. Equ. Appl.* **2011**, *17*, 445–456. [CrossRef]
15. Cabada, A.; Dimitrov, N. Nontrivial solutions of non-autonomous Dirichlet fractional discrete problems. *Fract. Calc. Appl. Anal.* **2020**, *23*, 980–995. [CrossRef]
16. Chen, C.; Bohner, M.; Jia, B. Existence and uniqueness of solutions for nonlinear Caputo fractional difference equations. *Turk. J. Math.* **2020**, *44*, 857–869. [CrossRef]
17. Henderson, J.; Neugebauer, J.T. Existence of local solutions for fractional difference equations with left focal boundary conditions. *Fract. Calc. Appl. Anal.* **2021**, *24*, 324–331. [CrossRef]
18. Atici, F.M.; Eloe, P.W. Discrete fractional calculus with the nabla operator. *Electron. J. Qual. Theory Differ. Equ.* **2009**, *I*, 1–12. [CrossRef]
19. Cabada, A.; Dimitrov, N.D.; Jonnalagadda, J.M. Non-trivial solutions of non-autonomous nabla fractional difference boundary value problems. *Symmetry* **2021**, *13*, 1101. [CrossRef]
20. Dimitrov, N.D.; Jonnalagadda, J.M. Existence, uniqueness and stability of solutions of a nabla fractional difference equations. *Fractal Fract* **2024**, *8*, 591. [CrossRef]
21. Li, Q.; Liu, Y.; Zhou, L. Fractional boundary value problem with nabla difference equation. *J. Appl. Anal. Comput.* **2021**, *11*, 911–919. [CrossRef] [PubMed]

22. Jonnalagadda, J.M. An ordering on Green's function and a Lyapunov-type inequality for a family of nabla fractional boundary value problems. *Fract. Diff. Calc.* **2019**, *9*, 109–124. [CrossRef]
23. Agarwal, R.; Meehan, M.; O'Regan, D. *Fixed Point Theory and Applications*; Cambridge University Press: Cambridge, UK, 2001.

fractal and fractional

MDPI

Article

New Results on a Nonlocal Sturm–Liouville Eigenvalue Problem with Fractional Integrals and Fractional Derivatives

Yunyang Zhang, Shaojie Chen and Jing Li *

School of Mathematics and Statistics, Shandong University, Weihai 264209, China; 202417850@mail.sdu.edu.cn (Y.Z.); 202217791@mail.sdu.edu.cn (S.C.)
* Correspondence: xlijing@sdu.edu.cn

Abstract: In this paper, we investigate the eigenvalue properties of a nonlocal Sturm–Liouville equation involving fractional integrals and fractional derivatives under different boundary conditions. Based on these properties, we obtained the geometric multiplicity of eigenvalues for the nonlocal Sturm–Liouville problem with a non-Dirichlet boundary condition. Furthermore, we discussed the continuous dependence of the eigenvalues on the potential function for a nonlocal Sturm–Liouville equation under a Dirichlet boundary condition.

Keywords: nonlocal Sturm–Liouville problem; fractional derivative; fractional integral; continuous dependence of eigenvalues; two-parameter method

1. Introduction

This paper discuss the nonlocal Sturm–Liouville problem

$$-y'' + q(x)y + \mu(D_{1-}^{\alpha} I_{0+}^{\alpha} + I_{1-}^{\alpha} D_{0+}^{\alpha})y = \lambda y \tag{1}$$

subject to

$$y(0) = 0 = y(1) + dy'(1), \tag{2}$$

where D_{0+}^{α} (D_{1-}^{α}) denotes the left-sided (right-sided) Riemann–Liouville fractional derivatives of order α, and $I_{0+}^{\alpha}(I_{1-}^{\alpha})$ represents the left-sided (right-sided) Riemann–Liouville fractional integrals of order α, whose definitions are given later. Here, $0 < \alpha < 1$, $q(x) \in L^2(0,1)$ is a real-valued potential function, μ and d are real constants, and λ is the spectral parameter.

From the eigenvalue properties of a class of nonlocal Sturm–Liouville problems in [1], it is known that for $0 < \alpha < 1/2$

$$\begin{cases} -y''(x) + q(x)y(x) + \mu(D_{1-}^{\alpha} I_{0+}^{\alpha} + I_{1-}^{\alpha} D_{0+}^{\alpha})y(x) = \lambda y(x) \quad \text{on } (0,1), \\ y(0) = 0 = y(1). \end{cases} \tag{3}$$

has real algebraic simple and discrete eigenvalues under certain conditions. These eigenvalues satisfy

$$-\infty < \lambda_1(\mu) < \lambda_2(\mu) < \cdots < \lambda_n(\mu) < \cdots, \ \lambda_n(\mu) \sim \pi^2 n^2, \ n \to \infty, \tag{4}$$

where $\lambda_n(\mu)$ is the n-th eigenvalue of (3). Additionally, the associated eigenfunctions form a complete orthogonal basis. Furthermore, [1] discusses the number of zeros present in the eigenfunctions, as well as the characteristics of solutions to the nonlocal Sturm–Liouville equation under specific initial conditions.

Nonlocal Sturm–Liouville problems, which incorporate both left-sided and right-sided fractional derivatives, arise from the field of nonlocal continuum mechanics (please refer to [2–5] for more details). In reference [4], the equilibrium equation governing an elastic bar of finite length, L, which includes long-range interactions among non-adjacent particles, can be expressed as

$$\frac{d^2u(x)}{dx} - \frac{\eta}{E}\mathcal{D}^{\alpha}u(x) = -\frac{f(x)}{E}.$$

Here, $u(x)$ denotes the axial displacement of the bar at position x, while $f(x)$ represents the longitudinal force per unit volume and η is an opportune constant of proportionality. E signifies the longitudinal modulus, and $\mathcal{D}^{\alpha} = D^{\alpha}_{0+} + D^{\alpha}_{1-}$, where D^{α}_{0+} and D^{α}_{1-} correspond to the left and right Riemann–Liouville fractional derivatives of order α, respectively.

Generally, a nonlocal Sturm–Liouville problem is characterized as a Sturm–Liouville-type problem that contains both integer and fractional derivatives, a topic that was the subject of extensive investigation in [6–10]. The form explored in [6–10] can be summarized as follows:

$$-y'' + q(x)y + \mu T_{\alpha}y = \lambda y,$$

where T_{α} is a self-adjoint fractional differential operator with both left-sided and right-sided fractional derivatives, such as $T_{\alpha} = D^{\alpha}_{0+} + D^{\alpha}_{1-}$, or $T_{\alpha} = D^{\alpha}_{0+}\,{}^{c}D^{\alpha}_{1-}$.

Additionally, the fractional Sturm–Liouville problem, which is closely related to the nonlocal Sturm–Liouville problem, is often obtained by replacing the integer derivative operators in a classical Sturm–Liouville problem, $-(p(x)y')' + q(x)y = \lambda\omega(x)y$, by the fractional derivative operators, such as

$$\mathcal{L}_{\alpha}y + q(x)y = \lambda\omega(x)y,$$

where $\mathcal{L}_{\alpha} = {}^{c}D^{\alpha}_{b-}(p(x)D^{\alpha}_{a+})$, or $\mathcal{L}_{\alpha} = D^{\alpha}_{a+}(p(x){}^{c}D^{\alpha}_{b-})$. For more details, please refer to [11–23] and reference therein. In [23] the authors employ a change of variables to transform ${}^{c}D^{\alpha}_{b-}(p(x)D^{\alpha}_{a+}) + q(x)y = \lambda\omega(x)y$ into a modified version of a differential equation with a principal term structured in the classical form $-(p(x)z')' + D^{1-\alpha}_{b-}((q(x) - \lambda\omega(x))D^{1-\alpha}_{a+}z) = 0$. Thereafter, the resulting equation is similar to the one considered in this manuscript.

In this study, we present novel findings on the eigenvalue properties of (1)–(2). We first consider the eigenvalue problem of (1)–(2) with $d \neq 0$ in Section 3. We obtained results showing that the eigenvalues of (1)–(2) with $d \neq 0$ are real values, and the corresponding eigenfunctions are orthogonal. Moreover the geometric multiplicity of the eigenvalues is simple. Then we discuss the eigenvalue problem of (1)–(2) with $d = 0$ in Section 4. We introduced an auxiliary two-parameter nonlocal Sturm–Liouville problem in Section 4.1. With the aid of the eigenvalue properties of this two-parameter nonlocal Sturm–Liouville problem, we obtained the continuous dependence of eigenvalues on the potential function in Section 4.2.

2. Preliminaries

In this section, we give some preliminary knowledge from such topics as fractional calculus and the spectral theory of nonlocal Sturm–Liouville problems, which will be used later. More detailed information can be found in [1,24].

We denote by $AC[0,1]$ the set of all the absolutely continuous, complex-valued functions on [0,1]. Let $L^2 = L^2(0,1)$ be the Hilbert space, with the usual inner product $\langle f, g\rangle$ and the norm $||f|| = \langle f, f\rangle^{1/2}$.

Definition 1. ($cf.$ [24] p. 69) *The Riemann–Liouville fractional integrals $I^{\alpha}_{0+}f$ and $I^{\alpha}_{1-}f$ of order $\alpha \in \mathbb{C}$ ($R(\alpha) > 0$) are defined by*

$$(I^{\alpha}_{0+}f)(x) = \frac{1}{\Gamma(\alpha)}\int_0^x \frac{f(t)}{(x-t)^{1-\alpha}}dt,\ x \in (0,1];\ (I^{\alpha}_{1-}f)(x) = \frac{1}{\Gamma(\alpha)}\int_x^1 \frac{f(t)}{(t-x)^{1-\alpha}}dt,\ x \in [0,1),$$

where $\Gamma(\alpha)$ is the Gamma function. These integrals are called the left-sided and the right-sided fractional integrals.

Definition 2. ($cf.$ [24] p. 70) *Let $0 < \alpha < 1$, $D = d/dx$. The left-sided and right-sided Riemann–Liouville derivatives of order α are defined by (when they exist)*

$$(D^{\alpha}_{0+}f)(x) = D(I^{1-\alpha}_{0+}f)(x) = \frac{\frac{d}{dx}\left(\int_0^x \frac{f(t)}{(x-t)^{\alpha}}dt\right)}{\Gamma(1-\alpha)}, x \in (0,1];$$
$$(D^{\alpha}_{1-}f)(x) = (-D)(I^{1-\alpha}_{1-}f)(x) = \frac{-\frac{d}{dx}\left(\int_x^1 \frac{f(t)}{(t-x)^{\alpha}}dt\right)}{\Gamma(1-\alpha)}, x \in [0,1).$$

Proposition 1. ($cf.$ [1] Theorem 4.1) *If $|\mu| < \frac{\Gamma(2-\alpha)\Gamma(1+\alpha)}{e^{\int_0^1 |q(t)|dt}(1+6e^{\int_0^1 |q(t)|dt})}$, then the nonlocal initial value problem*

$$\begin{cases} -y''(x) + (q(x)-\lambda)y(x) + \mu(D^{\alpha}_{1-}I^{\alpha}_{0+} + I^{\alpha}_{1-}D^{\alpha}_{0+})y(x) = 0, \quad y \in \underline{D}, \\ y(0) = k_1,\ y'(0) = k_2, \end{cases} \tag{5}$$

has, at most, one solution, where μ, k_1, k_2, and $\lambda > 0$ are real constants, and $\underline{D} = \{y \in L^2 : y, y' \in AC[0,1]\}$.

Proposition 2. ($cf.$ [1] Theorem 3.11) *There exists $\mu_0 > 0$, such that for $|\mu| < \mu_0$, all the eigenvalues of $-y'' + q(x)y + \mu(D^{\alpha}_{1-}I^{\alpha}_{0+} + I^{\alpha}_{1-}D^{\alpha}_{0+})y = \lambda y$ subject to $y(0) = 0 = y(1)$ are simple and satisfy*

$$-\infty < \lambda_1(\mu) < \lambda_2(\mu) < \cdots < \lambda_n(\mu) < \cdots,\ \lambda_n(\mu) \sim \pi^2 n^2,\ n \to \infty. \tag{6}$$

Definition 3. ($cf.$ [25] p.375) *Let $\mathcal{C}(X,Y)$ denote the set of all closed operators from X to Y. A family, $T(\kappa) \in \mathcal{C}(X,Y)$, defined for κ in a domain D_0 of the complex plane, is said to be holomorphic of type (A) if*

(i) *$\mathcal{D}(T(\kappa)) = \mathcal{D}$ is independent of κ;*
(ii) *$T(\kappa)u$ is holomorphic for $\kappa \in \mathcal{D}_0$ for every $u \in \mathcal{D}$.*

Proposition 3. ($cf.$ [25] Theorem 2.6) *Let T be a closable operator from X to Y, with $\mathcal{D}(T) = \mathcal{D}$. Let $T^{(n)}, n = 1,2,\cdots$ be operators from X to Y with domains containing $\mathcal{D}$, and let there be constants $a, b, c \geq 0$ such that*

$$\|T^{(n)}u\| \leq c^{n-1}(a\|u\| + b\|Tu\|), u \in \mathcal{D}, n = 1,2,\cdots \tag{7}$$

Then the series

$$T(\kappa)u = Tu + \kappa T^{(1)}u + \kappa^2 T^{(2)}u + \cdots, u \in \mathcal{D}$$

defines an operator, $T(\kappa)$, with domain $\mathcal{D}$ for $|\kappa| < 1/c$. If $|\kappa| < \frac{1}{b+c}$, $T(\kappa)$ is closable and the closures $\widetilde{T}(\kappa)$ for such κ form a holomorphic family of type (A).

3. Eigenvalue Problem with Non-Dirichlet Boundary Condition and $0 < \alpha < 1$

In this section, we consider the eigenvalue problem

$$\begin{cases} -y''(x) + q(x)y(x) + \mu(D^{\alpha}_{1-}I^{\alpha}_{0+} + I^{\alpha}_{1-}D^{\alpha}_{0+})y(x) = \lambda y(x) \quad \text{on } (0,1), \\ y(0) = 0 = y(1) + dy'(1), \end{cases} \tag{8}$$

where $d \neq 0$ is a real constant, and $0 < \alpha < 1$.

The fractional operator $\widetilde{T}$, associated with (8), is defined by

$$\begin{aligned} &\widetilde{T}y = -y'' + qy + \mu T_{\alpha}y, T_{\alpha}y := (D^{\alpha}_{1-}I^{\alpha}_{0+} + I^{\alpha}_{1-}D^{\alpha}_{0+})y, y \in \mathcal{D}(\widetilde{T}), \\ &\mathcal{D}(\widetilde{T}) := \{y \in L^2 : y, y' \in AC[0,1], y(0) = 0 = y(1) + dy'(1)\}. \end{aligned} \tag{9}$$

Proposition 4. *For $y_1, y_2 \in \mathcal{D}(\widetilde{T})$, it holds that*

$$\int_0^1 y_1(x) \cdot \widetilde{T}y_2(x)dx = \int_0^1 y_2(x) \cdot \widetilde{T}y_1(x)dx. \tag{10}$$

Proof. If $y_1, y_2 \in \mathcal{D}(\widetilde{T})$, by the definition of operator $\widetilde{T}$, we have $y_1(0) = 0 = dy_1'(1) + y_1(1)$

$$\begin{aligned} &\int_0^1 y_1(x) \cdot \widetilde{T}y_2(x)dx = \int_0^1 y_1(x) \cdot [-y_2''(x) + q(x)y_2(x) + \mu T_{\alpha}y_2(x)]dx \\ &= y_1(0)y_2'(0) - y_1(1)y_2'(1) + \int_0^1 y_1'(x)y_2'(x)dx + \int_0^1 q(x)y_1(x)y_2(x)dx + \mu \int_0^1 y_1(x)T_{\alpha}y_2(x)dx \\ &= dy_1'(1)y_2'(1) + \int_0^1 y_1'(x)y_2'(x)dx + \int_0^1 q(x)y_1(x)y_2(x)dx + \mu \int_0^1 y_1(x)T_{\alpha}y_2(x)dx \end{aligned}$$

and

$$\begin{aligned} &\int_0^1 y_2(x) \cdot \widetilde{T}y_1(x)dx = \int_0^1 y_2(x) \cdot [-y_1''(x) + q(x)y_1(x) + \mu T_{\alpha}y_1(x)]dx \\ &= dy_2'(1)y_1'(1) + \int_0^1 y_2'(x)y_1'(x)dx + \int_0^1 q(x)y_2(x)y_1(x)dx + \mu \int_0^1 y_2(x)T_{\alpha}y_1(x)dx. \end{aligned}$$

It follows from $y_1, y_2 \in \mathcal{D}(\mathcal{L})$ that $y_1(0) = 0 = y_2(0)$. By integrating by parts and exchanging the order of integration, we get

$$\begin{aligned} &\int_0^1 y_1(x)T_{\alpha}y_2(x)dx = -\frac{1}{\Gamma(\alpha)\Gamma(1-\alpha)} \int_0^1 y_1(x)\frac{d}{dx}\left(\int_x^1 (t-x)^{-\alpha} \int_0^t \frac{y_2(s)}{(t-s)^{1-\alpha}}dsdt\right)dx \\ &+\frac{1}{\Gamma(\alpha)\Gamma(1-\alpha)} \int_0^1 y_1(x)\left(\int_x^1 (t-x)^{\alpha-1}\frac{d}{dt}\int_0^t \frac{y_2(s)}{(t-s)^{\alpha}}dsdt\right)dx \\ &= \frac{1}{\Gamma(\alpha)\Gamma(1-\alpha)} \int_0^1 \left(\int_0^t (t-s)^{\alpha-1}y_2(s)ds\right)\left(\int_0^t (t-x)^{-\alpha}y_1'(x)dx\right)dt \\ &+\frac{1}{\Gamma(\alpha)\Gamma(1-\alpha)} \int_0^1 \left(\int_0^t (t-x)^{\alpha-1}y_1(x)dx\right)\left(\int_0^t (t-s)^{-\alpha}y_2'(s)ds\right)dt \\ &= \int_0^1 y_2(x)T_{\alpha}y_1(x)dx, \end{aligned}$$

for $y_1, y_2 \in \mathcal{D}(\widetilde{T})$, which proves (10). □

Theorem 1. *The eigenvalues of the nonlocal Sturm–Liouville eigenvalue problem* (8) *are real numbers.*

Proof. Let λ be an eigenvalue for (8) corresponding to eigenfunction y. Then for y and its complex conjugate $\overline{y}$, we obtain

$$\widetilde{T}y = \lambda y,\ y(0) = 0 = y(1) + dy'(1), \tag{11}$$

and

$$\widetilde{T}\overline{y} = \overline{\lambda}\overline{y},\ \overline{y}(0) = 0 = \overline{y}(1) + d\overline{y}'(1). \tag{12}$$

Multiplying two sides of (11) by $\overline{y}$ and integrating on the interval $[0,1]$, we get

$$\int_0^1 \overline{y}(x)\widetilde{T}y(x)dx = \lambda \int_0^1 y(x)\overline{y}(x)dx. \tag{13}$$

A similar method for (12) leads to the relation

$$\int_0^1 y(x)\widetilde{T}\overline{y}(x)dx = \overline{\lambda} \int_0^1 y(x)\overline{y}(x)dx. \tag{14}$$

Using Proposition 4, the following identity is worked out using (13) and (14),

$$(\lambda - \overline{\lambda}) \int_0^1 y(x)\overline{y}(x)dx = (\lambda - \overline{\lambda}) \int_0^1 |y(x)|^2 dx = 0.$$

Since y is a nontrivial solution, $||y||^2 > 0$. Then $\lambda = \overline{\lambda}$ implies that the eigenvalue of (8) is a real number. □

Theorem 2. *The eigenfunctions of the nonlocal Sturm–Liouville eigenvalue problem* (8) *corresponding to the distinct eigenvalues are orthogonal on the interval* $[0,1]$.

Proof. Let λ_1 and λ_2 be two distinct eigenvalues and y_1 and y_2 be the corresponding eigenfunctions. Then we obtain

$$\widetilde{T}y_1 = \lambda_1 y_1, \tag{15}$$

and

$$\widetilde{T}y_2 = \lambda_2 y_2. \tag{16}$$

Multiplying both sides of (15) by y_2 and (16) by y_1 implies the identity

$$y_2(x)\widetilde{T}y_1(x) - y_1(x)\widetilde{T}y_2(x) = (\lambda_1 - \lambda_2)y_1(x)y_2(x). \tag{17}$$

Integrating (17) on the interval $[0,1]$, we obtain the relationship

$$\int_0^1 (y_2(x)\widetilde{T}y_1(x) - y_1(x)\widetilde{T}y_2(x))dx = (\lambda_1 - \lambda_2) \int_0^1 y_1(x)y_2(x)dx.$$

According to Proposition 4, the Formula (10) leads to the equation

$$(\lambda_1 - \lambda_2) \int_0^1 y_1(x)y_2(x)dx = 0,$$

which implies that $\int_0^1 y_1(x)y_2(x)dx = 0$ as $\lambda_1 \neq \lambda_2$. This is exactly what we want to prove. □

The following theorem obtained the geometric multiplicity of the eigenvalues for the nonlocal Sturm–Liouville problem (8).

Theorem 3. *The eigenvalues of the nonlocal Sturm–Liouville eigenvalue problem* (8) *are simple for* $|\mu| < \frac{1}{7}\Gamma(2-\alpha)(1+\alpha)$ *and* $\lambda > 0$.

Proof. Let $\psi_1(x)$ and $\psi_2(x)$ be the two eigenfunctions of the eigenvalue problem (8), with the corresponding eigenvalue being λ_0.

Denote

$$\psi(x) = \psi_1(x) - c\psi_2(x),$$

where c is an arbitrary constant.

It follows from (8) that $\psi(0) = 0$. One can check that $\psi'(x) = \psi_1'(x) - c\psi_2'(x)$.

Now we need to show that $\psi_2'(0) \neq 0$. If not, then $\psi_2(x)$ is a solution of the initial value problem (5), with $k_1 = k_2 = 0$. Hence, through Proposition 1, we conclude that $\psi_2 \equiv 0$, which is a contradiction.

Choose $c = \frac{\psi_1'(0)}{\psi_2'(0)}$. It follows that $\psi'(0) = 0$. That is, ψ satisfies the fractional initial value problem (5) with $k_1 = k_2 = 0$.

According to Proposition 1, if $|\mu| < \frac{\Gamma(2-\alpha)\Gamma(1+\alpha)}{e^{\int_0^1 |q(t)|dt}(1+6e^{\int_0^1 |q(t)|dt})} < \frac{1}{7}\Gamma(2-\alpha)(1+\alpha)$, one sees that $\psi(x) \equiv 0$ on $(0,1)$, which implies that $\psi_1(x)$ and $\psi_2(x)$ are linearly dependent on $(0,1)$, which completes the proof. □

4. Eigenvalue Problem with Dirichlet Boundary Condition and $0 < \alpha < 1/2$

Due to the limited results of the initial value theory for nonlocal Sturm–Liouville problems (1), it is not possible to study the continuous dependence of eigenvalues on potential functions using the initial value theory, as in references [26–28]. We will use the two-parameter method to conduct research below.

4.1. Eigenvalue Properties of a Two-Parameter Nonlocal Sturm–Liouville Problem

In this section, we discuss the properties of the eigenvalues of the following two-parameter nonlocal Sturm–Liouville problem

$$\begin{cases} -y''(x) + q(x)y(x) + \gamma(q_1(x) - q(x))y(x) + \mu(D_{1-}^{\alpha} I_{0+}^{\alpha} + I_{1-}^{\alpha} D_{0+}^{\alpha})y(x) = \lambda y(x), \\ y(0) = 0 = y(1), \end{cases} \tag{18}$$

where $0 < \alpha < 1/2$, $q_1, q \in L^2(0,1)$, $\gamma \in [0,1]$, λ is the spectral parameter, $\mu \in (-\mu_0, \mu_0)$ is fixed, and μ_0 is defined as in Proposition 2. These properties are important to get the continuous dependence of the eigenvalues on the potential function.

Define the fractional operator, T, by

$$Ty = -y'' + qy + \mu T_\alpha y, \ T_\alpha y := (D_{1-}^{\alpha} I_{0+}^{\alpha} + I_{1-}^{\alpha} D_{0+}^{\alpha})y, \ y \in \mathcal{D}, \tag{19}$$

where

$$\mathcal{D} := \{y \in L^2(0,1) : y, y' \in AC[0,1], -y'' + qy \in L^2(0,1), y(0) = 0 = y(1)\}. \tag{20}$$

For fixed $\mu \in (-\mu_0, \mu_0)$, assume that $\lambda_n(0)$ and $n \geq 1$ are the eigenvalues of the nonlocal Sturm–Liouville problem, $Ty = -y'' + q(x)y + \mu T_\alpha y = \lambda y$, $y(0) = 0 = y(1)$, $y \in \mathcal{D}$, which satisfies (6):

$$-\infty < \lambda_1(0) < \lambda_2(0) < \cdots < \lambda_n(0) < \cdots, \ \lambda_n(0) \sim \pi^2 n^2, \ n \to \infty.$$

Denote by $T(\gamma)$ the operator given in (18) as

$$T(\gamma)y := Ty + \gamma T_1 y = Ty + \gamma(q_1(x) - q(x))y,\ y \in \mathcal{D},\ \gamma > 0.$$

Let $\lambda_n(\gamma)$ and $n \geq 1$ be the eigenvalues of the two-parameter nonlocal Sturm–Liouville problem

$$T(\gamma)y = Ty + \gamma T_1 y = \lambda y,\ y(0) = 0 = y(1). \tag{21}$$

Theorem 4. *Let $\mu \in (-\mu_0, \mu_0)$ be fixed. There exists $\gamma_0 > 0$, such that for $0 < \gamma < \gamma_0$, all the eigenvalues of* (21) *are simple and satisfy*

$$-\infty < \lambda_1(\gamma) < \lambda_2(\gamma) < \cdots < \lambda_n(\gamma) < \cdots,\ \lambda_n(\gamma) \sim \pi^2 n^2,\ n \to \infty. \tag{22}$$

Proof. By virtue of Definition 3, Proposition 3, and discussions similar to Theorem 3.8 in [1], we can prove that $\{T(\gamma), \gamma \in \mathbb{R}\}$ is a self-adjoint holomorphic family of type (A). Then for fixed $\mu \in (-\mu_0, \mu_0)$, there exists exactly one simple eigenvalue $\lambda_n(\gamma)$ of $T(\gamma)$ near each unperturbed eigenvalue $\lambda_n(0)$ for suitably small γ, since $\lambda_n(0)$ is simple. Moreover,

$$||T_1 y|| \leq \|q_1 - q\| \|y\|.$$

Therefore, the perturbation expansion near each $\lambda_n(0)$ has a positive convergence radius, ρ_n.

According to (4.74) in ([25], p. 406), the following inequality holds

$$\rho_n \geq \left(\frac{2(a + b|\lambda_n|)}{d_n} + 2b \right)^{-1}. \tag{23}$$

Then we obtain

$$\rho_n \geq \frac{d_n}{2\|q_1 - q\|}. \tag{24}$$

Here $a = \|q_1 - q\|, b = 0$, and d_n is the isolation distance of the eigenvalue $\lambda_n(0)$, defined as

$$d_n = \min\{|\lambda_n(0) - \lambda_{n-1}(0)|, |\lambda_{n+1}(0) - \lambda_n(0)|\}. \tag{25}$$

Then, if $\gamma < \rho_n$, there exists exactly one eigenvalue $\lambda_n(\gamma)$ of $T(\gamma)$, such that

$$|\lambda_n(\gamma) - \lambda_n(0)| < d_n/2.$$

Now we will prove that there exists $\gamma_0 > 0$, such that $\rho_n \geq \gamma_0$ for all $n \geq 1$. According to Proposition 2, we have $\lambda_n(0) \sim n^2\pi^2$ as $n \to \infty$. Hence,

$$d_n \sim (2n-1)\pi^2, n \to \infty, \tag{26}$$

$$\rho_n \geq c_n := \frac{d_n}{2\|q_1 - q\|} \sim \frac{(n - \frac{1}{2})}{\|q_1 - q\|}\pi^2.$$

Let $\gamma < \delta_1$, where $\delta_1 = \frac{\pi^2}{4\|q_1 - q\|}$. Then there exists N, such that for $n > N$,

$$\rho_n \geq c_n > \delta_1 > \gamma.$$

Therefore, there exists exactly one simple eigenvalue $\lambda_n(\gamma)$ of $T(\gamma)$, such that

$$|\lambda_n(\gamma) - \lambda_n(0)| < d_n/2,\ n > N.$$

For $1 \le n \le N$, we choose

$$d_n = \min\{|\lambda_j(0) - \lambda_k(0)| : 1 \le j \ne k \le N\} := d. \tag{27}$$

By (24), we have

$$\rho_n \ge \frac{d}{2\|q_1 - q\|} := \delta_2,\ 1 \le n \le N.$$

Set $\gamma_0 = \min\{\delta_1, \delta_2\}$. Then

$$\rho_n \ge \gamma_0 \ \text{ for all } \ n \ge 1.$$

Denote by O_n the disc$|\lambda - \lambda_n(0)| < d_n/2,\ n \ge 1$. If $\gamma < \gamma_0$, then each O_n contains exactly one simple eigenvalue of $T(\gamma)$ for $n \ge 1$.

Let $\mathcal{A} = \cup_{n=1}^{\infty} O_n$. We need to prove that $\mathcal{A}$ contains all the eigenvalues of $T(\gamma)$.

Set $\widetilde{\mathcal{A}} = \mathbb{C} \setminus \mathcal{A}$. We will prove that for $\gamma < \gamma_0$, $\widetilde{\mathcal{A}} \subset P(T(\gamma))$, where $P(T(\gamma))$ is the resolvent of $T(\gamma)$.

Suppose $\lambda \in \widetilde{\mathcal{A}}$. If $\lambda \notin \mathbb{R}$, it follows from Theorem 3.8 in [1] that

$$\lambda \in P(T(\gamma)).$$

If $\lambda \in \mathbb{R}$, then for some $n \ge 1$, the following inequality holds

$$\lambda < \lambda_1(0) - d_1/2, \ \text{ or } \ \lambda_n(0) + d_n/2 < \lambda < \lambda_{n+1}(0) - d_{n+1}/2,$$

where d_n is defined as in (25) for $n > N$, and as in (27) for $1 \le n \le N$.

We now prove $\lambda \in P(T(\gamma))$.

Suppose, to the contrary, that λ is an eigenvalue of $T(\gamma)$. By Theorem 4.21 ([25], p. 408), there exist $0 < \delta < \gamma_0$ and $k \in \mathbb{N}$, such that if $\gamma < \delta$, the inequality $|\lambda - \lambda_k(0)| < d_k/2$ holds, which implies that there exists $k \in \mathbb{N}$ such that $\lambda \in O_k$.

Each O_k contains exactly one simple eigenvalue of $T(\gamma)$ for $k \ge 1$. Therefore, we obtain a contradiction. Hence, $\lambda \in P(T(\gamma))$.

For $\gamma < \gamma_0$, we obtain

$$-\infty < \lambda_n(\gamma) < \lambda_{n+1}(\gamma), n \ge 1.$$

By (25) and (27), we have

$$\lambda_n(\gamma) \sim n^2\pi^2.$$

□

4.2. The Continuous Dependence of the Eigenvalues on the Potential Function

In this section, by the aid of the two-parameter method, we investigate the continuous dependence of the eigenvalues of

$$\begin{cases} -y''(x) + q(x)y(x) + \mu(D_{1-}^{\alpha} I_{0+}^{\alpha} + I_{1-}^{\alpha} D_{0+}^{\alpha})y(x) = \lambda y(x) \quad \text{on } (0,1), \\ y(0) = 0 = y(1). \end{cases} \tag{28}$$

where $0 < \alpha < 1/2$, $q \in L^2(0,1)$, λ is the spectral parameter, $\mu \in (-\mu_0, \mu_0)$ is fixed, and μ_0 is defined as in Proposition 2.

When $\gamma = 0$, equation

$$-y''(x) + q(x)y(x) + \gamma(q_1(x) - q(x))y(x) + \mu(D_{1-}^{\alpha} I_{0+}^{\alpha} + I_{1-}^{\alpha} D_{0+}^{\alpha})y(x) = \lambda y(x)$$

degenerates into equation

$$-y''(x) + q(x)y(x) + \mu(D^{\alpha}_{1-}I^{\alpha}_{0+} + I^{\alpha}_{1-}D^{\alpha}_{0+})y(x) = \lambda y(x),$$

and when $\gamma = 1$, equation

$$-y''(x) + q(x)y(x) + \gamma(q_1(x) - q(x))y(x) + \mu(D^{\alpha}_{1-}I^{\alpha}_{0+} + I^{\alpha}_{1-}D^{\alpha}_{0+})y(x) = \lambda y(x)$$

can be transformed into

$$-y''(x) + q_1(x)y(x) + \mu(D^{\alpha}_{1-}I^{\alpha}_{0+} + I^{\alpha}_{1-}D^{\alpha}_{0+})y(x) = \lambda y(x).$$

Therefore, the continuous dependence of the eigenvalue of $-y''(x) + q(x)y(x) + \mu(D^{\alpha}_{1-}I^{\alpha}_{0+} + I^{\alpha}_{1-}D^{\alpha}_{0+})y(x)$ on the potential function $q(x)$ can be transformed into the continuous dependence of the eigenvalue of $-y''(x) + q(x)y(x) + \gamma(q_1(x) - q(x))y(x) + \mu(D^{\alpha}_{1-}I^{\alpha}_{0+} + I^{\alpha}_{1-}D^{\alpha}_{0+})y(x) = \lambda y(x)$ on the parameter γ.

Theorem 5. *Let $\mu \in (-\mu_0, \mu_0)$, $n \geq 1$, and $q_0 \in L^2(0,1)$ be fixed. For any $\varepsilon > 0$, there exists $\delta_n > 0$, such that if $||q_1 - q_0|| \leq \delta_n$ for any $q_1 \in L^2(0,1)$, then $|\lambda_{n,q_1} - \lambda_{n,q_0}| < \varepsilon$, where λ_{n,q_i} $(i = 0,1)$ are the n-th eigenvalue of $-y'' + q_i y + \mu T_\alpha y = \lambda y$ subject to $y(0) = 0 = y(1)$.*

Proof. For two-parameter nonlocal Sturm–Liouville problem

$$-y''(x) + q_0(x)y(x) + \gamma(q_1(x) - q_0(x))y(x) + \mu T_\alpha y(x) = \lambda y(x), y(0) = 0 = y(1), \quad (29)$$

$\lambda_n(\gamma)(n \geq 1)$ are corresponding eigenvalues.

It suffices to show that for any $\varepsilon > 0$, there exists $\delta_n > 0$, such that for any $q_1 \in L^2(0,1)$, if $\gamma < \delta_n$, then $|\lambda_n(\gamma) - \lambda_n(0)| < \varepsilon$.

For the sake of simplicity in writing, we dropped the variable x and the subscript n. By Theorem 4, each eigenvalue $\lambda(\gamma)$ is simple on $(0, \gamma_0)$. Choose $0 < |\Delta| \ll 1$, such that $0 < \gamma + \Delta < \gamma_0$. Assume $\lambda(\gamma)$ and $\lambda(\gamma + \Delta)$ are different eigenvalues of (29). Let eigenfunctions $\varphi(\gamma)$ and $\varphi(\gamma + \Delta)$ denote the corresponding normalized eigenfunctions of $\lambda(\gamma)$ and $\lambda(\gamma + \Delta)$, respectively. Then we obtain

$$\begin{cases} -\varphi''(\gamma) + q_0(x)\varphi(\gamma) + \gamma(q_1(x) - q_0(x))\varphi(\gamma) + \mu T_\alpha \varphi(\gamma) = \lambda(\gamma)\varphi(\gamma), \\ \varphi(0,\gamma) = 0 = \varphi(1,\gamma) \end{cases} \quad (30)$$

and

$$\begin{aligned} &-\varphi''(\gamma+\Delta) + q_0(x)\varphi(\gamma+\Delta) + (\gamma+\Delta)(q_1(x) - q_0(x))\varphi(\gamma+\Delta) + \mu T_\alpha \varphi(\gamma+\Delta) \\ &= \lambda(\gamma+\Delta)\varphi(\gamma+\Delta),\ \varphi(0,\gamma+\Delta) = 0 = \varphi(1,\gamma+\Delta). \end{aligned} \quad (31)$$

$(31)\times\varphi(\gamma) - (30)\times\varphi(\gamma+\Delta)$, and integrating on $[0, 1]$, we have

$$\begin{aligned} &(\lambda(\gamma+\Delta) - \lambda(\gamma)) \int_0^1 \varphi(\gamma)\varphi(\gamma+\Delta) \\ &= \Delta \int_0^1 (q_1(x) - q_0(x))\varphi(\gamma)\varphi(\gamma+\Delta) + \mu \int_0^1 (\varphi(\gamma)(T_\alpha\varphi(\gamma+\Delta)) - \varphi(\gamma+\Delta)(T_\alpha\varphi(\gamma))). \end{aligned} \quad (32)$$

Moreover, we obtain

$$\int_0^1 \varphi(\gamma)(T_\alpha\varphi(\gamma+\Delta)) = \int_0^1 \varphi(\gamma+\Delta)(T_\alpha\varphi(\gamma)).$$

Therefore,

$$\lambda'(\gamma) = \lim_{\Delta\to 0} \frac{\lambda(\gamma+\Delta)-\lambda(\gamma)}{\Delta} = \int_0^1 \tilde{q}\varphi^2(\gamma), \tag{33}$$

where $\tilde{q}(x) := q_1(x) - q_0(x)$.

Define

$$\tilde{Q}(x) = \int_0^x \tilde{q}(t)dt, x \in [0,1], \tilde{Q}_0 = \max_{x\in[0,1]} \{|\tilde{Q}(x)|\},$$

$$Q(x) = \int_0^x q_0(t)dt, x \in [0,1], Q_0 = \max_{x\in[0,1]} \{|Q(x)|\}.$$

Since $||\varphi(\gamma)|| = 1$, $\varphi(1,\gamma) = \varphi(0,\gamma) = 0$, then we obtain

$$|\int_0^1 \tilde{q}\varphi(\gamma)|^2 \le \frac{||\varphi'(\gamma)||^2}{4\gamma} + 4\tilde{Q}_0^2\gamma, \ |\int_0^1 q_0\varphi(\gamma)|^2 \le \frac{||\varphi'(\gamma)||^2}{4} + 4Q_0^2, \tag{34}$$

and

$$|\int_0^1 \tilde{q}\varphi(\gamma)|^2 \le \frac{||\varphi'(\gamma)||^2}{4} + 4\tilde{Q}_0^2, \tag{35}$$

Because $T_\alpha y = (D_{1-}^\alpha I_{0+}^\alpha + I_{1-}^\alpha D_{0+}^\alpha)y$, by Definitions 1 and 2, we get the relationship

$$T_\alpha y = M_\alpha \left(\frac{\int_0^1 \frac{y(s)}{(1-s)^{1-\alpha}} ds}{(1-x)^\alpha} - \int_x^1 \frac{\int_0^t \frac{\frac{d}{ds}y(s)}{(t-s)^{1-\alpha}} ds}{(t-x)^\alpha} dt + \int_x^1 \frac{\int_0^t \frac{\frac{d}{ds}y(s)}{(t-s)^{\alpha}} ds}{(t-x)^{1-\alpha}} dt \right),$$

where $M_\alpha = \frac{1}{\Gamma(\alpha)\Gamma(1-\alpha)}$. Therefore,

$$\begin{aligned} \| T_\alpha y \| \ &\le \ M_\alpha \left(\| \int_x^1 \frac{\int_0^t \frac{\frac{d}{ds}y(s)}{(t-s)^{1-\alpha}} ds}{(t-x)^\alpha} dt \| + \| \int_x^1 \frac{\int_0^t \frac{\frac{d}{ds}y(s)}{(t-s)^{\alpha}} ds}{(t-x)^{1-\alpha}} dt \| + \| \frac{\int_0^1 \frac{y(s)}{(1-s)^{1-\alpha}} ds}{(1-x)^\alpha} \| \right) \\ &= \ M_\alpha \left(\int_0^1 \left| \int_x^1 \frac{\int_0^t \frac{y'(s)}{(t-s)^{1-\alpha}} ds}{(t-x)^\alpha} dt \right|^2 dx \right)^{1/2} + M_\alpha \left(\int_0^1 \left| \int_x^1 \frac{\int_0^t \frac{y'(s)}{(t-s)^{\alpha}} ds}{(t-x)^{1-\alpha}} dt \right|^2 dx \right)^{1/2} \\ &\quad + M_\alpha \left(\int_0^1 \left| \frac{\int_0^1 \frac{y(s)}{(1-s)^{1-\alpha}} ds}{(1-x)^\alpha} \right|^2 dx \right)^{1/2}. \end{aligned}$$

Denoted by

$$C_1 = \left(\int_0^1 \left| \int_x^1 \frac{\int_0^t \frac{y'(s)}{(t-s)^{1-\alpha}} ds}{(t-x)^\alpha} dt \right|^2 dx \right)^{1/2}, \ C_2 = \left(\int_0^1 \left| \int_x^1 \frac{\int_0^t \frac{y'(s)}{(t-s)^{\alpha}} ds}{(t-x)^{1-\alpha}} dt \right|^2 dx \right)^{1/2},$$

$$C_3 = \left(\int_0^1 \left| \frac{\int_0^1 \frac{y(s)}{(1-s)^{1-\alpha}} ds}{(1-x)^\alpha} \right|^2 dx \right)^{1/2}.$$

It follows that

$$\| T_\alpha y \| \le M_\alpha (C_1 + C_2 + C_3).$$

Utilizing the Cauchy–Schwarz inequality in conjunction with the integration by parts formula many times yields the following results

$$\begin{aligned} C_1^2 &\le \int_0^1 \left(\int_x^1 (t-x)^{-\alpha} dt \right) \left(\int_x^1 \frac{\left| \int_0^t \frac{y'(s)ds}{(t-s)^{1-\alpha}} \right|^2}{(t-x)^\alpha} dt \right) dx, \\ &\le \frac{1}{1-\alpha} \int_0^1 \left(\int_0^t (t-x)^{-\alpha} dx \right) \left| \int_0^t \frac{y'(s)}{(t-s)^{1-\alpha}} ds \right|^2 dt \\ &\le \frac{1}{\alpha(1-\alpha)^2} \int_0^1 \int_0^t \frac{|y'(s)|^2}{(t-s)^{1-\alpha}} dsdt \le \frac{1}{\alpha^2(1-\alpha)^2} \parallel y' \parallel^2 \end{aligned}$$

$$\begin{aligned} C_2^2 &\le \left(\int_0^1 \left(\int_x^1 (t-x)^{\alpha-1} dt \right) \left(\int_x^1 \frac{\left| \int_0^t \frac{y'(s)ds}{(t-s)^\alpha} \right|^2}{(t-x)^{1-\alpha}} dt \right) dx \right)^{1/2} \\ &\le \frac{1}{\alpha^2(1-\alpha)} \int_0^1 \int_0^t \frac{|y'(s)|^2}{(t-s)^\alpha} dsdt \le \frac{1}{\alpha^2(1-\alpha)^2} \parallel y' \parallel^2 \end{aligned}$$

$$\begin{aligned} C_3 &= \left(\int_0^1 (1-x)^{-2\alpha} dx \right)^{1/2} \left| \int_0^1 \frac{y(s)}{(1-s)^{1-\alpha}} ds \right| \\ &= \frac{1}{\sqrt{1-2\alpha}} \left| \int_0^1 \frac{y(s)}{(1-s)^{1-\alpha}} ds \right| \\ &\le \frac{\parallel y' \parallel}{\alpha\sqrt{1-2\alpha}}. \end{aligned}$$

Hence,

$$\parallel T_\alpha y \parallel \le M_\alpha (C_1 + C_2 + C_3) \le C_\alpha \parallel y' \parallel,$$

where $C_\alpha = \frac{1-\alpha+2\sqrt{1-4\alpha^2}}{\Gamma(1+\alpha)\Gamma(2-\alpha)\sqrt{1-4\alpha^2}}$.

By calculation, we find that

$$| \langle T_\alpha \varphi(\gamma), \varphi(\gamma) \rangle | \le C_\alpha \parallel \varphi'(\gamma) \parallel \parallel \varphi(\gamma) \parallel \le \frac{1}{4|\mu|} \parallel \varphi'(\gamma) \parallel^2 + |\mu| C_\alpha^2 \parallel \varphi(\gamma) \parallel^2. \tag{36}$$

By (30), we have

$$||\varphi'(\gamma)||^2 + \int_0^1 q|\varphi(\gamma)|^2 + \gamma \int_0^1 \tilde{q}|\varphi(\gamma)|^2 + \mu \langle T_\alpha \varphi(\gamma), \varphi(\gamma) \rangle = \lambda(\gamma). \tag{37}$$

By means of (34), (36), and (37), we obtain

$$||\varphi'(\gamma)||^2 \le 4(\lambda(\gamma) + 4Q_0^2 + 4\tilde{Q}_0^2\gamma^2 + |\mu|^2 C_\alpha^2). \tag{38}$$

A combination of (33), (35), and (38) gives that

$$|\lambda'(\gamma)| = | \int_0^1 \tilde{q}\varphi(\gamma)|^2 \le \frac{||\varphi'(\gamma)||^2}{4} + 4\tilde{Q}_0^2 \le \lambda(\gamma) + c, \tag{39}$$

where $c = 4Q_0^2 + 4\tilde{Q}_0^2\gamma^2 + |\mu|^2 C_\alpha^2 + 4\tilde{Q}_0^2$. Solving the differential inequality (39), we have

$$\lambda(\gamma) + c \le e^\gamma (\lambda(0) + c).$$

Therefore,

$$|\lambda'(\gamma)| \leq e^{\gamma}(\lambda(0) + c).$$

Hence, for any $\varepsilon > 0$, and for any $q_1 \in L^2(0,1)$, if $|\gamma| < \delta_n = \min\{\gamma_0, \frac{\varepsilon}{e^{\gamma}(\lambda(0)+c)}\}$, we have

$$|\lambda(\gamma) - \lambda(0)| = |\int_0^{\gamma} \lambda'(t)dt| \leq |\gamma|e^{\gamma}(\lambda(0) + c) < \varepsilon,$$

which completes the proof. □

5. Conclusions

In this paper, we considered a nonlocal Sturm–Liouville problem (1)–(2) with fractional integrals and fractional derivatives. We obtained that the eigenvalues of (1)–(2) with $d \neq 0$ are real values, and the corresponding eigenfunctions are orthogonal; see Theorems 1 and 2. In Theorem 3, based on these properties, we obtained results that show the geometric multiplicity of the eigenvalues is simple. Thereafter, we discussed the eigenvalue problem of (1)–(2) with $d = 0$. We led into an auxiliary two-parameter nonlocal Sturm–Liouville problem (18). In Theorem 4, we derived that the corresponding eigenvalue problem consists of a countable number of real eigenvalues, and the algebraic multiplicity of each eigenvalue is simple. With the aid of the eigenvalue properties of this nonlocal problem, we came to the conclusion that the eigenvalues are continuous with respect to the potential function; see Theorem 5.

Author Contributions: Data curation, Y.Z. and S.C.; writing—original draft preparation, J.L.; writing—review and editing, Y.Z. and S.C.; funding acquisition, J.L. All authors have read and agreed to the published version of the manuscript.

Funding: This research was funded by the Natural Science Foundation of Shandong Province (ZR2024MA005) and National Nature Science Foundation of China (Grant Nos.12071254, 12271299).

Institutional Review Board Statement: Not applicable.

Informed Consent Statement: Not applicable.

Data Availability Statement: No data were used to support this study.

Acknowledgments: The authors are grateful to the referee for his/her valuable comments, which greatly improved the original manuscript of this paper. The authors are grateful to X. Yuan for his valuable suggestions.

Conflicts of Interest: The authors declare no conflicts of interest.

References

1. Li, J.; Wang, M.R. Spectral problem and initial value problem of a nonlocal Sturm–Liouville problem. *Qual. Theor. Dyn. Syst.* **2021**,*20*, 1–22. [CrossRef]
2. Cottone, G.; Paola, M.D.; Zingales, M. Dynamics of non-local systems handled by fractional calculus. In Proceedings of the 6th WESEAS International Conference, Cairo, Egypt, 29–31 December 2007; pp. 81–89.
3. Paola, M. Di; Zingales, M. Non-local continuum: Fractional Calculus approach. In Proceeding of the XVIII AIMETA, Brescia, Italy, 11–14 September 2007; pp. 11–16.
4. Paola, M.D.; Zingales, M. Long-range cohesive interactions of non-local continuum mechanics faced by fractional calculus. *Int. J. Solids Struct.* **2008**, *45*, 5642–5659. [CrossRef]
5. Carpinteri, A.; Cornetti, P.; Sapora, A. A fractional calculus approach to nonlocal elasticity. *Eur. R. Phys. J. Spec. Top.* **2011**, *193*, 193–204. [CrossRef]
6. Qi, J.G.; Chen, S.Z. Eigenvalue problems of the model from nonlocal continuum mechanics. *J. Math. Phys.* **2011**, 52, 073516. [CrossRef]
7. Li, J.; Qi, J.G. Eigenvalue problem for fractional differential equations with right and left fractional derivatives. *Appl. Math. Compu.* **2015**, *256*, 1–10. [CrossRef]

8. Li, J.; Qi, J.G. Note on a nonlocal Sturm–Liouville problem with both right and left fractional derivatives. *Appl. Math. Lett.* **2019**, *97*, 14–19. [CrossRef]
9. Li, J.; Qi, J.G. On a nonlocal Sturm–Liouville problem with composite fractional derivatives. *Math. Meth. Appl. Sci.* **2021**, *44*, 1931–1941. [CrossRef]
10. Li, J.; Qi, J.G. Continuous dependence of eigenvalues on potential functions for nonlocal Sturm–Liouville equations. *Math. Meth. Appl. Sci.* **2023**, *46*, 10617–10623. [CrossRef]
11. Klimek, M.; Agrawal, O.P. Fractional Sturm–Liouville problem. *Comput. Math. Appl.* **2013**, *66*, 795–812. [CrossRef]
12. Zayernouri, M.; Karniadakis, G.E. Fractional Sturm–Liouville eigen-problems: theory and numerical approximation. *J. Comput. Phys.* **2013**, *252*, 495–517. [CrossRef]
13. Bas, E.; Metin, F.; Fractional singular Sturm–Liouville operator for coulomb potential, *Adv. Differ. Equ.* **2013**, *1*, 300. [CrossRef]
14. Klimek, M.; Odzijewicz, T.; Malinowska, A.B. Variational methods for the fractonal Sturm–Liouville problem. *J. Math. Anal. Appl.* **2014)**, *416*, 402–426. [CrossRef]
15. Bas, E.; Ozarslan, R.; Baleanu, D.; Ercan, A. Comparative simulations for solutions of fractional Sturm–Liouville problems with non-singular operators. *Adv. Differ. Equ.* **2018**, *1*, 350. [CrossRef]
16. Aleroev, T.S.; Aleroeva, H.T. Problems of Sturm–Liouville type for differential equations with fractional derivatives, In *Volume 2 Fractional Differential Equations*; Kochubei, A., Luchko, Y. Eds.; De Gruyter: Berlin, Germany; Boston, MA, USA, 2019; pp. 21–46.
17. Derakhshan, M.H.; Ansari, A. Fractional Sturm–Liouville problems for weber fractional derivatives. *Int. J. Comput. Math.* **2019**, *96*, 217–237. [CrossRef]
18. Ozarslan, R.; Ercan, A.; Bas, E. β-type fractional Sturm–Liouville coulomb operator and applied results. *Math. Meth. Appl. Sci.* **2019**, *42*, 6648–6659. [CrossRef]
19. Dehghan, M.; Mingarelli, A.B. Fractional Sturm–Liouville eigenvalue problems, I. *RACSAM* **2020**, *114*, 46. [CrossRef]
20. Maralani, E.M.; Saei, F.D.; Akbarfam, A.J.; Ghanbari, K. Eigenvalues of fractional Sturm–Liouville problems by successive method. *Comput. Methods Differ. Equ.* **2021**, *9*, 1163–1175.
21. Dehghan, M.; Mingarelli, A.B. Fractional Sturm–Liouville eigenvalue problems, II. *Fractal Fract.* **2022**, *6*, 487. [CrossRef]
22. Al-Jararha, M.; Al-Refai, M.; Luchko, Y. A self-adjoint fractional Sturm–Liouville problem with the general fractional derivatives. *J. Differ. Equ.* **2024**, *413* , 110–128. [CrossRef]
23. Dehghan, M.; Mingarelli, A.B. Spectral and Oscillation Theory for an Unconventional Fractional Sturm–Liouville Problem. *Fractal Fract.* **2024**, *8*, 238. [CrossRef]
24. Kilbas, A.A.; Srivastava, H.M.; Trujillo, J.J. *Theory and Applications of Fractional Differential Equations*; Elsevier: Amsterdam, The Netherlands, 2006.
25. Kato, T. *Perturbation Theory for Linear Operators*; Springer: New York, NY, USA, 1966.
26. Kong, Q.; Zettl, A. Eigenvalues of regular Sturm–Liouville problem. *J. Diff. Equ.* **1996**, *131* , 1–19. [CrossRef]
27. Zettl, A. *Sturm–Liouville Theory*; American Mathematical Society: Providence, RI, USA, 2005; Volume 121.
28. Xie, B.; Guo, H.J.; Li, J. Continuity of eigenvalues in weak topology for regular Sturm–Liouville problems. *Dynam. Syst. Appl.* **2018**, *27*, 353–365. [CrossRef]

fractal and fractional

MDPI

Article

Positive Solution Pairs for Coupled p-Laplacian Hadamard Fractional Differential Model with Singular Source Item on Time Variable

Cheng Li [1] and Limin Guo [2,*]

[1] School of Automotive Engineering, Changzhou Institute of Technology, Changzhou 213002, China; licheng@czust.edu.cn

[2] School of Science, Changzhou Institute of Technology, Changzhou 213002, China

* Correspondence: guolm@czu.cn

Abstract: The mathematical theories and methods of fractional calculus are relatively mature, which have been widely used in signal processing, control systems, nonlinear dynamics, financial models, etc. The studies of some basic theories of fractional differential equations can provide more understanding of mechanisms for the applications. In this paper, the expression of the Green function as well as its special properties are acquired and presented through theoretical analyses. Subsequently, on the basis of these properties of the Green function, the existence and uniqueness of positive solutions are achieved for a singular p-Laplacian fractional-order differential equation with nonlocal integral and infinite-point boundary value systems by using the method of a nonlinear alternative of Leray–Schauder-type Guo–Krasnoselskii's fixed point theorem in cone, and the Banach fixed point theorem, respectively. Some existence results are obtained for the case in which the nonlinearity is allowed to be singular with regard to the time variable. Several examples are correspondingly provided to show the correctness and applicability of the obtained results, where nonlinear terms are controlled by the integrable functions $\frac{1}{\pi(\ln t)^{\frac{1}{2}}(1-\ln t)^{\frac{1}{2}}}$ and $\frac{1}{\pi(\ln t)^{\frac{3}{4}}(1-\ln t)^{\frac{3}{4}}}$ in Example 1, and by the integrable functions $\theta, \overline{\theta}$ and $\varphi(v), \psi(u)$ in Example 2, respectively. The present work may contribute to the improvement and application of the coupled p-Laplacian Hadamard fractional differential model and further promote the development of fractional differential equations and fractional differential calculus.

Keywords: Hadamard fractional; singular nonlinear term; coupled differential system; positive solution; integral and infinite-point boundary condition

MSC: 26A33; 34A37

1. Introduction

The p-Laplacian differential equation was first introduced by Leibenson [1] when he studied the turbulent flow in a porous medium. Later, differential equations containing p-Laplace operators have been widely used in many fields such as non-Newtonian mechanics, cosmic physics, plasma problems and elasticity theory [1–6]. The p-Laplacian operator L_p is defined as $L_p(s) = |s|^{p-2}s,\ p,\ q > 1,\ \frac{1}{p} + \frac{1}{q} = 1$. For recent developments in this regard, see [7–11].

Recently, more and more researchers have dedicated their research to the existence and number of solutions of fractional differential equations and the corresponding nonlinear deformation, flexural wave and vibration, and the coupled problem, which can be referred to in [2,4,12–21]. There are many approaches to studying fractional differential equations, such as the mixed monotone operator method [10], Banach's fixed point theorem [22], Leray–Schauder's alternative method [23,24], Hussein–Jassim's method [25], the comparison principle method [26] and so on. In recent years, some scientists have devoted themselves to studying the Hadamard fractional differential equation as well as related nonlinear dynamical differential systems [6,22,26–33]. The Hadamard fractional derivative of $\nu(\nu > 0)$ order of a continuous function $\Psi : (0, \infty) \to \mathbb{R}^1_+$ is given by

$$^{H}\mathscr{D}^{\nu}_{1^+}\hbar(t) = \frac{1}{\Gamma(n-\nu)}\left(t\frac{d}{dt}\right)^n \int_1^t \frac{\Psi(s)}{s(\ln\frac{t}{s})^{\nu-n+1}}ds,$$

where $n = [\alpha] + 1$, $[\alpha]$ denotes the integer part of the number α, provided that the right-hand side is pointwise defined on $(0, \infty)$. The Hadamard fractional integral of $\nu(\nu > 0)$ order of a function $\Psi : (0, \infty) \to \mathbb{R}^1_+$ is given by

$$^{H}I^{\nu}_{1^+}\hbar(t) = \frac{1}{\Gamma(\nu)}\int_1^t (\ln\frac{t}{s})^{\nu-1}\frac{\Psi(s)}{s}ds.$$

In order to better guide the practice, a large number of workers are devoted to the basic theoretical research of fractional differential equations, among which the structure of Hadamard fractional differential equations is one of them. It has been noticed that some of the structure of fractional differential equations is based on Hadamard fractional differential equations. In [18], the authors discussed the following Hadamard fractional equations:

$$\begin{aligned} &^{H}D^{q}_{1^+}u(t) + \mathscr{F}(t, u(t), v(t)) = 0,\ 1 < t < e, \\ &^{H}D^{q}_{1^+}v(t) + \overline{\mathscr{F}}(t, u(t), v(t)) = 0,\ 1 < t < e, \end{aligned}$$

with the following multi-point boundary conditions:

$$\begin{aligned} u(1) &= \delta u(1) = 0, u(e) = \sum_{j=1}^{m-1} a_j u(\xi_j), \\ v(1) &= \delta v(1) = 0, v(e) = \sum_{j=1}^{m-1} b_j u(\eta_j), \end{aligned}$$

where $q \in (2, 3]$ is a real number, and $^{H}D^{q}_{1^+}u$ is the standard Hadamard fractional derivative. $a_i, b_j \geq 0, \xi_i, \eta_j \in (1, e)$ with $\sum_{i=1}^{m-1} a_i(\log\xi_i)^{q-1} \in [0, 1)$, and $\sum_{j=1}^{m-1} b_j(\log\eta_j)^{q-1} \in [0, 1)$; $\mathscr{F}, \overline{\mathscr{F}} \in C([1, e] \times \mathbb{R}^+ \times \mathbb{R}^+ \times \mathbb{R}^+, \mathbb{R}^+)(\mathbb{R}^+ = [0, +\infty))$. The authors obtained a triple positive solution and a nontrivial solution by a fixed point theorem and through the relationship between nonlinear and linear operators. Ardjouni [15] studied the following Hadamard fractional differential equations:

$$^{H}D^{\alpha}_{1^+}u(t) + \phi(t, u(t)) =^{H} D^{\beta}_{1^+}\varphi(t, u(t)), 1 < t < e,$$

with integral boundary conditions:

$$u(1) = 0, u(e) = \frac{1}{\Gamma(\alpha-\beta)}\int_1^e (\log\frac{e}{s})^{\alpha-\beta-1}g(s, x(s))\frac{ds}{s},$$

where $1 < \alpha \leq 2, 0 < \beta \leq \alpha - 1$, $\varphi, \phi : [1, e] \times [0, \infty) \to [0, \infty)$ are given as continuous functions, ϕ does not require any monotone assumption and φ is non-decreasing on x. The authors obtained the existence and uniqueness of the positive solution by the method of upper and lower solutions and Schauder and Banach fixed point theorems. In [34], we consider the following singular Hadamard fractional differential equation:

$$^{H}D^{\alpha}_{1^+}\left(\varphi_p\left(^{H}D^{\gamma}_{1^+}u\right)\right)(t) + \hbar(t, u(t),^{H} D^{\mu}_{1^+}u(t)) = 0, 1 < t < e,$$

with the infinite-point boundary condition:

$$u^{(j+\mu)}(1) = 0, j = 0,1,2,\ldots,n-2; {}^H D^{r_1}_{1^+}u(e) = \sum_{j=1}^{\infty} \eta_j {}^H D^{r_2}_{1^+}u(\xi_j),$$

$${}^H D^{\gamma}_{1^+}u(1) = 0; \varphi_p({}^H D^{\gamma}_{1^+}u(e)) = \sum_{j=1}^{\infty} \zeta_j \varphi_p({}^H D^{\gamma}_{1^+}u(\xi_j)),$$

where $\alpha, \gamma, \mu \in \mathbb{R}^+ = [0, +\infty); 1 < \alpha \leq 2, n < \gamma \leq n+1 (n \geq 3); r_1, r_2 \in [2, n-2]; r_2 \leq r_1$; the p-Laplacian operator φ_p is defined as $\varphi_p(s) = |s|^{p-2}s,\ p,\ q > 1,\ \frac{1}{p} + \frac{1}{q} = 1, 0 < \mu \leq n-2$ and $0 < \eta_i, \zeta_i < 1, 1 < \xi_i < e (i = 1,2,\ldots,\infty)$; $\hbar \in C((1,e) \times \mathbb{R}^1_+ \times \mathbb{R}^1_+)(\mathbb{R}^1_+ = [0, +\infty))$ and may be singular at $t = 1, e$; and ${}^H D^{\alpha}_{1^+}u, {}^H D^{\gamma}_{1^+}u, {}^H D^{\mu}_{1^+}u,\ {}^H D^{r_i}_{1^+}u (i = 1,2)$ are the standard Hadamard fractional derivatives. The existence of positive solutions is investigated by spectral analysis by us. For the portion of the research results that include the fractional differential systems and the corresponding nonlinear deformation, flexural wave and vibration, please refer to [4,15–21,35].

Motivated by the excellent results above, we consider the following Hadamard fractional differential system (HFDS):

$$\begin{aligned} L_{p_1}({}^H D^{\nu}_{1^+}u(t)) + \mathscr{F}(t, v(t), {}^H D^{\varsigma}_{1^+}v(t)) = 0,\ 1 < t < e, \\ L_{p_2}({}^H D^{\iota}_{1^+}v(t)) + \overline{\mathscr{F}}(t, u(t), {}^H D^{\varsigma}_{1^+}u(t)) = 0,\ 1 < t < e, \end{aligned} \tag{1}$$

with nonlocal integral and infinite-point boundary conditions:

$$\begin{aligned} u^{(i)}(1) = 0, i = 0,1,2,\ldots,n-2, u(e) = \sum_{j=1}^{\infty} \eta_j u(\xi_j) + \int_1^e h(t)u(t)dB(t), \\ v^{(j)}(1) = 0, i = 0,1,2,\ldots,m-2, v(e) = \sum_{j=1}^{\infty} \overline{\eta}_j v(\overline{\xi}_j) + \int_1^e \overline{h}(t)v(t)d\overline{B}(t), \end{aligned} \tag{2}$$

where $n-1 < \nu \leq n, m-1 < \iota \leq m, 0 < \varsigma < \max\{\nu - 1, \iota - 1\}$; the p-Laplacian operator L_{p_i} is defined as $L_{p_i}(s) = |s|^{p_i-2}s,\ p_i,\ q_i > 1,\ \frac{1}{p_i} + \frac{1}{q_i} = 1 (i = 1,2); \eta_j, \overline{\eta}_j \geq 0, 1 < \xi_j < e$, $1 < \overline{\xi}_j < e\ (j = 1,2\cdots)$ are parameters; $B, \overline{B}$ are functions of bounded variation; $h(t), \overline{h}(t) \in L^1(1,e)$ $\int_1^e h(t)u(t)dB(t)$ and $\int_1^e \overline{h}(t)v(t)d\overline{B}(t)$ denote the Riemann–Stieltjes integral with respect to $B(t)$ and $\overline{B}(t)$; $\mathscr{F}, \overline{\mathscr{F}} \in C((1,e) \times (0, +\infty)^2, \mathbb{R}^1_+))$ and $\mathscr{F}(t, x_1, x_2)$, $\overline{\mathscr{F}}(t, x_1, x_2)$ have singularity at $t = 1,\ e$; and ${}^H D^{\nu}_{1^+}u, {}^H D^{\iota}_{1^+}u$ are the standard Hadamard fractional derivatives.

In this paper, we investigate the existence of positive solutions for a singular infinite-point coupled p-Laplacian boundary value system. Compared with [18,19], the nonlinear term is singular in regard to time variable in this study, fractional derivatives are involved in the nonlinear terms and infinite point is involved in boundary conditions for HFDS (1) and (2). However, the nonlinear term is continuous in the studies [18,19] and the nonlinear terms of reference [18,19] do not contain derivative terms. Compared with [19,36,37], the equation in this paper is a p-Laplacian boundary value system which is a great extension from the general fractional differential equation. Compared with the references, on the one hand, the equations we study are complex and the singular form of nonlinearity can simulate more complex systems; on the other hand, we obtain the existence and uniqueness of the solutions to the equations.

This paper is organized as follows: In Section 1, we explain the research background and necessity of studying such a fractional differential equation in the Introduction section. In Section 2, we introduce some definitions and lemmas which will be used later, and give the expression of the theorem of the Green function, provide the nature of the theorem of Green function, and prove the continuity and total continuity of operators. In Section 3, we obtain the main results by using the method of a nonlinear alternative of Leray–Schauder-type, Guo–Krasnoselskii's fixed point theorem in cone and the Banach fixed point theorem, respectively. In Section 4, we list three examples to illustrate the validity of the proposed theories. Finally, we summarize some conclusions with the current shortcomings and future research plans in Section 5.

2. Preliminaries and Lemmas

With respect to some essential definitions and lemmas of fractional calculus of the Hadamard type, the reader may consult the recent bibliography such as those in [5,38,39]. Only the parts are listed here.

For convenience in terms of presentation, we list herein some conditions to be used throughout the paper.

(H_0): $\mathscr{F},\overline{\mathscr{F}}:(1,e)\times\mathbb{R}^+\times\mathbb{R}^+\to\mathbb{R}^+$, and there exists a function $\theta(t),\overline{\theta}(t):(1,e)\to\mathbb{R}^+$ such that $\mathscr{F}(t,x_0,x_1)\leq\theta(t),\overline{\mathscr{F}}(t,x_0,x_1)\leq\overline{\theta}(t)$ for $\forall(x_0,x_1)\in E\times E$, and

$$\int_1^e L_{q_1}(\vartheta(s))\frac{ds}{s}<+\infty,\int_1^e L_{q_2}(\overline{\vartheta}(s))\frac{ds}{s}<+\infty.$$

(H_1)

$$\int_1^e h(t)(\ln t)^{\alpha-1}dB(t)<+\infty,\int_1^e \overline{h}(t)(\ln t)^{\beta-1}d\overline{B}(t)<+\infty.$$

Lemma 1 ([3,5]). *If $\nu,\iota>0$, then*

$${}^HI^{\nu}_{1^+}(\ln x)^{\iota-1}=\frac{\Gamma(\iota)}{\Gamma(\iota+\nu)}(\ln x)^{\iota+\nu-1},{}^H\mathscr{D}^{\nu}_{1^+}(\ln x)^{\iota-1}=\frac{\Gamma(\iota)}{\Gamma(\iota-\nu)}(\ln x)^{\iota-\nu-1}.$$

Lemma 2 ([3]). *Suppose that $\nu>0$ and $\Psi\in C[0,\infty)\cap L^1[0,\infty)$, then the solution of Hadamard fractional differential equation ${}^H\mathscr{D}^{\nu}_{1^+}\Psi(t)=0$ is*

$$\Psi(t)=\kappa_1(\ln t)^{\nu-1}+\kappa_2(\ln t)^{\nu-2}+\cdots+\kappa_n(\ln t)^{\nu-n},\kappa_i\in\mathbb{R}(i=0,1,\cdots,n),n=[\nu]+1.$$

Lemma 3 ([3]). *Suppose that $\nu>0,\nu$ is not a natural number, $\Psi\in C[1,\infty)\cap L^1[1,\infty)$, then*

$$\Psi(t)={}^HI^{\nu}_{1^+}{}^H\mathscr{D}^{\nu}_{1^+}\hbar(t)+\sum_{k=1}^{n}\kappa_k(\ln t)^{\nu-k},$$

for $t\in(1,e]$, where $\kappa_k\in\mathbb{R}(k=1,2,\cdots,n)$, and $n=[\nu]+1$.

Lemma 4. *Let E be a real Banach space, and $P\subset E$ be a cone. Let Ω_1,Ω_2 be two bounded open subsets in E such that $\theta\in\Omega_1$ and $\overline{\Omega}_1\subset\Omega_2$. Let the operator $T:(\overline{\Omega}_2\backslash\Omega_1)\cap P\to P$ be completely continuous. Suppose that one of the conditions is as follows:*

(i) If $\|Tx\|\leq\|x\|,\forall x\in P\cap\partial\Omega_1$, $\|Tx\|\geq\|x\|$ for all $x\in P\cap\partial\Omega_2$;

(ii) If $\|Tx\|\geq\|x\|,\forall x\in P\cap\partial\Omega_1$, $\|Tx\|\leq\|x\|$ for all $x\in P\cap\partial\Omega_2$ holds, then T has a fixed point in $(\overline{\Omega}_2\backslash\Omega_1)\cap P$.

Lemma 5. *Let E be a Banach space and $\Omega\subset E$ be closed and convex. Assume U is a relatively open subset of Ω with $\theta\in U$, and let operator $A:\overline{U}\to\Omega$ be a continuous compact map. Then, either one of the following occurs:*

(1) A has a fixed point in U;

(2) There exists $u\in\partial U$ and $\varphi\in(0,1)$ with $u=\varphi Au$.

Lemma 6 ([40], Theorem 1.2.7). *Let $\Theta\subset C^1[J,E]$, then Θ is a relatively compact set if and only if the following are true:*

(a) Θ' is equicontinuous and $\Theta'(t)$ is a relatively compact set for any $t\in J$ on E;

(b) There exists $t_0\in J$ such that $\Theta(t_0)$ is a relatively compact set on E.

Now, we consider the following linear fractional differential equations.

Theorem 1. *Given $y, \overline{y} \in L^1(1,e) \cap C(1,e)$, then the liner HFDE problems*

$$\begin{cases} L_{p_1}({}^H D_{1^+}^{\nu} u(t)) + y(t) = 0,\ 1 < t < e, \\ u^{(j)}(1) = 0, j = 0,1,2,\cdots,n-2; u(e) = \sum\limits_{j=1}^{\infty} \eta_j u(\xi_j) + \int_1^e h(t)u(t)dB(t), \end{cases} \tag{3}$$

$$\begin{cases} L_{p_2}(D_{1^+}^{\iota} v(t)) + \overline{y}(t) = 0,\ 1 < t < e, \\ v^{(j)}(1) = 0, j = 0,1,2,\cdots,m-2; v(e) = \sum\limits_{j=1}^{\infty} \overline{\eta}_j v(\overline{\xi}_j) + \int_1^e \overline{h}(t)v(t)d\overline{B}(t) \end{cases} \tag{4}$$

have integral representation

$$\begin{aligned} u(t) &= \int_1^e \mathscr{G}(t,s) \frac{\varphi_{q_1}(y(s))}{s} ds, \\ v(t) &= \int_1^e \mathscr{H}(t,s) \frac{\varphi_{q_2}(\overline{y}(s))}{s} ds, \end{aligned} \tag{5}$$

where

$$\mathscr{G}(t,s) = \mathscr{G}_1(t,s) + \mathscr{G}_2(t,s),$$
$$\mathscr{H}(t,s) = \mathscr{H}_1(t,s) + \mathscr{H}_2(t,s),$$

in which

$$\mathscr{G}_1(t,s) = \frac{1}{\Gamma(\nu)} \begin{cases} \mathscr{P}(s)\Gamma(\nu)(\ln t)^{\nu-1}(\ln \frac{e}{s})^{\nu-1} - \Delta(\ln \frac{t}{s})^{\nu-1}, & 1 \le s \le t \le e, \\ \mathscr{P}(s)\Gamma(\nu)(\ln t)^{\nu-1}(\ln \frac{e}{s})^{\nu-1}, & 1 \le t \le s \le e, \end{cases} \tag{6}$$

$$\mathscr{G}_2(t,s) = \frac{(\ln t)^{\nu-1}}{\Delta_1} \int_1^e h(t)\mathscr{G}_1(t,s)dB(t), \tag{7}$$

$$\Delta_1 = \Delta - \int_1^e h(t)(\ln t)^{\nu-1}dB(t), \Delta = 1 - \sum_{i=1}^{\infty} \eta_j (\ln \xi_j)^{\nu-1},$$

$$\mathscr{P}(s) = \frac{1}{\Gamma(\nu)} - \frac{1}{\Gamma(\nu)} \sum_{j=1}^{\infty} \eta_j \left(\frac{\ln \xi_j - \ln s}{\ln e - \ln s} \right)^{\nu-1},$$

$$\mathscr{H}_1(t,s) = \frac{1}{\Gamma(\iota)} \begin{cases} (\ln t)^{\iota-1}(\ln \frac{e}{s})^{\iota-1} - \overline{\Delta}(\ln \frac{t}{s})^{\iota-1}, & 1 \le s \le t \le e, \\ (\ln t)^{\iota-1}(\ln \frac{e}{s})^{\iota-1}, & 1 \le t \le s \le e, \end{cases} \tag{8}$$

$$\mathscr{H}_2(t,s) = \frac{(\ln t)^{\iota-1}}{\overline{\Delta}_1} \int_1^e \overline{h}(t)\mathscr{H}_1(t,s)d\overline{B}(t), \tag{9}$$

$$\overline{\Delta}_1 = \overline{\Delta} - \int_1^e \overline{h}(t)(\ln t)^{\iota-1}d\overline{B}(t), \overline{\Delta} = 1 - \sum_{i=1}^{\infty} \overline{\eta}_j (\ln \xi_j)^{\iota-1},$$

$$\overline{\mathscr{P}}(s) = \frac{1}{\Gamma(\iota)} - \frac{1}{\Gamma(\iota)} \sum_{j=1}^{\infty} \overline{\eta}_j \left(\frac{\ln \xi_j - \ln s}{\ln e - \ln s} \right)^{\iota-1}.$$

Proof. By using Lemma 3, Equation (3) can be reduced to an equivalent integral equation:

$$u(t) = -{}^H I_{1^+}^{\nu} L_{q_1}(y(t)) + \kappa_1(\ln t)^{\nu-1} + \kappa_2(\ln t)^{\nu-2} + \cdots + \kappa_n(\ln t)^{\nu-n},$$

for some $\kappa_1, \kappa_2, \cdots, \kappa_n \in \mathbb{R}^1$. Via $u(1) = 0$ of (2), one has $\kappa_n = 0$, then

$$u'(t) = -{}^H I_{1+}^{\nu-1} L_{q_1}(y(t)) + \kappa_1(\nu-1)(\ln t)^{\nu-2}\frac{1}{t} + \kappa_2(\nu-2)(\ln t)^{\nu-3}\frac{1}{t} + \ldots,$$

by means of $u'(t) = 0$, one obtains $\kappa_{n-1} = 0$; by the same means, one arrives at $\kappa_2 = \kappa_3 = \ldots = \kappa_{n-2} = 0$, and then

$$u(t) = -\int_1^t \frac{(\ln \frac{t}{s})^{\nu-1}}{\Gamma(\nu)} \frac{L_{q_1}(y(s))}{s} ds + \kappa_1 (\ln t)^{\nu-1}. \tag{10}$$

By simple calculation, we have

$$u(e) = -{}^H I_{1+}^{\nu} L_{q_1}(y(e)) + \kappa_1. \tag{11}$$

Substituting (11) into $u(e) = \sum_{j=1}^{\infty} \eta_j u(\xi_j) + \int_1^e h(t)u(t)dB(t)$, we have

$$\begin{aligned}\kappa_1 -{}^H I_{1+}^{\nu} L_{q_1}(y(e)) = &\sum_{i=1}^{\infty} \eta_j \Big(C_1 (\ln \xi_j)^{\nu-1} -{}^H I_{1+}^{\nu} L_{q_1}(y(\xi_j)) \Big) \\ &+ \int_1^e h(t)u(t)dB(t),\end{aligned}$$

then

$$\begin{aligned}\kappa_1 = &\int_1^e \frac{(\ln e - \ln s)^{\nu-1}}{\Gamma(\nu)\Delta} L_{q_1}(y(s))\frac{ds}{s} - \sum_{j=1}^{\infty} \eta_j \int_1^{\xi_j} \frac{(\ln \xi_j - \ln s)^{\nu-1}}{\Gamma(\nu)\Delta} L_{q_1}(y(s))\frac{ds}{s} \\ &+ \frac{1}{\Delta}\int_1^e h(t)u(t)dB(t) \\ = &\int_1^e \frac{(\ln e - \ln s)^{\nu-1}\mathscr{P}(s)}{\Delta} L_{q_1}(y(s))\frac{ds}{s} + \frac{1}{\Delta}\int_1^e h(t)u(t)dB(t).\end{aligned} \tag{12}$$

Incorporating (12) into (10), one has

$$\begin{aligned}u(t) = &-\frac{1}{\Gamma(\nu)}\int_1^t (\ln \frac{t}{s})^{\nu-1} \frac{L_{q_1}(y(s))}{s} ds \\ &+ (\ln t)^{\nu-1} \frac{\frac{1}{\Gamma(\nu)}\int_1^e (\ln \frac{e}{s})^{\nu-1}\frac{L_{q_1}(y(s))}{s}ds - \sum_{i=1}^{\infty}\eta_j \frac{1}{\Gamma(\nu)}\int_1^{\xi_j} \ln(\frac{\xi_j}{s})^{\nu-1}\frac{L_{q_1}(y(s))}{s}ds}{\Delta} \\ &+ \frac{(\ln t)^{\nu-1}}{\Delta}\int_1^e h(t)u(t)dB(t) \\ = &\int_1^e \mathscr{G}(t,s)\frac{L_{q_1}(y(s))}{s}ds + \frac{(\ln t)^{\nu-1}}{\Delta}\int_1^e h(t)u(t)dB(t).\end{aligned} \tag{13}$$

Multiplying Equation (13) by $h(t)$ and the Riemann–Stieltjes integral from 1 to e, one arrives at

$$\begin{aligned}\int_1^e h(t)u(t)dB(t) = &\int_1^e h(t)\left[\int_1^e \mathscr{G}(t,s)L_{q_1}(y(s))\frac{ds}{s}\right]dB(t) \\ &+ \frac{\int_1^e h(t)(\ln t)^{\alpha-1}dB(t)}{\Delta}\int_1^e h(t)u(t)dB(t);\end{aligned}$$

hence,

$$\int_1^e h(t)u(t)dB(t) = \frac{\Delta}{\Delta_1}\int_1^e h(t)\left[\int_1^e \mathscr{G}(t,s)L_{q_1}(y(s))\frac{ds}{s}\right]dB(t),$$

and then,

$$\begin{aligned} u(t) &= \int_1^e \mathscr{G}_1(t,s)L_{q_1}(y(s))\frac{ds}{s} + \frac{(\ln t)^{\nu-1}}{\Delta}\frac{\Delta}{\Delta_1}\int_1^e h(t)\left[\int_1^e \mathscr{G}(t,s)L_{q_1}(y(s))\frac{ds}{s}\right]dB(t) \\ &= \int_1^e \mathscr{G}_1(t,s)L_{q_1}(y(s))\frac{ds}{s} + \int_1^e \mathscr{G}_2(t,s)L_{q_1}(y(s))\frac{ds}{s} \\ &= \int_1^e \mathscr{G}(t,s)L_{q_1}(y(s))\frac{ds}{s}, \end{aligned}$$

where $\mathscr{G}(t,s), \mathscr{G}_1(t,s), \mathscr{G}_2(t,s), \Delta, \Delta_1$ are as (5)–(7). Moreover, by simple calculation, one arrives at

$$^{H}D^{\varsigma}_{1^+}\mathscr{G}(t,s) = ^{H}D^{\varsigma}_{1^+}\mathscr{G}_1(t,s) + \frac{\Gamma(\nu)}{\Delta_1\Gamma(\nu-\varsigma)}(\ln t)^{\nu-1-\varsigma}\int_1^e h(t)\mathscr{G}_1(t,s)dB(t), \qquad (14).$$

and

$$^{H}D^{\mu}_{1^+}\mathscr{G}_1(t,s) = \frac{1}{\Delta\Gamma(\nu-\mu)}\begin{cases} \mathscr{P}(s)\Gamma(\nu)(\ln t)^{\nu-1-\varsigma}(\ln\frac{e}{s})^{\nu-1} - \Delta(\ln\frac{t}{s})^{\nu-1-\varsigma}, \ 1 \le s \le t \le e, \\ \mathscr{P}(s)\Gamma(\nu)(\ln t)^{\nu-1-\varsigma}(\ln\frac{e}{s})^{\nu-1}, \ 1 \le t \le s \le e. \end{cases}$$

Similarly, when one has (8) and (9), we omit the detail here. Moreover, one arrives at

$$^{H}D^{\varsigma}_{1^+}\mathscr{H}(t,s) = ^{H}D^{\varsigma}_{1^+}\mathscr{H}_1(t,s) + \frac{\Gamma(\iota)}{\Delta_1\Gamma(\iota-\varsigma)}(\ln t)^{\iota-1-\varsigma}\int_1^e \overline{h}(t)\mathscr{H}_1(t,s)dB(t), \qquad (15)$$

and

$$^{H}D^{\varsigma}_{1^+}\mathscr{H}_1(t,s) = \frac{1}{\overline{\Delta}\Gamma(\iota-\varsigma)}\begin{cases} (\ln t)^{\iota-1-\varsigma}(\ln\frac{e}{s})^{\iota-1} - \overline{\Delta}(\ln\frac{t}{s})^{\iota-1-\varsigma}, \\ 1 \le s \le t \le e, \\ (\ln t)^{\iota-1-\varsigma}(\ln\frac{e}{s})^{\iota-1}, \ 1 \le t \le s \le e. \end{cases}$$

□

Theorem 2. *The functions $\mathscr{G}(t,s)$, $^{H}D^{\varsigma}_{1^+}\mathscr{G}(t,s)$, $\mathscr{H}(t,s)$, and $^{H}D^{\varsigma}_{1^+}\mathscr{H}(t,s)$ given by (5) have the following properties:*

(1) $\mathscr{G}(t,s)$, $^{H}D^{\varsigma}_{1^+}\mathscr{G}(t,s)$, $\mathscr{H}(t,s)$, and $^{H}D^{\varsigma}_{1^+}\mathscr{H}(t,s)$ are uniformly continuous on $[1,e] \times [1,e]$;

(2)

$$\mathscr{G}(t,s) \le \mathscr{G}_1(e,s)\Upsilon, \mathscr{G}(t,s) \ge (\ln t)^{\nu-1}\mathscr{G}_1(e,s)\overline{\Upsilon},$$
$$^{H}D^{\varsigma}_{1^+}\mathscr{G}(t,s) \le ^{H}D^{\varsigma}_{1^+}\mathscr{G}_1(e,s)\Upsilon, ^{H}D^{\varsigma}_{1^+}\mathscr{G}(t,s) \ge (\ln t)^{\nu-\varsigma-1}{}^{H}D_{1^+}{}^{\varsigma}\mathscr{G}_1(e,s)\overline{\Upsilon},$$

where

$$\Upsilon = 1 + \frac{1}{\Delta_1}\int_1^e h(t)dB(t), \overline{\Upsilon} = 1 + \frac{1}{\Delta_1}\int_1^e h(t)(\ln t)^{\nu-1}dB(t);$$

(3)

$$\mathscr{H}(t,s) \le \mathscr{H}_1(e,s)\Xi, \mathscr{H}(t,s) \ge (\ln t)^{\iota-1}\mathscr{H}_1(e,s)\overline{\Xi},$$
$$^{H}D^{\varsigma}_{1^+}\mathscr{H}(t,s) \le ^{H}D^{\varsigma}_{1^+}\mathscr{H}_1(e,s)\Upsilon, ^{H}D^{\varsigma}_{1^+}\mathscr{H}(t,s) \ge (\ln t)^{\iota-\varsigma-1}{}^{H}D_{1^+}{}^{\varsigma}\mathscr{H}_1(e,s)\overline{\Upsilon},$$

where

$$\Xi = 1 + \frac{(\ln t)^{\iota-1}}{\Delta_1}\int_1^e \overline{h}(t)d\overline{B}(t), \overline{\Xi} = 1 + \frac{1}{\Delta_1}\int_1^e \overline{h}(t)(\ln t)^{\iota-1}d\overline{B}(t).$$

Proof. (1) It is easy to check whether $\mathscr{G}(t,s)$, $^{H}D^{\varsigma}_{1^+}\mathscr{G}(t,s)$, $\mathscr{H}(t,s)$ and $^{H}D^{\varsigma}_{1^+}\mathscr{H}(t,s)$ have uniformly continuous properties on $[1,e] \times [1,e]$.

(2) By a similar method with [41], for $t,s \in [1,e]$, we obtain

$$(\ln t)^{\nu-1}\mathscr{G}_1(e,s) \leq \mathscr{G}_1(t,s) \leq \mathscr{G}_1(e,s);$$

hence, we have

$$\begin{aligned}\mathscr{G}(t,s) &= \mathscr{G}_1(t,s) + \mathscr{G}_2(t,s)\\ &\leq \mathscr{G}_1(e,s) + \frac{(\ln t)^{\alpha-1}}{\Delta_1}\int_1^e h(t)\mathscr{G}_1(e,s)dB(t)\\ &= \mathscr{G}_1(e,s)(1 + \frac{(\ln t)^{\alpha-1}}{\Delta_1}\int_1^e h(t)dB(t)) = \mathscr{G}_1(e,s)\Upsilon,\end{aligned}$$

$$\begin{aligned}\mathscr{G}(t,s) &= \mathscr{G}_1(t,s) + \mathscr{G}_2(t,s)\\ &= \mathscr{G}_1(t,s) + \frac{(\ln t)^{\nu-1}}{\Delta_1}\int_1^e h(t)\mathscr{G}_1(e,s)dB(t)\\ &\geq (\ln t)^{\nu-1}\mathscr{G}_1(e,s) + \frac{(\ln t)^{\nu-1}}{\Delta_1}\int_1^e h(t)(\ln t)^{\nu-1}\mathscr{G}_1(e,s)dB(t)\\ &\geq (\ln t)^{\nu-1}\mathscr{G}_1(e,s)(1 + \frac{1}{\Delta_1}\int_1^e h(t)(\ln t)^{\nu-1}dB(t))\\ &= (\ln t)^{\nu-1}\mathscr{G}_1(e,s)\overline{\Upsilon}.\end{aligned}$$

By the same method, for $t,s \in [1,e]$, we have

$${}^HD_{1^+}^{\varsigma}\mathscr{G}(t,s) \leq^H D_{1^+}^{\varsigma}\mathscr{G}_1(e,s)\Upsilon,^H D_{1^+}^{\varsigma}\mathscr{G}(t,s) \geq (\ln t)^{\nu-\varsigma-1H}D_{1^+}{}^{\varsigma}\mathscr{G}_1(e,s)\overline{\Upsilon},$$

and

$${}^HD_{1^+}^{\varsigma}\mathscr{H}(t,s) \leq^H D_{1^+}^{\varsigma}\mathscr{H}_1(e,s)\Xi,^H D_{1^+}^{\varsigma}\mathscr{H}(t,s) \geq (\ln t)^{\nu-\varsigma-1H}D_{1^+}{}^{\mu}\mathscr{H}_1(e,s)\overline{\Xi}.$$

Let $E = C^{\varsigma}[1,e]$, and

$$\|u\| = \max\{\|u\|_0, \|{}^HD_{1^+}^{\varsigma}u\|_0\}, \|v\| = \max\{\|v\|_0, \|{}^HD_{1^+}^{\varsigma}v\|_0\},$$

where

$$\begin{aligned}\|v\|_0 &= \max_{t\in[1,e]}|v(t)|, \|{}^HD_{1^+}^{\varsigma}v\|_0 = \max_{t\in[1,e]}|{}^HD_{1^+}^{\varsigma}v(t)|,\\ \|u\|_0 &= \max_{t\in[1,e]}|u(t)|, \|{}^HD_{1^+}^{\varsigma}u\|_0 = \max_{t\in[1,e]}|{}^HD_{1^+}^{\varsigma}u(t)|.\end{aligned}$$

Then, $(E, \|\cdot\|)$ is a real Banach space, and $E\times E$ is a Banach space with the norm $\|(u,v)\| = \max\{\|u\|,\|v\|\}$. Define $P_0 = \{u \in E : u(t) \geq 0,^H D_{1^+}^{\varsigma}u(t) \geq 0, \forall t \in (1,e)\}$, and let P be a cone on $E\times E$ and

$$P = \{(u,v) \in E\times E | u \in P_0, v \in P_0, t \in (1,e)\}.$$

The vector (u,v) is a solution of system (1) and (2) if and only if $(u,v) \in C(1,e) \times C(1,e)$ is a solution of the following nonlinear integral equation system:

$$\begin{Bmatrix} u(t) \\ v(t)\end{Bmatrix} = \begin{Bmatrix} \int_1^e \mathscr{G}(t,s)L_{q_1}\left(\mathscr{F}(s,v(s),^H D_{1^+}^{\varsigma}v(s)\right)\frac{ds}{s} \\ \int_1^e \mathscr{H}(t,s)L_{q_2}\left(\overline{\mathscr{F}}(s,u(s),^H D_{1^+}^{\overline{\varsigma}}u(s)\right)\frac{ds}{s}, \end{Bmatrix} = \begin{Bmatrix} A_1(v)(t) \\ A_2(u)(t)\end{Bmatrix},$$

for $\forall u, v \in P, t \in (1,e)$.

$$\begin{Bmatrix} {}^H D_{1^+}^{\varsigma} u(t) \\ {}^H D_{1^+}^{\overline{\mu}} v(t) \end{Bmatrix} = \begin{Bmatrix} \int_1^e {}^H D_{1^+}{}^{\varsigma} \mathscr{G}(t,s) L_{q_1}\left(\mathscr{F}(s, v(s), {}^H D_{1^+}^{\varsigma} v(s)\right) \frac{ds}{s} \\ \int_1^e {}^H D_{1^+}{}^{\overline{\varsigma}} \mathscr{H}(t,s) L_{q_2}\left(\overline{\mathscr{F}}(s, u(s), {}^H D_{1^+}^{\overline{\varsigma}} u(s)\right) \frac{ds}{s}, \end{Bmatrix} = \begin{Bmatrix} {}^H D_{1^+}^{\varsigma} A_1(v)(t) \\ {}^H D_{1^+}^{\overline{\varsigma}} A_2(u)(t) \end{Bmatrix}.$$

Now, an operator $A : P \to P$ is defined as follows:

$$A(u,v)(t) = (A_1(v)(t), A_2(u)(t)), (u,v) \in P, t \in (1,e).$$

Next, we show that the operators $A_i : P \to P (i = 1,2)$ and $A : P \to P$ are three completely continuous operators. □

Theorem 3. *Let* (H_0) *and* (H_1) *hold, then the operators* A_1 *and* A_2 *are continuous, that is,* A *is continuous.*

Proof. At first, by the properties of $\mathscr{G}$, $\mathscr{H}$ and (H_0), we have

$$\begin{aligned} A_1(v)(t) &= \int_1^e \mathscr{G}(t,s) L_{q_1}\left(\mathscr{F}(s, v(s), {}^H D_{1^+}^{\varsigma} v(s)\right) \frac{ds}{s} \\ &\leq \left(\frac{1}{\Gamma(\nu)} + \frac{1}{\Gamma(\nu)\Delta_1} \int_1^e h(t)(\ln t)^{\nu-1} dB(t)\right) \int_1^e L_{q_1}\left(\mathscr{F}(s, v(s), {}^H D_{1^+}^{\varsigma} v(s)\right) \frac{ds}{s} \\ &\leq \left(\frac{1}{\Gamma(\nu)} + \frac{1}{\Gamma(\nu)\Delta_1} \int_1^e h(t)(\ln t)^{\nu-1} dB(t)\right) \int_1^e L_{q_1}(\vartheta(s)) \frac{ds}{s} \\ &< +\infty, (v,u) \in P,\ t,s \in [1,e], \end{aligned} \tag{16}$$

$$\begin{aligned} A_2(u)(t) &= \int_1^e \mathscr{H}(t,s) L_{q_2}\left(\overline{\mathscr{F}}(s, u(s), {}^H D_{1^+}^{\varsigma} u(s)\right) \frac{ds}{s} \\ &\leq \left(\frac{1}{\Gamma(\iota)} + \frac{1}{\Gamma(\iota)\overline{\Delta}_1} \int_1^e \overline{h}(t)(\ln t)^{\iota-1} d\overline{B}(t)\right) \int_1^e L_{q_2}\left(\mathscr{F}(s, u(s), {}^H D_{1^+}^{\varsigma} u(s)\right) \frac{ds}{s} \\ &\leq \left(\frac{1}{\Gamma(\iota)} + \frac{1}{\Gamma(\iota)\overline{\Delta}_1} \int_1^e \overline{h}(t)(\ln t)^{\iota-1} d\overline{B}(t)\right) \int_1^e L_{q_2}(\overline{\vartheta}(s)) \frac{ds}{s} \\ &< +\infty, (v,u) \in P,\ t,s \in [1,e], \end{aligned} \tag{17}$$

so, we determine that $A(u,v)(t) = (A_1(v)(t), A_2(u)(t))$ is well defined on P.

Since $\mathscr{G}(t,s), {}^H D_{1^+}^{\varsigma} \mathscr{G}(t,s), \mathscr{H}(t,s), {}^H D_{1^+}^{\varsigma} \mathscr{H}(t,s)$ are uniformly continuous, there exists a large $\Upsilon > 0$ such that

$$\max\{\mathscr{G}(t,s), {}^H D_{1^+}^{\varsigma} \mathscr{G}(t,s), \mathscr{H}(t,s), {}^H D_{1^+}^{\varsigma} \mathscr{H}(t,s)\} \leq \Upsilon, t,s \in [1,e]. \tag{18}$$

Now, we show that $A : P \to P$ is continuous; let $(v_n, u_n) \to (v,u), ({}^H D_{1^+}^{\varsigma} v_n, {}^H D_{1^+}^{\varsigma} u_n) \to ({}^H D_{1^+}^{\varsigma} v, {}^H D_{1^+}^{\varsigma} u)$, which means that $v_n \to v, {}^H D_{1^+}^{\varsigma} v_n \to {}^H D_{1^+}^{\varsigma} v, u_n \to u, {}^H D_{1^+}^{\varsigma} u_n \to {}^H D_{1^+}^{\varsigma} u$ in $C^{\varsigma}[1,e]$. Since $v_n \to v, {}^H D_{1^+}^{\varsigma} v_n \to {}^H D_{1^+}^{\varsigma} v, u_n \to u, {}^H D_{1^+}^{\varsigma} u_n \to {}^H D_{1^+}^{\varsigma} u$, there exists a large enough $\Pi > 0$ such that $\|(v_n, u_n)\| \leq \Pi, \|({}^H \mathscr{D}_{1^+}^{\varsigma} v_n, {}^H \mathscr{D}_{1^+}^{\varsigma} u_n)\| \leq \Pi\ (n = 1,2,\cdots)$, and then $\|(v,u)\| \leq \Pi, \|({}^H \mathscr{D}_{1^+}^{\varsigma} v, {}^H \mathscr{D}_{1^+}^{\varsigma} u)\| \leq \Pi$, that is $\|v\| < \Pi, \|{}^H \mathscr{D}_{1^+}^{\varsigma} v\| < \Pi, \|u\| < \Pi, \|{}^H \mathscr{D}_{1^+}^{\varsigma} u\| < \Pi$.

Furthermore, by (H_0) and (18), we have

$$\left| \int_1^e \mathscr{G}(t,s) L_{q_1}\left(\mathscr{F}(s, v_n(s), {}^H D_{1^+}^{\varsigma} v_n(s))\right) \frac{ds}{s} \right| < \Upsilon \left| \int_1^e L_{q_1}(\theta(s)) \frac{ds}{s} \right| < +\infty, \tag{19}$$

$$\left| \int_1^e {}^H D_{1^+}^{\varsigma} \mathscr{G}(t,s) L_{q_1}\left(\mathscr{F}(s, v_n(s), {}^H D_{1^+}^{\varsigma} v_n(s))\right) \frac{ds}{s} \right| < \Upsilon \left| \int_1^e L_{q_1}(\theta(s)) \frac{ds}{s} \right| < +\infty, \tag{20}$$

$$\left|\int_1^e \mathscr{H}(t,s)L_{q_2}\left(\overline{\mathscr{F}}(s,u_n(s),{}^H D_{1^+}^{\varsigma}u_n(s))\right)\frac{ds}{s}\right| < \Upsilon\left|\int_1^e L_{q_2}(\overline{\theta}(s))\frac{ds}{s}\right| < +\infty. \quad (21)$$

$$\left|\int_1^e {}^H D_{1^+}^{\varsigma}\mathscr{H}(t,s)L_{q_2}\left(\overline{\mathscr{F}}(s,u_n(s),{}^H D_{1^+}^{\varsigma}u_n(s))\right)\frac{ds}{s}\right| < \Upsilon\left|\int_1^e L_{q_2}(\overline{\theta}(s))\frac{ds}{s}\right| < +\infty. \quad (22)$$

By (H_0), we know that $L_{q_1}(\theta(s))$, and $L_{q_2}(\overline{\theta}(s))$ is integrable. Hence, for any $t \in [1,e]$, $n > N$, by (19)–(22) and the Lebesgue control convergence theorem, we obtain

$$\begin{aligned}
&|(A_1v_n)(t) - (A_1v)(t)| \\
=&\left|\int_1^e \mathscr{G}(t,s)L_{q_1}\left(\mathscr{F}(s,v_n(s),{}^H D_{1^+}^{\varsigma}v_n(s)\right)\frac{ds}{s}\right. \\
&\left.-\int_1^e \mathscr{G}(t,s)L_{q_1}\left(\mathscr{F}(s,v(s),{}^H D_{1^+}^{\varsigma}v(s)\right)\frac{ds}{s}\right| \\
\leq&\varepsilon,
\end{aligned}$$

$$\begin{aligned}
&|{}^H D_{1^+}^{\varsigma}(A_1v_n)(t) - {}^H D_{1^+}^{\varsigma}(A_1v)(t)| \\
=&\left|\int_1^e {}^H D_{1^+}^{\varsigma}\mathscr{G}(t,s)L_{q_1}\left(\mathscr{F}(s,v_n(s),{}^H D_{1^+}^{\varsigma}v_n(s)\right)\frac{ds}{s}\right. \\
&\left.-\int_1^e {}^H D_{1^+}^{\varsigma}\mathscr{G}(t,s)L_{q_1}\left(\mathscr{F}(s,v(s),{}^H D_{1^+}^{\varsigma}v(s)\right)\frac{ds}{s}\right| \\
\leq&\varepsilon,
\end{aligned}$$

and

$$\begin{aligned}
&|(A_2u_n)(t) - (A_2u)(t)| \\
=&\left|\int_1^e \mathscr{H}(t,s)L_{q_2}\left(\overline{\mathscr{F}}(s,u_n(s),{}^H D_{1^+}^{\varsigma}u_n(s)\right)\frac{ds}{s}\right. \\
&\left.-\int_1^e \mathscr{H}(t,s)L_{q_2}\left(\overline{\mathscr{F}}(s,u(s),{}^H D_{1^+}^{\varsigma}u(s)\right)\frac{ds}{s}\right| \\
=&\left|\int_1^e \mathscr{H}(t,s)\left(L_{q_2}\left(\overline{\mathscr{F}}(s,u_n(s),{}^H D_{1^+}^{\varsigma}u_n(s)\right)\right.\right. \\
&\left.\left.-L_{q_2}\left(\mathscr{F}(s,u_n(s),{}^H D_{1^+}^{\varsigma}u_n(s)\right)\frac{ds}{s}\right| \\
\leq&\varepsilon,
\end{aligned}$$

$$\begin{aligned}
&|{}^H D_{1^+}^{\varsigma}(A_2u_n)(t) - {}^H D_{1^+}^{\varsigma}(A_2u)(t)| \\
=&\left|\int_1^e {}^H D_{1^+}^{\varsigma}\mathscr{H}(t,s)L_{q_2}\left(\overline{\mathscr{F}}(s,u_n(s),{}^H D_{1^+}^{\varsigma}u_n(s)\right)\frac{ds}{s}\right. \\
&\left.-\int_1^e {}^H D_{1^+}^{\varsigma}\mathscr{H}(t,s)L_{q_2}\left(\overline{\mathscr{F}}(s,u(s),{}^H D_{1^+}^{\varsigma}u(s)\right)\frac{ds}{s}\right| \\
=&\left|\int_1^e {}^H D_{1^+}^{\varsigma}\mathscr{H}(t,s)\left(L_{q_2}\left(\overline{\mathscr{F}}(s,u_n(s),{}^H D_{1^+}^{\varsigma}u_n(s)\right)\right.\right. \\
&\left.\left.-L_{q_2}\left(\mathscr{F}(s,u_n(s),{}^H D_{1^+}^{\varsigma}u_n(s)\right)\frac{ds}{s}\right| \\
\leq&\varepsilon,
\end{aligned}$$

and hence, we obtain $\|A_1v_n - A_1v\|_0 \to 0$, $\|{}^H D_{1^+}^{\varsigma}(A_1v_n) - {}^H D_{1^+}^{\varsigma}(Av_1)\|_0 \to 0$, $\|A_2u_n - A_2u\|_0 \to 0$, $\|{}^H D_{1^+}^{\varsigma}(A_2u_n) - {}^H D_{1^+}^{\varsigma}(A_2u)\|_0 \to 0$ $(n \to \infty)$. That is, $\|A_1v_n - A_1v\| \to 0$, $\|A_2u_n - A_2u\| \to 0$, $(n \to \infty)$, namely A is continuous in the space E. □

Theorem 4. *Let* (H_0) *and* (H_1) *hold, then the operators* A_1, A_2 *and* A *are completely continuous.*

Proof. From Theorem 2, we have $(Au)(t),{}^H D^{\mu}_{1+}(Au)(t),(Av)(t),{}^H D^{\mu}_{1+}(Av)(t) \geq 0, t \in [1,e]$, and thus, $A(P) \subset P$.

Now, we will prove that AV is relatively compact for bounded $V \subset P$. Since V is bounded, there exists $D > 0$ such that for any $(v,u) \in V$, $\|(v,u)\| \leq D$. For $t \in [1,e]$, $(v,u) \in V$, we have

$$\begin{aligned}
A_1(v)(t) &= \int_1^e \mathscr{G}(t,s)L_{q_1}\left(\mathscr{F}(s,v(s),{}^H D^{\varsigma}_{1+}v(s)\right)\frac{ds}{s} \\
&\leq \left(\frac{1}{\Gamma(\nu)}+\frac{1}{\Gamma(\nu)\Delta_1}\int_1^e h(t)(\ln t)^{\nu-1}dB(t)\right)\int_1^e L_{q_1}\left(\mathscr{F}(s,v(s),{}^H D^{\varsigma}_{1+}v(s)\right)\frac{ds}{s} \\
&\leq \left(\frac{1}{\Gamma(\nu)}+\frac{1}{\Gamma(\nu)\Delta_1}\int_1^e h(t)(\ln t)^{\nu-1}dB(t)\right)\int_1^e L_{q_1}(\vartheta(s))\frac{ds}{s} \\
&= \left(\frac{1}{\Gamma(\nu)}+\frac{1}{\Gamma(\nu)\Delta_1}\imath\right)\jmath < +\infty, (v,u) \in P, t,s \in [1,e],
\end{aligned} \tag{23}$$

$$\begin{aligned}
&{}^H D^{\varsigma}_{1+}A_1(v)(t) = \int_1^e {}^H D^{\varsigma}_{1+}\mathscr{G}(t,s)L_{q_1}\left(\mathscr{F}(s,v(s),{}^H D^{\varsigma}_{1+}v(s)\right)\frac{ds}{s} \\
&\leq \left(\frac{1}{\Gamma(\nu-\varsigma)}+\frac{1}{\Gamma(\nu-\varsigma)\Delta_1}\int_1^e h(t)(\ln t)^{\nu-1}dB(t)\right)\int_1^e L_{q_1}\left(\mathscr{F}(s,v(s),{}^H D^{\varsigma}_{1+}v(s)\right)\frac{ds}{s} \\
&\leq \left(\frac{1}{\Gamma(\nu-\varsigma)}+\frac{1}{\Gamma(\nu-\varsigma)\Delta_1}\int_1^e h(t)(\ln t)^{\nu-1}dB(t)\right)\int_1^e L_{q_1}(\vartheta(s))\frac{ds}{s} \\
&= \left(\frac{1}{\Gamma(\nu-\varsigma)}+\frac{1}{\Gamma(\nu-\varsigma)\Delta_1}\imath\right)\jmath < +\infty, (u,v) \in P, t,s \in [1,e],
\end{aligned} \tag{24}$$

where $\imath = \int_1^e h(t)(\ln t)^{\nu-1}dB(t), \jmath = \int_1^e \varphi_{q_1}(\vartheta(s))\frac{ds}{s}$. Similarly, for $t \in [1,e]$, $(v,u) \in V$, we derive

$$\begin{aligned}
A_2(u)(t) &= \int_1^e \mathscr{H}(t,s)L_{q_2}\left(\overline{\mathscr{F}}(s,u(s),{}^H D^{\varsigma}_{1+}u(s)\right)\frac{ds}{s} \\
&\leq \left(\frac{1}{\Gamma(\iota)}+\frac{1}{\Gamma(\beta)\overline{\Delta}_1}\int_1^e \overline{h}(t)(\ln t)^{\iota-1}d\overline{B}(t)\right)\int_1^e L_{q_2}\left(\mathscr{F}(s,u(s),{}^H D^{\varsigma}_{1+}u(s)\right)\frac{ds}{s} \\
&\leq \left(\frac{1}{\Gamma(\iota)}+\frac{1}{\Gamma(\iota)\overline{\Delta}_1}\int_1^e \overline{h}(t)(\ln t)^{\iota-1}d\overline{B}(t)\right)\int_1^e L_{q_2}(\overline{\vartheta}(s))\frac{ds}{s} \\
&= \left(\frac{1}{\Gamma(\iota)}+\frac{1}{\Gamma(\iota)\overline{\Delta}_1}\overline{\imath}\right)\overline{\jmath} < +\infty, (v,u) \in P, t,s \in [1,e],
\end{aligned} \tag{25}$$

$$\begin{aligned}
&{}^H D^{\mu}_{1+}A_2(u)(t) = \int_1^e {}^H D^{\varsigma}_{1+}\mathscr{H}(t,s)L_{q_2}\left(\overline{\mathscr{F}}(s,u(s),{}^H D^{\varsigma}_{1+}u(s)\right)\frac{ds}{s} \\
&\leq \left(\frac{1}{\Gamma(\iota-\varsigma)}+\frac{1}{\Gamma(\iota-\varsigma)\overline{\Delta}_1}\int_1^e \overline{h}(t)(\ln t)^{\iota-1}d\overline{B}(t)\right)\int_1^e L_{q_2}\left(\mathscr{F}(s,u(s),{}^H D^{\varsigma}_{1+}u(s)\right)\frac{ds}{s} \\
&\leq \left(\frac{1}{\Gamma(\iota-\varsigma)}+\frac{1}{\Gamma(\iota-\varsigma)\overline{\Delta}_1}\int_1^e \overline{h}(t)(\ln t)^{\iota-1}d\overline{B}(t)\right)\int_1^e L_{q_2}(\overline{\vartheta}(s))\frac{ds}{s} \\
&= \left(\frac{1}{\Gamma(\iota-\varsigma)}+\frac{1}{\Gamma(\iota-\varsigma)\overline{\Delta}_1}\overline{\imath}\right)\overline{\jmath} < +\infty, (u,v) \in P, t,s \in [1,e],
\end{aligned} \tag{26}$$

where $\bar{\imath} = \int_1^e \bar{h}(t)(\ln t)^{\iota-1} d\bar{B}(t), \bar{\jmath} = \int_1^e L_{q2}(\bar{\vartheta}(s))\frac{ds}{s}$, which shows that AV is bounded. Next, we will verify that ${}^H D_{1+}^{\varsigma}(AV)$ is equicontinuous. Let $t_1, t_2 \in [1,e], t_1 < t_2, (v,u) \in V$, we obtain

$$
\begin{aligned}
&|{}^H D_{1+}^{\varsigma}(A_1 v)(t_2) - {}^H D_{1+}^{\varsigma}(A_1 v)(t_1)| \\
=& \Big| \int_1^e {}^H D_{1+}^{\varsigma} \mathscr{G}(t_2,s) L_{q_1}\left(\mathscr{F}(s,v(s),{}^H D_{1+}^{\varsigma} v(s)\right)\frac{ds}{s} \\
&- \int_1^e {}^H D_{1+}^{\varsigma} \mathscr{G}(t_1,s) L_{q_1}\left(\mathscr{F}(s,v(s),{}^H D_{1+}^{\varsigma} v(s)\right)\frac{ds}{s}\Big| \\
=& |(\ln t_2)^{\nu-1-\varsigma} - (\ln t_1)^{\nu-1-\varsigma}| \int_1^e L_{q_1}\left(\mathscr{F}(s,v(s),{}^H D_{s+}^{\varsigma} v(s)\right)\frac{ds}{s} \\
&+ |(\ln t_2)^{\nu-1-\varsigma} - (\ln t_1)^{\nu-1-\varsigma}| \frac{\Gamma(\nu)\int_1^e h(t)\mathscr{G}(t,s)dB(t)}{\Delta_1 \Gamma(\alpha-\mu)} \int_1^e L_{q_1}\left(\mathscr{F}(s,v(s),{}^H D_{1+}^{\varsigma} v(s)\right)\frac{ds}{s} \\
&+ \frac{1}{\Gamma(\nu-\mu)} \int_1^{t_1} \left|(\ln t_1 - \ln s)^{\nu-1-\varsigma} - (\ln t_2 - \ln s)^{\nu-1-\varsigma}\right| L_{q_1}\left(\mathscr{F}(s,v(s),{}^H D_{1+}^{\varsigma} v(s)\right)\frac{ds}{s} \\
&+ \int_{t_1}^{t_2} (\ln t_1 - \ln s)^{\nu-1-\varsigma} L_{q_1}\left(\mathscr{F}(s,v(s),{}^H D_{1+}^{\varsigma} v(s)\right)\frac{ds}{s} \\
\le& \left|(\ln t_2)^{\nu-1-\varsigma} - (\ln t_1)^{\nu-1-\varsigma}\right| \frac{1}{\Gamma(\nu-\varsigma)} \int_1^e L_{q_1}(\vartheta(s))\frac{ds}{s} + \int_{t_1}^{t_2} (\ln t - \ln s)^{\nu-1-\varsigma} L_{q_1}(\vartheta(s))\frac{ds}{s} \\
&+ \frac{1}{\Gamma(\nu-\varsigma)} \int_1^{t_1} |(\ln t_1 - \ln s)^{\nu-1-\varsigma} - (\ln t_2 - \ln s)^{\nu-1-\varsigma}| L_{q_1}(\vartheta(s))\frac{ds}{s},
\end{aligned}
$$

$$
\begin{aligned}
&\left|{}^H D_{1+}^{\varsigma}(A_2 u)(t_2) - {}^H D_{1+}^{\varsigma}(A_2 u)(t_1)\right| \\
=& \Big| \int_1^e {}^H D_{1+}^{\varsigma} \mathscr{G}(t_2,s) L_{q2}\left(\mathscr{F}(s,u(s),{}^H D_{1+}^{\varsigma} u(s)\right)\frac{ds}{s} \\
&- \int_1^e {}^H D_{1+}^{\varsigma} \mathscr{G}(t_1,s) L_{q2}\left(\mathscr{F}(s,u(s),{}^H D_{1+}^{\varsigma} u(s)\right)\frac{ds}{s}\Big| \\
=& |(\ln t_2)^{\iota-1-\mu} - (\ln t_1)^{\iota-1-\varsigma}| \int_1^e L_{q_1}\left(\mathscr{F}(s,u(s),{}^H D_{1+}^{\varsigma} u(s)\right)\frac{ds}{s} \\
&+ |(\ln t_2)^{\iota-1-\varsigma} - (\ln t_1)^{\iota-1-\varsigma}| \frac{\Gamma(\iota)\int_1^e h(t)\mathscr{H}(t,s)dB(t)}{\Delta_1 \Gamma(\iota-\varsigma)} \int_1^e L_{q2}\left(\overline{\mathscr{F}}(s,u(s),{}^H D_{1+}^{\varsigma} u(s)\right)\frac{ds}{s} \\
&+ \frac{1}{\Gamma(\iota-\varsigma)} \int_1^{t_1} |(\ln t_1 - \ln s)^{\iota-1-\varsigma} - (\ln t_2 - \ln s)^{\iota-1-\varsigma}| L_{q2}\left(\overline{\mathscr{F}}(s,u(s),{}^H D_{1+}^{\varsigma} u(s)\right)\frac{ds}{s} \\
&+ \int_{t_1}^{t_2} (\ln t_1 - \ln s)^{\iota-1-\varsigma} L_{q2}\left(\overline{\mathscr{F}}(s,u(s),{}^H D_{1+}^{\varsigma} u(s)\right)\frac{ds}{s} \\
\le& \left|(\ln t_2)^{\iota-1-\varsigma} - (\ln t_1)^{\iota-1-\varsigma}\right| \frac{1}{\Gamma(\iota-\varsigma)} \int_1^e L_{q2}(\bar{\vartheta}(s))\frac{ds}{s} + \int_{t_1}^{t_2} (\ln t - \ln s)^{\iota-1-\varsigma} \varphi_{q2}(\bar{\vartheta}(s))\frac{ds}{s} \\
&+ \frac{1}{\Gamma(\iota-\varsigma)} \int_1^{t_1} \left|(\ln t_1 - \ln s)^{\iota-1-\varsigma} - (\ln t_2 - \ln s)^{\iota-1-\varsigma}\right| L_{q2}(\bar{\vartheta}(s))\frac{ds}{s} \\
&+ |(\ln t_2)^{\iota-1-\varsigma} - (\ln t_1)^{\iota-1-\varsigma}| \frac{\Gamma(\iota)\int_1^e h(t)\mathscr{H}(t,s)dB(t)}{\Delta_1 \Gamma(\iota-\varsigma)} \int_1^e L_{q2}(\bar{\vartheta}(s))\frac{ds}{s}.
\end{aligned}
$$

From the above and the uniform continuity of $(\ln t)^{\nu-1-\varsigma}, (\ln t - \ln s)^{\nu-1-\varsigma}, (\ln t)^{\iota-1-\varsigma}, (\ln t - \ln s)^{\iota-1-\varsigma}$, and together with Lemma 6, we can derive that AV is relatively compact in $C^{(\mu)}[1,e]$, and so, we determine that $A : P \to P$ is completely continuous. □

3. Main Results

Theorem 5. *Suppose that* (H_0) *and* (H_1) *hold, and there exist* $t_0 \in (0,1)$ *and two positive constants* $\rho, \xi, \rho > \xi$*; further, suppose the following are true:*

(i) For $\forall(t,x,y) \in [1,e] \times [0,\xi] \times [0,\xi]$,

$$L_{q_1}(\mathscr{F}(t,v(t),{}^H D^{\varsigma}_{1+}v(t))) \geq \xi \max\left\{\frac{1}{(\ln t_0)^{\nu-1}\Upsilon}\left(\int_{t_0}^{e}\mathscr{G}_1(t_0,s)\frac{ds}{s}\right)^{-1}, \frac{1}{(\ln t_0)^{\nu-\varsigma-1}\Upsilon}\left(\int_{t_0}^{e}{}^H D_{1+}{}^{\varsigma}\mathscr{G}_1(t_0,s)\frac{ds}{s}\right)^{-1}\right\},$$

$$L_{q_2}(\overline{\mathscr{F}}(t,u(t),{}^H D^{\varsigma}_{1+}u(t))) \geq \xi\left\{\frac{1}{(\ln t_0)^{\iota-1}\Xi}\left(\int_{t_0}^{e}\mathscr{H}_1(t_0,s)\frac{ds}{s}\right)^{-1}, \frac{1}{(\ln t_0)^{\iota-\varsigma-1}\Xi}\left(\int_{t_0}^{e}{}^H D_{1+}{}^{\mu}\mathscr{H}_1(t_0,s)\frac{ds}{s}\right)^{-1}\right\}.$$

(ii) For $\forall(t,x,y) \in [1,e] \times [0,\rho] \times [0,\rho]$, *we have*

$$\mathscr{F}(s,v(s),{}^H D^{\varsigma}_{1+}v(s)) \leq \theta(s)\rho^{\frac{1}{q_1-1}}, \overline{\mathscr{F}}(s,u(s),{}^H D^{\varsigma}_{1+}u(s)) \leq \overline{\theta}(s)\rho^{\frac{1}{q_2-1}},$$
$$\forall(t,x_0,x_1) \in [1,e] \times [0,+\infty) \times [0,+\infty),$$

and

$$\Upsilon\int_1^e \max\{\mathscr{G}(e,s),{}^H D^{\varsigma}_{1+}\mathscr{G}(e,s)\}L_{q_1}(\theta(s))\frac{ds}{s} < 1,$$

$$\Xi\int_1^e \max\{\mathscr{H}(e,s),{}^H D^{\varsigma}_{1+}\mathscr{H}(e,s)\}L_{q_2}(\overline{\theta}(s))\frac{ds}{s} < 1.$$

Then, BVPs (1) and (2) have at least one positive solution.

Proof. Let $\Omega_1 = \{(u,v) \in P \mid \|u\| < \xi, \|v\| < \xi\}$ such that $0 < u(t), v(t) \leq \xi$ for any $(u,v) \in P \cap \partial\Omega_1$ and for all $t \in [1,e]$. By condition (i) and Theorem 2, we have

$$\begin{aligned} A_1 v(t_0) &= \int_1^e \mathscr{G}(t_0,s)L_{q_1}\left(\mathscr{F}(s,v(s),{}^H D^{\varsigma}_{1+}v(s)\right)\frac{ds}{s} \\ &\geq \int_{t_0}^e \mathscr{G}_1(e,s)(\ln t_0)^{\nu-1}\Upsilon\frac{ds}{s}\frac{\xi}{(\ln t_0)^{\nu-1}\Upsilon}\left(\int_{t_0}^{e}\mathscr{G}_1(t_0,s)\frac{ds}{s}\right)^{-1} \\ &= \xi, \end{aligned}$$

$$\begin{aligned} {}^H D^{\varsigma}_{1+}A_1 v(t_0) &= \int_1^e {}^H D^{\varsigma}_{1+}\mathscr{G}(t_0,s)L_{q_1}\left(\mathscr{F}(s,v(s),{}^H D^{\varsigma}_{1+}v(s)\right)\frac{ds}{s} \\ &\geq \int_{t_0}^e ({}^H D^{\varsigma}_{1+}\mathscr{G}_1(e,s)(\ln t_0)^{\nu-\varsigma-1}\Upsilon\frac{ds}{s}\frac{\xi}{(\ln t_0)^{\nu-\varsigma-1}\Upsilon}\left(\int_{t_0}^{e}({}^H D^{\varsigma}_{1+}\mathscr{G}_1(t_0,s))\frac{ds}{s}\right)^{-1} \\ &= \xi, \end{aligned}$$

$$\begin{aligned} A_2 u(t_0) &= \int_1^e \mathscr{H}(t_0,s)L_{q_2}\left(\overline{\mathscr{F}}(s,u(s),{}^H D^{\varsigma}_{1+}u(s)\right)\frac{ds}{s} \\ &\geq \int_{t_0}^e \mathscr{H}_1(e,s)(\ln t_0)^{\beta-1}\Xi\frac{ds}{s}\frac{\xi}{(\ln t_0)^{\beta-1}\Xi}\left(\int_{t_0}^{e}\mathscr{H}_1(t_0,s)\frac{ds}{s}\right)^{-1} \\ &= \xi, \end{aligned}$$

$$\begin{aligned} {}^H D^{\varsigma}_{1+}A_2 u(t_0) &= \int_1^e {}^H D^{\varsigma}_{1+}\mathscr{H}(t_0,s)L_{q_2}\left(\overline{\mathscr{F}}(s,u(s),{}^H D^{\varsigma}_{1+}u(s)\right)\frac{ds}{s} \\ &\geq \int_{t_0}^e {}^H D_{1+}{}^{\varsigma}\mathscr{H}_1(e,s)(\ln t_0)^{\iota-\varsigma-1}\Xi\frac{ds}{s}\frac{\xi}{(\ln t_0)^{\iota-\varsigma-1}\Xi}\left(\int_{t_0}^{e}{}^H D_{1+}{}^{\varsigma}\mathscr{H}_1(t_0,s)\frac{ds}{s}\right)^{-1} \\ &= \xi. \end{aligned}$$

Hence,

$$\|A_1 v\| = \max\{\|A_1 v\|_0, \|^H D^{\varsigma}_{1+} A_1 v\|_0\} \geq \xi,$$

$$\|A_2 u\| = \max\{\|A_2 v\|_0, \|^H D^{\varsigma}_{1+} A_2 v\|_0\} \geq \xi, \forall (u,v) \in P \cap \partial\Omega_2.$$

So,

$$\|A(u,v)\| = \max\{\|A_1 v\|, \|A_2 u\|\} \geq \xi = \|(u,v)\|.$$

Let $\Omega_1 = \{(u,v) \in P | \|u\| < \rho, \|v\| < \rho\}$, where $\rho > \xi$. For any $(u,v) \in P \cap \partial\Omega_2, t \in [1,e]$, we have $0 < u(t), v(t) \leq \rho$. By condition (ii) and Theorem 2, we have

$$\begin{aligned} A_1 v(t) &= \int_1^e \mathscr{G}(t,s) L_{q_1}\left(\mathscr{F}(s, v(s), ^H D^{\varsigma}_{1+} v(s)\right) \frac{ds}{s} \\ &\leq \int_1^e \mathscr{G}_1(e,s) \Upsilon \rho L_{q_1}(\theta(s) \frac{ds}{s} = \rho \Upsilon \int_1^e \mathscr{G}(e,s) \varphi_{q_1}(\theta(s)) \frac{ds}{s} \\ &\leq \rho, \end{aligned}$$

$$\begin{aligned} {}^H D^{\varsigma}_{1+} A_1 v(t) &= \int_1^e {}^H D^{\varsigma}_{1+} \mathscr{G}(t,s) L_{q_1}\left(\mathscr{F}(s, v(s), ^H D^{\varsigma}_{1+} v(s)\right) \frac{ds}{s} \\ &\leq \int_1^e {}^H D^{\varsigma}_{1+} (\mathscr{G}_1(e,s) \Upsilon \rho L_{q_1}(\theta(s)) \frac{ds}{s} = \rho \Upsilon \int_1^e {}^H D^{\varsigma}_{1+} \mathscr{G}(e,s) L_{q_1}(\theta(s)) \frac{ds}{s} \\ &\leq \rho, \end{aligned}$$

$$\begin{aligned} A_2 u(t) &= \int_1^e \mathscr{H}(t,s) L_{q_1}\left(\mathscr{F}(s, u(s), ^H D^{\varsigma}_{1+} u(s)\right) \frac{ds}{s} \\ &\leq \int_1^e \mathscr{H}_1(e,s) \rho \Xi L_{q_2}(\overline{\theta}(s)) \frac{ds}{s} = \Xi \rho \int_1^e \mathscr{H}_1(e,s) L_{q_2}(\overline{\theta}(s)) \frac{ds}{s} \\ &\leq \rho, \end{aligned}$$

$$\begin{aligned} {}^H D^{\varsigma}_{1+} A_2 u(t) &= \int_1^e {}^H D^{\mu}_{1+} \mathscr{H}(t,s) L_{q_1}\left(\mathscr{F}(s, u(s), ^H D^{\varsigma}_{1+} u(s)\right) \frac{ds}{s} \\ &\leq \int_1^e {}^H D^{\varsigma}_{1+} \mathscr{H}_1(e,s) \rho L_{q_2}(\overline{\theta}(s)) \frac{ds}{s} = \Xi \rho \int_1^e {}^H D^{\varsigma}_{1+} \mathscr{H}_1(e,s) L_{q_2}(\overline{\theta}(s)) \frac{ds}{s} \\ &\leq \rho, \end{aligned}$$

then we have

$$\|A_1 v\| = \max\{\|A_1 v\|_0, \|^H D^{\varsigma}_{1+} A_1 v\|_0\} \leq \rho,$$

$$\|A_2 u\| = \max\{\|A_2 u\|_0, \|^H D^{\varsigma}_{1+} A_2 u\|_0\} \leq \rho, \forall (u,v) \in P \cap \partial\Omega_2.$$

Hence, $\|A(u,v)\| = \max\{\|A_1 v\|, \|A_2 u\|\} \leq \rho = \|(u,v)\|$. According to Theorem 4, operator $A : P \to P$ is completely continuous; thus, by Lemma 4, the proof is finished. □

Theorem 6. *Suppose that* (H_0) *and* (H_1) *hold, and there exist the functions* $\theta(t), \overline{\theta}(t)$ *and the non-decreasing functions* $\varphi, \psi : [0, +\infty) \to (0, +\infty)$ *such that*
(iii)

$$\begin{aligned} &\mathscr{F}(s, v(s), ^H D^{\varsigma}_{1+} v(s)) \leq \theta(s) \varphi^{\frac{1}{q_1 - 1}}(v), \overline{\mathscr{F}}(s, u(s), ^H D^{\varsigma}_{1+} u(s)) \leq \overline{\theta}(s) \psi^{\frac{1}{q_2 - 1}}(u), \\ &\forall (t, x_0, x_1) \in [1,e] \times [0, +\infty) \times [0, +\infty); \end{aligned}$$

(iv) *and there exists an* $r > 0$, *such that*

$$\frac{r}{\max\{\varphi(r)), \psi((r)|)\}} > \max\left\{ \int_1^e \mathscr{G}_1(e,s) \Upsilon L_{q_1}(\theta(s)) \frac{ds}{s}, \int_1^e \mathscr{H}_1(e,s) \Upsilon L_{q_2}(\overline{\theta}(s)) \frac{ds}{s} \right\}.$$

Then, the BVPs (1) and (2) have a positive solution.

Proof. Let $U = \{(u,v) \in P \| \|(u,v)\| < r\}$, then $U \subset P$. According to Theorems 3 and 4, we determine that operator $A : \overline{U} \to P$ is completely continuous. If there exists $(u,v) \in \partial U$ and $\widetilde{\lambda} \in (0,1)$, we obtain $(u,v) = \widetilde{\lambda} A(u,v)$, and then, by (iii) for $t \in [1,e]$, we have

$$\begin{aligned} v(t) = \widetilde{\lambda} A_1 v(t) =& \widetilde{\lambda} \int_1^e \mathscr{G}(t,s) L_{q_1}\left(\mathscr{F}(s, v(s), {}^H D_{1^+}^{\varsigma} v(s)\right) \frac{ds}{s} \\ <& \int_1^e \mathscr{G}(t,s) L_{q_1}\left(\mathscr{F}(s, v(s), {}^H D_{1^+}^{\varsigma} v(s)\right) \frac{ds}{s} \\ <& \int_1^e \mathscr{G}(t,s) L_{q_1}\left(\theta(s) L^{\frac{1}{q_1 - 1}}(v)\right) \frac{ds}{s} \\ \leq& \varphi(\|v\|) \int_1^e \mathscr{G}_1(e,s) \Upsilon L_{q_1}(\theta(s)) \frac{ds}{s} \\ \leq& \varphi(\|(u,v)\|) \int_1^e \mathscr{G}_1(e,s) \Upsilon L_{q_1}(\theta(s)) \frac{ds}{s}; \end{aligned}$$

hence,

$$\|v\| \leq \varphi(\|(u,v)\|) \int_1^e \mathscr{G}_1(e,s) \Upsilon L_{q_1}(\theta(s)) \frac{ds}{s},$$

that is,

$$\frac{\|v\|}{\varphi(\|(u,v)\|)} \leq \int_1^e \mathscr{G}_1(e,s) \Upsilon L_{q_1}(\theta(s)) \frac{ds}{s}.$$

Similarly,

$$\frac{\|u\|}{\psi(\|(u,v)\|)} \leq \int_1^e \mathscr{H}_1(e,s) \Upsilon L_{q_2}(\overline{\theta}(s)) \frac{ds}{s}.$$

Hence,

$$\begin{aligned} &\frac{\|(u,v)\|}{\max\{\varphi(\|(u,v)\|), \psi(\|(u,v)\|)\}} \\ &\leq \max\left\{ \int_1^e \mathscr{G}_1(e,s) \Upsilon L_{q_1}(\theta(s)) \frac{ds}{s}, \int_1^e \mathscr{H}_1(e,s) \Xi L_{q_2}(\overline{\theta}(s)) \frac{ds}{s} \right\}. \end{aligned}$$

By (iv), we have $\|(u,v)\| \neq r$, which means $(u,v) \notin \partial U$. Then, by Lemma 5, a fixed point $(u,v) \in U$ is obtained. Hence, the BVPs (1) and (2) have a positive solution.

In this section, we consider the equation under the condition of $\mathscr{F}(s, x_1, y_1)$ and $\overline{\mathscr{F}}(s, x_1, y_1)$ being continuous. □

Theorem 7. *Assume that functions $\mathscr{F}(s, x_1, y_1)$ and $\overline{\mathscr{F}}(s, x_1, y_1)$ are continuous, and there exist functions $\theta(t), \overline{\theta}(t)$ and non-decreasing functions $\varphi, \psi : [0, +\infty) \to (0, +\infty)$ such that*

$$|L_{q_1}(\mathscr{F}(s, x_1, y_1)) - L_{q_1}(\mathscr{F}(s, x_2, y_2))| \leq L_1 \theta_1(s) |x_1 - x_2| + L_2 \theta_2(s) |y_1 - y_2|,$$

$$|L_{q_2}(\overline{\mathscr{F}}(s, x_1, y_1)) - L_{q_2}(\overline{\mathscr{F}}(s, x_2, y_2))| \leq \overline{L}_1 \overline{\theta}_1(s) |x_1 - x_2| + \overline{L}_2 \overline{\theta}_2(s) |y_1 - y_2|,$$

and

$$\frac{1}{\Gamma(\nu)} \Upsilon(L_1 \theta_1(s) + L_2 \theta_1(s)) < 1,$$

$$\frac{1}{\Gamma(\iota)} \Xi(\overline{L}_1 \theta_1(s) + \overline{L}_2 \overline{\theta}_1(s)) < 1.$$

Then, the BVPs (1) and (2) have a unique solution. In addition, we can obtain the unique solution by constructing an iterative sequence and error estimate.

Proof. In this section, we will use the Banach fixed point theorem. For $\forall t \in [1,e], v_1, v_2, u_1, u_2 \in E$, we have

$$\begin{aligned}
&|A_1v_2(t) - A_1v_1(t)| \\
=&\left|\int_1^e \mathscr{G}(t,s)L_{q_1}\left(\mathscr{F}(s,v_2(s),{}^H D^{\varsigma}_{1+}v_2(s)\right)\frac{ds}{s} - \int_1^e \mathscr{G}(t,s)L_{q_1}\left(\mathscr{F}(s,v_1(s),{}^H D^{\varsigma}_{1+}v_1(s)\right)\frac{ds}{s}\right| \\
=&\int_1^e \mathscr{G}(t,s)|L_{q_1}\left(\mathscr{F}(s,v_2(s),{}^H D^{\varsigma}_{1+}v_2(s)\right) - L_{q_1}\left(\mathscr{F}(s,v_1(s),{}^H D^{\varsigma}_{1+}v_1(s)\right)|\frac{ds}{s} \\
\leq&\int_1^e \mathscr{G}_1(t,s)\Upsilon(L_1\theta_1(s)|v_2(s) - v_1(s)| + L_2\theta_1(s)|{}^H D^{\varsigma}_{1+}v_2(s) - {}^H D^{\varsigma}_{1+}v_1(s)|) \\
\leq&\frac{1}{\Gamma(\nu)}\|v_2 - v_1\|\Upsilon(L_1\theta_1(s) + L_2\theta_1(s)),
\end{aligned}$$

$$\begin{aligned}
&|A_2u_2(t) - A_2u_1(t)| \\
=&\left|\int_1^e \mathscr{H}(t,s)L_{q_2}\left(\overline{\mathscr{F}}(s,u_2(s),{}^H D^{\varsigma}_{1+}u_2(s)\right)\frac{ds}{s} - \int_1^e \mathscr{H}(t,s)L_{q_2}\left(\mathscr{F}(s,u_1(s),{}^H D^{\varsigma}_{1+}u_1(s)\right)\frac{ds}{s}\right| \\
=&\int_1^e \mathscr{H}(t,s)|L_{q_1}\left(\mathscr{F}(s,u_2(s),{}^H D^{\varsigma}_{1+}u_2(s)\right) - L_{q_1}\left(\mathscr{F}(s,u_1(s),{}^H D^{\varsigma}_{1+}u_1(s)\right)|\frac{ds}{s} \\
\leq&\int_1^e \mathscr{H}_1(e,s)\Xi(\overline{L}_1\overline{\theta}_1(s)|u_2(s) - u_1(s)| + \overline{L}_2\overline{\theta}_2(s)|{}^H D^{\varsigma}_{1+}u_2(s) - {}^H D^{\varsigma}_{1+}u_1(s)|) \\
\leq&\frac{1}{\Gamma(\iota)}|u_2(s) - u_1(s)|\Xi(\overline{L}_1\theta_1(s) + \overline{L}_2\overline{\theta}_1(s)) \\
\leq&\frac{1}{\Gamma(\iota)}\|u_2 - u_1\|\Xi(\overline{L}_1\theta_1(s) + \overline{L}_2\overline{\theta}_1(s)).
\end{aligned}$$

Hence, we have

$$\begin{aligned}
&\max_{t\in[1,e]} |A(u_2,v_2) - A(u_1,v_1)| \\
&= \|A(u_2,v_2) - A(u_1,v_1)\| = \|(A_1v_2, A_2u_2) - (A_1v_1, A_2u_1)\| \\
&= \|(A_1v_2 - A_1v_1, A_2u_2 - A_2u_1)\| \leq \widetilde{L}\|(v_2 - v_1, u_2 - u_1)\|,
\end{aligned}$$

where

$$\widetilde{L} = \max\left\{\frac{1}{\Gamma(\nu)}\Upsilon(L_1\theta_1(s) + L_2\theta_1(s)|), \frac{1}{\Gamma(\iota)}\Xi(\overline{L}_1\overline{\theta}_1(s) + \overline{L}_2\overline{\theta}_1(s)|)\right\} < 1.$$

BVPs (1) and (2) have a unique solution in E by the contraction mapping principle. □

4. Examples

Example 1. *Consider the following boundary value problem:*

$$\begin{cases}
L_3\left({}^H D^{\frac{5}{2}}_{1+}u\right)(t) + \mathscr{F}(t,v(t),{}^H D^{\varsigma}_{1+}v(t)) = 0,\ 1 < t < e, \\
L_2\left(D^{\frac{5}{2}}_{1+}v\right)(t) + \overline{\mathscr{F}}(t,u(t),{}^H D^{\varsigma}_{1+}u(t)) = 0,\ 1 < t < e, \\
u(1) = u'(1) = 0,\ u(e) = \sum\limits_{j=1}^{\infty}\eta_j u(e^{\frac{1}{j^2}}) + \int_1^e h(t)u(t)dB(t), \\
v(1) = v'(1) = 0, v(e) = \sum\limits_{j=1}^{\infty}\overline{\eta}_j v(e^{\frac{1}{j^2}}) + \int_1^e \overline{h}(t)v(t)d\overline{B}(t),
\end{cases} \tag{27}$$

where $\alpha = \frac{5}{2}, \beta = \frac{5}{2}, \eta_j = \overline{\eta}_j = \frac{1}{2j^3}, \xi_j = \overline{\xi}_j = e^{\frac{1}{j^2}}, \ p_1 = 3, q_1 = \frac{3}{2}, p_2 = 2, q_2 = \frac{1}{2},$ $h(t) = \overline{h}(t) = (\ln t)^{\frac{1}{2}},$

$$B(t) = \overline{B}(t) = \begin{cases} 0, t \in [0, \frac{e}{2}], \\ 4, t \in [\frac{e}{2}, \frac{3e}{4}], \\ 1, t \in [\frac{3e}{4}, e], \end{cases}$$

and

$$\mathscr{F}(t, v(t), {}^H D_{1^+}^{\frac{1}{2}} v(t)) = \begin{cases} \frac{1}{4\pi(\ln t)^{\frac{1}{2}}(1-\ln t)^{\frac{1}{2}}}(v^2 + ({}^H D_{1^+}^{\frac{1}{2}} v)^2)^2, \\ (t, v, {}^H D_{1^+}^{\frac{1}{2}} v) \in (1, e) \times [0,1] \times [0,1], \\ \frac{499^2}{4\pi(\ln t)^{\frac{1}{2}}(1-\ln t)^{\frac{1}{2}}}, \\ (t, v, {}^H D_{1^+}^{\frac{1}{2}} v) \in (1, e) \times (1, +\infty) \times (1, +\infty), \end{cases}$$

$$\overline{\mathscr{F}}(t, u(t), {}^H D_{1^+}^{\frac{1}{2}} u(t)) = \begin{cases} \frac{1}{4\pi(\ln t)^{\frac{3}{4}}(1-\ln t)^{\frac{3}{4}}}(u^2 + ({}^H D_{1^+}^{\frac{1}{2}} u)^2)^2, \\ (t, u, {}^H D_{1^+}^{\frac{1}{2}} u) \in (1, e) \times [0,1] \times [0,1], \\ \frac{499^2}{4\pi(\ln t)^{\frac{3}{4}}(1-\ln t)^{\frac{3}{4}}}, \\ (t, u, {}^H D_{1^+}^{\frac{1}{2}} u) \in (1, e) \times (1, +\infty) \times (1, +\infty). \end{cases}$$

Now, let us simplify the expression of $\mathscr{F}$ *to* $\mathscr{F}(t, x, y) = \frac{1}{4\pi(\ln t)^{\frac{1}{2}}(1-\ln t)^{\frac{1}{2}}}(x^2 + y^2)$ *for* $(t, x, y) \in (1, e) \times [0,1] \times [0,1]$*, and draw Figures 1 and 2 in order to reveal the influence of* $\mathscr{F}$*.*

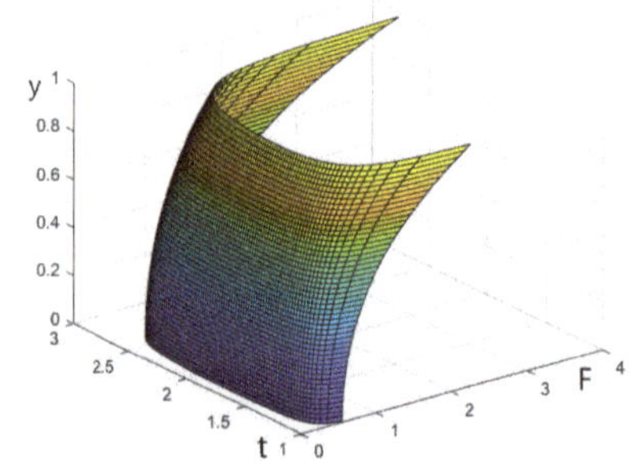

Figure 1. The first nonlinear function with singularity at points 1 and e (taking x = 1).

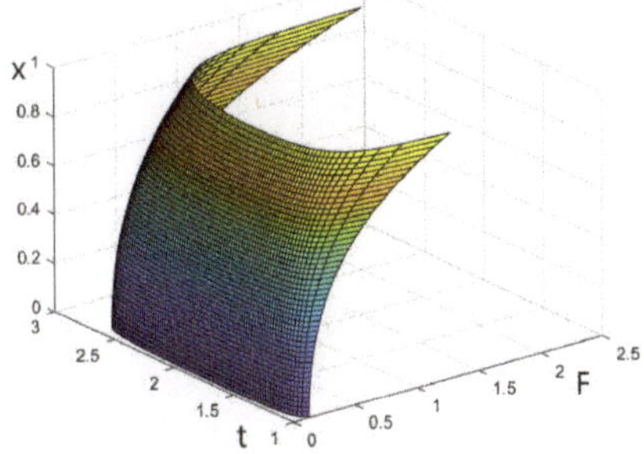

Figure 2. The first nonlinear function with singularity at points 1 and e (taking y = 0.5).

Figures 1 and 2 show a visualization of singular nonlinear terms of $\mathscr{F}$; note that $\overline{\mathscr{F}}$ is similar with $\mathscr{F}$, hence we omit the impact of $\mathscr{F}$ here. It is found that the nonlinearity is singular at $t = 1$ and e. Although the nonlinear term has significant singularity, it can be controlled by an integrable function, so the solutions of the equation are still stable and robust. By a simple calculation, we have

$$\Delta = \overline{\Delta} = 1 - \sum_{i=1}^{\infty} \eta_j (\ln \xi_j)^{\alpha-1} = 1 - \sum_{i=1}^{\infty} \frac{1}{2j^3} \frac{1}{j^3} = 1 - \frac{1}{2} \frac{\pi^6}{945} \approx 0.4913,$$

$$\begin{aligned}
\Delta_1 = \overline{\Delta}_1 &= \overline{\Delta} - \int_1^e \overline{h}(t)(\ln t)^{\beta-1} d\overline{B}(t) \\
&= \Delta - \int_1^e h(t)(\ln t)^{\alpha-1} dB(t) = \Delta - \int_1^e (\ln t)^2 dB(t) \\
&= 0.4913 - [4 \times (\ln \frac{e}{2})^2 - 3 \times (\ln \frac{3e}{4})^2] \approx 1.6369, \\
\Upsilon = 1 + \frac{1}{\Delta_1} \int_1^e h(t) dB(t) &= 1 + \frac{1}{1.6369} \int_1^e (\ln t)^{\frac{1}{2}} dB(t) \\
&= 1 + \frac{1}{1.6369} (4 \times (\ln \frac{e}{2})^{\frac{1}{2}} - 3 \times (\ln \frac{3e}{4})^{\frac{1}{2}}) \approx 0.8067,
\end{aligned}$$

and apparently,

$$\mathscr{F}(t, v(t), {}^H D_{1^+}^{\frac{1}{2}} v(t)) \leq \frac{1}{\pi (\ln t)^{\frac{1}{2}} (1 - \ln t)^{\frac{1}{2}}} = \theta(t),$$

$$\overline{\mathscr{F}}(t, v(t), {}^H D_{1^+}^{\frac{1}{2}} v(t)) \leq \frac{1}{\pi (\ln t)^{\frac{3}{4}} (1 - \ln t)^{\frac{3}{4}}} = \overline{\theta}(t).$$

Taking $\xi = \frac{3}{4}, t_0 = \frac{5}{4}$, then for $(t, x, y) \in [1, e] \times [0, \frac{3}{4}] \times [0, \frac{3}{4}]$,

$$L_3(\mathscr{F}(t, v(t), {}^H D_{1^+}^{\mu} v(t))) \to +\infty \geq \frac{\xi}{(\ln t_0)^{\alpha-1} \Upsilon} \left(\int_{t_0}^e (\mathscr{G}_1(t_0, s) \frac{ds}{s} \right)^{-1},$$

$$L_2(\overline{\mathscr{F}}(t, u(t), {}^H D_{1^+}^{\varsigma} u(t))) \to +\infty \geq \frac{\xi}{(\ln t_0)^{\beta-1} \Xi} \left(\int_{t_0}^e (\mathscr{H}_1(t_0, s) \frac{ds}{s} \right)^{-1}.$$

Moreover, for $(t,x,y)\in[1,e]\times[0,\rho]\times[0,\rho](\rho>\frac{3}{4})$,

$$\begin{aligned}
&\Upsilon\int_1^e \max\{\mathscr{G}(e,s),^H D_{1+}^{\varsigma}\mathscr{G}(e,s)\}L_{q_1}(\theta(s))\frac{ds}{s}\\
=&\Upsilon\int_1^e \max\{\mathscr{G}(e,s),^H D_{1+}^{\varsigma}\mathscr{G}(e,s)\}\frac{1}{\pi^{\frac{1}{2}}(\ln s)^{\frac{1}{4}}(1-\ln s)^{\frac{1}{4}}}\frac{ds}{s}\\
\leq&\frac{1}{\Gamma(v)}\Upsilon\frac{1}{\pi^{\frac{1}{2}}}\int_1^e\frac{1}{(\ln s)^{\frac{1}{4}}(1-\ln s)^{\frac{1}{4}}}\frac{ds}{s}\\
=&\frac{0.8067}{\Gamma(v)}\frac{1}{\pi^{\frac{1}{2}}}B(\frac{5}{4},\frac{5}{4})\approx 0.2116<1,
\end{aligned}$$

$$\begin{aligned}
&\Xi\int_1^e \max\{\mathscr{H}(e,s),^H D_{1+}^{\varsigma}\mathscr{H}(e,s)\}L_{q_2}(\overline{\theta}(s))\frac{ds}{s}\\
=&\Xi\int_1^e \max\{\mathscr{H}(e,s),^H D_{1+}^{\varsigma}\mathscr{H}(e,s)\}\frac{1}{\pi^{\frac{1}{2}}(\ln s)^{\frac{3}{8}}(1-\ln s)^{\frac{3}{8}}}\frac{ds}{s}\\
\leq&\frac{1}{\Gamma(\iota)}\Xi\frac{1}{\pi^{\frac{1}{2}}}\int_1^e\frac{1}{(\ln s)^{\frac{3}{8}}(1-\ln s)^{\frac{3}{8}}}\frac{ds}{s}\\
=&\frac{0.8067}{\Gamma(\iota)}\frac{1}{\pi^{\frac{1}{2}}}B(\frac{11}{8},\frac{11}{8})\approx 0.1682<1.
\end{aligned}$$

Hence, all the conditions of Theorem 5 are satisfied. Therefore, Equation (27) has at least one positive solution.

Example 2. *Consider the following boundary value problem:*

$$\begin{cases}
L_3\left({}^H D_{1+}^{\frac{5}{2}}u\right)(t)+\mathscr{F}(t,v(t),^H D_{1+}^{\varsigma}v(t))=0,\ 1<t<e,\\
L_2\left(D_{1+}^{\frac{5}{2}}v\right)(t)+\overline{\mathscr{F}}(t,u(t),^H D_{1+}^{\varsigma}u(t))=0,\ 1<t<e,\\
u(1)=u'(1)=0,\ u(e)=\sum\limits_{j=1}^{\infty}\eta_j u(\xi_j)+\int_1^e h(t)u(t)dB(t),\\
v(1)=v'(1)=0, v(e)=\sum\limits_{j=1}^{\infty}\overline{\eta}_j v(\overline{\xi}_j)+\int_1^e \overline{h}(t)v(t)d\overline{B}(t),
\end{cases}\tag{28}$$

$$\mathscr{F}(t,v(t),^H D_{1+}^{\frac{1}{2}}v(t))=\frac{1}{4\pi(\ln t)^{\frac{1}{2}}(1-\ln t)^{\frac{1}{2}}}(v^2+({}^H D_{1+}^{\frac{1}{2}}v)^2)^2,$$

$$\overline{\mathscr{F}}(t,u(t),^H D_{1+}^{\frac{1}{2}}u(t))=\frac{1}{4\pi(\ln t)^{\frac{3}{4}}(1-\ln t)^{\frac{3}{4}}}(u^2+({}^H D_{1+}^{\frac{1}{2}}u)^2)^2.$$

Apparently,

$$\mathscr{F}(s,v(s),^H D_{1+}^{\varsigma}v(s))\leq\theta(s)\varphi^{\frac{1}{q_1-1}}(v),\overline{\mathscr{F}}(s,u(s),^H D_{1+}^{\varsigma}u(s))\leq\overline{\theta}(s)\psi^{\frac{1}{q_2-1}}(u),$$
$$\forall(t,x_0,x_1)\in[1,e]\times[0,+\infty)\times[0,+\infty),$$

where

$$\theta(t)=\frac{1}{4\pi(\ln t)^{\frac{1}{2}}(1-\ln t)^{\frac{1}{2}}},\overline{\theta}(t)=\frac{1}{4\pi(\ln t)^{\frac{3}{4}}(1-\ln t)^{\frac{3}{4}}},$$

$$\varphi(v)=v^2+({}^H D_{1+}^{\frac{1}{2}}v)^2,\psi(u)=u^2+({}^H D_{1+}^{\frac{1}{2}}u)^2;$$

hence, (iii) holds. Taking $r = 1 > 0$,

$$\frac{r}{\max\{\varphi(r)), \psi((r)|)\}} = 1 > \max\left\{\int_1^e \mathcal{G}_1(e,s)\Upsilon L_{q_1}(\theta(s))\frac{ds}{s}, \int_1^e \mathcal{H}_1(e,s)\Upsilon L_{q_2}(\overline{\theta}(s))\frac{ds}{s}\right\}$$
$$= 0.1682,$$

so, (iv) holds. Hence, all the conditions of Theorem 6 hold, which implies that Equation (28) has at least one positive solution.

Example 3. *Consider the following boundary value problem:*

$$\begin{cases} L_3\left({}^H D_{1^+}^{\frac{5}{2}} u\right)(t) + \mathcal{F}(t, v(t), {}^H D_{1^+}^{\varsigma} v(t)) = 0,\ 1 < t < e, \\ L_2\left(D_{1^+}^{\frac{5}{2}} v\right)(t) + \overline{\mathcal{F}}(t, u(t), {}^H D_{1^+}^{\varsigma} u(t)) = 0,\ 1 < t < e, \\ u(1) = u'(1) = 0,\ u(e) = \sum_{j=1}^{\infty} \eta_j u(\xi_j) + \int_1^e h(t)u(t)dB(t), \\ v(1) = v'(1) = 0, v(e) = \sum_{j=1}^{\infty} \overline{\eta}_j v(\overline{\xi}_j) + \int_1^e \overline{h}(t)v(t)d\overline{B}(t), \end{cases} \tag{29}$$

where

$$\mathcal{F}(t, v(t), {}^H D_{1^+}^{\frac{1}{2}} v(t)) = 4\pi(\ln t)^{\frac{1}{2}}(1 - \ln t)^{\frac{1}{2}}(v + 2({}^H D_{1^+}^{\frac{1}{2}} v) + 1)^2,$$
$$\overline{\mathcal{F}}(t, u(t), {}^H D_{1^+}^{\frac{1}{2}} u(t)) = 4\pi(\ln t)^{\frac{3}{4}}(1 - \ln t)^{\frac{3}{4}}(u + 2({}^H D_{1^+}^{\frac{1}{2}} u) + 1)^2.$$

By some calculations, we have

$$\begin{aligned} &|L_{q_1}(\mathcal{F}(s, v_1(s), {}^H D_{1^+}^{\frac{1}{2}} v_1(s)) - L_{q_1}(\mathcal{F}(s, v_2(s), {}^H D_{1^+}^{\frac{1}{2}} v_2(s))| \\ =&|4\pi(\ln t)^{\frac{1}{2}}(1 - \ln t)^{\frac{1}{2}}(v_1 + 2({}^H D_{1^+}^{\frac{1}{2}} v_1) + 1) - 8\pi(\ln t)^{\frac{1}{2}}(1 - \ln t)^{\frac{1}{2}}(v_2 + 2({}^H D_{1^+}^{\frac{1}{2}} v_2) + 1)| \\ \leq&4\pi\frac{1}{3}(\ln t)^{\frac{1}{2}}(1 - \ln t)^{\frac{1}{2}}|v_1 - v_2| + 8\pi\frac{1}{3}(\ln t)^{\frac{1}{2}}(1 - \ln t)^{\frac{1}{2}}|{}^H D_{1^+}^{\frac{1}{2}} v_1 - {}^H D_{1^+}^{\frac{1}{2}} v_2| \\ \leq&L_1\theta_1(s)|x_1 - x_2| + L_2\theta_2(s)|y_1 - y_2|, \end{aligned}$$

where $L_1 = 1, L_2 = 2, \theta_1(s) = \frac{1}{3}4\pi(\ln t)^{\frac{1}{2}}(1 - \ln t)^{\frac{1}{2}}, \theta_2(s) = \frac{8}{3}\pi(\ln t)^{\frac{1}{2}}(1 - \ln t)^{\frac{1}{2}}$,

$$\begin{aligned} &|L_{q_2}(\overline{\mathcal{F}}(s, u_1(s), {}^H D_{1^+}^{\frac{1}{2}} u_1(s)) - L_{q_2}(\overline{\mathcal{F}}(s, u_2(s), {}^H D_{1^+}^{\frac{1}{2}} u_2(s))| \\ =&|4\pi(\ln t)^{\frac{1}{2}}(1 - \ln t)^{\frac{1}{2}}(u_1 + 2({}^H D_{1^+}^{\frac{1}{2}} u_1) + 1) - 8\pi(\ln t)^{\frac{1}{2}}(1 - \ln t)^{\frac{1}{2}}(u_2 + 2({}^H D_{1^+}^{\frac{1}{2}} u_2) + 1)| \\ \leq&4\pi\frac{1}{3}(\ln t)^{\frac{1}{2}}(1 - \ln t)^{\frac{1}{2}}|v_1 - v_2| + 8\pi\frac{1}{3}(\ln t)^{\frac{1}{2}}(1 - \ln t)^{\frac{1}{2}}|{}^H D_{1^+}^{\frac{1}{2}} v_1 - {}^H D_{1^+}^{\frac{1}{2}} v_2| \\ \leq&L_1\theta_1(s)|x_1 - x_2| + L_2\theta_2(s)|y_1 - y_2|, \end{aligned}$$

$$|L_{q_2}(\overline{\mathcal{F}}(s, x_1, y_1)) - L_{q_2}(\overline{\mathcal{F}}(s, x_2, y_2))| \leq \overline{L}_1\overline{\theta}_1(s)|x_1 - x_2| + \overline{L}_2\overline{\theta}_2(s)|y_1 - y_2|,$$

where $\overline{L}_1 = 1, \overline{L}_2 = 2, \overline{\theta}_1(s) = \frac{1}{3}4\pi(\ln t)^{\frac{3}{4}}(1 - \ln t)^{\frac{3}{4}}, \overline{\theta}_2(s) = \frac{8}{3}\pi(\ln t)^{\frac{3}{4}}(1 - \ln t)^{\frac{3}{4}}$, *and*

$$\frac{1}{\Gamma(\nu)}\Upsilon\left(L_1\theta_1(s) + L_2\theta_1(s)\frac{1}{\Gamma(\varsigma + 1)}\right) = \frac{1}{\Gamma(\frac{5}{2})}\frac{1}{3} \times 0.8067(1 + 2\frac{1}{\Gamma(\frac{3}{2})}) \approx 0.6588 < 1,$$

$$\frac{1}{\Gamma(\iota)}\Xi\left(\overline{L}_1\overline{\theta}_1(s) + \overline{L}_2\overline{\theta}_1(s)\frac{1}{\Gamma(\varsigma + 1)}\right)\frac{1}{\Gamma(\frac{5}{2})}\frac{1}{3} \times 0.8067(1 + 2\frac{1}{\Gamma(\frac{3}{2})}) \approx 0.6588 < 1.$$

Hence, all the conditions of Theorem 7 hold, which implies that Equation (29) has one unique solution.

It is worth mentioning that in this study, the nonlinear terms in the fractional-order differential equations exhibit a singularity that is one of the main innovations of the present research. Although singular nonlinear terms pose analytical difficulties, they can be controlled by an integrable function, which is why the solutions of the considered Hadamard fractional differential model are still stable and robust. Of course, in the future, we will strengthen the research on singular factors in practical engineering applications, especially in terms of solution stability or robustness.

5. Conclusions

The existence and uniqueness for positive solutions of a singular p-Laplacian Hadamard fractional-order differential equation with nonlocal integral and infinite-point boundary conditions are investigated. The methods used are a nonlinear alternative of Leray–Schauder-type Guo–Krasnoselskii's fixed point theorem in cone and the Banach fixed point theorem, respectively. First, we derive the expression of the Green function, and then determine some properties of the developed Green function. Subsequently, we demonstrate the existence of solutions of Hadamard fractional differential equation with nonlinear singular conditions by Leray–Schauder-type Guo–Krasnoselskii's fixed point theorem, respectively. Finally, we prove the uniqueness of the positive solution using Banach's fixed point theorem. The existence results of Theorems 5 and 6 are obtained under the condition of singular nonlinearity, while the nonlinear term is continuous in much of the previous literature (e.g., see [15,18]), which is one of the main contributions of the present study. Of course, there are also some limitations to this study, such as the absence of complete numerical solutions. We plan to conduct further research on numerical solution examples on this type of equation. Additionally, we will explore more complex boundary conditions, such as extending the present interval from $(1, e)$ to $(1, +\infty)$ or extending the study to other types of fractional differential equations, including Caputo–Hadamard, Atangana–Baleanu Caputo, and so on.

Author Contributions: Methodology, C.L.; Validation, C.L.; Formal analysis, C.L.; Investigation, C.L.; Resources, L.G.; Data curation, L.G.; Writing—original draft, C.L.; Writing—review & editing, L.G.; Project administration, L.G.; Funding acquisition, L.G. All authors have read and agreed to the published version of the manuscript.

Funding: This work was supported by the National Natural Science Foundation of China (Nos. 12272064 and 12101086), Natural Science Foundation of Jiangsu Province (No. BK20241773), Major Project of Basic Science (Natural Science) Research in Jiangsu Universities (Nos. 23KJA580001 and 24KJA120001), Changzhou Science and Technology Plan Project (No. CJ20241095).

Data Availability Statement: Data is contained within the article.

Acknowledgments: We thank the reviewers for their valuable comments.

Conflicts of Interest: The author declares that there are no conflicts of interest regarding the publication of this paper.

References

1. Leibenson, L. General problem of the movement of a compressible fluid in a porous medium. *Izv. Akad. Nauk Kirg. SSR Ser. Biol. Nauk.* **1983**, *9*, 7–10.
2. Cai, J.; Huang, W. Three-dimensional information storage of polymer doped with nano-silver. *Micr. Opt. Technol. Lett.* **2015**, *57*, 2662–2665. [CrossRef]
3. Kilbas, A.A.; Srivastava, H.M.; Trujillo, J.J. *Theory and Applications of Fractional Differential Equations*; Elsevier Science BV: Amsterdam, The Netherlands, 2006.
4. Li, C.; Zhu, C.; Zhang, N.; Sui, S.; Zhao, J. Free vibration of self-powered nanoribbons subjected to thermal-mechanical-electrical fields based on a nonlocal strain gradient theory. *Appl. Math. Model.* **2022**, *110*, 583–602. [CrossRef]
5. Ahmad, B.; Alsaedi, A.; Ntouyas, S.; Tariboon, J. *Hadamard-Type Fractional Differential Equations, Inclusions and Inequalities*; Springer: Cham, Switzerland, 2017.
6. Liu, W.; Liu, L. Properties of Hadamard Fractional Integral and Its Application. *Fractal Fract.* **2022**, *6*, 670. [CrossRef]

7. Chai, G. Positive solutions for boundary value problem of fractional differential equation with p -Laplacian operator. *Bound. Value Probl.* **2012**, *2012*, 18. [CrossRef]
8. Jong, K. Existence and uniqueness of positive solutions of a kind of multi-point boundary value problems for nonlinear fractional differential equations with p-Laplacian operator. *Mediterr. J. Math.* **2018**, *2018*, 129. [CrossRef]
9. Guo, L.; Liu, L. Maximal and minimal iterative positive solutions for singular infinite-point p-Laplacian fractional differential equations. *Nonlinear Anal. Model.Control* **2018**, *23*, 851–865. [CrossRef]
10. Guo, L.; Wang, Y.; Liu, H.; Li, C.; Zhao, J.; Chu, H. On iterative positive solutions for a class of singular infinite-point p-Laplacian fractional differential equation with singular source terms. *J. Appl. Anal. Comput.* **2023**, *13*, 1–16. [CrossRef]
11. Ciftci, C.; Deren, F. Analysis of p-Laplacian Hadamard fractional boundary value problems with the derivative term involved in the nonlinear term. *Math. Meth. Appl. Sci.* **2023**, *46*, 8945–8955. [CrossRef]
12. Huang, H.; Zhao, K.; Liu, X. On solvability of BVP for a coupled Hadamard fractional systems involving fractional derivative impulses. *AIMS Math.* **2022**, *7*, 19221–19236. [CrossRef]
13. Li, C.; Guo, L. Positive Solutions and Their Existence of a Nonlinear Hadamard Fractional-Order Differential Equation with a Singular Source Item Using Spectral Analysis. *Fractal Fract.* **2024**, *8*, 377. [CrossRef]
14. Guo, L.; Cai, J.; Xie, Z.; Li, C. Mechanical Responses of Symmetric Straight and Curved Composite Microbeams. *J. Vib. Eng. Technol.* **2024**, *12*, 1537–1549. [CrossRef]
15. Ardjouni, A. Positive solutions for nonlinear Hadamard fractional differential equations with integral boundary conditions. *AIMS Math.* **2019**, *4*, 1101–1113. [CrossRef]
16. Berhail, A.; Tabouche, N.; Boulares, H. Existence of Positive Solutions of Hadamard Fractional Differential Equations with Integral Boundary Conditions. *SSRN Electron. J.* **2019**. [CrossRef]
17. Zhang, K.; Wang, J.; Ma, W. Solutions for Integral Boundary Value Problems of Nonlinear Hadamard Fractional Differential Equations. *J. Func. Spaces* **2018**, *2018*. [CrossRef]
18. Xu, J.; Liu, L.; Bai, S.; Wu, Y. Solvability for a system of Hadamard fractional multi-point boundary value problems. *Nonlinear Anal. Model. Control* **2021**, *26*, 502–521. [CrossRef]
19. Ma, Y.; Maryam, M.; Riaz, U. Existence and Hyers-Ulam stability of Jerk-type Caputo and Hadamard mixed fractional differential equations. *Qual. Theory Dyn. Syst.* **2024**, *23*, 132. [CrossRef]
20. Wang, X.; Wang, G.; Chen, Z.; Lim, C.; Li, S.; Li, C. Controllable flexural wave in laminated metabeam with embedded multiple resonators. *J. Sound Vibr.* **2024**, *581*, 118386. [CrossRef]
21. Xie, Z.; Guo, L.; Li, C.; Shi, Y.; Han, B. Modeling the deformation of thin-walled circular tubes filled with metallic foam under two lateral loading patterns. *Structures* **2024**, *69*, 107289. [CrossRef]
22. Idrees, S.; Saeed, U. Generalized sine-cosine wavelet method for Caputo-Hadamard fractional differential equations. *Math. Meth. Appl. Sci.* **2022**, *45*, 9602–9621. [CrossRef]
23. Saha, K.; Sukavanam, N.; Pan, S. Existence and uniqueness of solutions to fractional differential equations with fractional boundary conditions. *Alex. Eng. J.* **2023**, *72*, 147–155. [CrossRef]
24. Ma, R.; Meng, Y.; Pang, H. The Existence Results of Solutions to the Nonlinear Coupled System of Hilfer Fractional Differential Equations and Inclusions. *Fractal Fract.* **2024**, *8*, 194. [CrossRef]
25. Jassim, H.K.; Abdulshareef Hussein, M. A New Approach for Solving Nonlinear Fractional Ordinary Differential Equations. *Mathematics* **2023**, *11*, 1565. [CrossRef]
26. Wang, G.; Pei, K.; Chen, Y. Stability analysis of nonlinear Hadamard fractional differential system. *J. Frankl. Inst.* **2019**, *356*, 6538–6546. [CrossRef]
27. Rahman, G.; Nisar, K.; Abdeljawad, T. Certain new proportional and Hadamard proportional fractional integral inequalities. *J. Inequalities Appl.* **2021**, *2021*, 71. [CrossRef]
28. Abdalla, B.; Abdeljawad, T. On the oscillation of Hadamard fractional differential equations. *Math. Meth. Appl. Sci.* **2018**, *2018*, 409. [CrossRef]
29. Istafa, G.; Rehman, M. Numerical solutions of Hadamard fractional differential equations by generalized Legendre functions. *Math. Meth. Appl. Sci.* **2023**, *46*, 6821–6842. [CrossRef]
30. Zhang, W.; Ni, J. New multiple positive solutions for Hadamard-type fractional differential equations with nonlocal conditions on an infinite interval. *Appl. Math. Lett.* **2021**, *118*, 107165. [CrossRef]
31. Nyamoradi, N.; Ahmad, B. Hadamard Fractional Differential Equations on an Unbounded Domain with Integro-initial Conditions. *Qual. Theory Dyn. Syst.* **2024**, *23*, 183. [CrossRef]
32. Ma, L.; Wu, B. Finite-time stability of Hadamard fractional differential equations in weighted Banach spaces. *Nonlinear Dyn.* **2022**, *107*, 3749–3766. [CrossRef]
33. Rao, Y.; Yussouf, M.; Farid, G.; Pecaric, J.; Tlili, I. Further generalizations of Hadamard and Fejer-Hadamard fractional inequalities and error estimates. *Adv. Differ. Equ.* **2020**, *2020*, 421. [CrossRef]
34. Guo, L.; Liu, H.; Li, C.; Zhao, J.; Xu, J. Existence of positive solutions for singular p-Laplacian Hadamard fractional differential equations with the derivative term contained in the nonlinear term. *Nonlinear Anal. Model. Control* **2023**, *28*, 491–515. [CrossRef]
35. Wang, Y.; Wang, P.; Meng, H. Dynamic performance and parameter optimization of a half-vehicle system coupled with an inerter-based X-structure nonlinear energy sink. *Appl. Math. Mech. Engl. Ed.* **2024**, *45*, 85–110. [CrossRef]

36. Alruwaily, Y.; Ahmad, B.; Ntouyas, S.; Alzaidi, A. Existence Results for Coupled Nonlinear Sequential Fractional Differential Equations with Coupled Riemann–Stieltjes Integro-Multipoint Boundary Conditions. *Fractal Fract.* **2022**, *6*, 123. [CrossRef]
37. Zhang, Q.; Li, C.; Zhou, L.; Li, L. Multipoint boundary value problems for higher-order Hadamard fractional neutral differential equations and inclusions. *Bound. Value Probl.* **2023**, *2023*, 11. [CrossRef]
38. Podlubny, I. *Fractional Differential Equations*; Academic Press: New York, NY, USA, 1999.
39. Hentenryck, P.; Bent, R.; Upfal, E. *An Introduction to the Fractional Calculus and Fractional Differential Equations*; Wiley: New York, NY, USA, 1993.
40. Guo, D.; Cho, Y.; Zhu, J. *Partial Ordering Methods in Nonlinear Problems*; Nov a Science Publishers: New York, NY, USA, 2004.
41. Zhang, X. Positive solutions for a class of singular fractional differential equation with infinite-point boundary value conditions. *Appl. Math. Lett.* **2015**, *39*, 22–27. [CrossRef]

fractal and fractional

MDPI

Article

Fractional Operators and Fractionally Integrated Random Fields on $\mathbb{Z}^\nu$

Vytautė Pilipauskaitė [1] and Donatas Surgailis [2,*]

1 Department of Mathematical Sciences, Aalborg University, Skjernvej 4A, 9220 Aalborg, Denmark; vypi@math.aau.dk
2 Faculty of Mathematics and Informatics, Vilnius University, Naugarduko 24, 03225 Vilnius, Lithuania
* Correspondence: donatas.surgailis@mif.vu.lt

Abstract: We consider fractional integral operators $(I-T)^d, d \in (-1,1)$ acting on functions $g : \mathbb{Z}^\nu \to \mathbb{R}, \nu \geq 1$, where T is the transition operator of a random walk on $\mathbb{Z}^\nu$. We obtain the sufficient and necessary conditions for the existence, invertibility, and square summability of kernels $\tau(s;d), s \in \mathbb{Z}^\nu$ of $(I-T)^d$. The asymptotic behavior of $\tau(s;d)$ as $|s| \to \infty$ is identified following the local limit theorem for random walks. A class of fractionally integrated random fields X on $\mathbb{Z}^\nu$ solving the difference equation $(I-T)^d X = \varepsilon$ with white noise on the right-hand side is discussed and their scaling limits. Several examples, including fractional lattice Laplace and heat operators, are studied in detail.

Keywords: fractional differentiation/integration operators; tempered fractional operators; fractional random field; random walk; limit theorems; long-range dependence; negative dependence; conditional autoregression

1. Introduction

Classical fractional differentiation/integration operators $(I-T)^d$, $d \in (-1,1)$, $d \neq 0$ acting on functions $g : \mathbb{Z} \to \mathbb{R}$, where $(I-T)g(t) = g(t) - g(t-1)$ is a 'discrete derivative' with respect to 'time' $t \in \mathbb{Z}$, are defined through the binomial expansion $(1-z)^d = \sum_{j=0}^{\infty} \psi_j(d) z^j$, $z \in \mathbb{C}$, $|z| < 1$, viz.:

$$(I-T)^d g(t) := \sum_{j=0}^{\infty} \psi_j(d) T^j g(t) = \sum_{j=0}^{\infty} \psi_j(d) g(t-j), \quad t \in \mathbb{Z} \tag{1}$$

with the coefficients

$$\psi_j(d) := \frac{\Gamma(j-d)}{\Gamma(j+1)\Gamma(-d)}, \quad j \in \mathbb{N}. \tag{2}$$

Here, Γ denotes the gamma function $\Gamma(z) := \int_0^\infty t^{z-1} \mathrm{e}^{-t} dt, z > 0$, and $\Gamma(z) := z^{-1}\Gamma(z+1)$, $-1 < z < 0$. Also, see the end of this section for all unexplained notation. The asymptotics

$$\psi_j(d) \sim \Gamma(-d)^{-1} j^{-d-1} \quad (j \to \infty), \quad 0 < |d| < 1 \tag{3}$$

(which follows by application of Stirling's formula to (2)) determines the class of functions g and the summability properties of (1).

Fractional operators in (1) play an important role in the theory of discrete-time stochastic processes—in particular, time series (see, e.g., the monographs [1–5] and the references therein). The autoregressive fractionally integrated moving-average ARFIMA$(0,d,0)$ process $\{X(t); t \in \mathbb{Z}\}$ is defined as a stationary solution of the stochastic difference equation

$$(I-T)^d X(t) = \sum_{j=0}^{\infty} \psi_j(d) X(t-j) = \varepsilon(t), \quad t \in \mathbb{Z} \tag{4}$$

with white noise (a sequence of standardized uncorrelated random variables (r.v.s)) $\{\varepsilon(t); t \in \mathbb{Z}\}$. For $d \in (-1/2, 1/2)$, the solution of (4) is obtained by applying the inverse operator, viz.:

$$X(t) = (I - T)^{-d}\varepsilon(t) = \sum_{j=0}^{\infty} \psi_j(-d)\varepsilon(t - j), \quad t \in \mathbb{Z}. \tag{5}$$

Since (3) implies $\sum_{j=0}^{\infty} \psi_j(d)^2 < \infty$ ($|d| < 1/2$), (5) is a well-defined stationary process with zero mean and finite variance. The ARFIMA$(0, d, 0)$ process is the basic parametric model in statistical inference for time series with a long memory property (also referred to as long-range dependence) (see [1–3,5,6] for a discussion of the ARFIMA$(0, d, 0)$ and its generalization ARFIMA(p, d, q) models). We note that the ARFIMA$(0, d, 0)$ process has an explicit covariance function and the spectral density

$$f(x) = (2\pi)^{-1}|1 - \mathrm{e}^{-\mathrm{i}x}|^{-2d}, \quad x \in \Pi := [-\pi, \pi]$$

which explodes or vanishes at the origin $x = 0$ as $(2\pi)^{-1}|x|^{-2d}$, depending on the sign of d.

In this paper, we extend fractional operators in (1) to functions g on a regular ν-dimensional lattice $\mathbb{Z}^\nu, \nu \geq 1$. Whereas generalization of our construction to irregular lattices or more abstract index sets is an interesting and challenging open problem, our choice of $\mathbb{Z}^\nu$ follows the traditional approach in random field theory, which heavily relies on the Fourier transform and spectral representation. We consider a rather general form of the operator T:

$$Tg(\boldsymbol{t}) = \sum_{\boldsymbol{u} \in \mathbb{Z}^\nu} g(\boldsymbol{t} + \boldsymbol{u})p(\boldsymbol{u}) = \mathrm{E}g(S_1 + \boldsymbol{t}), \quad \boldsymbol{t} \in \mathbb{Z}^\nu,$$

where $\{S_j; j \geq 0\}$ is a random walk on $\mathbb{Z}^\nu$ starting at $S_0 = \mathbf{0}$ with (1-step) probabilities $p = \{p(\boldsymbol{u}) := \mathrm{P}(S_1 = \boldsymbol{u}); \boldsymbol{u} \in \mathbb{Z}^\nu\}$. We assume that $p(\mathbf{0}) < 1$, i.e., the random walk is non-degenerate at $\mathbf{0}$. Clearly, $T^j g(\boldsymbol{t}) = \sum_{\boldsymbol{u} \in \mathbb{Z}^\nu} g(\boldsymbol{t} + \boldsymbol{u})p_j(\boldsymbol{u}) = \mathrm{E}g(S_j + \boldsymbol{t}), \boldsymbol{t} \in \mathbb{Z}^\nu$, where $p_j(\boldsymbol{u}) := \mathrm{P}(S_j = \boldsymbol{u}), \boldsymbol{u} \in \mathbb{Z}^\nu$ are the j-step probabilities, $j = 0, 1, 2, \cdots$ with $p_0(\boldsymbol{u}) = \mathbb{I}(\boldsymbol{u} = \mathbf{0})$. Similarly to (1), we define fractional operators $(I - T)^d, -1 < d < 1, d \neq 0$ acting on $g : \mathbb{Z}^\nu \to \mathbb{R}$ by

$$(I - T)^d g(\boldsymbol{t}) = \sum_{j=0}^{\infty} \psi_j(d) T^j g(\boldsymbol{t}) = \sum_{\boldsymbol{u} \in \mathbb{Z}^\nu} \tau(\boldsymbol{u}; d) g(\boldsymbol{t} + \boldsymbol{u}), \quad \boldsymbol{t} \in \mathbb{Z}^\nu$$

with coefficients

$$\tau(\boldsymbol{u}; d) := \sum_{j=0}^{\infty} \psi_j(d) p_j(\boldsymbol{u}), \tag{6}$$

expressed through the binomial coefficients $\psi_j(d)$ and random walk probabilities $p_j(\boldsymbol{u})$.

Let us describe the content and results of this paper in more detail. The main result of Section 2 is Theorem 1, which provides the sufficient condition

$$\int_{\Pi^\nu} |1 - \widehat{p}(\boldsymbol{x})|^{-2|d|} \mathrm{d}\boldsymbol{x} < \infty \tag{7}$$

for invertibility $(I - T)^d (I - T)^{-d} = I$ and the square summability of fractional coefficients in (6), in terms of the characteristic function $\widehat{p}(\boldsymbol{x}) := \mathrm{E}\exp\{\mathrm{i}\langle \boldsymbol{x}, S_1 \rangle\}$ (the Fourier transform) of the random walk. Section 2 also includes a discussion of the asymptotics of (6) as $|\boldsymbol{u}| \to \infty$, which is important in limit theorems and other applications of fractional integrated random fields. Using classical local limit theorems, Propositions 1 and 2 obtain 'isotropic' asymptotics of (6) for a large class of random walk $\{S_j\}$, showing that $\tau(\boldsymbol{u}; d)$ decay as $O(|\boldsymbol{u}|^{-\nu - 2d})$; hence, $\sum_{\boldsymbol{u} \in \mathbb{Z}^\nu} |\tau(\boldsymbol{u}; -d)| = \infty$ $(d > 0)$. The last fact is interpreted as the *long-range dependence* [3,4,7] of the fractionally integrated random field $\{X(\boldsymbol{t}); \boldsymbol{t} \in \mathbb{Z}^\nu\}$, defined as a stationary solution of the difference equation,

$$(I - T)^d X(\boldsymbol{t}) = \varepsilon(\boldsymbol{t}), \quad \boldsymbol{t} \in \mathbb{Z}^\nu \tag{8}$$

with white noise on the r.h.s. and it is studied in Section 3. Corollary 1 obtains conditions for the existence of the stationary solution of (8) given by the inverse operator $X(\boldsymbol{t}) = (I-T)^{-d}\varepsilon(\boldsymbol{t})$, which is detailed in Examples 1 and 2 for fractional Laplacian and fractional heat operators. Sections 2 and 3 also include a discussion of *tempered* fractional operators $(I-rT)^d, r \in (0,1)$ and *tempered* fractional random fields solving the analogous equation $(I-rT)^d X(\boldsymbol{t}) = \varepsilon(\boldsymbol{t})$, which generalize the class of tempered ARFIMA processes [8] and have *short-range dependence* and a summable covariance function.

Section 4 is devoted to the scaling limits of moving-average random fields on $\mathbb{Z}^\nu$ with coefficients satisfying Assumption 1, which includes 'isotropic' fractional coefficients $\tau(\boldsymbol{u};-d)$ as a special case. The scaling limits refer to the integrals $X_\lambda(\phi) = \int_{\mathbb{R}^\nu} X([\boldsymbol{t}])\phi(\boldsymbol{t}/\lambda)\mathrm{d}\boldsymbol{t}$ of random field $\{X(\boldsymbol{t}); \boldsymbol{t} \in \mathbb{Z}^\nu\}$ for each $\phi : \mathbb{R}^\nu \to \mathbb{R}$ from a class of (test) functions as scaling parameter $\lambda \to \infty$. The scaling limits are identified in Corollary 3 as self-similar Gaussian random fields with a Hurst parameter $H = (\nu - 4d)/2$. We note that limit theorems for random fields with long-range dependence or negative dependence have been studied in many works. The seminal paper [9] dealt with noncentral limit theorems for Gaussian subordinated fields. Anisotropic scaling limits of linear and subordinated random fields in dimensions $\nu = 2, 3$ were discussed in [10–16] and in the references therein, with particular focus on scaling transition arising under critical anisotropy exponents. Whereas most of the abovementioned works considered partial sums on rectangular domains, [17] studied the case of irregular summation regions and 'edge effects' arising under strong negative dependence. Statistical applications for random fields with long-range dependence were discussed in [2,18,19] and other works.

We expect that this study can be extended in several directions, including anisotropic scaling, infinite variance random fields, and fractional operators in $\mathbb{R}^\nu$ (see [20–25] for discussion and the properties of fractional random fields with the continuous argument $\boldsymbol{t} \in \mathbb{R}^\nu$).

Notation. In what follows, C denotes generic positive constants that may be different at different locations. We write $\xrightarrow{\mathrm{d}}$ and $\stackrel{\mathrm{d}}{=}$ for the weak convergence and equality of probability distributions. Denote by $|\cdot|$ the absolute-value norm on $\mathbb{K}$, where $\mathbb{K}$ is either $\mathbb{R}$ or $\mathbb{C}$ and the Euclidean norm on $\mathbb{R}^\nu$. $\langle \cdot, \cdot \rangle$ is the scalar product in $\mathbb{R}^\nu$. Denote by $\boldsymbol{e}_j$ the vector in $\mathbb{R}^\nu$ with 1 in the jth coordinate and 0's elsewhere. For $p \geq 1$, denote by $L^p(\mathbb{Z}^\nu)$ the space of functions $f : \mathbb{Z}^\nu \to \mathbb{K}$ for which $\sum_{\boldsymbol{u} \in \mathbb{Z}^\nu} |f(\boldsymbol{u})|^p < \infty$ and by $L^p(\mathbb{R}^\nu)$ the space of measurable functions $f : \mathbb{R}^\nu \mapsto \mathbb{K}$ for which the p-th power of the absolute value is integrable with respect to the Lebesgue measure $\mathrm{d}\boldsymbol{x}$ on $\mathbb{R}^\nu$: $\|f\|_{L^p(\mathbb{R}^\nu)} := (\int_{\mathbb{R}^\nu} |f(\boldsymbol{x})|^p \mathrm{d}\boldsymbol{x})^{1/p} < \infty$ with the identification of functions f, g, such that $f = g$ almost everywhere (a.e.). Denote by $L^\infty(\mathbb{R}^\nu)$ the space of measurable functions $f : \mathbb{R}^\nu \to \mathbb{K}$ for which $\|f\|_{L^\infty(\mathbb{R}^\nu)} := \inf\{C \geq 0 : |f| \leq C \text{ a.e.}\} < \infty$, with the identification of functions f, g, such that $f = g$ a.e. Write $\mathbb{I}(A)$ for the indicator function of a set A. Write $\lceil x \rceil$ for the smallest integer greater than or equal to $x \in \mathbb{R}$. $\mathrm{i} := \sqrt{-1} \in \mathbb{C}, \mathbb{Z}^\nu_0 := \mathbb{Z}^\nu \setminus \{\mathbf{0}\}$ and $\mathbb{N} := \{0, 1, 2, \dots\}$.

2. Invertibility and Properties of Fractional Operators

We start with the properties of the binomial coefficients in (2):

$$
\begin{aligned}
&\psi_j(d) < 0 \quad (j \geq 1), \quad \sum_{j=0}^{\infty} \psi_j(d) = 0 \quad \text{if } 0 < d < 1, \\
&\psi_j(d) > 0 \quad (j \geq 1), \quad \sum_{j=0}^{\infty} \psi_j(d) = \infty \quad \text{if } -1 < d < 0.
\end{aligned}
\tag{9}
$$

The identity $(1-z)^d(1-z)^{-d} = 1$ leads to

$$
1 = \sum_{j,k=0}^{\infty} \psi_j(d)\psi_k(-d) z^{j+k} = \sum_{n=0}^{\infty} z^n \sum_{j=0}^{n} \psi_j(d)\psi_{n-j}(-d)
$$

and the invertibility relation

$$\sum_{j=0}^{n} \psi_j(d)\psi_{n-j}(-d) = \mathbb{I}(n=0), \quad n \in \mathbb{N}. \tag{10}$$

The following lemma gives some basic properties of the fractional coefficients $\tau(\boldsymbol{u};d)$ in (6).

Lemma 1. *(i) Let $0 < d < 1$. Then, the series in (6) converges for every $\boldsymbol{u} \in \mathbb{Z}^\nu$ and*

$$\tau(\boldsymbol{0};d) > 0, \quad \tau(\boldsymbol{u};d) \le 0 \ (\boldsymbol{u} \neq \boldsymbol{0}), \quad \text{and} \quad \sum_{\boldsymbol{u}\in\mathbb{Z}^\nu} \tau(\boldsymbol{u};d) = 0. \tag{11}$$

(ii) Let $-1 < d < 0$. Then, $0 \le \tau(\boldsymbol{u};d) \le \infty$ for every $\boldsymbol{u} \in \mathbb{Z}^\nu$ and $\tau(\boldsymbol{0};d) \ge 1$ and

$$\sum_{\boldsymbol{u}\in\mathbb{Z}^\nu} \tau(\boldsymbol{u};d) = \infty.$$

Moreover, $\tau(\boldsymbol{0};d) < \infty$ implies $\tau(\boldsymbol{u};d) < \infty$ and

$$-\sum_{\boldsymbol{u}\neq\boldsymbol{0}} \tau(\boldsymbol{u};d)\tau(-\boldsymbol{u};-d) \le \tau(\boldsymbol{0};d) < \infty. \tag{12}$$

(iii) Let $0 < d < 1$ and $\tau(\boldsymbol{0};-d) < \infty$. Then,

$$\sum_{\boldsymbol{s}\in\mathbb{Z}^\nu} \tau(\boldsymbol{s};d)\tau(\boldsymbol{t}-\boldsymbol{s};-d) = \mathbb{I}(\boldsymbol{t}=\boldsymbol{0}), \quad \boldsymbol{t} \in \mathbb{Z}^\nu. \tag{13}$$

Proof. (i) From (6) and (9) we obtain

$$\tau(\boldsymbol{0};d) = 1 + \sum_{j=1}^{\infty} \psi_j(d)p_j(\boldsymbol{0}) > 1 + \sum_{j=1}^{\infty} \psi_j(d) = 0$$

since $p_j(\boldsymbol{0}) = 1 (\forall j \ge 1)$ is not possible. On the other hand, for $\boldsymbol{u} \neq \boldsymbol{0}$ we have $p_0(\boldsymbol{u}) = 0$ and

$$\tau(\boldsymbol{u};d) = \sum_{j=1}^{\infty} \psi_j(d)p_j(\boldsymbol{u}) \le 0 \tag{14}$$

in view of (9).
(ii) Since $\psi_j(d)p_j(\boldsymbol{u}) \ge 0$ is obvious from (9), it suffices to show (12), since it implies $\tau(\boldsymbol{u};d) < \infty$ by (11). We have

$$\begin{aligned}
\Sigma_0 := \sum_{\boldsymbol{u}\neq\boldsymbol{0}} \tau(\boldsymbol{u};d)(-\tau(-\boldsymbol{u};-d)) &= \sum_{\boldsymbol{u}\neq\boldsymbol{0}} \sum_{j,k=1}^{\infty} \psi_j(d)(-\psi_k(-d))p_j(\boldsymbol{u})p_k(-\boldsymbol{u}) \\
&= \sum_{n=2}^{\infty} \sum_{j=1}^{n-1} \psi_j(d)(-\psi_{n-j}(-d)) \sum_{\boldsymbol{u}\neq\boldsymbol{0}} p_j(\boldsymbol{u})p_{n-j}(-\boldsymbol{u})
\end{aligned}$$

where exchanging the order of summation is legitimate as all summands are non-negative. Hence, using $\sum_{\boldsymbol{u}\neq\boldsymbol{0}} p_j(\boldsymbol{u})p_{n-j}(-\boldsymbol{u}) \le p_n(\boldsymbol{0})$ and (10), we obtain

$$\begin{aligned}
\Sigma_0 &\le \sum_{n=2}^{\infty} p_n(\boldsymbol{0}) \sum_{j=1}^{n-1} \psi_j(d)(-\psi_{n-j}(-d)) = \sum_{n=2}^{\infty} p_n(\boldsymbol{0})(\psi_n(d) + \psi_n(-d)) \\
&\le \sum_{n=2}^{\infty} p_n(\boldsymbol{0})\psi_n(d) < \tau(\boldsymbol{0};d)
\end{aligned}$$

proving part (ii).
(iii) The convergence of the series in (13) and the equality follow as in (12):

$$\begin{aligned}\sum_{s\in\mathbb{Z}^\nu}\tau(s;d)\tau(t-s;-d) &= \sum_{j,k=0}^{\infty}\psi_j(d)\psi_k(-d)\sum_{s\in\mathbb{Z}^\nu}p_j(s)p_k(t-s)\\ &= \sum_{n=0}^{\infty}p_n(t)\sum_{j=0}^{n}\psi_j(d)\psi_{n-j}(-d)\\ &= p_0(t)=\mathbb{I}(t=0).\end{aligned}$$

Lemma 1 is proved. □

Remark 1. *Let* $0<d<1$. *Then, the inequalities are strict:* $\tau(u;d)<0$ *and* $\tau(u;-d)>0$, *if* $p_j(u)>0$ *for some* j, *i.e.,* u *is accessible from state* $\mathbf{0}$. *Moreover, if state* $\mathbf{0}$ *is transient, i.e., the probability of eventual return to* $\mathbf{0}$ *is strictly less than* 1, *which is equivalent to* $\sum_{j=0}^{\infty}p_j(\mathbf{0})<\infty$, *then* $\tau(\mathbf{0};-d)<\infty$.

The main result of this section is Theorem 1, which provides the necessary and sufficient conditions for the square summability of the fractional coefficients in (6), in terms of the characteristic function $\widehat{p}(x)$ (see (7)). Write $\widehat{f}$ for the Fourier transform of a function $f:\mathbb{Z}^\nu\to\mathbb{R}$. For $r\in(0,1), d\in(-1,1)$ introduce the *tempered fractional operators*

$$(I-rT)^d g(t)=\sum_{j=0}^{\infty}r^j\psi_j(d)T^j g(t)=\sum_{u\in\mathbb{Z}^\nu}\tau_r(u;d)g(t+u),\quad t\in\mathbb{Z}^\nu$$

with coefficients

$$\tau_r(u;d):=\sum_{j=0}^{\infty}r^j\psi_j(d)p_j(u),\tag{15}$$

and the Fourier transform $\widehat{\tau}_r(x;d)=(1-r\widehat{p}(x))^d$.

Theorem 1. *For* $-1<d<1$, *the following conditions are equivalent:*

$$\int_{\Pi^\nu}|1-\widehat{p}(x)|^{-2|d|}\mathrm{d}x<\infty,\tag{16}$$

$$\sum_{u\in\mathbb{Z}^\nu}\tau(u;-|d|)^2<\infty.\tag{17}$$

Either of these conditions implies

$$\widehat{\tau}(\cdot;-|d|)=(1-\widehat{p}(\cdot))^{-|d|}\quad in\ L^2(\Pi^\nu).\tag{18}$$

Moreover, for $0<d<1$, *the above conditions* (16)–(18) *hold with d in place of* $-|d|$.

Proof. Let $0<d<1$. Firstly, we consider $\tau(u;d)$ in (6). They satisfy $\sum_{u\in\mathbb{Z}^\nu}|\tau(u;d)|\le\sum_{j=0}^{\infty}|\psi_j(d)|<\infty$ because of (3) and $\sum_{u\in\mathbb{Z}^\nu}p_j(u)=1$ with $0\le p_j(u)\le 1$. Then, $\sum_{u\in\mathbb{Z}^\nu}\tau(u;d)^2<\infty$ is immediate. Moreover, we have the Fourier transform $\widehat{\tau}(x;d)=\sum_{j=0}^{\infty}\psi_j(d)\widehat{p}_j(x)$, where $\widehat{p}_j(x)=\widehat{p}(x)^j$ satisfies $|\widehat{p}(x)|\le 1$. We see that

$$\widehat{\tau}(x;d)=(1-\widehat{p}(x))^d,\quad x\in\Pi^\nu,\tag{19}$$

belongs to $L^2(\Pi^\nu)$.

Now let us prove the implication (16) ⇒ (17). We use approximation by the tempered fractional coefficients $\tau_r(u;-d)$ in (15) as $r\nearrow 1$. We ascertain that $\widehat{\tau}_r(x;-d)=(1-r\widehat{p}(x))^{-d}\to(1-\widehat{p}(x))^{-d}$ a.e. as $r\nearrow 1$. Next, for $z\in\mathbb{C}$, $|z|\le 1$, $0<r<1$ the inequality $|1-z|\le|1-rz|+|rz-z|\le|1-rz|+1-r$, where $1-r\le 1-|rz|\le|1-rz|$ becomes $|1-z|\le 2|1-rz|$. Using this, we obtain the domination for all $0<r<1$, $x\in\Pi^\nu$,

$$|\widehat{\tau}_r(x;-d)|\le\frac{1}{|1-r\widehat{p}(x)|^d}\le\frac{2^d}{|1-\widehat{p}(x)|^d}$$

by a function in $L^2(\Pi^\nu)$ according to (16). Hence, by the dominated convergence theorem (DCT), $\widehat{\tau}_r(\cdot;-d) \to (1-\widehat{p}(\cdot))^{-d}$ as $r \nearrow 1$ holds in $L^2(\Pi^\nu)$. As a consequence, $\widehat{\tau}_r(\cdot;-d), 0<r<1$ is a Cauchy sequence in $L^2(\Pi^\nu)$. By Parseval's theorem, the inverse Fourier transforms,

$$\tau_r(\boldsymbol{u};-d) = \frac{1}{(2\pi)^\nu}\int_{\Pi^\nu} \mathrm{e}^{-\mathrm{i}\langle \boldsymbol{u},\boldsymbol{x}\rangle}\widehat{\tau}_r(\boldsymbol{x};-d)\mathrm{d}\boldsymbol{x}, \quad \boldsymbol{u}\in\mathbb{Z}^\nu,\ 0<r<1,$$

are a Cauchy sequence in $L^2(\mathbb{Z}^\nu)$, and so $\tau_r(\cdot;-d)$ converges in $L^2(\mathbb{Z}^\nu)$ to some $f\in L^2(\mathbb{Z}^\nu)$ as $r\nearrow 1$. This f must be $\tau(\cdot;-d)$ because $\tau_r(\boldsymbol{u};-d)\nearrow\tau(\boldsymbol{u};-d)$ as $r\nearrow 1$ for all $\boldsymbol{u}$. We conclude that $\tau(\cdot;-d)\in L^2(\mathbb{Z}^\nu)$ or (17).

Let us turn to the implication (17) $\Rightarrow$ (16). From (17) and $\tau_r(\boldsymbol{u};-d)\nearrow\tau(\boldsymbol{u};-d)$ for all $\boldsymbol{u}$ it follows that $\tau_r(\cdot;-d)\to\tau(\cdot;-d)$ as $r\nearrow 1$ holds in $L^2(\mathbb{Z}^\nu)$. By Parseval's theorem, $\widehat{\tau}_r(\cdot;-d) = (1-r\widehat{p}(\cdot))^{-d}, 0<r<1$ is a Cauchy sequence in $L^2(\Pi^\nu)$. It follows that $\lim_{r\nearrow 1}\int_{\Pi^\nu}|\widehat{\tau}_r(\boldsymbol{x};-d)-g(\boldsymbol{x})|^2\mathrm{d}\boldsymbol{x}=0$ for some $g\in L^2(\Pi^\nu)$. We also have $\lim_{r\nearrow 1}(1-r\widehat{p}(\boldsymbol{x}))^{-d} = (1-\widehat{p}(\boldsymbol{x}))^{-d}$ for each $\boldsymbol{x}\in\Pi^\nu$, such that $\widehat{p}(\boldsymbol{x})\neq 1$. Since $\mathrm{Leb}_\nu(\boldsymbol{x}\in\Pi^\nu : \widehat{p}(\boldsymbol{x})=1)=0$ (see Lemma 2.3.2(a) in [26]) we conclude that $g(\cdot)=(1-\widehat{p}(\cdot))^{-d}$ a.e., proving (16).

The above argument also proves (18). On the one hand, $\widehat{\tau}(\cdot;-d)$ is the limit of $\widehat{\tau}_r(\cdot;-d)$ in $L^2(\Pi^\nu)$ as $r\nearrow 1$ because $\tau_r(\cdot;-d)$ converges in $L^2(\mathbb{Z}^\nu)$ to $\tau(\cdot;-d)$ as $r\nearrow 1$. On the other hand, $\widehat{\tau}_r(\cdot;-d)=(1-r\widehat{p}(\cdot))^{-d}\to(1-\widehat{p}(\cdot))^{-d}$ in $L^2(\Pi^\nu)$ as $r\nearrow 1$. We conclude that $\widehat{\tau}(\cdot;-d)=(1-\widehat{p}(\cdot))$ a.e. Theorem 1 is proved. □

Next, we turn to the asymptotics of the 'fractional coefficients' $\tau(\boldsymbol{u};d)$ in (6). The proof uses the local limit theorem in [26] for random walk probabilities $p_j(\boldsymbol{u})=\mathrm{P}(S_j=\boldsymbol{u})$. Following the latter work, we assume that

$$\mathrm{E}\mathrm{e}^{c|S_1|}<\infty \quad (\exists c>0) \quad \text{and } \{S_j\} \text{ is zero mean, aperiodic, irreducible.} \tag{20}$$

For example, if S_1 is symmetric, i.e., $S_1 \overset{\mathrm{d}}{=} -S_1$, and, moreover, has finite support that contains $\mathbf{0}, \boldsymbol{e}_i, i=1,\dots,\nu$, then the random walk satisfies our assumption (20). The conditions in (20) imply that the random walk has zero mean $\mathrm{E}S_1=\sum_{\boldsymbol{u}\in\mathbb{Z}^\nu}\boldsymbol{u}p(\boldsymbol{u})=\mathbf{0}$ and an invertible covariance matrix

$$\Gamma := \mathrm{E}S_1S_1'.$$

According to the classical (integral) CLT, the normalized sum $S_j/\sqrt{j}, j\to\infty$ approaches a Gaussian distribution on $\mathbb{R}^\nu$ with density

$$\phi(\boldsymbol{z}) := \frac{1}{(2\pi)^{\nu/2}\sqrt{\det\Gamma}}\mathrm{e}^{-\langle \boldsymbol{z},\Gamma^{-1}\boldsymbol{z}\rangle/2}, \quad \boldsymbol{z}\in\mathbb{R}^\nu.$$

Denote

$$\bar{p}_j(\boldsymbol{u}) := \frac{1}{(2\pi j)^{\nu/2}\sqrt{\det\Gamma}}\mathrm{e}^{-\langle \boldsymbol{u},\Gamma^{-1}\boldsymbol{u}\rangle/2j}, \quad \boldsymbol{u}\in\mathbb{R}^\nu.$$

Lemma 2 ([26] Theorem 2.3.11). *Under the conditions of* (20), *there exists* $C>0$, *such that*

$$|p_j(\boldsymbol{u})-\bar{p}_j(\boldsymbol{u})| \le C\bar{p}_j(\boldsymbol{u})\Big(\frac{1}{j^{1/2}}+\frac{|\boldsymbol{u}|^3}{j^2}\Big), \quad \forall\, |\boldsymbol{u}|<j^2,\ \boldsymbol{u}\in\mathbb{Z}^\nu. \tag{21}$$

For 'very atypical' values $|S_j|>j$ we use the following bound ([26], Proposition 2.1.2): for any $k\ge 1$ there exists $C>0$, such that

$$\mathrm{P}(|S_j|>z\sqrt{j}) \le Cz^{-k}, \quad \forall\, z>0. \tag{22}$$

Proposition 1. *Let* $p=\{p(\boldsymbol{u});\boldsymbol{u}\in\mathbb{Z}^\nu\}$ *satisfy* (20). *The coefficients in* (6) *are well-defined for any* $-(1\wedge\frac{\nu}{2})<d<1, d\neq 0$ *and satisfy*

$$\tau(u;d) = (B_1(d) + o(1))\langle u, \Gamma^{-1}u\rangle^{-(\nu/2)-d}, \quad |u| \to \infty, \tag{23}$$

where

$$B_1(d) := \frac{2^d \Gamma(d + (\nu/2))}{\pi^{\nu/2}\Gamma(-d)\sqrt{\det\Gamma}}.$$

Proof. Let us prove (23). Since Γ is positive-definite, $|u|_\Gamma := \sqrt{\langle u, \Gamma^{-1}u\rangle}$, $u \in \mathbb{R}^\nu$ is a norm. Note that it is equivalent to the Euclidean norm because any two norms are equivalent in finite-dimensional real vector space. In particular, the spectral decomposition $\Gamma^{-1} = U\Lambda U'$—where U is an orthogonal matrix whose columns are the real, orthonormal eigenvectors of Γ^{-1}, U' is the transpose of U, and Λ is a diagonal matrix whose entries are the eigenvalues of Γ^{-1} with $\lambda_{\max}, \lambda_{\min} > 0$ denoting the largest and smallest, respectively—gives $|u|_\Gamma = |\Lambda^{1/2}U'u|^2 \le \lambda_{\max}|u|^2$ and, similarly, $|u|^2_\Gamma \ge \lambda_{\min}|u|^2$. Using (6) for a large $K > 0$ we decompose $|u|_\Gamma^{\nu+2d}\tau(u;d) = \sum_{i=1}^3 J_i(u)$, where

$$\begin{aligned}
J_1(u) &:= |u|_\Gamma^{\nu+2d}\Gamma(-d)^{-1} \sum_{j>|u|^2_\Gamma/K} j^{-d-1}p_j(u),\\
J_2(u) &:= |u|_\Gamma^{\nu+2d} \sum_{j>|u|^2_\Gamma/K} (\psi_j(d) - \Gamma(-d)^{-1}j^{-d-1})p_j(u),\\
J_3(u) &:= |u|_\Gamma^{\nu+2d} \sum_{0\le j\le|u|^2_\Gamma/K} \psi_j(d)p_j(u).
\end{aligned}$$

It suffices to show that

$$\lim_{K\to\infty}\lim_{|u|\to\infty} J_1(u) = B_1(d), \quad \lim_{K\to\infty}\limsup_{|u|\to\infty} J_i(u) = 0, \quad i = 2, 3. \tag{24}$$

To show the first relation in (24), use (21). We have $J_1(u) = J_1'(u) + J_1''(u)$, where, for each $K > 0$ fixed, the main term $J_1'(u)$ and the remainder term $J_1''(u)$ asymptotically behave when $|u| \to \infty$ as

$$\begin{aligned}
J_1'(u) &:= |u|_\Gamma^{\nu+2d}\Gamma(-d)^{-1} \sum_{j>|u|^2_\Gamma/K} j^{-d-1}\bar p_j(u)\\
&= \frac{|u|_\Gamma^{\nu+2d}}{(2\pi)^{\nu/2}\Gamma(-d)\sqrt{\det\Gamma}} \int_0^\infty \mathbb{I}(|u|^2_\Gamma/K < [y])[y]^{-d-1-(\nu/2)}\mathrm{e}^{-|u|^2_\Gamma/2[y]}\mathrm{d}y\\
&\sim \frac{1}{(2\pi)^{\nu/2}\Gamma(-d)\sqrt{\det\Gamma}} \int_{1/K}^\infty x^{-d-1-(\nu/2)}\mathrm{e}^{-1/2x}\mathrm{d}x
\end{aligned}$$

and, for some constants $C, c > 0$,

$$\begin{aligned}
|J_1''(u)| &\le C|u|_\Gamma^{\nu+2d}K^{3/2} \sum_{j>|u|^2_\Gamma/K} j^{-d-3/2}\bar p_j(u)\\
&\le C|u|_\Gamma^{-1}K^{3/2}\int_0^\infty x^{-d-(3/2)-(\nu/2)}\mathrm{e}^{-c/x}\mathrm{d}x = o(1).
\end{aligned}$$

Hence, the first relation in (24) follows, using $\int_0^\infty x^{-1-\tau}\mathrm{e}^{-1/x}dx = \Gamma(\tau), \tau > 0$. In view of (3), the same argument also proves the second relation in (24) for $i = 2$.

Consider (24) for $i = 3$. Split $J_3(u) = J_3''(u) + J_3'(u)$ into two sums over $j > 0$, where $j^2 \le |u|$ and $j^2 > |u|$, respectively. In the sum $J_3'(u)$ we also have $j \le |u|^2_\Gamma/K \le |u|^2$, and Lemma 2 entails the bound

$$p_j(u) \le C\bar p_j(u)(\frac{|u|^3}{j^2}) \le C|u|^3 j^{-(\nu/2)-2}\mathrm{e}^{-c|u|^2/j}$$

for some constants $C, c > 0$. Hence,

$$|J_3'(u)| \le C|u|^{\nu+2d+3}\int_0^{|u|^2}[y]^{-d-3-(\nu/2)}e^{-c|u|^2/[y]}dy$$
$$\le C|u|^{-1}\int_0^1 x^{-d-3-(\nu/2)}e^{-c/x}dx = o(1)$$

since the last integral converges for any d. Finally, by (22), given a large enough $k > 0$, there exists $C > 0$, such that $p_j(u) \le Cj^{k/2}/|u|^k$, which implies $J_3''(u) = o(1)$. This proves (24) and completes the proof of Proposition 1. □

Lemma 2 does not apply to the simple random walk (which is not aperiodic), in which case the local CLT takes a somewhat different form (see [26], Theorem 2.1.3). The application of the latter result and the argument in the proof of Proposition 1 yields the following result:

Proposition 2. *Let $p(e_j) = p(-e_j) = \frac{1}{2\nu}, j = 1, \dots, \nu$. The coefficients in* (6) *are well-defined for any $-(1 \wedge \frac{\nu}{2}) < d < 1, d \ne 0$ and satisfy*

$$\tau(u;d) = (B(d) + o(1))|u|^{-\nu-2d}, \quad |u| \to \infty,$$

where

$$B(d) := \frac{2^d\Gamma(d+(\nu/2))}{\nu^d\Gamma(-d)}.$$

Proposition 1 and Lemma 2 do not apply to random walks with a non-zero mean, as in Example 2 below (fractional heat operator), in which case the fractional coefficients exhibit an anisotropic behavior different from (23). Such behavior is described in the following proposition. We assume that the underlying random walk factorizes into a deterministic drift by 1 in direction $-e_1$ and a random walk on $\mathbb{Z}^{\nu-1}$, as in Lemma 2:

$$p(u) = \begin{cases} 1-\theta, & u = -e_1, \\ \theta\tilde{q}(\tilde{u}), & u = -e_1 + (0, \tilde{u}), \end{cases} \tag{25}$$

where $\theta \in (0,1)$ and $\tilde{q}(\tilde{u})$ is a probability distribution concentrated on $\tilde{u} = (u_2, \dots, u_\nu) \in \mathbb{Z}^{\nu-1}$, such that $\tilde{u} \ne \mathbf{0}$. Write $\{S_j; j \ge 0\}$ for the random walk starting at $\mathbf{0}$ with j-step probabilities $\mathrm{P}(\tilde{S}_j = \tilde{u}|\tilde{S}_0 = \mathbf{0}) =: \tilde{q}_j(\tilde{u}), j = 0, 1, \dots,$ such that $\tilde{q}_1(\tilde{u}) := \tilde{q}(\tilde{u}), \tilde{u} \in \mathbb{Z}^{\nu-1}$. In order to apply Lemma 2, we make a similar assumption to (20):

$$\mathrm{E}e^{c|\tilde{S}_1|} < \infty \quad (\exists c > 0) \quad \text{and } \{\tilde{S}_j\} \text{ is zero mean, irreducible} \tag{26}$$

and we denote $\tilde{\Gamma} := \mathrm{E}\tilde{S}_1\tilde{S}_1'$, the respective covariance matrix. Let

$$\rho(x) := \left(x_1^2 + \langle\tilde{x}, \tilde{\Gamma}^{-1}\tilde{x}\rangle^2\right)^{1/2}, \quad x = (x_1, \tilde{x}) \in \mathbb{R}^\nu$$

be a positive function on $\mathbb{R}^\nu$ satisfying the homogeneity property, $\rho(\lambda x_1, \lambda^{1/2}\tilde{x}) = \lambda\rho(x)$, $\forall\lambda > 0$. As in Example 2, the fractional coefficients for $p(u)$ in (25) we write as

$$\tau(-u;d) = \psi_{u_1}(d)p_{u_1}(-u)\mathbb{I}(u_1 \ge 0), \quad u = (u_1, \tilde{u}) \in \mathbb{Z}^\nu. \tag{27}$$

Proposition 3. *Let* (26) *hold and $\theta \in (0,1)$. Then,*

$$\tau(-u;d) = \frac{u_1^{-d-(\nu+1)/2}}{\Gamma(-d)(2\pi\theta)^{(\nu-1)/2}\sqrt{\det\tilde{\Gamma}}}\exp\left\{-\frac{\langle\tilde{u}, \tilde{\Gamma}^{-1}\tilde{u}\rangle}{2\theta u_1}\right\}(1+o(1)) \tag{28}$$

as $u_1 \to \infty$ and $|\tilde{u}| \to \infty, |\tilde{u}| = o(u_1^{2/3})$. We also have

$$\tau(-u;d) = \rho(u)^{-d-(\nu+1)/2}\Big(L_0\big(\frac{u_1}{\rho(u)}\big) + o(1)\Big), \quad |u| \to \infty, \tag{29}$$

where $L_0(z), z \in [-1,1]$ is a continuous function on $[-1,1]$ given by

$$L_0(z) := \frac{z^{-d-(\nu+1)/2}}{\Gamma(-d)(2\pi\theta)^{(\nu-1)/2}\sqrt{\det\tilde{\Gamma}}} \exp\big\{-(1/2\theta)\sqrt{(1/z)^2-1}\big\}$$

for $z \in (0,1]$ and equals 0 for $z \in [-1,0]$.

Proof. Consider the following j-step probabilities of a random walk on $\mathbb{Z}^{\nu-1}$ starting at $\mathbf{0}$: $q_j(\tilde{u}) := p_j(u)$, where $u = (-j, \tilde{u})$ for $\tilde{u} \in \mathbb{Z}^{\nu-1}$, $j = 0, 1, \cdots$. Let us estimate these by $\bar{q}_j(\tilde{u}) := (2\pi j)^{-(\nu-1)/2}(\det\Gamma)^{-1/2}\exp\{-\langle\tilde{u}, \Gamma^{-1}\tilde{u}\rangle/2j\}$, where Γ is the covariance matrix of the 1-step distribution $q_1(\tilde{u}), \tilde{u} \in \mathbb{Z}^{\nu-1}$. Note $\Gamma = \theta\tilde{\Gamma}$. By Lemma 2,

$$|q_j(\tilde{u}) - \bar{q}_j(\tilde{u})| \le C\bar{q}_j(\tilde{u})\big(\frac{1}{j^{1/2}} + \frac{|\tilde{u}|^3}{j^2}\big), \quad \forall\, |\tilde{u}| < j^2,\ \tilde{u} \in \mathbb{Z}^{\nu-1}. \tag{30}$$

Relation (28) follows directly from (3), (27), and (30). Relation (29) is written as

$$\rho(u)^{d+(\nu+1)/2}\tau(-u;d) - L_0\big(\frac{u_1}{\rho(u)}\big) \to 0, \quad |u| \to \infty. \tag{31}$$

The asymptotics in (31) is immediate from (28) for $|u|$ tending to ∞ as in (28). The general case of (31) also follows from (28), using the continuity of L_0. For $\nu = 2$, the details can be found in [12] (proof of Proposition 4.1). □

Remark 2. The approximation in (28) compares with the kernel

$$h_{c,-d}(t) = c_1\, t_1^{-d-\frac{1+\nu}{2}} \exp\big\{-ct_1 - \frac{|\tilde{t}|^2}{4t_1}\big\}\mathbb{I}(t_1 > 0), \quad t = (t_1, \tilde{t}) \in \mathbb{R}^\nu \tag{32}$$

of the fractional heat operator $(c + \partial_1 - \widetilde{\Delta})^{-d}, \partial_1 - \widetilde{\Delta} := \partial/\partial t_1 - \sum_{i=2}^{\nu} \partial^2/\partial t_i^2$ for all $c > 0$, $d < 0$, and some $c_1 \in \mathbb{R}$. For $\nu = 2$, Ref. [25] Equation (3.7) has recently derived the analytic form in (32) of the kernel from the absolute square of its Fourier transform:

$$\begin{aligned} |\widehat{h}_{c,-d}(z)|^2 &= \Big|\int_{\mathbb{R}^\nu} \mathrm{e}^{\mathrm{i}\langle z,t\rangle} h_{c,-d}(t)\mathrm{d}t\Big|^2 \\ &= c_1^2(4\pi)^{\nu-1}\Gamma(-d)^2\big(z_1^2 + (c+|\tilde{z}|^2)^2\big)^d, \quad z = (z_1, \tilde{z}) \in \mathbb{R}^\nu, \end{aligned} \tag{33}$$

which is the implicit definition of this kernel in [22]. Similarly to derivations in [25], for $\nu \ge 2$, Equations (3.944.5-6) in the table of integrals [27] give

$$\begin{aligned} \widehat{h}_{c,-d}(z) &= c_1 \int_0^\infty \mathrm{e}^{\mathrm{i}z_1t_1 - ct_1} t_1^{d-\frac{1+\nu}{2}}\mathrm{d}t_1 \int_{\mathbb{R}^{\nu-1}} \exp\big\{\mathrm{i}\langle\tilde{z},\tilde{t}\rangle - \frac{|\tilde{t}|^2}{4t_1}\big\}\mathrm{d}\tilde{t} \\ &= c_1(4\pi)^{\frac{\nu-1}{2}} \int_0^\infty \mathrm{e}^{\mathrm{i}z_1t_1 - t_1(c+|\tilde{z}|^2)} t_1^{-d-1}\mathrm{d}t_1 \\ &= c_1(4\pi)^{\frac{\nu-1}{2}}\Gamma(-d)\big(z_1^2 + (c+|\tilde{z}|^2)^2\big)^{\frac{d}{2}} \exp\big\{-\mathrm{i}d\arctan\big(\frac{z_1}{c+|\tilde{z}|^2}\big)\big\}, \end{aligned}$$

yielding (33).

Finally, the tempered fractional coefficients in (15) are summable: $\sum_{u\in\mathbb{Z}^\nu} |\tau_r(u;d)| \le \sum_{j=0}^\infty r^j|\psi_j(d)| \le 2(1-r)^{-|d|} < \infty$ for any $d \in (-1,1), r \in (0,1)$ and *any* random walk $\{S_j\}$. Assuming the existence of the exponential moment $\mathrm{E}\mathrm{e}^{\kappa|S_1|} < \infty$ for some $\kappa > 0$, (15) decays exponentially,

$$|\tau_r(\boldsymbol{u};d)| \le C e^{-c|\boldsymbol{u}|}, \quad \boldsymbol{u} \in \mathbb{Z}^\nu, \tag{34}$$

for some $C, c > 0$. Indeed, Markov's inequality gives $r^j |\psi_j(d)| p_j(\boldsymbol{u}) \le P(|S_j| \ge |\boldsymbol{u}|) \le e^{-\kappa|\boldsymbol{u}|} E e^{\kappa|S_j|} \le e^{-\kappa|\boldsymbol{u}|}(E e^{\kappa|S_1|})^j \le e^{-(\kappa/2)|\boldsymbol{u}|}$ for any $0 \le j < c|\boldsymbol{u}|$ and large enough $|\boldsymbol{u}|$. Moreover, $\sum_{j \ge c|\boldsymbol{u}|} r^j |\psi_j(d)| p_j(\boldsymbol{u}) \le \sum_{j \ge c|\boldsymbol{u}|} r^j = r^{c|\boldsymbol{u}|}/(1-r)$, proving (34).

3. Fractionally Integrated Random Fields on $\mathbb{Z}^\nu$

Let $\{\varepsilon(\boldsymbol{t}); \boldsymbol{t} \in \mathbb{Z}^\nu\}$ be a white noise; in other words, a sequence of r.v.s with $E\varepsilon(\boldsymbol{t}) = 0$, $E\varepsilon(\boldsymbol{t})\varepsilon(\boldsymbol{s}) = \mathbb{I}(\boldsymbol{t} = \boldsymbol{s}), \boldsymbol{t}, \boldsymbol{s} \in \mathbb{Z}^\nu$. Given a sequence $a \in L^2(\mathbb{Z}^\nu)$ with the above noise we can associate a moving-average random field (RF),

$$X(\boldsymbol{t}) = \sum_{\boldsymbol{s} \in \mathbb{Z}^\nu} a(\boldsymbol{u})\varepsilon(\boldsymbol{t} - \boldsymbol{u}), \quad \boldsymbol{t} \in \mathbb{Z}^\nu \tag{35}$$

with zero mean and covariance $\mathrm{Cov}(X(\boldsymbol{t}), X(\boldsymbol{s})) = \sum_{\boldsymbol{u} \in \mathbb{Z}^\nu} a(\boldsymbol{u})a(\boldsymbol{t} - \boldsymbol{s} + \boldsymbol{u})$, which depends on $\boldsymbol{t} - \boldsymbol{s}$ alone and characterizes the dependence between values of X at distinct points $\boldsymbol{t} \ne \boldsymbol{s}$.

A moving-average RF X in (35) will be said to be

- long-range dependent (LRD) if $\sum_{\boldsymbol{u} \in \mathbb{Z}^\nu} |a(\boldsymbol{u})| = \infty$;
- short-range dependent (SRD) if $\sum_{\boldsymbol{u} \in \mathbb{Z}^\nu} |a(\boldsymbol{u})| < \infty$, $\sum_{\boldsymbol{u} \in \mathbb{Z}^\nu} a(\boldsymbol{u}) \ne 0$;
- negatively dependent (ND) if $\sum_{\boldsymbol{u} \in \mathbb{Z}^\nu} |a(\boldsymbol{u})| < \infty, \sum_{\boldsymbol{u} \in \mathbb{Z}^\nu} a(\boldsymbol{u}) = 0$.

The above classification is important in limit theorems and applications of random fields. It is not unanimous; several related but not equivalent classifications of dependence for stochastic processes can be found in [3,4,7,17] and other works.

Many RF models with discrete arguments are defined through linear difference equations involving white noise [28]. In this paper, we deal with fractionally integrated RFs X solving fractional equations on $\mathbb{Z}^\nu$,

$$(I - T)^d X(\boldsymbol{t}) = \sum_{\boldsymbol{s} \in \mathbb{Z}^\nu} \tau(\boldsymbol{s}; d) X(\boldsymbol{t} + \boldsymbol{s}) = \varepsilon(\boldsymbol{t}), \tag{36}$$

$$(I - rT)^d X(\boldsymbol{t}) = \sum_{\boldsymbol{s} \in \mathbb{Z}^\nu} \tau_r(\boldsymbol{s}; d) X(\boldsymbol{t} + \boldsymbol{s}) = \varepsilon(\boldsymbol{t}), \quad 0 < r < 1, \qquad \boldsymbol{t} \in \mathbb{Z}^\nu, \tag{37}$$

whose solutions are obtained by inverting these operators (see below).

Definition 1. *Let $d \in (-1, 1)$ and $\tau(\boldsymbol{u}; \pm d)$ in (6) be well-defined. By the stationary solution of equation (36) (respectively, (37)) we mean a stationary RF X, such that for each $\boldsymbol{t} \in \mathbb{Z}^\nu$ the series in (36) converges in mean square and (36) holds (respectively, the series in (37) converges in mean square and (37) holds).*

Corollary 1. *(i) Let $-1 < d < 1$. Then,*

$$X(\boldsymbol{t}) = (I - T)^{-d}\varepsilon(\boldsymbol{t}) = \sum_{\boldsymbol{u} \in \mathbb{Z}^\nu} \tau(\boldsymbol{u}; -d)\varepsilon(\boldsymbol{t} + \boldsymbol{u}), \quad \boldsymbol{t} \in \mathbb{Z}^\nu \tag{38}$$

is a stationary solution of equation (36) if condition (16) holds (for $0 < d < 1$, (16) is also necessary for the existence of the above X).
(ii) Let $0 < d < 1$ and (16) hold. Then, X in (38) is LRD. Moreover, it has a non-negative covariance function $\mathrm{Cov}(X(\mathbf{0}), X(\boldsymbol{t})) \ge 0$, and $\sum_{\boldsymbol{t} \in \mathbb{Z}^\nu} \mathrm{Cov}(X(\mathbf{0}), X(\boldsymbol{t})) = \infty$.
(iii) Let $-1 < d < 0$ and (16) hold. Then, X in (38) is ND; moreover, $\sum_{\boldsymbol{t} \in \mathbb{Z}^\nu} \mathrm{Cov}(X(\mathbf{0}), X(\boldsymbol{t})) = 0$.
(iv) Let $-1 < d < 1, 0 < r < 1$. Then,

$$X(\boldsymbol{t}) = (I - rT)^{-d}\varepsilon(\boldsymbol{t}) = \sum_{\boldsymbol{u} \in \mathbb{Z}^\nu} \tau_r(\boldsymbol{u}; -d)\varepsilon(\boldsymbol{t} + \boldsymbol{u}), \quad \boldsymbol{t} \in \mathbb{Z}^\nu \tag{39}$$

is a stationary solution of equation (37). Moreover, X in (39) is SRD. Furthermore, $\sum_{\boldsymbol{t} \in \mathbb{Z}^\nu} |\mathrm{Cov}(X(\mathbf{0}), X(\boldsymbol{t}))| < \infty$, $\sum_{\boldsymbol{t} \in \mathbb{Z}^\nu} \mathrm{Cov}(X(\mathbf{0}), X(\boldsymbol{t})) = (1 - r)^{-2d} > 0$.

Proof. (i) Let $0 < d < 1$. X in (38) is well-defined if and only if (17) holds, which is, therefore, a necessary condition. Let us show that X in (38) is a stationary solution of (36). We use the spectral representation of white noise,

$$\varepsilon(\boldsymbol{t}) = \int_{\Pi^\nu} \mathrm{e}^{\mathrm{i}\langle \boldsymbol{t},\boldsymbol{x}\rangle} Z(\mathrm{d}\boldsymbol{x}), \quad \boldsymbol{t} \in \mathbb{Z}^\nu, \tag{40}$$

where $Z(\mathrm{d}\boldsymbol{x})$ is a random complex-valued spectral measure on Π^ν with zero mean and variance $\mathrm{E}|Z(\mathrm{d}\boldsymbol{x})|^2 = \mathrm{d}\boldsymbol{x}/(2\pi)^\nu$. Then, $X(\boldsymbol{t})$ is written as

$$X(\boldsymbol{t}) = \int_{\Pi^\nu} \mathrm{e}^{\mathrm{i}\langle \boldsymbol{t},\boldsymbol{x}\rangle} \widehat{\tau}(\boldsymbol{x} - d) Z(\mathrm{d}\boldsymbol{x}) = \int_{\Pi^\nu} \mathrm{e}^{\mathrm{i}\langle \boldsymbol{t},\boldsymbol{x}\rangle} \frac{Z(\mathrm{d}\boldsymbol{x})}{(1-\widehat{p}(\boldsymbol{x}))^d} \tag{41}$$

see (18). Then, $(I-T)^d X(\boldsymbol{t}) = \int_{\Pi^\nu} \mathrm{e}^{\mathrm{i}\langle \boldsymbol{t},\boldsymbol{x}\rangle} \sum_{\boldsymbol{s}\in\mathbb{Z}^\nu} \tau(\boldsymbol{s};d) \mathrm{e}^{\mathrm{i}\langle \boldsymbol{s},\boldsymbol{x}\rangle} (1-\widehat{p}(\boldsymbol{x}))^{-d} Z(\mathrm{d}\boldsymbol{x}) = \varepsilon(\boldsymbol{t})$ follows by (19) and absolute summability $\sum_{\boldsymbol{s}\in\mathbb{Z}^\nu} |\tau(\boldsymbol{s};d)| < \infty$ (see (11) and (14)).

Next, let $-1 < d < 0$. Then, X in (38) is well-defined and is written as (41), due to $\sum_{\boldsymbol{s}\in\mathbb{Z}^\nu} |\tau(\boldsymbol{s};-d)| < \infty$. We need to show that the series in (36) converges in mean square towards $\varepsilon(\boldsymbol{t})$ if and only if (16) or (17) hold. The latter convergence writes as

$$\lim_{M\to\infty} \mathrm{E}|s_M - \varepsilon(\boldsymbol{t})|^2 = 0, \quad \text{where} \quad s_M := \sum_{|\boldsymbol{s}|\le M} \tau(\boldsymbol{s};d) X(\boldsymbol{t}+\boldsymbol{s}).$$

From (41),

$$\begin{aligned}
\mathrm{E}|s_M - \varepsilon(\boldsymbol{t})|^2 &= (2\pi)^{-\nu} \int_{\Pi^\nu} \Big| \sum_{|\boldsymbol{s}|\le M} \mathrm{e}^{\mathrm{i}\langle \boldsymbol{s},\boldsymbol{x}\rangle} \tau(\boldsymbol{s};d) - (1-\widehat{p}(\boldsymbol{x}))^d \Big|^2 |1-\widehat{p}(\boldsymbol{x})|^{2|d|} \mathrm{d}\boldsymbol{x} \\
&\le C \int_{\Pi^\nu} \Big| \sum_{|\boldsymbol{s}|\le M} \mathrm{e}^{\mathrm{i}\langle \boldsymbol{s},\boldsymbol{x}\rangle} \tau(\boldsymbol{s};d) - (1-\widehat{p}(\boldsymbol{x}))^d \Big|^2 \mathrm{d}\boldsymbol{x} \\
&= C \int_{\Pi^\nu} \Big| \sum_{|\boldsymbol{s}|> M} \mathrm{e}^{\mathrm{i}\langle \boldsymbol{s},\boldsymbol{x}\rangle} \tau(\boldsymbol{s};d) \Big|^2 \mathrm{d}\boldsymbol{x} \\
&= C \sum_{|\boldsymbol{s}|> M} \tau(\boldsymbol{s};-|d|)^2 \to 0 \quad (M\to\infty)
\end{aligned}$$

in view of (17). This proves part (i).
(ii) From (9), (6) we see $\tau(\boldsymbol{s};-d) \ge 0$ are non-negative and $\sum_{\boldsymbol{s}\in\mathbb{Z}^\nu} \tau(\boldsymbol{s};-d) = \sum_{j=0}^\infty \psi_j(-d) = \infty$. Thus, $\mathrm{Cov}(X(\mathbf{0}),X(\boldsymbol{t})) = \sum_{\boldsymbol{s}\in\mathbb{Z}^\nu} \tau(\boldsymbol{s};-d)\tau(\boldsymbol{t}+\boldsymbol{s};-d) \ge 0$ and $\sum_{\boldsymbol{t}\in\mathbb{Z}^\nu} \mathrm{Cov}(X(\mathbf{0}),X(\boldsymbol{t})) = \infty$.
(iii) As in the proof of (i), we obtain $\sum_{\boldsymbol{s}\in\mathbb{Z}^\nu} |\tau(\boldsymbol{s};-d)| \le 1 + \sum_{j=1}^\infty \sum_{\boldsymbol{s}\in\mathbb{Z}^\nu} |\psi_j(-d)| p_j(\boldsymbol{s}) = 1 + \sum_{j=1}^\infty |\psi_j(-d)| = 2$ (see (9)) and $\sum_{\boldsymbol{s}\in\mathbb{Z}^\nu} \tau(\boldsymbol{s};-d) = 0$, implying $\sum_{\boldsymbol{t}\in\mathbb{Z}^\nu} \mathrm{Cov}(X(\mathbf{0}),X(\boldsymbol{t})) = \sum_{\boldsymbol{t},\boldsymbol{s}\in\mathbb{Z}^\nu} \tau(\boldsymbol{s};-d)\tau(\boldsymbol{t}+\boldsymbol{s};-d) = 0$.
(iv) Using $\sum_{\boldsymbol{u}\in\mathbb{Z}^\nu} |\tau_r(\boldsymbol{u};d)| < \infty$, $\sum_{\boldsymbol{u}\in\mathbb{Z}^\nu} \tau_r(\boldsymbol{u};d) = \sum_{j=0}^\infty r^j \psi_j(d) = (1-r)^d$, the proof is similar to the above. Corollary 1 is proved. □

The ARFIMA(0,*d*,0) Equation (4) is autoregressive, since the best linear predictor (or conditional expectation in the Gaussian case) of $X(t)$, given the 'past' $X(s), s < t$, is a linear combination $\sum_{j=1}^\infty \psi_j(d) X(t-j)$ of the 'past' observations, due to the fact that $\mathrm{Cov}(X(s),\varepsilon(t)) = 0\ (s < t)$. For spatial equations, as in (36) or (37), an analogous property given the 'past' $X(\boldsymbol{s}), \boldsymbol{s} \ne \boldsymbol{t}$ does not hold, since $\mathrm{Cov}(X(\boldsymbol{s}),\varepsilon(\boldsymbol{t})) \ne 0\ (\boldsymbol{s} \ne \boldsymbol{t})$ as a rule. This issue is important in spatial statistics and has been discussed in the literature (see [29,30] and the references therein), distinguishing between 'simultaneous' and 'conditional autoregressive schemes'. A recent work [31] discusses some conditional autoregressive models with LRD property.

Definition 2. *Let X be an RF with $\mathrm{E}X(\boldsymbol{t})^2 < \infty$ for each $\boldsymbol{t} \in \mathbb{Z}^\nu$. We say that X has:*
(i) a simultaneous autoregressive representation with coefficients $b(\boldsymbol{s}), \boldsymbol{s} \in \mathbb{Z}^\nu_0$ if for each $\boldsymbol{t} \in \mathbb{Z}^\nu$

$$X(t) = \sum_{s \in \mathbb{Z}^\nu_0} b(s) X(t-s) + \xi(t),$$

where the series converges in mean square and the r.v.s $\xi(t), t \in \mathbb{Z}^\nu$ *satisfy* $\mathrm{Cov}(\xi(t), \xi(s)) = 0\, (\forall s \neq t)$.

(ii) a conditional autoregressive representation with coefficients $c(s), s \in \mathbb{Z}^\nu_0$ *if for each* $t \in \mathbb{Z}^\nu$

$$X(t) = \sum_{s \in \mathbb{Z}^\nu_0} c(s) X(t-s) + \eta(t), \tag{42}$$

where the series converges in mean square and the r.v.s $\eta(t), t \in \mathbb{Z}^\nu$ *satisfy* $\mathrm{Cov}(\eta(t), X(s)) = 0\, (\forall s \neq t)$.

Corollary 2. *(i) Let* $d \in (-1,1)$ *and X be a fractionally integrated RF in* (38) *and* (16) *holds. Then, X has a simultaneous autoregressive representation with coefficients* $b(s) = -\tau(-s;d)/\tau(0;d)$, $s \in \mathbb{Z}^\nu_0$ *and* $\xi(s) = \varepsilon(s)/\tau(0;d)$, $s \in \mathbb{Z}^\nu$;

(ii) Let $d \in (0,1)$, *X be a fractionally integrated RF in* (38) *and* (16) *holds. Then, X has a conditional autoregressive representation with coefficients* $c(s) = -\gamma^*(s)/\gamma^*(0), s \in \mathbb{Z}^\nu_0$ *and* $\eta(s) = \int_{\Pi^\nu} \mathrm{e}^{\mathrm{i}\langle s,x\rangle}(1-\widehat{p}(-x))^d Z(\mathrm{d}x)/\gamma^*(0)$, *where* $Z(\mathrm{d}x)$ *is a complex-valued random measure given in* (40) *with zero mean and variance* $\mathrm{E}|Z(\mathrm{d}x)|^2 = \mathrm{d}x/(2\pi)^\nu$ *and*

$$\gamma^*(s) := \frac{1}{(2\pi)^\nu} \int_{\Pi^\nu} \mathrm{e}^{-\mathrm{i}\langle s,x\rangle} |1-\widehat{p}(x)|^{2d} \mathrm{d}x, \quad s \in \mathbb{Z}^\nu;$$

(iii) Let $d \in (-1,1), 0 < r < 1$ *and X be a (tempered) fractionally integrated RF in* (39). *Then, X has a simultaneous autoregressive representation with* $b(s) = -\tau_r(-s;d)/\tau_r(0;d), \xi(t) = \varepsilon(t)/\tau_r(0;d)$ *and a conditional autoregressive representation with* $c(s) = -\gamma^*_r(s)/\gamma^*_r(0), \eta(t) = \int_{\Pi^\nu} \mathrm{e}^{\mathrm{i}\langle t,x\rangle}(1-r\widehat{p}(-x))^d Z(\mathrm{d}x)/\gamma^*_r(0)$, *with the same* $Z(\mathrm{d}x)$ *as in part (ii) and*

$$\gamma^*_r(s) := \frac{1}{(2\pi)^\nu} \int_{\Pi^\nu} \mathrm{e}^{-\mathrm{i}\langle s,x\rangle} |1-r\widehat{p}(x)|^{2d} \mathrm{d}x, \quad s \in \mathbb{Z}^\nu.$$

Proof. (i) is obvious from Corollary 1 and (36), $\tau(0;d) \neq 0$.

(ii) By (16), $c(s)$ and $\eta(t)$ are well-defined, $\eta(t) \in \mathbb{R}$ and $\mathrm{E}\eta(t)^2 < \infty$. The orthogonality relation $\mathrm{E}X(t)\eta(s) = 0\, (t \neq s)$ follows from the spectral representations in (40) and (41):

$$\begin{aligned}\mathrm{E}X(t)\eta(s) &= \frac{1}{(2\pi)^\nu \gamma^*(0)} \int_{\Pi^\nu} \mathrm{e}^{\mathrm{i}\langle t-s,x\rangle} \frac{\overline{(1-\widehat{p}(-x))^d}}{(1-\widehat{p}(x))^d} \mathrm{d}x \\ &= \frac{1}{(2\pi)^\nu \gamma^*(0)} \int_{\Pi^\nu} \mathrm{e}^{\mathrm{i}\langle t-s,x\rangle} \mathrm{d}x = 0 \quad (t \neq s).\end{aligned}$$

It remains to show (42), including the convergence of the series. In view of the definition of $c(s)$, this amounts to showing

$$\sum_{s \in \mathbb{Z}^\nu} X(t-s)\gamma^*(s) = \gamma^*(0)\eta(t)$$

or, in spectral terms, to the convergence of the Fourier series

$$\frac{1}{(1-\widehat{p}(x))^d} \sum_{s \in \mathbb{Z}^\nu} \mathrm{e}^{-\mathrm{i}\langle x,s\rangle} \gamma^*(s) = (1-\widehat{p}(-x))^d = \frac{|1-\widehat{p}(-x)|^{2d}}{(1-\widehat{p}(x))^d} \tag{43}$$

in $L^2(\Pi^\nu)$. Note $\gamma^*(s) = \mathrm{Cov}(X^*(0), X^*(s))$, where the RF $X^*(t) := (1-T)^d \varepsilon(t), t \in \mathbb{Z}^\nu$, results from application of the inverse operator. Since X^* has negative dependence (see (41) and the proof of Corollary 1 (iii)) the covariances $\gamma^*(s), s \in \mathbb{Z}^\nu$ are absolutely summable. Therefore, the Fourier series on the l.h.s. of (43) converges uniformly in $x \in \Pi^\nu$ to $|1-\widehat{p}(-x)|^{2d}$, proving (43).

(iii) The proof is analogous to (and simpler than) (i)–(ii), using $\sum_{u\in\mathbb{Z}^\nu}|\tau_r(u;d)| < \infty$. □

Example 1. *Fractional Laplacian. The (lattice) Laplace operator on $\mathbb{Z}^\nu$ is defined as*

$$[\Delta]g(t) := \frac{1}{2\nu}\sum_{j=1}^{\nu}(g(t+e_j) + g(t-e_j) - 2g(t)), \qquad t \in \mathbb{Z}^\nu$$

so that $[\Delta] = T - I$, where $Tg(t) = \frac{1}{2\nu}\sum_{j=1}^{\nu}(g(t+e_j) + g(t-e_j))$ is the transition operator of the simple random walk $\{S_j; j = 0, 1, \cdots\}$ on $\mathbb{Z}^\nu$ with equal one-step transition probabilities $1/2\nu$ to the nearest-neighbors $t \to t \pm e_j, j = 1, \cdots, \nu$. For $-1 < d < 1$, the fractional Laplace RF can be defined as a stationary solution of the difference equation

$$(-[\Delta])^d X(t) = \varepsilon(t), \quad t \in \mathbb{Z}^\nu \tag{44}$$

with weak white noise on the r.h.s., written as a moving-average RF:

$$X(t) = (-[\Delta])^{-d}\varepsilon(t) = \sum_{u\in\mathbb{Z}^\nu}\tau(u; -d)\varepsilon(t+u). \tag{45}$$

We find that $\widehat{p}(x) = (1/\nu)\sum_{j=1}^{\nu}\cos(x_j)$, $x = (x_1, \cdots, x_\nu) \in \Pi^\nu$ and

$$1 - \widehat{p}(x) = \frac{1}{\nu}\sum_{j=1}^{\nu}(1 - \cos(x_j)) \geq C|x|^2$$

for some $C > 0$ and $1 - \widehat{p}(x) \sim (1/2\nu)|x|^2$ $(|x| \to 0)$. Hence, condition (16) for (44) translates to

$$\int_{\Pi^\nu}\frac{dx}{|1 - \widehat{p}(x)|^{2|d|}} < \infty \quad \Longleftrightarrow \quad |d| < \frac{\nu}{4}.$$

In particular, a stationary solution of Equation (44) on $\nu \geq 4$ exists for all $-1 < d < 1$. Finally, recall that (16) is equivalent to condition (17). We could have verified the latter by using Corollary 2, which gives the asymptotics of coefficients $\tau(u; -d)$ in (45).

Example 2. *Fractional heat operator. For a parameter $0 < \theta < 1$, we can extend the definition of the (lattice) heat operator on $\mathbb{Z}^\nu$ from $\nu = 2$ in [12] to $\nu \geq 2$ as follows:*

$$\begin{aligned}\Delta_{1,2}g(t) &:= (1-\theta)(g(t) - g(t-e_1)) \\ &\quad - \frac{\theta}{2(\nu-1)}\sum_{j=2}^{\nu}(g(t-e_1+e_j) + g(t-e_1-e_j) - 2g(t)).\end{aligned}$$

Thus, $\Delta_{1,2} = I - T$ corresponds to the random walk on $\mathbb{Z}^\nu$ with 1-step distribution $p(-e_1) = 1-\theta, p(-e_1 \pm e_j) = \frac{\theta}{2(\nu-1)}, j = 2, \cdots, \nu$. We find that

$$|1 - \widehat{p}(x)|^2 = \Big(\cos(x_1) - 1 + \frac{\theta}{\nu-1}\sum_{j=2}^{\nu}(1 - \cos(x_j))\Big)^2 + \sin^2(x_1), \quad x = (x_1, \cdots, x_\nu) \in \Pi^\nu.$$

By the Taylor expansion,

$$|1 - \widehat{p}(x)|^2 \sim \Big(\frac{\theta}{2(\nu-1)}\Big)^2|\tilde{x}|^4 + x_1^2, \quad x \to 0, \quad \tilde{x} := (0, x_2, \cdots, x_\nu).$$

We also find that outside the origin $|1 - \widehat{p}(x)|^2 \geq C$ for some $C > 0$ since $0 < \theta < 1$. Therefore,

$$\int_{\Pi^\nu}\frac{dx}{|1 - \widehat{p}(x)|^{2|d|}} \leq C\int_0^1\int_0^1\frac{y^{\nu-2}dxdy}{(x^2 + y^4)^{|d|}} < \infty \quad \text{if } |d| < \frac{\nu+1}{4}$$

and $\int_{\Pi^\nu} |1-\widehat{p}(\boldsymbol{x})|^{-2|d|}\mathrm{d}\boldsymbol{x} = \infty$ *if* $|d| \ge \frac{\nu+1}{4}$. *The above result agrees with [12] for* $\nu = 2$, $0 < d < \frac{3}{4}$ *and extends it to the arbitrary* $\nu \ge 2$, $-1 < d < 1$.

Example 3. *Fractionally integrated time series models (case* $\nu = 1$*). As noted above, the* ARFIMA$(0, d, 0)$ *process is a particular case of* (38) *corresponding to the backward shift* $Tg(t) := g(t-1)$ *or the deterministic random walk* $t \to t-1$. *Another fractionally integrated time series model is given in Example 1 and corresponds to the symmetric nearest-neighbor random walk on* $\mathbb{Z}$ *with probabilities 1/2. It is of interest to compare these two processes and their properties. Let* $T_1 g(t) := g(t-1), T_2 g(t) := (1/2)(g(t+1) + g(t-1)), t \in \mathbb{Z}$ *be the corresponding operators,*

$$X_1(t) := (I - T_1)^{-d_1}\varepsilon(t) = \sum_{u=0}^{\infty} \psi_u(-d_1)\varepsilon(t-u),$$
$$X_2(t) := (I - T_2)^{-d_2}\varepsilon(t) = \sum_{u\in\mathbb{Z}} \tau(u; -d_2)\varepsilon(t+u), \quad t \in \mathbb{Z}.$$

For $|d_1| < 1/2$ *and* $|d_2| < 1/4$, *processes* X_1 *and* X_2 *are well-defined; moreover, they are stationary solutions of the respective equations* $(I - T_1)^{d_1} X(t) = \varepsilon(t)$ *and* $(I - T_2)^{d_2} X(t) = \varepsilon(t)$. *The spectral densities of* X_1 *and* X_2 *are given by*

$$f_1(x) = \frac{1}{2\pi|1 - \mathrm{e}^{-\mathrm{i}x}|^{2d_1}} = \frac{1}{2\pi \cdot 2^{d_1}|1 - \cos(x)|^{d_1}},$$
$$f_2(x) = \frac{1}{2\pi|1 - (1/2)(\mathrm{e}^{-\mathrm{i}x} + \mathrm{e}^{\mathrm{i}x})|^{2d_2}} = \frac{1}{2\pi|1 - \cos(x)|^{2d_2}}$$

We see that when $d_1 = 2d_2$ *the processes* X_1 *and* X_2 *have the same 2nd order properties up to a multiplicative constant, so that in the Gaussian case* X_2 *is a noncausal representation of the* ARFIMA$(0, 2d_2, 0)$.

4. Scaling Limits

As explained in the Introduction, the isotropic scaling limits refer to the limit distribution of the integrals

$$X_\lambda(\phi) := \int_{\mathbb{R}^\nu} X([\boldsymbol{t}])\phi(\boldsymbol{t}/\lambda)\mathrm{d}\boldsymbol{t}, \quad \text{as } \lambda \to \infty, \tag{46}$$

where $X = \{X(\boldsymbol{t}); \boldsymbol{t} \in \mathbb{Z}^\nu\}$ is a given stationary random field (RF) for each $\phi : \mathbb{R}^\nu \to \mathbb{R}$ from a class of (test) functions Φ. We choose the latter class to be

$$\Phi := L^1(\mathbb{R}^\nu) \cap L^\infty(\mathbb{R}^\nu).$$

In the following, X is a linear or moving-average RF on $\mathbb{Z}^\nu$:

$$X(\boldsymbol{t}) = \sum_{\boldsymbol{s}\in\mathbb{Z}^\nu} a(\boldsymbol{t}-\boldsymbol{s})\varepsilon(\boldsymbol{s}), \quad \boldsymbol{t} \in \mathbb{Z}^\nu, \tag{47}$$

where $\{\varepsilon(\boldsymbol{t}); \boldsymbol{t} \in \mathbb{Z}^\nu\}$ are independent identically distributed (i.i.d.) r.v.s, with $\mathrm{E}\varepsilon(\boldsymbol{t}) = 0$, $\mathrm{E}\varepsilon(\boldsymbol{t})^2 = 1$, and $a \in L^2(\mathbb{Z}^\nu)$ being deterministic coefficients. Obviously, stationary solution (38) of Equation (36) satisfying Corollary 1 is a particular case of linear RF with $a(\boldsymbol{t}) = \tau(-\boldsymbol{t}; -d)$. Our limits results assume an 'isotropic' behavior of $a(\boldsymbol{t})$ as $|\boldsymbol{t}| \to \infty$, detailed as follows. Let $C(\mathbb{S}_{\nu-1})$ denote the class of all continuous functions on $\mathbb{S}_{\nu-1} = \{\boldsymbol{t} \in \mathbb{R}^\nu : |\boldsymbol{t}| = 1\}$.

Assumption 1. *Let* $\{a(\boldsymbol{t}); \boldsymbol{t} \in \mathbb{Z}^\nu\}$ *be a sequence of real numbers satisfying the following properties:*
(i) Let $0 < d < \nu/4$. *Then,*

$$a(\boldsymbol{t}) = \frac{1}{|\boldsymbol{t}|^{\nu-2d}}\big(\ell(\frac{\boldsymbol{t}}{|\boldsymbol{t}|}) + o(1)\big), \quad |\boldsymbol{t}| \to \infty, \tag{48}$$

where $\ell(\cdot) \in C(\mathbb{S}_{\nu-1})$ is not identically zero.
(ii) Let $-\nu/4 < d < 0$. Then, $a(\boldsymbol{t})$ satisfies (48) with the same $\ell(\boldsymbol{t})$ and, moreover, $\sum_{\boldsymbol{t}\in\mathbb{Z}^\nu} a(\boldsymbol{t}) = 0$.
(iii) Let $d = 0$. Then, $\sum_{\boldsymbol{t}\in\mathbb{Z}^\nu} |a(\boldsymbol{t})| < \infty$ and $\sum_{\boldsymbol{t}\in\mathbb{Z}^\nu} a(\boldsymbol{t}) \neq 0$.

The class of RFs in (47) with coefficients satisfying Assumption 1 is related but not limited to the fractionally integrated RFs in (36) and (37). Note that the parameter d is no longer restricted to being in $(-1,1)$. By easy observation, Assumption 1 implies the LRD, ND, and SRD properties of Section 3 in the respective cases $d > 0, d < 0$, and $d = 0$. Following the terminology in time series [3], the parameter d in (48) may be called the *memory parameter* of the linear RF X in (47), except that for $\nu = 1$ the memory parameter is usually defined as $2d \in (-1/2, 1/2)$.

In particular, the covariance function $r(\boldsymbol{t}) := \mathrm{Cov}(X(\mathbf{0}), X(\boldsymbol{t}))$ of the linear RF X in (47) is written as

$$r(\boldsymbol{t}) = \sum_{\boldsymbol{u}\in\mathbb{Z}^\nu} a(\boldsymbol{u})a(\boldsymbol{t}+\boldsymbol{u}), \quad \boldsymbol{t} \in \mathbb{Z}^\nu$$

or the lattice convolution of $a(\boldsymbol{t})$ with itself. We will use the notation $[a_1 \star a_2]$ for the lattice convolution and $(a_1 \star a_2)$ for continuous convolution, viz.:

$$[a_1 \star a_2](\boldsymbol{t}) := \sum_{\boldsymbol{u}\in\mathbb{Z}^\nu} a_1(\boldsymbol{u})a_2(\boldsymbol{t}+\boldsymbol{u}), \quad \boldsymbol{t} \in \mathbb{Z}^\nu,$$

$$(a_1 \star a_2)(\boldsymbol{t}) := \int_{\mathbb{R}^\nu} a_1(\boldsymbol{u})a_2(\boldsymbol{t}+\boldsymbol{u})\mathrm{d}\boldsymbol{u}, \quad \boldsymbol{t} \in \mathbb{R}^\nu$$

which is well-defined for any $a_i \in L^2(\mathbb{Z}^\nu), i = 1,2$ (respectively, for any $a_i \in L^2(\mathbb{R}^\nu)$, $i = 1,2$).

Proposition 4. *Let $a_i \in L^2(\mathbb{Z}^\nu)$ satisfy Assumption 1 with $0 < d < \nu/4$ and some $\ell_i \in C(\mathbb{S}_{\nu-1}), i = 1,2$. Then,*

$$[a_1 \star a_2](\boldsymbol{t}) = |\boldsymbol{t}|^{4d-\nu}\big(L_{12}(\frac{\boldsymbol{t}}{|\boldsymbol{t}|}) + o(1)\big), \quad |\boldsymbol{t}| \to \infty, \tag{49}$$

where the (angular) function $L_{12}(\cdot) \in C(\mathbb{S}_{\nu-1})$ is given by

$$L_{12}(\boldsymbol{t}) := \int_{\mathbb{R}^\nu} \frac{\ell_1(\boldsymbol{s}/|\boldsymbol{s}|)\ell_2((\boldsymbol{t}-\boldsymbol{s})/|\boldsymbol{t}-\boldsymbol{s}|)}{|\boldsymbol{s}|^{\nu-2d}|\boldsymbol{t}-\boldsymbol{s}|^{\nu-2d}}\mathrm{d}\boldsymbol{s}, \quad \boldsymbol{t} \in \mathbb{S}_{\nu-1}.$$

Proof. The existence and continuity of L_{12} follow from the finiteness of the integrals $\int_{|\boldsymbol{s}|<1} |\boldsymbol{s}|^{2d-\nu}\mathrm{d}\boldsymbol{s} < \infty$, $\int_{|\boldsymbol{s}|>1} |\boldsymbol{s}|^{2(2d-\nu)}\mathrm{d}\boldsymbol{s} < \infty$. For (49), it suffices to show that

$$|\boldsymbol{t}|^{\nu-4d}[a_1 \star a_2](\boldsymbol{t}) - L_{12}(\boldsymbol{t}/|\boldsymbol{t}|) \to 0, \quad |\boldsymbol{t}| \to \infty. \tag{50}$$

Let $|\boldsymbol{t}|_+ := |\boldsymbol{t}| \vee 1$ and $a_i^0(\boldsymbol{t}) := |\boldsymbol{t}|_+^{2d-\nu}\ell_i(\boldsymbol{t}/|\boldsymbol{t}|_+), a_i^1(\boldsymbol{t}) := a_i(\boldsymbol{t}) - a_i^0(\boldsymbol{t}) = o(|\boldsymbol{t}|^{2d-\nu})$, $i = 1,2$ (see (48)). Then, $[a_1 \star a_2](\boldsymbol{t}) = \sum_{i,j=0}^1 [a_1^i \star a_2^j](\boldsymbol{t})$. Clearly, (50) follows from

$$|\boldsymbol{t}|^{\nu-4d}[a_1^0 \star a_2^0](\boldsymbol{t}) - L_{12}(\boldsymbol{t}/|\boldsymbol{t}|) \to 0, \quad |\boldsymbol{t}| \to \infty \tag{51}$$

and

$$[a_1^i \star a_2^j](\boldsymbol{t}) = o(|\boldsymbol{t}|^{4d-\nu}), \quad |\boldsymbol{t}| \to \infty, \quad (i,j) \neq (0,0),\ i,j = 0,1. \tag{52}$$

To prove (51), rewrite $[a_1^0 \star a_2^0](\boldsymbol{t}) = \int_{\mathbb{R}^\nu} a_1^0([\boldsymbol{u}])a_2^0(\boldsymbol{t} + [\boldsymbol{u}])\mathrm{d}\boldsymbol{u}$ as an integral and change the variable $\boldsymbol{u} \to |\boldsymbol{t}|\boldsymbol{u}$ in it. This leads to $|\boldsymbol{t}|^{\nu-4d}[a_1^0 \star a_2^0](\boldsymbol{t}) = \widetilde{L}_t(\boldsymbol{t}/|\boldsymbol{t}|)$, where

$$\widetilde{L}_t(\boldsymbol{z}) := \int_{\mathbb{R}^\nu} a_{1,t}(\tilde{\boldsymbol{u}})a_{2,t}(\boldsymbol{z}+\tilde{\boldsymbol{u}})\mathrm{d}\boldsymbol{u}, \quad \boldsymbol{z} \in \mathbb{S}_{\nu-1}, \tag{53}$$

where
$$a_{i,t}(\tilde{u}) := \frac{1}{(|t|^{-1} \vee |\tilde{u}|)^{\nu-2d}}\ell_i\Big(\frac{\tilde{u}}{|t|^{-1} \vee |\tilde{u}|}\Big), \quad \tilde{u} := \frac{[|t|u]}{|t|}.$$

Relation (51) follows once we prove the uniform convergence $\sup_{z\in\mathbb{S}_{\nu-1}} |\widetilde{L}_t(z) - L_{12}(z)| \to 0\ (|t| \to \infty)$. Since $\mathbb{S}_{\nu-1}$ is a compact set and L_{12} is continuous, the last relation is implied by the sequential convergence
$$|\widetilde{L}_t(z_t) - L_{12}(z)| \to 0 \quad (|t| \to \infty) \tag{54}$$
for any $z \in \mathbb{S}_{\nu-1}$ and any $\{z_t\}$ convergent to z: $|z_t - z| \to 0\ (|t| \to \infty)$. The proof of (54) uses the bound
$$|a_{i,t}(\tilde{u})| \le C|u|^{2d-\nu}, \quad u \in \mathbb{R}^\nu,\ i = 1,2, \tag{55}$$
which follows from the boundedness of ℓ_i and $|u| \le |\tilde{u}| + |u - \tilde{u}|$ with $|u - \tilde{u}| \le \nu^{1/2}/|t|$; hence, $|u| \le \nu^{1/2}(|\tilde{u}| + |t|^{-1}) \le 2\nu^{1/2}(|\tilde{u}| \vee |t|^{-1})$. Note $a_{1,t}(\tilde{u})a_{2,t}(z+\tilde{u}) \to a_1^0(u)a_2^0(z+u)$ $(|t| \to \infty)$ for any $u \ne \mathbf{0}, z$ and $|a_{1,t}(\tilde{u})a_{2,t}(z+\tilde{u})| \le C|u|^{2d-\nu}|z+u|^{2d-\nu}$ according to (55). Since $h(u) := C|u|^{2d-\nu}|z+u|^{2d-\nu}$ does not depend on t and $\int_{\mathbb{R}^\nu} h(u)\mathrm{d}u < \infty$, Pratt's lemma [32] applies to the integral in (53), resulting in (54) and (51). The proof of (52) is similar and simpler and is omitted. □

The question about the asymptotics of the variance of (46) arises, assuming the power-law asymptotics of the covariance admitting power-law behavior at large lags, which is tackled in the following proposition:

Proposition 5. *(i) For any $\beta > 0, \phi_i \in \Phi, i = 1,2$ as $\lambda \to \infty$*
$$\int_{\mathbb{R}^{2\nu}} |\phi_1(t_1/\lambda)\phi_2(t_2/\lambda)|(1 \wedge |t_1 - t_2|^{-\beta})\mathrm{d}t_1\mathrm{d}t_2 = \begin{cases} O(\lambda^\nu), & \beta > \nu, \\ O(\lambda^{2\nu-\beta}), & \beta < \nu, \\ O(\lambda^\nu \log\lambda), & \beta = \nu. \end{cases} \tag{56}$$

(ii) Let $r(t), t \in \mathbb{Z}^\nu$ satisfy
$$r(t) = |t|^{4d-\nu}\Big(L\big(\frac{t}{|t|}\big) + o(1)\Big), \quad |t| \to \infty, \tag{57}$$
where $0 < d < \nu/4$ and $L \in C(\mathbb{S}_{\nu-1})$. Then, for any $\phi_i \in \Phi, i = 1,2$
$$\lim_{\lambda\to\infty} \lambda^{-\nu-4d} \int_{\mathbb{R}^{2\nu}} \phi_1(t_1/\lambda)\phi_2(t_2/\lambda)r([t_1] - [t_2])\mathrm{d}t_1\mathrm{d}t_2 = c(\phi_1,\phi_2), \tag{58}$$
where
$$c(\phi_1,\phi_2) := \int_{\mathbb{R}^{2\nu}} \phi_1(t_1)\phi_2(t_2)L\Big(\frac{t_1 - t_2}{|t_1 - t_2|}\Big)\frac{\mathrm{d}t_1\mathrm{d}t_2}{|t_1 - t_2|^{\nu-4d}}. \tag{59}$$
(iii) Let $r \in L^1(\mathbb{Z}^\nu)$. Then, for any $\phi_i \in \Phi, i = 1,2,$
$$\lim_{\lambda\to\infty} \lambda^{-\nu} \int_{\mathbb{R}^{2\nu}} \phi_1(t_1/\lambda)\phi_2(t_2/\lambda)r([t_1] - [t_2])\mathrm{d}t_1\mathrm{d}t_2 = \int_{\mathbb{R}^\nu} \phi_1(t)\phi_2(t)\mathrm{d}t \times \sum_{s\in\mathbb{Z}^\nu} r(s). \tag{60}$$

Proof. (i) Write $I_{\lambda,\beta}$ for the l.h.s. of (56). First, let $\beta > \nu$. Then, $I_{\lambda,\beta} \le C\int_{\mathbb{R}^\nu} |\phi_1(t_1/\lambda)|\mathrm{d}t_1 \times \int_{\mathbb{R}^\nu} 1 \wedge |t_2 - t_1|^{-\beta}\mathrm{d}t_2 \le C\int_{\mathbb{R}^\nu} |\phi_1(t_1/\lambda)|\mathrm{d}t_1 = C\lambda^\nu \int_{\mathbb{R}^\nu} |\phi_1(t)|\mathrm{d}t = O(\lambda^\nu)$ as $\int_{\mathbb{R}^\nu} 1 \wedge |t|^{-\beta}\mathrm{d}t < \infty$. Next, let $\beta < \nu$; then, $I_{\lambda,\beta} \le \lambda^{2\nu-\beta}J_\beta$, where $J_\beta := \int_{\mathbb{R}^{2\nu}} |\phi_1(t_1)\phi_2(t_2)||t_1 - t_2|^{-\beta}\mathrm{d}t_1\mathrm{d}t_2 < \infty$ is followed by $J_\beta \le C\int_{\mathbb{R}^\nu} |\phi_1(t_1)|\mathrm{d}t_1 \int_{|t_2-t_1|\le 1} |t_2 - t_1|^{-\beta}\mathrm{d}t_2 + \int_{\mathbb{R}^{2\nu}} |\phi_1(t_1) \times \phi_2(t_2)|\mathrm{d}t\mathrm{d}t_2 < \infty$. Finally, for $\beta = \nu$ we have $I_{\lambda,\nu} = \lambda^\nu J_{\lambda,\nu}$, where $J_{\lambda,\nu} := \int_{\mathbb{R}^{2\nu}} |\phi_1(t_1) \times \phi_2(t_2)|(\lambda^{-1} \vee |t_1 - t_2|)^{-\nu}\mathrm{d}t_1\mathrm{d}t_2 = O(\log\lambda)$ follows similarly.

(ii) The convergence of the integral in (59) follows from that of J_β in part (i), with $\beta = \nu - 4d$. Let $c_\lambda(\phi_1, \phi_2)$ denote the integral on the l.h.s. of (58). By a change of variables,

$$\frac{c_\lambda(\phi_1, \phi_2)}{\lambda^{\nu+4d}} = \int_{\mathbb{R}^{2\nu}} \frac{\phi(t_1)\phi(t_2)}{|t_1 - t_2|^{\nu-4d}} \tilde{L}_\lambda(t_1, t_2) \mathrm{d}t_1 \mathrm{d}t_2,$$

where $\tilde{L}_\lambda(t_1, t_2) \to L((t_1 - t_2)/|t_1 - t_2|)$ $(\lambda \to \infty)$ for any $t_1 \neq t_2$. Using Pratt's lemma [32], it suffices to prove (58) for $L \equiv 1$. In the latter case, and with $\tilde{t}_i := [\lambda t_i]/\lambda, i = 1,2$, we see that $|\tilde{L}_\lambda(t_1, t_2)| \le C(|t_1 - t_2|/(|\tilde{t}_1 - \tilde{t}_2| \vee (1/\lambda)))^{\nu-4d} \le C$ as in the proof of Proposition 4. Thus, (58) follows from the DCT.
(iii) Let $c_\lambda(\phi_1, \phi_2)$ be the same as in the proof of (ii). For a large $K > 0$, write $c_\lambda(\phi_1, \phi_2) = \sum_{i=1}^3 c_{i,\lambda}$, where $c_{3,\lambda} := \int_{|t_1 - t_2| \le K} \phi_1(t_1/\lambda)(\phi_2(t_2/\lambda) - \phi_2(t_1/\lambda)) r([t_1] - [t_2]) \mathrm{d}t_1 \mathrm{d}t_2$, and $c_{2,\lambda} := \int_{|t_1 - t_2| \le K} \phi_1(t_1/\lambda)\phi_2(t_1/\lambda) r([t_1] - [t_2]) \mathrm{d}t_1 \mathrm{d}t_2$, and $c_{1,\lambda} := \int_{|t_1 - t_2| > K} \phi_1(t_1/\lambda) \times \phi_2(t_2/\lambda) r([t_1] - [t_2]) \mathrm{d}t_1 \mathrm{d}t_2$. Here, $\lambda^{-\nu}|c_{1,K}| \le C\lambda^{-\nu} \int_{\mathbb{R}^\nu} |\phi_1(t/\lambda)| \mathrm{d}t \times \sum_{|s|>K} |r(s)| \le C \sum_{|s|>K} |r(s)|$ can be made arbitrarily small uniformly in $\lambda \ge 1$ by choosing K large enough. Next,

$$\lambda^{-\nu}|c_{3,\lambda}| \le C \int_{\mathbb{R}^\nu} |\phi_1(t)| \mathrm{d}t \int_{|s| \le K} |\phi_2(t + \frac{s}{\lambda}) - \phi_2(t)| \mathrm{d}s.$$

By the boundedness of ϕ_2, we see that the integral $\int_{|s| \le K} |\phi_2(t + \frac{s}{\lambda}) - \phi_2(t)| \mathrm{d}s \to 0$ $(\lambda \to \infty)$ a.e. in $\mathbb{R}^\nu$, and is bounded in $t \in \mathbb{R}^\nu$. Then, since $\phi_1 \in L^1(\mathbb{R}^\nu)$ we conclude $\lim_{\lambda\to\infty} \lambda^{-\nu}|c_{3,\lambda}| = 0$ by the DCT. Finally, $\lambda^{-\nu} c_{2,\lambda} = \int_{\mathbb{R}^\nu} \phi_1(t)\phi_2(t) \mathrm{d}t \int_{|s + [\lambda t] - \lambda t| \le K} r(-[s]) \mathrm{d}s$, and we can replace the last integral by the r.h.s. of (60) uniformly in λ provided K is large enough. □

Proposition 5 does not apply to ND covariances satisfying (57) with negative $d < 0$. This case is more delicate, since it requires additional regularity conditions of the test functions and the occurrence of 'edge effects'. A detailed analysis of this issue in dimension $\nu = 2$ and for indicator (test) functions of rectangles in $\mathbb{R}^2_+$ can be found in [16]. Below, we present a result in this direction and sufficient conditions on $d, \phi_i, i = 1,2$ when the limits take a similar form to (58). We introduce a subclass of test functions:

$$\Phi_- := \Big\{\phi \in \Phi : \int_{\mathbb{R}^\nu} \Big(\int_{\mathbb{R}^\nu} |\phi(t + s) - \phi(s)|^2 \mathrm{d}s\Big)^{1/2} |t|^{2d-\nu} \mathrm{d}t < \infty\Big\}. \tag{61}$$

Proposition 6. *Let $a \in L^2(\mathbb{Z}^\nu)$ satisfy Assumption 1 with $-\nu/4 < d < 0$. Then, for any $\phi_i \in \Phi_-, i = 1,2$ we have*

$$\lim_{\lambda\to\infty} \lambda^{-\nu-4d} \int_{\mathbb{R}^{2\nu}} \phi_1(t_1/\lambda)\phi_2(t_2/\lambda)[a \star a]([t_1] - [t_2]) \mathrm{d}t_1 \mathrm{d}t_2 = c_-(\phi_1, \phi_2), \tag{62}$$

where

$$c_-(\phi_1, \phi_2) := \int_{\mathbb{R}^\nu} \prod_{i=1}^2 \Big(\int_{\mathbb{R}^\nu} (\phi_i(t + s) - \phi_i(s)) |t|^{2d-\nu} \ell(\frac{t}{|t|}) \mathrm{d}t\Big) \mathrm{d}s. \tag{63}$$

Proof. The convergence of the integral on the r.h.s. of (63) follows from (61) and the Minkowski integral inequality: $\{\int_{\mathbb{R}^\nu}(\int_{\mathbb{R}^\nu} |\phi(t + s) - \phi(s)||t|^{2d-\nu} \mathrm{d}t)^2 \mathrm{d}s\}^{1/2} \le \int_{\mathbb{R}^\nu} \|\phi(t + \cdot) - \phi(\cdot)\|_{L^2(\mathbb{R}^\nu)} \times |t|^{2d-\nu} \mathrm{d}t$.

The proof of the convergence in (62) resembles that of (58). Write $c_\lambda(\phi_1, \phi_2)$ for the integral on the l.h.s. of (62). Using $\sum_{s\in\mathbb{Z}^\nu} a(s) = 0$ we rewrite $\int_{\mathbb{R}^\nu} \phi_i(t_i/\lambda) a([t_i] - [s]) \mathrm{d}t_i = \int_{\mathbb{R}^\nu} (\phi_i((t_i + s)/\lambda) - \phi_i(s/\lambda)) a([t_i + s] - [s]) \mathrm{d}t_i, i = 1,2, s \in \mathbb{R}^\nu$, and

$$\frac{c_\lambda(\phi_1, \phi_2)}{\lambda^{\nu+4d}} = \int_{\mathbb{R}^\nu} \mathrm{d}s \prod_{i=1}^2 \int_{\mathbb{R}^\nu} (\phi_i(t_i + s) - \phi_i(s)) \lambda^{\nu-2d} a([\lambda(t_i + s)] - [\lambda s]) \mathrm{d}t_i,$$

where the inner integrals tend to those on the r.h.s. of (63) at each s, such that $\int_{\mathbb{R}^\nu} |\phi_i(t+s)-\phi_i(s)||t|^{2d-\nu}\mathrm{d}t < \infty$, $i=1,2$. The remaining details are similar to (58) and are omitted. □

Remark 3. *The restriction $d > -\nu/4$ in Proposition 6 is not necessary for* (63)*. Indeed, if $\phi \in \Phi$ satisfies the uniform Lipschitz condition $|\phi(t)-\phi(s)| < C(|t| < 1, s \in \mathbb{R}^\nu)$ then the integral in* (61) *converges for $0 > d > -\nu/2$, implying $\phi \in \Phi_-$. On the other hand, for the indicator functions $\phi(t) = \mathbb{I}(t \in A)$ of a bounded Borel set $A \subset \mathbb{R}^\nu$ with a 'regular' boundary, we typically have $\|\phi(t+\cdot)-\phi(\cdot)\|_{L^2(\mathbb{R}^\nu)} = O(|t|^{1/2})$ leading to $d > -\nu/4$.*

Relation (48) entails the existence of the scaling limit

$$\lim_{\lambda\to\infty} \lambda^{\nu-2d} a([\lambda t]) = a_\infty(t) := |t|^{2d-\nu}\ell\Big(\frac{t}{|t|}\Big), \qquad \lambda \to \infty, \quad \forall t \in \mathbb{R}^\nu \setminus \{0\}, \tag{64}$$

which is a continuous homogeneous function on $\mathbb{R}^\nu$: for any $\lambda > 0$ we have

$$a_\infty(\lambda t) = \lambda^{2d-\nu} a_\infty(t), \quad t \in \mathbb{R}^\nu \setminus \{0\}. \tag{65}$$

With the limit function in (64) we associate a Gaussian RF:

$$W_d(\phi) := \begin{cases} \int_{\mathbb{R}^\nu} (a_\infty \star \phi)(u) W(\mathrm{d}u), & 0 < d < \nu/4, \phi \in \Phi \\ \int_{\mathbb{R}^\nu} (a_\infty \star \phi)_{\mathrm{reg}}(u) W(\mathrm{d}u), & -\nu/4 < d < 0, \phi \in \Phi_-, \\ \int_{\mathbb{R}^\nu} \phi(u) W(\mathrm{d}u), & d = 0, \phi \in \Phi, \end{cases} \tag{66}$$

where $W(\mathrm{d}u)$ is a real-valued Gaussian white noise (also called the real-valued Gaussian random measure) with zero mean and where variance $\mathrm{d}u$, $(a_\infty \star \phi)(u) = \int_{\mathbb{R}^\nu} a_\infty(t)\phi(t+u)\mathrm{d}t$ is the usual and

$$(a_\infty \star \phi)_{\mathrm{reg}}(u) := \int_{\mathbb{R}^\nu} a_\infty(t)(\phi(t+u)-\phi(u))\mathrm{d}t, \quad u \in \mathbb{R}^\nu$$

the 'regularized' convolution. For the indicator test function $\phi(t) = \mathbb{I}(t \in B)$ of a Borel set $B \subset \mathbb{R}^\nu$ (belonging to Φ_-) we see that the latter convolution equals

$$(a_\infty \star \phi)_{\mathrm{reg}}(u) = \begin{cases} \int_B a_\infty(t-u)\mathrm{d}t, & u \notin B, \\ -\int_{\mathbb{R}^\nu \setminus B} a_\infty(t-u)\mathrm{d}t, & u \in B. \end{cases}$$

This paper uses the elementary properties of the white noise integrals in (66) only. Namely, $\int_{\mathbb{R}^\nu} \phi(u) W(\mathrm{d}u)$ is well-defined for each $\phi \in L^2(\mathbb{R}^\nu)$ and has a Gaussian distribution with zero mean and variance $\|\phi\|^2_{L^2(\mathbb{R}^\nu)}$ (see, e.g., [5,7]), implying that $\int_{\mathbb{R}^\nu} \phi(u/\lambda) W(\mathrm{d}u) \overset{\mathrm{d}}{=} \lambda^{\nu/2} \int_{\mathbb{R}^\nu} \phi(u) W(\mathrm{d}u)$ for each $\lambda > 0$. The interested reader is referred to [24] on white noise calculus on the Schwartz space and to [33] for fractional calculus with respect to fractional Brownian motion. The existence of stochastic integrals in (66) follows from Propositions 5 and 6. Particularly, the variances $\mathrm{E}W_d^2(\phi) = c(\phi,\phi)$ $(0 < d < \nu/4)$ and $\mathrm{E}W_d^2(\phi) = c_-(\phi,\phi)$ $(-\nu/4 < d < 0)$ agree with (59) and (63).

Let $\mathcal{S}(\mathbb{R}^\nu)$ be the Schwartz space of all infinitely differentiable rapidly decreasing functions $\phi : \mathbb{R}^\nu \to \mathbb{R}$, i.e., for each $p \in \mathbb{N}$ and each multi-index $\alpha = (\alpha_1, \ldots, \alpha_\nu) \in \mathbb{N}^\nu$,

$$\sup_{x \in \mathbb{R}^\nu} (1+|x|)^p |\partial^\alpha \phi(x)| < \infty,$$

where $\partial^\alpha \phi(x) := \partial^{\sum_{i=1}^\nu \alpha_i}\phi(x) / \prod_{i=1}^\nu \partial x_i$ (see, e.g., [34] (Section 7) for the properties of $\mathcal{S}(\mathbb{R}^\nu)$ and the dual space $\mathcal{S}'(\mathbb{R}^\nu)$ of tempered Schwartz distributions). Following [35], we say that a generalized RF $Y = \{Y(\phi); \phi \in \mathcal{S}(\mathbb{R}^\nu)\}$ is *stationary* if $Y(\phi) \overset{\mathrm{d}}{=} Y(\phi(\cdot + a))$ $(\forall \phi \in \mathcal{S}(\mathbb{R}^\nu), a \in \mathbb{R}^\nu)$ and *H-self-similar* $(H \in \mathbb{R})$ if $Y(\phi) \overset{\mathrm{d}}{=} \lambda^{H-\nu} Y(\phi(\cdot/\lambda))$

$(\forall\phi \in \mathcal{S}(\mathbb{R}^\nu), \lambda > 0)$. As noted in Remark 3, $\mathcal{S}(\mathbb{R}^\nu) \subset \Phi_- \subset \Phi$; hence, (66) is well-defined for any $\phi \in \mathcal{S}(\mathbb{R}^\nu)$ and represents stationary generalized RFs on $\mathcal{S}(\mathbb{R}^\nu)$. By the scaling property in (65) and a change of variables, we see that $W_d(\phi) \stackrel{d}{=} \lambda^{H(d)-\nu} W_d(\phi(\cdot/\lambda))$ $(\forall\phi \in \mathcal{S}(\mathbb{R}^\nu))$; hence, RF W_d in (66) is $H(d)$-self-similar, with

$$H(d) := (\nu - 4d)/2 \in (0, \nu), \quad -\nu/4 < d < \nu/4.$$

The RF in (66) appear as scaling limits in the following corollary:

Corollary 3. *Let X be a linear RF satisfying Assumption 1 and $X_\lambda(\phi)$ be defined in* (46). *Then,*

$$\lambda^{-(\nu+4d)/2} X_\lambda(\phi) \xrightarrow{d} \begin{cases} W_d(\phi), & 0 < d < \nu/4,\ \forall\phi \in \Phi, \\ W_d(\phi), & -\nu/4 < d < 0,\ \forall\phi \in \Phi_-, \\ \sigma W_0(\phi), & d = 0,\ \forall\phi \in \Phi, \end{cases}$$

where $\sigma^2 := \big(\sum_{t\in\mathbb{Z}^\nu} a(t)\big)^2$.

Proof. Since (46) writes as a linear form $X_\lambda(\phi) = \sum_{u\in\mathbb{Z}^\nu} \varepsilon(u) \int_{\mathbb{R}^\nu} \phi(t/\lambda) a([t] - u) \mathrm{d}t$ in i.i.d. r.v.s, we can use the Lindeberg-type condition (see also [3] (Corollary 4.3.1)). Accordingly, it suffices to show that

$$\sup_{u\in\mathbb{Z}^\nu} \Big| \int_{\mathbb{R}^\nu} \phi(t/\lambda) a([t] - u) \mathrm{d}t \Big| = o\big(\sqrt{\mathrm{Var}(X_\lambda(\phi))}\big), \quad \lambda \to \infty \tag{67}$$

holds in each case, $d > 0, d < 0, d = 0$, of the corollary. The behavior of the last variance is detailed in Propositions 5 and 6, and it grows to infinity in each case of d. On the other hand, the l.h.s. of (67) does not exceed $\|\phi\|_{L^\infty(\mathbb{R}^\nu)} \|a\|_{L^1(\mathbb{Z}^\nu)}$, which is bounded in cases $d < 0$ and $d = 0$. Finally, in case $d > 0$ we see that the l.h.s. of (67) does not exceed $\|\phi(\cdot/\lambda)\|_{L^2(\mathbb{R}^\nu)} \|a\|_{L^2(\mathbb{Z}^\nu)} = O(\lambda^{\nu/2})$ and (67) holds, since $d > 0$. □

Author Contributions: Conceptualization, D.S.; investigation, V.P.; writing—original draft preparation, D.S. and V.P.; writing—review and editing, D.S. and V.P. All authors have read and agreed to the published version of the manuscript.

Funding: This research received no external funding.

Data Availability Statement: Not applicable.

Acknowledgments: We thank two anonymous referees for useful comments. We are grateful to Maria Eulalia Vares for helpful reference and Rajendra Bhansali for drawing our attention to some issues discussed in this work.

Conflicts of Interest: The authors declare no conflict of interest.

References

1. Brockwell, P.J.; Davis, R.A. *Time Series: Theory and Methods*; Springer: New York, NY, USA, 1991.
2. Doukhan, P.; Oppenheim, G.; Taqqu, M.S. (Eds.) *Theory and Applications of Long-Range Dependence*; Birkhäuser: Boston, MA, USA, 2003.
3. Giraitis, L.; Koul, H.L.; Surgailis, D. *Large Sample Inference for Long Memory Processes*; Imperial College Press: London, UK, 2012.
4. Pipiras, V.; Taqqu, M.S. *Long-Range Dependence and Self-Similarity*; Cambridge University Press: Cambridge, UK, 2017.
5. Samorodnitsky, G.; Taqqu, M.S. *Stable Non-Gaussian Random Processes*; Chapman and Hall: New York, NY, USA, 1994.
6. Beran, J. *Statistics for Long-Memory Processes*; Monographs on Statistics and Applied Probability; Chapman and Hall: New York, NY, USA, 1994; Volume 61.
7. Samorodnitsky, G. *Stochastic Processes and Long Range Dependence*; Springer: New York, NY, USA, 2016.
8. Sabzikar, F.; Surgailis, D. Invariance principles for tempered fractionally integrated processes. *Stoch. Processes Appl.* **2018**, *128*, 3419–3438. [CrossRef]
9. Dobrushin, R.L.; Major, P. Non-central limit theorems for non-linear functionals of Gaussian fields. *Z. Wahrscheinlichkeitstheor. Verwandte Geb.* **1979**, *50*, 27–52. [CrossRef]

10. Damarackas, J.; Paulauskas, V. Spectral covariance and limit theorems for random fields with infinite variance. *J. Multivar. Anal.* **2017**, *153*, 156–175. [CrossRef]
11. Damarackas, J.; Paulauskas, V. On Lamperti type limit theorem and scaling transition for random fields. *J. Math. Anal. Appl.* **2021**, *497*, 124852. [CrossRef]
12. Pilipauskaitė, V.; Surgailis, D. Scaling transition for nonlinear random fields with long-range dependence. *Stoch. Processes Appl.* **2017**, *127*, 2751–2779. [CrossRef]
13. Pilipauskaitė, V.; Surgailis, D. Scaling limits of linear random fields on $\mathbb{Z}^2$ with general dependence axis. In *In and Out of Equilibrium 3: Celebrating Vladas Sidoravicius*; Vares, M.E., Fernandez, R., Fontes, L.R., Newman, C.M., Eds.; Progress in Probability; Birkhäuser: Basel, Switzerland, 2021; pp. 683–710.
14. Maini, L., Nourdin, I. Spectral central limit theorem for additive functionals of isotropic and stationary Gaussian fields. *Ann. Probab* **2024**, *52*, 737–763. [CrossRef]
15. Surgailis, D. Anisotropic scaling limits of long-range dependent linear random fields on $\mathbb{Z}^3$. *J. Math. Anal. Appl.* **2019**, *472*, 328–351. [CrossRef]
16. Wang, Y. An invariance principle for fractional Brownian sheets.. *J. Theoret. Probab.* **2014**, *27*, 1124–1139. [CrossRef]
17. Lahiri, S.N.; Robinson, P.M. Central limit theorems for long range dependent spatial linear processes. *Bernoulli* **2016**, *22*, 345–375. [CrossRef]
18. Boissy, Y.; Bhattacharyya, B.B.; Li, X.; Richardson, G.D. Parameter estimates for fractional autoregressive spatial processes. *Ann. Statist.* **2005**, *33*, 2533–2567. [CrossRef]
19. Koul, H.L.; Mimoto, N.; Surgailis, D. Goodness-of-fit tests for marginal distribution of linear random fields with long memory. *Metrika* **2016**, *79*, 165–193. [CrossRef]
20. Anh, V.V.; Leonenko, N.N.; Ruiz-Medina, M.D. Macroscaling limit theorems for filtered spatiotemporal random fields. *Stoch. Anal. Appl.* **2013**, *31*, 460–508. [CrossRef]
21. Cohen, S.; Istas, J. *Fractional Fields and Applications*; Mathématiques et Applications; Springer: Berlin/Heidelberg, Germany, 2013; Volume 73.
22. Kelbert, M.Y.; Leonenko, N.N.; Ruiz-Medina, M.D. Fractional random fields associated with stochastic fractional heat equations. *Adv. Appl. Prob.* **2005**, *37*, 108–133. [CrossRef]
23. Leonenko, N.N.; Ruiz-Medina, M.D.; Taqqu, M.S. Fractional elliptic, hyperbolic and parabolic random fields. *Electron. J. Probab.* **2011**, *16*, 1134–1172. [CrossRef]
24. Lodhia, A.; Scheffield, S.; Sun, X.; Watson, S.S. Fractional Gaussian fields: A survey. *Probab. Surv.* **2016**, *13*, 1–56. [CrossRef]
25. Pilipauskaitė, V.; Surgailis, D. Local scaling limits of Lévy driven fractional random fields. *Bernoulli* **2022**, *28*, 2833–2861. [CrossRef]
26. Lawler, G.F.; Limic, V. *Random Walk: A Modern Introduction*; Cambridge University Press: Cambridge, UK, 2012.
27. Gradshteyn, I.S.; Ryzhik, I.M. *Tables of Integrals, Series and Products*; Academic Press: New York, NY, USA, 2000.
28. Gaetan, C.; Guyon, X. *Spatial Statistics and Modeling*; Springer Series in Statistics; Springer: New York, NY, USA, 2010.
29. Besag, J. Spatial interaction and the statistical analysis of lattice systems (with Discussion). *J. R. Stat. Soc. B* **1974**, *36*, 192–236. [CrossRef]
30. Besag, J.; Kooperberg, C. On conditional and intrinsic autoregressions. *Biometrika* **1995**, *82*, 733–746.
31. Ferretti, A.; Ippoliti, L.; Valentini, P.; Bhansali, R.J. Long memory conditional random fields on regular lattices. *Environmetrics* **2023**, *34*, e2817. [CrossRef]
32. Pratt, J.W. On interchanging limits and integrals. *Ann. Math. Statist.* **1960**, *31*, 74–77. [CrossRef]
33. Pipiras, V.; Taqqu, M.S. Fractional calculus and its connections to fractional Brownian motion. In *Long Range Dependence: Theory and Applications*; Doukhan, P., Oppenheim, G., Taqqu, M.S., Eds.; Birkhäuser: Boston, MA, USA, 2003; pp. 165–201.
34. Rudin, W. *Functional Analysis*; McGraw-Hill: New York, NY, USA, 1973.
35. Dobrushin, R.L. Gaussian and their subordinated self-similar random generalized fields. *Ann. Prob.* **1979**, *7*, 1–28. [CrossRef]

fractal and fractional

MDPI

Article

Theoretical and Numerical Analysis of the $\mathbb{SIR}$ Model and Its Symmetric Cases with Power Caputo Fractional Derivative

Mohamed S. Algolam [1], Mohammed Almalahi [2,3], Khaled Aldwoah [4,*], Amira S. Awaad [5], Muntasir Suhail [6,*], Fahdah Ayed Alshammari [7] and Bakri Younis [8]

1 Department of Mathematics, College of Science, University of Ha'il, Ha'il 55473, Saudi Arabia
2 Department of Mathematics, College of Computer and Information Technology, Al-Razi University, Sana'a 12544, Yemen; dralmalahi@gmail.com
3 Jadara University Research Center, Jadara University, Irbid 00962, Jordan
4 Department of Mathematics, Faculty of Science, Islamic University of Madinah, Madinah 42351, Saudi Arabia
5 Department of Mathematics, College of Science and Humanities, Al-Kharj Prince Sattam Bin Abdulaziz University, Al-Kharj 11942, Saudi Arabia
6 Department of Mathematics, College of Science, Qassim University, Buraydah 51452, Saudi Arabia
7 Department of Biology, College of Science, Northern Border University, Arar 73241, Saudi Arabia
8 Department of Mathematics, Faculty of Arts and Science, Elmagarda, King Khalid University, Abha 61421, Saudi Arabia
* Correspondence: aldwoah@iu.edu.sa (K.A.); m.suhail@qu.edu.sa (M.S.)

Abstract: This paper introduces a novel fractional Susceptible-Infected-Recovered ($\mathbb{SIR}$) model that incorporates a power Caputo fractional derivative (PCFD) and a density-dependent recovery rate. This enhances the model's ability to capture memory effects and represent realistic healthcare system dynamics in epidemic modeling. The model's utility and flexibility are demonstrated through an application using parameters representative of the COVID-19 pandemic. Unlike existing fractional $\mathbb{SIR}$ models often limited in representing diverse memory effects adequately, the proposed PCFD framework encompasses and extends well-known cases, such as those using Caputo–Fabrizio and Atangana–Baleanu derivatives. We prove that our model yields bounded and positive solutions, ensuring biological plausibility. A rigorous analysis is conducted to determine the model's local stability, including the derivation of the basic reproduction number ($\mathbf{R}_0$) and sensitivity analysis quantifying the impact of parameters on $\mathbf{R}_0$. The uniqueness and existence of solutions are guaranteed via a recursive sequence approach and the Banach fixed-point theorem. Numerical simulations, facilitated by a novel numerical scheme and applied to the COVID-19 parameter set, demonstrate that varying the fractional order significantly alters predicted epidemic peak timing and severity. Comparisons across different fractional approaches highlight the crucial role of memory effects and healthcare capacity in shaping epidemic trajectories. These findings underscore the potential of the generalized PCFD approach to provide more nuanced and potentially accurate predictions for disease outbreaks like COVID-19, thereby informing more effective public health interventions.

Keywords: $\mathbb{SIR}$ model; generalized power fractional derivative; stability; simulations; numerical analysis

1. Introduction

The study of infectious diseases is a critical area in epidemiology, where mathematical models serve as essential tools for understanding disease spread dynamics, predicting outbreaks, and evaluating the effectiveness of interventions. The Susceptible-Infected-Recovered ($\mathbb{SIR}$) model, a cornerstone of epidemiological modeling, classifies populations into susceptible ($\mathbb{S}$), infected ($\mathbb{I}$), and recovered ($\mathbb{R}$) compartments. Its simplicity and versatility have allowed for extensive adaptations to incorporate real-world factors. For example, Marinov [1] employed an adaptive $\mathbb{SIRV}$ model with time-dependent rates to analyze the dynamics of COVID-19, integrating data from various national contexts to capture transmission variations and to evaluate vaccination strategies. Similarly, Balderrama et al. [2] explored optimal control strategies for a $\mathbb{SIR}$ epidemic model under quarantine limitations, highlighting the trade-offs between quarantine stringency and economic or social disruption. Further illustrating the adaptability of the $\mathbb{SIR}$ model, El Khalifi [3] investigated an extended $\mathbb{SIR}$ model with gradually waning immunity, acknowledging individual heterogeneity in immune system responses and demonstrating the impact of duration of immunity on long-term disease prevalence. These studies highlight the ability of the $\mathbb{SIR}$ model to address real-world complexities, while also suggesting limitations in capturing the influence of past events on current disease dynamics.

However, traditional $\mathbb{SIR}$ models often simplify disease dynamics by assuming instantaneous interactions and neglecting historical factors, such as the influence of past infection rates on current immunity levels. To address these limitations, fractional-order derivatives, which extend the concept of differentiation to non-integer orders [4–7], have emerged as a powerful tool. In contrast to integer-order derivatives, fractional derivatives inherently incorporate memory effects and long-range interactions, leading to more accurate representations of biological processes like disease transmission and recovery. This characteristic has led to several applications in the context of $\mathbb{SIR}$ models, which offer potentially more accurate predictions of epidemic spread. For example, Alqahtani [8] analyzed a fractional-order $\mathbb{SIR}$ model that incorporates the capacity of the healthcare system, showing an improved fit of the model to the observed infection data compared to its integer-order counterpart. Kim [9] introduced a normalized time-fractional $\mathbb{SIR}$ model using a novel fractional derivative designed to improve understanding of the influence of fractional-order on epidemiological dynamics and disease prediction accuracy, specifically demonstrating a reduction in prediction error when forecasting peak infection rates. Riabi et al. [10] investigated a fractional $\mathbb{SIR}$ epidemic model with the Atangana–Baleanu–Caputo operator, utilizing the homotopy perturbation method to obtain a series solution and demonstrating an increased number of immunized individuals compared to other methods. Alazman et al. [11] introduced a diffusion component into a fractional $\mathbb{SIR}$ model and analyzed its impact using a general fractional derivative, illustrating the effects of diffusion on the model's dynamics, revealing how diffusion can alter the spatial distribution of the infected population, a feature absent in traditional models. Beyond epidemiology, fractional calculus shows promise in areas like modeling drug delivery in pharmacokinetics, where non-local tissue interactions affect drug distribution, and in neuroscience for capturing memory effects in neuronal signaling. However, challenges remain in the widespread adoption of fractional-order models, including the computational cost of solving fractional differential equations and the difficulty in directly interpreting fractional-order parameters in terms of underlying biological mechanisms. Nevertheless, the ability of fractional calculus to capture memory and non-local effects makes it a valuable tool for enhancing the realism and predictive power of models in diverse biological systems exhibiting delayed responses or cumulative effects.

The utility of fractional calculus extends far beyond epidemiological modeling, with applications across various scientific fields. These applications leverage fractional calculus's ability to capture complex dynamics and memory effects often observed in real-world phenomena. Examples include physics and polymer technology, where fractional calculus aids in modeling complex material behaviors [12], and electrical circuits, enabling the incorporation of fractional-order elements for enhanced circuit representation [13]. In bioengineering, fractional calculus is utilized to model biological processes [14], while in robotics, it facilitates the design of fractional-order controllers for improved performance [15]. Its utility extends to fluid mechanics, where it helps model non-Newtonian fluid behavior [16], and electrodynamics of complex media, aiding in describing materials with memory effects [17]. Control theory benefits from fractional-order controllers, offering advantages over traditional methods [18], and, as discussed previously, disease modeling leverages fractional calculus to capture memory effects and non-local interactions in epidemiological models [19]. This widespread applicability underscores the power of fractional calculus in capturing complex behaviors not adequately represented by traditional integer-order calculus.

Within epidemiological modeling, the application of fractional calculus to the $\mathbb{SIR}$ framework has been explored using various fractional derivatives, including Caputo, Caputo–Fabrizio, and Atangana–Baleanu. These derivatives incorporate memory effects and non-local interactions, leading to more realistic representations of the spread of infectious diseases [20–22]. The Caputo fractional derivative is well suited for systems with well-defined initial conditions, while the Caputo–Fabrizio derivative is useful for systems with less-defined initial states. The Atangana–Baleanu derivative, with its non-singular kernel, provides advantages in modeling complex dynamics with crossovers. However, many studies focus on specific fractional derivatives, potentially limiting the exploration of generalized operators that can encompass a wider range of behaviors and simulate diseases with diverse memory characteristics. The selection of an appropriate fractional derivative is a crucial consideration, as it can significantly influence the model's properties, such as stability and the existence of solutions. While fractional $\mathbb{SIR}$ models have been applied to various diseases, a more thorough investigation of their qualitative and quantitative properties is still needed. Many previous studies have concentrated on numerical simulations, often lacking in-depth exploration of the theoretical foundations, such as the boundedness, positivity, and stability of solutions. Furthermore, rigorous comparisons between different fractional derivatives are often absent.

To address these gaps, we extend the classical $\mathbb{SIR}$ framework [23] by considering the incidence rate as $\frac{2\beta\mathbb{SI}}{N}$, which suggests a closed population with density-dependent interactions influenced by the total population size N ($N = \mathbb{S} + \mathbb{I} + \mathbb{R}$). Furthermore, we incorporate a $\delta\mathbb{R}$ term, representing the rate at which recovered individuals lose immunity and return to the susceptible compartment. Crucially, we employ a Power Caputo fractional derivative (PCFD) [24], which generalizes well-known fractional derivatives like Caputo–Fabrizio [25], Atangana–Baleanu [26], weighted Atangana–Baleanu [27], and weighted Hattaf fractional derivatives [28]. The PCFD provides a flexible and adaptable modeling framework capable of capturing diverse memory and non-local effects within disease dynamics. This work primarily focuses on the theoretical development, mathematical analysis, and numerical simulation of the PCFD SIR model to demonstrate its properties and potential. We use parameters representative of the COVID-19 pandemic to demonstrate the behavior of our novel PCFD SIR model. The construction of this paper is as follows: In Section 2, we present the construction of the proposed fractional $\mathbb{SIR}$ model. In Section 3, we recall the necessary mathematical foundations, detailing the power Caputo fractional derivative. Section 4 presents a rigorous qualitative analysis that demonstrates the boundedness and positivity of the solutions, which is critical to ensuring biological feasibility and applicability in the real world. In this section, we also investigate the stability of the disease-free equilibrium (DFE), deriving the basic reproduction number $\mathbf{R}_0$, a key epidemiological parameter for assessing the potential for disease spread. In addition, sensitivity analysis identifies influential parameters, revealing factors affecting disease transmission and recovery. In Section 5, we introduce a two-step Lagrange interpolation polynomial-based numerical method for approximating solutions to the fractional $\mathbb{SIR}$ model. Then, in Section 4.2, we explore symmetric model cases, including Caputo–Fabrizio, Atangana–Baleanu, and weighted Hattaf. Finally, Section 7 provides the biological interpretation of our results and conclusions.

2. Mathematical $\mathbb{SIR}$ Model

In this section, we extend the classical $\mathbb{SIR}$ model [23], given by

$$\begin{cases} \frac{d}{dz}\mathbb{S}(z) = \Lambda - \frac{\beta\mathbb{SI}}{\mathbb{S}+\mathbb{I}} - \mu\mathbb{S}, \\ \frac{d}{dz}\mathbb{I}(z) = \frac{\beta\mathbb{SI}}{\mathbb{S}+\mathbb{I}} - \left[\alpha_0 + (\alpha_1 - \alpha_0)\frac{b}{b+\mathbb{I}}\right]\mathbb{I} - \gamma\mathbb{I} - \mu\mathbb{I}, \\ \frac{d}{dz}\mathbb{R}(z) = \left[\alpha_0 + (\alpha_1 - \alpha_0)\frac{b}{b+\mathbb{I}}\right]\mathbb{I} - \mu\mathbb{R}, \end{cases}$$

by considering the incidence rate $\frac{2\beta\mathbb{SI}}{N}$. This suggests a closed population where interactions are density-dependent and influenced by the total population size N ($N = \mathbb{S} + \mathbb{I} + \mathbb{R}$). We assume that the total population size N is constant throughout the duration of the epidemic, which is justified by the relatively short timescale of the epidemic compared to demographic processes such as birth and death. Also, we add $\delta\mathbb{R}$ term, which represents the rate at which recovered individuals lose immunity and return to the susceptible compartment. We incorporate a power Caputo fractional-order dynamics and various important parameters related to disease transmission, recovery, and mortality. The fractional derivatives introduce memory effects and non-local interactions into the dynamics. The following model strength lies in its adaptability according to power parameters p in ${}^{\mathbb{PC}}_{a}\mathbf{D}^{\zeta,\psi,p}_{z,w}$, allowing for the exploration of diverse scenarios related to intervention and disease:

$$\begin{cases} {}^{\mathbb{PC}}_{a}\mathbf{D}^{\zeta,\psi,p}_{z,w}\mathbb{S}(z) = \Lambda - \frac{2\beta\mathbb{SI}}{N} - \mu\mathbb{S} + \delta\mathbb{R}, \\ {}^{\mathbb{PC}}_{a}\mathbf{D}^{\zeta,\psi,p}_{z,w}\mathbb{I}(z) = \frac{2\beta\mathbb{SI}}{N} - \left[\alpha_0 + (\alpha_1 - \alpha_0)\frac{b}{b+\mathbb{I}}\right]\mathbb{I} - (\gamma + \mu)\mathbb{I}, \\ {}^{\mathbb{PC}}_{a}\mathbf{D}^{\zeta,\psi,p}_{z,w}\mathbb{R}(z) = \left[\alpha_0 + (\alpha_1 - \alpha_0)\frac{b}{b+\mathbb{I}}\right]\mathbb{I} - (\mu + \delta)\mathbb{R}, \end{cases} \tag{1}$$

with initial conditions $\mathbb{S}(0) \geq 0, \mathbb{I}(0) \geq 0$ and $\mathbb{R}(0) \geq 0$. The definitions of parameters are presented in Table 1. The $\mathbb{SIR}$ model (1) contains three equations as follows:

Table 1. Description of Model Parameters.

Parameter	Description	Units
Λ	Recruitment rate	Individual/Time
β	Transmission rate	(Individual · Time)$^{-1}$
μ	Natural death rate	Time^{-1}
δ	Rate of loss of immunity	Time^{-1}
α_0	Baseline recovery rate attributable to healthcare intervention	Time^{-1}
α_1	Maximum recovery rate when healthcare resources are sufficient	Time^{-1}
b	Density dependence influence parameter	Individual
γ	Infection-induced death rate	Time^{-1}
N	Total population size	Individual

Susceptible Population Dynamics ($\mathbb{S}$)

$${}^{\mathbb{PC}}_{a}\mathbf{D}^{\zeta,\psi,p}_{z,w}\mathbb{S}(z) = \Lambda - \frac{2\beta\mathbb{SI}}{N} - \mu\mathbb{S} + \delta\mathbb{R},$$

where Λ represents the birth rate or influx of new susceptible individuals into the population. The term $\frac{2\beta\mathbb{S}\mathbb{I}}{N}$ represents the rate at which susceptible individuals become infected, β is the transmission rate, $\mathbb{S}$ is the number of susceptible individuals, $\mathbb{I}$ is the number of infected individuals, N is the total population size ($N = \mathbb{S} + \mathbb{I} + \mathbb{R}$), assumed constant (as shown in Figure 1).

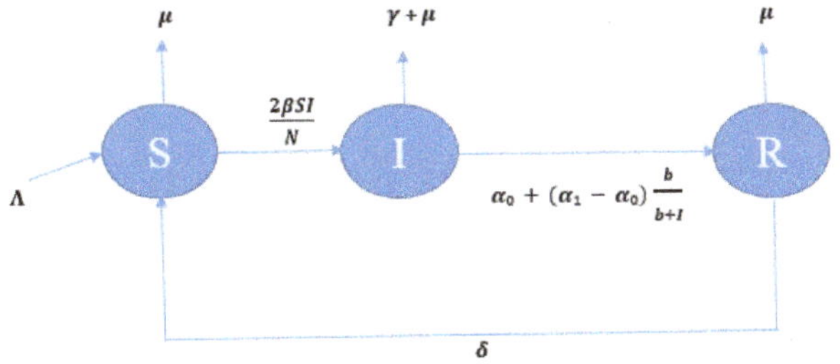

Figure 1. Schematic diagram of the modified $\mathbb{SIR}$ model.

This form modifies the incidence rate $\frac{\beta\mathbb{S}\mathbb{I}}{N}$ to account for saturation effects, emphasizing that the infection rate depends on the number of individuals in $\mathbb{S}$ and $\mathbb{I}$ without relying on the recovered population $\mathbb{R}$. The factor of '2' accounts for the increased contact rates within households of two individuals, where the probability of transmission is higher [29]. The term $\mu\mathbb{S}$ represents the number of susceptible individuals dying per unit time, where μ is the natural death rate. The term $\delta\mathbb{R}$ represents the rate at which recovered individuals lose immunity and return to the susceptible compartment.

Infected Population Dynamics ($\mathbb{I}$)

$$ {}^{\mathbb{PC}}_{a}\mathbf{D}^{\zeta,\psi,p}_{z,w}\mathbb{I}(z) = \frac{2\beta\mathbb{S}\mathbb{I}}{N} - \left[\alpha_0 + (\alpha_1 - \alpha_0)\frac{b}{b+\mathbb{I}}\right]\mathbb{I} - (\gamma + \mu)\mathbb{I}, $$

The term $\frac{2\beta\mathbb{S}\mathbb{I}}{N}$ represents the same infection process as in the susceptible equation. The term $\left[\alpha_0 + (\alpha_1 - \alpha_0)\frac{b}{b+\mathbb{I}}\right]\mathbb{I}$ represents the rate at which infected individuals recover through healthcare intervention and leave the infected compartment. Here, α_0 is the baseline recovery rate attributable to healthcare intervention, α_1 is the maximum recovery rate when healthcare resources are sufficient, b is a constant modulating the recovery rate based on the infected population [30]. The fraction $\frac{b}{b+\mathbb{I}}$ models the effect of healthcare resource constraints: When $\mathbb{I}$ is small, the recovery rate approaches α_1, when $\mathbb{I}$ is large, the recovery rate asymptotically approaches α_0. This reflects the real-world scenario in which a surge in infections can overwhelm healthcare systems, reducing the quality and availability of care for each infected individual. The term $\gamma\mathbb{I}$ represents the rate at which infected individuals die from infection. The term $\mu\mathbb{I}$ represents the number of infected individuals who die per unit time from natural causes.

Recovered Population Dynamics ($\mathbb{R}$)

$$ {}^{\mathbb{PC}}_{a}\mathbf{D}^{\zeta,\psi,p}_{z,w}\mathbb{R}(z) = \left[\alpha_0 + (\alpha_1 - \alpha_0)\frac{b}{b+\mathbb{I}}\right]\mathbb{I} - (\mu + \delta)\mathbb{R}. $$

The term $\left[\alpha_0 + (\alpha_1 - \alpha_0)\frac{b}{b+\mathbb{I}}\right]\mathbb{I}$ represents the rate at which infected individuals recover through healthcare intervention and enter the recovered compartment, as described in the infected population equation. The term $(\mu + \delta)\mathbb{R}$ accounts for the removal of recovered individuals due to: Natural death (μ), loss of immunity (δ), causing individuals to re-enter the susceptible compartment.

3. Basic Concepts

Definition 1 ([24]). *For $\zeta \in [0,1)$, with $\psi, p > 0$, and $\mathbb{X} \in H^1(a,b)$, where $H^1(a,b)$ is Sobolev space. The PCFD of order ζ, of a function $\mathbb{X}$ w.r.t the weight function w, $0 < w \in C^1([a,b])$, is defined by*

$$ {}^{\mathbb{PC}}_{a}\mathbf{D}^{\zeta,\psi,p}_{z,w}\mathbb{X}(z) = \frac{\mathbb{PC}(\zeta)}{1-\zeta}\frac{1}{w(z)}\int_a^z {}^{p}\mathbb{E}_{\psi,1}\left(-\frac{\zeta}{1-\zeta}(z-s)^{\psi}\right)(w\mathbb{X})'(s)ds, \quad (2) $$

where ${}^{p}\mathbb{E}_{\psi,1}$ is the Power Mittag-Leffler function given by

$$ {}^{p}\mathbb{E}_{\psi,1}(s) = \sum_{n=0}^{+\infty}\frac{(s\ln p)^n}{\Gamma(kn+l)}, s \in \mathbb{C}, and\ k,l,p > 0, $$

and $\mathbb{PC}(\zeta)$ is the normalization positive function satisfying $\mathbb{PC}(0) = \mathbb{PC}(1) = 1$.

Definition 2 ([24]). *The Power fractional integral with order ζ, of a function $\mathbb{X}$, w.r.t the non-decreasing weight function w,$0 < w \in C^1([a,b])$, is defined by*

$$ {}^{\mathbb{PC}}_{a}\mathbf{I}^{\zeta,\psi,p}_{z,w}\mathbb{X}(z) = \frac{1-\zeta}{\mathbb{PC}(\zeta)}\mathbb{X}(z) + \ln p\frac{\zeta}{\mathbb{PC}(\zeta)}\,{}^{\mathbb{RL}}\mathbf{I}^{\psi}_{a,w}\mathbb{X}(z), $$

where ${}^{\mathbb{RL}}\mathbf{I}^{\psi}_{a,w}\mathbb{X}(z)$ is the standard weighted R–L fractional integral of order ψ given by

$$ {}^{\mathbb{RL}}\mathbf{I}^{\psi}_{a,w}\mathbb{X}(z) = \frac{1}{\Gamma(\psi)}\frac{1}{w(z)}\int_a^z (z-s)^{\psi-1}(w\mathbb{X})(s)ds. $$

Remark 1. *The power Caputo fractional derivative, as given by Definition 1, generalizes some fractional derivatives as follows:*

(1) If $p = e, w(z) = 1$ and $\zeta = \psi$. Then, the Definition 1 reduced to the following definition of ABC fractional derivative [26]

$$ {}^{\mathbb{PC}}_{a}\mathbf{D}^{\zeta,e}_{z,1}\mathbb{X}(z) = \frac{\mathbb{PC}(\zeta)}{1-\zeta}\int_a^z {}^{e}\mathbb{E}_{\zeta,1}\left(-\frac{\zeta}{1-\zeta}(z-s)^{\zeta}\right)(\mathbb{X})'(s)ds. $$

(2) If $p = e, w(z) = 1$ and $\psi = 1$. Then, the Definition 1 reduced to the following definition of CF fractional derivative [25]

$$ {}^{\mathbb{PC}}_{a}\mathbf{D}^{\zeta,1,e}_{z,1}\mathbb{X}(z) = \frac{\mathbb{PC}(\zeta)}{1-\zeta}\int_a^z {}^{e}\mathbb{E}_{1,1}\left(-\frac{\zeta}{1-\zeta}(z-s)\right)(\mathbb{X})'(s)ds. $$

(3) If $p = e$ and $\zeta = \psi$. Then, the Definition 1 reduced to the following definition of weighted ABC fractional derivative [27]

$$ {}^{\mathbb{PC}}_{a}\mathbf{D}^{\zeta,e}_{z,w}\mathbb{X}(z) = \frac{\mathbb{PC}(\zeta)}{1-\zeta}\frac{1}{w(z)}\int_a^z {}^{p}\mathbb{E}_{\zeta,1}\left(-\frac{\zeta}{1-\zeta}(z-s)^{\zeta}\right)(w\mathbb{X})'(s)ds. $$

(4) If $p = e$. Then, the Definition 1 reduced to the following definition of weighted generalized Hattaf fractional derivative [28]

$$ {}^{\mathbb{PC}}_{a}\mathbf{D}^{\zeta,\psi,e}_{z,w}\mathbb{X}(z) = \frac{\mathbb{PC}(\zeta)}{1-\zeta}\frac{1}{w(z)}\int_a^z {}^{p}\mathbb{E}_{\psi,1}\left(-\frac{\zeta}{1-\zeta}(z-s)^{\psi}\right)(w\mathbb{X})'(s)ds. $$

4. Behavioral Characteristics of the $\mathbb{SIR}$ Model (1)

This section undertakes a rigorous analysis of the $\mathbb{SIR}$ model defined in model (1), focusing on its fundamental properties. We will establish the boundedness and positivity of the model solutions, determine the stability of the DFE, derive the basic reproduction number $\boldsymbol{R}_0$, and quantify the sensitivity of $\boldsymbol{R}_0$ to variations in model parameters, thereby revealing the key drivers of disease transmission.

4.1. Analysis of Solution Boundedness

Theorem 1. *The $\mathbb{SIR}$ PCFD Model (1) yields solutions $(\mathbb{S}, \mathbb{I}, \mathbb{R})$ that are guaranteed to be physically and mathematically feasible, lying within the region Ω, where*

$$\Omega = \left\{ (\mathbb{S}, \mathbb{I}, \mathbb{R}); \mathbb{S} + \mathbb{I} + \mathbb{R} \leq \frac{\Lambda}{\mu} \right\}.$$

Proof. The critical condition for the model to be biologically and mathematically feasible is that the total population size must be bounded. Thus, we have

$$\begin{aligned}
{}^{\mathbb{PC}}_{a}\mathbf{D}^{\zeta,\psi,p}_{z,w}N(z &= {}^{\mathbb{PC}}_{a}\mathbf{D}^{\zeta,\psi,p}_{z,w}\mathbb{S}(z) + {}^{\mathbb{PC}}_{a}\mathbf{D}^{\zeta,\psi,p}_{z,w}\mathbb{I}(z) + {}^{\mathbb{PC}}_{a}\mathbf{D}^{\zeta,\psi,p}_{z,w}\mathbb{R}(z) \\
&= \Lambda - \tfrac{2\beta\mathbb{SI}}{N} - \mu\mathbb{S} + \delta\mathbb{R} + \tfrac{2\beta\mathbb{SI}}{N} \\
&\quad - \left[\alpha_0 + (\alpha_1 - \alpha_0)\tfrac{b}{b+\mathbb{I}}\right]\mathbb{I} - (\gamma + \mu)\mathbb{I} \\
&\quad + \left[\alpha_0 + (\alpha_1 - \alpha_0)\tfrac{b}{b+\mathbb{I}}\right]\mathbb{I} - (\mu + \delta)\mathbb{R} \\
&= \Lambda - \mu N(z) - \gamma\mathbb{I},
\end{aligned}$$

where

$$N(z) = \mathbb{S}(z) + \mathbb{I}(z) + \mathbb{R}(z).$$

Clearly

$$\Lambda - \mu N(z) - \gamma\mathbb{I} \leq \Lambda - \mu N(z).$$

This implies that

$${}^{\mathbb{PC}}_{a}\mathbf{D}^{\zeta,\psi,p}_{z,w}N(z) \leq \Lambda - \mu N(z). \tag{3}$$

Applying the Laplace transform of PCFD [24] on both sides of (3), we obtain

$$\mathcal{L}\left(w(z){}^{\mathbb{PC}}_{a}\mathbf{D}^{\zeta,\psi,p}_{z,w}N(z)\right) \leq \mathcal{L}[w(z)(\Lambda - \mu N(z))].$$

This implies that,

$$\begin{aligned}
N(z) \leq{}& \tfrac{\Lambda}{\mu} + \tfrac{\mathbb{PC}(\zeta)w(a)}{[\mathbb{PC}(\zeta)-(1-\zeta)\mu]w(z)}\left(N(0) - \tfrac{\Lambda}{\mu}\right){}^{p}\mathbb{E}_{\psi,1}\left(\tfrac{\zeta\mu}{[\mathbb{PC}(\zeta)-(1-\zeta)\mu]}z^{\zeta}\right) \\
&- \tfrac{\mathbb{PC}(\zeta)\mu}{[\mathbb{PC}(\zeta)-(1-\zeta)\mu]w(z)}{}^{p}\mathbb{E}_{\psi,1}\left(\tfrac{\zeta\mu}{[\mathbb{PC}(\zeta)-(1-\zeta)\mu]}z^{\zeta}\right) * w'(z).
\end{aligned}$$

Consequently, $N(z)$ bounded by $\frac{\Lambda}{\mu}$. According to the fact $N(z) = \mathbb{S}(z) + \mathbb{I}(z) + \mathbb{R}(z)$, we deduce that $(\mathbb{S}, \mathbb{I}, \mathbb{R})$ are bounded in Ω. This means ensuring the biological feasibility of the model. This boundedness result ensures that the model predicts realistic population sizes and prevents unbounded growth. □

4.2. Nonnegativity of Solutions

Theorem 2. *The $\mathbb{SIR}$ PCFD Model (1), with initial conditions ($\mathbb{S}(0) > 0, \mathbb{I}(0) > 0$, and $\mathbb{R}(0) > 0$), guarantees non-negative solutions for all time.*

Proof. To biological relevance of our model, all state variables must remain non-negative. We will mathematically justify this by showing that each state variable is strictly positive for all $z \in [a, T]$. This justification will be based on the analysis of the third equation in model (1), presented below:

$$ {}_{a}^{\mathbb{PC}}\mathbf{D}_{z,w}^{\zeta,\psi,p}\mathbb{R}(z) = \left[\alpha_0 + (\alpha_1 - \alpha_0)\frac{b}{b+\mathbb{I}}\right]\mathbb{I} - (\mu+\delta)\mathbb{R}. $$

Then, we have

$$ {}_{a}^{\mathbb{PC}}\mathbf{D}_{z,w}^{\zeta,\psi,p}\mathbb{R}(z) \geq -(\mu+\delta)\mathbb{R}. \tag{4} $$

Applying Laplace transform of PCFD [24] on both sides of (4), we have

$$ \mathcal{L}\left[w(z){}_{a}^{\mathbb{PC}}\mathbf{D}_{z,w}^{\zeta,\psi,p}\mathbb{R}(z)\right] \geq -(\mu+\delta)\mathcal{L}[w(z)\mathbb{R}(z)](s). $$

Thus, we obtain

$$ \mathbb{R}(z) \geq \frac{\mathbb{PC}(\zeta)w(a)\mathbb{R}(0)}{[\mathbb{PC}(\zeta)-(1-\zeta)(\mu+\delta)]w(z)}\,{}^{p}\mathbb{E}_{\psi,1}\left(\frac{\zeta(\mu+\delta)}{[\mathbb{PC}(\zeta)-(1-\zeta)(\mu+\delta)]}z^{\zeta}\right). $$

Since $\mathbb{R}(0) > 0$ and $0 \leq^{p} E_{\psi,1} \leq 1$, we determine that $\mathbb{R}(z)$ is positive for all $z \in [a, T]$. Using an analogous argument, we can show that $\mathbb{S}$ and $\mathbb{I}$ are also positive, thereby establishing the model's biological feasibility. Consequently, the population compartments ($\mathbb{S}$, $\mathbb{I}$, $\mathbb{R}$) are guaranteed to remain non-negative, reflecting the biological reality that populations cannot have negative sizes. □

4.3. Disease-Free Equilibrium Point (DFE)

In the context of a $\mathbb{SIR}$ model, an equilibrium point is a state where the system is not changing. Mathematically, this means that the time derivatives of all the state variables are equal to zero. In this case, we are looking for values of $\mathbb{S}$, $\mathbb{I}$, and $\mathbb{R}$ where:

- ${}_{a}^{\mathbb{PC}}\mathbf{D}_{z,w}^{\zeta,\psi,p}\mathbb{S}(z) = 0$ (The rate of change of susceptible individuals is zero).
- ${}_{a}^{\mathbb{PC}}\mathbf{D}_{z,w}^{\zeta,\psi,p}\mathbb{I}(z) = 0$ (The rate of change of infected individuals is zero).
- ${}_{a}^{\mathbb{PC}}\mathbf{D}_{z,w}^{\zeta,\psi,p}\mathbb{R}(z) = 0$ (The rate of change of recovered individuals is zero).

Thus, we obtain

$$ \begin{cases} \Lambda - \frac{2\beta\mathbb{SI}}{N} - \mu\mathbb{S} + \delta\mathbb{R} = 0, \\ \frac{2\beta\mathbb{SI}}{N} - \left[\alpha_0 + (\alpha_1 - \alpha_0)\frac{b}{b+\mathbb{I}}\right]\mathbb{I} - (\gamma+\mu)\mathbb{I} = 0, \\ \left[\alpha_0 + (\alpha_1 - \alpha_0)\frac{b}{b+\mathbb{I}}\right]\mathbb{I} - (\mu+\delta)\mathbb{R} = 0. \end{cases} $$

By solving the above equilibrium equations, one can easily obtain the DFE point, ℓ_0, for model (1) as follows:

$$ \ell_0 = (\mathbb{S}(0), \mathbb{I}(0), \mathbb{R}(0)) = \left(\frac{\Lambda}{\mu}, 0, 0\right). $$

4.4. Basic Reproduction Number

To derive the basic reproduction number, $\boldsymbol{R}_0$, we first consider the equations governing the dynamics of the susceptible ($\mathbb{S}$) and infected ($\mathbb{I}$) compartments, which are given by:

$$ \begin{aligned} {}_{a}^{\mathbb{PC}}\mathbf{D}_{z,w}^{\zeta,\psi,p}\mathbb{S}(z) &= \Lambda - \tfrac{2\beta\mathbb{SI}}{N} - \mu\mathbb{S} + \delta\mathbb{R}, \\ {}_{a}^{\mathbb{PC}}\mathbf{D}_{z,w}^{\zeta,\psi,p}\mathbb{I}(z) &= \tfrac{2\beta\mathbb{SI}}{N} - \left[\alpha_0 + (\alpha_1 - \alpha_0)\tfrac{b}{b+\mathbb{I}}\right]\mathbb{I} - (\gamma+\mu)\mathbb{I}. \end{aligned} $$

The Disease-Free Equilibrium (DFE) is $\ell_0 = (\mathbb{S} = \Lambda/\mu, \mathbb{I} = 0, \mathbb{R} = 0)$. We assume a constant population size, $N = \mathbb{S} + \mathbb{I} + \mathbb{R}$, and that at equilibrium, the birth rate balances the death rate, i.e., $\Lambda \approx \mu N$. This system of equations can be expressed in a compact form as:

$$ {}^{\mathbb{PC}}_{a}\mathbf{D}^{\zeta,\psi,p}_{z,w} \begin{bmatrix} \mathbb{S}(z) \\ \mathbb{I}(z) \end{bmatrix} = F(z) - V(z), $$

where $F(z)$ represents the rate of new infections and $V(z)$ represents the rate of transfer out of the infected population. These are defined as:

$$ F(z) = \begin{bmatrix} -\frac{2\beta\mathbb{S}\mathbb{I}}{N} \\ \frac{2\beta\mathbb{S}\mathbb{I}}{N} \end{bmatrix}, $$

and

$$ V(z) = \begin{bmatrix} \mu\mathbb{S} - \Lambda + \delta\mathbb{R} \\ \left[\alpha_0 + (\alpha_1 - \alpha_0)\frac{b}{b+\mathbb{I}}\right]\mathbb{I} + (\gamma + \mu)\mathbb{I} \end{bmatrix}, $$

The Jacobian matrices of $F(z)$ and $V(z)$, evaluated at the DFE ($\ell_0 = (\mathbb{S} = \Lambda/\mu, \mathbb{I} = 0, \mathbb{R} = 0)$), denoted by $\mathcal{F}$ and $\mathcal{V}$, respectively, are:

$$ \mathcal{F} = \begin{bmatrix} 0 & -\frac{2\beta\Lambda}{N\mu} \\ 0 & \frac{2\beta\Lambda}{N\mu} \end{bmatrix}, \mathcal{V} = \begin{bmatrix} \mu & 0 \\ 0 & \alpha_1 + \gamma + \mu \end{bmatrix}. $$

Using the fact that $\boldsymbol{R}_0$ is the spectral radius of the next generation matrix $\mathcal{F}\mathcal{V}^{-1}$, and substituting $\Lambda = \mu N$, the basic reproduction number $\boldsymbol{R}_0$ for model (1) is given by

$$ \boldsymbol{R}_0 = \frac{2\beta}{\alpha_1 + \gamma + \mu}. $$

4.5. Stability Analysis

The stability of the Disease-Free Equilibrium (DFE) is critical in epidemiology. A locally stable DFE prevents sustained epidemics, as pathogens diminish due to low reproductive capacity. An unstable DFE risks outbreaks, even with minimal pathogen introduction. Understanding DFE stability guides public health interventions, enabling targeted control strategies to prevent disease spread.

Theorem 3. *The DFE of the $\mathbb{SIR}$ model (1) exhibits local asymptotic stability for $\boldsymbol{R}_0 < 1$, whereas values of $\boldsymbol{R}_0 > 1$ leads to instability in this equilibrium.*

Proof. The model (1) is linearized at the no-disease equilibrium to examine its local stability. This procedure leads to the Jacobian matrix, $J(\ell_0)$, which governs the dynamics of the linearized model.

$$ J^{[0]} = \begin{bmatrix} -\mu & -2\beta & 0 \\ 0 & 2\beta - (\alpha_1 + \gamma + \mu) & 0 \\ 0 & \alpha_1 & -\mu \end{bmatrix}. $$

The eigenvalues of the above matrix are $\lambda_1 = -\mu$ (this eigenvalue has multiplicity 2) and $\lambda_2 = 2\beta - (\alpha_1 + \gamma + \mu)$. For the DFE to be locally asymptotically stable, all eigenvalues of the Jacobian matrix evaluated at the equilibrium must have strictly negative real parts. Since $\lambda_1 = -\mu$, where μ is a positive parameter (death rate), it is always negative. Therefore, the stability is determined by the sign of λ_2. The DFE is stable if $\lambda_2 < 0$, that is: $2\beta -$

$(\alpha_1+\gamma+\mu) < 0$. This can be rearranged as $2\beta < (\alpha_1+\gamma+\mu)$. Dividing both sides by $(\alpha_1+\gamma+\mu)$, we obtain

$$\frac{2\beta}{\alpha_1+\gamma+\mu} < 1.$$

This means that the DFE of the model (1) exhibits local asymptotic stability for $\boldsymbol{R}_0 < 1$.

If $\lambda_2 > 0$, then the DFE is unstable. This corresponds to $2\beta - (\alpha_1+\gamma+\mu) > 0$. Which, following the same steps as above leads to $\frac{2\beta}{\alpha_1+\gamma+\mu} > 1$. Thus, the DFE is locally asymptotically stable when $\boldsymbol{R}_0 < 1$, and unstable when $\boldsymbol{R}_0 > 1$. □

4.6. Sensitivity Analysis

This section is devoted to the application of sensitivity analysis of the basic reproduction number, $\boldsymbol{R}_0$ with the model parameters. The derived indices elucidate the significance of individual parameters in the context of disease emergence and transmission processes. Furthermore, this sensitivity analysis serves to gauge the model's resilience to alterations in parameter values. The following formula is used to ascertain the sensitivity indices:

$$\mathbf{SEN}_{\ell}^{\boldsymbol{R}_0} = \frac{\ell}{\boldsymbol{R}_0}\left[\frac{\partial \boldsymbol{R}_0}{\partial \ell}\right].$$

Applying the above formula, we obtain the sensitivity indices of the parameters as follows:

- $\mathbf{SEN}_{\beta}^{\boldsymbol{R}_0} = 1,$
- $\mathbf{SEN}_{\alpha_1}^{\boldsymbol{R}_0} = -0.3556,$
- $\mathbf{SEN}_{\gamma}^{\boldsymbol{R}_0} = -0.1531,$
- $\mathbf{SEN}_{\mu}^{\boldsymbol{R}_0} = -0.6436.$

The sensitivity analysis indicates that controlling the transmission rate β is essential to mitigate disease spread, as the basic reproduction number ($\boldsymbol{R}_0$) exhibits the highest sensitivity to this parameter. While increasing the infected rate $(\gamma, \alpha_0, \alpha_1, \alpha_2)$ also helps lower $\boldsymbol{R}_0$ by increasing the recovery rate, its impact is comparatively less pronounced. The natural death rate (μ) also influence $\boldsymbol{R}_0$, though indirectly. Consequently, interventions that directly target transmission remain the most effective for controlling the disease within the model's framework, followed by strategies that enhance recovery. Figure 2 presented the sensitivity of $\boldsymbol{R}_0$ to each parameter in the model.

4.7. Scenario Analysis

Beyond the isolated impact of individual parameters on $\boldsymbol{R}_0$, investigating the interplay between parameter pairs unlocks a more nuanced comprehension of the model's complex dynamics. This pairwise analysis reveals how synergistic effects and countervailing influences between parameters jointly shape disease transmission, a phenomenon often obscured when considering single-parameter variations alone. The 3D contour plots shown in Figure 3 effectively visualize the responses of $\boldsymbol{R}_0$ across these multifaceted parameter landscapes, thus illuminating the sensitivity of the basic reproduction number to changes in joint parameters. In addition, Figure 4 shows the contour plots of $\boldsymbol{R}_0$ as combinations of pairs of two parameters, illustrating the basic reproduction number.

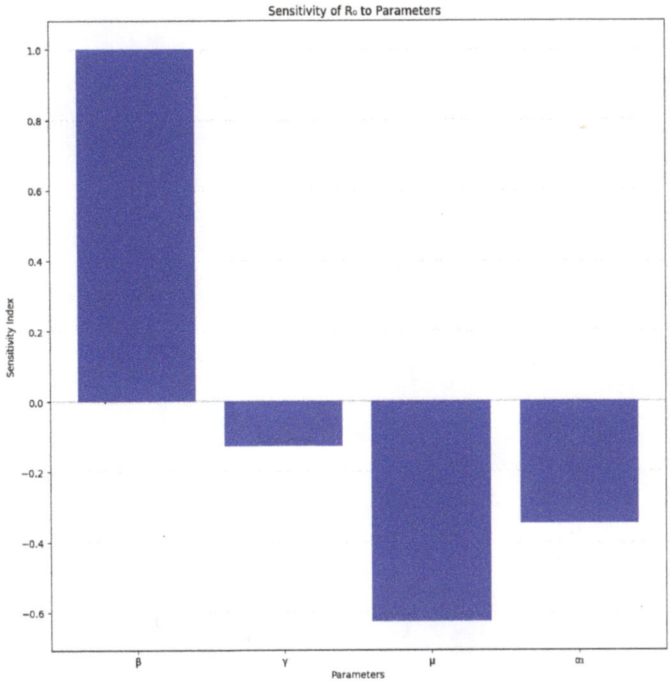

Figure 2. Sensitivity indices of $\mathbb{SIR}$ model parameters.

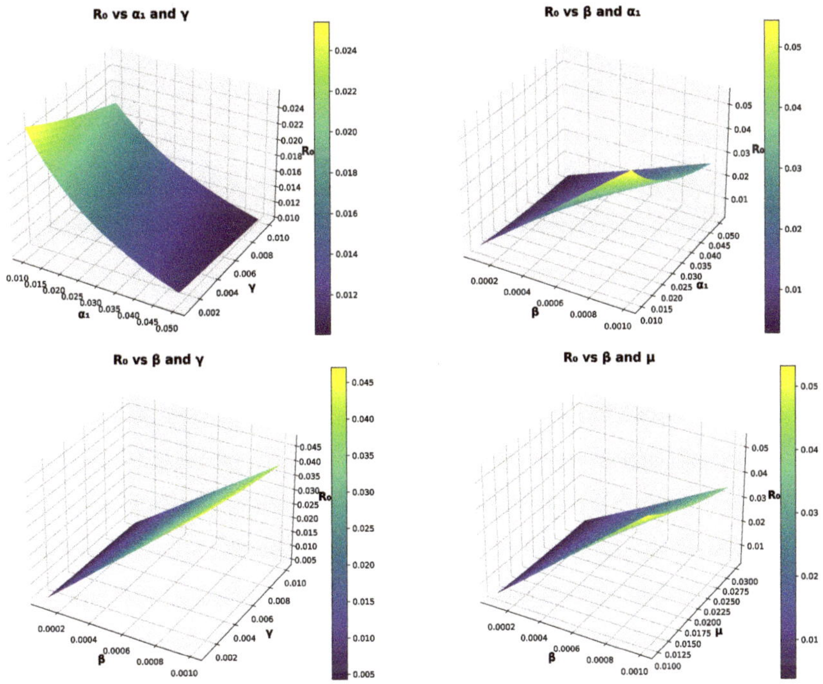

Figure 3. Contour 3D plots for illuminating the basic reproduction number R_0 sensitivity to joint parameter changes.

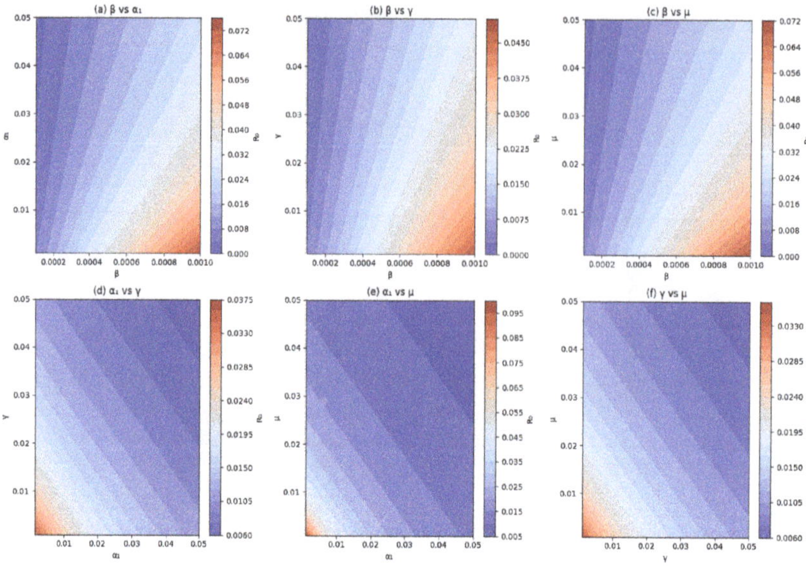

Figure 4. Contour 2D plots for illuminating the basic reproduction number R_0 sensitivity to joint parameter changes.

4.8. Lipschitz Property

By Lemma 4 in [31], we can convert the PCFD model (1) as the following equivalent integral equations:

$$\begin{bmatrix}\mathbb{S}(z)\\ \mathbb{I}(z)\\ \mathbb{R}(z)\end{bmatrix} = \frac{w(0)}{w(z)}\begin{bmatrix}\mathbb{S}_0\\ \mathbb{I}_0\\ \mathbb{R}_0\end{bmatrix} + {}_0^{\mathrm{PC}}\mathbf{I}_{z,w}^{\zeta,\psi,p}\begin{bmatrix}\mathbb{K}_1(z,\mathbb{S})\\ \mathbb{K}_2(z,\mathbb{I})\\ \mathbb{K}_3(z,\mathbb{R})\end{bmatrix}, \tag{5}$$

where

$$\begin{aligned}
\mathbb{K}_1(z,\mathbb{S}) &= \Lambda - \tfrac{2\beta\mathbb{S}\mathbb{I}}{N} - \mu\mathbb{S} + \delta\mathbb{R},\\
\mathbb{K}_2(z,\mathbb{I}) &= \tfrac{2\beta\mathbb{S}\mathbb{I}}{N} - \left[\alpha_0 + (\alpha_1-\alpha_0)\tfrac{b}{b+\mathbb{I}}\right]\mathbb{I} - (\gamma+\mu)\mathbb{I},\\
\mathbb{K}_3(z,\mathbb{R}) &= \left[\alpha_0 + (\alpha_1-\alpha_0)\tfrac{b}{b+\mathbb{I}}\right]\mathbb{I} - (\mu+\delta)\mathbb{R}.
\end{aligned}$$

Theorem 4. *Let $\mathbb{S},\mathbb{I},\mathbb{R},\hat{\mathbb{S}},\hat{\mathbb{I}},\hat{\mathbb{R}}$ be continuous functions in $L^1[0,1]$. Define positive constants x_1, x_2 and x_3 such that*

$$\parallel \mathbb{S} \parallel = \max_{\imath\in\mathcal{J}}|\mathbb{S}(\imath)| < x_1, \parallel \mathbb{I} \parallel = \max_{\imath\in\mathcal{J}}|\mathbb{I}(\imath)| < x_2, \parallel \mathbb{R} \parallel = \max_{\imath\in\mathcal{J}}|\mathbb{R}(\imath)| < x_3.$$

Then, the following kernels

$$\begin{aligned}
\mathbb{K}_1(z,\mathbb{S}) &= \Lambda - \tfrac{2\beta\mathbb{S}\mathbb{I}}{N} - \mu\mathbb{S} + \delta\mathbb{R},\\
\mathbb{K}_2(z,\mathbb{I}) &= \tfrac{2\beta\mathbb{S}\mathbb{I}}{N} - \left[\alpha_0 + (\alpha_1-\alpha_0)\tfrac{b}{b+\mathbb{I}}\right]\mathbb{I} - (\gamma+\mu)\mathbb{I},\\
\mathbb{K}_3(z,\mathbb{R}) &= \left[\alpha_0 + (\alpha_1-\alpha_0)\tfrac{b}{b+\mathbb{I}}\right]\mathbb{I} - (\mu+\delta)\mathbb{R},
\end{aligned}$$

satisfy Lipschitz conditions with Lipschitz constant $k = \max_{i=1}^{3}\{\mathcal{L}_{\mathbb{K}_i}\} > 0$*, such that*

$$\begin{aligned} \mathcal{L}_{\mathbb{K}_1} &= \left(\tfrac{2\beta x_2}{N} + \mu\right), \\ \mathcal{L}_{\mathbb{K}_2} &= \left(\tfrac{2\beta x_1}{N} + \left[\alpha_0 + (\alpha_1 - \alpha_0)\tfrac{b}{b+\mathbb{I}}\right] + (\gamma + \mu)\right), \\ \mathcal{L}_{\mathbb{K}_3} &= (\mu + \delta). \end{aligned}$$

Proof. For $\mathbb{K}_1(z,\mathbb{S}) = \Lambda - \frac{2\beta\mathbb{S}\mathbb{I}}{N} - \mu\mathbb{S} + \delta\mathbb{R}$, let $\mathbb{S}, \hat{\mathbb{S}} \in L^1[0,1]$. Thus,

$$\begin{aligned} \| \mathbb{K}_1(z,\mathbb{S}) - \mathbb{K}_1\left(z,\hat{\mathbb{S}}\right) \| &= \| \left(\Lambda - \tfrac{2\beta\mathbb{S}\mathbb{I}}{N} - \mu\mathbb{S} + \delta\mathbb{R}\right) - \left(\Lambda - \tfrac{2\beta\hat{\mathbb{S}}\mathbb{I}}{N} - \mu\hat{\mathbb{S}} + \delta\mathbb{R}\right) \| \\ &\leq \tfrac{2\beta\|\mathbb{I}\|}{N} \| \left(\mathbb{S} - \hat{\mathbb{S}}\right) \| + \mu \| \left(\mathbb{S} - \hat{\mathbb{S}}\right) \| \\ &\leq \left(\tfrac{2\beta x_2}{N} + \mu\right) \| \mathbb{S}_1 - \hat{\mathbb{S}}_1 \|. \end{aligned}$$

Put $\mathcal{L}_{\mathbb{K}_1} = \left(\frac{2\beta x_2}{N} + \mu\right) > 0$. Thus, we get

$$\| \mathbb{K}_1(z,\mathbb{S}_1) - \mathbb{K}_1\left(z,\hat{\mathbb{S}}_1\right) \| \leq \mathcal{L}_{\mathbb{K}_1} \| \mathbb{S}_1 - \hat{\mathbb{S}}_1 \|.$$

To further demonstrate the concept, we can obtain the following:

$$\| \mathbb{K}_2(z,\mathbb{S}_2) - \mathbb{K}_2\left(z,\hat{\mathbb{S}}_2\right) \| \leq \mathcal{L}_{\mathbb{K}_2} \| \mathbb{S}_2 - \hat{\mathbb{S}}_2 \|,$$

and

$$\| \mathbb{K}_3(z,\mathbb{R}) - \mathbb{K}_3\left(z,\hat{\mathbb{R}}\right) \| \leq \mathcal{L}_{\mathbb{K}_5} \| \mathbb{R} - \hat{\mathbb{R}} \|.$$

Let

$$k = \max_{i=1}^{3}\{\mathcal{L}_{\mathbb{K}_i}\} > 0.$$

Thus, the kernels $\mathbb{K}_i, i = 1,2,3$ are Lipschitz continuous with a Lipschitz constant $k > 0$. □

4.9. Existence of Solution via Recursive Sequences

In this section, we aim to prove the existence of a solution to the following model using a recursive sequence approach. We will use the contraction mapping theorem to show that the sequence converges to a unique solution. By (5) the solution of the model (1) is given by

$$\begin{bmatrix} \mathbb{S}(z) \\ \mathbb{I}(z) \\ \mathbb{R}(z) \end{bmatrix} = \frac{w(0)}{w(z)} \begin{bmatrix} \mathbb{S}_0 \\ \mathbb{I}_0 \\ \mathbb{R}_0 \end{bmatrix} + \frac{1-\zeta}{\mathbb{PC}(\zeta)} \begin{bmatrix} \mathbb{K}_1(z,\mathbb{S}) \\ \mathbb{K}_2(z,\mathbb{I}) \\ \mathbb{K}_3(z,\mathbb{R}) \end{bmatrix} + \ln p \frac{\zeta}{\mathbb{PC}(\zeta)} \, {}^{\mathbb{RL}}\mathbf{I}_{a,w}^{\psi} \begin{bmatrix} \mathbb{K}_1(z,\mathbb{S}) \\ \mathbb{K}_2(z,\mathbb{I}) \\ \mathbb{K}_3(z,\mathbb{R}) \end{bmatrix}.$$

Let's represent the given system in a compact operator form. Define:

$$\mathbf{X}(z) = \begin{bmatrix} \mathbb{S}(z) \\ \mathbb{I}(z) \\ \mathbb{R}(z) \end{bmatrix}, \mathbf{X}_0 = \begin{bmatrix} \mathbb{S}_0 \\ \mathbb{I}_0 \\ \mathbb{R}_0 \end{bmatrix},$$

and

$$\mathbf{F}(z,\mathbf{X}(z)) = \begin{bmatrix} \mathbb{K}_1(z,\mathbb{S}) \\ \mathbb{K}_2(z,\mathbb{I}) \\ \mathbb{K}_3(z,\mathbb{R}) \end{bmatrix}.$$

Thus, the original system can be written as:

$$\mathbf{X}(z) = \frac{w(0)}{w(z)}\mathbf{X}_0 + \frac{1-\zeta}{\mathbb{PC}(\zeta)}\mathbf{F}(z,\mathbf{X}(z)) + \ln p \frac{\zeta}{\mathbb{PC}(\zeta)}\,{}^{\mathbb{RL}}\mathbf{I}^{\psi}_{a,w}\mathbf{F}(z,\mathbf{X}(z)).$$

Define the operator

$$\mathbf{H}(\mathbf{X}(z)) = \frac{w(0)}{w(z)}\mathbf{X}_0 + \frac{1-\zeta}{\mathbb{PC}(\zeta)}\mathbf{F}(z,\mathbf{X}(z)) + \ln p \frac{\zeta}{\mathbb{PC}(\zeta)}\,{}^{\mathbb{RL}}\mathbf{I}^{\psi}_{a,w}\mathbf{F}(z,\mathbf{X}(z)).$$

We define a recursive sequence of vector functions $\{\mathbf{X}_n(z)\}, n = 0, 1, 2, \cdots$ as follows:

$$\mathbf{X}_{n+1}(z) = \frac{w(0)}{w(z)}\mathbf{X}_0 + \frac{w(0)}{w(z)}\mathbf{X}_0 + \frac{1-\zeta}{\mathbb{PC}(\zeta)}\mathbf{F}(z,\mathbf{X}_n(z)) + \ln p \frac{\zeta}{\mathbb{PC}(\zeta)}\,{}^{\mathbb{RL}}\mathbf{I}^{\psi}_{a,w}\mathbf{F}(z,\mathbf{X}_n(z)).$$

Theorem 5. *Assume that $w(z) \neq 0$ for all z in the considered interval $[0,T]$ and the components of $\mathbf{F}(z,\mathbf{X}(z))$ are continuous and bounded for all $\mathbf{X}$ and z in the interval $[0,T]$. Then, the model (1) possesses a solution provided that:*

$$k\left[\frac{1-\zeta}{|\mathbb{PC}(\zeta)|} + \frac{|\ln(p)|\zeta}{|\mathbb{PC}(\zeta)|}\frac{T^{\psi}}{\Gamma(\psi+1)}\right] < 1,$$

where k is the Lipschitz constant defined in Theorem 4.

Proof. Let us define the operator $\mathbf{H}: \mathbf{C}([0,T]) \to \mathbf{C}([0,T])$ as follows

$$\mathbf{H}(\mathbf{X}(z)) = \frac{w(0)}{w(z)}\mathbf{X}_0 + \frac{1-\zeta}{\mathbb{PC}(\zeta)}\mathbf{F}(z,\mathbf{X}(z)) + \ln p \frac{\zeta}{\mathbb{PC}(\zeta)}\,{}^{\mathbb{RL}}\mathbf{I}^{\psi}_{a,w}\mathbf{F}(z,\mathbf{X}(z)).$$

For all $\mathbf{X}, \mathbf{Y} \in \mathbf{C}([0,T])$ and $z \in [0,T]$, we have

$$\begin{aligned}\| \mathbf{H}(\mathbf{X}) - \mathbf{H}(\mathbf{Y}) \| \leq & \frac{1-\zeta}{\mathbb{PC}(\zeta)} \| \mathbf{F}(z,\mathbf{X}(z)) - \mathbf{F}(z,\mathbf{Y}(z)) \| \\ & + \ln p \frac{\zeta}{\mathbb{PC}(\zeta)}\,{}^{\mathbb{RL}}\mathbf{I}^{\psi}_{a,w} \| \mathbf{F}(z,\mathbf{X}(z)) - \mathbf{F}(z,\mathbf{Y}(z)) \|,\end{aligned}$$

By Theorem 4, $\mathbf{F}(z,\mathbf{X}(z))$ satisfies the Lipschitz condition $k = \max_{i=1}^{3}\{\mathcal{L}_{\mathbb{K}_i}\} > 0$. Thus, we obtain that

$$\begin{aligned}\| \mathbf{H}(\mathbf{X}) - \mathbf{H}(\mathbf{Y}) \| \leq & \frac{1-\zeta}{\mathbb{PC}(\zeta)} k \| \mathbf{X} - \mathbf{Y} \| \\ & + \ln p \frac{\zeta}{\mathbb{PC}(\zeta)} k \| \mathbf{X} - \mathbf{Y} \| {}^{\mathbb{RL}}\mathbf{I}^{\psi}_{0,w}(1)z \\ \leq & k\left[\frac{1-\zeta}{|\mathbb{PC}(\zeta)|} + \frac{|\ln(p)|\zeta}{|\mathbb{PC}(\zeta)|}\frac{T^{\psi}}{\Gamma(\psi+1)}\right] \| \mathbf{X} - \mathbf{Y} \|.\end{aligned}$$

Thus, by the Banach fixed point theorem, we have that $\mathbf{H}$ is a contraction operator. Since $\mathbf{H}$ is a contraction mapping, the sequence $\{\mathbf{X}_n(z)\}$ converges to a limit, which we denote by $\mathbf{X}(z)$. This means that:

$$\lim_{n\to\infty} \mathbf{X}_n(z) = \mathbf{X}(z).$$

And since $\mathbf{X}_{n+1}(z) = \mathbf{H}(\mathbf{X}_n(z))$, taking limits as $n \to \infty$, and since $\mathbf{H}$ is a continuous operator. We have that:

$$\lim_{n\to\infty} \mathbf{X}_{n+1}(z) = \lim_{n\to\infty} \mathbf{H}(\mathbf{X}_n(z)) = \mathbf{H}\Big(\lim_{n\to\infty} \mathbf{X}_n(z)\Big).$$

and

$$\mathbf{X}(z) = \mathbf{H}(\mathbf{X}(z)).$$

That means the limit $\mathbf{X}(z)$ is a fixed point of the operator $\mathbf{H}$. Therefore, $\mathbf{X}(z)$ satisfies:

$$\mathbf{X}(z) = \frac{w(0)}{w(z)}\mathbf{X}_0 + \frac{1-\zeta}{\mathbb{PC}(\zeta)}\mathbf{F}(z,\mathbf{X}(z)) + \ln p \frac{\zeta}{\mathbb{PC}(\zeta)}\, {}^{\mathbb{RL}}\mathbf{I}^{\psi}_{a,w}\mathbf{F}(z,\mathbf{X}(z)).$$

Thus, a recursive sequence of functions $\mathbf{X}_n(z)$ approaches the solution. This sequence converges to a unique function $\mathbf{X}(z)$, which represents the solution to the given system, according to the contraction mapping theorem. Therefore, a solution exists for the given system. □

5. Numerical Scheme with Power Caputo Fractional Derivative

We will now introduce a numerical method, based on the two-step Lagrange interpolation polynomial [32], to approximate the solution of model (1). This approach is chosen for its ability to achieve a balance between computational efficiency and accuracy in approximating solutions to systems of ordinary differential equations. The two-step nature of the method allows for the inclusion of previous solution values, improving the approximation in each iteration, while the use of a Lagrange interpolation polynomial ensures that the approximation fits the known solution points well. From (5), the solution of (1) is given by

$$\mathbb{S}(z) = \begin{cases} \frac{w(a)}{w(z)}\mathbb{S}_0 + \frac{1-\zeta}{|\mathbb{PC}(\zeta)|}\Big(\Lambda - \frac{2\beta\mathbb{S}\mathbb{I}}{N} - \mu\mathbb{S} + \delta\mathbb{R}\Big) \\ + \frac{|\ln(p)|\zeta}{|\mathbb{PC}(\zeta)|\Gamma(\psi)w(z)}\int_a^z (z-s)^{\psi-1}w(s)\Big(\Lambda - \frac{2\beta\mathbb{S}\mathbb{I}}{N} - \mu\mathbb{S} + \delta\mathbb{R}\Big)ds, \end{cases}$$

$$\mathbb{I}(z) = \begin{cases} \frac{w(a)}{w(z)}\mathbb{I}_0 + \frac{1-\zeta}{|\mathbb{PC}(\zeta)|}\Big(\frac{2\beta\mathbb{S}\mathbb{I}}{N} - \Big[\alpha_0 + (\alpha_1-\alpha_0)\frac{b}{b+\mathbb{I}}\Big]\mathbb{I} - (\gamma+\mu)\mathbb{I}\Big) \\ + \frac{|\ln(p)|\zeta}{|\mathbb{PC}(\zeta)|\Gamma(\psi)w(z)}\int_a^z (z-s)^{\psi-1}w(s)\times \\ \Big(\frac{2\beta\mathbb{S}\mathbb{I}}{N} - \Big[\alpha_0 + (\alpha_1-\alpha_0)\frac{b}{b+\mathbb{I}}\Big]\mathbb{I} - (\gamma+\mu)\mathbb{I}\Big)ds, \end{cases}$$

$$\mathbb{R}(z) = \begin{cases} \frac{w(0)}{w(z)}\mathbb{I}_0 + \frac{1-\zeta}{|\mathbb{PC}(\zeta)|}\Big(\Big[\alpha_0 + (\alpha_1-\alpha_0)\frac{b}{b+\mathbb{I}}\Big]\mathbb{I} + \gamma\mathbb{I} - (\mu+\delta)\mathbb{R}\Big) \\ + \frac{|\ln(p)|\zeta}{|\mathbb{PC}(\zeta)|\Gamma(\psi)w(z)}\int_a^z (z-s)^{\psi-1}w(s)\Big(\Big[\alpha_0 + (\alpha_1-\alpha_0)\frac{b}{b+\mathbb{I}}\Big]\mathbb{I} - (\mu+\delta)\mathbb{R}\Big). \end{cases}$$

Let $z_m = a + mh$ with $m \in \mathbb{N}$ and h are the discretization step. One has

$$\mathbb{S}(z_{m+1}) = \begin{cases} \frac{w(a)}{w(z_m)}\mathbb{S}_0 + \frac{1-\zeta}{|\mathbb{PC}(\zeta)|}\Big(\Lambda - \frac{2\beta\mathbb{S}\mathbb{I}}{N} - \mu\mathbb{S} + \delta\mathbb{R}\Big)(m) \\ + \frac{|\ln(p)|\zeta}{|\mathbb{PC}(\zeta)|\Gamma(\psi)w(z_m)}\int_a^{z_{m+1}} (z_{m+1}-s)^{\psi-1}w(s)\Big(\Lambda - \frac{2\beta\mathbb{S}\mathbb{I}}{N} - \mu\mathbb{S} + \delta\mathbb{R}\Big)ds, \end{cases}$$

$$\mathbb{I}(z_{m+1}) = \begin{cases} \frac{w(a)}{w(z_m)}\mathbb{I}_0 + \frac{1-\zeta}{|\mathbb{PC}(\zeta)|}\Big(\frac{2\beta\mathbb{S}\mathbb{I}}{N} - \Big[\alpha_0 + (\alpha_1-\alpha_0)\frac{b}{b+\mathbb{I}}\Big]\mathbb{I} - (\gamma+\mu)\mathbb{I}\Big)(m) \\ + \frac{|\ln(p)|\zeta}{|\mathbb{PC}(\zeta)|\Gamma(\psi)w(z_m)}\int_a^{z_{m+1}} (z_{m+1}-s)^{\psi-1}w(s)\times \\ \Big(\frac{2\beta\mathbb{S}\mathbb{I}}{N} - \Big[\alpha_0 + (\alpha_1-\alpha_0)\frac{b}{b+\mathbb{I}}\Big]\mathbb{I} - (\gamma+\mu)\mathbb{I}\Big)ds, \end{cases}$$

$$\mathbb{R}(z_{m+1}) = \begin{cases} \frac{w(0)}{w(z_m)}\mathbb{I}_0 + \frac{1-\zeta}{|\mathbb{PC}(\zeta)|}\Big(\Big[\alpha_0 + (\alpha_1-\alpha_0)\frac{b}{b+\mathbb{I}}\Big]\mathbb{I} - (\mu+\delta)\mathbb{R}\Big)(m) \\ + \frac{|\ln(p)|\zeta}{|\mathbb{PC}(\zeta)|\Gamma(\psi)w(z_m)}\int_a^{z_{m+1}} (z_{m+1}-s)^{\psi-1}w(s)\Big(\Big[\alpha_0 + (\alpha_1-\alpha_0)\frac{b}{b+\mathbb{I}}\Big]\mathbb{I} - (\mu+\delta)\mathbb{R}\Big)ds, \end{cases}$$

which yields

$$\mathbb{S}(z_{m+1}) = \begin{cases} \frac{w(a)}{w(z_m)}\mathbb{S}_0 + \frac{1-\zeta}{|\mathbb{PC}(\zeta)|}\Big(\Lambda - \frac{2\beta\mathbb{SI}}{N} - \mu\mathbb{S} + \delta\mathbb{R}\Big)(m) \\ +\frac{|\ln(p)|\zeta}{|\mathbb{PC}(\zeta)|\Gamma(\psi)w(z_m)}\sum_{l=0}^{m}\int_{z_l}^{z_{l+1}}(z_{l+1}-s)^{\psi-1}w(s)\times \\ \Big(\Lambda - \frac{2\beta\mathbb{SI}}{N} - \mu\mathbb{S} + \delta\mathbb{R}\Big)ds, \end{cases}$$

$$\mathbb{I}(z_{m+1}) = \begin{cases} \frac{w(a)}{w(z_m)}\mathbb{I}_0 + \frac{1-\zeta}{|\mathbb{PC}(\zeta)|}\Big(\frac{2\beta\mathbb{SI}}{N} - \Big[\alpha_0 + (\alpha_1-\alpha_0)\frac{b}{b+\mathbb{I}}\Big]\mathbb{I} - (\gamma+\mu)\mathbb{I}\Big)(m) \\ +\frac{|\ln(p)|\zeta}{|\mathbb{PC}(\zeta)|\Gamma(\psi)w(z_m)}\sum_{l=0}^{m}\int_{z_l}^{z_{l+1}}(z_{l+1}-s)^{\psi-1}w(s)\times \\ \Big(\frac{2\beta\mathbb{SI}}{N} - \Big[\alpha_0 + (\alpha_1-\alpha_0)\frac{b}{b+\mathbb{I}}\Big]\mathbb{I} - (\gamma+\mu)\mathbb{I}\Big)ds, \end{cases}$$

$$\mathbb{R}(z_{m+1}) = \begin{cases} \frac{w(0)}{w(z_m)}\mathbb{I}_0 + \frac{1-\zeta}{|\mathbb{PC}(\zeta)|}\Big(\Big[\alpha_0 + (\alpha_1-\alpha_0)\frac{b}{b+\mathbb{I}}\Big]\mathbb{I} + \gamma\mathbb{I} - (\mu+\delta)\mathbb{R}\Big)(m) \\ +\frac{|\ln(p)|\zeta}{|\mathbb{PC}(\zeta)|\Gamma(\psi)w(z_m)}\sum_{l=0}^{m}\int_{z_l}^{z_{l+1}}(z_{l+1}-s)^{\psi-1}w(s)\times \\ \Big(\Big[\alpha_0 + (\alpha_1-\alpha_0)\frac{b}{b+\mathbb{I}}\Big]\mathbb{I} + \gamma\mathbb{I} - (\mu+\delta)\mathbb{R}\Big)ds. \end{cases}$$

By Lagrange interpolation polynomial through the points $(z_{l-1}, \mathbb{S}(z_{l-1}), \mathbb{I}(z_{l-1}), \mathbb{R}(z_{l-1}))$ and $(z_l, \mathbb{S}(z_l), \mathbb{I}(z_l), \mathbb{R}(z_l)), l = 1, 2, 3, \cdots, m$ and $h = z_{l-1} - z_l$, we obtain

$$\mathbb{S}(z_{m+1}) = \begin{cases} \frac{w(a)}{w(z_m)}\mathbb{S}_0 + \frac{1-\zeta}{|\mathbb{PC}(\zeta)|}\Big(\Lambda - \frac{2\beta\mathbb{SI}}{N} - \mu\mathbb{S} + \delta\mathbb{R}\Big)(m) \\ +\frac{|\ln(p)|\zeta}{|\mathbb{PC}(\zeta)|\Gamma(\psi)w(z_m)}\sum_{l=1}^{m}\Bigg[\frac{w(l-1)\Big(\Lambda - \frac{2\beta\mathbb{SI}}{N} - \mu\mathbb{S} + \delta\mathbb{R}\Big)(l-1)}{h}\times \\ \int_{z_l}^{z_{l+1}}(z_{l+1}-s)^{\psi-1}(z_l-s)ds + \frac{w(l)\Big(\Lambda - \frac{2\beta\mathbb{SI}}{N} - \mu\mathbb{S} + \delta\mathbb{R}\Big)(l)}{h}\times \\ \int_{z_l}^{z_{l+1}}(z_{l+1}-s)^{\psi-1}(s-z_{l-1})ds\Bigg], \end{cases} \quad (6)$$

$$\mathbb{I}(z_{m+1}) = \begin{cases} \frac{w(a)}{w(z_m)}\mathbb{I}_0 + \frac{1-\zeta}{|\mathbb{PC}(\zeta)|}\Big(\frac{2\beta\mathbb{SI}}{N} - \Big[\alpha_0 + (\alpha_1-\alpha_0)\frac{b}{b+\mathbb{I}}\Big]\mathbb{I} - (\gamma+\mu)\mathbb{I}\Big)(m) \\ +\frac{|\ln(p)|\zeta}{|\mathbb{PC}(\zeta)|\Gamma(\psi)w(z_m)}\sum_{l=1}^{m}\Bigg[\frac{w(l-1)\Big(\frac{2\beta\mathbb{SI}}{N} - \Big[\alpha_0+(\alpha_1-\alpha_0)\frac{b}{b+\mathbb{I}}\Big]\mathbb{I} - (\gamma+\mu)\mathbb{I}\Big)(l-1)}{h}\times \\ \int_{z_l}^{z_{l+1}}(z_{l+1}-s)^{\psi-1}(z_l-s)ds + \frac{w(l)\Big(\frac{2\beta\mathbb{SI}}{N} - \Big[\alpha_0+(\alpha_1-\alpha_0)\frac{b}{b+\mathbb{I}}\Big]\mathbb{I} - (\gamma+\mu)\mathbb{I}\Big)(l)}{h}\times \\ \int_{z_l}^{z_{l+1}}(z_{l+1}-s)^{\psi-1}(s-z_{l-1})ds\Bigg] \end{cases} \quad (7)$$

$$\mathbb{R}(z_{m+1}) = \begin{cases} \frac{w(0)}{w(z_m)}\mathbb{I}_0 + \frac{1-\zeta}{|\mathbb{PC}(\zeta)|}\Big(\Big[\alpha_0 + (\alpha_1-\alpha_0)\frac{b}{b+\mathbb{I}}\Big]\mathbb{I} - (\mu+\delta)\mathbb{R}\Big)(m) \\ +\frac{|\ln(p)|\zeta}{|\mathbb{PC}(\zeta)|\Gamma(\psi)w(z_m)}\sum_{l=1}^{m}\Bigg[\frac{w(l-1)\Big(\Big[\alpha_0+(\alpha_1-\alpha_0)\frac{b}{b+\mathbb{I}}\Big]\mathbb{I} - (\mu+\delta)\mathbb{R}\Big)(l-1)}{h}\times \\ \int_{z_l}^{z_{l+1}}(z_{l+1}-s)^{\psi-1}(z_l-s)ds + \frac{w(l)\Big(\Big[\alpha_0+(\alpha_1-\alpha_0)\frac{b}{b+\mathbb{I}}\Big]\mathbb{I} - (\mu+\delta)\mathbb{R}\Big)(l)}{h}\times \\ \int_{z_l}^{z_{l+1}}(z_{l+1}-s)^{\psi-1}(s-z_{l-1})ds\Bigg] \end{cases} \quad (8)$$

Furthermore, we have

$$\int_{z_l}^{z_{l+1}}(z_{m+1}-s)^{\psi-1}(z_l-s)ds = \frac{h^{\psi+1}}{\psi(\psi+1)}\Big[(m-l)^{\psi}(m-l+1+\psi) - (m-l+1)^{\psi+1}\Big], \quad (9)$$

and

$$\int_{z_l}^{z_{l+1}}(z_{m+1}-s)^{\psi-1}(s-z_{l-1})ds = \frac{h^{\psi+1}}{\psi(\psi+1)}\begin{bmatrix}(m-l+1)^{\psi}(m-l+2+\psi) \\ -(m-l)^{\psi}(m-l+2+2\psi)\end{bmatrix}. \quad (10)$$

Thus, by (9) and (10), the Equations (6)–(8) becomes as follows

$$\mathbb{S}(z_{m+1}) = \begin{cases} \frac{w(a)}{w(z_m)}\mathbb{S}_0 + \frac{1-\zeta}{|\mathbb{PC}(\zeta)|}\wp_1(z_m, \mathbb{S}(z_m))(m) \\ + \frac{|\ln(p)|h^{\psi}}{|\mathbb{PC}(\zeta)|\Gamma(\psi+2)w(z_m)} \sum_{l=1}^{m} \Big[w(l-1)\wp_1(z_{l-1}, \mathbb{S}(z_{l-1}))\mathcal{A}^{\psi}_{m,l} \\ + w(l)\wp_1(z_l, \mathbb{S}(z_l))(l)\mathcal{B}^{\psi}_{m,l} \Big], \end{cases} \tag{11}$$

$$\mathbb{I}(z_{m+1}) = \begin{cases} \frac{w(a)}{w(z_m)}\mathbb{I}_0 + \frac{1-\zeta}{|\mathbb{PC}(\zeta)|}\wp_2(z_m, \mathbb{I}(z_m)) \\ + \frac{|\ln(p)|h^{\psi}}{|\mathbb{PC}(\zeta)|\Gamma(\psi+2)w(z_m)} \sum_{l=1}^{m} \Big[w(l-1)\wp_2(z_{l-1}, \mathbb{I}(z_{l-1}))\mathcal{A}^{\psi}_{m,l} \\ + w(l)\wp_2(z_l, \mathbb{I}(z_l))(l)\mathcal{B}^{\psi}_{m,l} \Big] \end{cases} \tag{12}$$

$$\mathbb{R}(z_{m+1}) = \begin{cases} \frac{w(0)}{w(z_m)}\mathbb{I}_0 + \frac{1-\zeta}{|\mathbb{PC}(\zeta)|}\wp_3(z_m, \mathbb{R}(z_m)) \\ + \frac{|\ln(p)|h^{\psi}}{|\mathbb{PC}(\zeta)|\Gamma(\psi+2)w(z_m)} \sum_{l=1}^{m} \Big[w(l-1)\wp_3(z_{l-1}, \mathbb{R}(z_{l-1}))\mathcal{A}^{\psi}_{m,l} \\ + w(l)\wp_3(z_l, \mathbb{R}(z_l))(l)\mathcal{B}^{\psi}_{m,l} \Big] \end{cases} \tag{13}$$

where

$$\begin{aligned} \wp_1(z, \mathbb{S}(z)) &= \Lambda - \frac{2\beta\mathbb{S}(z)\mathbb{I}(z)}{N} - \mu\mathbb{S}(z) + \delta\mathbb{R}(z), \\ \wp_2(z, \mathbb{I}(z)) &= \frac{2\beta\mathbb{S}(z)\mathbb{I}(z)}{N} - \Big[\alpha_0 + (\alpha_1 - \alpha_0)\frac{b}{b+\mathbb{I}}\Big]\mathbb{I}(z) - (\gamma + \mu)\mathbb{I}(z), \\ \wp_3(z, \mathbb{R}(z)) &= \Big[\alpha_0 + (\alpha_1 - \alpha_0)\frac{b}{b+\mathbb{I}}\Big]\mathbb{I}(z) - (\mu + \delta)\mathbb{R}(z), \\ \mathcal{A}^{\psi}_{m,l} &= (m-l)^{\psi}(m-l+1+\psi) - (m-l+1)^{\psi+1}, \\ \mathcal{B}^{\psi}_{m,l} &= (m-l+1)^{\psi}(m-l+2+\psi) - (m-l)^{\psi}(m-l+2+2\psi). \end{aligned}$$

6. SIR Model on COVID-19

A key strength of this model lies in its enhanced capabilities to simulate a range of real-world infectious disease scenarios. Specifically, the model incorporates the $\delta\mathbb{R}$ term (where δ represents the rate of immunity loss), thereby enabling the capture of diseases where protection following infection is not lifelong, such as influenza. In such cases, the model can effectively investigate the initial propagation of novel strains within a susceptible population, and providing insights into the effectiveness of early intervention strategies. Furthermore, the PCFD employs a flexible framework for capturing diverse memory and non-local effects within disease dynamics according to its power parameter p, and generalizes well-known fractional derivatives. Moreover, a density-dependent recovery rate, represented mathematically by $\Big[\alpha_0 + (\alpha_1 - \alpha_0)\frac{b}{b+\mathbb{I}}\Big]$, accounts for the impact of healthcare resource limitations, a feature particularly relevant for simulating outbreaks where access to medical care significantly influences outcomes. In this section, we illustrate the application and behavior of the SIR model using parameters representative of the COVID-19 pandemic (Table 2) to provide a concrete real-world example and motivate the use of this advanced fractional framework.

Here, we consider $z \in [0, 1000]$, and the values of parameters as in Table 2 with initial conditions $(\mathbb{S}_0, \mathbb{I}_0, \mathbb{R}_0) = (90, 40, 30)$. The complete code of simulations is provided in a GitHub repository via the link: https://github.com/Almalahi/COMPLETE-CODE-SIR-MODEL (accessed on 29 March 2025).

Table 2. Values of Model Parameters.

Parameter	Value	Units	Ref.
Λ	1.75	Individual/Time	[29]
β	0.01	(Individual · Time)$^{-1}$	[33]
μ	0.005	Time^{-1}	[29]
δ	0.04	Time^{-1}	[34]
α_0	0.2	Time^{-1}	[29]
α_1	0.21	Time^{-1}	[23]
b	0.3	Individual	[29]
γ	0.2	Time^{-1}	[35]

By these values, with PCFD model (1), we have Figures 5–7 present a graphical depiction of the $\mathbb{S}$, $\mathbb{I}$ and $\mathbb{R}$ with different fractional order of the PCFD model (1).

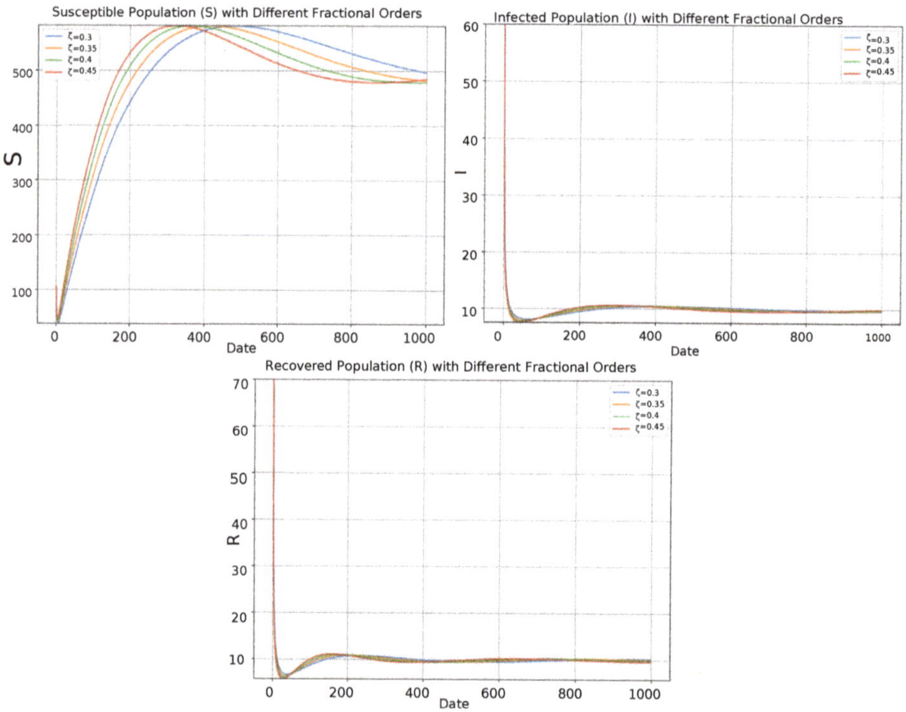

Figure 5. Graphical depiction of the Susceptible $\mathbb{S}$, Infected $\mathbb{I}$ and Recovered $\mathbb{R}$ classes with $p = 10$, $\psi = 2$ and $\zeta = 0.3, 0.35, 0.4, 0.45$ of the power-law Caputo fractional model.

These visualizations offer a direct view into the dynamic interplay of the three epidemiological classes in different cases, illustrating their temporal evolution.

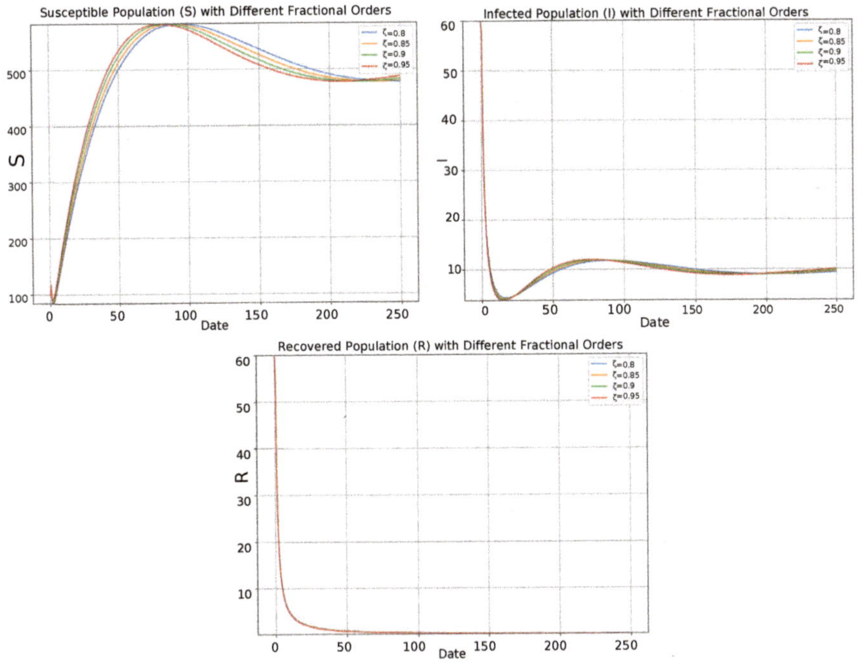

Figure 6. Graphical depiction of the Susceptible $\mathbb{S}$, Infected $\mathbb{I}$ and Recovered $\mathbb{R}$ classes with $p = 100$, $\psi = 2.5$ and $\zeta = 0.8, 0.85, 0.9, 0.95$ of the power-law Caputo fractional model.

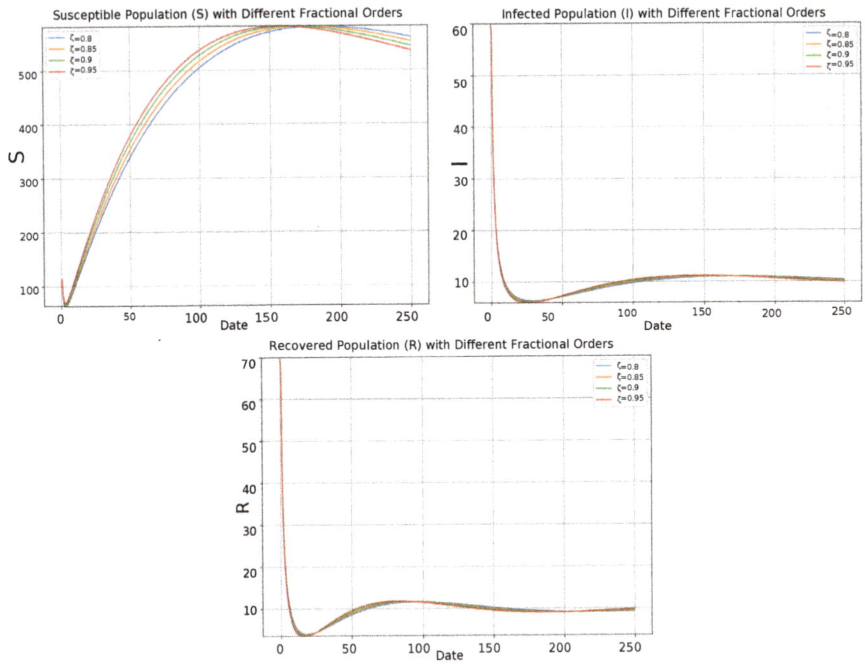

Figure 7. Graphical depiction of the Susceptible $\mathbb{S}$, Infected $\mathbb{I}$ and Recovered $\mathbb{R}$ classes with $p = 10$, $\psi = 2.5$ and $\zeta = 0.8, 0.85, 0.9, 0.95$ of the power-law Caputo fractional model.

7. Symmetric Cases of Model (1)

The fractional derivative employed within model (1) offers a high degree of generalization, encompassing several symmetric cases contingent upon the specific choices of its parameters ζ, ψ, the fractional derivative's power, p, and the weighting function, $w(z)$. In the ensuing subsections, we will explore and analyze simulations of these distinct symmetric scenarios, for comparison, to highlight the flexibility of the PCFD and illustrate the versatility and richness of the fractional model using the COVID-19 representative parameter set.

$\mathbb{SIR}$ COVID-19 Model with Caputo–Fabrizio Fractional Approach

If $w(z) = 1, p = e, \psi = 1$. Then, the model (1) reduce to the Caputo–Fabrizio fractional COVID-19 model given by

$$\begin{cases} {}^{\mathbb{PC}}_{a}\mathbf{D}^{\zeta,1,e}_{z,1}\mathbb{S}(z) = \Lambda - \frac{2\beta\mathbb{S}\mathbb{I}}{N} - \mu\mathbb{S} + \delta\mathbb{R}, \\ {}^{\mathbb{PC}}_{a}\mathbf{D}^{\zeta,1,e}_{z,1}\mathbb{I}(z) = \frac{2\beta\mathbb{S}\mathbb{I}}{N} - \left[\alpha_0 + (\alpha_1 - \alpha_0)\frac{b}{b+\mathbb{I}}\right]\mathbb{I} - (\gamma + \mu)\mathbb{I}, \\ {}^{\mathbb{PC}}_{a}\mathbf{D}^{\zeta,1,e}_{z,1}\mathbb{R}(z) = \left[\alpha_0 + (\alpha_1 - \alpha_0)\frac{b}{b+\mathbb{I}}\right]\mathbb{I} - (\mu + \delta)\mathbb{R}. \end{cases} \tag{14}$$

With the same parameter values in Table 2, the graphs of approximate solutions in case of Caputo–Fabrizio model (14) are given as follows:

Figures 8 and 9 provide a detailed graphical representation of the classes $\mathbb{S}$, $\mathbb{I}$, and $\mathbb{R}$, with $w(z) = 1, p = e, \psi = 1$. in different fractional order of the Caputo–Fabrizio fractional model (14).

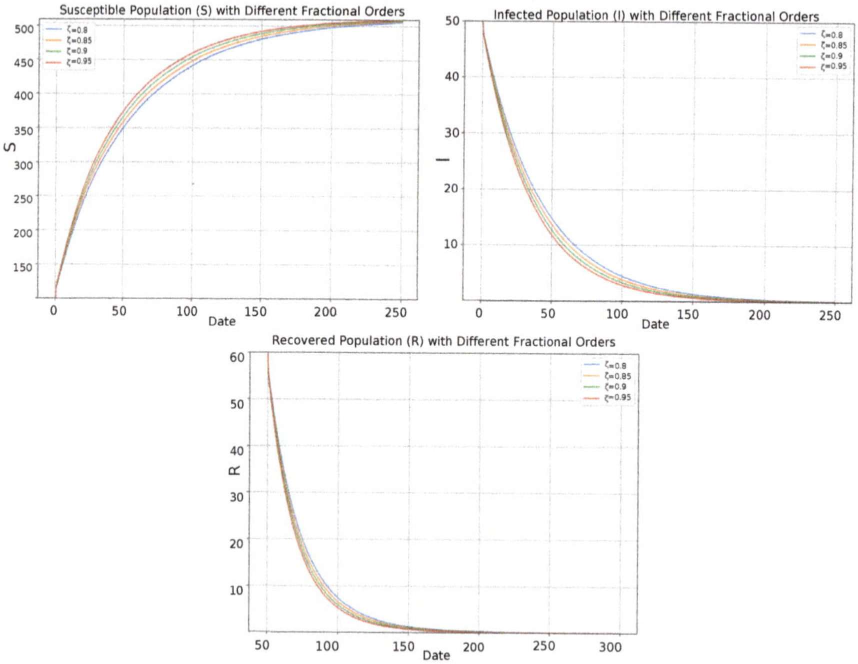

Figure 8. Graphical depiction of the Susceptible $\mathbb{S}$, Infected $\mathbb{I}$ and Recovered $\mathbb{R}$ classes as simulated by the Caputo–Fabrizio fractional model (14) with $w(z) = 1, p = e, \psi = 1$. and $\zeta = 0.8, 0.85, 0.9, 0.95$.

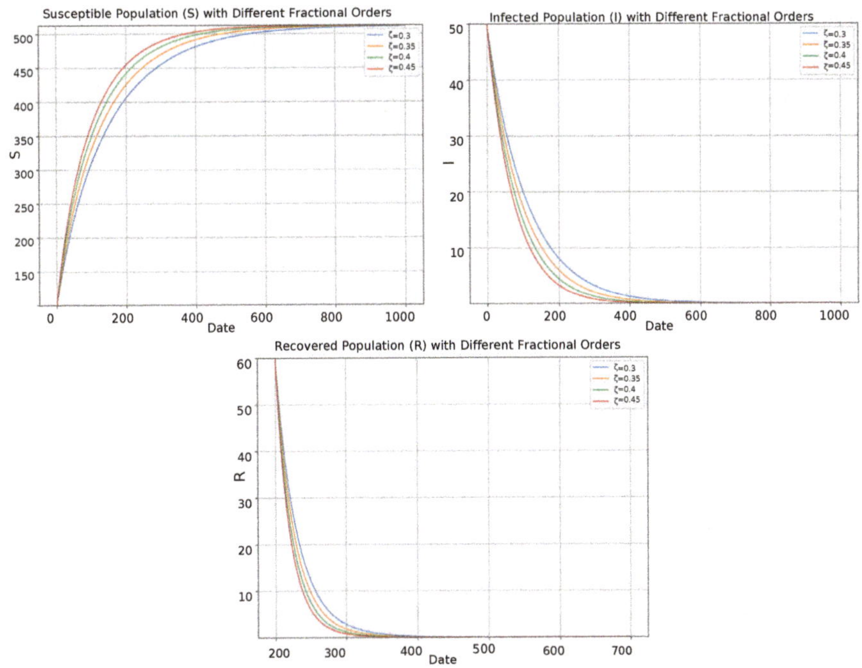

Figure 9. Graphical depiction of the Susceptible $\mathbb{S}$, Infected $\mathbb{I}$ and Recovered $\mathbb{R}$ classes as simulated by the Caputo–Fabrizio fractional model (14) with $w(z) = 1, p = e, \psi = 1.$ and $\zeta = 0.3, 0.35, 0.4, 0.45$.

$\mathbb{SIR}$ COVID-19 Model with Atangana–Baleanu Fractional Approach

If $w(z) = 1, p = e, \zeta = \psi$. Then, the model (1) reduce to the Atangana–Baleanu fractional COVID-19 model given by

$$\begin{cases} {}^{\mathbb{PC}}_{a}\mathbf{D}^{\zeta,\zeta,e}_{z,1}\mathbb{S}(z) = \Lambda - \frac{2\beta\mathbb{SI}}{N} - \mu\mathbb{S} + \delta\mathbb{R}, \\ {}^{\mathbb{PC}}_{a}\mathbf{D}^{\zeta,\zeta,e}_{z,1}\mathbb{I}(z) = \frac{2\beta\mathbb{SI}}{N} - \left[\alpha_0 + (\alpha_1 - \alpha_0)\frac{b}{b+\mathbb{I}}\right]\mathbb{I} - (\gamma + \mu)\mathbb{I}, \\ {}^{\mathbb{PC}}_{a}\mathbf{D}^{\zeta,\zeta,e}_{z,1}\mathbb{R}(z) = \left[\alpha_0 + (\alpha_1 - \alpha_0)\frac{b}{b+\mathbb{I}}\right]\mathbb{I} - (\mu + \delta)\mathbb{R}. \end{cases} \tag{15}$$

The graphs of approximate solutions of Atangana–Baleanu fractional model (15) are given as follows:

- Figure 10 provide a detailed graphical depiction of $\mathbb{S}$, $\mathbb{I}$, and $\mathbb{R}$ populations as simulated by the Atangana–Baleanu fractional model (15) with $w(z) = 1, p = e, \zeta = \psi$ and $\zeta = 0.3, 0.35, 0.4, 0.45$.

$\mathbb{SIR}$ COVID-19 Model with Weighted Atangana–Baleanu Fractional Approach

If $p = e, \zeta = \psi$. Then, the model (1) reduce to the weighted Atangana–Baleanu fractional model given by

$$\begin{cases} {}^{\mathbb{PC}}_{a}\mathbf{D}^{\zeta,\zeta,e}_{z,w}\mathbb{S}(z) = \Lambda - \frac{2\beta\mathbb{SI}}{N} - \mu\mathbb{S} + \delta\mathbb{R}, \\ {}^{\mathbb{PC}}_{a}\mathbf{D}^{\zeta,\zeta,e}_{z,w}\mathbb{I}(z) = \frac{2\beta\mathbb{SI}}{N} - \left[\alpha_0 + (\alpha_1 - \alpha_0)\frac{b}{b+\mathbb{I}}\right]\mathbb{I} - (\gamma + \mu)\mathbb{I}, \\ {}^{\mathbb{PC}}_{a}\mathbf{D}^{\zeta,\zeta,e}_{z,w}\mathbb{R}(z) = \left[\alpha_0 + (\alpha_1 - \alpha_0)\frac{b}{b+\mathbb{I}}\right]\mathbb{I} - (\mu + \delta)\mathbb{R}. \end{cases} \tag{16}$$

The graphs of approximate solutions of weighted Atangana–Baleanu fractional model (16) are given as follows:

- Figures 11 and 12 provide a detailed graphical depiction of $\mathbb{S}$, $\mathbb{I}$, and $\mathbb{R}$ populations as simulated by the weighted Atangana–Baleanu fractional model (16) with $w(z) = z+1$, $p = e, \zeta = \psi$ with different fractional order.

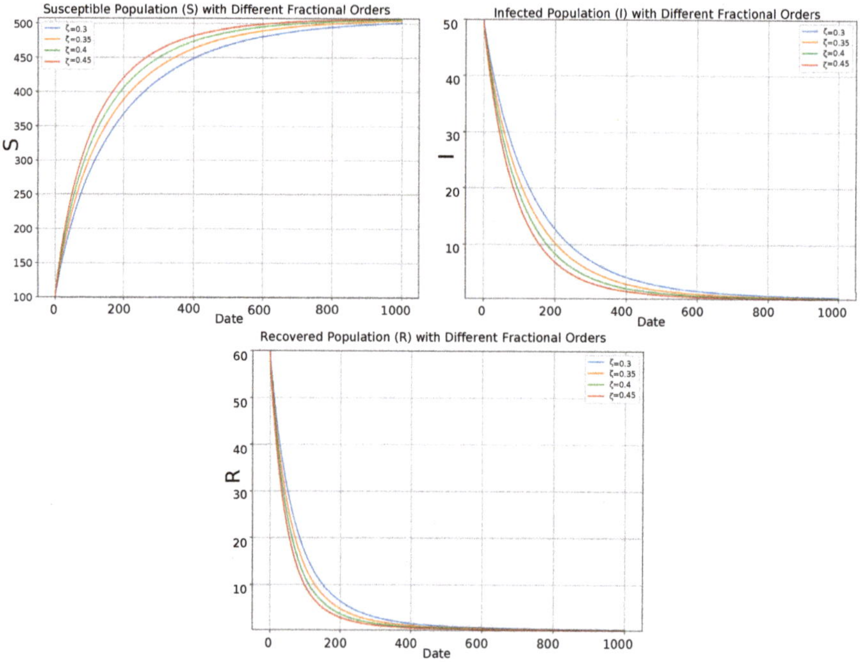

Figure 10. Graphical depiction of the Susceptible $\mathbb{S}$, Infected $\mathbb{I}$ and Recovered $\mathbb{R}$ classes as simulated by the Atangana–Baleanu fractional model (15) with $w(z) = 1, p = e, \zeta = \psi$ and $\zeta = 0.3, 0.35, 0.4, 0.45$.

$\mathbb{SIR}$ COVID-19 Model with Weighted Generalized Hattaf Fractional Approach

If $p = e$. Then, the model (1) reduce to the weighted generalized Hattaf fractional model given by

$$\begin{cases} {}^{\mathbb{PC}}_{a}\mathbf{D}^{\zeta,\psi,e}_{z,w}\mathbb{S}(z) = \Lambda - \frac{2\beta\mathbb{SI}}{N} - \mu\mathbb{S} + \delta\mathbb{R}, \\ {}^{\mathbb{PC}}_{a}\mathbf{D}^{\zeta,\psi,e}_{z,w}\mathbb{I}(z) = \frac{2\beta\mathbb{SI}}{N} - \left[\alpha_0 + (\alpha_1 - \alpha_0)\frac{b}{b+\mathbb{I}}\right]\mathbb{I} - (\gamma + \mu)\mathbb{I}, \\ {}^{\mathbb{PC}}_{a}\mathbf{D}^{\zeta,\psi,e}_{z,w}\mathbb{R}(z) = \left[\alpha_0 + (\alpha_1 - \alpha_0)\frac{b}{b+\mathbb{I}}\right]\mathbb{I} - (\mu + \delta)\mathbb{R}. \end{cases} \tag{17}$$

The graphs of approximate solutions of weighted generalized Hattaf fractional model (17) are given as follows:

Figures 13 and 14 provide a detailed graphical depiction of $\mathbb{S}$, $\mathbb{I}$, and $\mathbb{R}$ classes as simulated by the weighted generalized Hattaf fractional model (17) with $w(z) = z+1, p = e$ with different fractional order.

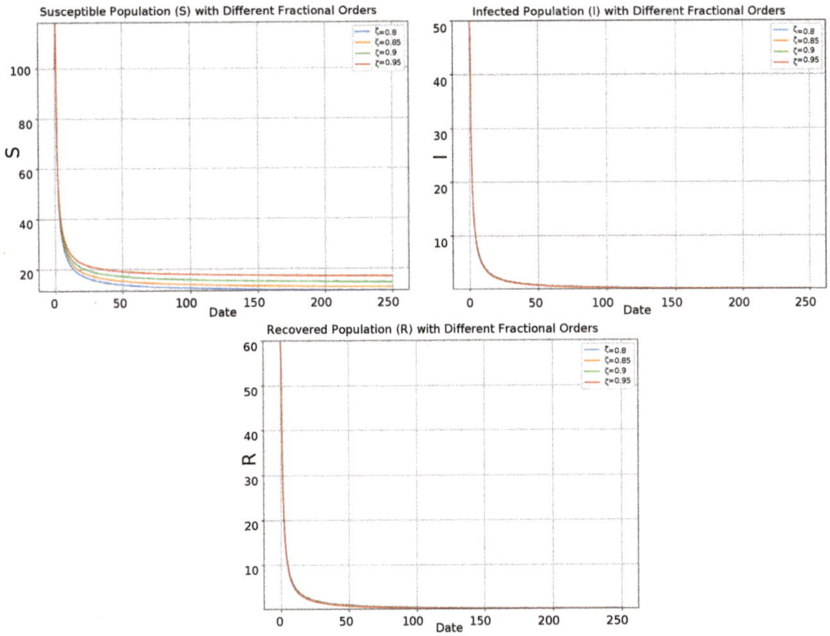

Figure 11. Graphical depiction of the Susceptible $\mathbb{S}$, Infected $\mathbb{I}$ and Recovered $\mathbb{R}$ classes as simulated by the weighted Atangana–Baleanu fractional model (16) with $w(z) = z + 1, p = e, \zeta = \psi$ and $\zeta = 0.8, 0.85, 0.9, 0.95$.

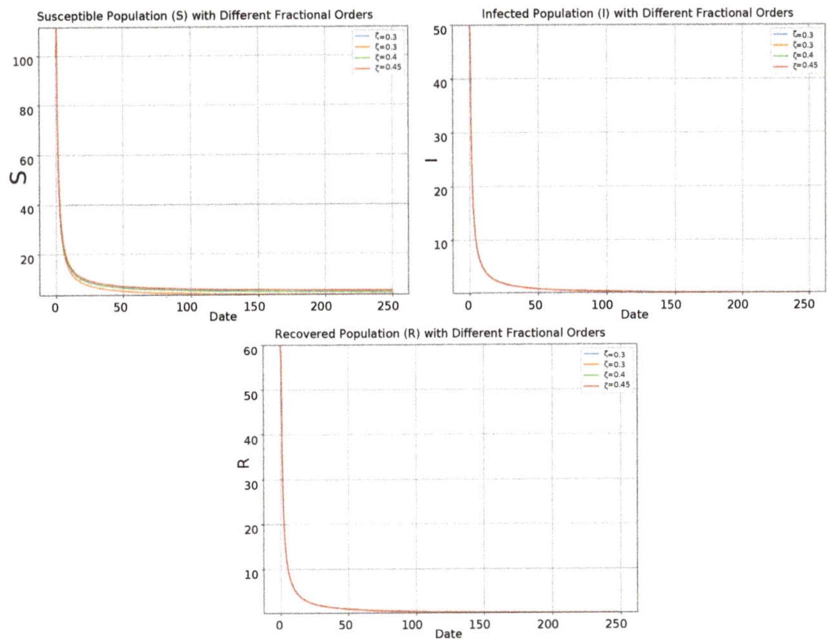

Figure 12. Graphical depiction of the Susceptible $\mathbb{S}$, Infected $\mathbb{I}$, and Recovered $\mathbb{R}$ classes as simulated by the weighted Atangana–Baleanu fractional model (16) with $p = e, \zeta = \psi$.

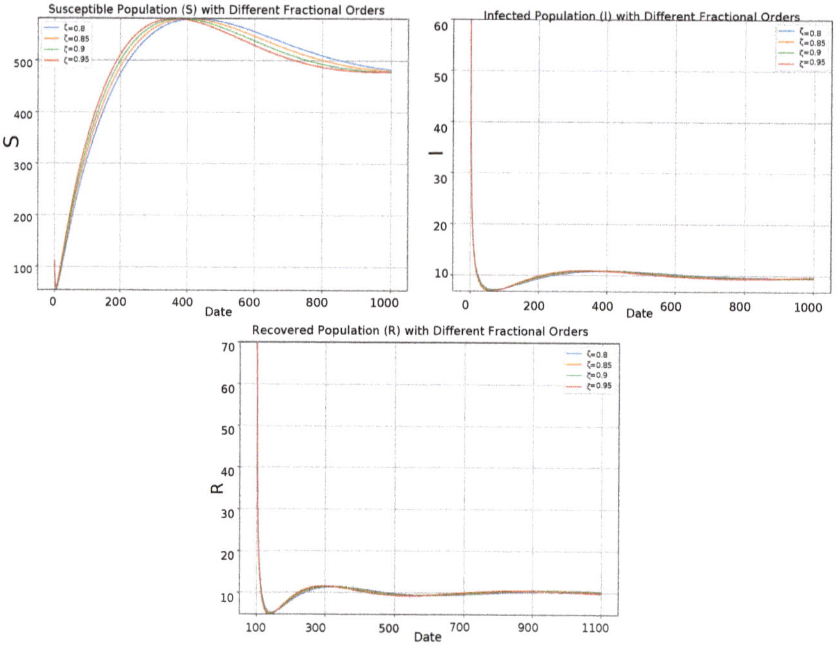

Figure 13. Graphical depiction of the Susceptible $\mathbb{S}$, Infected $\mathbb{I}$ and Recovered $\mathbb{R}$ classes as simulated by the weighted generalized Hattaf fractional model (17) with $w(z) = z+1, p = e$ and and $\zeta = 0.8, 0.85, 0.9, 0.95$.

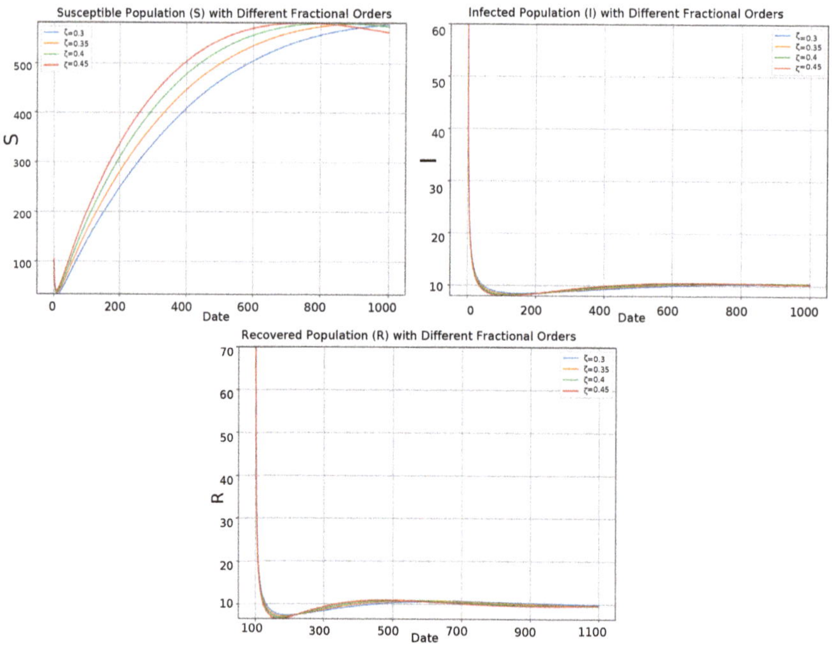

Figure 14. Graphical depiction of the Susceptible $\mathbb{S}$, Infected $\mathbb{I}$ and Recovered $\mathbb{R}$ classes as simulated by the weighted generalized Hattaf fractional model (17) with $w(z) = z+1, p = e$ and and $\zeta = 0.3, 0.35, 0.4, 0.45$.

Tables 3–7 address the comparison of fractional models and the standard integer-order SIR model against the "Actual COVID-19 Trend" characteristics.

Table 3. Comparative Evaluation Between Classical and power Fractional SIR Models vs. Actual COVID-19 Data (Duration for $\zeta = 0.85$ adjusted based on visual inspection of Figures 6 and 7).

Model Type	**Peak Inf. Time (days)**	**Max Infected Individuals**	**Epidemic Duration (days)**	**Alignment with Real Data**
Integer-order SIR [23,29]	35	48	~90	Moderate
Fractional SIR ($\zeta = 0.85$)	50	40	~150	High
Actual COVID-19 Trend [36]	50–55	~39–42	~130–140	—

Table 4. Caputo–Fabrizio SIR Model ($w(z) = 1, p = e, \psi = 1.$) vs. Actual COVID-19 Data.

Model Type	**Peak Inf. Time (days, approx.)**	**Max Infected (I_{max}, approx.)**	**Epidemic Duration (days, approx.)**	**Alignment with Real Data**
Integer-order SIR [23,29]	35	48	~90	Moderate
Fractional SIR (Caputo–Fabrizio, $\zeta = 0.85$) Figures 8 and 9	~40	~39	~130	High
Actual COVID-19 Trend [36]	50–55	~39–42	~130–140	—

Table 5. Atangana–Baleanu SIR Model ($w(z) = 1, p = e, \zeta = \psi.$) vs. Actual COVID-19 Data.

Model Type	**Peak Inf. Time (days, approx.)**	**Max Infected (I_{max}, approx.)**	**Epidemic Duration (days, approx.)**	**Alignment with Real Data**
Integer-order SIR [23,29]	35	48	~90	Moderate
Fractional SIR (Atangana–Baleanu, $\zeta = 0.45$) Figure 10	~35	~38	~250	Low to Moderate
Actual COVID-19 Trend [36]	50–55	~39–42	~130–140	—

Table 6. Weighted Atangana–Baleanu SIR Model ($w(z) = z + 1, p = e, \zeta = \psi$) vs. Actual COVID-19 Data.

Model Type	**Peak Inf. Time (days, approx.)**	**Max Infected (I_{max}, approx.)**	**Epidemic Duration (days, approx.)**	**Alignment with Real Data**
Integer-order SIR [23,29]	35	48	~90	Moderate
Fractional SIR (Weighted AB, $\zeta = 0.80$) Figures 11 and 12	~22	~40	~110	Low
Fractional SIR (Weighted AB, $\zeta = 0.45$) Figures 11 and 12	~45	~30	~250	Low
Actual COVID-19 Trend [36]	50–55	~39–42	~130–140	—

Table 7. Weighted Generalized Hattaf SIR Model ($w(z) = z + 1, p = e$) vs. Actual COVID-19 Data.

Model Type	**Peak Inf. Time (days, approx.)**	**Max Infected (I_{max}, approx.)**	**Epidemic Duration (days, approx.)**	**Alignment with Real Data**
Integer-order SIR [23,29]	35	48	~90	Moderate
Fractional SIR (Weighted Hattaf, $\zeta = 0.95$) Figures 13 and 14	~50	~40	~130	High
Actual COVID-19 Trend [36]	50–55	~39–42	~130–140	—

8. Discussion and Biological Interpretation

This study introduced a novel SIR model incorporating a generalized PCFD and applied it using parameters representative of the COVID-19 pandemic (Table 2) to provide a concrete real-world example and illustrate the potential of this advanced fractional framework. The simulation results, presented in Figures 5–14 and summarized comparatively in Tables 3–7, offer significant insights into how fractional calculus, particularly the flexible PCFD approach, can capture diverse epidemic dynamics. This section discusses the biological interpretation of these findings, evaluating the performance of different fractional derivatives against the standard integer-order model and benchmark characteristics derived from actual COVID-19 trends, thereby addressing the need to demonstrate the model's relevance and potential advantages through illustrative simulations.

Our analysis reveals that the choice of fractional derivative and its associated parameters $(\zeta, p, \psi, w(z))$ profoundly influences the predicted epidemic trajectory, even when using the same underlying parameter set (Table 2). This is clearly demonstrated in Tables 4–7, where different symmetric cases of the PCFD yield markedly different alignments with the benchmark COVID-19 trend. This highlights the importance of selecting an appropriate modeling framework and tuning its parameters carefully for specific applications. The fractional order, ζ, is particularly influential, primarily modulating the "memory" embedded in the system—how strongly past events influence present dynamics. The ability to adjust this memory effect via ζ is key to potentially achieving improved alignment with real-world data. For instance, compared to the baseline integer-order model which showed only moderate alignment (Tables 4–7), specific fractional models like Caputo–Fabrizio ($\zeta = 0.85$, Table 4) and Weighted Hattaf ($\zeta = 0.95$, Table 7) demonstrated high alignment, successfully capturing the peak timing, magnitude, and duration characteristics of the benchmark trend much more closely. This improved fit, as summarized in the overall comparison (Table 3), suggests that the memory effects implicit in these specific fractional orders better represent the underlying dynamics of the illustrative COVID-19 scenario than the standard derivative. Conversely, other fractional derivatives like Atangana–Baleanu (Table 5) and Weighted Atangana–Baleanu (Table 6) showed low alignment for the tested parameters, emphasizing that simply using any fractional derivative does not guarantee superiority.

The PCFD model, by its generalized nature encompassing these various forms, allows for tuning these elements, offering enhanced flexibility to potentially match specific disease characteristics more accurately than restrictive models. We now examine the behavior of each population compartment, interpreting the simulation results (Figures 5–14) in light of the comparative evaluation Tables:

- Susceptible Population ($\mathbb{S}$): As expected, $\mathbb{S}$ initially declines in all simulations. However, the rate of decline and subsequent recovery or stabilization varies significantly, impacting the overall epidemic duration and alignment score. Models achieving high alignment (Tables 4 and 7) exhibit $\mathbb{S}$ dynamics consistent with the benchmark epidemic duration (130–140 days), showing significant depletion by the peak infection time (e.g., $S \approx 220$ for CF, $S \approx 200$ for WGH at peak) and partial recovery towards the end ($S \approx 200$ for CF, $S \approx 180$ for WGH). In contrast, models with lower alignment, such as Atangana–Baleanu (Table 5), show dynamics (e.g., $S \approx 150$ at end) reflecting the much longer predicted epidemic duration ($\sim$250 days). The diversity in S-dynamics across Figures 5–14 illustrates the PCFD framework's capacity to represent varied scenarios, including those with potentially faster (e.g., Figure 11, WAB) or slower (e.g., Figure 10, AB) susceptibility changes compared to the benchmark.
- Infected Population ($\mathbb{I}$): The dynamics of the $\mathbb{I}$ compartment are central to the comparative evaluation. The benchmark trend showed a peak around 50–55 days with

a relative magnitude of ∼39–42 individuals. The integer-order model predicted an earlier (35 days) and higher (48 individuals) peak (Tables 4–7). Significantly, the Caputo–Fabrizio ($\zeta = 0.85$, Table 4) and Weighted Hattaf ($\zeta = 0.95$, Table 7) models closely matched the benchmark peak time (∼40/∼50 days) and magnitude (∼39/∼40 individuals). This successful replication highlights the potential of these fractional approaches (summarized in Table 3). In contrast, the Atangana–Baleanu model (Table 5) predicted an early peak (∼35 days), and the Weighted Atangana–Baleanu model (Table 6) predicted either a very early peak (∼22 days for $\zeta = 0.80$) or a lower peak magnitude (∼30 for $\zeta = 0.45$), both failing to align well with the benchmark $\mathbb{I}$ curve characteristics. The PCFD's ability to generalize allows it, in principle, to capture dynamics ranging from the well-aligned cases (like WGH) to the less aligned ones (like AB), depending on the chosen parameters $(p, \psi, w(z), \zeta)$. The modulation of peak characteristics via the fractional definition, combined with the density-dependent recovery term [30], is crucial for realistic simulation.

- Recovered Population ($\mathbb{R}$): The accumulation of the $\mathbb{R}$ population reflects the progression towards the end of the epidemic wave. In models with high alignment (Tables 4 and 7), the $\mathbb{R}$ curve rises steadily and approaches its plateau around the benchmark duration of 130–140 days (reaching $R \approx 160$ for CF, $R \approx 180$ for WGH). This contrasts sharply with models showing poor duration alignment, like Atangana–Baleanu (Table 5), where the $\mathbb{R}$ population continues to rise significantly beyond 140 days, reaching $R \approx 210$ only around 250 days. The diverse shapes of the R curves in Figures 5–14 again showcase the flexibility conferred by the fractional derivative choice, influencing factors like apparent recovery speed and the final proportion recovered within a given timeframe, relevant to understanding immunity accumulation [33].

In conclusion, this section explicitly addressed the need for demonstrating the real-world relevance and motivation of the proposed PCFD SIR model through comparative evaluation (Table 3). By applying the model using COVID-19 representative parameters (Table 2) and comparing the outcomes against a benchmark trend (Tables 4–7), we have shown that specific fractional derivatives generalized by the PCFD (namely Caputo–Fabrizio and Weighted Hattaf under the tested conditions) can offer superior alignment compared to the standard integer-order model. The primary motivation for using the generalized PCFD framework lies in its inherent flexibility to capture a wider spectrum of dynamics—particularly varying memory effects influencing transmission, peak characteristics, and recovery patterns—than is possible with standard integer-order models or single fixed fractional derivatives. The results clearly indicate that the choice of fractional derivative significantly impacts predicted epidemic dynamics, and careful selection or fitting is crucial. The comparative tables strongly suggest that the PCFD approach offers a valuable and adaptable tool for exploring.

9. Conclusions

This study introduced and analyzed a novel fractional Susceptible-Infected-Recovered (SIR) model incorporating PCFD and a density-dependent recovery rate reflecting healthcare capacity constraints. We proved solutions' boundedness and positivity, analysed the stability of the disease-free equilibrium, derived an explicit formula for the basic reproduction number (R_0), and conducted a sensitivity analysis. The analysis confirms the biological plausibility of the model and reveals the dominant influence of the transmission rate (β) on R_0. Numerical simulations vividly demonstrate the significant impact of the fractional order (ζ) on crucial epidemic characteristics, such as peak timing and severity. This highlights a core strength and challenge of fractional modeling: the choice of derivative and its associated parameters—the fractional order ζ, the power parameters p and ψ, and the weighting function $w(z)$—collectively determine the type and strength of memory embedded within the model. These choices profoundly influence predicted epidemic dynamics in simulation, modulating how past events shape current infection rates, recovery processes, and mortality, thereby substantially altering projections of epidemic spread, peak characteristics, and overall duration. For instance, lower fractional orders generally emphasize longer-term historical dynamics, while higher orders prioritize more recent events. The PCFD framework's generality, encompassing specific derivatives like Caputo–Fabrizio, Atangana–Baleanu, and generalized Hattaf (including weighted variants) as special cases, offers significant flexibility. However, this underscores the critical importance of selecting or fitting these fractional parameters appropriately for specific disease contexts, as different choices lead to distinct predictions in model outputs. Furthermore, the model's inclusion of detailed recovery pathways (both dependent on and independent of healthcare intervention) and an infection-induced death rate enhances its realism in representing diverse disease outcomes and the impact of healthcare systems. The comparison Tables 3–7 demonstrates that models incorporating fractional derivatives—particularly the Caputo–Fabrizio (CF) and weighted generalized Hattaf (WGH) cases—yield predictions that are more consistent with observed data in terms of peak infection timing and total case count. The advantage of fractional-order derivatives over classical models lies in their inherent ability to capture memory and hereditary properties of the infection dynamics. This allows the model to account for the influence of historical infection rates on current behavior—something integer-order models fundamentally lack. As seen in our simulations and comparative analysis, fractional models adjust more effectively to real-world outbreak patterns, thereby offering superior descriptive and predictive power. One of the unique strengths of our approach is the use of the Power Caputo Fractional Derivative (PCFD), which serves as a unifying operator encompassing various well-known fractional derivatives as special cases. This flexibility not only provides a broader mathematical foundation but also allows the model to be calibrated based on specific memory kernels suited to different types of epidemics. Such generality enhances the model's adaptability across a spectrum of diseases with varying temporal characteristics.. Future work will focus on extending this model to incorporate spatial dynamics and age-structured populations, as well as calibrating and validating the model against specific real-world epidemiological time-series data, aiming to further enhance its utility for detailed epidemic forecasting and control.

Author Contributions: Conceptualization, M.S.A. and M.A.; methodology, M.A.; software, M.A.; formal analysis, M.S.; investigation, A.S.A. and F.A.A.; writing—original draft preparation, M.A.; writing—review and editing, M.S., K.A. and B.Y.; visualization, F.A.A.; supervision, M.A. and K.A.; project administration, K.A.; funding acquisition, M.S. All authors have read and agreed to the published version of the manuscript.

Funding: This research received no external funding.

Data Availability Statement: All data used in this work are contained within the article.

Acknowledgments: The Researchers would like to thank the Deanship of Graduate Studies and Scientific Research at Qassim University for financial support (QU-APC-2025).

Conflicts of Interest: There are no conflicts of interest declared by the authors.

References

1. Marinov, T.T.; Marinova, R.S. Adaptive SIR model with vaccination: Simultaneous identification of rates and functions illustrated with COVID-19. *Sci. Rep.* **2022**, *12*, 15688. [CrossRef]
2. Balderrama, R.; Peressutti, J.; Pinasco, J.P.; Vazquez, F.; Vega, C.S.D.L. Optimal control for a SIR epidemic model with limited quarantine. *Sci. Rep.* **2022**, *12*, 12583. [CrossRef] [PubMed]
3. El Khalifi, M.; Britton, T. SIRS epidemics with individual heterogeneity of immunity waning. *J. Theor. Biol.* **2022**, *587*, 111815. [CrossRef]
4. Podlubny, I. *Fractional Differential Equations*; Academic Press: San Diego, CA, USA, 1999.
5. Samko, S.G.; Kilbas, A.A.; Marichev, O.I. *Fractional Integrals and Derivatives*; Gordon & Breach: Yverdon, Switzerland, 1993.
6. Magin, R.L. *Fractional Calculus in Bioengineering*; Begell House: Redding, CA, USA, 2006.
7. Kilbas, A.A.; Srivastava, H.M.; Trujillo, J.J. *Theory and Applications of Fractional Differential Equations. North-Holland Mathematics Studies*; Elsevier: Amsterdam, The Netherlands, 2006.
8. Alqahtani, R.T. Mathematical model of SIR epidemic system (COVID-19) with fractional derivative: Stability and numerical analysis. *Adv. Differ. Equ.* **2021**, *2021*, 2. [CrossRef] [PubMed]
9. Kim, J. Influence of fractional order on the behavior of a normalized time-fractional SIR model. *Mathematics* **2024**, *12*, 3081. [CrossRef]
10. Riabi, L.; Hamdi Cherif, M.; Cattani, C. An Efficient Approach to Solving the Fractional SIR Epidemic Model with the Atangana–Baleanu-Caputo Fractional Operator. *Fractal Fract.* **2023**, *7*, 618. [CrossRef]
11. Alazman, I.; Mishra, M.N.; Alkahtani, B.S.; Dubey, R.S. Analysis of infection and diffusion coefficient in an sir model by using generalized fractional derivative. *Fractal Fract.* **2024**, *8*, 537. [CrossRef]
12. Hilfer, R. (Ed.) *Applications of Fractional Calculus in Physics*; World Scientific: Singapore, 2000.
13. Das, S. Application of generalized fractional calculus in electrical circuit analysis and electromagnetics. In *Functional Fractional Calculus*; Springer: Berlin/Heidelberg, Germany, 2011; pp. 387–436.
14. Oldham, K.B. Fractional differential equations in electrochemistry. *Adv. Eng. Softw.* **2010**, *41*, 9–12. [CrossRef]
15. Chávez-Vázquez, S.; Gómez-Aguilar, J.F.; Lavín-Delgado, J.E.; Escobar-Jiménez, R.F.; Olivares-Peregrino, V.H. Applications of fractional operators in robotics: A review. *J. Intell. Robot. Syst.* **2022**, *104*, 63. [CrossRef]
16. Ali, Z.; Nia, S.N.; Rabiei, F.; Shah, K.; Tan, M.K. A Semianalytical Approach to the Solution of Time-Fractional Navier-Stokes Equation. *Adv. Math. Phys.* **2021**, *2021*, 5547804. [CrossRef]
17. Tarasov, V.E. *Fractional Dynamics: Applications of Fractional Calculus to Dynamics of Particles, Fields and Media*; Springer Science and Business Media: Berlin, Germany, 2011.
18. Matušů, R. Application of fractional-order calculus to control theory. *Int. J. Math. Model. Methods Appl. Sci.* **2011**, *5*, 1162–1169.
19. Ali, Z. Theoretical and Computational Study of Fractional-Order Mathematical Models for Infectious Diseases. Doctoral Dissertation, Monash University, Melbourne, Australia, 2023.
20. Aldwoah, K.A.; Almalahi, M.A.; Shah, K. Theoretical and numerical simulations on the hepatitis B virus model through a piecewise fractional order. *Fractal Fract.* **2023**, *7*, 844. [CrossRef]
21. Alraqad, T.; Almalahi, M.A.; Mohammed, N.; Alahmade, A.; Aldwoah, K.A.; Saber, H. Modeling Ebola Dynamics with a Φ-Piecewise Hybrid Fractional Derivative Approach. *Fractal Fract.* **2024**, *8*, 596. [CrossRef]
22. Saber, H.; Almalahi, M.A.; Albala, H.; Aldwoah, K.; Alsulami, A.; Shah, K.; Moumen, A. Investigating a Nonlinear Fractional Evolution Control Model Using W-Piecewise Hybrid Derivatives: An Application of a Breast Cancer Model. *Fractal Fract.* **2024**, *8*, 735. [CrossRef]
23. Alshammari, F.S.; Khan, M.A. Dynamic behaviors of a modified SIR model with nonlinear incidence and recovery rates. *Alex. Eng. J.* **2021**, *60*, 2997–3005. [CrossRef]
24. Lotfi, E.M.; Zine, H.; Torres, D.F.; Yousfi, N. The power fractional calculus: First definitions and properties with applications to power fractional differential equations. *Mathematics* **2022**, *10*, 3594. [CrossRef]
25. Caputo, M.; Fabrizio, M. A new definition of fractional derivative without singular kernel. *Prog. Fract. Differ. Appl.* **2015**, *1*, 73–85.
26. Atangana, A.; Baleanu, D. New fractional derivatives with non-local and non-singular kernel: Theory and application to heat transfer model. *Therm. Sci.* **2016**, *20*, 763–769. [CrossRef]
27. Al-Refai, M. On weighted Atangana–Baleanu fractional operators. *Adv. Differ. Equ.* **2020**, *2020*, 3. [CrossRef]
28. Hattaf, K. A new generalized definition of fractional derivative with non-singular kernel. *Computation* **2020**, *8*, 49. [CrossRef]
29. Chawla, S.R.; Ahmad, S.; Khan, A.; Albalawi, W.; Nisar, K.S.; Ali, H.M. Stability analysis and optimal control of a generalized SIR epidemic model with harmonic mean type of incidence and nonlinear recovery rates. *Alex. Eng. J.* **2024**, *97*, 44–60. [CrossRef]
30. Shan, C.; Zhu, H. Bifurcations and complex dynamics of an SIR model with the impact of the number of hospital beds. *J. Differ. Equ.* **2014**, *257*, 1662–1688. [CrossRef]
31. Zitane, H.; Torres, D.F. A class of fractional differential equations via power non-local and non-singular kernels: Existence, uniqueness and numerical approximations. *Phys. D Nonlinear Phenom.* **2024**, *457*, 133951. [CrossRef]

32. Gassem, F.; Almalahi, M.; Osman, O.; Muflh, B.; Aldwoah, K.; Kamel, A.; Eljaneid, N. Nonlinear Fractional Evolution Control Modeling via Power Non-Local Kernels: A Generalization of Caputo–Fabrizio, Atangana–Baleanu, and Hattaf Derivatives. *Fractal. Fract.* **2025**, *9*, 104.
33. Lipsitch, M.; Krammer, F.; Regev-Yochay, G.; Lustig, Y.; Balicer, R.D. SARS-CoV-2 breakthrough infections in vaccinated individuals: Measurement, causes and impact. *Nat. Rev. Immunol.* **2022**, *22*, 57–65. [CrossRef]
34. Cromer, D.; Steain, M.; Reynaldi, A.; Schlub, T.E.; Wheatley, A.K.; Juno, J.A.; Kent, S.J.; Triccas, J.A.; Khoury, D.S.; Davenport, M.P. Neutralizing antibody titres as predictors of protection against SARS-CoV-2 variants and the impact of boosting: A meta-analysis. *Lancet Microbe* **2022**, *3*, e52–e61. [CrossRef] [PubMed]
35. Verity, R.; Okell, L.C.; Dorigatti, I.; Winskill, P.; Whittaker, C.; Imai, N.; Ferguson, N.M. Estimates of the severity of COVID-19 disease. *Lancet Infect. Dis.* **2020**, *20*, 669–677. [CrossRef] [PubMed]
36. World Health Organization. WHO COVID-19 Dashboard-WHO Data. Available online: https://data.who.int/dashboards/covid19/cases (accessed on 23 March 2025).

fractal and fractional

MDPI

Article

Pell and Pell–Lucas Sequences of Fractional Order

Jagan Mohan Jonnalagadda [1] and Marius-F. Danca [2,3,*]

1 Department of Mathematics, Birla Institute of Technology & Science Pilani, Hyderabad 500078, Telangana, India; jjaganmohan@hyderabad.bits-pilani.ac.in
2 STAR-UBB Institute, Babes-Bolyai University, 400084 Cluj-Napoca, Romania
3 Romanian Institute of Science and Technology, 400487 Cluj-Napoca, Romania
* Correspondence: m.f.danca@gmail.com

Abstract: The purpose of this paper is to introduce the fractional Pell numbers, together with several properties, via a Grünwald–Letnikov fractional operator of orders $q \in (0,1)$ and $q \in (1,2)$. This paper also explores the fractional Pell–Lucas numbers and their properties. Due to the long-term memory property, fractional Pell sequences and fractional Pell–Lucas sequences present potential applications in modeling and computation. The closed form is deduced, and the numerical schemes are determined. The fractional characteristic equation is introduced, and it is shown that its solutions include a fractional silver ratio depending on the fractional order. In addition, the tiling problem and the concept of the fractional silver spiral are considered. A MATLAB program for applying the use of the fractional silver ratio is presented.

Keywords: Grünwald–Letnikov fractional operator; fractional Pell numbers; fractional Pell–Lucas numbers; fractional characteristic equation; fractional silver ratio

1. Introduction

The Pell numbers are named after English mathematician John Pell (1611–1685). Details about Pell can be found in, e.g., [1–3], while some properties can be found in [4]. Pell numbers may be calculated by means of a recurrence relation similar to that for the Fibonacci numbers. Pell–Lucas numbers, or companion Pell numbers, are defined similarly to the Pell numbers by recurrence relation, the difference consisting of the initial condition.

Background on fractional calculus and fractional differences can be found in, e.g., [5–8], while an appropriate bibliography for the fractional q-calculus is provided in [9].

This paper continues the work started in [10], where the Fibonacci's numbers of fractional order were introduced and analyzed.

The Fibonacci numbers are the most famous example of a linear recurrence relation. Both the Fibonacci and Pell sequences are interesting recursively defined sequences, but they differ significantly in their prominence and application across different fields. So, compared with Pell sequences that arise in number theory, particularly in Pell's equation $x^2 - 2y^2 = 1$, or continuous fractions of square roots, Fibonacci sequences have far wider and deeper mathematical exposure (e.g., in number theory, combinatorics, algebra, and geometry). Also, in computer science, Fibonacci's numbers are common in algorithm design and data structures and used in teaching recursion, dynamic programming, and time complexity, while Pell's numbers might be used only in niche recurrence problems compared to Fibonacci's numbers. These sequences serve as benchmarks for solving recurrence relations (e.g., via characteristic equations). They illustrate the impact of initial conditions and coefficients on closed-form solutions. However, in domains like number theory, continuous fractions, cryptography, algebraic number theory, and theoretical physics,

Fibonacci sequences are more widespread. Fractional Pell sequences serve as recursive structures for developing fractional difference methods with better accuracy in modeling anomalous dynamics. They can help to generate generalized orthogonal polynomials for spectral methods, which are helpful in numerical PDE solvers. Fractional Pell sequences possess long-term memory due to fractional-order recursions. So, they can be applied in viscoelastic materials, anomalous diffusion, fractional-order delay systems, wave propagation in fractal media, biological growth and branching processes, as well as in neural networks, viscoelastic materials, epidemiology, and finance. These sequences can also solve fractional dynamic equations on time scales, giving rise to new special functions and stability behaviors. Introducing fractional versions of Fibonacci and Pell numbers enables new analytical tools and models in discrete fractional calculus. However, their usefulness would depend on whether they provide meaningful insights or solve problems that classical discrete sequences cannot.

Some of the properties of Pell's numbers have been shown to be demonstrable by the fractional approach, such as the property that the silver ratio can be expressed as the ratio of two consecutive Pell numbers, the deduction of the characteristic equation generating the fractional silver ratio, or the deduction of the closed (explicit) form of fractional Pell numbers. Similarly to the fractional golden ratio determined via the fractional Fibonacci numbers, where the fractional golden spiral is used to cover the tiling with fractional Fibonacci numbers, the fractional Pell numbers are used to generate the fractional silver spiral covering a square tiling. While previous studies [11,12] showed that the generalization of discrete systems via a fractional approach breaks the symmetry, in this article, it is shown that the symmetry is not destroyed by the use of a silver ratio or golden ratio of fractional order.

Among the various definitions for fractional differences, the most widely used are the Grünwald–Letnikov, the Riemann–Liouville, and the Caputo definitions. Among the three definitions, the Grünwald–Letnikov definition, which stems from the limitation of integer-order difference, plays an outstanding role in numerical calculation. It also provides the discrete approximation of a fractional derivative. Moreover, the definitions for fractional sum and differences can be expressed in a unified manner. The Caputo approach is equivalent to the Grünwald–Letnikov approach in the case of homogeneous initial conditions. However, in the case of inhomogeneous initial conditions, both approaches are not the same (in the context of fractional sequences and their applications; see, e.g., [13–19]).

This paper is structured as follows: Section 2 presents the utilized notions in the paper; Section 3 introduces the fractional Pell numbers with the closed explicit form, the numerical scheme, the fractional silver ratio, and some related properties; Section 4 deals with the fractional Pell–Lucas numbers, explicit form, and numerical scheme; Section 5 concludes the manuscript; and Appendix A presents a MATLAB (https://www.mathworks.com/products/matlab.html, accessed on 21 June 2025) script generating a pinecone.

2. Preliminaries

We shall use the following fundamentals of discrete fractional calculus throughout the article. For any $a \in \mathbb{R}$, denote by $\mathbb{N}_a = \{a, a+1, a+2, \ldots\}$.

Definition 1 ([20])**.** *The Pell numbers are defined by the recurrence relation*

$$P(0) = 0, \quad P(1) = 1, \tag{1}$$
$$P(n+2) = P(n) + 2P(n+1), \quad n \in \mathbb{N}_0. \tag{2}$$

The first terms are

$$0, 1, 2, 5, 12, 29, 70, 169, 408, 985, 2378, 5741, 13860, \ldots$$

Definition 2 ([20])**.** *The Pell–Lucas numbers are defined by the recurrence relation*

$$Q(0) = 2, \quad Q(1) = 2, \tag{3}$$
$$Q(n+2) = Q(n) + 2Q(n+1), \quad n \in \mathbb{N}_0, \tag{4}$$

with the first terms

$$2, 2, 6, 14, 34, 82, 198, 478, 1154, 2786, 6726, 16238, 39202, \ldots$$

Definition 3 ([21])**.** *Let $u : \mathbb{N}_a \to \mathbb{R}$. The first-order nabla difference of u is defined by*

$$\nabla u(n) = u(n) - u(n-1), \quad n \in \mathbb{N}_{a+1},$$

and the second-order nabla difference of u is defined by

$$\nabla^2 u(n) = u(n) - 2u(n-1) + u(n-2), \quad n \in \mathbb{N}_{a+2}.$$

Definition 4 ([7])**.** *The Euler gamma function is defined by*

$$\Gamma(z) = \int_0^\infty e^{-s} s^{z-1} ds, \quad \Re(z) > 0.$$

Using the reduction formula

$$\Gamma(z+1) = z\Gamma(z), \quad \Re(z) > 0,$$

the Euler gamma function can also be extended to the half-plane $\Re(z) \leq 0$, except for $z \in \{\ldots, -2, -1, 0\}$.

Definition 5 ([22])**.** *Let $u : \mathbb{N}_a \to \mathbb{R}$ and $\nu \in \mathbb{R}$. The νth Grünwald–Letnikov fractional difference/sum of u based on a is given by*

$$\nabla_a^\nu u(n) = \frac{1}{\Gamma(-\nu)} \sum_{s=a}^{n} \frac{\Gamma(n-s-\nu)}{\Gamma(n-s+1)} u(s), \quad n \in \mathbb{N}_a.$$

3. Fractional Pell Sequence

A two-dimensional system of linear difference equations that describes (2) is

$$\begin{pmatrix} P(n+2) \\ P(n+1) \end{pmatrix} = \begin{pmatrix} 2 & 1 \\ 1 & 0 \end{pmatrix} \begin{pmatrix} P(n+1) \\ P(n) \end{pmatrix}, \quad n \in \mathbb{N}_0.$$

Then,

$$\begin{pmatrix} \nabla P(n+2) \\ \nabla P(n+1) \end{pmatrix} = \begin{pmatrix} 1 & 1 \\ 1 & -1 \end{pmatrix} \begin{pmatrix} P(n+1) \\ P(n) \end{pmatrix}, \quad n \in \mathbb{N}_0.$$

Consequently, we have the following initial value problem

$$\nabla \bar{P}(n) = A\bar{P}(n-1), \quad n \in \mathbb{N}_1, \tag{5}$$

$$\bar{P}(0) = \bar{P}_0, \tag{6}$$

associated with the Pell numbers. Here,

$$\bar{P}(n) = \begin{pmatrix} P(n+1) \\ P(n) \end{pmatrix},$$

$$A = \begin{pmatrix} 1 & 1 \\ 1 & -1 \end{pmatrix},$$

$$\bar{P}_0 = \begin{pmatrix} P(1) \\ P(0) \end{pmatrix} = \begin{pmatrix} 1 \\ 0 \end{pmatrix}.$$

Now, for $0 < q < 1$, we consider the qth-order difference equation

$$\nabla_0^q \bar{x}(n) = A\bar{x}(n-1), \quad n \in \mathbb{N}_1, \tag{7}$$

together with the initial condition

$$\bar{x}(0) = \begin{pmatrix} 1 \\ 0 \end{pmatrix}, \tag{8}$$

analogous to (5) and (6). Here,

$$\bar{x}(n) = \begin{pmatrix} x(n+1) \\ x(n) \end{pmatrix}, \quad A = \begin{pmatrix} 1 & 1 \\ 1 & -1 \end{pmatrix}.$$

3.1. *The Solution of the Initial Value Problem (7) and (8)*

Theorem 1. *The unique solution of (7) and (8) is given by*

$$\bar{x}(n) = \sum_{k=0}^{n} A^k \frac{\Gamma(n-k+kq+q)}{\Gamma(n-k+1)\Gamma(kq+q)} \bar{x}(0), \quad n \in \mathbb{N}_0. \tag{9}$$

Proof. Denote by

$$u(n) = \sum_{k=0}^{n} A^k \frac{\Gamma(n-k+kq+q)}{\Gamma(n-k+1)\Gamma(kq+q)}, \quad n \in \mathbb{N}_0.$$

First, we show that u satisfies the fractional difference equation

$$\nabla_0^q u(n) = Au(n-1), \quad n \in \mathbb{N}_1. \tag{10}$$

To see this, for $n \in \mathbb{N}_1$, consider

$$\begin{aligned}
\nabla_0^q u(n) &= \frac{1}{\Gamma(-q)} \sum_{s=0}^{n} \frac{\Gamma(n-s-q)}{\Gamma(n-s+1)} u(s) \quad \text{(By Definition 5)} \\
&= \frac{1}{\Gamma(-q)} \sum_{s=0}^{n} \frac{\Gamma(n-s-q)}{\Gamma(n-s+1)} \left[\sum_{k=0}^{s} A^k \frac{\Gamma(s-k+kq+q)}{\Gamma(s-k+1)\Gamma(kq+q)} \right] \\
&= \sum_{k=0}^{n} A^k \left[\sum_{s=k}^{n} \frac{\Gamma(n-s-q)}{\Gamma(n-s+1)\Gamma(-q)} \frac{\Gamma(s-k+kq+q)}{\Gamma(s-k+1)\Gamma(kq+q)} \right] \\
&= \sum_{k=0}^{n} A^k \frac{\Gamma(n-k+kq)}{\Gamma(n-k+1)\Gamma(kq)} \\
&= \sum_{k=1}^{n} A^k \frac{\Gamma(n-k+kq)}{\Gamma(n-k+1)\Gamma(kq)} \\
&= A \sum_{k=0}^{n-1} A^k \frac{\Gamma(n-1-k+kq+q)}{\Gamma(n-1-k+1)\Gamma(kq+q)} \\
&= Au(n-1),
\end{aligned}$$

implying that (10) holds. Therefore, any solution of (7) is of the form

$$\bar{x}(n) = u(n)c, \quad n \in \mathbb{N}_0,$$

where c is any constant vector. Since $u(0) = I$, we obtain $c = \bar{x}(0)$. Thus, the unique solution of the initial value problem (7) and (8) is given by (9). □

3.2. Closed-Form Expression of Fractional Pell Sequence

The following result is the generalization of Binet's formula for the fractional Pell numbers.

Theorem 2. *The closed-form expression of the fractional Pell sequence is given by*

$$x(n) = \frac{1}{2\varphi} \sum_{k=0}^{n} \left[\varphi^k - (-\varphi)^k \right] \frac{\Gamma(n-k+kq+q)}{\Gamma(n-k+1)\Gamma(kq+q)}, \quad n \in \mathbb{N}_0.$$

Here, $\varphi = \sqrt{2}$.

Proof. The eigenvalues of A are φ and $-\varphi$. The corresponding eigenvectors are $\begin{pmatrix} 1 \\ \varphi - 1 \end{pmatrix}$ and $\begin{pmatrix} 1 \\ -\varphi - 1 \end{pmatrix}$, respectively. Now, we diagonalize the matrix A through the use of its eigendecomposition:

$$A = S\Omega S^{-1},$$

and

$$A^k = S\Omega^k S^{-1}, \quad k = 1, 2, \cdots, n,$$

where

$$\Omega = \begin{pmatrix} \varphi & 0 \\ 0 & -\varphi \end{pmatrix}, \quad S = \begin{pmatrix} 1 & 1 \\ \varphi - 1 & -\varphi - 1 \end{pmatrix}.$$

Consequently, from (9), we have

$$\bar{x}(n) = \sum_{k=0}^{n} \left[S\Omega^k S^{-1} \bar{x}(0) \right] \frac{\Gamma(n-k+kq+q)}{\Gamma(n-k+1)\Gamma(kq+q)}, \quad n \in \mathbb{N}_0.$$

For $k = 0, 1, \cdots, n$, consider

$$\begin{aligned} S\Omega^k S^{-1} &= \begin{pmatrix} 1 & 1 \\ \varphi - 1 & -\varphi - 1 \end{pmatrix} \begin{pmatrix} \varphi & 0 \\ 0 & -\varphi \end{pmatrix}^k \begin{pmatrix} 1 & 1 \\ \varphi - 1 & -\varphi - 1 \end{pmatrix}^{-1} \\ &= -\frac{1}{2\varphi} \begin{pmatrix} 1 & 1 \\ \varphi - 1 & -\varphi - 1 \end{pmatrix} \begin{pmatrix} \varphi^k & 0 \\ 0 & (-\varphi)^k \end{pmatrix} \begin{pmatrix} -\varphi - 1 & -1 \\ -\varphi + 1 & 1 \end{pmatrix}. \end{aligned}$$

Since $\bar{x}(n) = \begin{pmatrix} x(n+1) \\ x(n) \end{pmatrix}$, the closed form, which is an explicit expression for the nth element in the fractional Pell sequence, is given by

$$x(n) = \frac{1}{2\varphi} \sum_{k=0}^{n} \left[\varphi^k - (-\varphi)^k \right] \frac{\Gamma(n-k+kq+q)}{\Gamma(n-k+1)\Gamma(kq+q)},$$

for $n \in \mathbb{N}_0$. □

Remark 1. *For $q = 1$, we obtain the expression of the closed integer-order (IO) form for the nth element in Pell sequences* (1) *and* (2) *as follows:*

$$\begin{aligned} x(n) &= \frac{1}{2\varphi} \sum_{k=0}^{n} \left[\varphi^k - (-\varphi)^k \right] \frac{\Gamma(n+1)}{\Gamma(n-k+1)\Gamma(k+1)} \\ &= \frac{1}{2\varphi} \sum_{k=0}^{n} \binom{n}{k} \varphi^k - \frac{1}{2\varphi} \sum_{k=0}^{n} \binom{n}{k} (-\varphi)^k \\ &= \frac{1}{2\varphi} (1+\varphi)^n - \frac{1}{2\varphi} (1-\varphi)^n \\ &= \frac{1}{2\sqrt{2}} \left[\left(1+\sqrt{2}\right)^n - \left(1-\sqrt{2}\right)^n \right], \end{aligned}$$

for $n \in \mathbb{N}_0$.

Theorem 3. *$x(n) > 0$ for all $n \in \mathbb{N}_1$.*

Proof. Clearly, $x(1) = 1 > 0$. From (7), we have

$$\nabla_0^q x(n+1) = x(n) + x(n-1), \quad n \in \mathbb{N}_1. \tag{11}$$

Expanding the left-hand side of (11) using Definition 5 and rearranging the terms, we get

$$\begin{aligned} x(n+1) &= x(n) + x(n-1) - \frac{1}{\Gamma(-q)} \sum_{j=0}^{n} \frac{\Gamma(n-j-q+1)}{\Gamma(n-j+2)} x(j) \\ &= x(n) + x(n-1) + \frac{q}{\Gamma(1-q)} \sum_{j=0}^{n} \frac{\Gamma(n-j-q+1)}{\Gamma(n-j+2)} x(j), \end{aligned}$$

for $n \in \mathbb{N}_1$. Since $\Gamma(1-q) > 0$, $\Gamma(n-j-q+1) > 0$ and $\Gamma(n-j+2) > 0$ for all $0 \leq j \leq n$ and $n \in \mathbb{N}_1$, it successively follows that $x(n+1) > 0$ for all $n \in \mathbb{N}_1$. □

3.3. Numerical Scheme for the Fractional Pell Sequence

To obtain the numerical integral for the fractional Pell sequence, one rewrites (2) in the normal form, one replaces the classical ∇ difference operator with the Grünwald–Letnikov fractional difference operator, one expands the Grünwald–Letnikov fractional difference operator, and, finally, one rearranges the terms to express $x(n)$.

Using Definition 3, (2) can be rewritten as

$$\nabla^2 P(n) = f(P(n-1), P(n-2)), \quad n \in \mathbb{N}_2, \tag{12}$$

where

$$f(P(n-1), P(n-2)) = 2P(n-2), \quad n \in \mathbb{N}_2.$$

Now, for $1 < q < 2$, we consider the qth-order difference equation

$$\nabla_0^q x(n) = f(x(n-1), x(n-2)), \quad n \in \mathbb{N}_2, \tag{13}$$

together with the initial condition

$$x(0) = 0, \quad x(1) = 1,$$

analogous to (1)–(12).

Theorem 4. *The numerical scheme for the fractional Pell sequence is given by*

$$x(n) = qx(n-1) + \left[2 - \frac{q(q-1)}{2}\right] x(n-2) - \sum_{j=0}^{n-3} \frac{\Gamma(n-j-q)}{\Gamma(n-j+1)\Gamma(-q)} x(j), \quad n \in \mathbb{N}_2. \tag{14}$$

Proof. From Definition 5, we have

$$\begin{aligned}
\nabla_0^q x(n) &= \sum_{j=0}^{n} \frac{\Gamma(n-j-q)}{\Gamma(n-j+1)\Gamma(-q)} x(j) \\
&= x(n) - qx(n-1) + \frac{q(q-1)}{2} x(n-2) + \sum_{j=0}^{n-3} \frac{\Gamma(n-j-q)}{\Gamma(n-j+1)\Gamma(-q)} x(j).
\end{aligned} \tag{15}$$

Using (15) in (13) and rearranging the terms, we obtain

$$\begin{aligned}
x(n) = f(x(n-1), x(n-2)) + qx(n-1) - \frac{q(q-1)}{2} x(n-2) \\
- \sum_{j=0}^{n-3} \frac{\Gamma(n-j-q)}{\Gamma(n-j+1)\Gamma(-q)} x(j), \quad n \in \mathbb{N}_2.
\end{aligned}$$

That is,

$$x(n) = qx(n-1) + \left[2 - \frac{q(q-1)}{2}\right] x(n-2) - \sum_{j=0}^{n-3} \frac{\Gamma(n-j-q)}{\Gamma(n-j+1)\Gamma(-q)} x(j), \quad n \in \mathbb{N}_2.$$

□

In Table 1, the fractional Pell sequences are presented for $q = 1.99$, $q = 1.995$, $q = 1.999$, and $q = 2$ (IO), respectively.

Table 1. Fractional Pell sequences for $q = 1.99$, $q = 1.995$, $q = 1.999$, and IO ($q = 2$), respectively.

#	$q = 1.99$	$q = 1.995$	$q = 1.999$	IO
1	0	0	0	0
2	1	1	1	1
3	1.99000000000	1.99500000000	1.99900000000	2
4	4.97505000000	4.98751250000	4.99750050000	5
5	11.92008817890	11.96001913091	11.99199983283	12
6	28.77036010178	28.88507358306	28.97699771786	29
7	69.35116600455	69.67521980455	69.93498596635	70
8	167.20881853340	168.10317529800	168.82043801696	169
9	403.13188359617	405.56193312317	407.51174632077	408
10	971.93524756072	978.45500806016	983.68898580072	985
11	2343.28804106191	2360.60539480727	2374.51490469204	2378
12	5649.51967020207	5695.14417610542	5731.81033968845	5741
13	13620.45119203567	13739.88521182454	13835.92258701109	13860
14	32836.32193044393	33147.66861641826	33398.17489180408	33461
15	79147.45145012428	79961.75170649997	80617.47387422606	80782

Remark 2. *We make the following observations:*

(i) *For $n \in \mathbb{N}_3$ and $0 \le j \le n-3$, consider*

$$\frac{\Gamma(n-j-q)}{\Gamma(n-j+1)\Gamma(-q)} = q(q-1)\frac{\Gamma(n-j-q)}{\Gamma(n-j+1)\Gamma(2-q)}.$$

Clearly, by [7], $\Gamma(n-j-q) > 0$, $\Gamma(n-j+1) > 0$, and $\Gamma(2-q) > 0$, implying that

$$\frac{\Gamma(n-j-q)}{\Gamma(n-j+1)\Gamma(-q)} > 0, \quad 0 \le j \le n-3, \quad n \in \mathbb{N}_3;$$

(ii) *For $q = 2$, the numerical scheme* (14) *reduces to the IO form of Pell's numbers* (2).

Lemma 1. *Denote by*

$$\lim_{n\to\infty} \frac{x(n+1)}{x(n)} = \Lambda. \tag{16}$$

Then, $\Lambda \le \dfrac{q+\sqrt{(4-q)(2+q)}}{2}$.

Proof. Corresponding to (14), the numerical scheme is

$$x(n+1) = qx(n) + \left[2 - \frac{q(q-1)}{2}\right]x(n-1) - \sum_{j=1}^{n-1} \frac{\Gamma(n-j-q+2)}{\Gamma(n-j+3)\Gamma(-q)} x(j-1), \quad n \in \mathbb{N}_1. \tag{17}$$

Clearly,

$$\lim_{n\to\infty} \frac{x(n-1)}{x(n)} = \frac{1}{\Lambda}. \tag{18}$$

From (17), we have

$$\frac{x(n+1)}{x(n)} = q + \left[2 - \frac{q(q-1)}{2}\right]\frac{x(n-1)}{x(n)} - \sum_{j=1}^{n-1} \frac{\Gamma(n-j-q+2)}{\Gamma(n-j+3)\Gamma(-q)} \frac{x(j-1)}{x(n)}, \quad n \in \mathbb{N}_1. \quad (19)$$

For $n \in \mathbb{N}_1$ and $0 \le j \le n-1$, consider

$$\frac{\Gamma(n-j-q+2)}{\Gamma(n-j+3)\Gamma(-q)} = q(q-1)\frac{\Gamma(n-j-q+2)}{\Gamma(n-j+3)\Gamma(2-q)}.$$

Clearly, by [7], $\Gamma(n-j-q+2) > 0, \Gamma(n-j+3) > 0$, and $\Gamma(2-q) > 0$, implying that

$$\frac{\Gamma(n-j-q+2)}{\Gamma(n-j+3)\Gamma(-q)} > 0, \quad 0 \le j \le n-1, \quad n \in \mathbb{N}_1.$$

Also, $2 - \frac{q(q-1)}{2} > 0$, $\frac{x(n-1)}{x(n)} > 0$, and

$$\frac{x(j-1)}{x(n)} \ge 0, \qquad 1 \le j \le n-1, \quad n \in \mathbb{N}_1.$$

Then, from (19), we have

$$\frac{x(n+1)}{x(n)} \le q + \left[2 - \frac{q(q-1)}{2}\right]\frac{x(n-1)}{x(n)}, \quad n \in \mathbb{N}_1. \quad (20)$$

Setting $n \to \infty$ on both sides of (20) and using (16) and (18), we obtain

$$\Lambda \le q + \left[2 - \frac{q(q-1)}{2}\right]\frac{1}{\Lambda}. \quad (21)$$

Let us define A and B to simplify the inequality: $A = q$ and $B = \left[2 - \frac{q(q-1)}{2}\right]$. Then, (21) is equivalent to

$$\Lambda^2 - A\Lambda - B \le 0. \quad (22)$$

Also, let

$$\lambda_1 = \frac{A + \sqrt{A^2 + 4B}}{2}, \quad \lambda_2 = \frac{A - \sqrt{A^2 + 4B}}{2}.$$

Clearly, $\lambda_1 > 0$ and $\lambda_2 < 0$. Then, from (22), we obtain

$$\Lambda \le \lambda_1.$$

That is,

$$\lim_{n\to\infty} \frac{x(n+1)}{x(n)} \le \frac{q + \sqrt{(4-q)(2+q)}}{2}. \quad (23)$$

□

If one denotes $E(q) = \frac{q+\sqrt{(4-q)(2+q)}}{2}$, Figure 1 verifies the inequality $\frac{x(n+1)}{x(n)} < E(q)$ for $q = 1.9$ and $n = 1, 2, \ldots, 15$.

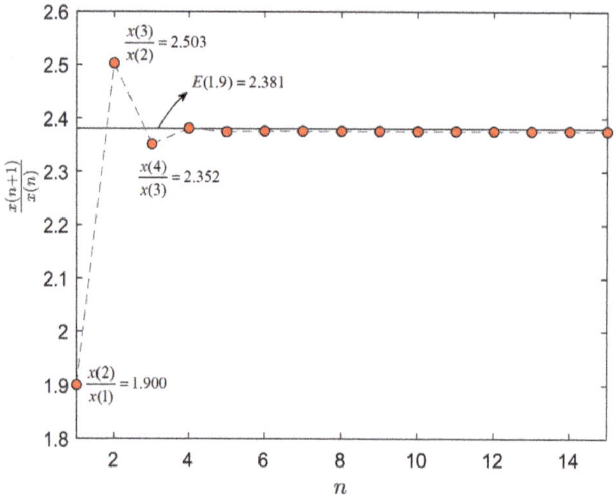

Figure 1. Numerical verification of the inequality (23) for $q = 1.9$, $n = 1, 2, \ldots, 15$. E represents the line $\frac{2+\sqrt{(4-q)(2+q)}}{2}$ in (23) for $q = 1.9$.

Remark 3. *We now examine the special case when $q = 2$. We have*

$$\frac{\Gamma(n-j-q+2)}{\Gamma(n-j+3)\Gamma(-q)} = 0, \quad 0 \le j \le n-1, \quad n \in \mathbb{N}_1.$$

Then, from (19)*, we have*

$$\frac{x(n+1)}{x(n)} = q + \left[2 - \frac{q(q-1)}{2}\right]\frac{x(n-1)}{x(n)}, \quad n \in \mathbb{N}_1.$$

Consequently, we obtain

$$\Lambda = \lim_{n\to\infty} \frac{P(n+1)}{P(n)} = \lambda_1 = \frac{2+\sqrt{(4-2)(2+2)}}{2} = 1+\sqrt{2},$$

i.e., the known result for the integer order (IO) Pell's numbers, $\delta = 1+\sqrt{2}$ being the silver ratio.

3.4. Fractional Silver Ratio and Tiling Obtained with Fractional Pell's Numbers

3.4.1. Fractional Silver Ratio

Definition 6 ([23])**.** *Let $v : \mathbb{N}_0 \to \mathbb{R}$. The Z-transform of u is a complex function given by*

$$\bar{u}(z) = Z[u(n)] = \sum_{k=0}^{\infty} u(k)z^{-k},$$

where z is a complex number for which this series converges absolutely.

Theorem 5. *The generalized characteristic equation for the fractional Pell sequence for $q \in (1,2)$ is given by*

$$z^2\left(1-\frac{1}{z}\right)^q - 2 = 0. \tag{24}$$

Proof. Denote by $Z[x(n)] = \bar{x}(z)$. Then,

$$Z[x(n+1)] = z\bar{x}(z) - zx(0),$$

and

$$Z[x(n+2)] = z^2\bar{x}(z) - z^2x(0) - zx(1).$$

Also, for $1 < q < 2$, by using Definitions 5 and 6, we have

$$\begin{aligned}
Z\left[\nabla_0^q x(n)\right] &= \sum_{k=0}^{\infty} \nabla_0^q x(k) z^{-k} \\
&= \sum_{k=0}^{\infty}\left[\sum_{j=0}^{k} \frac{\Gamma(k-j-q)}{\Gamma(k-j+1)\Gamma(-q)} x(j)\right] z^{-k} \\
&= \sum_{j=0}^{\infty}\left[\sum_{k=j}^{\infty} \frac{\Gamma(k-j-q)}{\Gamma(k-j+1)\Gamma(-q)} z^{-k}\right] x(j) \\
&= \sum_{j=0}^{\infty}\left[\sum_{k=0}^{\infty} \frac{\Gamma(k-q)}{\Gamma(k+1)\Gamma(-q)} z^{-k-j}\right] x(j) \\
&= \sum_{j=0}^{\infty}\left[\sum_{k=0}^{\infty} \frac{\Gamma(k-q)}{\Gamma(k+1)\Gamma(-q)} z^{-k}\right] z^{-j} x(j) \\
&= \sum_{j=0}^{\infty}\left[\left(1-\frac{1}{z}\right)^{q}\right] z^{-j} x(j) \\
&= \left(1-\frac{1}{z}\right)^{q} \sum_{j=0}^{\infty} x(j) z^{-j} \\
&= \left(1-\frac{1}{z}\right)^{q} \bar{x}(z).
\end{aligned}$$

Take

$$y(n) = \nabla_0^q x(n) = \sum_{j=0}^{n} \frac{\Gamma(n-j-q)}{\Gamma(n-j+1)\Gamma(-q)} x(j), \quad n \in \mathbb{N}_0.$$

Then, $y(0) = x(0) = 0$ and $y(1) = -qx(0) + x(1) = 1$. Denote by $Z[y(n)] = \bar{y}(z)$. Then,

$$\begin{aligned}
Z\left[\nabla_0^q x(n+2)\right] &= Z[y(n+2)] \\
&= z^2\bar{y}(z) - z^2y(0) - zy(1) \\
&= z^2 Z[y(n)] - z \\
&= z^2 Z\left[\nabla_0^q x(n)\right] - z \\
&= z^2\left(1-\frac{1}{z}\right)^{q} \bar{x}(z) - z.
\end{aligned}$$

The equivalent form of the fractional Pell sequence is given by

$$\nabla_0^q x(n+2) = 2x(n), \quad n \in \mathbb{N}_0. \tag{25}$$

Taking the Z-transform of (25) and rearranging the terms, we get

$$z^2\left(1-\frac{1}{z}\right)^{q} \bar{x}(z) - z = 2\bar{x}(z).$$

That is,

$$\bar{x}(z) = \frac{z}{z^2\left(1-\frac{1}{z}\right)^{q} - 2}.$$

Consequently, the fractional characteristic equation for the fractional Pell sequence is

$$z^2\left(1-\frac{1}{z}\right)^q - 2 = 0.$$

□

If one denotes with $\delta = \Re(z)$ the real part of z, then the characteristic equation becomes

$$\delta^2\left(1-\frac{1}{\delta}\right)^q - 2 = 0,$$

whose solutions are fractional silver ratio as function of q, $\delta = \delta(q)$.

For $q = 1.5$, the generalized characteristic equation has the solution $\delta = 2.2$; for $q = 1.1$, one obtains $\delta = 2.05$, while, for $q = 2$, one obtains the characteristic equation of IO

$$\delta^2 - 2\delta - 1 = 0,$$

with the known silver ratio solution $\delta = 1 + \sqrt{2}$ (see also Remark 2 (ii)).

To determine the solutions graphically, denote the surface determined by the characteristic polynomial by $\Sigma(\delta, q) := \delta^2\left(1-\frac{1}{\delta}\right)^q - 2$, the surface $\bar{z} = \Sigma(\delta, q)$ being drawn in Figure 2. The intersection between Σ and the plane $\bar{z} = 0$, denoted by Γ (red plot), represents the curve of solutions of the fractional characteristic equation. For example, for $q = 1.5$, the numerical solution of the characteristic Equation (24) is $\delta = 2.217$, which matches with the graphical solution; the intersection between the plane $q = 1.5$ and Γ (point $P(2.217, 1.5)$ in the plane $\bar{z} = 0$).

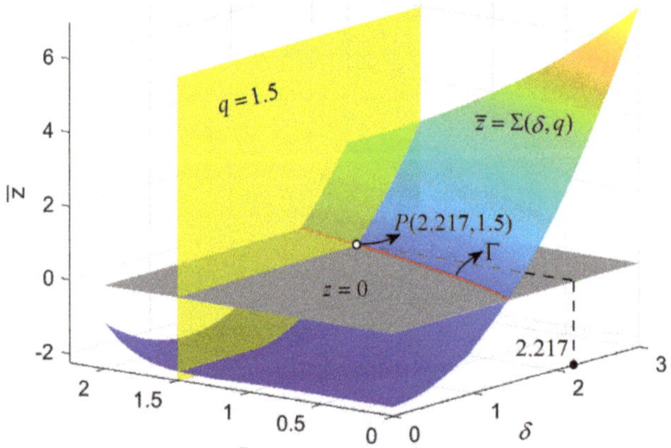

Figure 2. The curve Γ representing the solutions of the characteristic Equation (24) (red plot) as intersection between the plane $\bar{z}$ and the surface Σ. For $q = 1.5$, to obtain the solution of the characteristic equation, one crosses the curve Γ of the solution, with the plane $q = 1.5$ and the point $P(2.217, 1.5)$. The solution $\delta = 2.217$ represents the fractional silver ratio for $q = 1.5$.

3.4.2. Fractional Pell's Tiling

As known, a domino tiling with Pell's numbers is a tessellation of some region by dominoes by using rectangular tiles. For example, the kth rectangular tile has the length $P(k)$ and the width $2 \times P(k-1) + P(k-2)$ (see, e.g., [24,25]). In Figure 3 the case of domino tiling with 8 Pell's numbers is presented (the zoomed rectangle reveals the tiling steps).

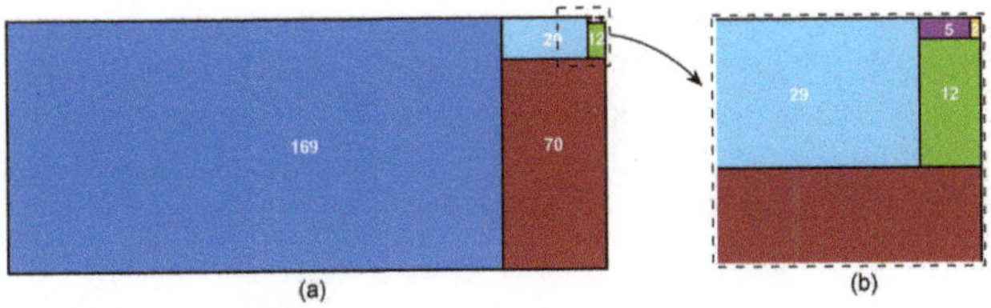

Figure 3. (**a**) Domino tiling with IO Pell's numbers; (**b**) zoomed detail reveals the construction of the tiling.

Also, the tiling can be generated with squares of Pell sequence lengths. To construct this tiling, start with the first square of size 1×1 , i.e., $P(1)$ ($P(0)$ is omitted, and then continue to the right with a square of size 2×2, which means $P(2)$, then up with square of size 5×5, i.e., $P(3)$, next left with a square of 12×12, i.e., $P(5)$, down with a square 29×29, i.e., $P(6)$, and so on, the rule being the rotation counterclockwise of each new rectangle, with 90 °C. Next, if one draws a quarter-circle arc inside each new square connecting opposite corners, one obtains the silver spiral (red plot in Figure 4a for a visual representation, where the IO case is considered).

Considering now 8 fractional Pell's numbers, the spiral and fractional silver spiral, plotted over the tiling for $q = 1.995$ and $q = 1.9$, are presented in Figure 4b and Figure 4c, respectively. For $q = 1.995$, the fractional tiling and the fractional silver spiral are similar to the case of IO in Figure 4a; for $q = 1.9$, the fitting differences become visible.

Figure 4d shows fractional silver spirals for $q = 1 + i \times 0.1$ for $i = 0, \ldots, 10$.

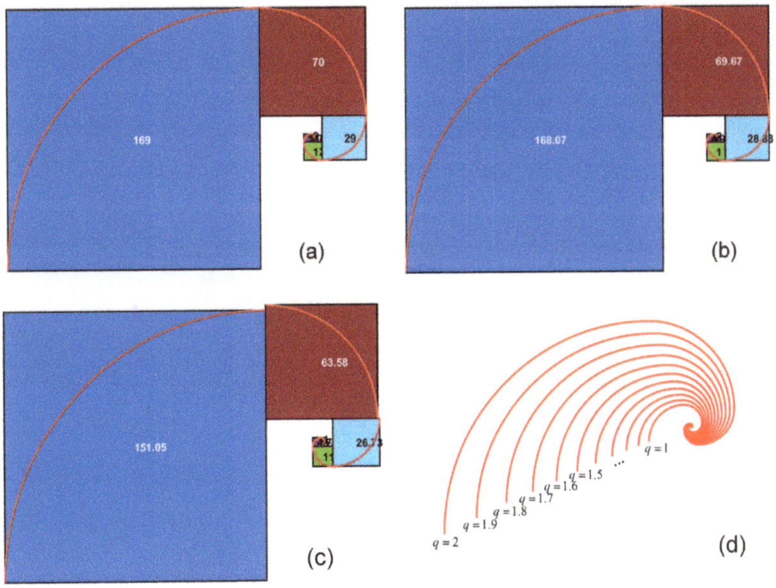

Figure 4. Silver spiral with 8 Pell numbers: (**a**) IO silver spiral; (**b**) fractional silver spiral for $q = 1.995$; (**c**) fractional silver spiral for $q = 1.9$; (**d**) fractional silver spiral for $q = 1 + 10 \times 0.1$ (for $q = 2$, one obtains the IO silver spiral).

While in [11,12] it was shown that the fractional approach of discrete systems can break the symmetry, the fractional silver ratio introduced in this paper and also the fractional golden ratio (introduced in [10]) do not break the symmetry and the beauty of the perfection of nature. It is certainly known that the root mechanism that generates patterns in plants via the golden ratio, can be considered as an optimal packing, a fact first discovered by the German botanist Werner Hoffmeister in 19th century (see Figure 5). However, the fractional silver ratio generates artistic representations too. Thus, Figure 5 presents artistic representations of a pinecone using the MATLAB script presented in the appendix (the script can be found in [26]). The script, originally written to run with the golden ratio sequence as a factor of π (see highlighted line 25), is easily adapted here to use the fractional silver ratio. In Figure 5a, the case of the IO silver ratio of IO is presented, in Figure 5b the case of fractional silver ratio $\delta = 2.22$, corresponding to $q = 1.5$, and in Figure 5c the case of the fractional silver ratio $\delta = 2.05$, corresponding to $q = 1.1$.

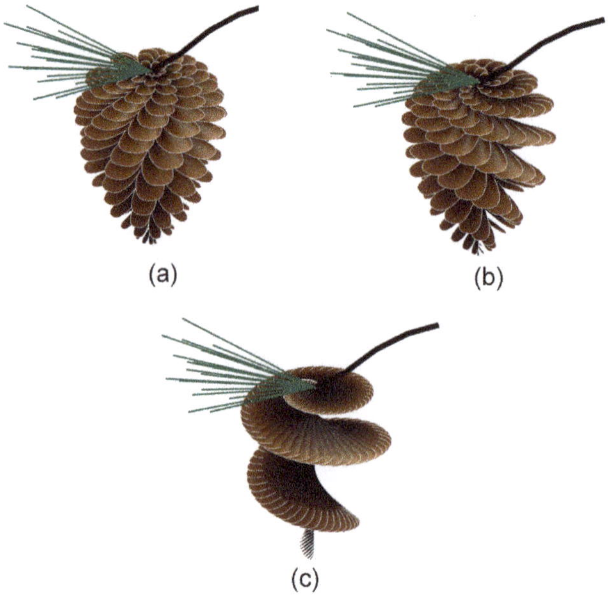

Figure 5. Artistic fractional pinecone obtained with the script [26] for (**a**) IO silver ratio, $\delta = 1 + \sqrt{2}$; (**b**) fractional silver ratio, $\delta = 2.22$, corresponding to $q = 1.5$; (**c**) fractional silver ratio, $\delta = 2.05$, corresponding to $q = 1.1$.

4. Fractional Pell–Lucas Sequence

A two-dimensional system of linear difference equations describing the Pell–Lucas sequence (4) is

$$\begin{pmatrix} Q(n+2) \\ Q(n+1) \end{pmatrix} = \begin{pmatrix} 2 & 1 \\ 1 & 0 \end{pmatrix} \begin{pmatrix} Q(n+1) \\ Q(n) \end{pmatrix}, \quad n \in \mathbb{N}_0.$$

Then,

$$\begin{pmatrix} \nabla Q(n+2) \\ \nabla Q(n+1) \end{pmatrix} = \begin{pmatrix} 1 & 1 \\ 1 & -1 \end{pmatrix} \begin{pmatrix} Q(n+1) \\ Q(n) \end{pmatrix}, \quad n \in \mathbb{N}_0.$$

Consequently, we have the following initial value problem

$$\nabla \bar{Q}(n) = A\bar{Q}(n-1), \quad n \in \mathbb{N}_1, \tag{26}$$

$$\bar{Q}(0) = \bar{Q}_0, \tag{27}$$

associated with the Pell–Lucas numbers. Here,

$$\bar{Q}(n) = \begin{pmatrix} Q(n+1) \\ Q(n) \end{pmatrix},$$

$$A = \begin{pmatrix} 1 & 1 \\ 1 & -1 \end{pmatrix},$$

$$\bar{Q}_0 = \begin{pmatrix} Q(1) \\ Q(0) \end{pmatrix} = \begin{pmatrix} 2 \\ 2 \end{pmatrix}.$$

We observe that the matrix A in (26) is same as in (5). Now, for $0 < q < 1$, we consider the qth-order difference equation

$$\nabla_0^q \bar{y}(n) = A\bar{y}(n-1), \quad n \in \mathbb{N}_1,$$

together with the initial condition

$$\bar{y}(0) = \begin{pmatrix} 2 \\ 2 \end{pmatrix},$$

analogous to (26) and (27). Here,

$$\bar{y}(n) = \begin{pmatrix} y(n+1) \\ y(n) \end{pmatrix}, \quad A = \begin{pmatrix} 1 & 1 \\ 1 & -1 \end{pmatrix}.$$

4.1. Closed Form of the Fractional Pell–Lucas Sequence

With the help of Theorem 1, we mimic the proof of Theorem 2 to obtain the following statement, the generalized Binet's formula for fractional Pell–Lucas sequence.

Theorem 6. *The closed-form expression of the fractional Pell–Lucas sequence is given by*

$$y(n) = \sum_{k=0}^{n} \left[\varphi^k + (-\varphi)^k\right] \frac{\Gamma(n-k+kq+q)}{\Gamma(n-k+1)\Gamma(kq+q)}, \quad n \in \mathbb{N}_0.$$

Remark 4. *For $q = 1$, we obtain the closed IO form expression for the nth element in Pell–Lucas sequences (3) and (4) as follows:*

$$\begin{aligned} y(n) &= \frac{1}{\varphi} \sum_{k=0}^{n} \left[\varphi^k + (-\varphi)^k\right] \frac{\Gamma(n+1)}{\Gamma(n-k+1)\Gamma(k+1)} \\ &= \sum_{k=0}^{n} \binom{n}{k} \varphi^k + \sum_{k=0}^{n} \binom{n}{k} (-\varphi)^k \\ &= (1+\varphi)^n + (1-\varphi)^n \\ &= \left(1+\sqrt{2}\right)^n + \left(1-\sqrt{2}\right)^n, \end{aligned}$$

for $n \in \mathbb{N}_0$.

Theorem 7. $y(n) > 0$ *for all $n \in \mathbb{N}_0$.*

Proof. The proof is similar to the proof of Theorem 3. So, we omit it. □

4.2. Numerical Scheme for the Fractional Pell–Lucas Sequence

Following the steps from the start of Section 3.3 and by considering (4) instead of (2), the numerical integral for the fractional Pell–Lucas sequence can be obtained.

Using Definition 3, (4) can be rewritten as

$$\nabla^2 Q(n) = f(Q(n-1), Q(n-2)), \quad n \in \mathbb{N}_2, \tag{28}$$

where

$$f(Q(n-1), Q(n-2)) = 2Q(n-2), \quad n \in \mathbb{N}_2.$$

Now, for $1 < q < 2$, we consider the qth-order difference equation

$$\nabla_0^q y(n) = f(y(n-1), y(n-2)), \quad n \in \mathbb{N}_2,$$

together with the initial condition

$$y(0) = 2, \quad y(1) = 2,$$

analogous to (3)–(28).

Theorem 8. *The numerical scheme for the fractional Pell–Lucas sequence is given by*

$$y(n) = qy(n-1) + \left[2 - \frac{q(q-1)}{2}\right] y(n-2) - \sum_{j=0}^{n-3} \frac{\Gamma(n-j-q)}{\Gamma(n-j+1)\Gamma(-q)} y(j), \quad n \in \mathbb{N}_2. \tag{29}$$

Proof. The proof is similar to the proof of Theorem 4. So, we omit it. □

Remark 5. *For $q = 2$, the numerical scheme* (29) *reduces to the IO definition of the Pell–Lucas numbers.*

For example, the first 15 fractional Pell–Lucas numbers displayed with 4 decimals for $q = 1.999$ are

$$2, 2, 6.0099, 13.9999, 33.9940, 81.9739, 197.9108, 477.72047, 1153.17036, 2783.6227, 6719.3551, 16219.7623, 39152.61760, 94509.48860, 228129.71839.$$

By mimicking the proof of Lemma 1, we obtain the following statement:

Lemma 2. $\lim\limits_{n\to\infty} \dfrac{y(n+1)}{y(n)} \leq \dfrac{q + \sqrt{(4-q)(2+q)}}{2}$.

Remark 6. *Similar to Remark 3, for $q = 2$, we obtain*

$$\lim_{n\to\infty} \frac{Q(n+1)}{Q(n)} = 1 + \sqrt{2}.$$

Theorem 9. *The characteristic equation for the fractional Pell–Lucas sequence is given by* (24).

Proof. The proof is similar to the proof of Theorem 5. So, we omit it. □

5. Conclusions

In this paper, the fractional generalization of Pell and Pell–Lucas numbers is introduced by considering the Grünwald–Letnikov fractional operator of orders $q \in (0, 1)$ and $q \in (1, 2)$. Several properties of integer-order Pell and Pell–Lucas numbers extend naturally to the fractional case. The fractional silver ratio is deduced from the characteristic equation of the fractional Pell numbers as a function of the fractional order q. The numerical tests show that the fractional Pell numbers can be used to tile a region, and the fractional silver spiral fits the tiling, demonstrating that the fractional silver spiral aligns well with the fractional tiling pattern. This work, which continues the study in [10], offers a new perspective on the use of fractional calculus in recurrence-defined numbers.

Author Contributions: Software, M.-F.D.; Formal analysis, M.-F.D.; Investigation, J.M.J.; Writing—original draft, M.-F.D.; Writing—review and editing, M.-F.D.; Visualization, M.-F.D.; Supervision, M.-F.D. All authors have read and agreed to the published version of the manuscript.

Funding: This research received no external funding.

Data Availability Statement: The original contributions presented in this study are included in the article. Further inquiries can be directed to the corresponding author.

Acknowledgments: The authors are grateful to Eric Ludlam and Adam Danz from MathWorks for the permission to use the MATLAB script to generate the pinecone, as provided in Appendix A.

Conflicts of Interest: The authors declare no conflicts of interest.

Appendix A

MATLAB script for pinecone.

```
% Copyright 2024, Eric M. Ludlam;
figure
nscales = 140; %Number of scales
height = 2.5; %Height of inner part of pinecone
swt = 0.3; %Scale width in theta
sth = 0.2; %Scale thickness (as a curve in height)
stilt = 1.2; %From inside to outside, tile of each scale
nn = 18; %Number of needles
% Exponents for curves
hexp = 2.8; %scale density over height
rexp = 2; %radius shape across height
scexp = 3; %scale rounded shape (end)
suexp = 3; %scale roundness in height
stexp = 2.1; %scale tilt for height
stuexp = 2; %scale thickness of U by height
cexp = 2; %color gradient
% Colors
brown1 = [0 0 0]; %Dark center color
brown2 = [0.470 0.240 0.010]; % Brighter outer color
edge = [1 1 1]; %Scale edging
green = [0.060 0.590 0.400]; % Pine Needles
% Resolution
vps = 17; % verts per scale : An odd number so 1 vert is in center
vpr = 20; % verts per radius
% Scale locations
```

```
FP = 2.05 * (1:nscales) ;%FP = Golden/Silver Ratio sequence as factor of pi
H = linspace(0, 1, nscales).^hexp * height; %Height of the root of each scale
R = 1 - abs(linspace(-1, 1, nscales).^rexp); %Radius of pinecone over height
U = 1 - abs(linspace(-1, 1, nscales).^stuexp); %Thickness of scale U shape by height
% Geometry of the scales at the locations
ST = reshape((linspace(-0.5, 0.5, vps) * swt + FP')', 1, []); %Scale Theta
SR = reshape(((1 - abs(linspace(-1, 1, vps).^scexp)).*R')', 1, []); %Scale Radii
SH = reshape((ones(1, vps).*H' + abs(linspace(-1, 1, vps).^suexp.*U') * sth)', 1, []); %Scale Height
MR = linspace(0, 1, vpr)'.*SR;
% Compute final geometry of the pinecone.
X = cospi(ST).*MR;
Y = sinpi(ST).*MR;
Z = SH.*ones(vpr, 1) + MR.*linspace(0, 1, vps * nscales).^stexp * stilt;
C=linspace(0,1,vpr).^cexp'.*ones(1,vps*nscales);
% Plot pinecone
set(gcf, 'Color', '#fffafa'); %Snow
plot3(X(end, :), Y(end, :), -Z(end, :), '-', 'Color', edge);
surface(X, Y, -Z, C, 'EdgeColor', 'none');
shading interp
% Dark center to Brown colormap
colormap(interp1([1 256], [brown1; brown2], 1:256));
% Branch
bx = [0 0.5 1 1.5 2];
by = [0 0 0 0 0];
bz = [0 0.05 0.2 0.25 0.2];
line('XData', bx, 'YData', by, 'ZData', bz, 'Color', brown1, 'LineWidth', 5);
% Pine Needles
NT = linspace(0, 5, nn)';
NR = linspace(0.1, 0.8, nn)';
NV = [0 0 0 - ones(nn, 1) * 2, cospi(NT).*NR, sinpi(NT).*NR + 0.9];
NF = [ones(nn, 1) (1 : nn)' + 1];
patch('Vertices', NV, 'Faces', NF, 'EdgeColor', green, 'FaceColor', 'none', 'LineWidth', 1.5);
% Setup Axes
set(gca, 'Position', [0 0 1 1], 'Clipping', 'off');
daspect([1 1 1]);
axis([-1.3 1.3 -1.3 1.3 -height + 0.2 0.5], 'off')
material([0.6 1 0.3])
lighting gouraud
light('Position',[13.2 7.2 16.5]);
```

References

1. Bicknell, N. A primer on the Pell sequence and related sequence. *Fibonacci Q.* **1975**, *13*, 345–349. [CrossRef]
2. Dasdemir, A. On the Pell, Pell-Lucas and modified Pell numbers by matrix method. *Appl. Math. Sci.* **2011**, *64*, 3173–3181.
3. Horadam, A.F. Applications of modified Pell numbers to representations. *Ulam Q.* **1994**, *3*, 34–53.
4. Murty, M.N. Some facts about Silver Ratio and its relation with Pell numbers and Silver Rectangle. *IOSR J. Math.* **2023**, *19*, 40–45.
5. Atici, F.M.; Chang, S.; Jonnalagadda, J.M. Grünwald–Letnikov fractional operators: From past to present. *Fract. Differ. Calc.* **2021**, *11*, 147–159.
6. Ferreira, R.A.C. *Discrete Fractional Calculus and Fractional Difference Equations*; Springer: Cham, Switzerland, 2022.
7. Goodrich, C.; Peterson, A.C. *Discrete Fractional Calculus*; Springer: Cham, Switzerland, 2015.
8. Gray, H.L.; Zhang, N.F. On a new definition of the fractional difference. *Math. Comput.* **1988**, *50*, 513–529. [CrossRef]
9. Atici, F.M.; Eloe, P.W. Fractional q-calculus on a time scale. *J. Nonlinear Math. Phys.* **2007**, *14*, 333–344. [CrossRef]
10. Jonnalagadda, J.M.; Danca, M.-F. Notes on Fibonacci numbers of fractional order. *Int. J. Bifurc. Chaos* **2025**. [CrossRef]
11. Danca, M.F.; Jonnalagadda, J.M. Fractional order curves. *Symmetry* **2025**, *17*, 455. [CrossRef]
12. Danca, M.F. Symmetry-breaking and bifurcation diagrams of fractional-order maps. *Commun. Nonlinear Sci. Numer.* **2023**, *116*, 106760. [CrossRef]
13. Wei, Y.; Yin, W.; Zhao, Y.; Wang, Y. A new insight into the Grünwald-Letnikov discrete fractional calculus. *J. Comput. Nonlinear Dyn.* **2019**, *14*, 041008. [CrossRef]
14. Chen, C.; Bohner, M.; Jia, B. Caputo fractional continuous cobweb models. *J. Comput. Appl. Math.* **2020**, *374*, 112734. [CrossRef]
15. Yang, S.Y.; Wu, G.C. Discrete Gronwall's inequality for Ulam stability of delay fractional difference equations. *Math. Model. Anal.* **2025**, *30*, 169–185. [CrossRef]
16. Wu, G.C.; Abdeljawad, T.; Liu, J.; Baleanu, D.; Wu, K.T. Mittag–Leffler stability analysis of fractional discrete-time neural networks via fixed point technique. *Nonlinear Anal. Model. Control* **2019**, *24*, 919–936. [CrossRef]
17. Liu, X.; Du, F.; Anderson, D.; Jia, B. Monotonicity results for nabla fractional h-difference operators. *Math. Methods Appl. Sci.* **2021**, *44*, 1207–1218. [CrossRef]
18. Ricci, P.E.; Srivastava, R.; Caratelli, D. Laguerre-type Bernoulli and Euler Numbers and related fractional polynomials. *Mathematics* **2024**, *12*, 381. [CrossRef]
19. Caratelli, D.; Natalini, P.; Ricci, P.E. Fractional Bernoulli and Euler Numbers and Related Fractional Polynomials—A Symmetry in Number Theory. *Symmetry* **2023**, *15*, 1900. [CrossRef]
20. Cull, P.; Flahive, M.; Robson, R. *Difference Equations. From Rabbits to Chaos*; Springer: New York, NY, USA, 2005.
21. Kelley, W.G.; Peterson, A.C. *Difference Equations. An Introduction with Applications*, 2nd ed.; Harcourt/Academic Press: San Diego, CA, USA, 2001.
22. Wei, Y.; Cao, J.; Li, C.; Chen, Y. How to empower Grünwald-Letnikov fractional difference equations with available initial condition? *Nonlinear Anal. Model. Control* **2022**, *27*, 650–668. [CrossRef]
23. Elaydi, S. *An Introduction to Difference Equations*, 3rd ed.; Springer: New York, NY, USA, 2005.
24. Benjamin, A.T.; Plott, S.S.; Sellers, J. Tiling proofs of recent sum identities involving Pell numbers. *Ann. Comb.* **2008**, *12*, 271–278. [CrossRef]
25. Sellers, J.A. Domino tilings and products of Fibonacci and Pell numbers. *J. Integer Seq.* **2002**, *5*, 02.1.2.
26. Ludlam, E. Pinecone. *GitHub Repos.* 2024. Available online: https://github.com/zappo2/digital-art-with-matlab/tree/master/pinecone (accessed on 4 April 2025).

fractal and fractional

MDPI

Article

Fractal-Fractional-Order Modeling of Liver Fibrosis Disease and Its Mathematical Results with Subinterval Transitions

Amjad E. Hamza [1], Osman Osman [2,*], Arshad Ali [3], Amer Alsulami [4], Khaled Aldwoah [5,*], Alaa Mustafa [6] and Hicham Saber [1]

1 Department of Mathematics, College of Science, University of Ha'il, Ha'il 55473, Saudi Arabia
2 Department of Mathematics, College of Science, Qassim University, Buraydah 52571, Saudi Arabia
3 Department of Mathematics, University of Malakand, Chakdara 18000, Khyber Pakhtunkhwa, Pakistan; arshad.swatpk@gmail.com
4 Department of Mathematics, Turabah University College, Taif University, Taif 21944, Saudi Arabia
5 Department of Mathematics, Faculty of Science, Islamic University of Madinah, Madinah 42351, Saudi Arabia
6 Department of Mathematics, Faculty of Science, Northern Border University, Arar 73213, Saudi Arabia
* Correspondence: o.osman@qu.edu.sa (O.O.); aldwoah@iu.edu.sa (K.A.)

Abstract: In this paper, we study human liver disease with a different approach of interval-based investigation by introducing subintervals. This investigation may be referred to as a short memory investigation. Such concepts are useful in problems where a transition is observed when transitioning from one subinterval to the other one. We use the classical and fractal-fractional-order derivative in each subinterval. We study the existence of solutions by using Banach's and Krasnoselskii's fixed-point theorems. Their stability is analyzed by adopting the Hyers–Ulam (H-U) stability approach. Also, using the extended Adams–Bashforth–Moulton (ABM) method, we simulate the results that visually present the numerical solutions for different fractal-fractional-order values.

Keywords: fibrosis disease; subinterval transitions; fractional derivatives; fractal-fractional derivatives; fixed point; stability and numerical analyses

1. Introduction

The liver, a crucial organ similar in importance to the heart and brain, is roughly triangular in shape and extends across the abdominal cavity [1]. It plays a pivotal role in various physiological processes, including hemostasis, blood clotting, and blood volume regulation. Additionally, the liver metabolizes drugs, detoxifies harmful substances like alcohol, and supports the immune system. It also contributes significantly to the regulation of glucose levels in the body.

Liver diseases, such as alcoholic and nonalcoholic liver diseases, hepatocellular carcinoma, cirrhosis, hepatitis B, and hepatitis C [2], have a substantial global impact. A 2017 review reported that cirrhosis alone resulted in over 1,320,000 deaths worldwide between 1990 and 2017. Notably, Sub-Saharan Africa, the lowest-income area, experienced the highest age-standardized death rate, while high-income areas had the lowest. Egypt recorded the highest age-standardized death rate during the same period [3].

Health professionals utilize liver profile tests to assess liver function comprehensively. These tests, which include measurements such as aspartate aminotransferase, serum bilirubin, alanine aminotransferase, alpha-fetoprotein, alkaline phosphatase, ceruloplasmin, and 50 nucleotidase, offer valuable insights. Thorough examination of liver biochemical substances and indicators enables doctors to take proactive measures to enhance patient care. Furthermore, the use of bromsulphthalein (BSP) is instrumental in identifying liver damage [4,5].

The concept of the existence theory is fundamental in mathematical analysis, particularly in differential equations (DEs) and dynamical systems. This theory is essential as it determines whether a system of DEs has a solution, providing a basis for further analysis. Additionally, the unique result guarantees the predictability of the solution. On the other hand, stability analysis stands as one of the most crucial and highly specialized areas of research. It has demonstrated its utility as a powerful tool in linear and nonlinear analysis, optimization theory, and qualitative theory. We can draw on various fixed-point and stability results to support these assertions [6–10].

Several attempts have been made to model the function and performance of the mentioned organ, but these attempts have been limited to classical differential equations. The works of ČelechovskáL [11], Calvetti and Kuceyeski [12], Repetto and Tweedy [13], and Friedman and Hao [14] are fundamental.

In [11], the author considered the following classical human liver model:

$$\begin{cases} \frac{dX}{dt} = -aX(t) + bY(t), \\ \frac{dY}{dt} = aX(t) - (b+c)Y(t), \\ \frac{dZ}{dt} = cY(t), \\ X(0) = h > 0, Y(0) = 0, Z(0) = 0, \end{cases} \tag{1}$$

where the variables X, Y, and Z, and the parameters a, b, c, and h are defined in Table 1. The use of fractional calculus has proven to be an enormously good tool in this regard. A suitable mathematical model can better describe its performance. Some researchers have made great efforts and attempts to model it in a more realistic and accurate way using the non-integer-order calculus. In modeling various diseases and other phenomena, it has proven to be good; see, for instance [15–19]. It can change the model enormously in how we view it and manage its outcomes to compare them with the actual data. It is remarkably noticed that in the case of various classical models, the estimated amounts of BSP deviate from clinical data, but in the case of the fractional-order model, it shows closeness to the actual data. The additional inheritance and memory qualities of FDEs make them effective in analyzing and replicating actual occurrences. In fact, fractional differential equations (FDEs) possess memory and the analytical capabilities to comprehend actual evidence; this is one of its many valuable aspects (see [20]). In [21], Ameen et al. formulated a human liver model with modified parameters in the sense of a Caputo fractional derivative (CFD). The advancement in fractional calculus has proven to be more beneficial for developing our understanding of many phenomena and processes. The Caputo–Fabrizio (CF) fractional derivative [22] and the Atangana–Baleanu–Caputo (ABC) fractional derivative [23] were recently introduced and are highly used in the modeling of many processes and phenomena (see [24]). Similarly, many of the previous models have been reformulated in the sense of CF and ABC derivatives. In [25], fractals to fractional derivatives are integral to predicting complex systems. This approach gained importance from researchers and has been applied in many research problems; see [26–29]. In [30], Baleanu et al. used the CF derivative to study a human liver.

It is observed that many real-world phenomena show transitions when they are changing or shifting from one interval to another. In such a case, the phenomena cannot be accurately modeled via usual methods. To overcome this situation, Atangana and Araz [31] introduced the piecewise concept of derivatives and integrals. This concept is different from the conventional methods of modeling. In this approach, the phenomena are studied in subintervals of the whole time interval, with discontinuity at a point. Unlike traditional fractional derivatives, this approach has proven to be good in the mathematical description of crossover effects among various forms [32,33].

In this research paper, we consider a human liver model given in [11] and study it with subinterval transitions via the fractal-fractional Caputo derivative (FFCD). We reformulate the mode as

$$\begin{cases} {}^{p}D^{r,\xi}X(t) = -aX(t) + bY(t), \\ {}^{p}D^{r,\xi}Y(t) = aX(t) - (b+c)Y(t), \\ {}^{p}D^{r,\xi}Z(t) = cY(t), \\ X(0) = h, Y(0) = 0, Z(0) = 0, \end{cases} \tag{2}$$

where the variables X, Y, and Z, and parameters a, b, c, and h are the same as those given in (1). Our model is dimensional as the case of the basic classical model in [11].

Table 1. Parameters and their description.

Parameters	Parameter Definition
$X(t)$	BSP quantity in the blood at time t.
$Y(t)$	BSP quantity in the the liver at time t.
$Z(t)$	BSP quantity in the bile at time t.
a	transferring rate of BSP from the blood to the liver.
b	transferring rate of BSP from liver to the bile.
c	refluxing rate of BSP from the liver into the blood.
h	positive bounded real number.

In (2), looking at the terms, it is obvious that by adding the equations, we obtain

$${}^{p}D^{r,\xi}X(t) + {}^{p}D^{r,\xi}Y(t) + {}^{p}D^{r,\xi}Z(t) = 0 \tag{3}$$

and

$$X(0) + Y(0) + Z(0) = h. \tag{4}$$

This implies that

$$X(t) + Y(t) + Z(t) = h, \quad \forall\, t \geq 0. \tag{5}$$

This means that

$$Z(t) = h - X(t) - Y(t), \quad \forall\, t \geq 0. \tag{6}$$

The value of Z can be calculated from the values of X and Y. Thus, it is enough to take the lower dimensional system of DEs as

$$\begin{cases} {}^{p}D^{r,\xi}X(t) = -aX(t) + bY(t), \\ {}^{p}D^{r,\xi}Y(t) = aX(t) - (b+c)Y(t), \\ X(0) = h, Y(0) = 0. \end{cases} \tag{7}$$

As in [11], we find the equilibrium points of system (7) by solving the following algebraic system:

$$\begin{aligned} -aX(t) + bY(t) &= 0, \\ aX(t) - (b+c)Y(t) &= 0. \end{aligned} \tag{8}$$

The parameters a, b, and c in system (2) express the rates of decay of BSP from the blood and the liver. Hence, they have to be positive. Therefore, we assume that $a > 0$, $b > 0$, and $c > 0$. Under this assumption, there is only one equilibrium point: $P = (0,0)$. Similarly, to find the steady state of our proposed system, we compare the right-hand side of the system of equations equal to 0, which, by a similar argument of the parameters $a, b, c > 0$, we obtain $(X_\infty, Y_\infty, Z_\infty) = (0,0,0)$. Now, we study the stability of system (7) at the equilibrium point. The matrix of the parameters of system (7) is

$$M = \begin{pmatrix} -a & b \\ a & -b-c \end{pmatrix}. \tag{9}$$

Its characteristic values are given by the algebraic equation

$$det(M - \lambda I) = \lambda^2 + \lambda(a + b + c) + ad = 0, \tag{10}$$

as

$$\lambda_{1,2} = \frac{-(a+b+c) \pm \sqrt{(a+b+c)^2 - 4ad}}{2}. \tag{11}$$

Since $a, b,$ and c are assumed to be positive,

$$|a + b + c|^2 > (a + b + c)^2 - 4ad \geq 0. \tag{12}$$

Thus, the characteristic values $\lambda_{1,2}$ are negative, which means that the solution $X(t) = 0$, $Y(t) = 0$ at the equilibrium point of (7) is globally asymptotically stable. Also, it is stable at the steady state: $(X_\infty, Y_\infty, Z_\infty) = (0, 0, 0)$. This means that the human liver model has a unique and stable steady state at the equilibrium and steady point.

To investigate the local stability of system (2), we analyze the eigenvalues of the Jacobian matrix. Compute the Jacobian matrix by taking partial derivatives of the model equations with respect to X, Y, and Z:

$$J = \begin{pmatrix} -a & b & 0 \\ a & -b-c & 0 \\ 0 & c & 0 \end{pmatrix} \tag{13}$$

Find the eigenvalues (λ) by solving the characteristic equation:

$$det(J - \lambda I) = 0, \tag{14}$$

where I is the identity matrix. Solving (14) for (λ), we obtain $\lambda_1 = -a$, $\lambda_2 = -(b + c)$, $\lambda_3 = 0$. For local stability, all the eigenvalues must have negative real parts, but here, $Re(\lambda_3) = 0$. This zero eigenvalue indicates a neutrally stable direction. In such a case, the Center Manifold Theory can be applied, which confirms the local stability of the proposed system.

The system of Equation (2) may be written as

$${}^{p}D^{r,\xi}\psi(t) = \begin{cases} v(t, \psi(t)), \\ \psi(0) = \psi_0, \quad t \in [0, \mathscr{T}], \end{cases} \tag{15}$$

where the vector $\psi(t) = (X, Y, Z)$ denotes the variable, ψ_0 is a given initial condition, and the variable function v is given by

$$v(t, \psi(t)) = \begin{bmatrix} \Phi_1(t, X, Y, Z) \\ \Phi_2(t, X, Y, Z) \\ \Phi_3(t, X, Y, Z) \end{bmatrix}, \tag{16}$$

$$\psi(t) = \begin{bmatrix} X(t) \\ Y(t) \\ Z(t) \end{bmatrix} = \begin{bmatrix} -aX(t) + bY(t) \\ aX(t) - (b+c)Y(t) \\ cY(t) \end{bmatrix}, \ \psi_0 = \begin{bmatrix} X_0 \\ Y_0 \\ Z_0 \end{bmatrix}. \tag{17}$$

In view of (16) and (17), problem (15) may be written as

$$\begin{aligned} {}^{p}D^{r,\xi}X(t) &= \Phi_1(t, X, Y, Z) \\ {}^{p}D^{r,\xi}Y(t) &= \Phi_2(t, X, Y, Z) \\ {}^{p}D^{r,\xi}Z(t) &= \Phi_3(t, X, Y, Z), \end{aligned} \tag{18}$$

where $\Phi_1, \Phi_2, \Phi_3 : [0, \mathscr{T}] \times \mathscr{R}^3 \to \mathscr{R}$ are piecewise continuous. The recent set of equations takes the compact form as follows:

$$
{}^{p}D^{r,\xi}\psi(t) = \begin{cases} \Phi_1(t, \psi(t)) \\ \Phi_2(t, \psi(t)) \\ \Phi_3(t, \psi(t)), \\ \psi(0) = \psi_0, \quad t \in [0, \mathscr{T}]. \end{cases} \tag{19}
$$

This research work is innovative in that it gives an accurate prediction of the variation in the amount of $X(t)$, $Y(t)$, and $Z(t)$ in a time interval $[0, \mathscr{T}]$ in the human liver and can study the process of the BSP test more accurately. The findings of this work will be useful in the fields of drug theory, biochemistry, health care, computational chemistry, computational biology, and others.

This paper is structured in the following manner: In Section 2, the basic definitions with preliminary results are provided. Section 3 is allocated for the existence of unique solution and stability results. In Section 4, a numerical scheme for numerical solutions is developed. In Section 5, the numerical solutions are simulated, which graphically present the main outcomes. In Section 6, we discuss and illustrate the simulated results. In Section 7, we give a conclusion of the established results.

2. Elementary Results

Let the sup norm denoted by $\|.\|_{[0,\mathscr{T}]}$ be described by

$$
\|g(t)\|_{[0,\mathscr{T}]} = \sup_{[0,\mathscr{T}]} \|g(t)\|, \quad g(t) \in C([0, \mathscr{T}], R^3). \tag{20}
$$

Here, $C([0, \mathscr{T}], R^3) := \mathbb{I}$ with the norm $\|.\|_{[0,\mathscr{T}]}$ is Banach space. We give the following definitions adopted from [20,25,31].

Definition 1. *Let y be a continuous and fractal differentiable mapping on $[0, \mathscr{T}]$, then the interval-based integral is defined by*

$$
{}^{p}I^{r}y(t) = \begin{cases} I^{r}y(t), & if\, t \in [0, t_1], \\ {}^{FF}I^{r,\xi}y(t), & t \in [t_1, t_2], \\ I^{r}y(t), & if\, t \in [t_2, t_3], \\ {}^{FF}I^{r,\xi}y(t), & t \in [t_3, \mathscr{T}], \end{cases} \tag{21}
$$

where I^r is a classical integral while ${}^{FF}I^{r,\xi}$ is a fractal-fractional integral in the Riemann–Liouville sense, which is defined as follows.

Definition 2.

$$
\begin{cases} I^{r}y(t) = \int_a^t y(\theta)d\theta, \\ {}^{FF}I^{r,\xi}y(t) = \dfrac{\xi}{\Gamma(r)} \int_a^t \theta^{\xi-1}(t-\theta)^{r-1}y(\theta)d\theta. \end{cases} \tag{22}
$$

Definition 3. *For $y \in C[0, \mathscr{T}]$, the interval-based derivative is defined by*

$$
{}^{p}D^{r}y(t) = \begin{cases} D^{r}y(t), & if\, t \in [0, t_1], \\ {}^{FFC}D^{r,\xi}y(t), & 0 < r, \xi \le 1, \quad t \in [t_1, t_2], \\ D^{r}y(t), & if\, t \in [t_2, t_3], \\ {}^{FFC}D^{r,\xi}y(t), & 0 < r, \xi \le 1, \quad t \in [t_3, \mathscr{T}], \end{cases} \tag{23}
$$

where D^r is a classical derivative of order r and ${}^{FFC}D^{r,\xi}$ is a fractal-fractional Caputo derivative of fractal dimension ξ and fractional order r, which is defined as follows.

Definition 4. *For $y \in C[0, \mathcal{T}]$, the classical and fractal-fractional Caputo derivatives are defined by*

$$\begin{cases} D^r y(t) = \dfrac{dy}{dt}, \\ {}^{FFC}D^{r,\xi} y(t) = \dfrac{1}{\Gamma(1-r)} \displaystyle\int_a^t (t-\theta)^{-r} \frac{d}{dt^{\xi}} y(\theta) d\theta, \quad 0 < r, \xi \leq 1. \end{cases} \tag{24}$$

Definition 5. *The ABM for ordinary problems is formulated as*

$$z_{n+1} = z_n + h \sum_{i=1}^{r} b_i f(\tau_n + ih, z_n + ih),$$

where z_n, h, $f(z, \tau)$, and b_i represent the approximate solution, the step size, ODE, and the coefficients, respectively.

3. Existence and Stability Analysis

This section is divided into two subsections. In the first subsection, we provide a lemma and a corollary result and investigate the existence of a unique solution of the proposed model. In the second subsection, using the H-U concept of stability, we analyze the stability results.

3.1. Existence of a Unique Solution

Lemma 1. *The solution of*

$$\begin{aligned} {}^{P}D^r \psi(t) &= h(t), \quad r \in (0, 1], \\ \psi(0) &= \psi_0, \quad \psi(t_1) = \psi_{t_1}, \quad \psi(t_2) = \psi_{t_2}, \quad \psi(t_3) = \psi_{t_3} \end{aligned}$$

is given by

$$\psi(t) = \begin{cases} \psi_0 + \displaystyle\int_0^t h(\theta) d\theta, \quad if\ t \in [0, t_1], \\ \psi_{t_1} + \dfrac{\xi}{\Gamma(r)} \displaystyle\int_{t_1}^t \theta^{\xi-1} (t-\theta)^{r-1} h(\theta) d\theta, \quad t \in [t_1, t_2] \\ \psi_{t_2} + \displaystyle\int_{t_2}^t h(\theta) d\theta, \quad if\ t \in [t_2, t_3], \\ \psi_{t_3} + \dfrac{\xi}{\Gamma(r)} \displaystyle\int_{t_3}^t \theta^{\xi-1} (t-\theta)^{r-1} h(\theta) d\theta, \quad t \in [t_3, \mathcal{T}]. \end{cases} \tag{25}$$

Proof. As it is easy to prove, we thus omit it. □

Corollary 1. *The equivalent integral equations of problem* (15) *are given, via Lemma 1, as*

$$\psi(t) = \begin{cases} \psi_0 + \displaystyle\int_0^t v(\theta, \psi(\theta)) d\theta, \quad if\ t \in [0, t_1], \\ \psi_{t_1} + \dfrac{\xi}{\Gamma(r)} \displaystyle\int_{t_1}^t \theta^{\xi-1} (t-\theta)^{r-1} v(\theta, \psi(\theta)) d\theta, \quad t \in [t_1, t_2] \\ \psi_{t_2} + \displaystyle\int_{t_2}^t v(\theta, \psi(\theta)) d\theta, \quad if\ t \in [t_2, t_3], \\ \psi_{t_3} + \dfrac{\xi}{\Gamma(r)} \displaystyle\int_{t_3}^t \theta^{\xi-1} (t-\theta)^{r-1} v(\theta, \psi(\theta)) d\theta, \quad t \in [t_3, \mathcal{T}]. \end{cases} \tag{26}$$

We define an operator $\mathscr{P} : \mathbb{I} \to \mathbb{I}$ by

$$\mathscr{P}(\psi) = \begin{cases} \psi_0 + \int_0^t v(\theta, \psi(\theta))d\theta, & if\ t \in [0, t_1], \\ \psi_{t_1} + \frac{\xi}{\Gamma(r)} \int_{t_1}^t \theta^{\xi-1}(t-\theta)^{r-1} v(\theta, \psi(\theta))d\theta, & t \in [t_1, t_2] \\ \psi_{t_2} + \int_{t_2}^t v(\theta, \psi(\theta))d\theta, & if\ t \in [t_2, t_3], \\ \psi_{t_3} + \frac{\xi}{\Gamma(r)} \int_{t_3}^t \theta^{\xi-1}(t-\theta)^{r-1} v(\theta, \psi(\theta))d\theta, & t \in [t_3, \mathscr{T}]. \end{cases} \tag{27}$$

Let the following given assumptions hold true:

(D_1) Let there be, for $\psi, \bar{\psi} \in \mathbb{I}$, $\mathscr{K}_v > 0$, satisfying

$$|v(t, \psi(t)) - v(t, \bar{\psi}(t))| \le \mathscr{K}_v |\psi(t) - \bar{\psi}(t)|.$$

(D_2) The real values $\mathscr{N}_0, \mathscr{N}_1 > 0$, satisfy

$$|v(t, \psi(t))| \le \mathscr{N}_0 + \mathscr{N}_1 |\psi(t)|.$$

Theorem 1. *Under the assumption* (D_1) *and if* $\max\left(t_1\mathscr{K}_v, t_3\mathscr{K}_v, \zeta_1\mathscr{K}_v\beta(r,\xi), \zeta_2\mathscr{K}_v\beta(r,\xi)\right) < 1$ *holds, then problem* (15) *has a unique solution.*

Proof. For this result, we take two cases:

Case-I: If t lies in the first interval, i.e., $[0, t_1]$, then

$$|\mathscr{P}(\psi)(t) - \mathscr{P}(\overline{\psi})(t)| \le \int_0^t |v(\theta, \psi(\theta)) - v(\theta, \overline{\psi}(\theta))| d\theta. \tag{28}$$

Using assumption (D_1) and applying the norm, we have

$$\|\mathscr{P}(\psi) - \mathscr{P}(\overline{\psi})\| \le t_1 \mathscr{K}_v \|\psi - \bar{\psi}\|. \tag{29}$$

Case-II: $t \in [t_1, t_2]$.

$$\begin{aligned} |\mathscr{P}(\psi)(t) - \mathscr{P}(\overline{\psi})(t)| &\le \frac{\xi}{\Gamma(r)} \int_{t_1}^t \theta^{\xi-1}(t-\theta)^{r-1} |v(\theta, \psi(\theta)) - v(\theta, \overline{\psi}(\theta))| d\theta \\ &\le \frac{\xi \mathscr{K}_v}{\Gamma(r)} \int_{t_1}^t \theta^{\xi-1}(t-\theta)^{r-1} \|\psi - \bar{\psi}\| d\theta. \end{aligned} \tag{30}$$

Consider the integral $\int_{t_1}^t \theta^{\xi-1}(t-\theta)^{r-1} d\theta$. Let $\theta = tw$. This implies that $d\theta = tdw$. If $\theta = t_1$, then $w = \frac{t_1}{t}$, and if $\theta = t$, then $w = 1$. Thus, we have

$$\begin{aligned} \int_{t_1}^t \theta^{\xi-1}(t-\theta)^{r-1} d\theta &= t^{\xi+r-1} \int_{\frac{t_1}{t}}^1 w^{\xi-1}(1-w)^{r-1} dw \le t^{\xi+r-1} \int_0^1 w^{\xi-1}(1-w)^{r-1} dw \\ &= t^{\xi+r-1} \beta(r, \xi), \end{aligned} \tag{31}$$

where $\beta(r, \xi)$ is a beta function. Hence, from (30), we obtain

$$\begin{aligned} |\mathscr{P}(\psi)(t) - \mathscr{P}(\overline{\psi})(t)| &\le \frac{\xi \mathscr{K}_v t^{\xi+r-1}}{\Gamma(r)} \beta(r, \xi) \|\psi - \bar{\psi}\| \\ &\le \frac{\xi \mathscr{K}_v {t_2}^{\xi+r-1}}{\Gamma(r)} \beta(r, \xi) \|\psi - \bar{\psi}\|. \end{aligned} \tag{32}$$

Let us denote $\frac{\xi t_2^{\xi+r-1}}{\Gamma(r)}$ by ζ_1. Then,

$$|\mathscr{P}(\psi)(t) - \mathscr{P}(\overline{\psi})(t)| \leq \zeta_1 \mathscr{K}_v \beta(r,\xi) \|\psi - \bar{\psi}\|. \tag{33}$$

Case-III: $t \in [t_2, t_3]$.

$$|\mathscr{P}(\psi)(t) - \mathscr{P}(\overline{\psi})(t)| \leq \int_{t_2}^{t} |v(\theta, \psi(\theta)) - v(\theta, \overline{\psi}(\theta))| d\theta. \tag{34}$$

Using assumption (D_1) and applying the norm, we have

$$\|\mathscr{P}(\psi) - \mathscr{P}(\overline{\psi})\| \leq t_3 \mathscr{K}_v \|\psi - \bar{\psi}\|. \tag{35}$$

Case—IV: $t \in [t_3, \mathscr{T}]$. By an analysis similar to Case-II, we obtain

$$|\mathscr{P}(\psi)(t) - \mathscr{P}(\overline{\psi})(t)| \leq |\mathscr{P}(\psi)(t) - \mathscr{P}(\overline{\psi})(t)| \leq \zeta_2 \mathscr{K}_v \beta(r,\xi) \|\psi - \bar{\psi}\|. \tag{36}$$

where $\zeta_2 = \frac{\xi \mathscr{T}^{\xi+r-1}}{\Gamma(r)}$. Now, $\max\left(t_1 \mathscr{K}_v, t_3 \mathscr{K}_v, \zeta_1 \mathscr{K}_v \beta(r,\xi), \zeta_2 \mathscr{K}_v \beta(r,\xi)\right) < 1$. Therefore, from (29), (33), (35), and (36), we deduce that the fixed point of the operator $\mathscr{P}$ is unique. □

Theorem 2. *Under the assumed conditions* (D_1), *problem* (15) *has one or more solutions.*

Proof. To carry out this result, let us define two operators, namely $\mathscr{P}_1$ and $\mathscr{P}_2$, such that $\mathscr{P} = \mathscr{P}_1 + \mathscr{P}_2$ as

$$\mathscr{P}_1(\psi) = \begin{cases} \psi_0 + \int_0^t v(\theta, \psi(\theta)) d\theta, & if\ t \in [0, t_1], \\ 0, & if\ t \in [t_1, t_2], \\ \psi(t_2) + \int_{t_2}^t v(\theta, \psi(\theta)) d\theta, & if\ t \in [t_2, t_3], \\ 0, & if\ t \in [t_3, \mathscr{T}] \end{cases} \tag{37}$$

and

$$\mathscr{P}_2(\psi) = \begin{cases} 0, & if\ t \in [0, t_1], \\ \psi(t_1) + \frac{\xi}{\Gamma(r)} \int_{t_1}^t \theta^{\xi-1} (t-\theta)^{r-1} v(\theta, \psi(\theta)) d\theta, & if\ t \in [t_1, t_2] \\ 0, & if\ t \in [t_2, t_3] \\ \psi(t_3) + \frac{\xi}{\Gamma(r)} \int_{t_3}^t \theta^{\xi-1} (t-\theta)^{r-1} v(\theta, \psi(\theta)) d\theta, & if\ t \in [t_3, \mathscr{T}]. \end{cases} \tag{38}$$

We take a closed ball $\mho_\delta = \{\psi \in \mathbb{I} : \|\psi\| \leq \delta\}$, satisfying

$$\delta \geq \max\Big\{ \|\psi(0)\| + \mathscr{N}_0 t_1 + \mathscr{N}_1 \delta t_1, \|\psi(2)\| + \mathscr{N}_0 t_3 + \mathscr{N}_1 \delta t_3,$$
$$\|\psi(t_1)\| + \frac{\xi t_2^{\xi+r-1} \beta(r,\xi)}{\Gamma(r)} (N_0 + \mathscr{N}_1 \delta), \|\psi(t_3)\| + \frac{\xi \mathscr{T}^{\xi+r-1} \beta(r,\xi)}{\Gamma(r)} (N_0 + \mathscr{N}_1 \delta) \Big\}.$$

We now present a number of steps to complete the proof.

Step 1:

$\mathscr{P}_1\psi(t)+\mathscr{P}_2\psi(t)\in \mho_\delta$. For $t\in[0,t_1]$, $\psi\in\mho_\delta$, we have

$$\begin{aligned}|\mathscr{P}_1\psi(t)+\mathscr{P}_2\psi(t)| &= \left|\psi_0+\int_0^t v(\theta,\psi(\theta))d\theta\right| \\ &\leq |\psi_0|+\int_0^t |v(\theta,\psi(\theta))|d\theta \\ &\leq |\psi_0|+\int_0^t (\mathscr{N}_0+\mathscr{N}_1|\psi(t)|)d\theta.\end{aligned} \tag{39}$$

Using (D_2), we obtain

$$\begin{aligned}|\mathscr{P}_1\psi(t)+\mathscr{P}_2\psi(t)| &\leq |\psi_0|+\int_0^t (\mathscr{N}_0+\mathscr{N}_1|\psi(t)|)d\theta \\ &\leq |\psi_0|+\sup_{t\in[0,t_1]}\mathscr{N}_0 t+\sup_{t\in[0,t_1]}\mathscr{N}_1|\psi(t)|t \\ &\leq |\psi_0|+\mathscr{N}_0 t_1+\mathscr{N}_1\delta t_1\leq\delta.\end{aligned} \tag{40}$$

Hence,

$$\|\mathscr{P}_1\psi+\mathscr{P}_2\psi\|\leq\|\psi(0)\|+\mathscr{N}_0 t_1+\mathscr{N}_1\delta t_1\leq\delta. \tag{41}$$

Similarly, for $t\in[t_2,t_3]$, we obtain

$$\|\mathscr{P}_1\psi+\mathscr{P}_2\psi\|\leq\|\psi(2)\|+\mathscr{N}_0 t_3+\mathscr{N}_1\delta t_3\leq\delta. \tag{42}$$

For $t\in[t_1,t_2]$, taking $\psi\in\mho_\delta$, we have

$$\begin{aligned}|\mathscr{P}_1\psi(t)+\mathscr{P}_2\psi(t)| &= \left|\psi(t_1)+\frac{\xi}{\Gamma(r)}\int_{t_1}^t \theta^{\xi-1}(t-\theta)^{r-1}v(\theta,\psi(\theta))d\theta\right| \\ &\leq |\psi(t_1)|+\frac{\xi}{\Gamma(r)}\int_{t_1}^t \theta^{\xi-1}(t-\theta)^{r-1}|v(\theta,\psi(\theta))|d\theta \\ &\leq |\psi(t_1)|+\frac{\xi}{\Gamma(r)}\int_{t_1}^t \theta^{\xi-1}(t-\theta)^{r-1}(\mathscr{N}_0+\mathscr{N}_1|\psi(t)|)d\theta.\end{aligned} \tag{43}$$

As in (31), using the transformation

$$\begin{aligned}&\int_{t_1}^t \theta^{\xi-1}(t-\theta)^{r-1}d\theta = t^{\xi+r-1}\int_{\frac{t_1}{t}}^1 w^{\xi-1}(1-w)^{r-1}dw\leq t^{\xi+r-1}\int_0^1 w^{\xi-1}(1-w)^{r-1}dw \\ &= t^{\xi+r-1}\beta(r,\xi),\end{aligned}$$

from (43), we have

$$|\mathscr{P}_1\psi(t)+\mathscr{P}_2\psi(t)|\leq|\psi(t_1)|+\frac{\xi t^{\xi+r-1}\mathscr{N}_0}{\Gamma(r)}\beta(r,\xi)+\frac{\xi t^{\xi+r-1}\mathscr{N}_1\delta}{\Gamma(r)}\beta(r,\xi)\leq\delta. \tag{44}$$

This implies that

$$\|\mathscr{P}_1\psi+\mathscr{P}_2\psi\|\leq\|\psi(t_1)\|+\frac{\xi {t_2}^{\xi+r-1}\beta(r,\xi)}{\Gamma(r)}(N_0+\mathscr{N}_1\delta)\leq\delta. \tag{45}$$

Similarly, for $t\in[t_3,\mathscr{T}]$, we obtain

$$\|\mathscr{P}_1\psi+\mathscr{P}_2\psi\|\leq\|\psi(t_3)\|+\frac{\xi \mathscr{T}^{\xi+r-1}\beta(r,\xi)}{\Gamma(r)}(N_0+\mathscr{N}_1\delta)\leq\delta. \tag{46}$$

Therefore, $\mathscr{P}_1\psi(t)+\mathscr{P}_2\psi(t)\in\mho_\delta$.

Step 2:

$\mathscr{P}_1$ is a contraction.

Let $\psi, \overline{\psi} \in \mho_\delta$. First, we consider the result for $t \in [0, t_1]$.

$$|\mathscr{P}_1(\psi)(t) - \mathscr{P}_1(\overline{\psi})(t)| \leq \int_0^t |v(\theta, \psi(\theta)) - v(\theta, \overline{\psi}(\theta))| d\theta. \tag{47}$$

Using assumption (D_1) and applying the norm, we have

$$\|\mathscr{P}_1(\psi) - \mathscr{P}_1(\overline{\psi})\| \leq t_1 \mathscr{K}_v \|\psi - \bar{\psi}\|. \tag{48}$$

Similarly, for $t \in [t_2, t_3]$, we have

$$\|\mathscr{P}_1(\psi) - \mathscr{P}_1(\overline{\psi})\| \leq t_3 \mathscr{K}_v \|\psi - \bar{\psi}\|. \tag{49}$$

Thus, $\mathscr{P}_1$ is a contraction in $[0, t_1]$ and $[t_2, t_3]$. Also, the result is obvious for $t \in [t_1, t_2]$ and $t \in [t_3, \mathscr{T}]$. Therefore, $\mathscr{P}_1$ is a contraction in $[0, \mathscr{T}]$.

Step 3:

In the third step, we need to show that the sub-operator $\mathscr{P}_2$ is relatively compact. As $v(t, \psi(t))$ is continuous, $\mathscr{P}_2$ is thus also continuous.

Next, we need to show that $\mathscr{P}_2$ is uniformly bounded on the closed ball $\mho_\delta$. For $t \in [0, t_1]$, $t \in [t_2, t_3]$, the case is obvious. Hence, we consider for $t \in [t_1, t_2]$ and $t \in [t_3, \mathscr{T}]$.

For $t \in [t_1, t_2]$, $\psi \in \mho_\delta$.

$$|\mathscr{P}_2\psi(t)| \leq |\psi(t_1)| + \sup_{t \in (t_1, \mathscr{T}]} \frac{\xi}{\Gamma(r)} \int_{t_1}^t \theta^{\xi-1}(t-\theta)^{r-1} |v(\theta, \psi(\theta))| d\theta.$$

Using assumption (D_2) and the transformation given in (31), we have

$$\begin{aligned} |\mathscr{P}_2\psi(t)| &\leq |\psi(t_1)| + \frac{\xi t_2{}^{\xi+r-1}(\mathscr{N}_0 + \mathscr{N}_1\delta)}{\Gamma(r)} \beta(r, \xi) \leq \delta \\ &\leq \|\psi(t_1)\| + \frac{\xi.\mathscr{T}^{\xi+r-1}(\mathscr{N}_0 + \mathscr{N}_1\delta)}{\Gamma(r)} \beta(r, \xi) \leq \delta. \end{aligned}$$

Similarly, for $t \in [t_3, \mathscr{T}]$, we obtain

$$|\mathscr{P}_2\psi(t)| \leq \|\psi(t_3)\| + \frac{\xi.\mathscr{T}^{\xi+r-1}(\mathscr{N}_0 + \mathscr{N}_1\delta)}{\Gamma(r)} \beta(r, \xi) \leq \delta.$$

Thus, $\mathscr{P}_2$ is uniformly bounded on the closed ball $\mho_\delta$. Now, it remains to show that $\mathscr{P}_2$ is equi-continuous. For $\psi \in \mho_\delta$ and any $t_a, t_b \in [0, t_1]$, $t_a, t_b \in [t_2, t_3]$, with $t_a < t_b$, the case is obvious. We consider the result for $t_a, t_b \in [t_1, t_2]$ and $t_a, t_b \in [t_3, \mathscr{T}]$, with, $t_a < t_b$ and $\psi \in \mho_\delta$.

$$\begin{aligned} &|\mathscr{P}_2\psi(t_b) - \mathscr{P}_2\psi(t_a)| \\ &\leq \left| \frac{\xi}{\Gamma(r)} \left(\int_{t_1}^{t_b} \theta^{\xi-1}(t_b-\theta)^{r-1} v(\theta, \psi(\theta)) d\theta - \int_{t_1}^{t_a} \theta^{\xi-1}(t_a-\theta)^{r-1} v(\theta, \psi(\theta)) d\theta \right) \right|. \end{aligned} \tag{50}$$

In the integral $\int_{t_1}^{t_b} \theta^{\xi-1}(t_b-\theta)^{r-1} d\theta$, let $\theta = t_b x$. Then, $d\theta = t_b dx$. We obtain $x = \frac{t_1}{t_b}$ for $\theta = t_1$ and $x = 1$ for $\theta = t_b$. The integral transforms into the form $t_b{}^{\xi+r-1} \int_{\frac{t_1}{t_b}}^1 x^{\xi-1}(1-x)^{r-1} dx$. Similarly, in integral $\int_{t_1}^{t_a} \theta^{\xi-1}(t_a-\theta)^{r-1} v(\theta, \psi(\theta)) d\theta$, by taking $\theta = t_a x$, the integral obtains the form ${t_a}^{\xi+r-1}\int_{\frac{t_1}{t_a}}^{1} x^{\xi-1}(1-x)^{r-1}dx$. Using these transformations and assumption (D_2), (50) takes the form

$$\begin{aligned}
&|\mathscr{P}_2\psi(t_b)-\mathscr{P}_2\psi(t_a)| \\
&\leq \left|\frac{\xi(\mathcal{N}_0+\mathcal{N}_1\delta)}{\Gamma(r)}\left({t_b}^{\xi+r-1}\int_{\frac{t_1}{t_b}}^{1} x^{\xi-1}(1-x)^{r-1}dx - {t_a}^{\xi+r-1}\int_{\frac{t_1}{t_a}}^{1} x^{\xi-1}(1-x)^{r-1}dx\right)\right| \\
&\to 0 \text{ as } t_a \to t_b.
\end{aligned} \tag{51}$$

Similarly, for $t_a, t_b \in [t_3, \mathscr{T}]$, with, $t_a < t_b$ and $\psi \in \mho_\delta$, we obtain

$$\begin{aligned}
&|\mathscr{P}_2\psi(t_b)-\mathscr{P}_2\psi(t_a)| \\
&\leq \left|\frac{\xi(\mathcal{N}_0+\mathcal{N}_1\delta)}{\Gamma(r)}\left({t_b}^{\xi+r-1}\int_{\frac{t_3}{t_b}}^{1} x^{\xi-1}(1-x)^{r-1}dx - {t_a}^{\xi+r-1}\int_{\frac{t_3}{t_a}}^{1} x^{\xi-1}(1-x)^{r-1}dx\right)\right| \\
&\to 0 \text{ as } t_a \to t_b.
\end{aligned} \tag{52}$$

This proves the equi-continuity of the sub-operator $\mathscr{P}_2$. Therefore, using the Arzelá–Ascoli theorem and the above steps, the relative compactness and, consequently, the complete continuity of $\mathscr{P}$ are proven. Therefore, by Krasnoselskii's fixed-point theorem, there is one or more solutions of the proposed problem (15). □

3.2. Stability Results

In this section, we use the H-U approach of the stability analysis to derive stable criteria for the proposed problem. We have adopted the following definitions of stability from [34].

Definition 6. *The model* (15) *is H-U-stable if there exists a real number* $\mathbb{C} = \max\{\mathbb{C}_1, \mathbb{C}_2, \mathbb{C}_3\} > 0$ *such that for each* $\epsilon = \max\{\epsilon_1, \epsilon_2, \epsilon_3\} > 0$*, there is a solution* $\overline{\psi} \in \mathbb{I}$ *of* (53)

$$\left|{}^{p}D^{r,\xi}\overline{\psi}(t) - v(t, \overline{\psi}(t))\right| \leq \epsilon, t \in J \tag{53}$$

corresponding to a unique solution $\psi \in \mathbb{I}$ *of model* (15)*, such that*

$$\|\overline{\psi} - \psi\| \leq \mathbb{C}\epsilon, \qquad t \in J,$$

where

$$\overline{\psi}(t) = \begin{bmatrix} \overline{\psi}_1 \\ \overline{\psi}_2 \\ \overline{\psi}_3 \end{bmatrix} = \begin{bmatrix} -a\overline{X}(t) + b\overline{Y}(t) \\ a\overline{X}(t) - (b+c)\overline{Y}(t) \\ c\overline{Y}(t) \end{bmatrix},$$

$$v(t, \overline{\psi}(t)) = \begin{bmatrix} \overline{\Phi}_1(t, \overline{X}, \overline{Y}, \overline{Z}) \\ \overline{\Phi}_2(t, \overline{X}, \overline{Y}, \overline{Z}) \\ \overline{\Phi}_3(t, \overline{X}, \overline{Y}, \overline{Z}) \end{bmatrix}, \overline{\psi}_0 = \begin{bmatrix} \overline{X}_0 \\ \overline{Y}_0 \\ \overline{Z}_0 \end{bmatrix}.$$

Remark 1. *The function* $\overline{\psi} \in \mathbb{I}$ *is a solution of the inequality*

$$\left|{}^{p}D^{r,\xi}\overline{\psi}(t) - v(t, \overline{\psi}(t))\right| \leq \epsilon, t \in J,$$

if and only if there is a small perturbation $\aleph \in \mathbb{I}$ *that satisfies the following:*

(i) $|\aleph(t)| \leq \epsilon, t \in J$;

(ii) ${}^{p}D^{r,\xi}\overline{\psi}(t) = v(t, \overline{\psi}(t)) + \aleph(t), t \in J$,

where $\aleph(t) = (t, \aleph_1(t), \aleph_2(t), \aleph_3(t))$.

By Remark 1, we have the following problem with a small perturbation function $\aleph(t)$,

$$ {}^{p}D^{r,\xi}\overline{\psi}(t)=\begin{cases} v(t,\overline{\psi}(t))+\aleph(t), & r\in(0,1],\\ \overline{\psi}(0)=\overline{\psi}_0, \quad \overline{\psi}(t_1)=\overline{\psi}_{t_1}, \quad \overline{\psi}(t_2)=\overline{\psi}_{t_2}, \quad \overline{\psi}(t_3)=\overline{\psi}_{t_3}. \end{cases} \tag{54} $$

Lemma 2. *Problem* (54) *with the perturbation function* $\aleph(t)$ *has the following solution:*

$$ \overline{\psi}(t)=\begin{cases} \overline{\psi}_0+\int_0^t (v(\theta,\overline{\psi}(\theta))+\aleph(\theta))d\theta, \quad if\ t\in[0,t_1],\\ \overline{\psi}_{t_1}+\frac{\xi}{\Gamma(r)}\int_{t_1}^t \theta^{\xi-1}(t-\theta)^{r-1}(v(\theta,\overline{\psi}(\theta))+\aleph(\theta))d\theta, \quad t\in[t_1,t_2]\\ \overline{\psi}_{t_2}+\int_{t_2}^t (v(\theta,\overline{\psi}(\theta))+\aleph(\theta))d\theta, \quad if\ t\in[t_2,t_3],\\ \overline{\psi}_{t_3}+\frac{\xi}{\Gamma(r)}\int_{t_3}^t \theta^{\xi-1}(t-\theta)^{r-1}(v(\theta,\overline{\psi}(\theta))+\aleph(\theta))d\theta, \quad t\in[t_3,\mathscr{T}]. \end{cases} \tag{55} $$

Theorem 3. *Under the assumption* (D_1) *and if* $\max\left(t_1\mathscr{K}_v,\xi\mathscr{K}_v\beta(r,\xi)\right)<1$ *holds, then problem* (15) *is H-U-stable.*

Proof. For any solution $\overline{\psi}\in\mathbb{I}$ of inequality (53) and unique solution $\psi\in\mathbb{I}$ of model (15), we consider, for this result, two cases:

Case-I : For $t\in[0,t_1]$, we have

$$ |\overline{\psi}(t)-\psi(t)|\leq\int_0^t|v(\theta,\overline{\psi}(\theta))-v(\theta,\psi(\theta))|d\theta+\int_0^t\aleph(\theta)d\theta. \tag{56} $$

Using assumption (D_1), part (i) of Remark 1 and applying the norm, we have

$$ \|\overline{\psi}-\psi\|\leq t_1\mathscr{K}_v\|\overline{\psi}(t)-\psi(t)\|+t_1\epsilon. \tag{57} $$

This implies that

$$ \|\overline{\psi}(t)-\psi(t)\|\leq\frac{t_1}{1-t_1\mathscr{K}_v}\epsilon. \tag{58} $$

Similarly, for $t\in[t_2,t_3]$, we obtain

$$ \|\overline{\psi}(t)-\psi(t)\|\leq\frac{t_3}{1-t_3\mathscr{K}_v}\epsilon. \tag{59} $$

Case-II : $t\in[t_1,t_2]$.

$$ \begin{aligned} |\overline{\psi}(t)-\psi(t)| &\leq\frac{\xi}{\Gamma(r)}\int_{t_1}^t\theta^{\xi-1}(t-\theta)^{r-1}|v(\theta,\overline{\psi}(\theta))-v(\theta,\psi(\theta))|d\theta\\ &+\frac{\xi}{\Gamma(r)}\int_{t_1}^t\theta^{\xi-1}(t-\theta)^{r-1}|\aleph(\theta)|d\theta\\ &\leq\frac{\xi\mathscr{K}_v}{\Gamma(r)}\int_{t_1}^t\theta^{\xi-1}(t-\theta)^{r-1}|\bar{\psi}(\theta)-\psi(\theta)|d\theta\\ &+\frac{\xi\epsilon}{\Gamma(r)}\int_{t_1}^t\theta^{\xi-1}(t-\theta)^{r-1}d\theta. \end{aligned} \tag{60} $$

Using the transformation given in (31), the last inequality implies that

$$\begin{aligned} |\overline{\psi}(t)-\psi(t)| &\leq \frac{\xi\mathscr{K}_v}{\Gamma(r)}t^{\xi+r-1}\beta(r,\xi)|\bar{\psi}(\theta)-\psi(\theta)| \\ &+\frac{\xi\epsilon}{\Gamma(r)}t^{\xi+r-1}\beta(r,\xi) \\ &\leq \frac{\xi\mathscr{K}_v}{\Gamma(r)}t_2{}^{\xi+r-1}\beta(r,\xi)|\bar{\psi}(\theta)-\psi(\theta)| \\ &+\frac{\xi\epsilon}{\Gamma(r)}t_2{}^{\xi+r-1}\beta(r,\xi). \end{aligned} \tag{61}$$

Denote $\frac{\xi}{\Gamma(r)}t_2{}^{\xi+r-1}$ by ζ_1, and then we have

$$|\overline{\psi}(t)-\psi(t)| \leq \zeta_1\mathscr{K}_v\beta(r,\xi)|\bar{\psi}(t)-\psi(t)|+\zeta_1\beta(r,\xi)\epsilon. \tag{62}$$

Taking the maximum and simplifying the result, we have

$$\|\overline{\psi}-\psi\| \leq \frac{\zeta_1\beta(r,\xi)}{1-\zeta_1\mathscr{K}_v\beta(r,\xi)}\epsilon. \tag{63}$$

Similarly, for $t\in[t_3,\mathscr{T}]$, we obtain

$$\|\overline{\psi}-\psi\| \leq \frac{\zeta_2\beta(r,\xi)}{1-\zeta_2\mathscr{K}_v\beta(r,\xi)}\epsilon, \tag{64}$$

where $\mathbb{C}>0$ is chosen, such that

$$\mathbb{C}=\begin{cases} \frac{t_1}{1-t_1\mathscr{K}_v}, & if\ t\in[0,t_1], \\ \frac{\zeta_1\beta(r,\xi)}{1-\zeta_1\mathscr{K}_v\beta(r,\xi)}, & if\ t\in[t_1,t_2] \\ \frac{t_3}{1-t_3\mathscr{K}_v}, & if\ t\in[t_2,t_3], \\ \frac{\zeta_2\beta(r,\xi)}{1-\zeta_2\mathscr{K}_v\beta(r,\xi)}, & if\ t\in[t_3,\mathscr{T}]. \end{cases}$$

Hence,

$$\|\overline{\psi}-\psi\| \leq \mathbb{C}\epsilon. \tag{65}$$

Therefore, model (15) is H-U-stable. □

4. Numerical Scheme

In this section, we will establish a numerical scheme for the proposed human liver model under piecewise FFCD by using the extended ADM numerical method and Lagrangian piecewise interpolation [35]. This method has increasingly been applied to approximate the solutions of nonlinear fractal-fractional-order problems. This method has also extensively been used in epidemic models; see [36,37]. Its convergence depends on fractional order, time step size, and spatial grid size.

First, we present the equivalent integral form of our proposed problem at $t=t_{q+1}$ as

$$\begin{cases} X^{q+1} = \begin{cases} X(0) + \int_0^{t_{q+1}} \Phi_1(\theta, X, Y, Z) d\theta, & if\ t_{q+1} \in [0, t_1], \\ X(t_1) + \frac{\xi}{\Gamma(r)} \int_{t_1}^{t_{q+1}} \theta^{\xi-1}(t_{q+1}-\theta)^{r-1} \Phi_1(\theta, X, Y, Z) d\theta, & t_{q+1} \in [t_1, t_2], \\ X(t_2) + \int_{t_2}^{t_{q+1}} \Phi_1(\theta, X, Y, Z) d\theta, & if\ t_{q+1} \in [t_2, t_3], \\ X(t_3) + \frac{\xi}{\Gamma(r)} \int_{t_3}^{t_{q+1}} \theta^{\xi-1}(t_{q+1}-\theta)^{r-1} \Phi_1(\theta, X, Y, Z) d\theta, & t_{q+1} \in [t_3, \mathscr{T}], \end{cases} \\ Y^{q+1} = \begin{cases} Y(0) + \int_0^{t_{q+1}} \Phi_2(\theta, X, Y, Z) d\theta, & if\ t_{q+1} \in [0, t_1], \\ Y(t_1) + \frac{\xi}{\Gamma(r)} \int_{t_1}^{t_{q+1}} \theta^{\xi-1}(t_{q+1}-\theta)^{r-1} \Phi_2(\theta, X, Y, Z) d\theta, & t_{q+1} \in [t_1, t_2], \\ Y(t_2) + \int_{t_2}^{t_{q+1}} \Phi_2(\theta, X, Y, Z) d\theta, & if\ t_{q+1} \in [t_2, t_3], \\ Y(t_3) + \frac{\xi}{\Gamma(r)} \int_{t_3}^{t_{q+1}} \theta^{\xi-1}(t_{q+1}-\theta)^{r-1} \Phi_2(\theta, X, Y, Z) d\theta, & t_{q+1} \in [t_3, \mathscr{T}], \end{cases} \\ Z^{q+1} = \begin{cases} Z(0) + \int_0^{t_{q+1}} \Phi_3(\theta, X, Y, Z) d\theta, & if\ t_{q+1} \in [0, t_1], \\ Z(t_1) + \frac{\xi}{\Gamma(r)} \int_{t_1}^{t_{q+1}} \theta^{\xi-1}(t_{q+1}-\theta)^{r-1} \Phi_3(\theta, X, Y, Z) d\theta, & t_{q+1} \in [t_1, t_2], \\ Z(t_2) + \int_{t_2}^{t_{q+1}} \Phi_3(\theta, X, Y, Z) d\theta, & if\ t_{q+1} \in [t_2, t_3], \\ Z(t_3) + \frac{\xi}{\Gamma(r)} \int_{t_3}^{t_{q+1}} \theta^{\xi-1}(t_{q+1}-\theta)^{r-1} \Phi_3(\theta, X, Y, Z) d\theta, & t_{q+1} \in [t_3, \mathscr{T}]. \end{cases} \end{cases} \tag{66}$$

An approximation of the system of equations (66) is given as

$$\begin{cases} X^{q+1} = \begin{cases} X(0) + \int_0^{t_{q+1}} \Phi_1(\theta, X, Y, Z) d\theta, & if\ t_{q+1} \in [0, t_1], \\ X(t_1) + \frac{\xi}{\Gamma(r)} \sum_{\varrho=1}^{q} \int_{t_\varrho}^{t_{q+1}} \theta^{\xi-1}(t_{q+1}-\theta)^{r-1} \Phi_1(\theta, X, Y, Z) d\theta, & t_{q+1} \in [t_1, t_2], \\ X(t_2) + \int_{t_2}^{t_{q+1}} \Phi_1(\theta, X, Y, Z) d\theta, & if\ t_{q+1} \in [t_2, t_3], \\ X(t_3) + \frac{\xi}{\Gamma(r)} \sum_{\varrho=3}^{q} \int_{t_\varrho}^{t_{q+1}} \theta^{\xi-1}(t_{q+1}-\theta)^{r-1} \Phi_1(\theta, X, Y, Z) d\theta, & t_{q+1} \in [t_3, \mathscr{T}], \end{cases} \\ Y^{q+1} = \begin{cases} Y(0) + \int_0^{t_{q+1}} \Phi_2(\theta, X, Y, Z) d\theta, & if\ t_{q+1} \in [0, t_1], \\ Y(t_1) + \frac{\xi}{\Gamma(r)} \sum_{\varrho=1}^{q} \int_{t_\varrho}^{t_{q+1}} \theta^{\xi-1}(t_{q+1}-\theta)^{r-1} \Phi_2(\theta, X, Y, Z) d\theta, & t_{q+1} \in [t_1, t_2], \\ Y(t_2) + \int_{t_2}^{t_{q+1}} \Phi_2(\theta, X, Y, Z) d\theta, & if\ t_{q+1} \in [t_2, t_3], \\ Y(t_3) + \frac{\xi}{\Gamma(r)} \sum_{\varrho=3}^{q} \int_{t_\varrho}^{t_{q+1}} \theta^{\xi-1}(t_{q+1}-\theta)^{r-1} \Phi_2(\theta, X, Y, Z) d\theta, & t_{q+1} \in [t_3, \mathscr{T}], \end{cases} \\ Z^{q+1} = \begin{cases} Z(0) + \int_0^{t_{q+1}} \Phi_3(\theta, X, Y, Z) d\theta, & if\ t_{q+1} \in [0, t_1], \\ Z(t_1) + \frac{\xi}{\Gamma(r)} \sum_{\varrho=1}^{q} \int_{t_\varrho}^{t_{q+1}} \theta^{\xi-1}(t_{q+1}-\theta)^{r-1} \Phi_3(\theta, X, Y, Z) d\theta, & t_{q+1} \in [t_1, t_2], \\ Z(t_2) + \int_{t_2}^{t_{q+1}} \Phi_3(\theta, X, Y, Z) d\theta, & if\ t_{q+1} \in [t_2, t_3], \\ Z(t_3) + \frac{\xi}{\Gamma(r)} \sum_{\varrho=3}^{q} \int_{t_\varrho}^{t_{q+1}} \theta^{\xi-1}(t_{q+1}-\theta)^{r-1} \Phi_3(\theta, X, Y, Z) d\theta, & t_{q+1} \in [t_3, \mathscr{T}]. \end{cases} \end{cases} \tag{67}$$

We now use the Lagrangian polynomial piecewise interpolation in the interval $[t_q, t_{q+1}]$ to approximate the kernels within the integrals as follows:

$$\begin{cases} \mathscr{U}_q(\theta) = \dfrac{\theta - t_{q-1}}{t_q - t_{q-1}} t_q^{\xi-1} \Phi_1(t^q, X^q, Y^q, Z^q), \\ -\dfrac{\theta - t_q}{t_q - t_{q-1}} t_{q-1}^{\xi-1} \Phi_1(t^{q-1}, X^{q-1}, Y^{q-1}, Z^{q-1}), \\ \mathscr{V}_q(\theta) = \dfrac{\theta - t_{q-1}}{t_q - t_{q-1}} t_q^{\xi-1} \Phi_2(t^q, X^q, Y^q, Z^q), \\ -\dfrac{\theta - t_q}{t_q - t_{q-1}} t_{q-1}^{\xi-1} \Phi_2(t^{q-1}, X^{q-1}, Y^{q-1}, Z^{q-1}), \\ \mathscr{W}_q(\theta) = \dfrac{\theta - t_{q-1}}{t_q - t_{q-1}} t_q^{\xi-1} \Phi_3(t^q, X^q, Y^q, Z^q), \\ -\dfrac{\theta - t_q}{t_q - t_{q-1}} t_{q-1}^{\xi-1} \Phi_3(t^{q-1}, X^{q-1}, Y^{q-1}, Z^{q-1}). \end{cases} \tag{68}$$

By using these approximations, the system of Equation (67), takes the form

$$\begin{cases} X^{q+1} = \begin{cases} X(0) + \int_0^{t_{q+1}} \Phi_1(\theta, X, Y, Z) d\theta, \quad if\ t_{q+1} \in [0, t_1], \\ X(t_1) + \frac{\xi}{\Gamma(r)} \sum_{\varrho=1}^{q} \int_{t_\varrho}^{t_{q+1}} \theta^{\xi-1} (t_{q+1} - \theta)^{r-1} \mathscr{U}_q(\theta) d\theta, \quad t_{q+1} \in [t_1, t_2], \\ X(t_2) + \int_{t_2}^{t_{q+1}} \Phi_1(\theta, X, Y, Z) d\theta, \quad if\ t_{q+1} \in [t_2, t_3], \\ X(t_3) + \frac{\xi}{\Gamma(r)} \sum_{\varrho=3}^{q} \int_{t_\varrho}^{t_{q+1}} \theta^{\xi-1} (t_{q+1} - \theta)^{r-1} \mathscr{U}_q(\theta) d\theta, \quad t_{q+1} \in [t_3, \mathscr{T}], \end{cases} \\ Y^{q+1} = \begin{cases} Y(0) + \int_0^{t_{q+1}} \Phi_2(\theta, X, Y, Z) d\theta, \quad if\ t_{q+1} \in [0, t_1], \\ Y(t_1) + \frac{\xi}{\Gamma(r)} \sum_{\varrho=1}^{q} \int_{t_\varrho}^{t_{q+1}} \theta^{\xi-1} (t_{q+1} - \theta)^{r-1} \mathscr{V}_q(\theta) d\theta, \quad t_{q+1} \in [t_1, t_2], \\ Y(t_2) + \int_{t_2}^{t_{q+1}} \Phi_2(\theta, X, Y, Z) d\theta, \quad if\ t_{q+1} \in [t_2, t_3], \\ Y(t_3) + \frac{\xi}{\Gamma(r)} \sum_{\varrho=3}^{q} \int_{t_\varrho}^{t_{q+1}} \theta^{\xi-1} (t_{q+1} - \theta)^{r-1} \mathscr{V}_q(\theta) d\theta, \quad t_{q+1} \in [t_3, \mathscr{T}], \end{cases} \\ Z^{q+1} = \begin{cases} Z(0) + \int_0^{t_{q+1}} \Phi_3(\theta, X, Y, Z) d\theta, \quad if\ t_{q+1} \in [0, t_1], \\ Z(t_1) + \frac{\xi}{\Gamma(r)} \sum_{\varrho=1}^{q} \int_{t_\varrho}^{t_{q+1}} \theta^{\xi-1} (t_{q+1} - \theta)^{r-1} \mathscr{W}_q(\theta) d\theta, \quad t_{q+1} \in [t_1, t_2], \\ Z(t_2) + \int_{t_2}^{t_{q+1}} \Phi_3(\theta, X, Y, Z) d\theta, \quad if\ t_{q+1} \in [t_2, t_3], \\ Z(t_3) + \frac{\xi}{\Gamma(r)} \sum_{\varrho=3}^{q} \int_{t_\varrho}^{t_{q+1}} \theta^{\xi-1} (t_{q+1} - \theta)^{r-1} \mathscr{W}_q(\theta) d\theta, \quad t_{q+1} \in [t_3, \mathscr{T}]. \end{cases} \end{cases} \tag{69}$$

Using the Lagrangian polynomial piecewise interpolation and integration, we derive the numerical scheme for the proposed problem as follows:

$$
\begin{cases}
X^{q+1} = \begin{cases}
X(0) + \frac{3\Delta t}{2}\Phi_1(t_q, X^q, Y^q, Z^q) - \frac{\Delta t}{2}\Phi_1(t_{q-1}, X^{q-1}, Y^{q-1}, Z^{q-1}); \; t_q, t_{q-1} \in [0, t_1], \\
X(t_1) + \frac{\xi h^r}{\Gamma(r+2)} \sum_{\varrho=1}^{q} \Big[t_\varrho^{\xi-1} \Phi_1(t_\varrho, X^\varrho, Y^\varrho, Z^\varrho) \Big((q+1-\varrho)^r (q-\varrho+2+r) \\
-(q-\varrho)^r (q-\varrho+2+2r) \Big) - t_{\varrho-1}^{\xi-1} \Phi_1(t_{\varrho-1}, X^{\varrho-1}, Y^{\varrho-1}, Z^{\varrho-1}) \\
\times \Big((q-\varrho+1)^{r-1} - (q-\varrho)^r (q-\varrho+1+r) \Big) \Big]; \quad t_\varrho, t_{\varrho-1} \in [t_1, t_2], \\
X(t_2) + \frac{3\Delta t}{2}\Phi_1(t_q, X^q, Y^q, Z^q) - \frac{\Delta t}{2}\Phi_1(t_{q-1}, X^{q-1}, Y^{q-1}, Z^{q-1}); \; t_q, t_{q-1} \in [t_2, t_3], \\
X(t_3) + \frac{\xi h^r}{\Gamma(r+2)} \sum_{\varrho=3}^{q} \Big[t_\varrho^{\xi-1} \Phi_1(t_\varrho, X^\varrho, Y^\varrho, Z^\varrho) \Big((q+1-\varrho)^r (q-\varrho+2+r) \\
-(q-\varrho)^r (q-\varrho+2+2r) \Big) - t_{\varrho-1}^{\xi-1} \Phi_1(t_{\varrho-1}, X^{\varrho-1}, Y^{\varrho-1}, Z^{\varrho-1}) \\
\times \Big((q-\varrho+1)^{r-1} - (q-\varrho)^r (q-\varrho+1+r) \Big) \Big]; \quad t_\varrho, t_{\varrho-1} \in [t_3, \mathscr{T}],
\end{cases} \\
Y^{q+1} = \begin{cases}
Y(0) + \frac{3\Delta t}{2}\Phi_2(t_q, X^q, Y^q, Z^q) - \frac{\Delta t}{2}\Phi_2(t_{q-1}, X^{q-1}, Y^{q-1}, Z^{q-1}); \; t_q, t_{q-1} \in [0, t_1], \\
Y(t_1) + \frac{\xi h^r}{\Gamma(r+2)} \sum_{\varrho=1}^{q} \Big[t_\varrho^{\xi-1} \Phi_2(t_\varrho, X^\varrho, Y^\varrho, Z^\varrho) \Big((q+1-\varrho)^r (q-\varrho+2+r) \\
-(q-\varrho)^r (q-\varrho+2+2r) \Big) - t_{\varrho-1}^{\xi-1} \Phi_2(t_{\varrho-1}, X^{\varrho-1}, Y^{\varrho-1}, Z^{\varrho-1}) \\
\times \Big((q-\varrho+1)^{r-1} - (q-\varrho)^r (q-\varrho+1+r) \Big) \Big]; \quad t_\varrho, t_{\varrho-1} \in [t_1, t_2], \\
Y(t_2) + \frac{3\Delta t}{2}\Phi_2(t_q, X^q, Y^q, Z^q) - \frac{\Delta t}{2}\Phi_2(t_{q-1}, X^{q-1}, Y^{q-1}, Z^{q-1}); \; t_q, t_{q-1} \in [t_2, t_3], \\
Y(t_3) + \frac{\xi h^r}{\Gamma(r+2)} \sum_{\varrho=3}^{q} \Big[t_\varrho^{\xi-1} \Phi_2(t_\varrho, X^\varrho, Y^\varrho, Z^\varrho) \Big((q+1-\varrho)^r (q-\varrho+2+r) \\
-(q-\varrho)^r (q-\varrho+2+2r) \Big) - t_{\varrho-1}^{\xi-1} \Phi_2(t_{\varrho-1}, X^{\varrho-1}, Y^{\varrho-1}, Z^{\varrho-1}) \\
\times \Big((q-\varrho+1)^{r-1} - (q-\varrho)^r (q-\varrho+1+r) \Big) \Big]; \quad t_\varrho, t_{\varrho-1} \in [t_3, \mathscr{T}],
\end{cases} \\
Z^{q+1} = \begin{cases}
Z(0) + \frac{3\Delta t}{2}\Phi_3(t_q, X^q, Y^q, Z^q) - \frac{\Delta t}{2}\Phi_3(t_{q-1}, X^{q-1}, Y^{q-1}, Z^{q-1}); \; t_q, t_{q-1} \in [0, t_1], \\
Y(t_1) + \frac{\xi h^r}{\Gamma(r+2)} \sum_{\varrho=1}^{q} \Big[t_\varrho^{\xi-1} \Phi_3(t_\varrho, X^\varrho, Y^\varrho, Z^\varrho) \Big((q+1-\varrho)^r (q-\varrho+2+r) \\
-(q-\varrho)^r (q-\varrho+2+2r) \Big) - t_{\varrho-1}^{\xi-1} \Phi_3(t_{\varrho-1}, X^{\varrho-1}, Y^{\varrho-1}, Z^{\varrho-1}) \\
\times \Big((q-\varrho+1)^{r-1} - (q-\varrho)^r (q-\varrho+1+r) \Big) \Big]; \quad t_\varrho, t_{\varrho-1} \in [t_1, t_2], \\
Z(t_2) + \frac{3\Delta t}{2}\Phi_3(t_q, X^q, Y^q, Z^q) - \frac{\Delta t}{2}\Phi_3(t_{q-1}, X^{q-1}, Y^{q-1}, Z^{q-1}); \; t_q, t_{q-1} \in [t_2, t_3], \\
Z(t_3) + \frac{\xi h^r}{\Gamma(r+2)} \sum_{\varrho=3}^{q} \Big[t_\varrho^{\xi-1} \Phi_3(t_\varrho, X^\varrho, Y^\varrho, Z^\varrho) \Big((q+1-\varrho)^r (q-\varrho+2+r) \\
-(q-\varrho)^r (q-\varrho+2+2r) \Big) - t_{\varrho-1}^{\xi-1} \Phi_3(t_{\varrho-1}, X^{\varrho-1}, Y^{\varrho-1}, Z^{\varrho-1}) \\
\times \Big((q-\varrho+1)^{r-1} - (q-\varrho)^r (q-\varrho+1+r) \Big) \Big]; \quad t_\varrho, t_{\varrho-1} \in [t_3, \mathscr{T}],
\end{cases}
\end{cases} \tag{70}
$$

5. Simulations of the Numerical Results

In this portion of the manuscript, simulations of the numerical results derived in Section 4 are performed. We take the initial values as $X(0) = 250,\ Y(0) = 0,\ Z(0) = 0,$

and $a = 0.054736$, $b = 0.0152704$, $c = 0.0093906$ [11]. We present the numerical results graphically in Figures 1–3 for different fractional orders using the fractal order $\xi = 1$.

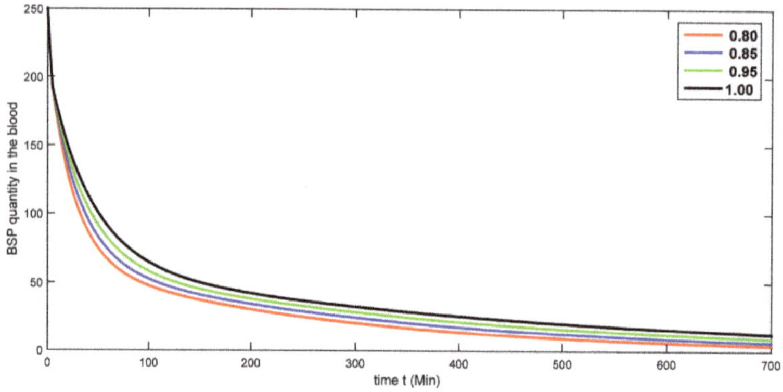

Figure 1. Simulation of BSP quantity in blood over time, corresponding to different fractional-order values using fractal order $\xi = 1$.

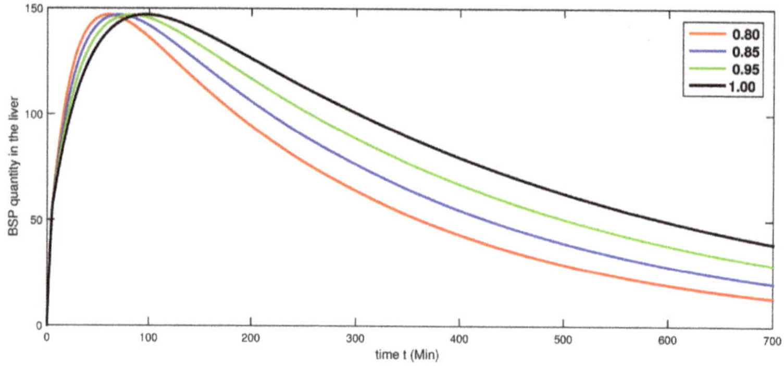

Figure 2. Simulation of BSP quantity in the liver over time, corresponding to different fractional-order values using fractal order $\xi = 1$.

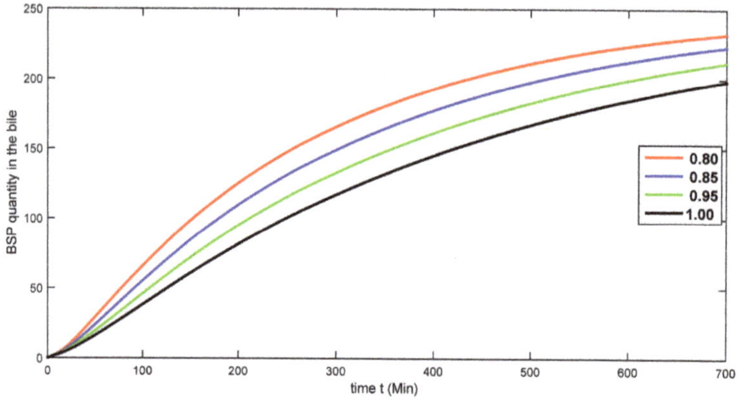

Figure 3. Simulation of BSP quantity in bile over time, corresponding to different fractional-order values using fractal order $\xi = 1$.

Here, we present the numerical solutions for various classes of the proposed model against different fractal-fractional-order values in Figures 4–6.

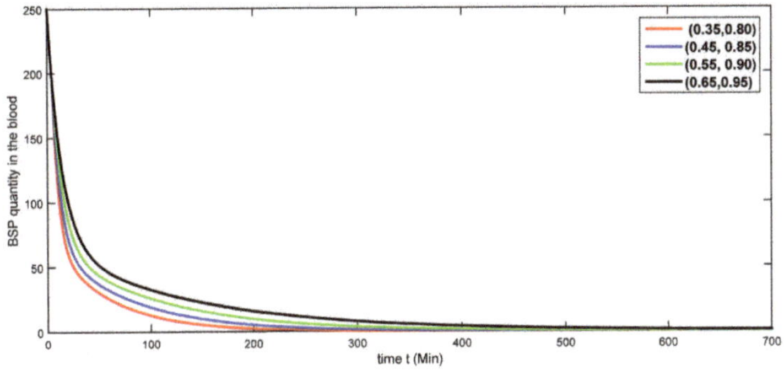

Figure 4. Simulation of BSP quantity in blood over time, corresponding to different fractal-fractional-order values.

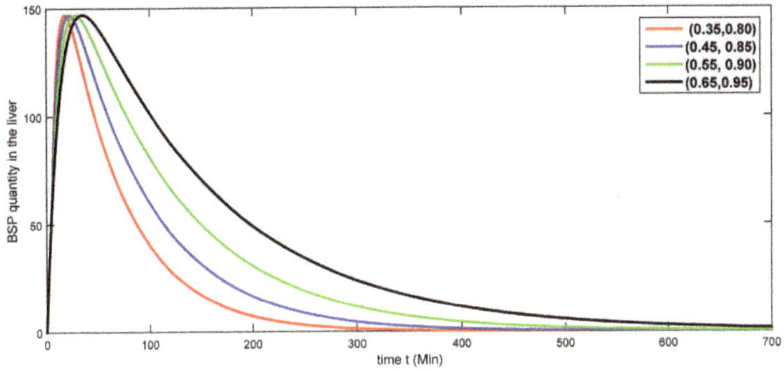

Figure 5. Simulation of BSP quantity in the liver over time, corresponding to different fractal-fractional-order values.

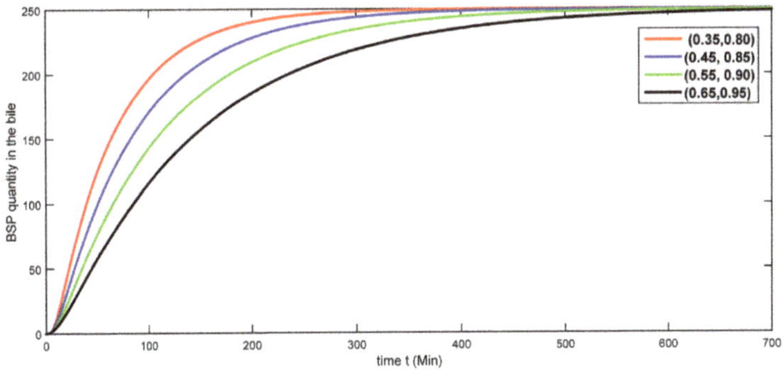

Figure 6. Simulation of BSP quantity in bile over time, corresponding to different fractal-fractional-order values.

Here, we present the numerical solutions for various classes of the proposed model against different fractal-fractional-order values in Figures 7–9.

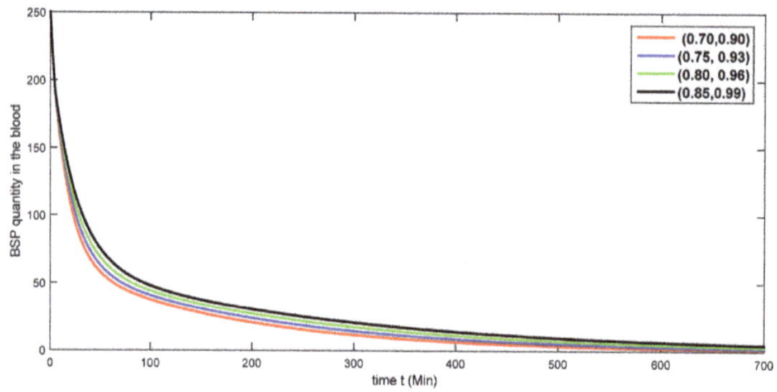

Figure 7. Simulation of BSP quantity in blood over time, corresponding to different fractal-fractional-order values.

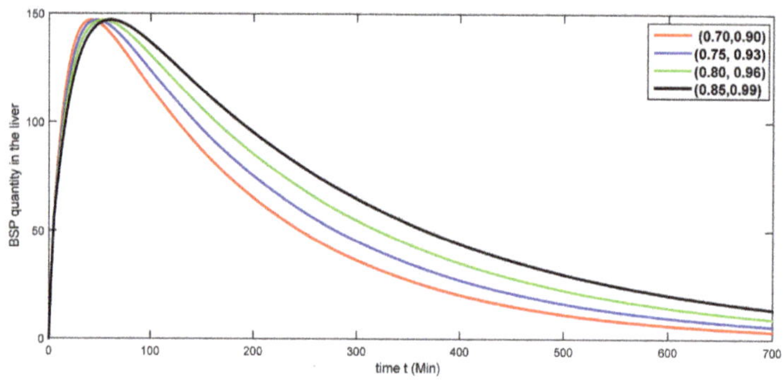

Figure 8. Simulation of BSP quantity in the liver over time, corresponding to different fractal-fractional-order values.

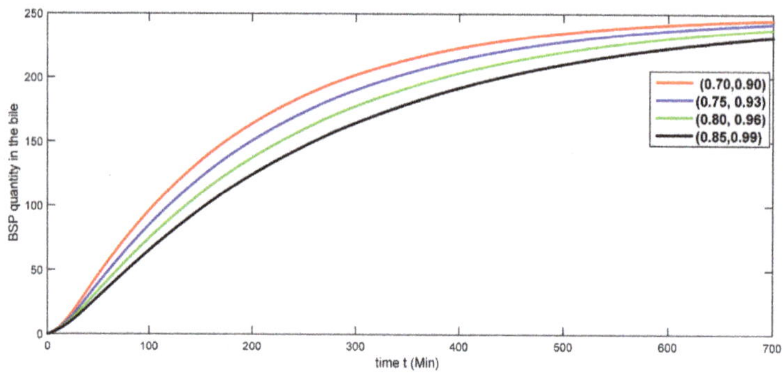

Figure 9. Simulation of BSP quantity in bile over time, corresponding to different fractal-fractional-order values.

To make a comparison between the proposed fractal-fractional model and its equivalent integer-order variant, we present the plots for integer order as follows.

6. Discussion

We used a numerical method based on the procedure of the Adam Bashforth method. This method has increasingly been applied to approximate the solutions of nonlinear fractal-fractional-order problems. This method has also extensively been used in epidemic models. However, this method has some limitations as well. For instance, in the case of oscillatory phenomena, the proposed numerical method suffers from instability like RK-4 (the Runge–Kutta method of order 4). In such a situation, short time intervals should be used. Moreover, this method does not converge unconditionally. Its convergence depends on fractional order, time step size, and spatial grid size.

We take different values of fractal-fractional order to simulate and illustrate the result as shown in the figures. In Figures 1–3, BSP levels in blood, liver, and bile are graphically shown for a fixed fractal order $\xi = 1$ and various fractional orders. In Figures 4–9, BSP levels in blood, liver, and bile are graphically shown for various sets of fractal-fractional orders. From these simulations, we observe the crossover effects in the BSP level at some instants of the given time intervals for various values of fractal dimension and fractional order. In Figure 1, we see that the BSP level in blood quickly decreases in the first 50 min and then it suddenly changes towards stability. In Figure 4, we observe a fast decline in the quantity of BSP levels in blood for varying ξ in the interval $(0, 1)$ and taking the same fractional order as in Figure 1. In Figure 2, we see that the quantity of the BSP level in the liver first increases and then shows a decline after observing crossover effects for a fixed fractal order $\xi = 1$ and various fractional orders. In Figure 5, we observe a fast decline in the quantity of the BSP level in the liver for varying ξ in the interval $(0, 1)$ and taking the same fractional order as in Figure 3. In Figure 3, we see that the quantity of the BSP level in bile smoothly increases and reaches its peak at point 700 for a fixed fractal order $\xi = 1$ and various fractional orders. In Figure 6, we observe that the quantity of the BSP level in bile reaches its peak earlier for varying ξ in the interval $(0, 1)$ and taking the same fractional order as in Figure 3. From Figures 4–9, it is obvious that the decay process is faster at a lower-order fractional value and larger fractal values. In the same way, the growth process is faster at a higher fractional order and lower fractal values and vice versa.

We compare the proposed fractal-fractional model and its equivalent integer-order variant graphically. We see that in the integer-order plot given in Figure 10, there is only one option to be considered, while in the case of the fractal-fractional-order model, we obtain multiple choice graphs for each class of the considered model for various fractal-fractional values. The fractal-fractional values are arbitrary. We can choose any value to simulate the results. From this discussion and interpretation, the significance of fractal-fractional order derivatives is obvious.

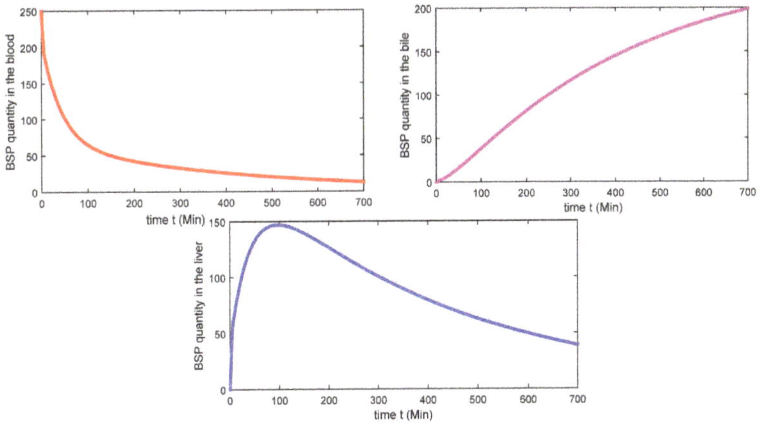

Figure 10. Numerical simulations of the integer-order model for all three classes of the considered model.

7. Conclusions

In this research paper, we extended the concept of piecewise fractal-fractional derivative to a human liver model that was previously studied in various forms. Conditions for unique solutions and stability results are carried out for the model under consideration. We established numerical schemes for both classical and power law kernels of the proposed problem by using the extended method of ABM and Lagrangian polynomial piecewise interpolation and simulated the numerical results that visually represent the numerical solutions at different fractal and fractional values. Our obtained results have the property of crossover and memory effects that make the results interesting.

In the future, a more realistic model can be considered by adding the recruitment rate to the model and by modifying the parameters involved in the proposed model.

Author Contributions: Conceptualization, O.O.; Software, A.M.; Formal analysis, A.A. (Amer Alsulami); Investigation, A.A. (Amer Alsulami); Writing—original draft, A.A. (Arshad Ali); Writing—review & editing, A.E.H., K.A. and H.S.; Project administration, K.A.; Funding acquisition, O.O. All authors have read and agreed to the published version of the manuscript.

Funding: This research received no external funding.

Data Availability Statement: All data are included in paper.

Acknowledgments: The researchers would like to thank the Deanship of Graduate Studies and Scientific Research at Qassim University for financial support (QU-APC-2024-9/1).

Conflicts of Interest: The authors declare no conflicts of interest.

References

1. Abdel-Misih, S.R.Z.; Bloomston, M. Liver anatomy. *Surg. Clin. N. Am.* **2010**, *90*, 643–653. [PubMed]
2. Sepanlou, S.G.; Safiri, S.; Bisignano, C.; Ikuta, K.S.; Merat, S.; Saberifiroozi, M.; Padubidri, J.R. The global, regional, and national burden of cirrhosis by cause in 195 countries and territories, 1990–2017: A systematic analysis for the Global Burden of Disease Study 2017. *Lancet Gastroenterol. Hepatol.* **2020**, *5*, 245–266. [CrossRef] [PubMed]
3. Lehman, E.M.; Wilson, M.L. Epidemiology of hepatitis viruses among hepatocellular carcinoma cases and healthy people in Egypt: A systematic review and meta-analysis. *Int. J. Cancer* **2009**, *124*, 690–697. [CrossRef] [PubMed]
4. Lumeij, J.T. Avian clinical biochemistry. In *Clinical Biochemistry of Domestic Animals*; Academic Press: Cambridge, MA, USA, 1997; pp. 857–883.
5. Islam, R.; Alam, M.J. Evaluation of liver protective activity of Moringa oleifera bark extract in paracetamol induced hepatotoxicity in rats. *BioRxiv* **2019**, 513002.
6. Latrach, K.; Taoudi, M.A.; Zeghal, A. Some fixed point theorems of the Schauder and the Krasnosel'skii type and application to nonlinear transport equations. *J. Differ. Equ.* **2006**, *221*, 256–271. [CrossRef]
7. Ahmad, B.; Ntouyas, S.K.; Alsaedi, A. New existence results for nonlinear fractional differential equations with three-point integral boundary conditions. *Adv. Differ. Equ.* **2011**, *2011*, 107384.
8. Dhage, B.C.; Dhage, S.B.; Buvaneswari, K. Existence of mild solutions of nonlinear boundary value problems of coupled hybrid fractional integro differential equations. *J. Fract. Calc. Appl.* **2019**, *10*, 191–206.
9. Devi, A.; Kumar, A. Hyers-Ulam stability and existence of solution for hybrid fractional differential equation with p-Laplacian operator. *Chaos Solitons Fractals* **2022**, *156*, 111859. [CrossRef]
10. Vu, H.; Rassias, J.M.; Hoa, N.V. Hyers-Ulam stability for boundary value problem of fractional differential equations with ψ-Caputo fractional derivative. *Math. Methods Appl. Sci.* **2023** *46*, 438–460. [CrossRef]
11. Čelechovská, L. A simple mathematical model of the human liver. *Appl. Math.* **2004**, *49*, 227–246. [CrossRef]
12. Calvetti, D.; Kuceyeski, A.; Somersalo, E. A mathematical model of liver metabolism: From steady state to dynamic. *J. Phys. Conf. Ser.* **2008**, *124*, 012012. [CrossRef]
13. Repetto, R.; Tweedy, J.H. Mathematical modelling of the circulation in the liver lobule. *J. Biomech. Eng.* **2010**, *132*, 111011.
14. Friedman, A.; Hao, W. Mathematical modelling of liver fibrosis. *Math. Biosci. Eng.* **2017**, *14*, 143–164. [CrossRef]
15. Shah, K.; Alqudah, M.A.; Jarad, F.; Abdeljawad, T. Semi-analytical study of Pine Wilt Disease modelwith convex rate under Caputo-Febrizio fractional order derivative. *Chaos Soliton Fractals* **2020**, *135*, 109754. [CrossRef]
16. Khan, H.; Alzabut, J.; Shah, A.; He, Z.Y.; Etemad, S.; Rezapour, S.; Zada, A. On fractal-fractional waterborne disease model: A study on theoretical and numerical aspects of solutions via simulations. *Fractals* **2023**, *31*, 2340055. [CrossRef]
17. Aldwoah, K.A.; Almalahi, M.A.; Shah, K. Theoretical and Numerical Simulations on the Hepatitis B Virus Model through a Piecewise Fractional Order. *Fractal Fract.* **2023**, *7*, 844. [CrossRef]
18. Aldwoah, K.A.; Almalahi, M.A.; Hleili, M.; Alqarni, F.A.; Aly, E.S.; Shah, K. Analytical study of a modified-ABC fractional order breast cancer model. *J. Appl. Math. Comput.* **2024**, *70*, 3685–3716. [CrossRef]

19. Aldwoah, K.A.; Almalahi, M.A.; Shah, K.; Awadalla, M.; Egami, R.H. Dynamics analysis of dengue fever model with harmonic mean type under fractal-fractional derivative. *AIMS Math.* **2024**, *9*, 13894–13926. [CrossRef]
20. Podlubny, L. Fractional Differential Equations. In *An Introduction to Fractional Derivatives, Fractional Differential Equations, to Methods of Their Solution and Some of Their Applications*; Academic Press: San Diego, CA, USA, 1999; Volume 198.
21. Ameen, I. G.; Sweilam, N.H.; Ali, H.M. A fractional-order model of human liver: Analytic-approximate and numerical solutions comparing with clinical data. *Alex. Eng. J.* **2021**, *60*, 4797–4808. [CrossRef]
22. Caputo, M.; Fabrizio, M. A new definition of fractional derivative without singular kernel. *Prog. Fract. Differ. Appl.* **2015**, *1*, 73–85.
23. Atangana, A.; Baleanu, D. New fractional derivative with non-local and non-singular kernel. *Therm. Sci.* **2016**, *20*, 757–763. [CrossRef]
24. Rezapour, S.; Etemad, S.; Mohammadi, H. A mathematical analysis of a system of Caputo-Fabrizio fractional differential equations for the anthrax disease model in animals. *Adv. Diff. Equ.* **2020**, *2020*, 481. [CrossRef]
25. Atangana, A. Fractal-fractional differentiation and integration: Connecting fractal calculus and fractional calculus to predict complex system. *Chaos Solitons Fractals* **2017**, *102*, 396–406. [CrossRef]
26. Shah, K.; Abdeljawad, T. Study of radioactive decay process of uranium atoms via fractals-fractional analysis. *S. Afr. J. Chem. Eng.* **2024**, *48*, 63–70. [CrossRef]
27. Khan, H.; Aslam, M.; Rajpar, A.E.H.; Chu, Y.M.; Etemad, S.; Rezapour, S.; Ahmad, H. A new fractal-fractional hybrid model for studying climate change on coastal ecosystems from the mathematical point of view. *Fractals* **2024**, *32*, 2440015. [CrossRef]
28. Shah, A.; Khan, H.; De la Sen, M.; Alzabut, J.; Etemad, S.; Deressa, C.T.; Rezapour, S. On non-symmetric fractal-fractional modeling for ice smoking: Mathematical analysis of solutions. *Symmetry* **2022**, *15*, 87. [CrossRef]
29. Alraqad, T.; Almalahi, M.A.; Mohammed, N.; Alahmade, A.; Aldwoah, K.A.; Saber, H. Modeling Ebola Dynamics with a Piecewise Hybrid Fractional Derivative Approach. *Fractal Fract.* **2024**, *8*, 596. [CrossRef]
30. Baleanu, D.; Jajarmi, A.; Mohammadi, H.; Rezapour, S. A new study on the mathematical modelling of human liver with Caputo-Fabrizio fractional derivative. *Chaos Solitons Fractals* **2020**, *134*, 109705. [CrossRef]
31. Atangana, A.; Araz, S.I. New concept in calculus: Piecewise differential and integral operators. *Chaos Solitons Fractals* **2021**, *145*, 110638. [CrossRef]
32. Atangana, A.; Araz, S.I. Piecewise derivatives versus short memory concept: Analysis and application. *AIMs Math.* **2022**, *19*, 8601–8620.
33. Ansari, K.J.; Asma; Ilyas, F.; Shah, K.; Khan, A.; Abdeljawad, T. On new updated concept for delay differential equations with piecewise Caputo fractional-order derivative. *Waves Random Complex Media* **2023**, *2023*, 1–20. [CrossRef]
34. Rus, I.A. Ulam stabilities of ordinary differential equations in a Banach space. *Carpath. J. Math.* **2010**, *26*, 103–107.
35. Khan, M.A.; Atangana, A. *Numerical Methods for Fractal-Fractional Differential Equations and Engineering Simulations and Modeling*; Simulations and Modeling; CRC Press: Boca Raton, FL, USA, 2023.
36. Riaz, M.; Alqarni, F.A.; Aldwoah, K.; Birkea, F.M.O.; Hleili, M. Analyzing a Dynamical System with Harmonic Mean Incidence Rate Using Volterra-Lyapunov Matrices and Fractal-Fractional Operators. *Fractal Fract.* **2024**, *8*, 321. [CrossRef]
37. Arfan, M.; Alrabaiah, H.; Rahman, M.U.; Yu-Liang Sun, Y.L.; Hashim, A.S.; Pansera, B.A.; Ahmadian, A.; Salahshour, S. Investigation of fractal-fractional order model of COVID-19 in Pakistan under Atangana-Baleanu Caputo (ABC) derivative. *Results Phys.* **2021**, *24*, 104046. [CrossRef]

fractal and fractional

MDPI

Article

Application of Fractional-Order Multi-Wing Chaotic System to Weak Signal Detection

Hongcun Mao, Yuling Feng, Xiaoqian Wang, Chao Gao and Zhihai Yao *

Physics Department, Changchun University of Science and Technology, Changchun 130022, China; 2020200021@mails.cust.edu.cn (H.M.); fyl0819@aliyun.com (Y.F.); xqwang21@cust.edu.cn (X.W.); gaoc@cust.edu.cn (C.G.)

* Correspondence: yaozh@cust.edu.cn; Tel.:+86-1350-432-3954

Abstract: This work investigates a fractional-order multi-wing chaotic system for detecting weak signals. The influence of the order of fractional calculus on chaotic systems' dynamical behavior is examined using phase diagrams, bifurcation diagrams, and SE complexity diagrams. Then, the principles and methods for determining the frequencies and amplitudes of weak signals are examined utilizing fractional-order multi-wing chaotic systems. The findings indicate that the lowest order at which this kind of fractional-order multi-wing chaotic system appears chaotic is 2.625 at $a = 4$, $b = 8$, and $c = 1$, and that this value decreases as the driving force increases. The four-wing and double-wing change dynamics phenomenon will manifest in a fractional-order chaotic system when the order exceeds the lowest order. This phenomenon can be utilized to detect weak signal amplitudes and frequencies because the system parameters control it. A detection array is built to determine the amplitude using the noise-resistant properties of both four-wing and double-wing chaotic states. Deep learning images are then used to identify the change in the array's wing count, which can be used to determine the test signal's amplitude. When frequencies detection is required, the MUSIC method estimates the frequencies using chaotic synchronization to transform the weak signal's frequencies to the synchronization error's frequencies. This solution adds to the contact between fractional-order calculus and chaos theory. It offers suggestions for practically implementing the chaotic weak signal detection theory in conjunction with deep learning.

Keywords: multi-wing chaotic system; fractional calculus; weak signal detection; deep learning; MUSIC algorithm

1. Introduction

As a nonlinear signal detection method, chaotic weak signal detection has been studied for over thirty years. The difference between the chaotic system method and other classical signal processing techniques is that chaotic systems can resist noise through iteration. This allows the noise to be much larger than weak signals and achieve a negative signal-to-noise ratio, which is already superior to the most common amplification methods. Among numerous weak signal detection methods that can handle noise, the detection performance of chaotic detection methods is related to the design of chaotic systems. By increasing the effective number of control parameters in chaotic systems, weaker, smaller signals can be detected, resulting in higher detection performance limits. Since Birx [1] proved in 1992 that the Duffing chaotic system can be used for weak signal detection, he is considered the pioneer of the theory of chaotic weak signal detection. Wang [2] continued his work on Birx by showing how to detect weak signals using the initial value sensitivity property of the Duffing system and gave a complete procedure for doing so. In recent years, researchers have kept a close eye on Duffing systems for weak signal detection, and several novel theories for gauging the signal detection capability have emerged [3–7]. Meanwhile, many practical problems have been resolved by applying chaotic weak signal detection approaches [8–10]. This shows that the subject of chaos-based weak signal identification has gained popularity in engineering applications and can potentially tackle problems that are not well-suited for linear signal detection.

Researchers have employed more chaotic systems to detect signals and have also found solutions to a few real-world issues to enhance the detection performance further [11–18]. Furthermore, the multi-wing chaotic system has a distinct attractor topology beyond these additional systems. As a result, this chaotic system likewise displays extremely complicated features [19–24], which naturally prompts researchers to think of using it for the detection of weak signals. Li [25] created a nonlinear feedback controller from chaotic synchronization, stabilized the chaotic system with many wings to the equilibrium point, and then used the chaotic system's synchronized state to detect weak signals with multiple frequencies. In Yan's [26] study of a multi-wing chaotic system with an infinite number of equilibrium points, he found that weak signals might be identified by comparing the fluctuations between four-wing and two-wing chaotic attractors. The viability and superiority of employing a multi-wing chaotic system for weak signal identification are amply illustrated by these works.

Due to advancements in chaos theory, fractional-order chaotic systems have grown in importance within the field of chaos. Additionally, fractional-order calculus has introduced new features to the field, making fractional-order chaotic systems highly relevant as a research hotspot with significant potential for engineering applications [27–31]. In all chaotic applications, fractional-order chaotic systems for the detection of weak signals have emerged as a state-of-the-art part of chaotic weak signal detection [32–36].

Although fractional-order multi-wing systems have been partially studied and applied [37–40], research on how to use such systems for weak signal detection is rare, especially in demonstrating the advantages of fractional calculus. Secondly, how to apply the existing theory of chaotic weak signal detection to practical device design is also a major obstacle to the development of this theory. Finally, deep learning image recognition is a very mature technology, and in the state criteria of chaotic systems, the attractor graph method is a classic method. However, the development of combining the attractor graph method with deep learning image recognition and introducing deep learning into chaotic weak signal detection is still blank.

Therefore, in order to address the above issues, in this paper, we researched the application of fractional-order multi-wing chaotic systems in weak signal detection. Firstly, the multi-wing chaotic system will be rewritten into the fractional-order form, because the fractional-order system is more consistent with the actual physical model. Then the influence of order parameters in fractional-order calculus on the characteristics of chaotic systems is analyzed. Lastly, weak signal detection was accomplished using this fractional-order chaotic system. Using the difference in the number of four-wing and two-wing chaotic attractor wings, a chaotic array represents the difference between weak signals while detecting their amplitude. In determining the frequency of the weak signal, a fractional-order multi-wing chaotic synchronization system is designed which is built using the drive–response method. If the weak signal is added to the driving part, the synchronization error of this system will vary with different frequencies of the weak signal. This system then uses a multi-signal classification (MUSIC) algorithm to estimate the weak signal frequencies by converting the weak signal frequencies into a chaotic synchronization error.

The remainder of the paper is summarized as follows after the introduction: Section 2 presents the system model of the fractional-order multi-wing chaotic system and employs phase diagrams, equilibrium points, bifurcation diagrams, complexity, and other techniques to assess the dynamics features. Section 3 covers the identification of weak signals using a fractional-order multi-wing chaotic system. It divides the procedure into two parts: amplitude detection and frequency detection. It also provides the detection principle and discusses using the chaotic array and MUSIC methods for processing data in real-world scenarios. Section 4 concludes the paper at the end.

2. Fractional-Order Multi-Wing Chaotic System Model and Dynamic Characteristics Analysis

2.1. Fractional-Order Multi-Wing Chaotic System Model

A non-autonomous, multi-wing chaotic system was proposed by Yan [26]. It has complicated dynamical features, including the generation of symmetric attractors, an infinite number of equilibrium points, and a driving amplitude that affects the number of wings. The following is the equation:

$$\begin{cases} \dot{x} = -ax + byz \\ \dot{y} = cy - xz \\ \dot{z} = -z + xy + G \end{cases} \tag{1}$$

where G is the external driving force signal, a, b and c are positive parameters, x, y, and z are state variables, and the amplitude r and frequency ω are often included in G. As a result, this system can be employed as a weak signal detection system. Nevertheless, there are still issues with this detection system. The main one is that the frequency and amplitude r do not regulate the appearance of chaos in the numerical region of all standard weak signals, which leads to the creation of detection blind zones and lowers the detection performance.

Therefore, using fractional-order calculus, Equation (1) is enhanced in this study to create a new 3D fractional-order system that is more suited for weak signal detection. This new system can be stated as:

$$\begin{cases} D^q x = -ax + byz \\ D^q y = cy - xz \\ D^q z = -z + xy + G \end{cases} \tag{2}$$

where G is the external driving force signal, x, y, and z are the state variables, a, b, and c are the positive parameters, and q is the derivative order. D is the fractional-order differential established by Caputo. A few fundamental characteristics of system Equation (2) are examined next.

2.2. Dissipativity and the Existence of an Attractor

The divergence can be used to calculate the dissipativity of the chaotic equations [41], and the exponential constraint rate of system Equation (2) is:

$$\Delta V = \frac{\partial \dot{x}}{\partial x} + \frac{\partial \dot{y}}{\partial y} + \frac{\partial \dot{z}}{\partial z} \tag{3}$$

For the proposed system, ΔV is $-a + c - 1$, and for the chosen set of parameters, it is equal to -4. This result means that all system orbits will eventually be confined to a subset of zero volume, i.e., system Equation (2) is dissipative. This dissipative nature of the system guarantees the existence of an attractor for the system.

So the numerical approximate solution of the fractional-order multi-wing chaotic system can be obtained through calculation, which can be used to draw the attractor phase diagram. For the approximate solution, we use the Grünwald–Letnikov approximation formula based on the Riemann–Liouville definition. The general numerical solution expression for fractional differential equations using this method is:

$$\begin{cases} {}_aD_t^q y(t) = f(y(t), t) \\ y(t_k) = f(y(t_k), t_k) \times h^q - \sum\limits_{j=v}^{k} c_j^{(q)} y(t_{k-j}) \end{cases} \tag{4}$$

where

$$c_0^{(q)} = 1, c_j^{(q)} = (1 - \frac{1+q}{j}) \times c_{j-1}^{(q)}. \tag{5}$$

According to the existing studies on chaotic systems of integer order, let $q = 0.95$, $a = 4, b = 8, c = 1, G = r \times sin(\omega \times t)$; take $r = 1.126$, and $\omega = 1$. The initial values are taken as $[x, y, z] = [0.1; 0.1; 0.1]$. This chaotic system forms a four-wing chaotic attractor as shown in Figure 1.

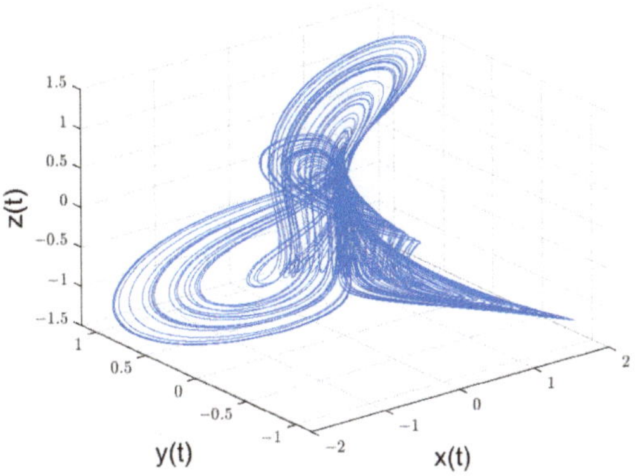

Figure 1. If $q = 0.95$, $a = 4$, $b = 8$, $c = 1$, $G = r \times \sin(\omega \times t), r = 1.126, \omega = 1$, and the starting value of $(x, y, z) = [0.1; 0.1; 0.1]$, then a fractional-order multi-wing chaotic system has four wings in its attractor.

2.3. Equilibrium Analysis

Drive force signal G governs system Equation (2), which is non-autonomous. As a result, the left side of system Equation (2) must be set to zero to compute the equilibrium point.

$$\begin{cases} 0 = -ax + byz \\ 0 = cy - xz \\ 0 = -z + xy + G \end{cases} \tag{6}$$

Then, we may determine that, at this moment, the equilibrium points of Equations (1) and (2) are the same and that infinite equilibrium points exist with infinite driving signal G values. Consequently, as indicated in Table 1, they are grouped to obtain five different types of equilibrium points.

Table 1. Equilibrium points of system Equation (2).

Equilibrium Point	State Variable x	State Variable y	State Variable z
S_0	0	0	0
S_1	$\sqrt{1-\sqrt{2}G}$	$\sqrt{\frac{1-\sqrt{2}G}{2}}$	$\sqrt{\frac{1}{2}}$
S_2	$-\sqrt{1-\sqrt{2}G}$	$-\sqrt{\frac{1-\sqrt{2}G}{2}}$	$\sqrt{\frac{1}{2}}$
S_3	$-\sqrt{1+\sqrt{2}G}$	$\sqrt{\frac{1+\sqrt{2}G}{2}}$	$-\sqrt{\frac{1}{2}}$
S_4	$\sqrt{1+\sqrt{2}G}$	$-\sqrt{\frac{1+\sqrt{2}G}{2}}$	$-\sqrt{\frac{1}{2}}$

To get the Jacobian matrix, linearize system Equation (2) at the equilibrium points (x^*, y^*, z^*):

$$J = \begin{bmatrix} -4 & 8z^* & 8y^* \\ -z^* & 1 & -x^* \\ y^* & x^* & -1 \end{bmatrix}. \tag{7}$$

Let $det(\lambda E - J) = 0$; obtain the corresponding characteristic polynomial as:

$$\lambda^3 + A_2\lambda^2 + A_1\lambda + A_0 = 0. \tag{8}$$

where

$$\begin{aligned} A_2 =& 4, \\ A_1 =& -1 - 8(y^*)^2 + 8(x^*)^2 + (z^*)^2, \\ A_0 =& -4 + 16x^*y^*z^* + 8(y^*)^2 + 4(x^*)^2 + 8(z^*)^2. \end{aligned} \tag{9}$$

The eigenvalues of the equilibrium point fulfill $Re[\lambda] < 0$ if it is stable. According to the Routh–Hurwitz criterion, the equilibrium point is only stable when $A_2 > 0, A_0 > 0$ and $A_2 \times A_1 - A_0 > 0$. Given the conditions of this paper, we select $G = 0, 1$, and 5, respectively, because the size of G impacts each equilibrium point, and G also affects the system's ability to identify weak signals. Table 2 displays the equilibrium point's stability.

Table 2. Stability of equilibrium points of system Equation (2).

Value of Driving Signal G	Eigenvalues at Equilibrium Point S_0	Eigenvalues at Equilibrium Point S_1 S_2	Eigenvalues at Equilibrium Point S_3 S_4
0	$-4, -1, 1$ Unstable Saddle Point	$-4.7186, 0.3593 \pm 1.8060i$ Unstable Saddle Point	$-4.7186, 0.3593 \pm 1.8060i$ Unstable Saddle Point
1	$-1, -1.5 \pm 1.3229i$ stable Focus	$0.8128, -2.4064 \pm 1.5374i$ Unstable Saddle Point	$-5.8526, 0.9263 \pm 2.3962i$ Unstable Saddle Point
5	$-1, -1.5 \pm 13.9194i$ stable Focus	$2.5574, -3.2787 \pm 5.2185i$ Unstable Saddle Point	$-8.3744, 2.1872 \pm 3.2614i$ Unstable Saddle Point

According to Table 2, the equilibrium point S_0 belongs to the first class of saddle points, whereas the saddle points S_1, S_2, S_3, and S_4 belong to the second class. The first class of saddle points connects the rings of chaotic attractors that were created around the second class of saddle points.

M. S. Tavazoei [42] provides the condition for the system to appear as a locally asymptotically stable equilibrium point, which can be computed to determine the minimal fractional calculus order in which chaos can arise. The results are as follows:

$$|arg(eig(J))| < \frac{q\pi}{2}.$$

As shown in Table 2, the necessary condition for the existence of chaotic attractors in system Equation (2) at $a = 4$, $b = 8$, and $c = 1$ is $q > 0.875$, which means the total order is 2.625, and this value decreases with the increase of G.

2.4. Dynamic Characteristics under the Influence of Order

The integer-order chaotic system can be considered a specific fractional-order system by the theory of fractional-order calculus. Except for order, the remaining parameters of a fractional-order chaotic system then influence the chaotic system in a way comparable to the law of an integer-order system. As a result, we solely consider how the additional order parameter affects the fractional-order multi-wing chaotic system's dynamic properties. A bifurcation diagram and SE complexity diagram are used for this. The result is shown in Figure 2:

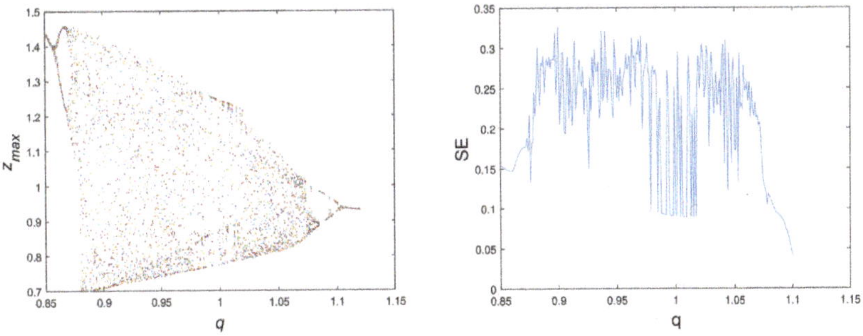

Figure 2. Bifurcation diagram and SE complexity diagram of the fractional-order multi-wing chaotic system Equation (2) varying with parameter q, where $a = 4$, $b = 8$, $c = 1$, $\omega = 1$, $G = r \times \sin(\omega \times t)$, $r = 1.126$, and $\omega = 1$. The value range of q is from 0.85 to 1.15.

The chaotic phenomenon is evident in the range of $[0.85, 1.05]$ in Figure 2, which is consistent with the results computed in the preceding section. Furthermore, the chaotic system ceases to be chaotic when the order exceeds 1.05, demonstrating how differing fractional-order calculus orders alter the remaining parameters' control range. Thus, the advantage of the fractional-order chaotic system is demonstrated by the fact that, by altering the order, it can gain a more extensive chaos interval or period window than the integer-order chaotic system's fixed influence range of each parameter.

Next, taking orders of 0.9 and 0.95 as examples, we will compare the influence of G values on the state of chaotic systems at different orders. The results are shown in Figure 3:

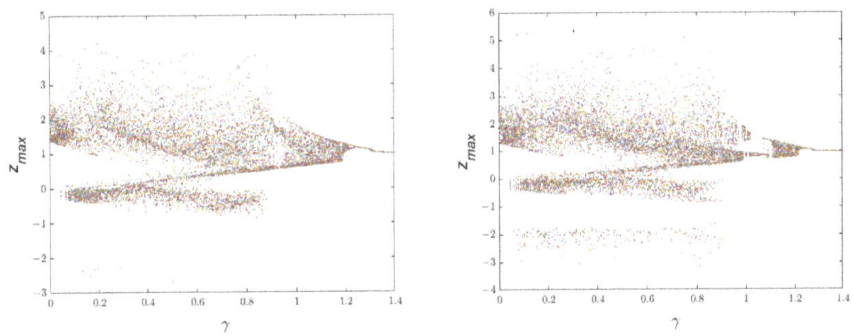

Figure 3. Bifurcation diagram of the fractional-order multi-wing chaotic system Equation (2) varying with parameter r, where $G = r \times \sin(\omega \times t)$, $a = 4$, $b = 8$, $c = 1$, $\omega = 1$, and $q = 0.9$ in the left panel, $q = 0.95$ in the right panel, and the value range of r is from 0 to 1.4.

From Figure 3, it can be seen that after changing the order value from 1, the length of the chaotic region becomes significantly longer, and the number of occurrences of the period window becomes less. This suggests fewer blind spots for detection and a more comprehensive detection range for weak signal detection with this technique.

3. Weak Signal Detection

The study that is now available indicates that the multi-wing chaotic system Equation (1) has the property of having switchable numbers of wings, which is achieved by varying the driving force G. Consequently, this property of the fractional-order chaotic system remains. Furthermore, this chaotic system possesses the properties of a single-parameter chaotic system with rapid state change, which is compatible with the chaotic system properties required in the field of chaotic weak signal detection. Consequently, it is possible to convert the information of weak signals into fractional-order multi-wing chaotic systems' dynamical phenomena and thereafter identify the weak signals.

3.1. Amplitudes Detection of Weak Signals

According to the conventional theory of chaotic weak signal detection, adding a weak signal will cause the chaotic system to enter a periodic state. At this time, the chaotic system will undergo chaotic control to revert to its chaotic state, offsetting the added weak signals and the altered control parameter to obtain the signal for measurement. In this process, the chaotic state has a higher noise resistance than the periodic state. Therefore, to circumvent the periodic state's low robustness to noise, we used the difference between the four-winged and the two-winged chaotic states in this study to detect the weak signals.

First, we considered the case of a single fractional-order chaotic system as a detection system when the equations of the system are:

$$\begin{cases} D^q x = -ax + byz \\ D^q y = cy - xz \\ D^q z = -z + xy + G + M(t) \end{cases} \tag{10}$$

where $M(t) = g + Nosie$ is the addition of a mixed signal made up of noise and the signal that has to be measured. A portion of the signal to be measured must be known in advance; g is the same form of the weak signal to be calculated as the drive signal. Considering Gaussian white noise as the noise and a sinusoidal weak signal with a frequency of 1 rad/s, $M(t)$ represents the weak signal. The question is how to determine the amplitude of the weak signal at this particular instant. With $q = 0.9$, $a = 4$, $b = 8$, $c = 1$, and $G = r{\times}\sin(t)$, the attractor of Equation (10) is displayed as follows when r is between the critical values of 1.12939796 and 1.12939797.

Figure 4 shows that the attractor of the chaotic system Equation (10) will vary if the control parameters are altered by 0.00000001. Consequently, it is possible to determine the variation pattern of control parameters by tracking changes in attractors. The influence of the signal to be tested is similar to altering the control parameters because both the form of G and the signal $M(t)$ to be tested are consistent. This allows the attractor's change to determine the amplitude of the weak signal that needs to be measured. Numerous studies have examined the effects of various noise on chaotic systems [43,44], and fractional-order multi-wing chaotic systems have the inherent ability to withstand noise.

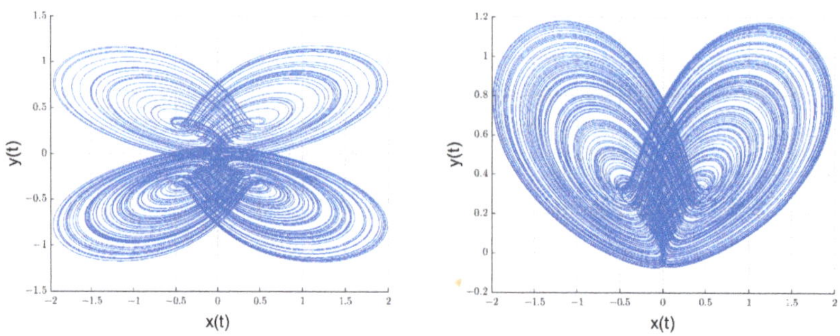

Figure 4. Using the G-algorithm for the numerical approximation of Riemann–Liouville, the attractor of Equation (10) is projected in the x-y plane, where the parameters are $a = 4, b = 8, c = 1, w = 1$, and the time interval is 0.01; $r = 1.12939796$ on the left, and $r = 1.12939797$ on the right.

In terms of the performance of individual chaotic detection, there is no essential difference between fractional-order chaotic systems and integer-order chaotic systems. However, when establishing a chaotic oscillator array, multiple arrays with order differences can be established by changing the fractional order. That is why this paper discusses the use of chaotic oscillator arrays for weak signal detection. It should be noted that fractional-order chaotic systems can use distinct fractional-order systems to form arrays, unlike integer-order systems, which can only modify one parameter. Consequently, the array's dimensionality has increased. Once the array is established, variations can be used to determine the amplitude information of weak signals. Several arrays can be built to increase precision because this paper's fractional-order multi-wing chaotic system can display chaotic events in fractional orders between 0.875 and 1. Here, taking the order equal to 0.9 as an example, we explain how to use a chaotic oscillator array for detection.

Figure 5 shows that the interval over which the four-wing chaos phenomenon occurs has a few complex windows. When utilizing an array to detect signals instead of a single chaotic oscillator, these windows can prevent errors from occurring. The chaotic array alters due to the addition of various weak signals, as seen in Figure 6.

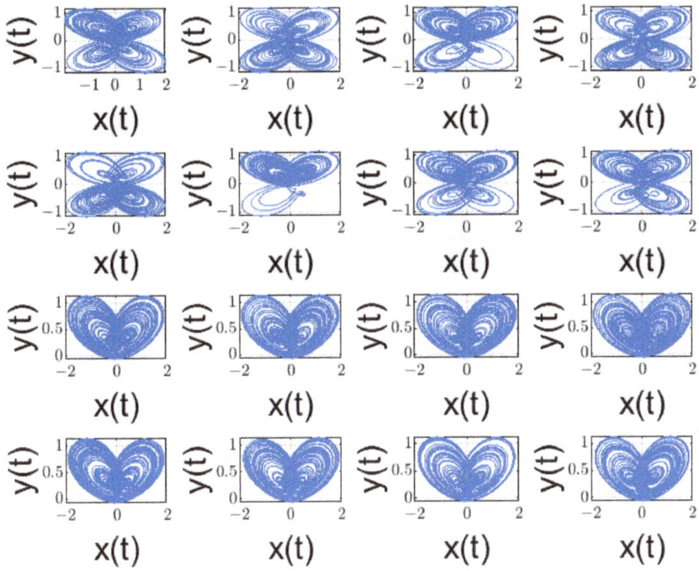

Figure 5. Chaos oscillator detection array, where the value of r ranges from 1.122 to 1.137, simulation time is 500, and calculation step size is 0.005.

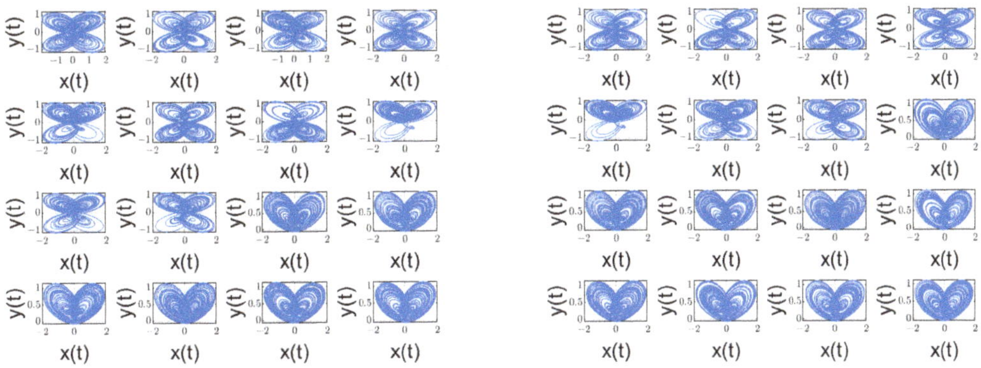

Figure 6. Chaos oscillator detection array, where the weak signal added on the left is $-0.02\sin(t)$, and on the right it is $0.01\sin(t)$.

Figure 6 illustrates how the addition of weak signals altered the chaotic array's properties, with the direction of the change varying according to whether the signal was positive or negative. The chaotic array's wing count will decrease with the addition of a positive weak signal and rise with the addition of a negative weak signal. Thus, in real-world applications, the measured signal's amplitude can be acquired as long as the chaotic array is located.

From the above analysis, it can be seen that in order to use chaotic arrays to detect weak signals, it is necessary to identify the state of the chaotic array and obtain information on the changes in the chaotic array. If the common Lyapunov exponent method is used, each oscillator needs to be calculated, and the 4×4 size in this article requires 16 calculations. If the chaotic phase diagram method is used for discrimination, it reduces the calculation time and number of calculations, but there is no universally recognized criterion for qualitative analysis. Therefore, we consider using deep learning image recognition to recognize and distinguish chaotic phase diagrams.

The manuscript introduces deep learning image recognition into the theory of chaotic weak signal detection, which is used to quickly identify information in chaotic arrays. This method has been rare in previous research, and it uses the multi-wing features of the attractor to simultaneously identify the entire array, reducing the judgment time. In addition, the main problem of detecting weak signals with chaos is the need to judge the chaotic state, so currently, commonly used methods make it difficult to design actual signal detection devices. By establishing a chaotic array to transform weak signals into image changes in a chaotic array and then using more mature deep learning image recognition for processing, this design makes the emergence of actual signal detection devices possible.

There are many mature models for deep learning image recognition, and the T-Rex2 model is used in this manuscript. It is open-source and can be used on online websites. T-Rex2 is an interactive object counting model designed to first detect and then count any objects. It formulates object counting as an open-set object detection task with the integration of visual prompts. Users can specify the objects of interest by marking points or boxes on a reference image, and T-Rex2 then detects all objects with a similar pattern. Guided by the visual feedback from T-Rex2, users can also interactively refine the counting results by identifying missing or falsely detected objects.

As a result, we may learn the attractor graph based on two wings by using Figure 4 as sample data. Equation (7) presents the findings.

From Figure 7, it can be seen that the deep learning image recognition method can successfully obtain the number of wings of the chaotic attractor based on the number of samples. So the number of wings of the chaotic arrays in Figures 5 and 6 are 21, 23, and 20, respectively. It is possible to determine the precise amplitude of the extra-weak signal by comparing the wing numbers. The actual amplitudes of the weak signals can be determined to be $0.01 \times -2 = -0.02$ and $0.01 \times 1 = 0.01$, respectively, based on the order of magnitude involved in building a chaotic oscillator array.

Next, we will consider the detection performance of fractional-order multi-wing chaotic systems under the conditions selected for this paper. The lowest detectable signal-to-noise ratio is used to represent the performance, with the specific condition that when the noise is too large and the attractor phase diagram changes to the point where deep learning cannot recognize it, it is considered undetectable. When the noise levels are 0.329 and 0.330, respectively, the results of deep learning image recognition using chaotic attractors are shown in Figure 8.

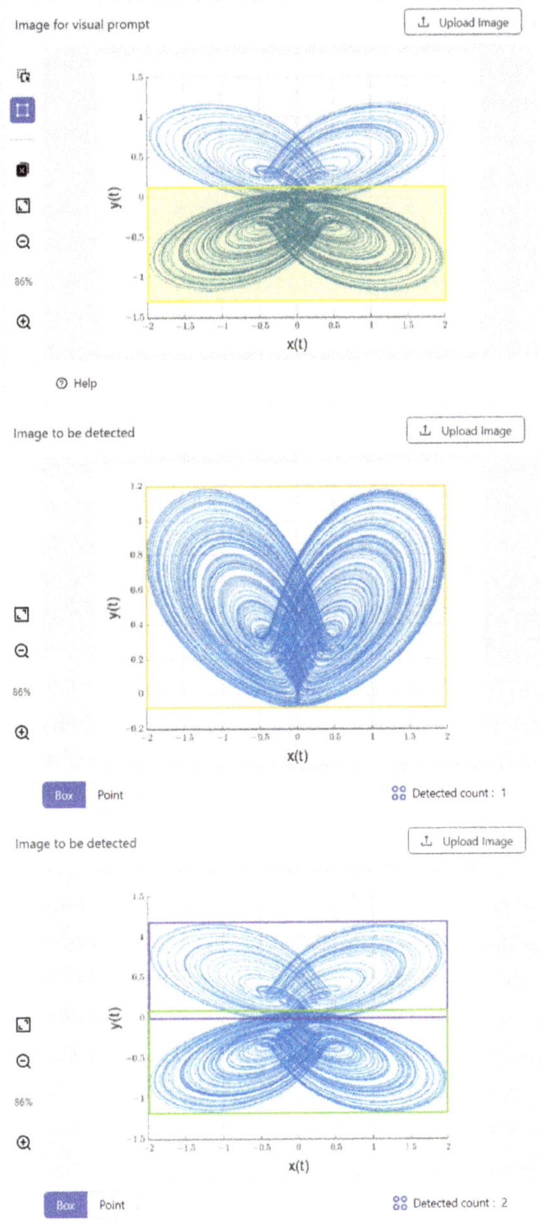

Figure 7. The yellow solid box indicates that users prompt once on one image. This article selects the double-wing part of the four-wing chaotic attractor. Other different color boxes are automatically annotated by T-Rex2 and display other images with similar object patterns to the prompt image. Using the left half of the four-wing attractor as an example, deep learning image recognition results were able to correctly identify both biplane and four-wing attractors.

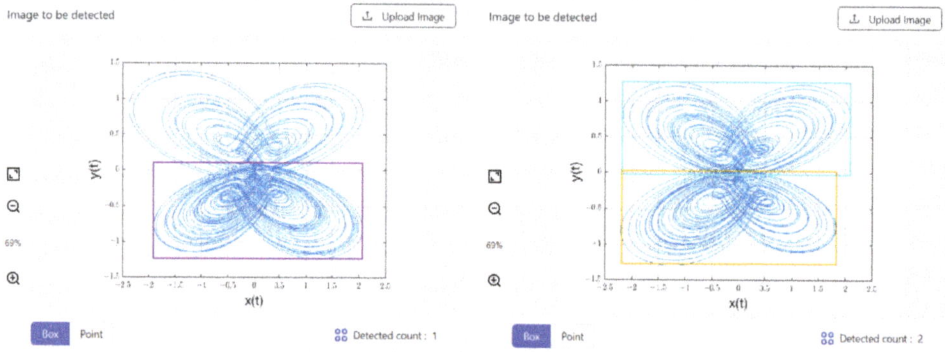

Figure 8. The results of chaotic attractors obtained by adding different levels of noise in deep learning image recognition.

So according to the formula, the minimum detectable signal-to-noise ratio of a fractional-order multi-wing chaotic system under the selected conditions is:

$$SNR = 10 * log(0.01/0.329) = -34.93db.$$

3.2. Frequencies Detection of Weak Signals

Currently, frequencies detection can be considered using the sweeping method, but this method is time-consuming and consumes many hardware resources. Therefore, researchers have proposed using the method of chaotic synchronization to detect the frequencies of weak signals. This is because the current research on chaos synchronization has been very in-depth, and many different synchronization methods have been proposed [45,46]. The drive–response method is a very classic chaos synchronization method. The use of the drive–response chaotic system to detect the frequencies of weak signals is based on the principle of using an applied weak signal to change the synchronization error of the chaotic system, and this error is linearly correlated with the applied weak signal. Therefore, the frequencies of the weak signal can be obtained by calculating the frequencies of the error value. The designed driving and controlled response systems are shown in Equations (11) and (12).

$$\begin{cases} D^q x = -ax_1 + by_1 z_1 \\ D^q y = cy_1 - x_1 z_1 \\ D^q z = -z_1 + x_1 y_1 + G \end{cases} \tag{11}$$

$$\begin{cases} D^q x = -ax_2 + by_2 z_2 - u_x \\ D^q y = cy_2 - x_2 z_2 - u_y \\ D^q z = -z_2 + x_2 y_2 + G - u_z \end{cases} \tag{12}$$

The terms u_x, u_y, and u_z in system Equation (12) are nonlinear controllers. Let the synchronization error between system Equation (11) and system Equation (12) be $e_x = x_2 - x_1$, $e_y = y_2 - y_1$, and $e_z = z_2 - z_1$. Then the synchronization error is the difference between Equations (11) and (12). That is, the following synchronization error of fractional-order chaotic systems is obtained:

$$\begin{cases} D^q e_x = -ae_x + b(e_y e_z + e_y z_1 + e_z y_1) - u_x \\ D^q e_y = ce_y - (e_x e_z + e_x z_1 + e_z x_1) - u_y \\ D^q e_z = -e_z + e_x e_y + e_x y_1 + e_y x_1 - u_z \end{cases} \tag{13}$$

The synchronization controller is designed as follows:

$$\begin{cases} u_x = b(e_y e_z + e_y z_1 + e_z y_1) \\ u_y = c e_y - (e_x e_z + e_x z_1 + e_z x_1) + k_y e_y \\ u_z = e_x e_y + e_x y_1 + e_y x_1 \end{cases} \tag{14}$$

Bringing system Equation (14) into system Equation (13) yields the final synchronization error, as shown in system Equation (15).

$$\begin{cases} D^q e_x = -a e_x \\ D^q e_y = k_y e_y \\ D^q e_z = -e_z \end{cases} \tag{15}$$

Since the fractional-order order $0 < q < 1$ in this paper, the Lyapunov function E is constructed according to the sufficient condition for stability of fractional-order systems [47,48]:

$$E(e_x, e_y, e_z) = \frac{1}{2}(e_x^2 + e_y^2 + e_z^2).$$

The derivative is then obtained as:

$$\dot{E} = \dot{e_x} e_x + \dot{e_y} e_y + \dot{e_z} e_z = -a e_x^2 - k e_y^2 - e_z^2.$$

It is obvious that the synchronization error is asymptotically stable; thus, we are able to show that the drive and response systems Equations (11) and (12) are synchronized, as shown in Figure 9.

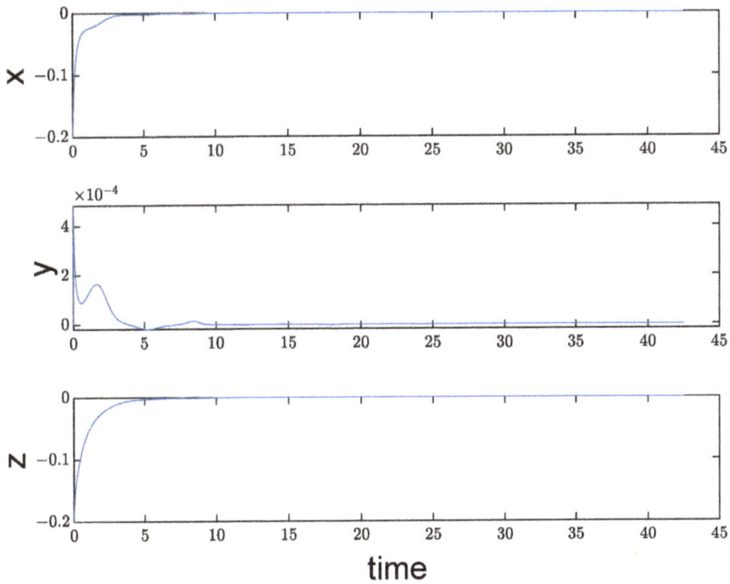

Figure 9. The synchronization error of the state variables x, y, and z when the system Equations (11) and (12) are synchronized.

Therefore, synchronization errors can be used to observe changes in the drive–response system when detecting the signal's frequencies. For instance, the equation for driving the system becomes as follows when a mixed signal, $S(t)$, is added to the third component in system Equation (11):

$$\begin{cases} D^q x = -ax + byz \\ D^q y = cy - xz \\ D^q z = -z + xy + G + S(t) \end{cases} \tag{16}$$

Thus, $S(t)$ will enter the chaotic system's iteration in system (16), and $S(t)$ will not change the chaotic system's dynamic properties. On the other hand, if $S(t)$ has the same form as G, then altering the system's parameters equals modifying the chaotic system's dynamic properties. As seen in Figure 10, this will modify the chaotic synchronization system's synchronization error.

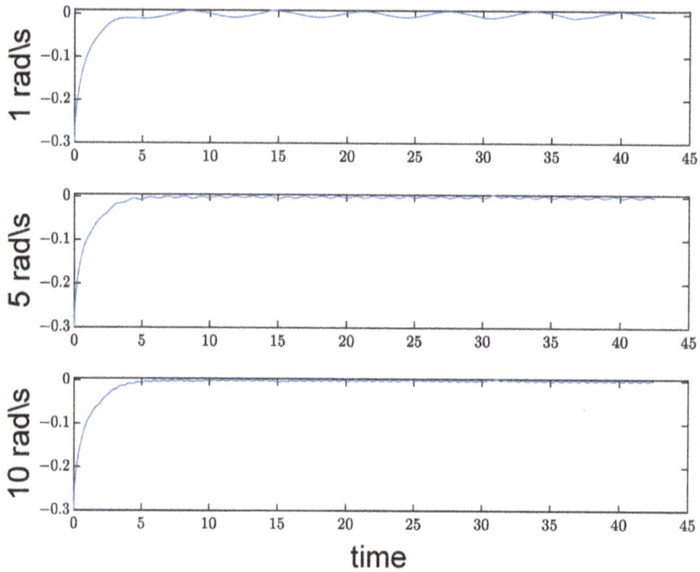

Figure 10. After adding $S(t)$ of different frequencies to system Equation (16), the error between the selected state variables z in the figure show the synchronization error of the chaotic synchronization system , where $S(t) = 0.01\sin(\omega * t)$, where ω is 1, 5, and 10 rad/s.

Figure 10 illustrates this point. While the chaotic system is stable, varying $S(t)$ will result in varying synchronization errors, and the frequencies of fluctuations in synchronization errors is equal to that of $S(t)$. Thus, it is possible to determine the frequencies of $S(t)$ by computing the frequencies of synchronization mistakes. Additionally, a weak signal frequencies was found. The frequencies inside the synchronization error can be obtained in various ways. Schmidt [49] proposed the MUSIC algorithm, which is used in this paper. This algorithm can assess the signal's frequencies and successfully withstand noise. The following are the primary steps:

1. Use N data points stabilized by the synchronization error, then extract $N - M$ data points from them as the sample matrix.

2. Find the covariance matrix of the constructed sample. $R = \frac{1}{N-M}\sum_{n=1}^{N-M} X(n)X^H(n)$.

3. Perform eigenvalue decomposition of the covariance matrix R. The eigenvalues are arranged from small to large, and the first m corresponding eigenvectors are taken to construct the signal eigenmatrix $U_S = [v_1, v_2, \ldots v_m]$. The rest are used to construct the noise characteristic matrix $U_N = [v_{m+1}, v_{m+2}, \ldots v_M]$.

4. Using the frequencies estimation formula, $P(f) = \frac{1}{G(f)' U_N U_N' G(f)}$, where $G(f) = [1, e^{-2\pi fj}, \ldots, e^{-2\pi(M-1)fj}]$, the maximum value of $P(f)$ calculated is the frequencies of the synchronization error.

Using the above steps, calculate the synchronization error of Figure 10 and obtain Figure 11.

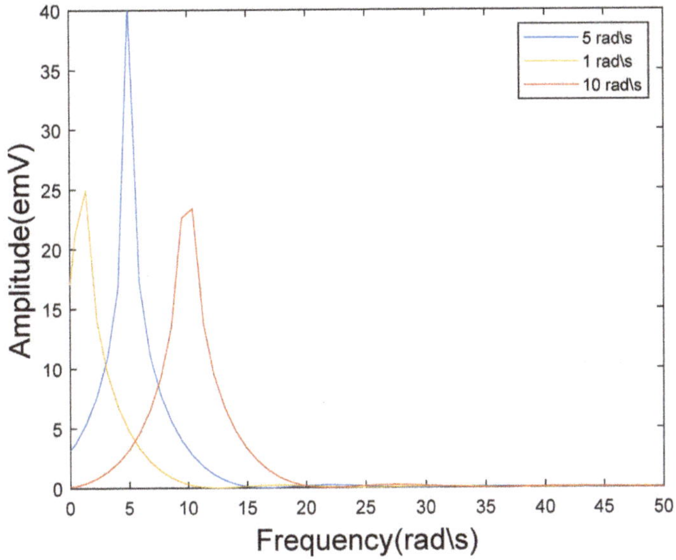

Figure 11. The result graph of frequencies estimation using the MUSIC algorithm for the stable synchronization error shows three peaks around 1, 5, and 10 rad/s.

From Figure 11, it can be seen that the three peaks in the resulting graph are around 1, 5, and 10 rad/s, which is consistent with the frequencies of the weak signal we input. This result indicates that using a synchronous fractional-order multi-wing chaotic system to detect the frequencies of weak signals is feasible.

4. Conclusions

This paper addresses the potential application of fractional-order multi-wing chaotic systems for weak signal detection. First, the impact of order in fractional calculus on the dynamic properties of chaotic systems is examined. Based on the findings, a 0.9 fractional-order multi-wing chaotic system is chosen as the weak signal detection system. In the case of amplitude detection, the various features of chaotic array detection and single detection oscillators are examined independently. Suppose that frequencies detection of weak signals is required. In that case, a fractional-order multi-wing chaotic system with drive–response synchronization is devised to detect the frequencies of the measured signal through changes in the synchronization error. When processing data, the MUSIC technique measures the synchronization error and subsequently estimates the frequencies of weak signals. Deep learning image recognition is used to process the number of wings of chaotic arrays.

The novelty of the work in this paper consists of the following: First, the creation of chaotic oscillator detection arrays highlights the advantages of fractional-order chaotic systems. Secondly, using the difference between four-winged chaotic states and double-winged chaotic states for detection makes both states resistant to noise. Finally, the states of the chaotic array are identified using deep learning images: a method that significantly reduces the judgment time compared to the usual Lyapunov method.

This paper still requires some prior knowledge to identify weak signals. Furthermore, this paper's correctness could still be enhanced. Therefore, the main problem of chaotic weak signal detection theory remains how to detect the frequencies and amplitude of weak signals simultaneously. The primary issue is that high accuracy increases the approximate calculation error of fractional calculus and complicates the construction of chaotic arrays and synchronization. Consequently, the engineering implementation of the suggested signal detection technique will be the main focus of future research.

Author Contributions: Conceptualization, H.M. and Z.Y.; Data curation, X.W.; Formal analysis, H.M.; Funding acquisition, C.G.; Investigation, H.M.; Methodology, H.M.; Project administration, Z.Y.; Resources, Y.F.; Software, H.M.; Supervision, Y.F., C.G. and Z.Y.; Validation, H.M., Y.F. and Z.Y.; Visualization, Z.Y.; Writing—original draft, H.M.; Writing—review and editing, X.W. All authors have read and agreed to the published version of the manuscript.

Funding: This research was funded by grants from the Key Science and Technology Research Projects in Jilin Province (grant No. 20160204020GX) and the Jilin Province Science and Technology Development Plan Project (grant No. 20190201135JC).

Institutional Review Board Statement: Not applicable.

Informed Consent Statement: Not applicable.

Data Availability Statement: The raw data supporting the conclusions of this article will be made available by the authors on request.

Conflicts of Interest: The authors declare no conflicts of interest.

Abbreviations

The following abbreviations are used in this manuscript:

MUSIC	Multi-signal classification

References

1. Birx, D.L.; Pipenberg, S.J. Chaotic oscillators and complex mapping feed forward networks(CMFFNs) for signal detection in noisy environments. In Proceedings of the [Proceedings 1992] IJCNN International Joint Conference on Neural Networks, Baltimore, MD, USA, 7–11 June 1992.
2. Wang, G.Y.; He, S. Quantitative study on detection and estimation of weak signals by using chaotic duffifing oscillators. *IEEE Trans. Circuits Syst. I* **2003**, *50*, 945–953. [CrossRef]
3. Wang, Q.B.; Yang, Y.J.; Zhang, X. Weak signal detection based on Mathieu-Duffing oscillator with time-delay feedback and multiplicative noise. *Chaos Solitons Fractals* **2020**, *137*, 109832. [CrossRef]
4. Jiao, S.B.; Jiang, W.; Lei, S.; Huang, W.C.; Zhang, Q. Research on detection method of multi-frequency weak signal based on stochastic resonance and chaos characteristics of Duffing system. *Chin. J. Phys.* **2020**, *64*, 333–347.
5. Zhao, Z.H.; Yang, S. Application of van der Pol-Duffing oscillator in weak signal detection. *Comput. Electr. Eng.* **2015**, *41*, 1–8.
6. Li, Q.Y.; Shi, S. Research on weak signal detection method based on duffing oscillator in narrowband noise. In Proceedings of the Artificial Intelligence for Communications and Networks: Second EAI International Conference, Virtual Event, 19–20 December 2020.
7. Akilli, M.; Yilmaz, N.; Gediz Akdeniz, K. Automated system for weak periodic signal detection based on Duffing oscillator. *IET Signal Process.* **2020**, *14*, 710–716. [CrossRef]
8. Li, C.S.; Qu, L.S. Applications of chaotic oscillator in machinery fault diagnosis. *Mech. Syst. Signal Process.* **2007**, *21*, 257–269. [CrossRef]
9. Chen, H.Y.; Lv, J.T.; Zhang, S.Q.; Zhang, L.G.; Li, J. Chaos weak signal detecting algorithm and its application in the ultrasonic Doppler bloodstream speed measuring. *J. Phys. Conf. Ser.* **2005**, *13*, 320. [CrossRef]
10. Hu, G.; Wang, K.J.; Liu, L.L. Detection Line Spectrum of Ship Radiated Noise Based on a New 3D Chaotic System. *Sensors* **2021**, *21*, 1610. [CrossRef] [PubMed]
11. Xiong, L.; Qi, L.W.; Teng, S.F.; Wang, Q.S.; Wang, L.; Zhang, X.G. A simplest Lorenz-like chaotic circuit and its applications in secure communication and weak signal detection. *EPJ-Spec. Top.* **2021**, *230*, 1933–1944. [CrossRef]
12. Shi, M.; Jin, C.L. Applying Improved Chaos System to Weak Signal Detection. In Proceedings of the 2015 International Industrial Informatics and Computer Engineering Conference, Xi'an, China, 10–11 January 2015.
13. Li, G.Z.; Tan, N.L.; Su, S.Q.; Zhang, C. Unknown frequency weak signal detection based on Lorenz chaotic synchronization system. *J. Vib. Shock* **2019**, *38*, 155–161.
14. Li, G.Z.; Zhang, B. A Novel Weak Signal Detection Method via Chaotic Synchronization Using Chua's Circuit. *IEEE Trans. Ind. Electron.* **2017**, *64*, 2255–2265. [CrossRef]
15. Li, Y.; Li, F.G.; Lyu, S.X.; Xu, M.; Wang, S.Y. Blind extraction of ECG signals based on similarity in the phase space. *Chaos Solitons Fractals* **2021**, *147*, 110950. [CrossRef]

16. Li, S.Y.; Lin, Y.C.; Tam, L.M. A smart detection technology for personal ECG monitoring via chaos-based data mapping strategy. *Multimed. Tools Appl.* **2021**, *80*, 6397–6412. [CrossRef]
17. Yin, C.; Jiang, S.B.; Zhang, Y.N. A Photoacoustic Spectrum Detection System Based on Chaos Detection of Weak Signal. In Proceedings of the 2021 IEEE 5th Advanced Information Technology, Electronic and Automation Control Conference, Chongqing, China, 12–14 March 2021.
18. Soong, C.Y.; Huang, W.T.; Lin, F.P.; Tzeng, P.Y. Controlling chaos with weak periodic signals optimized by a genetic algorithm. *Phys. Rev. E* **2004**, *70*, 016211. [CrossRef] [PubMed]
19. Yang, Y.; Huang, L.L.; Xiang, J.H.; Bao, H.; Li, H.Z. Generating multi-wing hidden attractors with only stable node-foci via non-autonomous approach. *Phys. Scr.* **2021**, *96*, 125220. [CrossRef]
20. Wu, Q.J.; Hong, Q.H.; Liu, X.Y.; Wang, X.P.; Zeng, Z.G. A novel amplitude control method for constructing nested hidden multi-butterfly and multiscroll chaotic attractors. *Chaos Solitons Fractals* **2020**, *134*, 109727. [CrossRef]
21. Sahoo, S.; Roy, B.K. Design of multi-wing chaotic systems with higher largest Lyapunov exponent. *Chaos Solitons Fractals* **2022**, *157*, 111926. [CrossRef]
22. Peng, X.N.; Zeng, Y.C. A simple method for generating mirror symmetry composite multiscroll chaotic attractors . *Int. J. Bifurc. Chaos* **2020**, *30*, 2050220. [CrossRef]
23. Yan, D.W.; Ji'e, M.; Wang, L.D.; Duan, S.K.; Du, X.Y. Generating novel multi-scroll chaotic attractors via fractal transformation. *Nonlinear Dyn.* **2022**, *107*, 3919–3944. [CrossRef]
24. Hong, Q.H.; Wu, Q.J.; Wang, X.P.; Zeng, Z.G. Novel Nonlinear Function Shift Method for Generating Multiscroll Attractors Using Memristor-Based Control Circuit. *IEEE Trans. Very Large Scale Integr. (VLSI) Syst.* **2019**, *27*, 1174–1185. [CrossRef]
25. Li, W.J.; Li, P.; Jia, M.M. Chaos control and chaos synchronization of a multi-wing chaotic system and its application in multi-frequency weak signal detection. *AIP Adv.* **2021**, *11*, 095003. [CrossRef]
26. Yan, S.H.; Sun, X.; Wang, Q.Y.; Ren, Y.; Shi, W.L.; Wang, E. A novel double-wing chaotic system with infinite equilibria and coexisting rotating attractors: Application to weak signal detection. *Phys. Scr.* **2021**, *96*, 125216. [CrossRef]
27. Hammouch, Z.; Yavuz, M.; Ozdemir, N. Numerical Solutions and Synchronization of a Variable-Order Fractional Chaotic System. *Math. Model. Numer. Simul. Appl.* **2021**, *1*, 11–23. [CrossRef]
28. Chen, L.P.; Yin, H.; Huang, T.W.; Yuan, L.G.; Zheng, S.; Yin, L.S. Chaos in fractional-order discrete neural networks with application to image encryption. *Neural Netw.* **2020**, *125*, 174–184. [CrossRef] [PubMed]
29. Baleanu, D.; Zibaei, S.; Namjoo, M.; Jajarmi, A. A nonstandard finite difference scheme for the modeling and nonidentical synchronization of a novel fractional chaotic system. *Adv. Differ. Equ.* **2021**, *2021*, 308. [CrossRef]
30. Wang, S.J.; He, S.B.; Yousefpour, A.; Jahanshahi, H.; Repnik, R.; Perc, M. Chaos and complexity in a fractional-order financial system with time delays. *Chaos Solitons Fractals* **2020**, *131*, 109521. [CrossRef]
31. Sayed, S.; Amir, A.; Emile Franc Doungmo Goufo. Investigation of complex behaviour of fractal fractional chaotic attractor with mittag-leffler Kernel. *Chaos Solitons Fractals* **2021**, *152*, 111332.
32. He, Y.Z.; Fu, Y.X.; Qiao, Z.J.; Kang, Y.M. Chaotic resonance in a fractional-order oscillator system with application to mechanical fault diagnosis. *Chaos Solitons Fractals* **2021**, *142*, 110536. [CrossRef]
33. Huang, P.F.; Chai, Y.; Chen, X.L. Multiple dynamics analysis of Lorenz-family systems and the application in signal detection. *Chaos Solitons Fractals* **2022**, *156*, 111797. [CrossRef]
34. Li, G.H.; Xie, R.T.; Yang, H. Detection method of ship-radiated noise based on fractional-order dual coupling oscillator. *Nonlinear Dyn.* **2024**, *112*, 2091–2118. [CrossRef]
35. Qiao, Z.J.; He, Y.B.; Liao, C.R.; Zhu, R.H. Noise-boosted weak signal detection in fractional nonlinear systems enhanced by increasing potential-well width and its application to mechanical fault diagnosis. *Chaos Solitons Fractals* **2023**, *175*, 113960. [CrossRef]
36. Dong, K.F.; Xu, K.; Zhou, Y.Y.; Zuo, C.; Wang, L.M.; Zhang, C.; Jin, F.; Song, J.; Mo, W.; Hui, Y. A memristor-based chaotic oscillator for weak signal detection and its circuitry realization. *Nonlinear Dyn.* **2022**, *109*, 2129–2141. [CrossRef]
37. Zhang, S.; Zeng, Y.C.; Li, Z.J. One to four-wing chaotic attractors coined from a novel 3D fractional-order chaotic system with complex dynamics. *Chin. J. Phys.* **2018**, *56*, 793–806. [CrossRef]
38. Cai, H.; Sun, J.Y.; Gao, Z.B.; Zhang, H. A novel multi-wing chaotic system with FPGA implementation and application in image encryption. *J.-Real-Time Image Process.* **2022**, *19*, 775–790. [CrossRef]
39. Wang, C.H. Dynamic Behavior Analysis and Robust Synchronization of a Novel Fractional-Order Chaotic System with Multiwing Attractors. *J. Mathematics.* **2021**, *2021*, 6684906. [CrossRef]
40. Zhang, S.; Zeng, Y.C.; Li, J.Z. A Novel Four-Dimensional No-Equilibrium Hyper-Chaotic System With Grid Multiwing Hyper-Chaotic Hidden Attractors. *J. Comput. Nonlinear Dynam.* **2018**, *13*, 090908. [CrossRef]
41. Sahoo, S.; Roy, B.K. A new multi-wing chaotic attractor with unusual variation in the number of wings. *Chaos Solitons Fractals* **2022**, *164*, 112598. [CrossRef]
42. Tavazoei, M.S.; Haeri, M. A necessary condition for double scroll attractor existence in fractional-order systems. *Phys. Lett. A* **2007**, *367*, 102–113. [CrossRef]
43. Nie, C.Y.; Wang, Z.W. Application of Chaos in Weak Signal Detection. In Proceedings of the 2011 Third International Conference on Measuring Technology and Mechatronics Automation, Shanghai, China, 6–7 January 2011.

44. Faber, J.; Bozovic, D. Noise-induced chaos and signal detection by the nonisochronous Hopf oscillator. *Chaos* **2019**, *29*, 043132. [CrossRef] [PubMed]
45. Wang, S.F. Finite-time synchronization of fractional multi-wing chaotic system. *Phys. Scr.* **2023**, *98*, 115224. [CrossRef]
46. Kumar, V.; Heiland, J.; Benner, P. Projective lag quasi-synchronization of coupled systems with mixed delays and parameter mismatch: A unified theory. *Neural Comput. Applic.* **2023**, *35*, 23649--23665. [CrossRef]
47. Matignon, D. Stability Results For Fractional Differential Equations With Applications To Control Processing. *Comput. Eng. Syst. Appl.* **1997**, *2*, 963–968.
48. Hu, J.B.; Han, Y.; Zhao, L.D. A novel stablility theorem for fractional systems and its applying in synchronizing fractional chaotic system based on back-stepping approach. *Acta Phys. Sin.* **2009**, *58*, 2235–2239.
49. Schmidt, R. Multiple emitter location and signal parameter estimation. *IEEE Trans. Antennas Propag.* **1986**, *34*, 276–280. [CrossRef]

fractal and fractional

MDPI

Article

An Optimal Control Theory-Based Study for Fractional Smoking Model Using Bernoulli Wavelet Method

Sanowar Ahasan [1], Sunil Kumar [1,2,*] and Shaher Momani [2,3]

1 Department of Mathematics, National Institute of Technology Jamshedpur, Jamshedpur 831014, Jharkhand, India; sanowar.bolpur@gmail.com
2 Nonlinear Dynamics Research Center (NDRC), Ajman University, Ajman P.O. Box 346, United Arab Emirates; shahermm@yahoo.com
3 Department of Mathematics, University of Jordan, Amman P.O. Box 11942, Jordan
* Correspondence: skumar.math@nitjsr.ac.in; Tel.: +91-7870102516

Abstract: This paper introduces a dynamic model that explores smoking and optimal control strategies. It shows how fractional-order (FO) analysis has uncovered hidden parts of complex systems and provides information about previously ignored elements. This paper uses the Bernoulli wavelet operational matrix method and the Adam–Bashforth–Moulton (ABM) method to analyse this model numerically. The mathematical model is segmented into five sub-classes: susceptible smokers, ingestion class, unusual smokers, regular smokers, and ex-smokers. It considers four optimal control measures: an anti-smoking education campaign, distribution of anti-smoking gum, administration of anti-nicotine drugs, and governmental restrictions on smoking in public areas. We show in this model how to control smoking in society strategically.

Keywords: fractional-order model; Caputo derivative; Bernoulli wavelet method; operational matrix; residual-error analysis; fractional optimum control problem (FOCP)

1. Introduction

Fractional calculus (FC) is a branch of mathematical analysis that studies several possibilities for defining the differentiation and integration operator's real or complex number powers. Fractional derivatives are useful for understanding the memory and characteristics of different processes and materials. Models based on classical integer order often overlook or disregard the significant impacts of these effects [1]. FO derivatives and integrals possess non-local characteristics. In the context of these properties, the future state of a model is influenced not only by its current state but also by all of its preceding states [2]. Multiple definitions of fractional derivatives exist. Various researchers have proposed different approaches to define fractional derivatives. Riemann and Liouville introduced a power-law-based concept, while Caputo and Fabrizio introduced a derivative with FO based on the exponential law. Additionally, Atangana and Baleanu suggested an alternative version of the FO derivative utilizing the generalized Mittag–Leffler function, which incorporates a non-local and non-singular kernel with strong memory properties. FO derivatives provide a novel approach for modeling the dynamics of complex phenomena. FC's many applications in engineering and the mathematical modeling of physical systems have attracted much attention recently. FC has applications in mathematics, engineering, physics, bio-engineering, and economics. Several systems have been described more precisely and smoothly by fractional differential equations (FDEs).

A wavelet originates from a zero point, undergoes alternating periods of rising and falling, and eventually returns to zero, repeating this pattern one or more times [3]. The term "omelette", the French equivalent for wavelet that translates to "small wave", was initially introduced by Haar in 1909 and adopted by Morlet and Grossmann in 1984 [4]. Wavelet theory has real-world applications in many exciting fields of science and technology. The following are several domains where it finds use: music, optics, signal and image processing, radar technology, nuclear engineering, earthquake prediction, physics, geology, astronomy, and more [5–12]. Numerical analysis is a branch of mathematics used to investigate and estimate answers to problems that have not been solved analytically [13]. There are two classifications of wavelets: continuous and discrete. A wavelet transform represents a function that uses the wavelet technique. It is primarily characterized by a function called the "mother wavelet". This is scaled and shifted to generate the various wavelets. Wavelet analysis allows wavelets to be applied in various areas or domains using a collection of orthonormal and comparable basis functions defined in time and space. Consequently, the concept of wavelets was introduced, employing basis functions localized within finite domains. When compared to other numerical methods, wavelets provide a better approximation due to their ability to identify both sharp irregularities and smooth perturbations, due to their localization. Consequently, wavelet analysis offers a more precise description of function properties compared to Fourier analysis [14] and can accurately represent various operators and functions, as well as being compatible with quick numerical techniques [15]. In this model, we use the Bernoulli wavelet method (BWM). The Bernoulli wavelet is preferred over other wavelets, such as Haar, Legendre, Bernstein, Hermite, etc., for several reasons:

1. It is efficient for representing piecewise smooth functions due to its basis on Bernoulli polynomials.
2. It has a more straightforward implementation with lower computational complexity.
3. It handles boundary conditions well due to its compact support.
4. It provides smooth approximations compared to Haar's piecewise constant approximations.
5. It is accurate for solving numerical problems and significant differential equations.
6. It offers practical multi-resolution analysis for analyzing signals at various scales.

Owing to these properties, Bernoulli wavelets are particularly well-suited for engineering and computational tasks that demand smooth, efficient, and accurate function representations.

Mathematical modeling involves examining a specific aspect of a real-life problem using mathematical language and concepts [16]. Understanding how the world and its mechanisms function requires modeling. It involves representing the world in simplified models and forms, collaborating with engineers and scientists to address real-world problems effectively. Furthermore, it has helped reveal various new aspects of issues. The observer's viewpoint is critical in the modeling process. It is important to be able to visualize models mentally. Engineers and scientists employ such techniques to model and design upcoming technologies. In conjunction with this procedure, prototypes are frequently employed. A prototype serves as a scaled-down representation of a functional model. Prototypes are utilized in various situations where there is a requirement to test or analyze a model without causing any impact or harm to the actual one. Additionally, using models, one may understand how atoms and particles behave, imagine how our environment will change, and create a vast range of products, from toy vehicles to actual cars. Within the realm of nonlinear dynamics and applied sciences, the exploration of mathematical modeling for infectious diseases in ecology and biology is a captivating field of study. Within this discipline, there exist abundant opportunities to acquire the skills necessary for characterizing the behavior of infectious disease models and assessing their dynamic properties [17,18]. Mathematical modeling has widespread applications in applied sciences, particularly FC.

Smoking stands as one of the most significant global health concerns in contemporary times. A considerable number of individuals lose their lives due to smoking during the years of most excellent output, as per a report by the World Health Organization (WHO) on the global smoking epidemic. The adverse effects of this on different physiological processes contribute to over 5 million deaths annually across the globe, with projections indicating a potential increase to around 8 million by the year 2030. Smokers face a 70% elevated likelihood of experiencing a heart attack in comparison to individuals who do not smoke. The detrimental health impacts of smoking go beyond the individual who smokes, affecting others as well. Secondhand smoke comprises harmful substances from both the smoke exhaled and the immediate smoke emitted by burning tobacco, in addition to the smoke that the smoker directly inhales. Individuals who do not smoke but are regularly exposed to secondhand smoke have a higher likelihood of being susceptible to various diseases, such as lung cancer and cardiovascular conditions, similar to smokers [19]. Numerous scientific studies indicate that smoking further heightens the risk of acquiring ailments such as cancer, cardiovascular disorders, stroke, respiratory conditions, diabetes, and chronic obstructive pulmonary disease. In addition, smoking increases the risk of tuberculosis, various ocular conditions, and immune system disorders like rheumatoid arthritis. There are still social and economic repercussions from smoking, even in nations with low death rates where its incidence has peaked. It also includes elevated levels of suffering, illness, and death, the subsequent decline in productivity, and the associated healthcare expenses [20].

A limited amount of research has been conducted on FOCPs [21,22]. As the need for practical, precise, and highly accurate systems increases, so does the requirement for optimal control theories and the corresponding analytical and numerical methods to solve the associated equations. This study uses the CF and the benefits of FC to provide a valuable examination of the dynamical behavior of a mathematical model for smoking [23]. Through numerical exploration using the Homotopy Perturbation Method (HPM) and the Laplace transform combined with the Adomian Decomposition Method (LADM), the study yields consistent and robust numerical results, providing strong validation for the model with arbitrary-order derivatives. The findings highlight the significant influence of various parameters within the model, concluding that FO systems exhibit more complex dynamics than those with integer-order derivatives. The research supports a system of smoking, indicating that different psychological and physiological processes are involved in initiating smoking compared to developing a regular smoking habit [24]. They employed the constant proportional Caputo–Fabrizio (CPCF) operator to construct a FO system that captures the harmful effects of smoking on society. Additionally, they conducted qualitative and quantitative evaluations of the suggested methodology and thoroughly examined the CPCF operator. Also, they applied the iterative Laplace transform method to develop a numerical simulation for a specific set of FDEs.

As per the findings of this study, the application of the BWM to the smoking model has yet to be explored. Therefore, our objective is to observe the model's behavior when this method is employed. This research uses the Bernoulli wavelet's operational matrix approach to compute the nonlinear FO smoking model. A comparative analysis is conducted between the outcomes obtained through the fractional ABM numerical method and those derived from various scenarios. This study fills this gap using the optimal control technique and offering a numerical approach. The ABM method offers significant benefits in fractional systems due to its higher accuracy, enhanced stability, and adaptability. It balances computational efficiency and precision by using a correction step to refine predictions, making it ideal for fractional dynamics with memory effects. Despite these strengths, the ABM method has more complex implementation requirements, relies on precise initial values, and may be less effective for highly stiff systems. Then, we use optimal control theory in this model. This study's other achievement is the introduction of four controls designed to effectively decrease the number of individuals who smoke and simultaneously boost the number of people who successfully quit smoking for good. To the author's knowledge, thinking methods have yet to be utilized to solve the proposed model thus far. This paper's remaining sections are organized as follows: A thorough description of derivatives with non-integer order is given in Section 2. We analyze the fractional smoking system in Section 3. The fundamental idea of the Bernoulli wavelet's operational matrix (BWOM) is summed up in Section 4. We apply BWM and ABM to the smoking system in Section 5 to obtain an approximate solution. The formulation of optimal controls and their solution are covered in Section 6. Section 7 displays the simulation results and the following discussion. The concluding section summarizes the research findings and concludes.

2. Preliminaries

This section explores the fundamental ideas and symbols associated with FC. $\mathbb{N}$ represents the natural number set.

Definition 1 ([25]). *The description of the Riemann–Liouville arbitrary integral of order $\sigma > 0$ for a function S_s is as follows:*

$$J_0^{\sigma} S_s(t) = \frac{1}{\Gamma(\sigma)} \int_0^t (t-\xi)^{\sigma-1} S_s(\xi) d\xi, \ t > 0, \tag{1}$$

where the symbol $\Gamma(.)$ denotes the Gamma function.

Definition 2 ([25,26]). *Consider the range where $0 < m-1 < \sigma < m$, with m belonging to the set of natural numbers. The Caputo derivative of order σ for a function S_s is defined as follows:*

$$\begin{aligned} {}^{C}D_0^{\sigma} S_s(t) &= J_0^{m-\sigma}\left(\frac{d^m S_s}{dt^m}\right)(t), \\ {}^{C}D_0^{\sigma} S_s(t) &= \frac{1}{\Gamma(m-\sigma)} \int_0^t (t-\xi)^{m-\sigma-1} \frac{d^m S_s}{d\xi^m}(\xi) d\xi. \end{aligned} \tag{2}$$

These are the essential characteristics we have:

$${}^{C}D_0^{\sigma}(J_0^{\sigma} S_s)(t) = S_s(t),$$

and

$$J_0^{\sigma}\left({}^{C}D_0^{\sigma} S_s\right)(t) = S_s(t) - \sum_{k=0}^{m-1} \frac{d^k S_s}{dt^k}(0^+)\frac{t^k}{k!}.$$

3. FO Smoking Model

The choice of a fractional derivative is essential when studying memory-dependent dynamics, such as addiction processes, relapse mechanisms, and long-term behavioural changes in smoking. Both the Caputo and Riemann–Liouville (RL) definitions are mathematically sound, but for several important reasons, the Caputo derivative is more appropriate for simulating real-world behavioural systems:

1. The RL derivative of a constant is not zero. This leads to fractional initial conditions, which do not translate well to real-world measurements. However, the Caputo

derivative vanishes for constants, and its initial conditions are standard, making it easier to match with actual data.

2. The Riemann–Liouville (RL) approach calculates the average of past cravings first, then looks at how this average changes. This has sometimes given too much weight to old cravings in unrealistic ways. In contrast, the Caputo method looks at how cravings change moment-to-moment first, then considers how these changes build up over time. This makes more sense for addiction because people do not respond to their average past craving—they react to sudden changes, like a bad withdrawal day or stressful event, triggering stronger urges.
3. RL derivatives have produced unrealistic singularities at $t = 0$. For finite initial conditions, Caputo guarantees smooth solutions. Because Caputo has well-posed initial conditions, the statistical fitting of fractional models to clinical data is more stable.

For these reasons, the manuscript employs the Caputo framework to capture memory-dependent smoking dynamics accurately [24].

$$\begin{aligned}
{}_0^C D_t^\sigma S_s(t) &= e_1 - e_2 S_s(t) I_c(t) + e_3 R_s(t) - e_4 S_s(t),\\
{}_0^C D_t^\sigma I_c(t) &= e_2 S_s(t) I_c(t) - e_5 I_c(t) U_s(t) - (e_6 + e_4) I_c(t),\\
{}_0^C D_t^\sigma U_s(t) &= e_5 I_c(t) U_s(t) - (e_7 + e_8 + e_4) U_s(t),\\
{}_0^C D_t^\sigma R_s(t) &= e_7 U_s(t) - (e_9 + e_4 + e_3) R_s(t),\\
{}_0^C D_t^\sigma E_s(t) &= e_9 R_s(t) - e_4 E_s(t).
\end{aligned} \tag{3}$$

The initial conditions are given as [23],

$$S_s(0) = \zeta_1,\ \ I_c(0) = \zeta_2,\ \ U_s(0) = \zeta_3,\ \ R_s(0) = \zeta_4,\ \ E_s(0) = \zeta_5, \tag{4}$$

where

$$\zeta_1 \ = \ 68,\ \zeta_2 = 40,\ \zeta_3 = 30,\ \zeta_4 = 20,\ \zeta_5 = 15. \tag{5}$$

Here, $0 < \sigma \leq 1$, ${}^C D_0^\sigma$ Caputo derivative σ. The different type of smokers are susceptible smokers S_s, ingestion class I_c, unusual smokers U_s, regular smokers R_s, and ex-smokers E_s.

e_1 is the enlistment rate, e_2 is the rate at which S_s transitions to I_c, e_5 is the rate at which I_c transitions to U_s, e_7 is the rate at which U_s transitions to R_s, e_9 is the migration rate, e_4 is the natural fatality rate, and e_3 is the recovery rate, while e_6 and e_8 represent the fatality rates due to snuffing and smoking, respectively.

4. Characteristics and Function Approximation of the Bernoulli Wavelet

Wavelets are a category of functions generated by consistently altering both the translation, denoted as 'b', and the dilation, represented by 'a', of a single function $\Xi(t)$, which is referred to as the mother wavelet. When both the translation and dilation parameters are in constant flux, the resulting wavelet family is as follows [27]:

$$\Xi_{a,b}(t) = \mid a \mid^{-1/2} \Xi\left(\frac{t-b}{a}\right), \quad a, b \in \mathbb{R}, a \neq 0. \tag{6}$$

If we limit the values of the parameters a and b to discrete values, we get $a = a_0^{-k}$, $b = nb_0 a_0^{-k}$, $a_0 > 1$, $b_0 > 0$, where n and k are positive integers, The discrete wavelet family that we have is as follows:

$$\Xi_{k,n}(t) = \mid a \mid^{k/2} \Xi\left(a_0^k t - nb_0\right).$$

The wavelet basis in the $L^2(\mathbb{R})'s$ space is constructed using $\Xi_{k,n}(t)$. Particularly, when $a_0 = 2$ and $b_0 = 1$, $\Xi_{k,n}(t)$ constitute an orthonormal basis.

Bernoulli wavelets, denoted as $\Xi_{n,m}(t) = \Xi(k,n,m,t)$, possess four parameters: $n = 0,1,2,3,\ldots,2^{k-1}-1$, where k is any positive integer. These wavelets are associated with Bernoulli polynomials of degree m, and t represents the normalized time degree. Their definition pertains to the semi-interval $[0,1)$.

$$\Xi_{n,m}(t) = \begin{cases} 2^{\frac{k-1}{2}}\tilde{\beta}_m\left(2^{k-1}t-n\right), & \frac{n}{2^{k-1}} \le t < \frac{n+1}{2^{k-1}}, \\ 0, & \text{otherwise}. \end{cases} \tag{7}$$

Here,

$$\tilde{\beta}_m(t) = \begin{cases} 1, & m=0, \\ \frac{1}{\sqrt{\frac{(-1)^{m-1}(m!)^2}{(2m)!}\beta_{2m}}}\beta_m(t), & m>0, \end{cases} \tag{8}$$

and $m = 0,1,2,\ldots,M-1$, where $\beta_m(t)$ denotes the Bernoulli polynomials with order m, which are described on interval $[0,1]$ as [28]

$$\beta_m(t) = \sum_{i=0}^{m}({}^mC_i)\beta_{m-i}t^i. \tag{9}$$

In addition, we obtain polynomials of these particular types, where $\beta_i = \beta_i(0)$, $i = 0,1,2,\ldots,m$ and these β_i values correspond to Bernoulli numbers.

$$\beta_0(t) = 1,\ \beta_1(t) = t - \frac{1}{2},\ \beta_2(t) = t^2 - t + \frac{1}{6},\ \beta_3(t) = t^3 - \frac{3}{2}t^2 + \frac{1}{2}t.$$

A function f defined within the interval $[0,1)$ can be expressed using Bernoulli wavelets in the following manner:

$$f(t) = \sum_{n=0}^{\infty}\sum_{m=0}^{\infty} c_{n,m}\Xi_{n,m}(t). \tag{10}$$

If the series in Equation (10) is not finite and is truncated, it has been expressed in the following alternative form:

$$f(t) \simeq f_{\hat{m}}(t) = \sum_{n=0}^{2^{k-1}-1}\sum_{m=0}^{M-1} c_{n,m}\Xi_{n,m}(t) = C^T\Xi(t), \tag{11}$$

where C and $Y(t)$ are $\hat{m} \times 1\left(\hat{m} = 2^{k-1} \times M\right)$ column vectors and T represents transposition.

Now,

$$\begin{aligned} C =& \left[c_{0,0}, c_{0,1}, c_{0,2}, \ldots, c_{0,M-1}, \ldots, c_{2^{k-1}-1,0}, c_{2^{k-1}-1,1}, \ldots, c_{2^{k-1}-1,M-1}\right]^T, \\ =& [c_1, c_2, c_3, \ldots, c_{\hat{m}}]^T, \end{aligned} \tag{12}$$

and

$$\begin{aligned} \Xi(t) =& \left[\Xi_{0,0}(t), \Xi_{0,1}(t), \ldots, \Xi_{0,M-1}(t), \ldots, \Xi_{2^{k-1}-1,0}(t), \Xi_{2^{k-1}-1,1}(t), \ldots, \Xi_{2^{k-1}-1,M-1}(t)\right]^T, \\ =& [\Xi_1(t), \Xi_2(t), \ldots, \Xi_{\hat{m}}(t)]^T. \end{aligned} \tag{13}$$

In this section, we present the Bernoulli Wavelet matrix denoted as $\phi_{\hat{m}\times\hat{m}}$, which is defined as $\phi_{\hat{m}\times\hat{m}} = [\Xi\left(\frac{2i-1}{2\hat{m}}\right)],\ i = 1,2,3,\ldots,2^{k-1}M$.

$$\phi_{12*12} = \begin{bmatrix} 2 & 2 & 2 & 0 & 0 & 0 & 0 & 0 & 0 & 0 & 0 & 0 \\ 0 & 0 & 0 & 2 & 2 & 2 & 0 & 0 & 0 & 0 & 0 & 0 \\ 0 & 0 & 0 & 0 & 0 & 0 & 2 & 2 & 2 & 0 & 0 & 0 \\ 0 & 0 & 0 & 0 & 0 & 0 & 0 & 0 & 0 & 2 & 2 & 2 \\ -2.3094 & 0 & 2.3094 & 0 & 0 & 0 & 0 & 0 & 0 & 0 & 0 & 0 \\ 0 & 0 & 0 & -2.3094 & 0 & 2.3094 & 0 & 0 & 0 & 0 & 0 & 0 \\ 0 & 0 & 0 & 0 & 0 & 0 & -2.3094 & 0 & 2.3094 & 0 & 0 & 0 \\ 0 & 0 & 0 & 0 & 0 & 0 & 0 & 0 & 0 & -2.3094 & 0 & 2.3094 \\ 0.7454 & -2.2361 & 0.7454 & 0 & 0 & 0 & 0 & 0 & 0 & 0 & 0 & 0 \\ 0 & 0 & 0 & 0.7454 & -2.2361 & 0.7454 & 0 & 0 & 0 & 0 & 0 & 0 \\ 0 & 0 & 0 & 0 & 0 & 0 & 0.7454 & -2.2361 & 0.7454 & 0 & 0 & 0 \\ 0 & 0 & 0 & 0 & 0 & 0 & 0 & 0 & 0 & 0.7454 & -2.2361 & 0.7454 \end{bmatrix}.$$

We have now obtained the Bernoulli wavelet matrix $\phi_{\hat{m}\times\hat{m}}$ for a specific set of collocation points given by $\frac{2i-1}{2\hat{m}}$, where $k = 3, \ M = 3$.

4.1. Utilizing the Block-Pulse Function, We Can Construct BWOM

In this section, we present the operational matrix for both non-integer and integer orders of the Bernoulli wavelet, which holds significant importance in our proposed system for addressing the nonlinear, non-integer-order smoking dynamic model.

With the assistance of the block-pulse function

Block-pulse functions have been outlined within the given time frame $[0, t_l)$, [25]

$$b_j(t) = \begin{cases} 1, & \frac{jt_l}{\hat{m}} \le t < \frac{(j+1)t_l}{\hat{m}}, \\ 0, & \text{otherwise,} \end{cases}$$

where $j = 0, 1, \ldots, m$ and $B_{\hat{m}} = [b_1, b_2, .., b_m]$. In this study, the block-pulse function demonstrates beneficial properties. We shall use its characteristics to determine the Bernoulli wavelet's operational matrix.

$$(J_t^\sigma B_{\hat{m}})(t) \cong F^\sigma B_{\hat{m}}(t),$$

$$F^\sigma = \frac{t_l^\sigma}{m^\sigma(\Gamma(\sigma+2))} \begin{bmatrix} 1 & \zeta_1 & \zeta_2 & \cdots & \zeta_{\hat{m}-1} \\ 0 & 1 & \zeta_1 & \cdots & \zeta_{\hat{m}-2} \\ 0 & 0 & 1 & \zeta_1 & \vdots \\ \vdots & \vdots & \vdots & \ddots & \vdots \\ 0 & 0 & 0 & 0 & 1 \end{bmatrix},$$

where,

$$\zeta_l = (l+1)^{\sigma+1} - 2l^{\sigma+1} + (l-1)^{\sigma+1}, \ l = 1, 2, 3, \ldots, \hat{m} - 1.$$

We are currently in the process of constructing BWOM to address fractional-order integration denoted as P^σ,

$$(J_t^\sigma \varphi)(t) \cong P^\sigma \varphi(t),$$

then, we get

$$(J_t^\sigma \varphi)(t) \cong (J_t^\sigma \varphi B_{\hat{m}})(t) = \varphi(J_t^\sigma B_{\hat{m}})(t) \approx \varphi F^\sigma B_{\hat{m}}.$$

Therefore,

$$P^\sigma \varphi(t) \cong \varphi(t) F^\sigma B_{\hat{m}},$$

$$P^\sigma = \phi_{\hat{m}*\hat{m}} F^\sigma \phi_{\hat{m}*\hat{m}}^{-1}.$$

Using the previous equations, we have derived the operational matrix P^{σ}. Finally, considering specific values $k = 2, M = 3, \sigma = 0.65$ and utilizing collocation points $\frac{2i-1}{2m}$, we acquired the operational matrix that is shown below:

$$P^{0.65} = \begin{bmatrix} 0.6694 & 0.7697 & 0.2839 & -0.1021 & -0.0318 & 0.0263 \\ 0 & 0.6694 & 0 & 0.2839 & 0 & -0.0318 \\ -0.2297 & 0.0931 & 0.1895 & -0.0467 & 0.1821 & 0.0191 \\ 0 & -0.2297 & 0 & 0.1895 & 0 & 0.1821 \\ -0.0832 & -0.0819 & -0.1364 & 0.0021 & 0.1302 & -0.0023 \\ 0 & -0.0832 & 0 & -0.1364 & 0 & 0.1302 \end{bmatrix}.$$

The BWOM has been obtained for any arbitrary order in the $0 < \sigma \leq 1$ range.

4.2. Convergence Analysis

This section is dedicated to providing detailed information on analyzing the convergence of the Bernoulli wavelet function approximation [29].

Theorem 1. *As per* (11), *it is clear that any function* $Q(t) \in L^2[0,1]$ *has been approximated using Bernoulli wavelets in the following manner.*

$$Q(t) \approx \sum_{n=0}^{2^{k-1}-1} \sum_{m=0}^{M-1} c_{n,m} \Xi_{n,m}(t). \tag{14}$$

Now, we take M=3 here,

$$Q(t) \approx \sum_{n=0}^{2^{k-1}-1} \sum_{m=0}^{2} c_{n,m} \Xi_{n,m}(t). \tag{15}$$

So,

$$\begin{aligned} ||\varepsilon|| &= ||error(Q(t))|| \\ &= \left|\left| \sum_{n=0}^{\infty} \sum_{m=0}^{2} c_{n,m} \Xi_{n,m}(t) - \sum_{n=0}^{2^{k-1}-1} \sum_{m=0}^{2} c_{n,m} \Xi_{n,m}(t) \right|\right| \to 0,\ (k \to \infty). \end{aligned} \tag{16}$$

Proof. The orthogonal properties of Bernoulli wavelets, as demonstrated in [30], lead us to the following conclusion

$$||\varepsilon||^2 = \left|\left| \sum_{n=0}^{\infty} \sum_{m=0}^{2} c_{n,m} \Xi_{n,m}(t) - \sum_{n=0}^{2^{k-1}-1} \sum_{m=0}^{2} c_{n,m} \Xi_{n,m}(t) \right|\right|^2. \tag{17}$$

By utilizing the norm property of the polynomial $Q(t) \in L^2[0,1]$, we have established the following

$$\begin{aligned}
||\varepsilon||^2 =& \left\langle \sum_{n=0}^{\infty}\sum_{m=0}^{2} c_{n,m}\Xi_{n,m}(t) - \sum_{n=0}^{2^{k-1}-1}\sum_{m=0}^{2} c_{n,m}\Xi_{n,m}(t), \sum_{n=0}^{\infty}\sum_{m=0}^{2} c_{n,m}\Xi_{n,m}(t) \right. \\
& \left. - \sum_{n=0}^{2^{k-1}-1}\sum_{m=0}^{2} c_{n,m}\Xi_{n,m}(t) \right\rangle \\
=& \int_0^1 \left(\sum_{n=0}^{\infty}\sum_{m=0}^{2} c_{n,m}\Xi_{n,m}(t) - \sum_{n=0}^{2^{k-1}-1}\sum_{m=0}^{2} c_{n,m}\Xi_{n,m}(t) \right)^2 dt \\
=& \int_0^1 \left(\sum_{n=2^{k-1}}^{\infty}\sum_{m=0}^{2} c_{n,m}\Xi_{n,m}(t) \right)^2 dt \qquad (18) \\
=& \int_0^1 \sum_{n=2^{k-1}}^{\infty}\sum_{m=0}^{2} c_{n,m}^2\Xi_{n,m}^2(t) \\
=& \sum_{n=2^{k-1}}^{\infty}\sum_{m=0}^{2} c_{n,m}^2, \qquad c_{n,m} = \langle Q(t), \Xi_{n,m}(t) \rangle.
\end{aligned}$$

Given that $Q(t)$ is continuous on $[0,1]$, we can find a value $\gimel > 0$ such that the following condition holds,

$$|Q(t)| < \gimel, \quad \forall t \in [0,1].$$

When $m = 0$, we have derived the following from the definition of Bernoulli wavelets

$$\begin{aligned}
c_{n,m} =& \langle Q(t), \Xi_{n,m}(t) \rangle \\
=& \int_0^1 Q(t)\Xi_{n,m}(t)dt \\
=& \int_{\frac{n}{2^{k-1}}}^{\frac{n+1}{2^{k-1}}} Q(t)2^{\frac{k-1}{2}}dt \qquad (19) \\
<& 2^{\frac{k-1}{2}} \int_{\frac{n}{2^{k-1}}}^{\frac{n+1}{2^{k-1}}} \gimel dt \\
=& \frac{\gimel}{2^{\frac{k-1}{2}}}.
\end{aligned}$$

In the given examples, this condition is satisfied only when $m = 0$. However, when $m \neq 0$, the following cases apply

$$\begin{aligned}
c_{n,m} =& \langle Q(t), \Xi_{n,m}(t) \rangle \\
=& \int_0^1 Q(t)\Xi_{n,m}(t)dt \qquad (20) \\
=& \int_{\frac{n}{2^{k-1}}}^{\frac{n+1}{2^{k-1}}} Q(t)2^{\frac{k-1}{2}} \frac{1}{\sqrt{\frac{(-1)^{m-1}(m!)^2}{(2m)!}\beta_{2m}}} \beta_m\left(2^{k-1}t - n\right)dt.
\end{aligned}$$

First, we select the value 2^{k-1} so that $2^{k-1}t - n = u$, which gives us $t = \frac{u+n}{2^{k-1}}$. Therefore, $dt = \frac{1}{2^{k-1}}\,du$. By following a similar approach, we have derived the following.

$$c_{n,m} = \int_0^1 Q\left(\frac{u+n}{2^{k-1}}\right)2^{\frac{k-1}{2}} \frac{1}{\sqrt{\frac{(-1)^{m-1}(m!)^2}{(2m)!}\beta_{2m}}} \frac{1}{2^{k-1}}\beta_m(u)du$$
$$< \frac{\daleth}{2^{\frac{k-1}{2}}} \frac{1}{\sqrt{\frac{(-1)^{m-1}(m!)^2}{(2m)!}\beta_{2m}}} \int_0^1 \beta_m(u)du \to 0. \quad (21)$$

For every positive integer Y, the following statement is true:

$$\sum_{n=2^{k-1}}^{2^{k-1}+Y} \sum_{m=0}^{2} c_{n,m}^2 < \frac{3(Y+1)\daleth^2}{2^{k-1}} \to 0, \ (k \to \infty). \quad (22)$$

$$\sum_{n=2^{k-1}}^{\infty} \sum_{m=0}^{2} c_{n,m}^2 \to 0, \ (k \to \infty). \quad (23)$$

$$||\varepsilon|| = \left(\sum_{n=2^{k-1}}^{\infty} \sum_{m=0}^{2} c_{n,m}^2 \right)^{\frac{1}{2}}, \ (k \to \infty). \quad (24)$$

□

5. Proposed Method

The primary goal of this section is to formulate a smoking model with FO dynamics by employing the ABM in conjunction with the BWM.

5.1. *Experiment of Bernoulli Wavelet Approach on Smoking Model*

According to the study's findings, no investigation has been conducted into applying the BWM to the smoking model. Thus, we aim to see how the model behaves using this approach. The nonlinear FO smoking model is calculated in this study using the operational matrix approach of the Bernoulli wavelet. Let us consider a smoking model (3) with the initial condition (4). Further, we consider the higher-order derivatives in terms of Bernoulli wavelet with unknown coefficients, and we get

$$\begin{aligned}
{}^{C}D_0^{\sigma} S_s(t) &= \daleth_1^T \Xi(t), \\
{}^{C}D_0^{\sigma} I_c(t) &= \daleth_2^T \Xi(t), \\
{}^{C}D_0^{\sigma} U_s(t) &= \daleth_3^T \Xi(t), \\
{}^{C}D_0^{\sigma} R_s(t) &= \daleth_4^T \Xi(t), \\
{}^{C}D_0^{\sigma} E_s(t) &= \daleth_5^T \Xi(t),
\end{aligned} \quad (25)$$

where,

$$\begin{aligned}
\beth_1^T &= \left[(\beth_1)_{1,0}, (\beth_1)_{1,1}, \ldots, (\beth_1)_{1,M-1}, \ldots, (\beth_1)_{2^{k-1},0}, (\beth_1)_{2^{k-1},1}, \ldots, (\beth_1)_{2^{k-1},M-1}\right]^T, \\
\beth_2^T &= \left[(\beth_2)_{1,0}, (\beth_2)_{1,1}, \ldots, (\beth_2)_{1,M-1}, \ldots, (\beth_2)_{2^{k-1},0}, (\beth_2)_{2^{k-1},1}, \ldots, (\beth_2)_{2^{k-1},M-1}\right]^T, \\
\beth_3^T &= \left[(\beth_3)_{1,0}, (\beth_3)_{1,1}, \ldots, (\beth_3)_{1,M-1}, \ldots, (\beth_3)_{2^{k-1},0}, (\beth_3)_{2^{k-1},1}, \ldots, (\beth_3)_{2^{k-1},M-1}\right]^T, \\
\beth_4^T &= \left[(\beth_4)_{1,0}, (\beth_4)_{1,1}, \ldots, (\beth_4)_{1,M-1}, \ldots, (\beth_4)_{2^{k-1},0}, (\beth_4)_{2^{k-1},1}, \ldots, (\beth_4)_{2^{k-1},M-1}\right]^T, \\
\beth_5^T &= \left[(\beth_5)_{1,0}, (\beth_5)_{1,1}, \ldots, (\beth_5)_{1,M-1}, \ldots, (\beth_5)_{2^{k-1},0}, (\beth_5)_{2^{k-1},1}, \ldots, (\beth_5)_{2^{k-1},M-1}\right]^T,
\end{aligned}$$

and

$$S_s(0) = \zeta_1, \; I_c(0) = \zeta_2, \; U_s(0) = \zeta_3, \; R_s(0) = \zeta_4, \; E_s(0) = \zeta_5.$$

the vectors denoted as "unknown" and the function $\Xi(t)$ have already been provided. We are currently utilizing the Riemann–Liouville fractional operator, as deduced from the subtraction of Equations (3) and (4).

$$\begin{aligned}
\left(J_0^{\sigma\,C}D_0^{\sigma}\right)S_s(t) &= S_s(t) - S_s(0) = S_s(t) - \zeta_1 = \beth_1^T P^{\sigma}\Xi(t), \\
\left(J_0^{\sigma\,C}D_0^{\sigma}\right)I_c(t) &= I_c(t) - I_c(0) = I_c(t) - \zeta_2 = \beth_2^T P^{\sigma}\Xi(t), \\
\left(J_0^{\sigma\,C}D_0^{\sigma}\right)U_s(t) &= U_s(t) - U_s(0) = U_s(t) - \zeta_3 = \beth_3^T P^{\sigma}\Xi(t), \\
\left(J_0^{\sigma\,C}D_0^{\sigma}\right)R_s(t) &= R_s(t) - R_s(0) = R_s(t) - \zeta_4 = \beth_4^T P^{\sigma}\Xi(t), \\
\left(J_0^{\sigma\,C}D_0^{\sigma}\right)E_s(t) &= E_s(t) - E_s(0) = E_s(t) - \zeta_5 = \beth_5^T P^{\sigma}\Xi(t).
\end{aligned} \tag{26}$$

Now, we use (25)–(26) we derive from Equation (3)

$$\begin{aligned}
\beth_1^T\Xi(t) =& e_1 - e_2\left(\beth_1^T P^{\sigma}\Xi(t) + \zeta_1\right)\left(\beth_2^T P^{\sigma}\Xi(t) + \zeta_2\right) \\
&+ e_3\left(\beth_4^T P^{\sigma}\Xi(t) + \zeta_4\right) - e_4\left(\beth_1^T P^{\sigma}\Xi(t) + \zeta_1\right), \\
\beth_2^T\Xi(t) =& e_2\left(\beth_1^T P^{\sigma}\Xi(t) + \zeta_1\right)\left(\beth_2^T P^{\sigma}\Xi(t) + \zeta_2\right) \\
&- e_5\left(\beth_2^T P^{\sigma}\Xi(t) + \zeta_2\right)\left(\beth_3^T P^{\sigma}\Xi(t) + \zeta_3\right) \\
&- (e_6 + e_4)\left(\beth_2^T P^{\sigma}\Xi(t) + \zeta_2\right), \\
\beth_3^T\Xi(t) =& e_5\left(\beth_2^T P^{\sigma}\Xi(t) + \zeta_2\right)\left(\beth_3^T P^{\sigma}\Xi(t) + \zeta_3\right) \\
&- (e_7 + e_8 + e_4)\left(\beth_3^T P^{\sigma}\Xi(t) + \zeta_3\right), \\
\beth_4^T\Xi(t) =& e_7\left(\beth_3^T P^{\sigma}\Xi(t) + \zeta_3\right) \\
&- (e_9 + e_4 + e_3)\left(\beth_4^T P^{\sigma}\Xi(t) + \zeta_4\right), \\
\beth_5^T\Xi(t) =& e_9\left(\beth_4^T P^{\sigma}\Xi(t) + \zeta_4\right) \\
&- e_4\left(\beth_5^T P^{\sigma}\Xi(t) + \zeta_5\right).
\end{aligned} \tag{27}$$

Then, we utilize the collocation point (27), which has been written as

$$\begin{aligned}
\beth_1^T \Xi(t_i) =& e_1 - e_2\left(\beth_1^T P^\sigma \Xi(t_i) + \zeta_1\right)\left(\beth_2^T P^\sigma \Xi(t_i) + \zeta_2\right) \\
&+ e_3\left(\beth_4^T P^\sigma \Xi(t_i) + \zeta_4\right) - e_4\left(\beth_1^T P^\sigma \Xi(t_i) + \zeta_1\right), \\
\beth_2^T \Xi(t_i) =& e_2\left(\beth_1^T P^\sigma \Xi(t_i) + \zeta_1\right)\left(\beth_2^T P^\sigma \Xi(t_i) + \zeta_2\right) \\
&- e_5\left(\beth_2^T P^\sigma \Xi(t_i) + \zeta_2\right)\left(\beth_3^T P^\sigma \Xi(t_i) + \zeta_3\right) \\
&- (e_6 + e_4)\left(\beth_2^T P^\sigma \Xi(t_i) + \zeta_2\right), \\
\beth_3^T \Xi(t_i) =& e_5\left(\beth_2^T P^\sigma \Xi(t_i) + \zeta_2\right)\left(\beth_3^T P^\sigma \Xi(t_i) + \zeta_3\right) \\
&- (e_7 + e_8 + e_4)\left(\beth_3^T P^\sigma \Xi(t_i) + \zeta_3\right),
\end{aligned}$$

$$\begin{aligned}
\beth_4^T \Xi(t_i) =& e_7\left(\beth_3^T P^\sigma \Xi(t_i) + \zeta_3\right) \\
&- (e_9 + e_4 + e_3)\left(\beth_4^T P^\sigma \Xi(t_i) + \zeta_4\right), \\
\beth_5^T \Xi(t_i) =& e_9\left(\beth_4^T P^\sigma \Xi(t_i) + \zeta_4\right) \\
&- e_4\left(\beth_5^T P^\sigma \Xi(t_i) + \zeta_5\right).
\end{aligned} \tag{28}$$

$\forall\ i = 1, 2, \ldots, m$. By transforming Equation (28) into a nonlinear system involving 5 m unknown vectors, we employ an iterative approach using Matlab to solve this system of nonlinear equations. Since (28) is reduced, we obtain approximate solutions of the system of Equation (3).

5.2. ABM Scheme for the Smoking Model

The ABM scheme is the most popular numerical method for solving fractional initial-value problems of any type [31]. The ABM method's increased accuracy, stability, and adaptability make it a valuable tool for fractional systems. It is perfect for fractional dynamics with memory effects because it compromises accuracy and computational efficiency by refining predictions through a corrective step. A comparison is made between the results from different scenarios and the fractional ABM numerical technique results. Let us consider that the following FDE is

$$\begin{aligned}
{}_0^C D_t^\sigma x_j(t) = f_j(t, x_j(t)),\ \ x_j^k(0) = x_{j0}^k, \\
k = 0, 1, 2, \cdots, \lceil \sigma \rceil, j \in N,
\end{aligned} \tag{29}$$

where x_{j0}^k is the arbitrary real number, $\sigma > 0$ and ${}_0^C D_t^\sigma$ is the fractional differential operator in Caputo sense. We analyze the results of the non-linear fractional smoking model using the ABM to obtain its numerical solution. Now, let $h = \frac{T}{\hat{m}}, \;\; t_n = nh, \;\; n = 0,1,2,\cdots,\hat{m};$ then, the corrector values are defined as,

$$
\begin{aligned}
(S_s)_{n+1} =& \zeta_1 + \frac{h^\sigma}{\Gamma(\sigma+2)}(e_1 - e_2(S_s)^p_{n+1}(I_c)^p_{n+1} + e_3(R_s)^p_{n+1} - e_4(S_s)^p_{n+1}) \\
&+ \frac{h^\sigma}{\Gamma(\sigma+2)}\sum_{j=0}^{n}\sigma_{j,n+1}(e_1 - e_2(S_s)_j(I_c)_j + e_3(R_s)_j - e_4(S_s)_j), \\
(I_c)_{n+1} =& \zeta_2 + \frac{h^\sigma}{\Gamma(\sigma+2)}(e_2(S_s)^p_{n+1}(I_c)^p_{n+1} - e_5(I_c)^p_{n+1}(U_s)^p_{n+1} - (e_6+e_4)(I_c)^p_{n+1}) \\
&+ \frac{h^\sigma}{\Gamma(\sigma+2)}\sum_{j=0}^{n}\sigma_{j,n+1}(e_2(S_s)_j(I_c)_j - e_5(I_c)_j(U_s)_j - (e_6+e_4)(I_c)_j), \\
(U_s)_{n+1} =& \zeta_3 + \frac{h^\sigma}{\Gamma(\sigma+2)}(e_5(I_c)^p_{n+1}(U_s)^p_{n+1} - (e_7+e_8+e_4)(U_s)^p_{n+1}) \\
&+ \frac{h^\sigma}{\Gamma(\sigma+2)}\sum_{j=0}^{n}\sigma_{j,n+1}(e_5(I_c)_j(U_s)_j - (e_7+e_8+e_4)(U_s)_j), \\
(R_s)_{n+1} =& \zeta_4 + \frac{h^\sigma}{\Gamma(\sigma+2)}(e_7(U_s)^p_{n+1} - (e_9+e_4+e_3)(R_s)^p_{n+1}) \\
&+ \frac{h^\sigma}{\Gamma(\sigma+2)}\sum_{j=0}^{n}\sigma_{j,n+1}(e_7(U_s)_j - (e_9+e_4+e_3)(R_s)_j), \\
(E_s)_{n+1} =& \zeta_5 + \frac{h^\sigma}{\Gamma(\sigma+2)}(e_9(R_s)^p_{n+1} - e_4(E_s)^p_{n+1}) \\
&+ \frac{h^\sigma}{\Gamma(\sigma+2)}\sum_{j=0}^{n}\sigma_{j,n+1}(e_9(R_s)_j - e_4(E_s)_j,
\end{aligned}
\tag{30}
$$

the corresponding predictor values are given as:

$$
\begin{aligned}
(S_s)^p_{n+1} =& \zeta_1 + \frac{1}{\Gamma(\sigma)}\sum_{j=0}^{n}\Theta_{j,n+1}(e_1 - e_2(S_s)_j(I_c)_j + e_3(R_s)_j - e_4(S_s)_j), \\
(I_c)^p_{n+1} =& \zeta_2 + \frac{1}{\Gamma(\sigma)}\sum_{j=0}^{n}\Theta_{j,n+1}(e_2(S_s)_j(I_c)_j - e_5(I_c)_j(U_s)_j - (e_6+e_4)(I_c)_j), \\
(U_s)^p_{n+1} =& \zeta_3 + \frac{1}{\Gamma(\sigma)}\sum_{j=0}^{n}\Theta_{j,n+1}(e_5(I_c)_j(U_s)_j - (e_7+e_8+e_4)(U_s)_j), \\
(R_s)^p_{n+1} =& \zeta_4 + \frac{1}{\Gamma(\sigma)}\sum_{j=0}^{n}\Theta_{j,n+1}(e_7(U_s)_j - (e_9+e_4+e_3)(R_s)_j), \\
(E_s)^p_{n+1} =& \zeta_5 + \frac{1}{\Gamma(\sigma)}\sum_{j=0}^{n}\Theta_{j,n+1}(e_9(R_s)_j - e_4(E_s)_j),
\end{aligned}
\tag{31}
$$

where

$$
\sigma_{j,n+1} = \begin{cases} n^{\sigma+1} - (n-\sigma)(n+1)^\sigma, & j=0 \\ (n-j+2)^{\sigma+1} + (n-j)^{\sigma+1} - 2(n-j+1)^{\sigma+1}, & 0 \le j \le n \\ 1, & j=1 \end{cases}
$$

and

$$
\Theta_{j,n+1} = \frac{h^\sigma}{\sigma}((n+1-j)^\sigma - (n-j)^\sigma), \; 0 \le j \le n.
$$

5.3. Remark

The stability of the ABM approach has been confirmed in reference [32], and it has been effectively used in the solution of differential equations with fixed FO. Therefore, there is no necessity to restate these findings here.

6. The Fractional Optimal Control Problem (FOCP)

FOCPs have not been the subject of much research. The need for optimum control theories and the related analytical and numerical techniques to solve the associated equations grows along with the demand for realistic, accurate, and exact systems. This study closes this gap by providing a numerical approach and utilising the optimal control technique. Here, the aim is to maximize the population of ex-smokers and control the smoking habit in society. This section discusses an optimal control approach appropriate for the system dynamics (3). Four controls have been considered in this study, constructed in (3), which have been represented as follows [33]:

$$\begin{aligned}
&{}_0^C D_t^{\sigma}(S_s)(t) = e_1 - e_2(S_s)(t)(I_c)(t) + e_3(R_s)(t) - (e_4 + w_1)(S_s)(t),\\
&{}_0^C D_t^{\sigma}(I_c)(t) = e_2(S_s)(t)(I_c)(t) - e_5(I_c)(t)(U_s)(t) - (e_6 + e_4 + w_2)(I_c)(t),\\
&{}_0^C D_t^{\sigma}(U_s)(t) = e_5(I_c)(t)(U_s)(t) - (e_7 + e_8 + e_4 + w_3)(U_s)(t),\\
&{}_0^C D_t^{\sigma}(R_s)(t) = e_7(U_s)(t) - (e_9 + e_4 + e_3 + w_4)(R_s)(t),\\
&{}_0^C D_t^{\sigma}(E_s)(t) = (e_9 + w_4)(R_s)(t) - e_4(E_s)(t) + w_1(S_s)(t) + w_2(I_c)(t) + w_3(U_s)(t).
\end{aligned} \tag{32}$$

By implementing the appropriate laws, the number of smokers and the pool of potential smokers have been brought down to more controllable levels. On the other hand, the number of smokers and potential smokers will rise while the number of persons quitting will fall if these four limitations are not implemented. When formulating the objective function, we took into account the control issues outlined in Equation (32). The following objective function has been derived:

$$\begin{aligned}
J(w(t)) = \quad & \int_0^{t_f} (R_s(t) - E_s(t) + \tfrac{1}{2}(k_1 w_1^2(t) + k_2 w_2^2(t)\\
& + k_3 w_3^2(t) + k_4 w_4^2(t)))dt.
\end{aligned} \tag{33}$$

This study's main objective is to reduce $J(w(t))$ while respecting its restrictions using the optimum control method.

6.1. Optimal Control Solutions

Let optimal control Equations (32) and (33) be written with a Hamiltonian function as follows:

$$H = L + \sum_{j=1}^{5} \lambda j(t) g_j, \tag{34}$$

where the Lagrangian function can be written as:

$$\begin{aligned}
L(R_s, E_s, w_i) = \quad & R_s(t) - E_s(t) + \tfrac{1}{2}(k_1 w_1^2(t) + k_2 w_2^2(t)\\
& + k_3 w_3^2(t) + k_4 w_4^2(t)),
\end{aligned} \tag{35}$$

and

$$
\begin{aligned}
{}_0^C D_t^{\sigma} S_s(t) &= g_1(t),\\
{}_0^C D_t^{\sigma} I_c(t) &= g_2(t),\\
{}_0^C D_t^{\sigma} U_s(t) &= g_3(t),\\
{}_0^C D_t^{\sigma} R_s(t) &= g_4(t),\\
{}_0^C D_t^{\sigma} E_s(t) &= g_5(t).
\end{aligned} \tag{36}
$$

The adjoint system, with λ as the adjoint vector, is given by:

$$
{}_0^C D_{t_f}^{\sigma} \lambda = \frac{\partial L}{\partial x} + \lambda^T \frac{\partial g}{\partial x}, \quad \lambda(t_f) = 0. \tag{37}
$$

The optimal control $w^*(t)$ satisfies the following equation:

$$
\frac{\partial L}{\partial w^*} + \lambda^T \frac{\partial g}{\partial w^*} = 0. \tag{38}
$$

The Euler–Lagrange optimality conditions for the FOCP with Caputo fractional derivatives are given by (36)–(38). Note, when $\sigma = 1$, the above FOCP becomes a classical optimal control problem.

Here, $\lambda = (\lambda_1, \lambda_2, \lambda_3, \lambda_4, \lambda_5)$, $g = (g_1, g_2, g_3, g_4, g_5)$, $i = 1, 2, 3, 4, 5$ are the right sides of system (32). The state system was already given by (32). Using the relations above, the adjoint system is derived as:

$$
\begin{aligned}
&D_{t_f}^{\sigma} \lambda_1 = \lambda_1(-e_2 I_c - (e_4 + w_1)) + \lambda_2(e_2 I_c) + \lambda_5 w_1,\\
&D_{t_f}^{\sigma} \lambda_2 = \lambda_1(-e_2 S_s) + \lambda_2(e_2 S_s - e_5 U_s - (e_6 + e_4 + w_2)) + \lambda_3(e_5 U_s) + \lambda_5 w_2,\\
&D_{t_f}^{\sigma} \lambda_3 = \lambda_2(-e_5 I_c) + \lambda_3(e_5 I_c - (e_7 + e_8 + e_4 + w_3)) + \lambda_4(e_7) + \lambda_5 w_3,\\
&D_{t_f}^{\sigma} \lambda_4 = 1 + \lambda_1 e_3 - \lambda_4(e_9 + e_4 + e_3 + w_4) + \lambda_5(e_9 + w_4),\\
&D_{t_f}^{\sigma} \lambda_5 = -1 - e_4 \lambda_5,
\end{aligned} \tag{39}
$$

with the boundary conditions $\lambda_i = 0,$, where $i = 1, 2, 3, 4, 5$. From the Equations (34)–(38), the expression for optimal control function is obtained as:

$$
\begin{aligned}
w_1^*(t) =& \frac{(\lambda_1 - \lambda_5) S_s}{k_1},\\
w_2^*(t) =& \frac{(\lambda_2 - \lambda_5) I_c}{k_2},\\
w_3^*(t) =& \frac{(\lambda_3 - \lambda_5) U_s}{k_3},\\
w_4^*(t) =& \frac{(\lambda_4 - \lambda_5) R_s}{k_4}.
\end{aligned} \tag{40}
$$

For the boundedness of the optimal control, we get the following forms of the above expression:

$$\begin{aligned} w_1^*(t) &= \max\left\{\min\left\{\frac{(\lambda_1-\lambda_5)S_s}{k_1},1\right\},0\right\}, \\ w_2^*(t) &= \max\left\{\min\left\{\frac{(\lambda_2-\lambda_5)I_c}{k_2},1\right\},0\right\}, \\ w_3^*(t) &= \max\left\{\min\left\{\frac{(\lambda_3-\lambda_5)U_s}{k_3},1\right\},0\right\}, \\ w_4^*(t) &= \max\left\{\min\left\{\frac{(\lambda_4-\lambda_5)R_s}{k_4},1\right\},0\right\}, \end{aligned} \tag{41}$$

replacing $w_i(t)$ by $w_i^*(t), i = 1,2,3,4,5$ in system (32) and (39), we got desire FOCP .

6.2. Existence of Optimal Control Solution

The methodology was employed to showcase the suitability of implementing optimal control for the model [34,35]. The assumption was made that the control system described in Equation (32) has been reformulated as follows:

$$\xi_t = C\xi + F(\xi). \tag{42}$$

In this context, the state variable vector is defined as: $\xi = [S_s(t), I_c(t), U_s(t), R_s(t), E_s(t)]^T$ and

$$C = \begin{bmatrix} -a & 0 & 0 & b & 0 \\ 0 & -c & 0 & 0 & 0 \\ 0 & 0 & -d & 0 & 0 \\ 0 & 0 & p & -f & 0 \\ i & j & m & g & -h \end{bmatrix},$$

where
$a = e_4 + w_1, b = e_3, c = e_4 + e_6 + w_2, d = e_7 + e_8 + e_4 + w_3, p = e_7,$
$f = e_9 + e_4 + e_3, g = e_9 + w_4, h = e_4, i = w_1, j = w_2, m = w_3,$

$$F(\xi) = (e_1 - e_2 S_s I_c, e_2 S_s I_c - e_5 I_c U_s, e_5 I_c U_s, 0, 0)^T.$$

Equation (42) is a nonlinear FDE with bounded coefficients, where ξ_t is the time derivative of ξ. Now,

$$B(\xi) = C\xi + F(\xi),$$

$$\begin{aligned} F(\xi_1) - F(\xi_2) = (&-e_2(S_s)_1(I_c)_1 + e_2(S_s)_2(I_c)_2, \\ &e_2(S_s)_1(I_c)_1 - e_2(S_s)_2(I_c)_2 - e_5(I_c)_1(U_s)_1 + e_5(I_c)_2(U_s)_2, \\ &e_5(I_c)_1(U_s)_1 - e_5(I_c)_2(U_s)_2, 0, 0)^T. \end{aligned}$$

Therefore,

$$
\begin{aligned}
|F(\xi_1) - F(\xi_2)| &= |-e_2(S_s)_1(I_c)_1 + e_2(S_s)_2(I_c)_2| \\
&+ |e_2(S_s)_1(I_c)_1 - e_2(S_s)_2(I_c)_2 - e_5(I_c)_1(U_s)_1 + e_5(I_c)_2(U_s)_2| \\
&+ |e_5(I_c)_1(U_s)_1 - e_5(I_c)_2(U_s)_2| \\
&\leq 2e_2|(S_s)_1(I_c)_1 + (S_s)_2(I_c)_2| + 2e_5|(I_c)_1(U_s)_1 + (I_c)_2(U_s)_2| \\
&\leq 2e_2|(S_s)_1[(I_c)_1 - (I_c)_2] + (I_c)_2[(S_s)_1 - (S_s)_2]| \\
&+ 2e_5|(I_c)_1[(U_s)_1 - (U_s)_2] + (U_s)_2[(I_c)_1 - (I_c)_2]| \\
&\leq 2e_2|(I_c)_2||(S_s)_1 - (S_s)_2| \\
&+ [2e_2|(S_s)_1| + 2e_5|(U_s)_2|]|(I_c)_1 - (I_c)_2| \\
&+ 2e_5|(I_c)_1||(U_s)_1 - (U_s)_2| \\
&\leq 2e_2\frac{e_1}{e_4}|(S_s)_1 - (S_s)_2| + (2e_2 + 2e_5)\frac{e_1}{e_4}|(I_c)_1 - (I_c)_2| \\
&+ 2e_5\frac{e_1}{e_4}|(U_s)_1 - (U_s)_2|.
\end{aligned}
$$

So, $|B(\xi_1) - B(\xi_2)| \leq Z|\xi_1 - \xi_2|$. Here,

$$
Z = \max\left\{\tfrac{(2e_2+2e_5)e_1}{e_4}, ||C||\right\} < \infty,
$$

observing that $B(\xi)$ is uniformly Lipschitz continuous, we have deduced, based on the definition of w_i, that a solution to the controlled model (32) does indeed exist.

7. Numerical Result and Discussion

In this part, we provide numerical solutions for the nonlinear fractional-order smoking model using the ABM approach and Bernoulli wavelet techniques. The Forward Euler method is a simple and versatile numerical technique for solving ordinary and fractional differential equations. It offers several advantages, including ease of implementation, low computational cost, and suitability for short-term predictions. However, it has some limitations, such as low accuracy for fractional models, stability issues, and inefficiency for long-term simulations. While the method is a good starting point, more advanced techniques like implicit schemes or fractional-specific methods may be more suitable for addressing these limitations in fractional models. The ABM is highly beneficial for fractional systems due to its superior accuracy, stability, and adaptability. Improving forecasts with a correction step successfully strikes a compromise between computing cost and accuracy, which makes it ideal for fractional dynamics with memory effects. However, it has implementation complexity and dependency on accurate initial values, and it could be more suitable for highly stiff systems. We will also illustrate the graphical patterns of this model for different values of the order σ. Then, by using control theory, we observe how to restrain and reduce this negative impact on society. In this paper, we utilize a numerical method optimal control technique and analyse the result [36–42]. Additionally, we examine the nonlinear FO smoking model with the subsequent parameter values from Table 1:

Table 1. Parameter values of system (3).

Parameters	Value	Source
e_1	0.1	[23]
e_2	0.003	[23]
e_3	0.003	[23]
e_4	0.002	[23]
e_5	0.002	[23]
e_6	0.003	[23]
e_7	0.05	[23]
e_8	0.003	[23]
e_9	0.05	[23]

$$\begin{aligned}&e_1 = 0.1, e_2 = 0.003, e_3 = 0.003, e_4 = 0.002, e_5 = 0.002, e_6 = 0.003,\\&e_7 = 0.05, e_8 = 0.003, e_9 = 0.05,\end{aligned}$$

and

$$S_s(0) = 68, I_c(0) = 40, U_s(0) = 30, R_s(0) = 20, E_s(0) = 15.$$

Applying the Laplace and inverse Laplace transforms in Equation (3) allows us to derive the following result.

$$\begin{aligned}S_s(t) =& S_s(0) + L^{-1}\left[\frac{1}{s^\sigma}L\{e_1 - e_2 S_s(t) I_c(t) + e_3 R_s(t) - e_4 S_s(t)\}\right],\\I_c(t) =& I_c(0) + L^{-1}\left[\frac{1}{s^\sigma}L\{e_2 S_s(t) I_c(t) - e_5 I_c(t) U_s(t) - (e_6 + e_4) I_c(t)\}\right],\\U_s(t) =& U_s(0) + L^{-1}\left[\frac{1}{s^\sigma}L\{e_5 I_c(t) U_s(t) - (e_7 + e_8 + e_4) U_s(t)\}\right],\\R_s(t) =& R_s(0) + L^{-1}\left[\frac{1}{s^\sigma}L\{e_7 U_s(t) - (e_9 + e_4 + e_3) R_s(t)\}\right],\\E_s(t) =& E_s(0) + L^{-1}\left[\frac{1}{s^\sigma}L\{e_9 R_s(t) - e_4 E_s(t)\}\right].\end{aligned} \tag{43}$$

Additionally, the iterative scheme is as follows:

$$\begin{aligned}(S_s)_n(t) =& S_s(0) + L^{-1}\Big[\frac{1}{s^\sigma}L\{e_1 - e_2 (S_s)_{n-1}(t)(I_c)_{n-1}(t) + e_3 (R_s)_{n-1}(t)\\&- e_4 (S_s)_{n-1}(t)\}\Big],\\(I_c)_n(t) =& I_c(0) + L^{-1}\Big[\frac{1}{s^\sigma}L\{e_2 (S_s)_{n-1}(t)(I_c)_{n-1}(t) - e_5 (I_c)_{n-1}(t) U_s(t)\\&- (e_6 + e_4)(I_c)_{n-1}(t)\}\Big],\\(U_s)_n(t) =& U_s(0) + L^{-1}\Big[\frac{1}{s^\sigma}L\{e_5 (I_c)_{n-1}(t)(U_s)_{n-1}(t)\\&- (e_7 + e_8 + e_4)(U_s)_{n-1}(t)\}\Big],\\(R_s)_n(t) =& R_s(0) + L^{-1}\left[\frac{1}{s^\sigma}L\{e_7 (U_s)_{n-1}(t) - (e_9 + e_4 + e_3)(R_s)_{n-1}(t)\}\right],\\(E_s)_n(t) =& E_s(0) + L^{-1}\left[\frac{1}{s^\sigma}L\{e_9 (R_s)_{n-1}(t) - e_4 (E_s)_{n-1}(t)\}\right].\end{aligned} \tag{44}$$

In Equation (44), we have derived an approximate solution as the value of n approaches infinity.

$$(S_s(t), I_c(t), U_s(t), R_s(t), E_s(t)) = \lim_{n\to\infty}((S_s)_n(t), (I_c)_n(t), (U_s)_n(t), (R_s)_n(t), (E_s)_n(t)).$$

Using the initial condition, we have computed the numerical outcome of Equation (3). We have expressed this result approximately as follows, and more details are available in [29]:

$$\begin{aligned}
(S_s)_1(t) &= 68 - (8.1360)t,\\
(I_c)_1(t) &= 40 + (5.5600)t,\\
(U_s)_1(t) &= 30 + (0.7500)t,\\
(R_s)_1(t) &= 20 + (0.4000)t,\\
(E_s)_1(t) &= 15 + (0.9700)t,\\
(S_s)_2(t) &= -8.1360 - 0.1404t + 0.1357t^2,\\
(I_c)_2(t) &= 5.5600 - 0.2635t - 0.1440t^2,\\
(U_s)_2(t) &= 0.7500 + 0.3523t + 0.0083t^2,\\
(R_s)_2(t) &= 0.4000 + 0.0155t,\\
(E_s)_2(t) &= 0.9700 + 0.0181t,\\
&\vdots
\end{aligned}$$

Ultimately, the approximate solution is derived by utilizing Equations (3) and (4). To showcase the effectiveness and precision of the approach, residual errors are employed in the following manner.

$$\begin{aligned}
E_{n+1,S_s}(t) &= (S_s)'_{n+1}(t) - [e_1 - e_2 S_s(t) I_c(t) + e_3 R_s(t) - e_4 S_s(t)],\\
E_{n+1,I_c}(t) &= (I_c)'_{n+1}(t) - [e_2 S_s(t) I_c(t) - e_5 I_c(t) U_s(t) - (e_6 + e_4) I_c(t)],\\
E_{n+1,U_s}(t) &= (U_s)'_{n+1}(t) - [e_5 I_c(t) U_s(t) - (e_7 + e_8 + e_4) U_s(t)],\\
E_{n+1,R_s}(t) &= (R_s)'_{n+1}(t) - [e_7 U_s(t) - (e_9 + e_4 + e_3) R_s(t)],\\
E_{n+1,E_s}(t) &= (E_s)'_{n+1}(t) - [e_9 R_s(t) - e_4 E_s(t)].
\end{aligned}$$

Figure 1 presents the graphical behavior of susceptible smokers $S_s(t)$, ingestion class $I_c(t)$, unusual smokers $U_s(t)$, regular smokers $R_s(t)$, and ex-smokers $E_s(t)$ using numerical techniques with $m = 96$, $t_l = 2$ days, and $\sigma = 1$. Figure 2 displays the graphical behavior of susceptible smokers $S_s(t)$, ingestion class $I_c(t)$, unusual smokers $U_s(t)$, regular smokers $R_s(t)$, and ex-smokers $E_s(t)$ using numerical techniques with $m = 96$, $t_l = 60$ days, and $\sigma = 1$. In Figure 3, a 2D plot illustrates susceptible smokers $S_s(t)$, ingestion class $I_c(t)$, unusual smokers $U_s(t)$, regular smokers $R_s(t)$, and ex-smokers $E_s(t)$ with different values of σ using the BWM. Figure 4 demonstrates a 3D plot of susceptible smokers $S_s(t)$, ingestion class $I_c(t)$, unusual smokers $U_s(t)$, regular smokers $R_s(t)$, and ex-smokers $E_s(t)$ at $m = 96$, and $\sigma = 0.5$. Figures 5 and 6 display residual-error graphs with $n = 1$ and $n = 2$. The simulation results were obtained after 2.959 seconds. Figures 7 and 8 present a comparison graph of different system components using various numerical techniques for $\sigma = 1$ and $\sigma = 0.92$. Figure 9 depicts the relationship between susceptible smokers and other components of the smoking model for $\sigma = 0.89$. Figure 9a shows that after ten days, both lines converge at a point; subsequently, the ingestion class increases until 20 days and then decreases. Figure 9b illustrates that both lines meet at a point after ten days, after which the number of unusual smokers increases until 30 days and then decreases. In Figure 9c, both lines intersect at a point after ten days, following which the number of regular smokers increases until 40 days and then decreases. Figure 9d demonstrates that both lines meet at a point after ten days. Figure 10a displays the relationship between ingestion class and regular smokers. After 20 days, both lines converge at a single point. The number of regular smokers increases until 40 days and then slightly decreases, while the ingestion class line grows initially until ten days in and then decreases. Figure 10b showcases the graphical behavior of regular and unusual smokers. Both lines meet at a single point after 50 days.

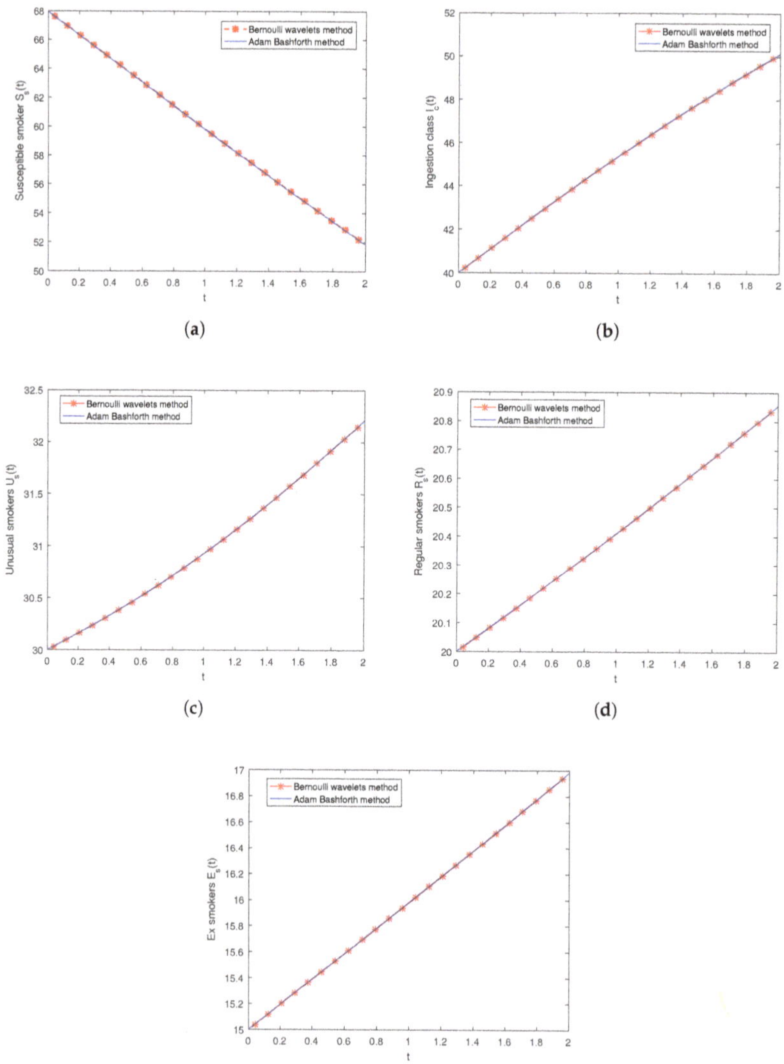

(e)

Figure 1. Comparison graphs of (**a**) Susceptible smokers, (**b**) Ingestion class, (**c**) Unusual smokers, (**d**) Regular smokers, (**e**) Ex smokers with $\sigma = 1, m = 96$.

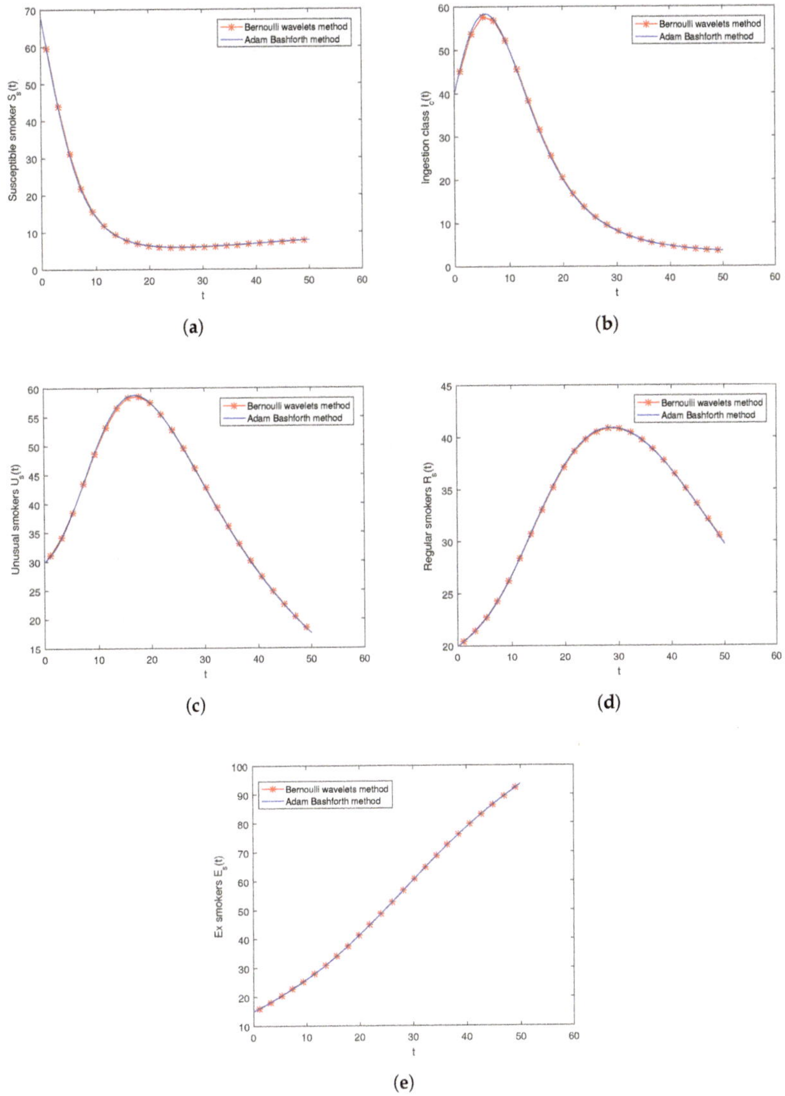

Figure 2. Comparison graphs of (**a**) Susceptible smokers, (**b**) Ingestion class, (**c**) Unusual smokers, (**d**) Regular smokers, (**e**) Ex smokers with $\sigma = 1, m = 96$.

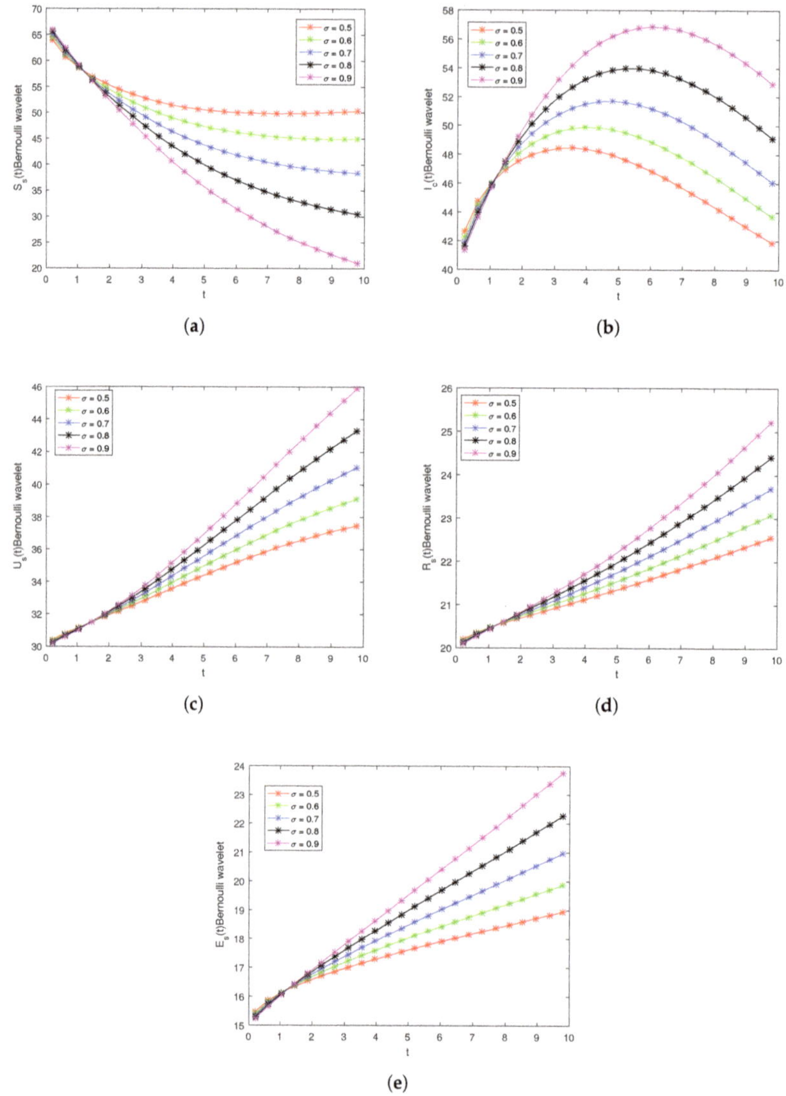

Figure 3. Time-series graphs of (**a**) Susceptible smokers, (**b**) Ingestion class, (**c**) Unusual smokers, (**d**) Regular smokers, (**e**) Ex smokers when σ varies using BWM, where $m = 96$.

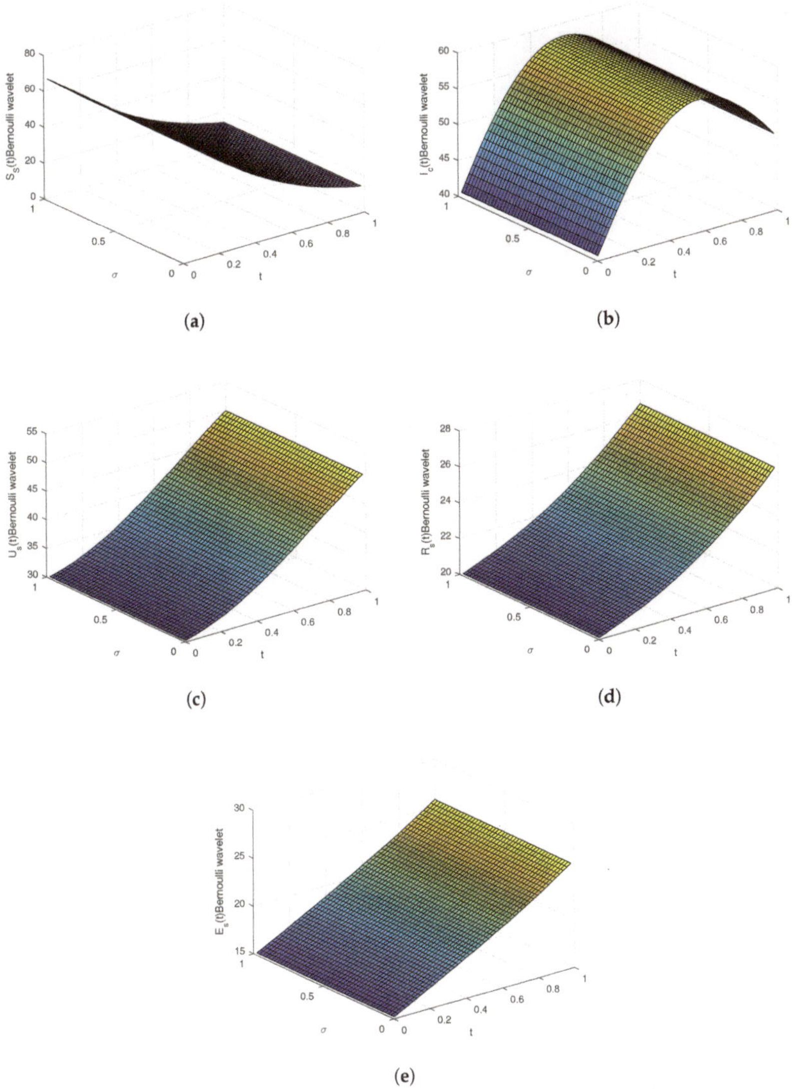

Figure 4. Three-dimensional graphs (**a**) Susceptible smokers, (**b**) Ingestion class, (**c**) Unusual smokers, (**d**) Regular smokers, (**e**) Ex smokers with BWM, where $m = 96$.

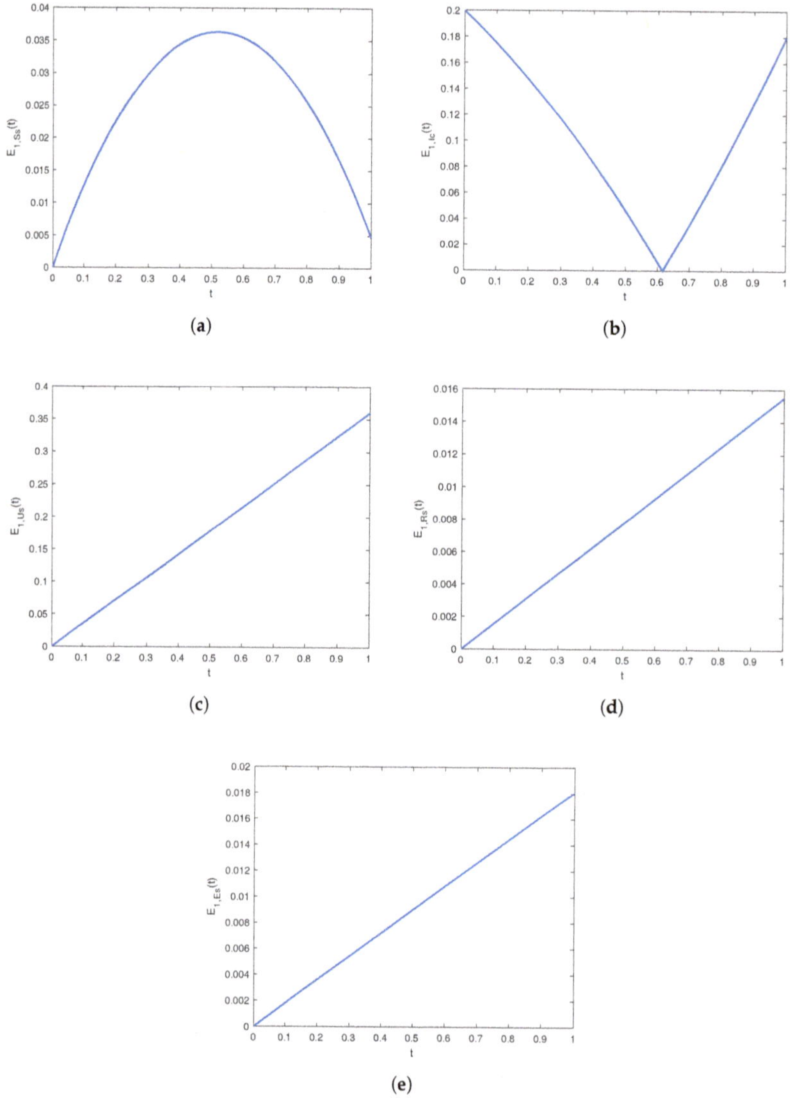

Figure 5. Graphs of residual error of (**a**) Susceptible smokers, (**b**) Ingestion class, (**c**) Unusual smokers, (**d**) Regular smokers, (**e**) Ex smokers with $n = 1, \sigma = 0.9$.

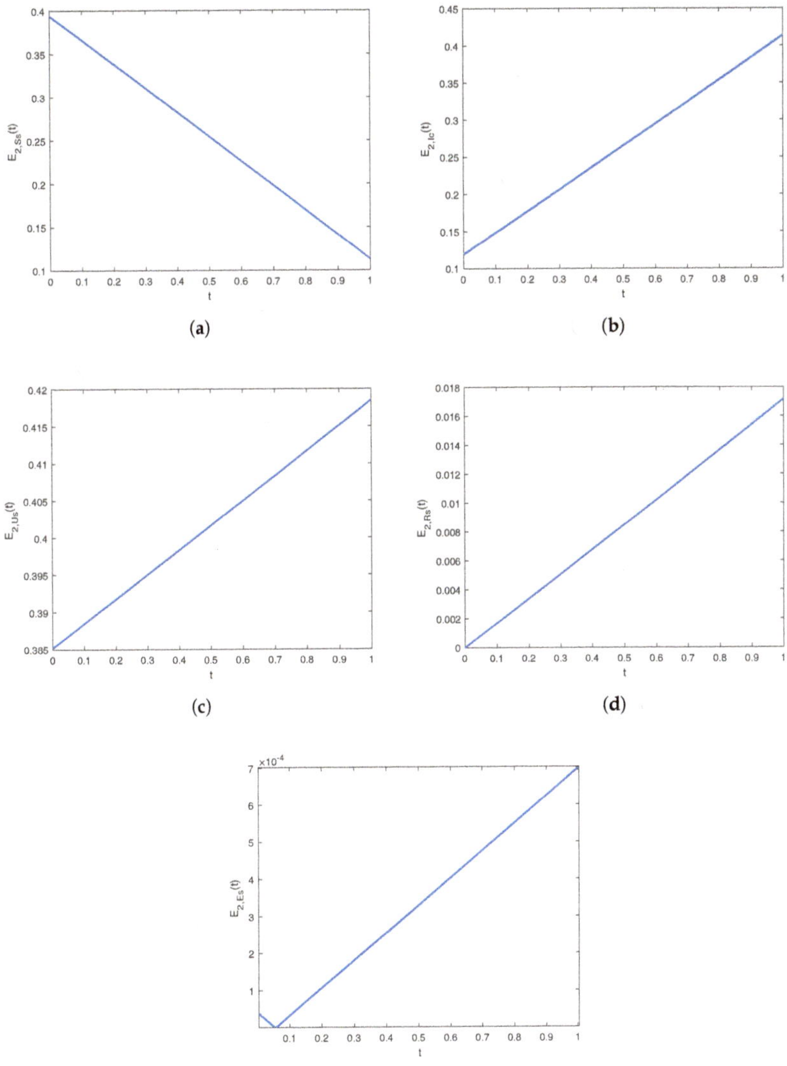

Figure 6. Graphs of residual error of (**a**) Susceptible smokers, (**b**) Ingestion class, (**c**) Unusual smokers, (**d**) Regular smokers, (**e**) Ex smokers with $n = 2, \sigma = 0.9$.

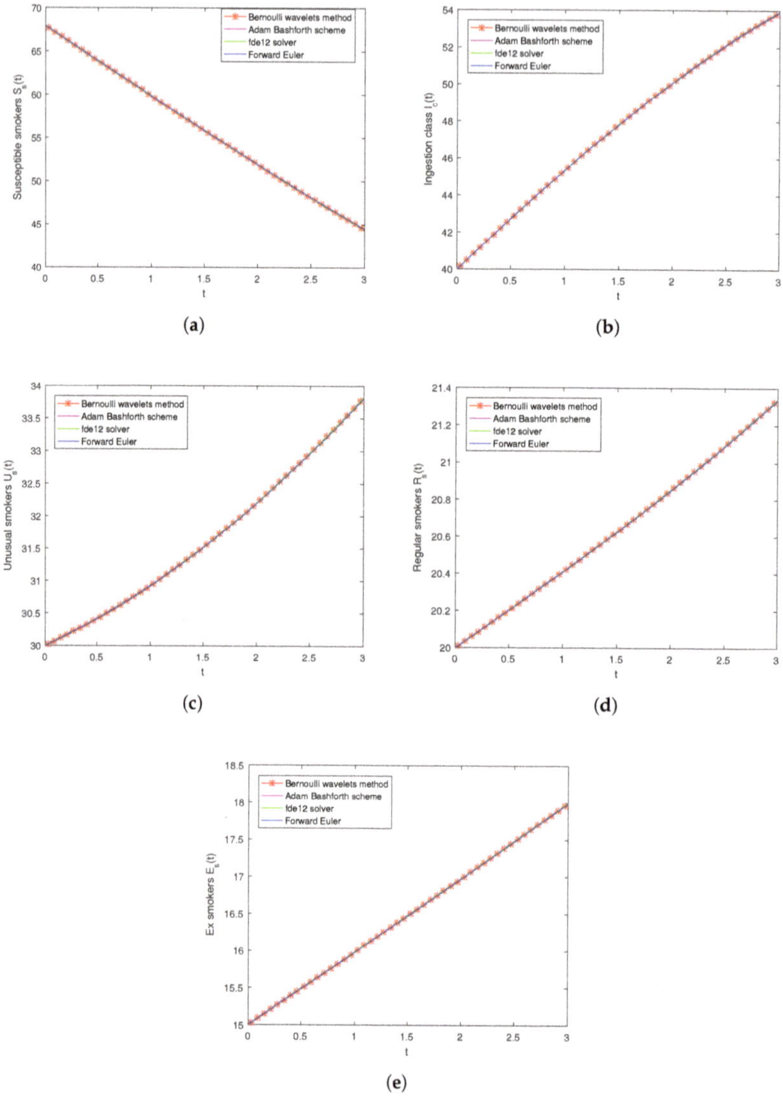

Figure 7. Comparison graphs of (**a**) Susceptible smokers, (**b**) Ingestion class, (**c**) Unusual smokers, (**d**) Regular smokers, (**e**) Ex smokers when $k = 5, M = 3$ and $\sigma = 1$.

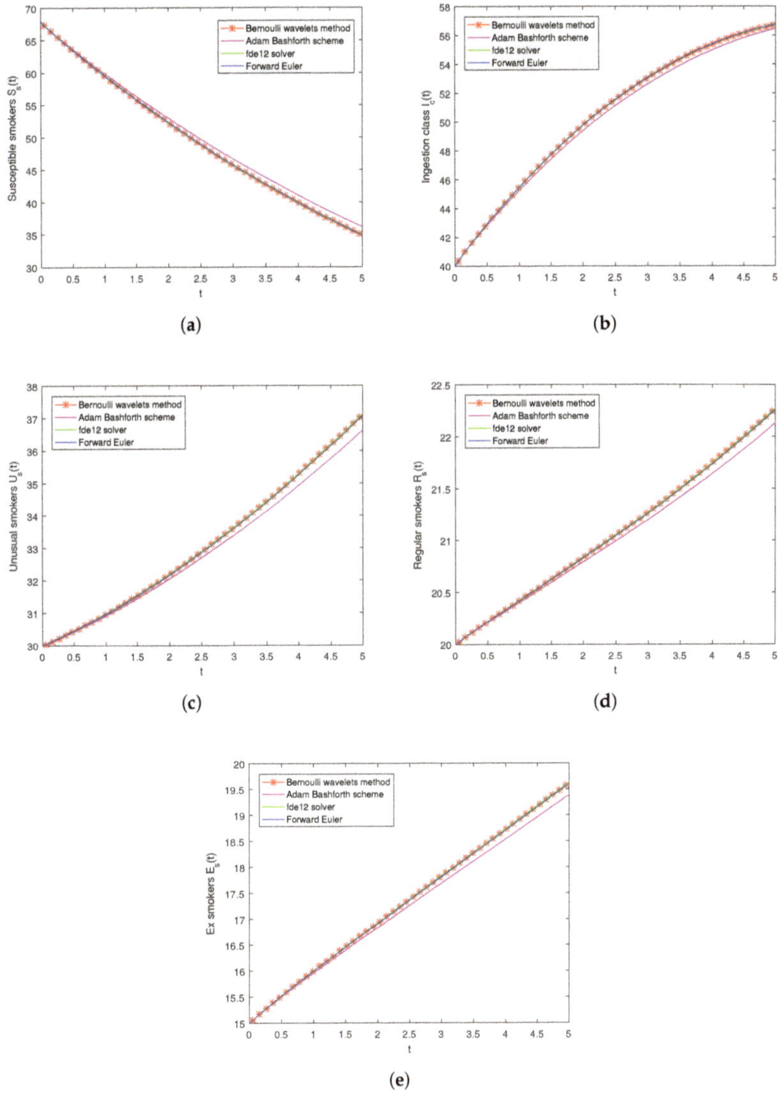

Figure 8. Comparison graphs of (**a**) Susceptible smokers, (**b**) Ingestion class, (**c**) Unusual smokers, (**d**) Regular smokers, (**e**) Ex smokers when $k = 5, M = 3$ and $\sigma = 0.92$.

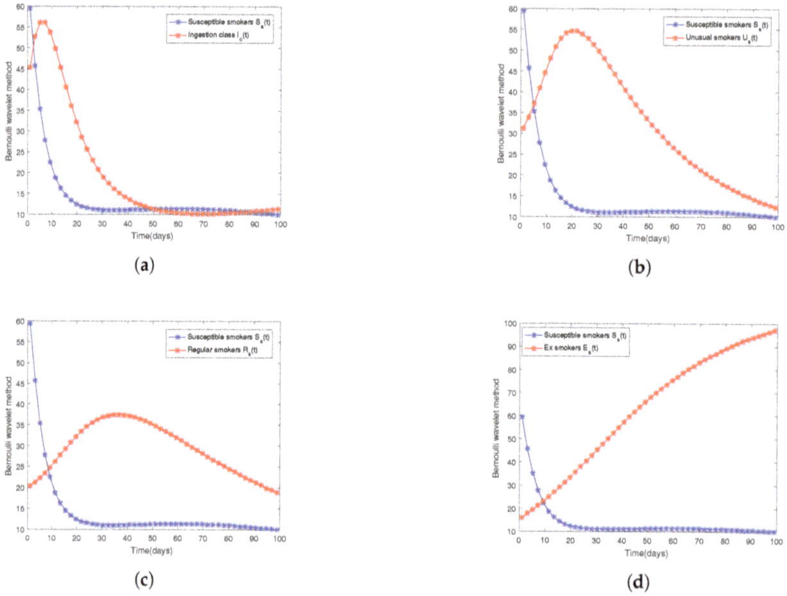

Figure 9. Combination graphs of (**a**) $S_s(t)$ and $I_c(t)$; (**b**) $S_s(t)$ and $U_s(t)$; (**c**) $S_s(t)$ and $R_s(t)$; and (**d**) $S_s(t)$ and $E_s(t)$ for $k = 5, M = 3$, and $\sigma = 0.89$.

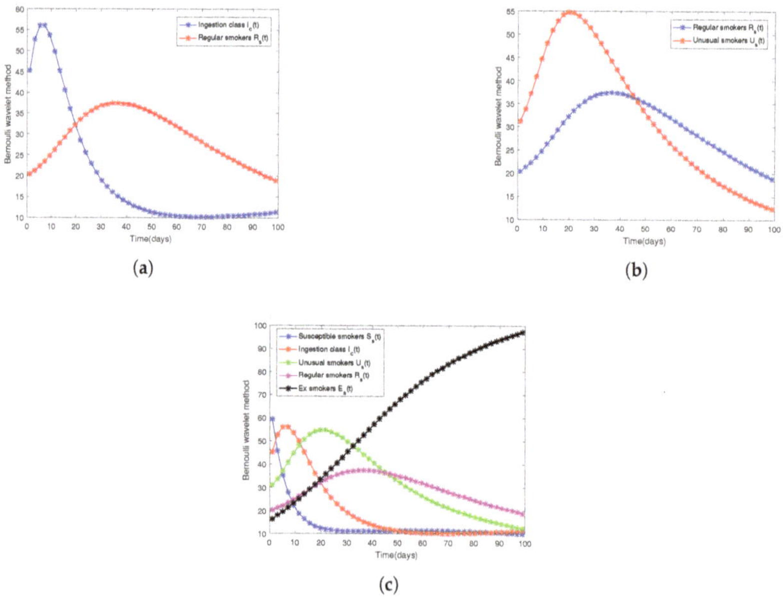

Figure 10. (**a**) Combination of $I_c(t)$ and $R_s(t)$; (**b**) $R_s(t)$ and $U_s(t)$; and (**c**) all components of system for $k = 5$, $M = 3$, and $\sigma = 0.89$.

The line for regular smokers increases until 40 days and then decreases; the line for unusual smokers increases until 30 days and then decreases. Figure 10c depicts the relationship between all system components. This figure reveals a drastic decrease in the population of susceptible smokers to zero. The number of those in the ingestion class, unusual smokers, and regular smokers initially increases, then decreases to zero. Lastly, the number of ex-smokers exhibits an increase. Figure 10 portrays the above relation for $\sigma = 0.89$. In Figures 11 and 12, the same relation is shown for $\sigma = 1$ as in Figures 9 and 10. In Figure 12c, the susceptible smokers' population decreases, stabilizing after some time. The number of ingestion class, unusual smokers, and regular smokers initially increases but gradually decreases. Finally, the number of ex-smokers exhibits an increase. In Figure 13, we can observe the impact of parameter e_2 on the fractional smoking system. A lower value of this parameter leads to a slower decrease in the susceptible population. Similarly, for the ingestion class, regular smokers, and unusual smokers, a lower value of e_2 results in a slower increase in these populations. However, as time progresses, the influence of parameter e_2 becomes minimal when these three system components decrease. In the case of ex-smokers, a lower value of e_2 leads to a slower increase in their population. Figure 14 illustrates the effect of parameter e_3 on the smoking model. For susceptible smokers, the ingestion class, and unusual smokers, the population decreases significantly for a low value of e_3. As for regular smokers, a slightly low value of e_3 substantially increases their population. Subsequently, as these populations decrease over time, the rate of decrease is low for a comparable low value of e_3. In the case of ex-smokers, the population increase rate is higher for a lower value of e_3. Figure 15 showcases the impact of parameter e_9 on the model. Evidently, this parameter significantly affects regular and ex-smokers—a slight change in its value results in a rapid effect. For a low value of e_9, the rate of increase in regular smokers is substantial. When the population decreases, the rate of decrease is low for a lower value of this parameter. In the case of ex-smokers, the rate of increase is high for a higher value of e_9. The study focused on administering an anti-nicotine medication over 35 days. This approach was chosen due to the potential risks associated with prolonged drug treatment and the optimal timing for vaccination likely occurring during the initial phases of an illness. Figures 16a and 17a illustrate the portion of the non-smoking demographic that can transition into becoming smokers for $\sigma = 1$ and $\sigma = 0.95$. On the initial day, a notable decline was observed within this population. Following the implementation of the control, there was a minor uptick in the count of potential smokers by the 25th day, as contrasted with the pre-control period. This observation suggests that the decrease will likely persist if this population is subjected to the same control over an extended duration. Figures 16b and 17b depict the demography of the ingestion class for $\sigma = 1$ and $\sigma = 0.95$. The population experienced a notable increase in the initial days, followed by a substantial decrease. Subsequently, after implementing control measures, the number of people in the ingestion class decreased from the initial days. Regarding the subset of the population characterised by occasional smoking, proactive control measures were put in place. These measures included distributing anti-smoking gum and enforcing government regulations prohibiting smoking in public areas. As illustrated in Figures 16c and 17c, there was a significant increase in the initial days, followed by a slight decrease. After implementing these control measures, the population of unusual smokers showed a substantial decline. Figures 16d and 17d depict the population of active smokers under controlled conditions and without such measures. Governmental prohibitions on smoking in public places and anti-nicotine medication therapy are the suggested strategies for controlling this population. From the beginning to the end of the simulation period, the number of active smokers decreased, according to the simulations. Additionally, the population under control measures demonstrated a more notable fall compared to the time before controls were implemented. Consequently, the applied measures produced positive outcomes in this instance. Based on the study's findings, it is recommended to provide a range of control measures, including an anti-smoking education campaign,

$w_1(t)$; anti-smoking gum, $w_2(t)$; anti-nicotine drug treatment, $w_3(t)$; and government prohibition of smoking in public spaces, $w_4(t)$. The simulations showed a significant rise in people quitting smoking for good, particularly if control mechanisms were put in place. This approach highlights the effectiveness of implementing control measures. Figures 18 and 19 show the impact of control parameters on the smoking system by varying these parameters. If $w_1(t) \neq 0, w_2(t) \neq 0, w_3(t) = 0, w_4(t) = 0$, then the ex-smoker population significantly increase, while other state variables decrease in Figure 18. In Figure 19, $w_1 \neq 0, w_2(t) = 0, w_3(t) \neq 0, w_4(t) = 0$, then we get a greater number of ex-smokers, where the other compartments decrease. Figure 20 illustrates the graphical representation of these parameters. We see how the smoking system has been solved more easily using BWM and how the system's behaviour changes when we alter specific parameter values. By implementing certain control measures, we can also reduce the number of smokers in society.

We compare the solutions of the smoking model using BWM with other numerical techniques for $\sigma = 1$, which are shown in Tables 2–6. Tables 7–11 show the comparison of solutions between BWM and other numerical techniques of the model above for $\sigma = 0.92$. Tables 12 and 13 show RMSE and MAE values of the given system using BWM and ABM, respectively.

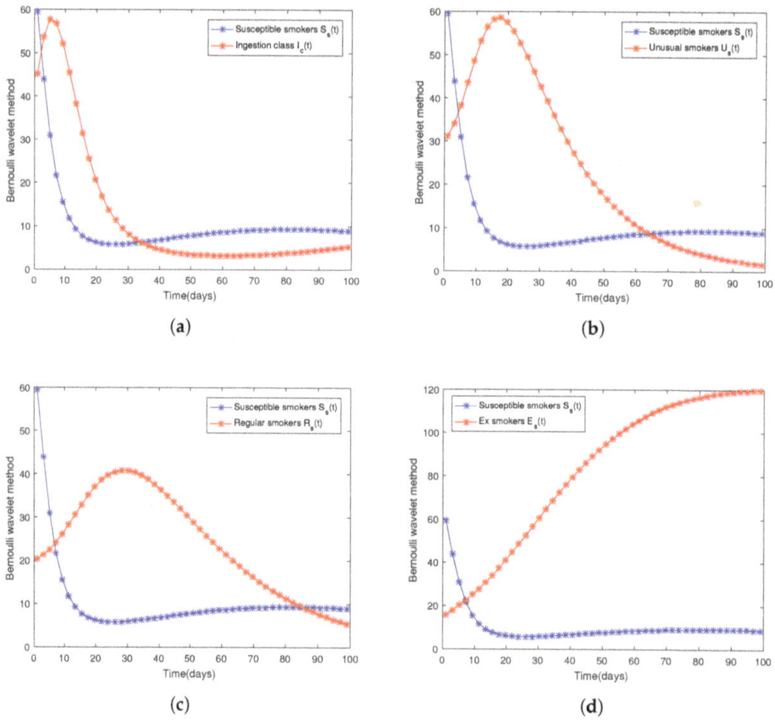

Figure 11. Combination of (**a**) $S_s(t)$ and $I_c(t)$; (**b**) $S_s(t)$ and $U_s(t)$; (**c**) $S_s(t)$ and $R_s(t)$; and (**d**) $S_s(t)$ and $E_s(t)$ for $k = 5, M = 3$ and $\sigma = 1$.

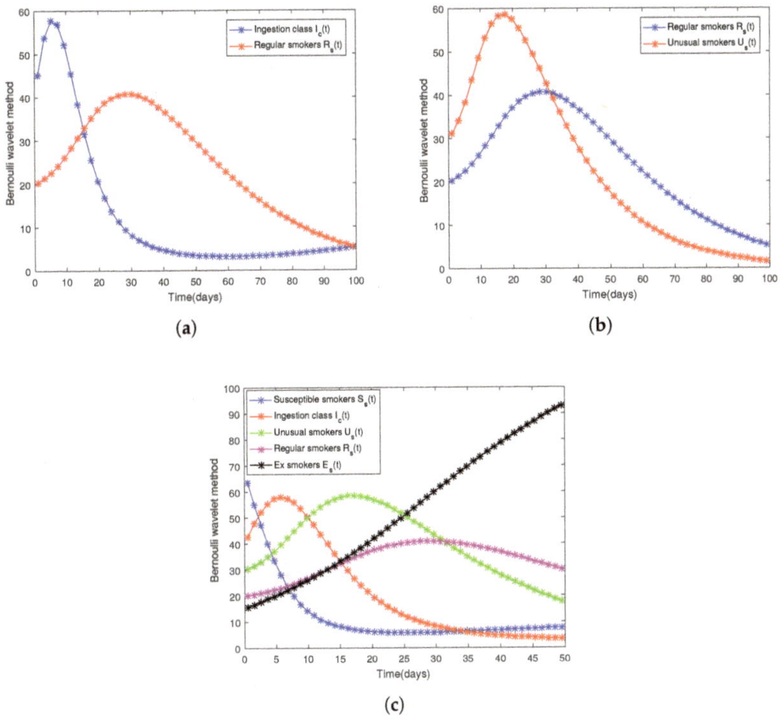

Figure 12. (**a**) Combination of $I_c(t)$ and $R_s(t)$; (**b**) $R_s(t)$ for $k = 5$ and $M = 3$, and $\sigma = 0.89$ and $U_s(t)$; and (**c**) all components of system for $k = 5$, $M = 3$, and $\sigma = 1$.

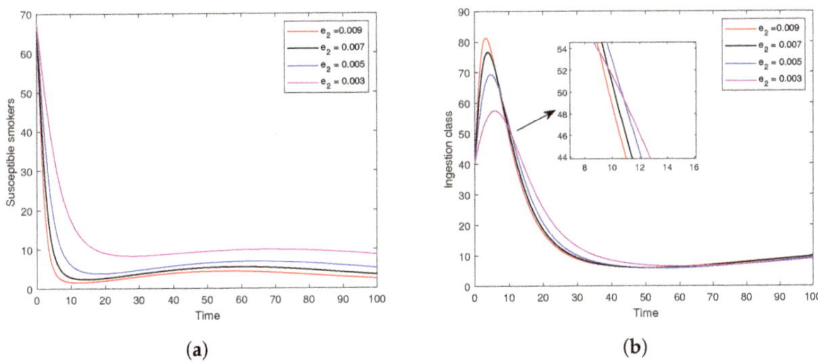

Figure 13. *Cont.*

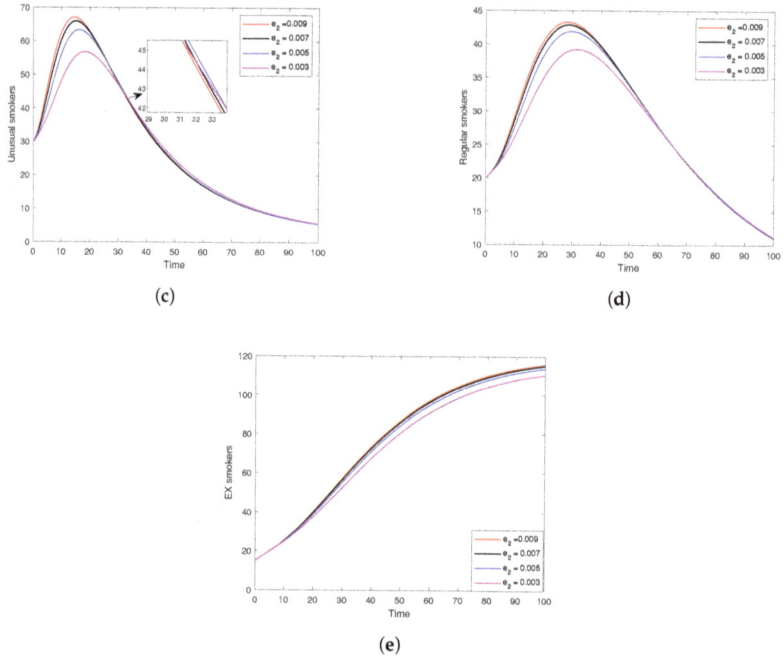

Figure 13. Time-series graphs of (**a**) Susceptible smokers, (**b**) Ingestion class, (**c**) Unusual smokers, (**d**) Regular smokers, (**e**) Ex smokers when e_2 varies.

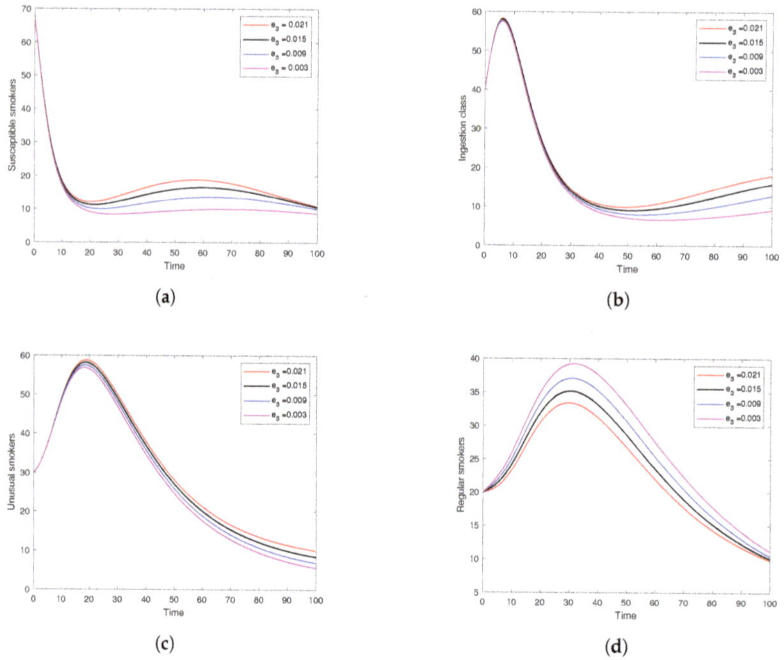

Figure 14. *Cont.*

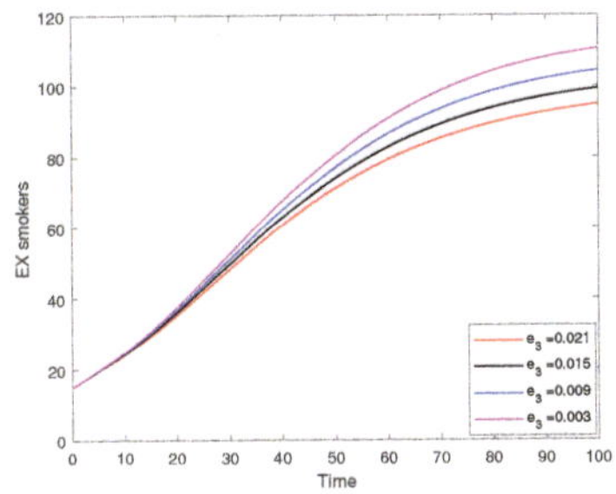

(**e**)

Figure 14. Time-series graphs of (**a**) Susceptible smokers, (**b**) Ingestion class, (**c**) Unusual smokers, (**d**) Regular smokers, (**e**) Ex smokers when e_3 varies.

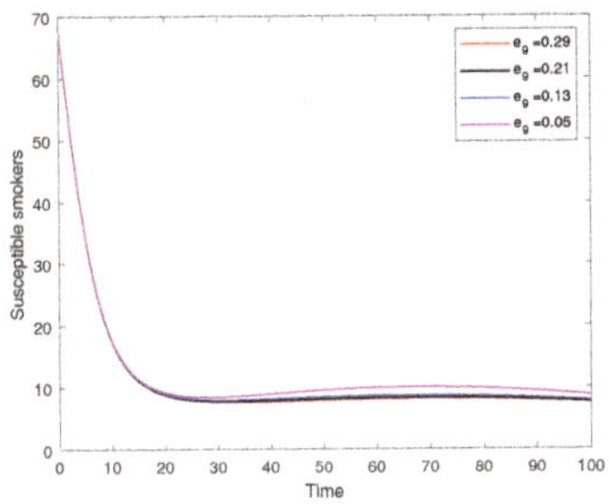

(**a**)

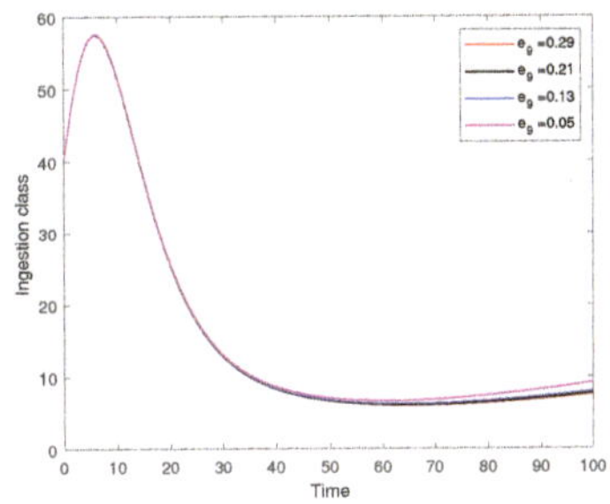

(**b**)

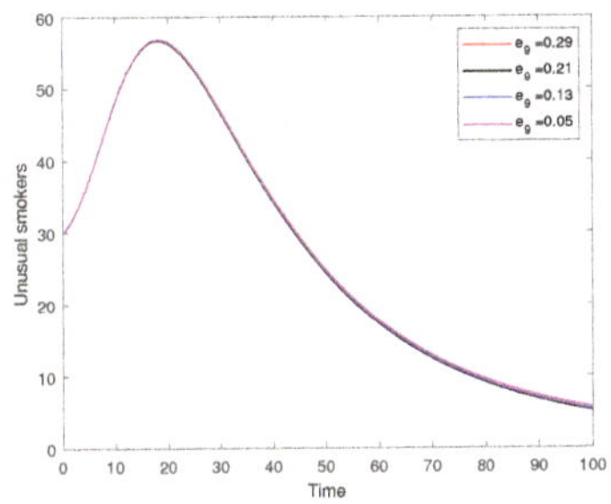

(**c**)

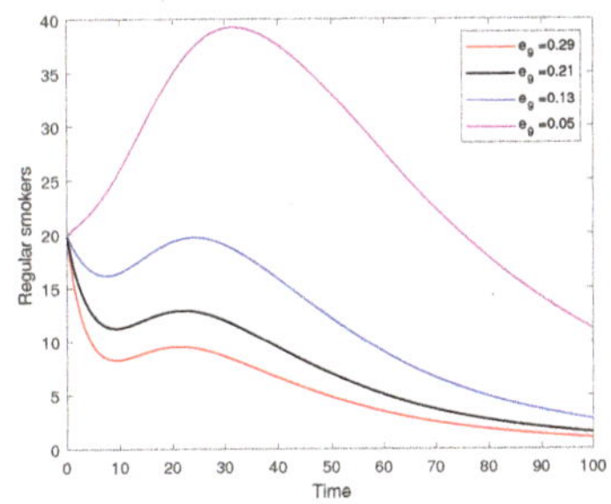

(**d**)

Figure 15. *Cont.*

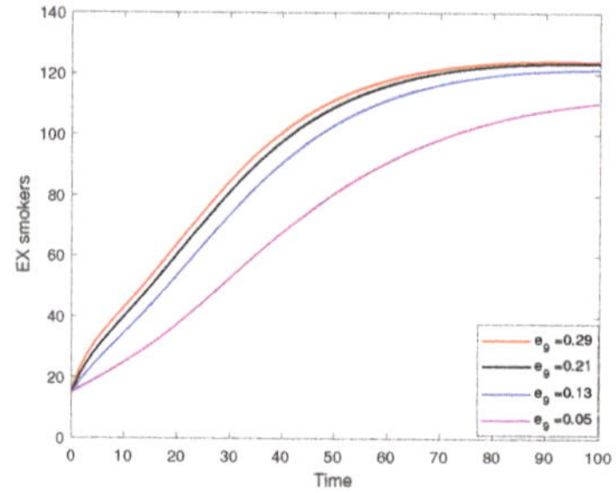

(**e**)

Figure 15. Time-series graphs of (**a**) Susceptible smokers, (**b**) Ingestion class, (**c**) Unusual smokers, (**d**) Regular smokers, (**e**) Ex smokers when e_9 varies.

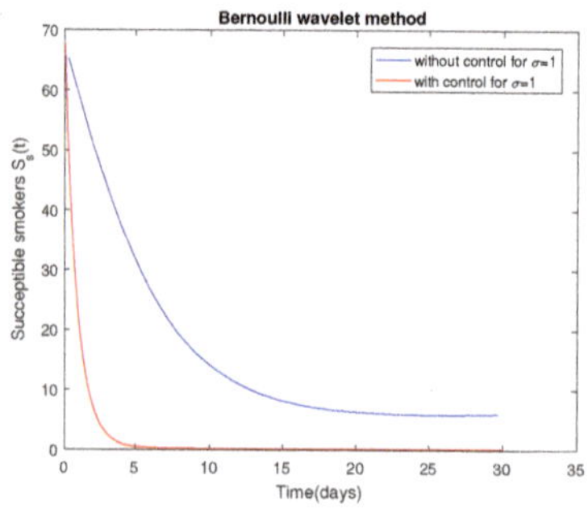

(**a**)

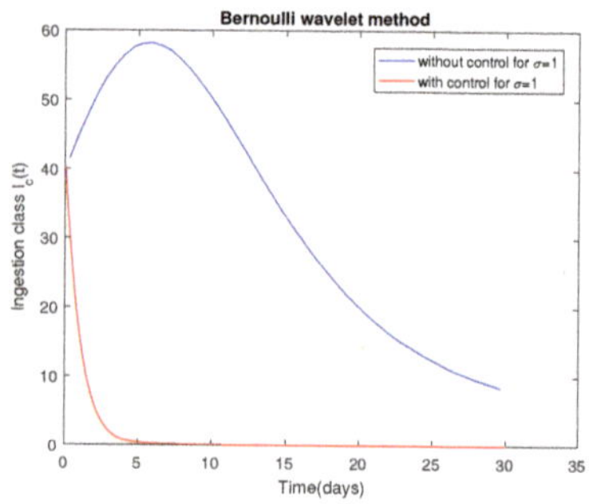

(**b**)

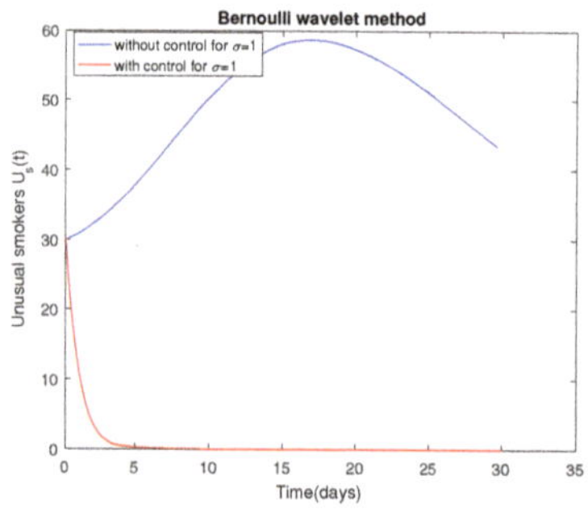

(**c**)

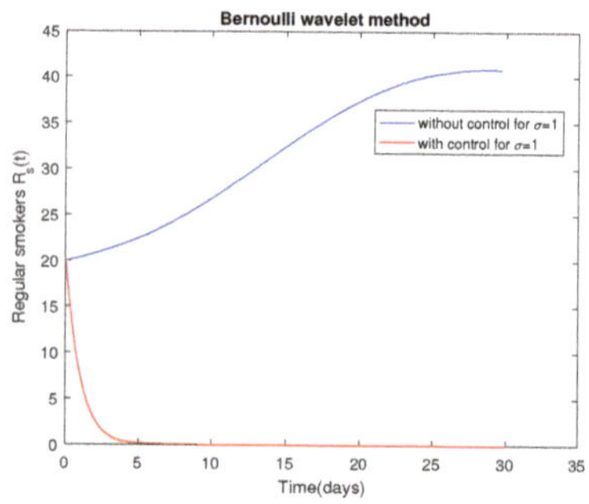

(**d**)

Figure 16. *Cont.*

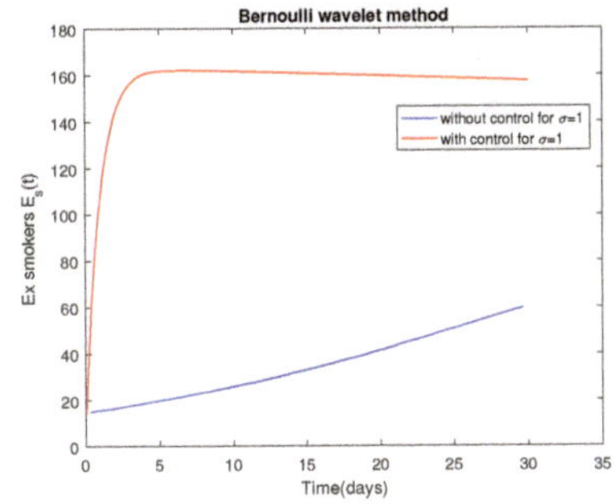

(e)

Figure 16. Dynamic of (**a**) Susceptible smokers, (**b**) Ingestion class, (**c**) Unusual smokers, (**d**) Regular smokers, (**e**) Ex smokers with and without control for $\sigma = 1$.

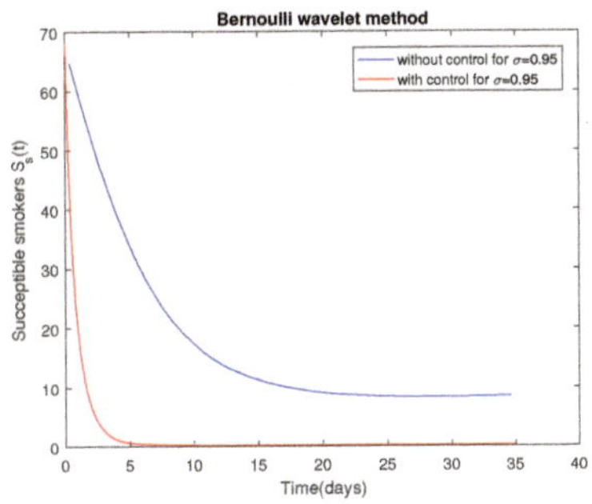

(**a**)

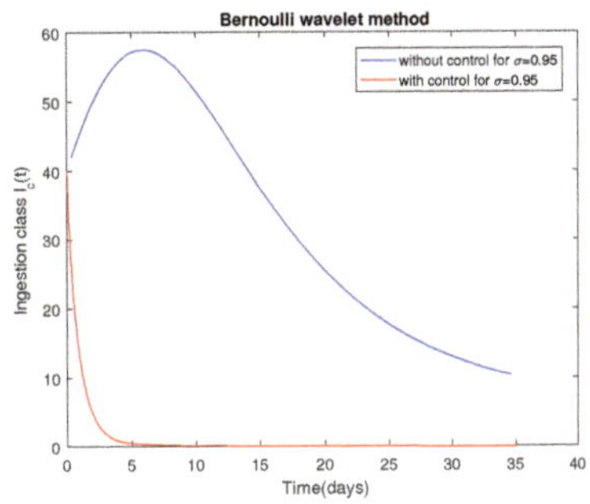

(**b**)

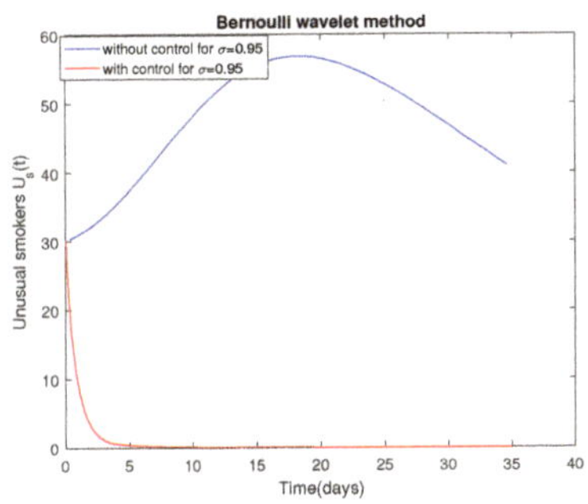

(**c**)

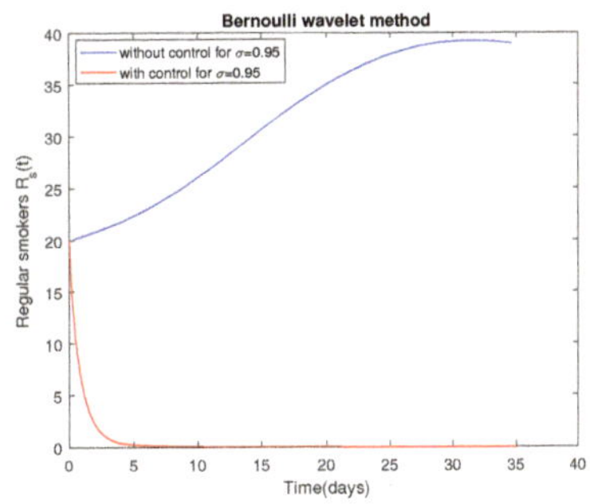

(**d**)

Figure 17. *Cont.*

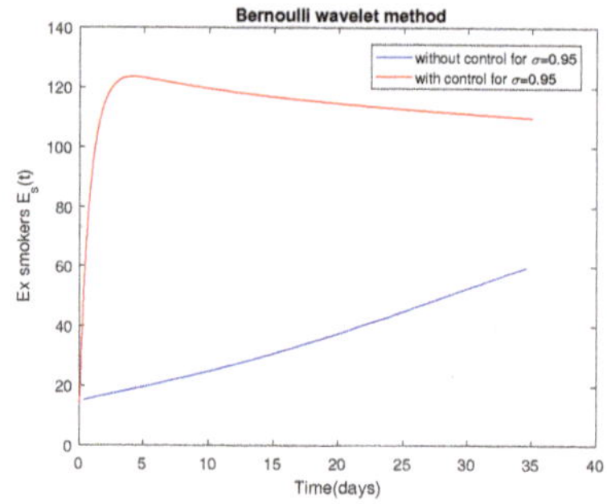

(**e**)

Figure 17. Dynamic of (**a**) Susceptible smokers, (**b**) Ingestion class, (**c**) Unusual smokers, (**d**) Regular smokers, (**e**) Ex smokers with and without control for $\sigma = 0.95$.

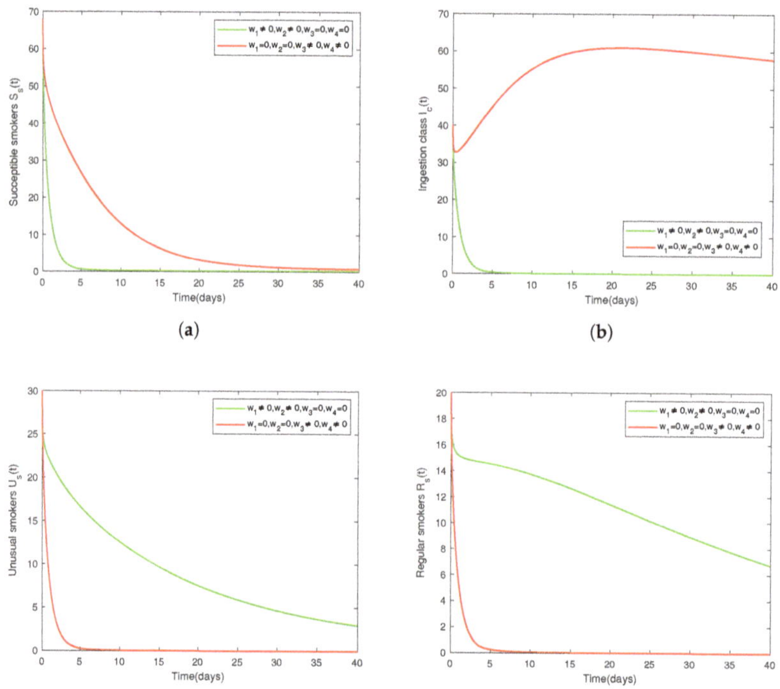

(**a**) (**b**)

(**c**) (**d**)

Figure 18. *Cont.*

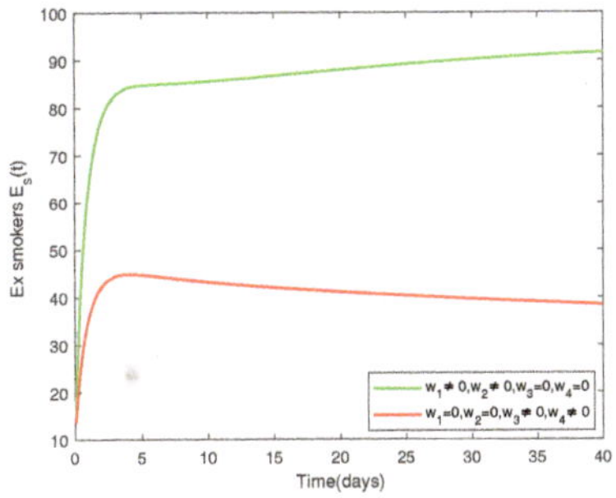

(**e**)

Figure 18. Dynamic of (**a**) Susceptible smokers, (**b**) Ingestion class, (**c**) Unusual smokers, (**d**) Regular smokers, (**e**) Ex smokers by varying control parameters for $\sigma = 0.95$.

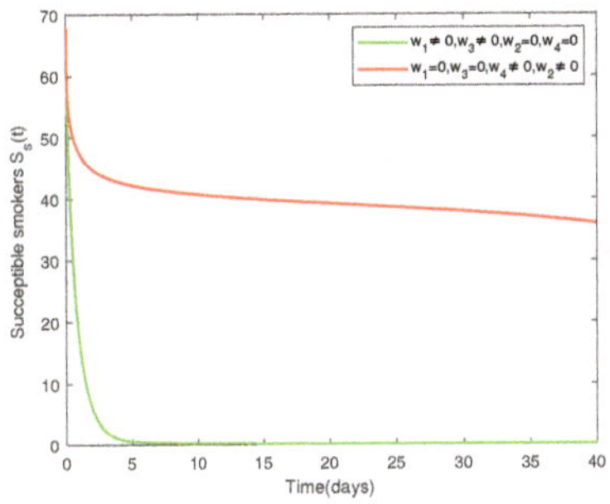

(**a**)

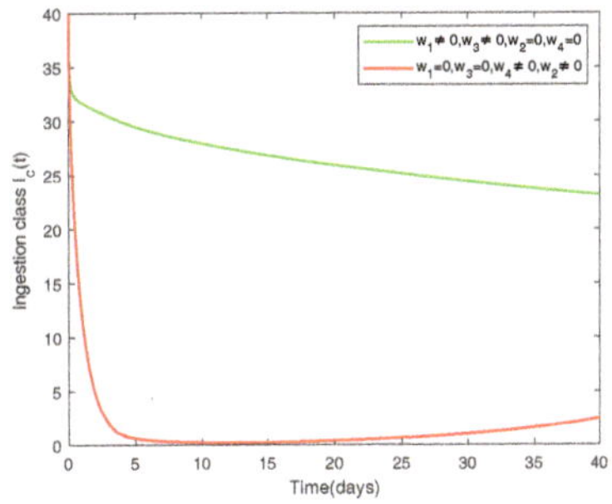

(**b**)

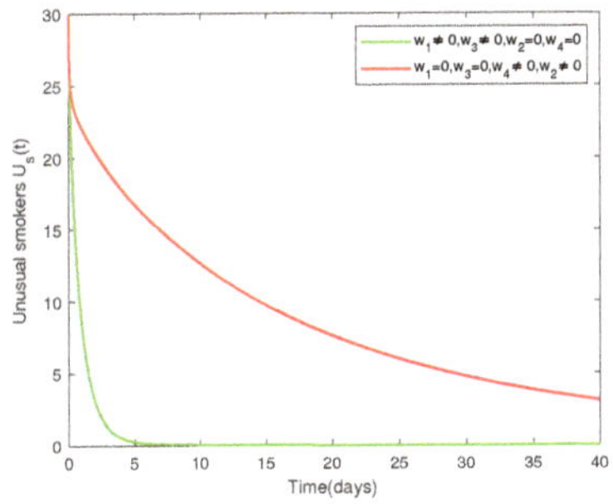

(**c**)

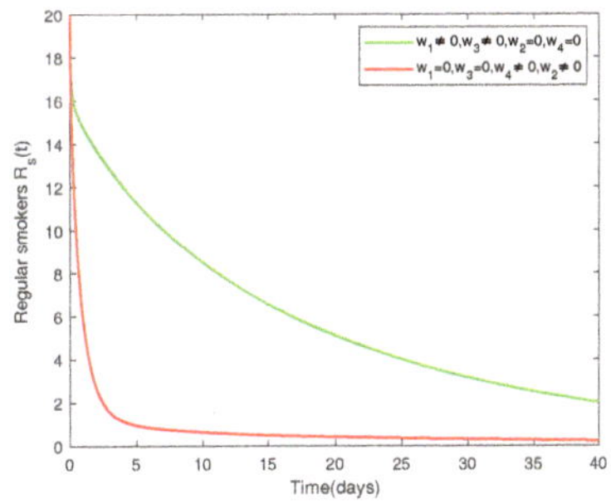

(**d**)

Figure 19. *Cont.*

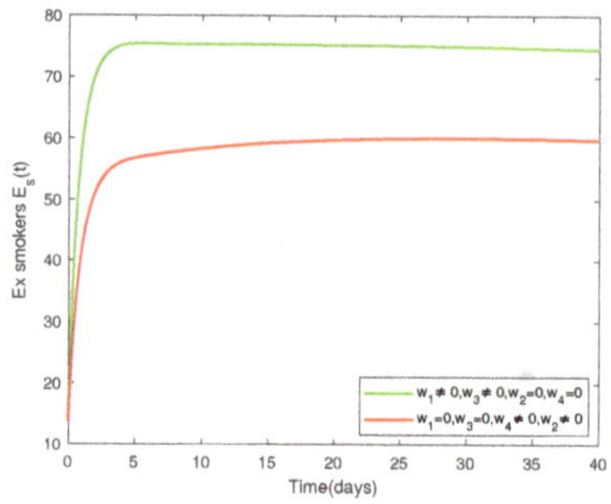

(**e**)

Figure 19. Dynamic of (**a**) Susceptible smokers, (**b**) Ingestion class, (**c**) Unusual smokers, (**d**) Regular smokers, (**e**) Ex smokers by varying control parameters for $\sigma = 0.95$.

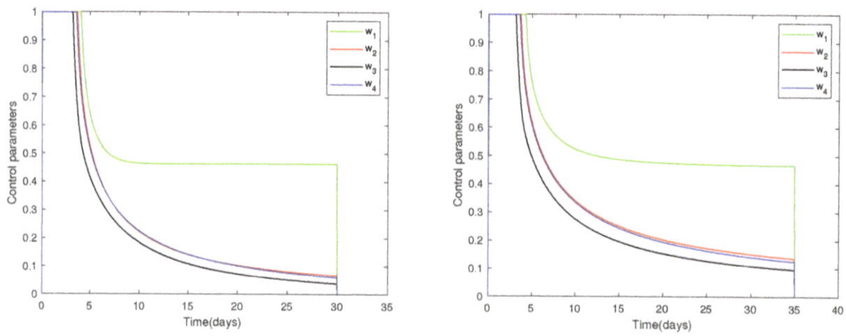

(**f**) (**g**)

Figure 20. Control profile is plotted as a function of time for (a) $\sigma = 1$; (b) $\sigma = 0.95$.

Table 2. Comparing the solutions of susceptible smokers at $\sigma = 1.0$, $k = 5$, and $M = 3$.

Sr.	*t*	BWM	ABM	Fde12	Forward Euler
1	0	67.7456	67.7152	67.7455	67.7559
2	0.1	67.2366	67.1858	67.2364	67.2673
3	0.2	66.2175	66.1665	66.3705	66.2278
4	0.3	65.7074	65.6769	65.7073	65.6769
5	0.4	64.6870	64.6564	64.7380	64.6973
6	0.5	63.6665	63.6359	62.6663	63.6564
7	0.6	63.1565	63.1055	63.1562	63.1667
8	0.7	62.1373	62.0864	62.1371	62.1882
9	0.8	61.6283	61.5978	61.6281	61.6384
10	0.9	60.6119	60.5814	60.6118	60.6015
11	1.0	59.5981	59.5677	59.5979	59.8712

Table 3. Comparing the solutions of the ingestion class at $\sigma = 1.0$, $k = 5$, and $M = 3$.

Sr.	t	BWM	ABM	Fde12	Forward Euler
1	0	40.1735	40.1944	40.1734	40.1667
2	0.1	40.5199	40.5546	40.5192	40.4994
3	0.2	41.2091	41.2436	41.2091	41.2027
4	0.3	41.5518	41.5725	41.5517	41.5728
5	0.4	42.2327	42.2532	42.2328	42.2266
6	0.5	42.9071	42.9275	42.9080	42.9148
7	0.6	43.2417	43.2753	43.2416	43.2361
8	0.7	43.9051	43.9383	43.9051	43.8735
9	0.8	44.2337	44.2536	44.2346	44.2287
10	0.9	44.8845	44.9041	44.8854	44.8928
11	1.0	45.5260	43.5454	45.5259	45.3558

Table 4. Comparing the solutions of unusual smokers at $\sigma = 1.0$, $k = 5$, and $M = 3$.

Sr.	t	BWM	ABM	Fde12	Forward Euler
1	0	30.0238	30.0265	30.0247	30.0226
2	0.1	30.0720	30.0768	30.0719	30.0688
3	0.2	30.1727	30.1777	30.1728	30.1712
4	0.3	30.2251	30.2281	30.2250	30.2277
5	0.4	30.3340	30.3372	30.3339	30.3322
6	0.5	30.4485	30.4519	30.4486	30.4488
7	0.6	30.5079	30.5137	30.5079	30.5057
8	0.7	30.6307	30.6368	30.6305	30.6233
9	0.8	30.6942	30.6979	30.6942	30.6917
10	0.9	30.8254	30.8293	30.8252	30.8254
11	1.0	30.9622	30.9662	30.9622	30.9232

Table 5. Comparing the solutions of regular smokers at $\sigma = 1.0$, $k = 5$ and $M = 3$.

Sr.	t	BWM	ABM	Fde12	Forward Euler
1	0	20.0125	20.0140	20.0127	20.0120
2	0.1	20.0376	20.0401	20.0333	20.0361
3	0.2	20.0879	20.0904	20.0876	20.0874
4	0.3	20.1132	20.1147	20.1133	20.1147
5	0.4	20.1640	20.1655	20.1640	20.1634
6	0.5	20.2151	20.2166	20.2150	20.2156
7	0.6	20.2408	20.2434	20.2407	20.2402
8	0.7	20.2926	20.2951	20.2926	20.2899
9	0.8	20.3186	20.3201	20.3186	20.3180
10	0.9	20.3709	20.3725	20.3709	20.3714
11	1.0	20.4238	20.4254	20.4238	20.4093

Table 6. Comparing the solutions of ex-smokers at $\sigma = 1.0$, $k = 5$, and $M = 3$.

Sr.	t	BWM	ABM	Fde12	Forward Euler
1	0	15.0303	15.0340	15.0308	15.0291
2	0.1	15.0910	15.0971	15.0911	15.0874
3	0.2	15.2126	15.2187	15.2125	15.2114
4	0.3	15.2735	15.2772	15.2733	15.2772
5	0.4	15.3956	15.3992	15.3956	15.3943
6	0.5	15.5179	15.5216	15.5176	15.5191
7	0.6	15.5792	15.5853	15.5796	15.5779
8	0.7	15.7019	15.7081	15.7019	15.6957
9	0.8	15.7634	15.7671	15.7632	15.7621
10	0.9	15.8866	15.8903	15.8866	15.8878
11	1.0	16.0101	16.0138	16.0102	15.9766

Table 7. Comparing the solutions of susceptible smokers at $\sigma = 0.92$, $k = 5$, and $M = 3$.

Sr.	t	BWM	ABM	Fde12	Forward Euler
1	0	67.4534	67.4465	67.4532	67.4936
2	0.1	66.4774	66.5203	66.4774	66.5690
3	0.2	65.5605	65.6449	65.5603	65.5835
4	0.3	64.6734	64.7971	64.6734	64.7349
5	0.4	63.8069	63.9686	63.8070	63.9044
6	0.5	62.9564	63.1552	62.9564	62.9872
7	0.6	62.1192	62.3923	62.1193	62.1847
8	0.7	61.2938	61.6019	61.2936	61.2943
9	0.8	60.4789	60.8215	60.4799	60.5130
10	0.9	56.6738	60.0501	56.6739	59.7405
11	1.0	58.8778	59.2874	58.8778	58.9763

Table 8. Comparing the solutions of the ingestion class at $\sigma = 0.92$, $k = 5$, and $M = 3$.

Sr.	t	BWM	ABM	Fde12	Forward Euler
1	0	40.3719	40.3774	40.3720	40.3455
2	0.1	41.0329	41.0046	41.0329	40.9724
3	0.2	41.6484	41.5926	41.6483	41.6347
4	0.3	42.2386	42.1573	42.2395	42.2001
5	0.4	42.8100	42.7044	42.8100	42.7486
6	0.5	43.3657	43.2369	43.3666	43.3488
7	0.6	43.9075	43.7320	43.9075	43.8690
8	0.7	44.4365	44.2403	44.4366	44.4404
9	0.8	44.9535	44.7374	44.9536	44.9368
10	0.9	45.4590	45.2240	44.4591	44.4227
11	1.0	45.9533	45.7003	45.9533	45.8984

Table 9. Comparing the solutions of unusual smokers at $\sigma = 0.92$, $k = 5$, and $M = 3$.

Sr.	t	BWM	ABM	Fde12	Forward Euler
1	0	30.0519	30.0519	30.0519	30.04732
2	0.1	30.1474	30.1425	30.1473	30.1370
3	0.2	30.2421	30.2326	30.2420	30.2381
4	0.3	30.3382	30.3240	30.3380	30.3295
5	0.4	30.4366	30.4174	30.4345	30.4230
6	0.5	30.5374	30.5129	30.5372	30.5310
7	0.6	30.6408	30.6061	30.6406	30.6295
8	0.7	30.7469	30.7063	30.7470	30.7434
9	0.8	30.8558	30.8090	30.8557	30.8473
10	0.9	30.9675	30.9143	30.9676	30.9538
11	1.0	31.0819	31.0221	31.0820	31.0629

Table 10. Comparing the solutions of regular smokers at $\sigma = 0.92$, $k = 5$, and $M = 3$.

Sr.	t	BWM	ABM	Fde12	Forward Euler
1	0	20.0269	20.0272	20.0270	20.0249
2	0.1	20.0751	20.0729	20.0752	20.0705
3	0.2	20.1206	20.1163	20.1206	20.1193
4	0.3	20.1648	20.1586	20.1650	20.1616
5	0.4	20.2083	20.2001	20.2083	20.2033
6	0.5	20.2514	20.2412	20.2523	20.2496
7	0.6	20.2941	20.2800	20.2941	20.2905
8	0.7	20.3366	20.3206	20.3375	20.3362
9	0.8	20.3790	20.3610	20.3791	20.3768
10	0.9	20.4213	20.4014	20.4213	20.4173
11	1.0	20.4637	20.4418	20.4638	20.4579

Table 11. Comparing the solutions of ex-smokers at $\sigma = 0.92$, $k = 5$, and $M = 3$.

Sr.	t	BWM	ABM	Fde12	Forward Euler
1	0	15.0652	15.0660	15.0652	15.0604
2	0.1	15.1816	15.1765	15.1816	15.1707
3	0.2	15.2911	15.2810	15.2912	15.2883
4	0.3	15.3973	15.3825	15.3974	15.3899
5	0.4	15.5012	15.4818	15.5013	15.4894
6	0.5	15.6035	15.5795	15.6036	15.5997
7	0.6	15.7045	15.6715	15.7043	15.6964
8	0.7	15.8045	15.7671	15.8044	15.8042
9	0.8	15.9037	15.8619	15.9038	15.8992
10	0.9	16.0021	15.9560	16.0022	15.9935
11	1.0	16.0999	16.0494	16.0999	15.0873

Table 12. Comparing the solutions of smoking system between initial data and BWM at $\sigma = 1.0$, $k = 5$, $t = 0$, and $M = 3$, and providing the Root Mean Square Error (RMSE) and Mean Absolute Error (MAE).

Component	BWM	Actual Data	Error	RMSE	MAE
Susceptible smokers	67.7456	68	−0.2544	0.2544	0.2544
Ingestion class	40.1735	40	0.1735	0.1735	0.1735
Unusual smokers	30.0238	30	0.0238	0.0238	0.0238
Regular smokers	20.0125	20	0.0125	0.0125	0.0125
Ex smokers	15.0303	15	0.0303	0.0303	0.0303

Table 13. Comparing the solutions of the smoking system between initial data and ABM at $\sigma = 1.0$ and $t = 0$, and providing the Root Mean Square Error (RMSE) and Mean Absolute Error (MAE) .

Component	ABM	Actual Data	Error	RMSE	MAE
Susceptible smokers	67.7152	68	−0.2848	0.2848	0.2848
Ingestion class	40.1944	40	0.1944	0.1944	0.1944
Unusual smokers	30.0265	30	0.0265	0.0265	0.0265
Regular smokers	20.0140	20	0.0140	0.0140	0.0140
Ex smokers	15.0340	15	0.0340	0.0340	0.0340

8. Conclusions

The research explores the innovative application of Bernoulli wavelets to effectively solve systems of any order. It begins with a comprehensive analysis of the convergence and numerical procedure, using the unique orthogonal characteristics of Bernoulli wavelets. These wavelets are then used to convert FDEs into algebraic equations, simplifying the numerical solving process. The study provides a detailed illustration of various dynamic behaviours for different FO, emphasizing the influence of parameters and derivative order on the behaviour of arbitrary-order smoking systems. In this study, it is observed that a lower value of e_2 results in a slower decline of the susceptible population and an increase in the number of regular and unusual smokers. This lower value also leads to slower population growth for ex-smokers. Furthermore, a lower value of e_3 causes a notable decline in susceptible individuals and those in the ingestion class, as well as in unusual smokers. Conversely, for regular smokers, a slightly lower value of e_3 leads to a significant increase. Additionally, it is illustrated that a lower value of e_9 significantly increases the growth rate of regular smokers and slows down the rate of decline when the population decreases. Conversely, a higher value of e_9 results in more rapid population growth for ex-smokers. An alternative numerical method known as ABM is introduced to demonstrate the precision and relevance of the suggested approach. The results are then compared with other numerical techniques like Fde12 and forward Euler to validate the approximation of the BWM. In this proposed model, four control variables are used: $w_1(t)$, $w_2(t)$, $w_3(t)$ and $w_4(t)$. Reducing the number of smokers and increasing the number of persons who permanently stop smoking are the two main objectives of the intervention. The simulation findings have led to the conclusion that the control variables employed have an effect consistent with the intended objectives. In conclusion, we observe how to solve the smoking system using BWM more smoothly, and if we change some parameters and control parameter values, then we see the system's behaviour change. We also observe how to control smoking populations in society by taking some control measures. This observation will help health policymakers and scientists to address this issue. Future research will involve using other differential operators like AB, FF, etc., on this system, analyzing and applying other wavelets like Hermite, Laguerre, Bernstein, etc., on this model and numerically investigating it.

Author Contributions: Conceptualization, S.A. and S.K.; Formal analysis, S.A.; Investigation, S.A. and S.K.; Methodology, S.A. and S.K.; Project administration, S.A. and S.K.; Software, S.A. and S.K.; Validation, S.A. and S.K.; Writing—original draft, S.A. and S.K.; Writing—review & editing, S.A., S.K. and S.M.; Data curation, S.K. and S.M.; Funding acquisition, S.K. and S.M.; Resources, S.K.; Supervision, S.K.; Visualization, S.K. All authors have read and agreed to the published version of the manuscript.

Funding: This research received no external funding

Data Availability Statement: Data is accessible upon request from the authors.

Acknowledgments: We acknowledged the support provided by Ajman University for covering the publication fee or any other relevant charges.

Conflicts of Interest: The authors state that they have no conflicts of interest.

References

1. Ghanbari, B.; Aguilar, J.F.G. Modeling the dynamics of nutrient–phytoplankton–zooplankton system with variable-order fractional derivatives. *Chaos Solitons Fractals* **2018**, *116*, 114–120. [CrossRef]
2. Delgado, V.F.M.; Aguilar, J.F.G.; Saad, K.; Jiménez, R.F.E. Application of the Caputo-Fabrizio and Atangana-Baleanu fractional derivatives to mathematical model of cancer chemotherapy effect. *Math. Methods Appl. Sci.* **2019**, *42*, 1167–1193. [CrossRef]
3. Amanullah; Yousaf, M.; Zeb, S.; Akram, M.; Hussain, S.M.; Ro, J.S. Hermite Wavelet Method for Approximate Solution of Higher Order Boundary Value Problems of Ordinary Differential Equations. *Fractals* **2023**, *31*, 2340032. [CrossRef]
4. Grossmann, A.; Morlet, J. Decomposition of Hardy functions into square integrable wavelets of constant shape. *SIAM J. Math. Anal.* **1984**, *15*, 723–736. [CrossRef]
5. Shih, W.C. *Time Frequency Analysis and Wavelet Transform Tutorial, Wavelet for Music Signals Analysis;* Graduate Institute of Communication Engineering National Taiwan University: Taipei, Taiwan, 2006.
6. Sandoz, P. Wavelet transform as a processing tool in white-light interferometry. *Opt. Lett.* **1997**, *22*, 1065–1067. [CrossRef] [PubMed]
7. Bultheel, A.; Huybrechs, D. *Wavelets with Applications in Signal and Image Processing;* Course Material University of Leuven: Leuven, Belgium, 2003.
8. Zhirnov, V.; Solonskaya, S.; Zima, I. Application of wavelet transform for generation of radar virtual images. *Telecommun. Radio Eng.* **2014**, *73*, 1533–1539. [CrossRef]
9. Cong, T.; Su, G.; Qiu, S.; Tian, W. Applications of ANNs in flow and heat transfer problems in nuclear engineering: A review work. *Prog. Nucl. Energy* **2013**, *62*, 54–71. [CrossRef]
10. Ali, A.; Ghazali, R.; Deris, M.M. The wavelet multilayer perceptron for the prediction of earthquake time series data. In Proceedings of the13th International Conference on Information Integration and Web-Based Applications and Services, Ho Chi Minh City, Vietnam, 5–7 December 2011; pp. 138–143.
11. Kui, L.; Jun, L.Z.; Wei, Z.J.; Feng, Z. Application of time-frequency analysis in geology. *World Geol.* **2000**, *19*, 282–285.
12. Starck, J.L. Multiscale methods in astronomy: Beyond wavelets. In Proceedings of the Astronomical Data Analysis Software and Systems XI, Victoria, BC, Canada, 30 September–3 October 2002; Volume 281, p. 391.
13. Khalid, A.; Rehan, A.; Osman, M. An extended 3rd-order B-spline strategy to solve linear BVPs rising in stability analysis of electrically conducting fluid in a magnetic field. *Int. J. Mod. Phys. C* **2022**, *33*, 2250153. [CrossRef]
14. Zhang, T.; Baehr, W.; Fu, Y. Chemical chaperone TUDCA preserves cone photoreceptors in a mouse model of Leber congenital amaurosis. *Investig. Ophthalmol. Vis. Sci.* **2012**, *53*, 3349–3356. [CrossRef]
15. Beylkin, G.; Coifman, R.; Rokhlin, V. Fast wavelet transforms and numerical algorithms I. *Commun. Pure Appl. Math.* **1991**, *44*, 141–183. [CrossRef]
16. Al Jawary, M.A.; Raham, R.K. A semi-analytical iterative technique for solving chemistry problems. *J. King Saud Univ.-Sci.* **2017**, *29*, 320–332. [CrossRef]
17. Naji, R.K.; Mustafa, A.N. The dynamics of an eco-epidemiological model with nonlinear incidence rate. *J. Appl. Math.* **2012**, *2012*, 852631. [CrossRef]

18. Zhang, F.; Chen, Y.; Li, J. Dynamical analysis of a stage-structured predator-prey model with cannibalism. *Math. Biosci.* **2019**, *307*, 33–41. [CrossRef] [PubMed]
19. Rezapour, S.; Etemad, S.; Sinan, M.; Alzabut, J.; Vinodkumar, A. A mathematical analysis on the new fractal-fractional model of second-hand smokers via the power law type kernel: Numerical solutions, equilibrium points, and sensitivity analysis. *J. Funct. Spaces* **2022**, *2022*, 3553021. [CrossRef]
20. Janssen, F. Similarities and differences between sexes and countries in the mortality imprint of the smoking epidemic in 34 low-mortality countries, 1950–2014. *Nicotine Tob. Res.* **2020**, *22*, 1210–1220. [CrossRef]
21. Agrawal, O.P. A general formulation and solution scheme for fractional optimal control problems. *Nonlinear Dyn.* **2004**, *38*, 323–337. [CrossRef]
22. Akbarian, T.; Keyanpour, M. A new approach to the numerical solution of fractional order optimal control problems. *Appl. Appl. Math. Int. J. (AAM)* **2013**, *8*, 12.
23. Anjam, Y.N.; Shafqat, R.; Sarris, I.E.; Rahman, M.U.; Touseef, S.; Arshad, M. A fractional order investigation of smoking model using Caputo-Fabrizio differential operator. *Fractal Fract.* **2022**, *6*, 623. [CrossRef]
24. Nisar, K.S.; Farman, M.; Hincal, E.; Shehzad, A. Modelling and analysis of bad impact of smoking in society with Constant Proportional-Caputo Fabrizio operator. *Chaos Solitons Fractals* **2023**, *172*, 113549. [CrossRef]
25. Agrawal, K.; Kumar, R.; Kumar, S.; Hadid, S.; Momani, S. Bernoulli wavelet method for non-linear fractional Glucose–Insulin regulatory dynamical system. *Chaos Solitons Fractals* **2022**, *164*, 112632. [CrossRef]
26. Kumar, P.; Kumar, A.; Kumar, S. A study on fractional order infectious chronic wasting disease model in deers. *Arab J. Basic Appl. Sci.* **2023**, *30*, 601–625. [CrossRef]
27. Keshavarz, E.; Ordokhani, Y.; Razzaghi, M. Bernoulli wavelet operational matrix of fractional order integration and its applications in solving the fractional order differential equations. *Appl. Math. Model.* **2014**, *38*, 6038–6051. [CrossRef]
28. Moghadam, A.S.; Arabameri, M.; Baleanu, D.; Barfeie, M. Numerical solution of variable fractional order advection-dispersion equation using Bernoulli wavelet method and new operational matrix of fractional order derivative. *Math. Methods Appl. Sci.* **2020**, *43*, 3936–3953.
29. Alkahtani, B.S.T.; Agrawal, K.; Kumar, S.; Alzaid, S.S. Bernoulli polynomial based wavelets method for solving chaotic behaviour of financial model. *Results Phys.* **2023**, *53*, 107011. [CrossRef]
30. Wang, J.; Xu, T.Z.; Wei, Y.Q.; Xie, J.Q. Numerical solutions for systems of fractional order differential equations with Bernoulli wavelets. *Int. J. Comput. Math.* **2019**, *96*, 317–336. [CrossRef]
31. Diethelm, K.; Ford, N.J. Multi-order fractional differential equations and their numerical solution. *Appl. Math. Comput.* **2004**, *154*, 621–640. [CrossRef]
32. Diethelm, K. *The Analysis of Fractional Differential Equations*; Springer: Berlin/ Heidelberg, Germany, 2010.
33. Ilmayasinta, N.; Purnawan, H. Optimal Control in a Mathematical Model of Smoking. *J. Math. Fundam. Sci.* **2021**, *53*, 380–394. [CrossRef]
34. Fleming, W.H.; Rishel, R.W. *Deterministic and Stochastic Optimal Control*; Springer Science & Business Media: Berlin/Heidelberg, Germany, 2012; Volume 1.
35. Lukes, D.L. *Differential Equations: Classical to Controlled*; Academic Press: New York, NY, USA, 1982.
36. Cao, X.; Datta, A.; Basir, F.A.; Roy, P.K. Fractional-order model of the disease psoriasis: A control based mathematical approach. *J. Syst. Sci. Complex.* **2016**, *29*, 1565–1584. [CrossRef]
37. Basir, F.A.; Roy, P.K. Stability analysis and optimal control of a fractional order model for HIV infection. *WSEAS Trans. Math.* **2017**, *16*, 152–62.
38. Abraha, T.; Basir, F.A.; Obsu, L.L.; Torres, D.F. Pest control using farming awareness: Impact of time delays and optimal use of biopesticides. *Chaos Solitons Fractals* **2021**, *146*, 110869. [CrossRef]
39. Roy, P.K.; Saha, S.; Basir, F.A. Effect of awareness programs in controlling the disease HIV/AIDS: An optimal control theoretic approach. *Adv. Differ. Equ.* **2015**, *2015*, 217. [CrossRef]
40. Basir, F.A.; Elaiw, A.M.; Kesh, D.; Roy, P.K. Optimal control of a fractional-order enzyme kinetic model. *Control Cybern.* **2015**, *44*, 443–461.
41. Basir, F.A.; Abraha, T. Mathematical Modelling and Optimal Control of Malaria Using Awareness-Based Interventions. *Mathematics* **2023**, *11*, 1687. [CrossRef]
42. Basir, F.A.; Rajak, B.; Rahman, B.; Hattaf, K. Hopf Bifurcation Analysis and Optimal Control of an Infectious Disease with Awareness Campaign and Treatment. *Axioms* **2023**, *12*, 608. [CrossRef]

fractal and fractional

MDPI

Article

Quantum Dynamics in a Comb Geometry: Green Function Solutions with Nonlocal and Fractional Potentials

Enrique C. Gabrick [1,*], Ervin K. Lenzi [2,3,4], Antonio S. M. de Castro [2,3], José Trobia [5] and Antonio M. Batista [2,5]

1 Institute of Physics, University of São Paulo, São Paulo 05508-090, SP, Brazil
2 Graduate Program in Science, State University of Ponta Grossa, Ponta Grossa 84030-900, PR, Brazil; eklenzi@uem.br (E.K.L.); asmcastro@uepg.br (A.S.M.d.C.); abatista@uepg.br (A.M.B.)
3 Department of Physics, State University of Ponta Grossa, Ponta Grossa 84030-900, PR, Brazil
4 Department of Physics, State University of Maringá, Maringá 87020-900, PR, Brazil
5 Department of Mathematics and Statistics, State University of Ponta Grossa, Ponta Grossa 84030-900, PR, Brazil; jtrobia@uepg.br
* Correspondence: gabrick@if.usp.br

Abstract: We investigate a generalized quantum Schrödinger equation in a comb-like structure that imposes geometric constraints on spatial variables. The model is extended by the introduction of nonlocal and fractional potentials to capture memory effects in both space and time. We consider four distinct scenarios: (i) a time-dependent nonlocal potential, (ii) a spatially nonlocal potential, (iii) a combined space–time nonlocal interaction with memory kernels, and (iv) a fractional spatial derivative, which is related to distributions asymptotically governed by power laws and to a position-dependent effective mass. For each scenario, we propose solutions based on the Green's function for arbitrary initial conditions and analyze the resulting quantum dynamics. Our results reveal distinct spreading regimes, depending on the type of non-locality and the fractional operator applied to the spatial variable. These findings contribute to the broader generalization of comb models and open new questions for exploring quantum dynamics in backbone-like structures.

Keywords: comb models; quantum dynamics; Green's function

1. Introduction

The Schrödinger equation represents an important breakthrough in describing non-relativistic quantum systems across various physical scenarios. It supports our understanding of microscopic phenomena and has become a cornerstone of modern quantum theory [1]. Initially formulated by Schrödinger in a series of seminal papers [2,3], the equation was derived from classical mechanics through a judicious choice of the action variable, leading to a variational principle that yields a partial differential equation: the Schrödinger equation. Its solutions, known as wave functions, describe the temporal evolution of quantum wave packets. However, obtaining analytical solutions is often challenging, especially for systems with complex or non-trivial potentials [4]. Once the wave function is determined, it enables the extraction of physical properties such as probability densities [5] and the diffusion behavior of quantum particles [6].

Despite its success, the Schrödinger equation has been extended in several directions to encompass experimental results. These extensions include anomalous relaxation processes [7,8], in which the wave function may exhibit stretched-exponential or power-law decay, instead of the exponential decay predicted by the traditional formalism [9,10]. An important class of generalizations introduces fractional derivatives into the Schrödinger equation [4,6,11–14], providing a compact and elegant framework to model memory effects, nonlocal correlations, and dissipative dynamics [7]. Another direction involves non-linear modifications, often motivated by connections to porous media equations and non-extensive statistical mechanics [15,16], particularly those based on Tsallis entropy [17–20]. The comb model is another intriguing extension to describe anomalous diffusion [21]. This model features a branched geometry that resembles a backbone with perpendicular fingers, where a particle that undergoes a random walk may enter and become temporarily trapped in the fingers before returning to the main axis. This structure gives rise to an anomalous diffusion, where the mean square displacement (MSD) scales as $\langle x^2(t)\rangle \sim t^{\mu}$, with $0 < \mu < 1$ (subdiffusive regime) or $\mu > 1$ (superdiffusive regime), depending on the configuration [22].

Further generalizations of the comb model [23] incorporate fractional time derivatives [24] and fractal geometries, as in the Refs. [25,26], which extended these ideas by incorporating linear reactions and stochastic resetting within a fractional comb framework [27,28]. From a biological perspective, comb-like geometries have been employed to model transport along spiny dendrites, which exhibit subdiffusive dynamics [29]. This diffusion regime arises from trapping mechanisms in the finger regions and is effectively described by time-fractional operators. Although comb structures have been extensively studied in classical diffusion, their quantum counterparts remain relatively unexplored [30–32]. In a quantum comb model, particle motion along the central axis (x) is confined to the line $y = 0$ due to a delta-function potential in the transverse (y) direction [30]. Notably, the fractional-time Schrödinger equation (FTSE) of order $1/2$ emerges naturally as a special case within this framework.

Here, we analyze a generalized Schrödinger equation that incorporates a backbone structure with branches (comb-like structure), fractional derivative in space [33,34], and a generic time-dependent external potential. To account these features, we write the Schrödinger equation in the following form

$$i\hbar\frac{\partial}{\partial t}\psi(\mathbf{r},t) = -\frac{\hbar^2}{2m}\left[\delta\left(\frac{y}{l_y}\right)D_x^{\mu,\eta}\psi(\mathbf{r},t) + \frac{\partial^2}{\partial y^2}\psi(\mathbf{r},t)\right] + \mathcal{V}[\psi(\mathbf{r},t)], \tag{1}$$

where $\mathcal{V}[\psi(\mathbf{r},t)]$ it is given by

$$\begin{aligned}\mathcal{V}[\psi(\mathbf{r},t)] = &\int_0^t dt' V_{xy}^{(1)}(x,y;t-t')\psi(\mathbf{r},t') + \int_0^t dt' V_{xy}^{(2)}(y;t-t')\psi(\mathbf{r},t') \\ &+ \int_0^t dt' \int_{-\infty}^{\infty} dx' V_{xy}^{(3)}(x-x',y,t-t')\psi(x',y,t')\,.\end{aligned} \tag{2}$$

We consider four configurations in Equation (2). First, we address a nonlocal dependence on time, i.e., the external potential is time-dependent and is expressed as a product of spatial delta functions. The second setup simultaneously incorporates nonlocal dependencies in both space and time. For this, we introduce two external potentials: one that has dependence on space variables and the other that is time-dependent. In the third scenario, we consider nonlocal dependence and memory kernels, i.e., we mix the previous scenarios by incorporating memory on time and a fractional derivative in space [33,34]. For the last configuration, we include a fractional spatial operator and nonlocal terms. For the posed problems, we obtain the corresponding solutions through Green's function and show that the diffusion is anomalous, exhibiting a super-diffusive regime.

This paper is organized as follows. Section 2 introduces the generalized Schrödinger equation of the comb, and the subsequent subsections present the particular problems. In Section 3, we present our discussions, findings, and outline potential future directions.

2. Schrödinger Equation in a Comb-Model

Let us now investigate Equation (1) in connection with Equation (2) by considering different cases.

2.1. Nonlocal Dependence on Time

First, let us consider the Schrödinger equation with the geometric constraints between the directions x and y subjected to external potentials, which may have a time dependence. For this case, we consider integer operators in spatial variables, where Equation (1) results in

$$\begin{aligned} i\hbar\frac{\partial}{\partial t}\psi(\mathbf{r},t) = & -\frac{\hbar^2}{2m}\left[\delta\left(\frac{y}{l_y}\right)\frac{\partial^2}{\partial x^2}\psi(\mathbf{r},t)+\frac{\partial^2}{\partial y^2}\psi(\mathbf{r},t)\right] \\ & +\int_0^t dt' V_{xy}^{(1)}(x,y;t-t')\psi(\mathbf{r},t')+\int_0^t dt' V_{xy}^{(2)}(y;t-t')\psi(\mathbf{r},t'), \end{aligned} \tag{3}$$

where $V_{xy}^{(1)}(x,y,t)=\mathfrak{K}_1(t)\delta(x/l_x)\delta(y/l_y)$ and $V_{xy}^{(2)}(y,t)=\mathfrak{K}_2(t)\delta(y/l_y)$ with the initial condition $\psi(\mathbf{r},0)=\varphi(\mathbf{r})$. Note that these terms have a nonlocal dependence on time, which results in a Schrödinger equation with nonlocal terms [35,36] or nonlocal potential [37,38].

To solve Equation (3), we use the Green function approach, leading to

$$\begin{aligned} i\hbar\frac{\partial}{\partial t}\mathcal{G}(\mathbf{r},\mathbf{r}',t) & - i\hbar\delta(x-x')\delta(y-y')\delta(t) = -\frac{\hbar^2}{2m}\left[\delta\left(\frac{y}{l_y}\right)\frac{\partial^2}{\partial x^2}\mathcal{G}(\mathbf{r},\mathbf{r}',t)+\frac{\partial^2}{\partial y^2}\mathcal{G}(\mathbf{r},\mathbf{r}',t)\right] \\ & + \int_0^t dt' V_{xy}^{(1)}(x,y;t-t')\mathcal{G}(\mathbf{r},\mathbf{r}',t')+\int_0^t dt' V_{xy}^{(2)}(y;t-t')\mathcal{G}(\mathbf{r},\mathbf{r}',t'), \end{aligned} \tag{4}$$

with $\mathbf{r}'=(x',y')$. By using the Fourier ($\mathfrak{F}\{\mathcal{G}(\mathbf{r},\mathbf{r}',t)\}=\widetilde{\mathcal{G}}(k_x,k_y,\mathbf{r}',t)$) and Laplace transforms ($\mathfrak{L}\{\mathcal{G}(\mathbf{r},\mathbf{r}',t)\}=\widehat{\mathcal{G}}(\mathbf{r},\mathbf{r}',s)$), we obtain

$$\begin{aligned} i\hbar s\widehat{\widetilde{\mathcal{G}}}(k_x,k_y,\mathbf{r}',s)-i\hbar e^{-ik_xx'}e^{-ik_yy'} = & \frac{\hbar^2}{2m}\left[l_yk_x^2\widehat{\widetilde{\mathcal{G}}}(k_x,0,\mathbf{r}',s)+k_y^2\widehat{\widetilde{\mathcal{G}}}(k_x,k_y,\mathbf{r}',s)\right] \\ & +\widehat{\mathfrak{K}}_1(s)l_xl_y\widehat{\mathcal{G}}(0,0,\mathbf{r}',s)+\widehat{\mathfrak{K}}_2(s)l_y\widehat{\widetilde{\mathcal{G}}}(k_x,0,\mathbf{r}',s), \end{aligned} \tag{5}$$

with $\widehat{\widetilde{\mathcal{G}}}(k_x,0,\mathbf{r}',s)=\widehat{\widetilde{\mathcal{G}}}(k_x,y=0,\mathbf{r}',s)$, and $\widehat{\mathfrak{K}}_i(s)$ $(i=1,2)$ is the Laplace transform of the time contribution of the respective potentials $V_{xy}^i(x,y,t)$. After performing algebraic manipulation in Equation (5), we get

$$\begin{aligned} \widehat{\widetilde{\mathcal{G}}}(k_x,k_y,\mathbf{r}',s) = & e^{-ik_xx'}e^{-ik_yy'}\widehat{\widetilde{\mathcal{G}}}_y(k_y,s)-\left[\frac{i\hbar}{2m}l_yk_x^2+\frac{i}{\hbar}\widehat{\mathfrak{K}}_x(s)l_y\right]\widehat{\widetilde{\mathcal{G}}}(k_x,0,\mathbf{r}',s)\widehat{\widetilde{\mathcal{G}}}_y(k_y,s) \\ & -\frac{i}{\hbar}\widehat{\mathfrak{K}}_1(s)l_xl_y\widehat{\mathcal{G}}(0,0,\mathbf{r}',s)\widehat{\widetilde{\mathcal{G}}}_y(k_y,s), \end{aligned} \tag{6}$$

with

$$\widehat{\widetilde{\mathcal{G}}}_y(k_y,s)=\frac{1}{s+i\hbar k_y^2/(2m)}. \tag{7}$$

The inverse Fourier transform in the y variables results in

$$\begin{aligned} \widehat{\widetilde{\mathcal{G}}}(k_x,y,\mathbf{r}',s) = & e^{-ik_xx'}\widehat{\mathcal{G}}_y(y-y',s)-\left[\frac{i\hbar}{2m}l_yk_x^2+\frac{i}{\hbar}\widehat{\mathfrak{K}}_2(s)l_y\right]\widehat{\widetilde{\mathcal{G}}}(k_x,0,\mathbf{r}',s)\widehat{\mathcal{G}}_y(y,s) \\ & -\frac{i}{\hbar}\widehat{\mathfrak{K}}_1(s)l_xl_y\widehat{\mathcal{G}}(0,0,\mathbf{r}',s)\widehat{\mathcal{G}}_y(y,s). \end{aligned} \tag{8}$$

From this equation, it is possible to show that

$$\widehat{\widetilde{\mathcal{G}}}(k_x,0,\mathbf{r}',s) = e^{-ik_xx'}\widehat{\widetilde{\mathcal{G}}}_x(k_x,s)\widehat{\mathcal{G}}_y(y',s) - \frac{i}{\hbar}\widehat{\mathfrak{K}}_1(s)l_xl_y\widehat{\mathcal{G}}(0,0,\mathbf{r}',s)\widehat{\mathcal{G}}_y(0,s)\widehat{\widetilde{\mathcal{G}}}_x^{(1)}(k_x,s), \tag{9}$$

with

$$\widehat{\widetilde{\mathcal{G}}}_x^{(1)}(k_x,s) = \frac{1}{1+\left(i\hbar k_x^2/(2m)+(i/\hbar)\widehat{\mathfrak{K}}_2(s)\right)l_y\widehat{\mathcal{G}}_y(0,s)}. \tag{10}$$

By performing the inverse of the Fourier transform in the x variable in the previous equation, we obtain

$$\widehat{\mathcal{G}}(0,0,\mathbf{r}',s) = \frac{\widehat{\mathcal{G}}_y(y',s)\widehat{\mathcal{G}}_x^{(1)}(x',s)}{1+(i/\hbar)\widehat{\mathfrak{K}}_1(s)l_xl_y\widehat{\mathcal{G}}_y(0,s)\widehat{\mathcal{G}}_x^{(1)}(0,s)}. \tag{11}$$

By using these results, it is possible to show that

$$\begin{aligned}\widehat{\widetilde{\mathcal{G}}}(k_x,0,\mathbf{r}',s) &= e^{-ik_xx'}\widehat{\widetilde{\mathcal{G}}}_x^{(1)}(k_x,s)\widehat{\mathcal{G}}_y(y',s)\\ &-\frac{i}{\hbar}\frac{\widehat{\mathfrak{K}}_1(s)l_xl_y\widehat{\mathcal{G}}_y(y',s)\widehat{\mathcal{G}}_x^{(1)}(x',s)}{1+(i/\hbar)\widehat{\mathfrak{K}}_1(s)l_xl_y\widehat{\mathcal{G}}_y(0,s)\widehat{\mathcal{G}}_x^{(1)}(0,s)}\widehat{\mathcal{G}}_y(0,s)\widehat{\widetilde{\mathcal{G}}}_x^{(1)}(k_x,s),\end{aligned} \tag{12}$$

and, consequently,

$$\begin{aligned}\widehat{\mathcal{G}}(x,y,\mathbf{r}',s) &= \delta(x-x')\left[\widehat{\mathcal{G}}_y(y-y',s)-\widehat{\mathcal{G}}_y(|y|+|y'|,s)\right]\\ &+\left[\widehat{\mathcal{G}}_x^{(1)}(x-x',s)-\widehat{\mathcal{G}}^{(1)}(|x|+|x'|,s)\right]\widehat{\mathcal{G}}_y(|y|+|y'|,s)\\ &+\frac{\widehat{\mathcal{G}}_y(|y|+|y'|,s)}{1+(i/\hbar)\widehat{\mathfrak{K}}_1(s)l_xl_y\widehat{\mathcal{G}}_y(0,s)\widehat{\mathcal{G}}_x^{(1)}(0,s)}\widehat{\mathcal{G}}_x^{(1)}(|x|+|x'|,s).\end{aligned} \tag{13}$$

The straightforward inverse Laplace in Equation (13) is challenging due to the last term. To solve this problem, we propose an expansion in this term, allowing us to rewrite Equation (13) equal to

$$\begin{aligned}\widehat{\mathcal{G}}(x,y,\mathbf{r}',s) &= \delta(x-x')\left[\widehat{\mathcal{G}}_y(y-y',s)-\widehat{\mathcal{G}}_y(|y|+|y'|,s)\right]\\ &+\left[\widehat{\mathcal{G}}_x^{(1)}(x-x',s)-\widehat{\mathcal{G}}^{(1)}(|x|+|x'|,s)\right]\widehat{\mathcal{G}}_y(|y|+|y'|,s)\\ &+\sum_{n=0}^{\infty}\left(-\frac{i}{\hbar}l_xl_y\right)^n\left[\widehat{\mathfrak{K}}_1(s)\widehat{\mathcal{G}}_y(0,s)\widehat{\mathcal{G}}_x^{(1)}(0,s)\right]^n\widehat{\mathcal{G}}_y(|y|+|y'|,s)\widehat{\mathcal{G}}_x^{(1)}(|x|+|x'|,s).\end{aligned} \tag{14}$$

From this expansion, we can obtain the inverse Laplace in Equation (14), which leads to

$$\begin{aligned}\mathcal{G}(x,y,\mathbf{r}',t) &= \delta(x-x')\Big[\mathcal{G}_y(y-y',t)-\mathcal{G}_y(|y|+|y'|,t)\Big] \\ &+\int_0^t dt'\Big[\mathcal{G}_x^{(1)}(x-x',t-t')-\mathcal{G}^{(1)}(|x|+|x'|,t-t')\Big]\mathcal{G}_y(|y|+|y'|,t') \\ &+\sum_{n=0}^{\infty}\Big(-\frac{i}{\hbar}l_x l_y\widehat{\mathcal{G}}_y(0,1)\widehat{\mathcal{G}}_x^{(1)}(0,1)\Big)^n\int_0^t dt_n\mathcal{I}(t-t_n)\int_0^{t_n}dt_{n-1}\mathcal{I}(t_n-t_{n-1})\cdots \\ &\times\int_0^{t_2}dt_1\mathcal{I}(t_2-t_1)\int_0^{t_1}dt'\mathcal{G}_y(|y|+|y'|,t_1-t')\mathcal{G}_x^{(1)}(|x|+|x'|,t')\,,\end{aligned} \tag{15}$$

with $\mathcal{I}(t)=(1/\Gamma(1/4))\int_0^t dt'\mathfrak{K}_1(t')/(t-t')^{3/4}$. From Equation (15), we obtain the wave function by using the following equation

$$\psi(\mathbf{r},\mathbf{r}',t)=\int_{-\infty}^{\infty}dx'\int_{-\infty}^{\infty}dy'\mathcal{G}(\mathbf{r},\mathbf{r}',t)\varphi(\mathbf{r}')\,, \tag{16}$$

subject to the initial condition previously defined.

To illustrate the behavior of solutions given by Equation (16), we set the configuration of the first problem (i) with an initial condition equal to $\varphi(\mathbf{r})=\delta(x)\delta(y)$ with $\mathfrak{K}_1(t)=(\mathfrak{K}_1/\tau)e^{-it/\tau}$ and $\mathfrak{K}_2(t)=0$. For this configuration, the behavior of the absolute value of the wave function $|\psi(x,y,t)|$ is displayed in Figure 1. The package that is initially centered in $(x,y)=(0,0)$ starts to spread along the space, exhibiting an oscillatory dynamic in one direction and a decay in another.

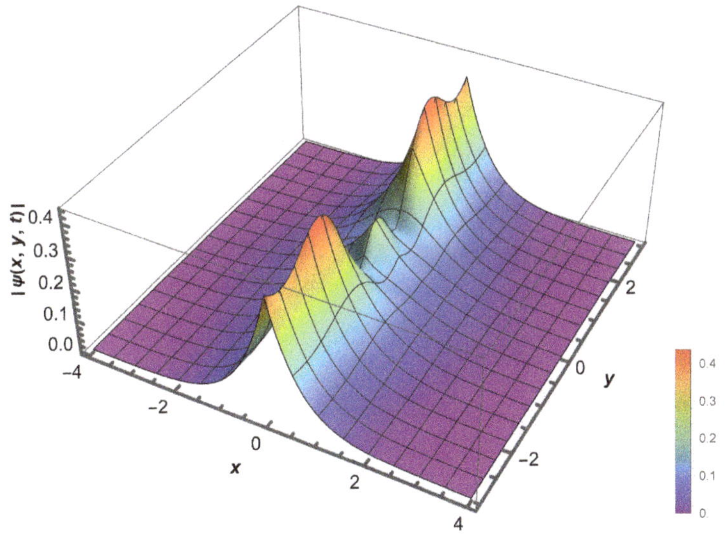

Figure 1. Behavior of the absolute value of the wave function for the initial condition $\varphi(\mathbf{r})=\delta(x)\delta(y)$ with $\mathfrak{K}_1(t)=(\mathfrak{K}_1/\tau)e^{-it/\tau}$ and $\mathfrak{K}_2(t)=0$. Without loss of generality, we consider $\tau=0.1$, $\mathfrak{K}_1/(\hbar\tau)=1$, $\hbar/m=1$, and $l_x=l_y=1$, in arbitrary unities.

To compare with the previous results, we set another parameter configuration (ii): $\varphi(\mathbf{r})=e^{-\mathbf{r}^2/2}/\sqrt{\pi}$ with $\mathfrak{K}_1(t)=\mathfrak{K}_1\delta(t)$ and $\mathfrak{K}_2(t)=0$, which represents a Gaussian package combined with a time delta potential. In the center of Figure 2, we observe a typical decay of an initial Gaussian package, which spreads along the space. However, this solution presents oscillatory waves that spread along the plane (x,y) due to the extra terms.

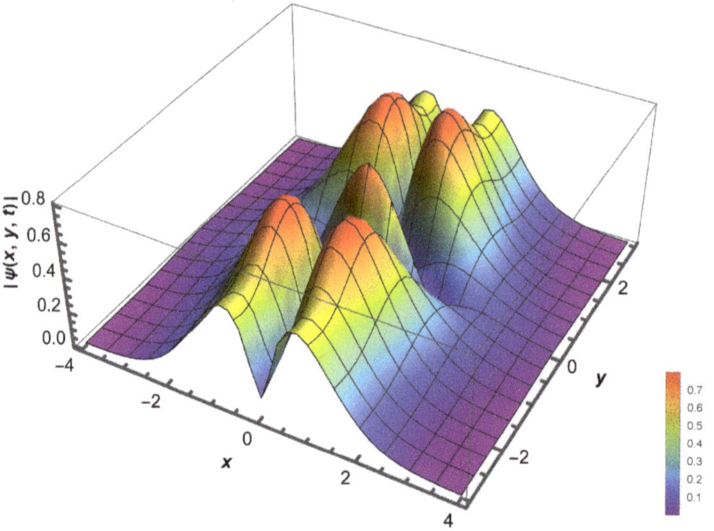

Figure 2. Behavior of the Green function the absolute value of the wave function for the initial condition $\varphi(\mathbf{r}) = e^{-\mathbf{r}^2/2}/\sqrt{\pi}$ with $\mathfrak{K}_1(t) = \mathfrak{K}_1\delta(t)$ and $\mathfrak{K}_2(t) = 0$. Without loss of generality, we consider $\mathfrak{K}_{xy}/\hbar = 1, \hbar/m = 1$, and $l_x = l_y = 1$, in arbitrary unities.

Additionally, we study the relaxation process for different scenarios: both the previously considered and the standard comb for two dimensions. The results are presented in Figure 3, characterized by the nonlocal terms for the initial condition and nonlocal dependence on time. By analyzing Figure 3, we verify different behaviors of the relaxation process for the wave function when memory effects are considered. Comparing our results (blue and black lines) with the standard comb model in two dimensions (orange line), we observe that both cases present a super-diffusive regime, where the former leads to $|\psi(0,0,t)|^{-2} \sim t^{2.5}$, while the latter leads to $|\psi(0,0,t)|^{-2} \sim t^{1.5}$. In this case, the additional terms, i.e., the nonlocal effects on time, make the relaxation process faster.

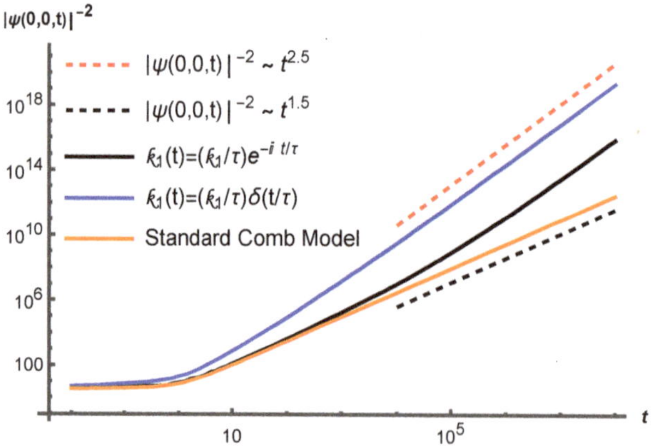

Figure 3. Behavior of the $|\psi(0,0,t)|^{-2}$ for the cases (*i*) $\varphi(\mathbf{r}) = \delta(x)\delta(y)$ with $\mathfrak{K}_1(t) = (\mathfrak{K}_1/\tau)e^{-it/\tau}$ and $\mathfrak{K}_x(t) = 0$) in the blue line; (*ii*) $\varphi(\mathbf{r}) = e^{-\mathbf{r}^2/2}/\sqrt{\pi}$ with $\mathfrak{K}_1(t) = (\mathfrak{K}_1/\tau)\delta(t/\tau)$ and $\mathfrak{K}_2(t) = 0$ in black line; and the standard two-dimensional comb model in orange line. Without loss of generality, we consider, for simplicity, $\mathfrak{K}_1/\hbar = 1, \hbar/m = 1$, and $l_x = l_y = 1$, in arbitrary unities.

2.2. Nonlocal Dependence on Space and Time

Now, we consider the nonlocal term with a spatial dependence on the variable x, instead of the nonlocal term at the origin with a nonlocal dependence on time, i.e., we consider the following Schrödinger equation:

$$\begin{aligned} i\hbar\frac{\partial}{\partial t}\psi(\mathbf{r},t) &= -\frac{\hbar^2}{2m}\left[\delta\left(\frac{y}{l_y}\right)\frac{\partial^2}{\partial x^2}\psi(\mathbf{r},t)+\frac{\partial^2}{\partial y^2}\psi(\mathbf{r},t)\right] \\ &+\int_0^t dt'\int_{-\infty}^{\infty}dx' V_{xy}^{(3)}(x-x',y,t-t')\psi(x',y,t')+\int_0^t dt' V_{xy}^{(2)}(y;t-t')\psi(\mathbf{r},t'), \end{aligned} \tag{17}$$

where $V_{xy}^{(3)}(x,y)=\mathfrak{K}_3(x,t)\delta(y/l_y)$ and $V_{xy}^{(2)}(y,t)=\mathfrak{K}_2(t)\delta(y/l_y)$ with the initial condition $\psi(\mathbf{r},0)=\varphi(\mathbf{r})$. In Equation (17), the kernel $\mathfrak{K}_3(x,t)$ introduces a nonlocal dependence on space and time, different from the previous case, which only considered a time dependence. It is worth noting that depending on the choice of the $\mathfrak{K}_3(x,t)$, we can relate this term with the fractional derivative in space such as the ones discussed in Refs. [39,40], which can be related to the Lévy distributions. One of them corresponds to the choice $\mathfrak{K}_3(x,t)=\mathfrak{K}(x)\delta(t)$ with $\mathfrak{F}\{\mathfrak{K}(x);k_x\}=-|k_x|^{\mu_x}$.

Analogously to the presented previous case, we solve Equation (17) through the Green function approach, yielding the following equation

$$\begin{aligned} i\hbar\frac{\partial}{\partial t}\mathcal{G}(\mathbf{r},\mathbf{r}',t)-i\hbar\delta(x-x')\delta(y-y')\delta(t) &= -\frac{\hbar^2}{2m}\left[\delta\left(\frac{y}{l_y}\right)\frac{\partial^2}{\partial x^2}\mathcal{G}(\mathbf{r},\mathbf{r}',t)+\frac{\partial^2}{\partial y^2}\mathcal{G}(\mathbf{r},\mathbf{r}',t)\right] \\ +\int_0^t dt'\int_{-\infty}^{\infty}dx' V_{xy}^{(3)}(x-x',y,t-t')\mathcal{G}(\mathbf{r},\mathbf{r}',t') &+\int_0^t dt' V_{xy}^{(2)}(y;t-t')\mathcal{G}(\mathbf{r},\mathbf{r}',t')\,. \end{aligned} \tag{18}$$

Now, using the Fourier and Laplace transforms, we obtain

$$\begin{aligned} i\hbar s\widehat{\widetilde{\mathcal{G}}}(k_x,k_y,\mathbf{r}',s)-i\hbar e^{-ik_xx'}e^{-ik_yy'} &= \frac{\hbar^2}{2m}\left[l_yk_x^2\widehat{\widetilde{\mathcal{G}}}(k_x,0,\mathbf{r}',s)+k_y^2\widehat{\widetilde{\mathcal{G}}}(k_x,k_y,\mathbf{r}',s)\right] \\ &+\widehat{\widetilde{\mathfrak{K}}}_3(k_x,s)l_y\widehat{\widetilde{\mathcal{G}}}(k_x,0,\mathbf{r}',s)+\widehat{\mathfrak{K}}_2(s)l_y\widehat{\widetilde{\mathcal{G}}}(k_x,0,\mathbf{r}',s), \end{aligned} \tag{19}$$

which can be written as

$$\begin{aligned} \widehat{\widetilde{\mathcal{G}}}(k_x,k_y,\mathbf{r}',s) &= e^{-ik_xx'}e^{-ik_yy'}\widehat{\widetilde{\mathcal{G}}}_y(k_y,s)-\left[\frac{i\hbar}{2m}l_yk_x^2+\frac{i}{\hbar}\widehat{\mathfrak{K}}_2(s)l_y\right]\widehat{\widetilde{\mathcal{G}}}(k_x,0,\mathbf{r}',s)\widehat{\widetilde{\mathcal{G}}}_y(k_y,s) \\ &-\frac{i}{\hbar}\widehat{\widetilde{\mathfrak{K}}}_3(k_x,s)l_y\widehat{\widetilde{\mathcal{G}}}(k_x,0,\mathbf{r}',s)\widehat{\widetilde{\mathcal{G}}}_y(k_y,s)\,. \end{aligned} \tag{20}$$

By applying the inverse of the Fourier transform in the y variable and performing some calculations, we obtain that

$$\begin{aligned} \widehat{\widetilde{\mathcal{G}}}(k_x,y,\mathbf{r}',s) &= e^{-k_xx'}\widehat{\widetilde{\mathcal{G}}}_y(y-y',s) \\ &-\left[\frac{i\hbar}{2m}l_yk_x^2+\frac{i}{\hbar}l_y\left(\widehat{\mathfrak{K}}_2(s)+\widehat{\widetilde{\mathfrak{K}}}_3(k_x,s)\right)\right]\widehat{\widetilde{\mathcal{G}}}(k_x,0,\mathbf{r}',s)\widehat{\mathcal{G}}_y(y,s)\,. \end{aligned} \tag{21}$$

From this equation, it is possible to show that

$$\widehat{\widetilde{\mathcal{G}}}(k_x,0,\mathbf{r}',s)=e^{-k_xx'}\widehat{\widetilde{\mathcal{G}}}_x^{(2)}(k_x,s)\widehat{\mathcal{G}}_y(y',s), \tag{22}$$

with

$$\widehat{\widetilde{\mathcal{G}}}_x^{(2)}(k_x,s)=\frac{1}{1+\left[i\hbar k_x^2/(2m)+(i/\hbar)\left(\widehat{\mathfrak{K}}_2(s)+\widehat{\widetilde{\mathfrak{K}}}_3(k_x,s)\right)\right]l_y\widehat{\mathcal{G}}_y(0,s)}\,. \tag{23}$$

By using these results, it is possible to show that

$$\begin{aligned}\widehat{\widetilde{\mathcal{G}}}(k_x,y,\mathbf{r}',s) &= e^{-k_x x'}\widehat{\mathcal{G}}_y(y-y',s) \\ &\quad - \left[\frac{i\hbar}{2m}l_y k_x^2 + \frac{i}{\hbar}l_y\left(\widehat{\mathfrak{K}}_2(s)+\widehat{\widetilde{\mathfrak{K}}}_3(k_x,s)\right)\right]e^{-k_x x'}\widehat{\widetilde{\mathcal{G}}}_x^{(2)}(k_x,s)\widehat{\mathcal{G}}_y(y',s)\widehat{\mathcal{G}}_y(y,s)\end{aligned} \tag{24}$$

and, consequently,

$$\begin{aligned}\widehat{\mathcal{G}}(x,y,\mathbf{r}',s) &= \delta(x-x')\left[\widehat{\mathcal{G}}_y(y-y',s)-\widehat{\mathcal{G}}_y(|y|+|y'|,s)\right] \\ &\quad + \widehat{\mathcal{G}}_x^{(2)}(x-x',s)\widehat{\mathcal{G}}_y(|y|+|y'|,s)\,.\end{aligned} \tag{25}$$

The inverse Laplace transform applied in Equation (25) formally results in

$$\begin{aligned}\mathcal{G}(x,y,\mathbf{r}',t) &= \delta(x-x')\left[\mathcal{G}_y(y-y',t)-\mathcal{G}_y(|y|+|y'|,t)\right] \\ &\quad + \int_0^t dt'\mathcal{G}_x^{(2)}(x-x',t-t')\mathcal{G}_y(|y|+|y'|,t')\,,\end{aligned} \tag{26}$$

which can be combined with Equation (16) to obtain the wave function related to this system.

The absolute value of the wave function, for $\varphi(\mathbf{r}) = e^{-\mathbf{r}^2/2}/\sqrt{\pi}$ for the case worked out in this section, is displayed in Figure 4. Now, observe that the nonlocal dependence on space and time leads the solution to a spread of a Gaussian package, without oscillation in the plane (x,y).

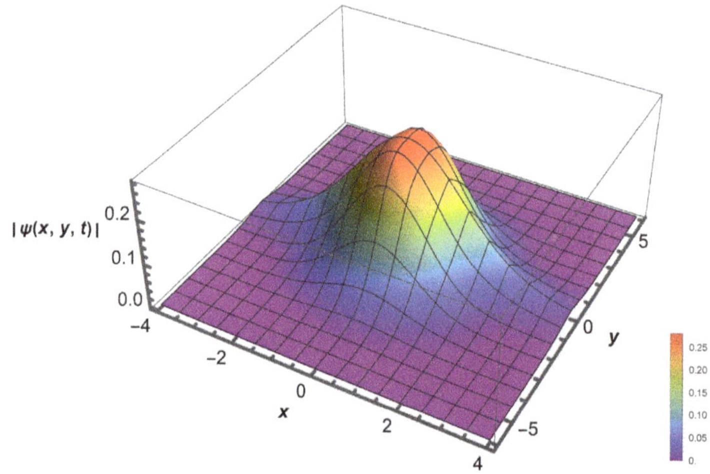

Figure 4. Behavior of the absolute value of the wave function for the initial condition $\varphi(\mathbf{r}) = e^{-\mathbf{r}^2/2}/\sqrt{\pi}$ with $\mathfrak{K}_3(t) = (\mathfrak{K}_3/\tau)\delta(t/\tau)\delta(x)$ and $\mathfrak{K}_2(t) = 0$. Without loss of generality, we consider $\mathfrak{K}_3/\hbar = 1$, $\hbar/m = 1$, $\tau = 1$, and $l_x = l_y = 1$, in arbitrary unities.

The wave function resulting from Equation (26) also leads the relaxation process in a super-diffusive regime for certain potential choices, as observed in Figure 5, where the blue line is for $\mathfrak{K}_2(t) = (\mathfrak{K}_2/\tau)\delta(t/\tau)$ and $\widetilde{\mathfrak{K}}_3(k_x,t) = \mathfrak{K}_3$ with $\varphi(\mathbf{r}) = \delta(x)\delta(y)$; and the black line is for $\mathfrak{K}_2(t) = (\mathfrak{K}_2/\tau)e^{-t/\tau}$ and $\widetilde{\mathfrak{K}}_3(k_x,t) = (\mathfrak{K}_3/\tau)k_x^2 e^{-t/\tau}$ with $\varphi(\mathbf{r}) = e^{-\mathbf{r}^2/2}/\sqrt{\pi}$. In the orange line, we show the $|\psi(0,0,t)|^{-2}$ associated with the standard comb model in two dimensions. In this case, we also verify a super-diffusive regime, which goes with $t^{1.5}$.

However, in our modification, we observe that the relaxation process is faster than in the standard case, going with $\sim t^3$.

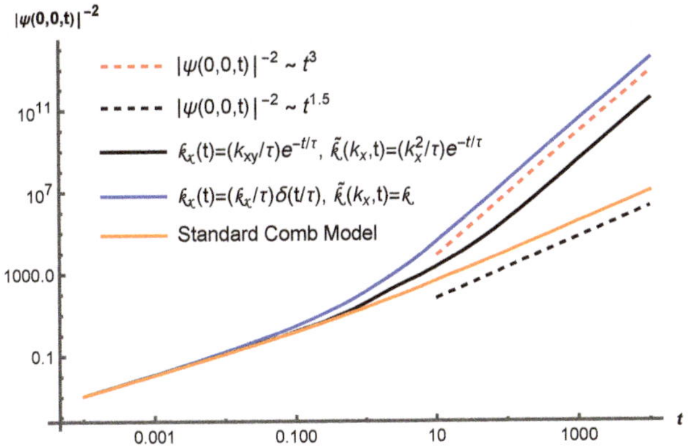

Figure 5. Behavior of the $|\psi(0,0,t)|^{-2}$ for $\mathfrak{K}_x(t) = (\mathfrak{K}_x/\tau)\delta(t/\tau)$ and $\mathfrak{K}(k_x,t) = k$ with $\varphi(\mathbf{r}) = \delta(x)\delta(y)$ in the blue line; $\mathfrak{K}_2(t) = (\mathfrak{K}_2/\tau)e^{-t/\tau}$ and $\widetilde{\mathfrak{K}}_3(k_x,t) = (\mathfrak{K}_3/\tau)k_x^2 e^{-t/\tau}$ with $\varphi(\mathbf{r}) = e^{-\mathbf{r}^2/2}/\sqrt{\pi}$ in the black line; and the standard comb model with orange line. Without loss of generality, we consider, for simplicity, $\mathfrak{K}_2/\hbar = 1$, $\mathfrak{K}_3/\hbar = 1$ $\hbar/m = 1$, and $l_x = l_y = 1$, in arbitrary unities.

2.3. Nonlocal Dependence and Memory Kernels

Following, we consider the mixing between the two previous cases, i.e., the memory kernels related to each case, in Equation (3), yielding

$$i\hbar\frac{\partial}{\partial t}\psi(\mathbf{r},t) = -\frac{\hbar^2}{2m}\left[\delta\left(\frac{y}{l_y}\right)\frac{\partial^2}{\partial x^2}\psi(\mathbf{r},t) + \frac{\partial^2}{\partial y^2}\psi(\mathbf{r},t)\right] + \int_0^t dt' V_{xy}^{(2)}(y;t-t')\psi(\mathbf{r},t') + \int_0^t dt' V_{xy}^{(1)}(x,y;t-t')\psi(\mathbf{r},t') + \int_{-\infty}^{\infty} dx' \int_0^t dt' V_{xy}^{(3)}(x-x',y;t-t')\psi(x',y,t'). \tag{27}$$

The Green function connected with this case can be obtained by solving the following equation

$$i\hbar\frac{\partial}{\partial t}\mathcal{G}(\mathbf{r},\mathbf{r}',t) - i\hbar\delta(x-x')\delta(y-y')\delta(t) = -\frac{\hbar^2}{2m}\left[\delta\left(\frac{y}{l_y}\right)\frac{\partial^2}{\partial x^2}\mathcal{G}(\mathbf{r},\mathbf{r}',t) + \frac{\partial^2}{\partial y^2}\mathcal{G}(\mathbf{r},\mathbf{r}',t)\right] + \int_0^t dt' \int_{-\infty}^{\infty} dx' \left[V_{xy}^{(1)}(x-x',y,t-t') + V_{xy}^{(3)}(x-x',y,t-t')\right]\mathcal{G}(\mathbf{r},\mathbf{r}',t') + \int_0^t dt' V_{xy}^{(2)}(y;t-t')\mathcal{G}(\mathbf{r},\mathbf{r}',t'), \tag{28}$$

which in the Fourier–Laplace space can be written as follows:

$$i\hbar s\widehat{\widetilde{\mathcal{G}}}(k_x,k_y,\mathbf{r}',s) - i\hbar e^{-ik_x x'}e^{-ik_y y'} = \frac{\hbar^2}{2m}\left[l_y k_x^2\widehat{\widetilde{\mathcal{G}}}(k_x,0,\mathbf{r}',s) + k_y^2\widehat{\widetilde{\mathcal{G}}}(k_x,k_y,\mathbf{r}',s)\right] + \widehat{\widetilde{\mathfrak{K}}}_3(k_x,s)l_y\widehat{\widetilde{\mathcal{G}}}(k_x,0,\mathbf{r}',s) + \widehat{\mathfrak{K}}_2(s)l_y\widehat{\widetilde{\mathcal{G}}}(k_x,0,\mathbf{r}',s) + \widehat{\mathfrak{K}}_1(s)l_x l_y\widehat{\mathcal{G}}(0,0,\mathbf{r}',s), \tag{29}$$

From this equation, it is possible to show that

$$\widehat{\widetilde{\mathcal{G}}}(k_x,0,\mathbf{r}',s) = e^{-ik_x x'}\widehat{\widetilde{\mathcal{G}}}_x(k_x,s)\widehat{\mathcal{G}}_y(y',s) - \frac{i}{\hbar}\widehat{\mathfrak{K}}_1(s)l_x l_y\widehat{\mathcal{G}}(0,0,\mathbf{r}',s)\widehat{\mathcal{G}}_y(0,s)\widehat{\widetilde{\mathcal{G}}}_x^{(2)}(k_x,s), \tag{30}$$

and, consequently,

$$\widehat{\mathcal{G}}(0,0,\mathbf{r}',s) = \frac{\widehat{\mathcal{G}}_y(y',s)\widehat{\mathcal{G}}_x^{(2)}(x',s)}{1 + (i/\hbar)\widehat{\mathfrak{K}}_1(s)l_x l_y\widehat{\mathcal{G}}_y(0,s)\widehat{\mathcal{G}}_x^{(2)}(0,s)}. \tag{31}$$

By using these results, it is possible to show that

$$\begin{aligned}\widehat{\widetilde{\mathcal{G}}}(k_x,0,\mathbf{r}',s) &= e^{-ik_x x'}\widehat{\widetilde{\mathcal{G}}}_x^{(2)}(k_x,s)\widehat{\mathcal{G}}_y(y',s)\\ &-\frac{i}{\hbar}\frac{\widehat{\mathfrak{K}}_1(s)l_x l_y\widehat{\mathcal{G}}_y(y',s)\widehat{\mathcal{G}}_x^{(2)}(x',s)}{1+(i/\hbar)\widehat{\mathfrak{K}}_1(s)l_x l_y\widehat{\mathcal{G}}_y(0,s)\widehat{\mathcal{G}}_x^{(2)}(0,s)}\widehat{\mathcal{G}}_y(0,s)\widehat{\widetilde{\mathcal{G}}}_x^{(2)}(k_x,s),\end{aligned} \tag{32}$$

and, therefore,

$$\begin{aligned}\widehat{\mathcal{G}}(x,y,\mathbf{r}',s) &= \delta(x-x')\left[\widehat{\mathcal{G}}_y(y-y',s)-\widehat{\mathcal{G}}_y(|y|+|y'|,s)\right]\\ &+\left[\widehat{\mathcal{G}}_x^{(2)}(x-x',s)-\widehat{\mathfrak{G}}^{(2)}(x,x',s)\right]\widehat{\mathcal{G}}_y(|y|+|y'|,s)\\ &+\frac{\widehat{\mathcal{G}}_y(|y|+|y'|,s)}{1+(i/\hbar)\widehat{\mathfrak{K}}_1(s)l_x l_y\widehat{\mathcal{G}}_y(0,s)\widehat{\mathcal{G}}_x^{(2)}(0,s)}\widehat{\mathfrak{G}}^{(2)}(x,x',s)\,,\end{aligned} \tag{33}$$

with

$$\widehat{\mathfrak{G}}^{(2)}(x,x',s)=\widehat{\mathcal{G}}_x^{(2)}(|x|,s)\widehat{\mathcal{G}}_x^{(2)}(|x'|,s)/\widehat{\mathcal{G}}_x^{(2)}(0,s) \tag{34}$$

Equation (33) can be formally written as Equation (13) when the equation $\widehat{\mathfrak{G}}^{(2)}(x,x',s)=\widehat{\mathcal{G}}_x^{(2)}(|x|+|x'|,s)$ is verified.

2.4. Fractional Spatial Operator and Nonlocal Terms

Another possibility considers a fractional operator applied to the spatial variable. In this case, we consider the following fractional operator [33,34] applied to the x variable:

$$\frac{1}{2}\int_{-\infty}^{\infty}dx\zeta_{\pm,\eta}(x,k_x)\left(D_x^{\mu,\eta}\psi(\mathbf{r},t)\right)\equiv-|k_x|^{\mu+\eta}\widetilde{\psi}_{\pm}(k_x,y,t), \tag{35}$$

with the integral transform given by:

$$\frac{1}{2}\int_{-\infty}^{\infty}dx\zeta_{\pm,\eta}(x,k)\psi(\mathbf{r},t)=\widetilde{\psi}_{\pm}(k_x,y,t)\,, \tag{36}$$

$$\frac{1}{2}\int_{-\infty}^{\infty}dk_x\zeta_{\pm,\eta}(x,k)\widetilde{\psi}_{\pm}(k_x,y,t)=\psi(\mathbf{r},t), \tag{37}$$

where

$$\zeta_{+,\eta}(x,k_x)=(|k_x||x|)^{\frac{1}{2}(1+\eta)}\mathrm{J}_{-\nu}\left(2(|k_x||x|)^{\frac{1}{2}(2+\eta)}/(2+\eta)\right)\quad\text{and} \tag{38}$$

$$\zeta_{-,\eta}(x,k_x)=xk_x(|k_x||x|)^{\frac{1}{2}(1+\eta)-1}\mathrm{J}_{\nu}\left(2(|k_x||x|)^{\frac{1}{2}(2+\eta)}/(2+\eta)\right), \tag{39}$$

where the sub-indexes $+$ and $-$ refer to the odd and even solutions, $\nu=(1+\eta)/(2+\eta)$, and $\mathrm{J}_\nu(x)$ is the Bessel function [7]. We stress that Equations (36) and (37) may be related to a generalized Hankel transform [41–44]. The Green function connected with this case can be obtained by solving the following equation

$$\begin{aligned}i\hbar\frac{\partial}{\partial t}\mathcal{G}(\mathbf{r},\mathbf{r}',t)-i\hbar\delta(x-x')\delta(y-y')\delta(t) &= -\frac{\hbar^2}{2m}\left[\delta\left(\frac{y}{l_y}\right)D_x^{\mu,\eta}\mathcal{G}(\mathbf{r},\mathbf{r}',t)+\frac{\partial^2}{\partial y^2}\mathcal{G}(\mathbf{r},\mathbf{r}',t)\right]\\ &+\int_0^t dt' V_{xy}^{(1)}(x,y;t-t')\mathcal{G}(\mathbf{r},\mathbf{r}',t')+\int_0^t dt' V_{xy}^{(2)}(y;t-t')\mathcal{G}(\mathbf{r},\mathbf{r}',t')\,,\end{aligned} \tag{40}$$

One noticeable point regarding this extension of the Schrödinger equation is that the behavior of the solutions can be characterized by power laws and stretched exponential. Additionally, the Schrödinger equation with an effective-position-dependent mass can directly relate with Equation (35), for example, $\mu=2$ results in the standard differential operators: $D_x^{2,\eta}(\cdots)\equiv\partial_x\left[|x|^{-\eta}\partial_x(\cdots)\right]$. This case allows us to relate the x - direction of Equation (40) with a Schrödinger equation with an effective-position dependent mass, i.e., $m(x)=m|x|^{\eta}$ [45–47], which has been analyzed by taking several situations such as hetero-structures [48] and/or heterogeneous media [49–51], into account. To solve Equation (40), we write the Green's as follows:

$$\mathcal{G}(\mathbf{r},\mathbf{r}',t) = \int_0^\infty dk_x k_x \left[\zeta_+(x,k_x)\widetilde{\mathcal{G}}_+(k_x,y,\mathbf{r}',t) + \zeta_-(x,k_x)\widetilde{\mathcal{G}}_-(k_x,y,\mathbf{r}',t)\right] \tag{41}$$

with

$$\widetilde{\mathcal{G}}_\pm(k_x,y,\mathbf{r}',t) = \frac{1}{2}\int_{-\infty}^\infty dx \zeta_\pm(x,k_x)\mathcal{G}(\mathbf{r},\mathbf{r}',t)\,, \tag{42}$$

where $\widetilde{\mathcal{G}}_\pm(k_x,y,\mathbf{r}',t)$ is determined by the Equation (40). By substituting Equation (41) in Equation (40) and using the orthogonality of the eigenfunction and the Fourier transform for the y variable, it is possible to show that

$$\begin{aligned}&\left(i\hbar\frac{\partial}{\partial t} - \frac{\hbar^2}{2m}|k_y|^2\right)\widetilde{\mathcal{G}}_\pm(k_x,k_y,\mathbf{r}',t) - i\hbar\zeta_\pm(x',k_x)e^{-ik_yy'}\delta(t) = \frac{\hbar^2}{2m}l_y|k_x|^{\mu+\eta}\widetilde{\mathcal{G}}_\pm(k_x,0,\mathbf{r}',t)\\ &\quad + l_y\int_0^t dt' k_2(t-t')\widetilde{\mathcal{G}}_\pm(k_x,0,\mathbf{r}',t') + l_y l_x\int_0^t dt' k_1(t-t')\mathcal{G}_\pm(0,0,\mathbf{r}',t')\,,\end{aligned} \tag{43}$$

By performing some calculations, it is possible to show that

$$\begin{aligned}\widehat{\widetilde{\mathcal{G}}}_\pm(k_x,k_y,\mathbf{r}',s) &= \zeta_\pm(x',k_x)e^{-ik_yy'}\widehat{\widetilde{\mathcal{G}}}_y(k_y,s) - \frac{i}{\hbar}l_y l_x\widehat{k}_1(s)\widehat{\widetilde{\mathcal{G}}}_y(k_y,s)\widehat{\mathcal{G}}_\pm(0,0,\mathbf{r}',t)\\ &\quad - \frac{i}{\hbar}\left[\frac{\hbar^2}{2m}l_y|k_x|^{\mu+\eta} + \widehat{k}_2(s)\right]\widehat{\widetilde{\mathcal{G}}}_y(k_y,s)\widehat{\widetilde{\mathcal{G}}}_\pm(k_x,0,\mathbf{r}',t)\end{aligned} \tag{44}$$

with

$$\begin{aligned}\widehat{\widetilde{\mathcal{G}}}_\pm(k_x,0,\mathbf{r}',s) &= \zeta_\pm(x',k_x)\widehat{\widetilde{\mathcal{G}}}^{(3)}_{\pm,x}(k_x,s)\widehat{\mathcal{G}}_y(y',s)\\ &\quad - \frac{i}{\hbar}\widehat{\mathfrak{K}}_1(s)l_x l_y\widehat{\mathcal{G}}_\pm(0,0,\mathbf{r}',s)\widehat{\mathcal{G}}_y(0,s)\widehat{\widetilde{\mathcal{G}}}^{(3)}_{\pm,x}(k_x,s),\end{aligned} \tag{45}$$

and, as a consequence,

$$\widehat{\widetilde{\mathcal{G}}}^{(3)}_{\pm,x}(k_x,s) = \frac{1}{1 + \left(i\hbar|k|_x^{\mu+\eta}/(2m) + (i/\hbar)\widehat{\mathfrak{K}}_2(s)\right)l_y\widehat{\mathcal{G}}_y(0,s)}\,. \tag{46}$$

By performing additional calculations, we can show that

$$\widehat{\mathcal{G}}_+(0,0,\mathbf{r}',s) = \frac{\widehat{\mathcal{G}}_y(y',s)\widehat{\mathfrak{G}}^{(3)}_{+,x}(0,x',s)}{1 + (i/\hbar)\widehat{\mathfrak{K}}_1(s)l_x l_y\widehat{\mathcal{G}}_y(0,s)[\widehat{\mathfrak{G}}^{(3)}_{+,x}(0,0,s)/\zeta_+(0,1)]}\,, \tag{47}$$

where

$$\widehat{\mathfrak{G}}^{(3)}_{\pm,x}(x,x',s) = \int_0^\infty dk_x\zeta_\pm(x',k_x)\zeta_\pm(x,k_x)\widehat{\widetilde{\mathcal{G}}}^{(3)}_{\pm,x}(k_x,s)\,. \tag{48}$$

For the initial condition $\varphi(x,y) = \delta(x)\delta(y)$, the evolution of the absolute Green function is displayed in Figure 6. For the sake of simplicity, we consider the absence of nonlocal terms to show the changes produced by the spatial operator incorporated in the Schrödinger equation with the backbone structure with branches. We observe that the presence of these operators changes the shape of the Green function when compared with the case of Figure 1 by introducing a different behavior connected with the spatial operator.

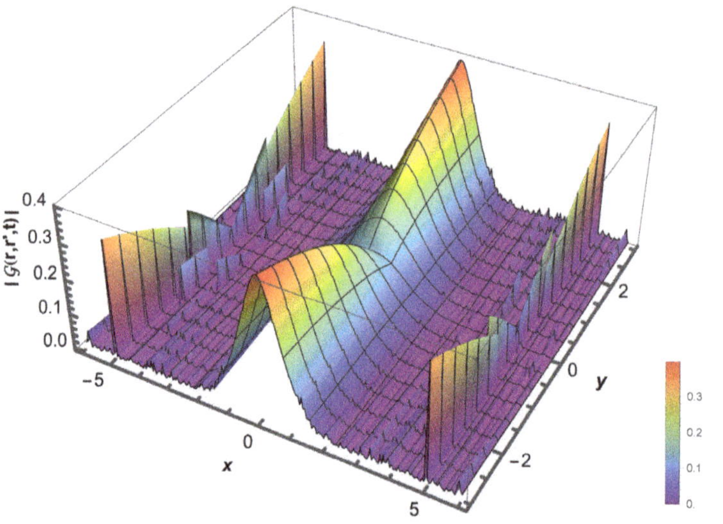

Figure 6. Behavior of the absolute Green function given by Equation (41) in absence of nonlocal terms, for $\mu = 1.8$ and $\eta = 1$. Without loss of generality, we consider $\hbar/m = 1$, $l_x = l_y = 1$, $\mathbf{r}' = 0$, and the initial condition $\varphi(x, y) = \delta(x)\delta(y)$, in arbitrary unities.

3. Discussion and Conclusions

We have analyzed a Schrödinger model with geometric constraints that couple the spatial variables x and y, under arbitrary time-dependent potentials. Our study considered four distinct cases: (i) a model with nonlocal dependence on time, (ii) a model with nonlocal spatial dependence, (iii) a mixed case that incorporates memory effects in both space and time through external potential kernels, and (iv) a formulation involving a fractional spatial derivative linked to a position-dependent effective mass. For each configuration, we constructed solutions using Green's function techniques, allowing us to determine wave functions for arbitrary initial conditions.

For the proposed solutions, we examined their behavior, which shows the evolution and spreading of wave packets under different nonlocal regimes. Our results show distinct scaling laws and dynamics depending on the nature of memory and spatial coupling. In particular, we observed that nonlocal terms and fractional operators can modify relaxation behavior. Furthermore, the cases explored here may be physically realized in engineered quantum systems such as optical lattices, photonic waveguides, and mesoscopic devices. For instance, comb-shaped waveguide arrays fabricated using femtosecond laser writing can emulate the geometry of a quantum comb, where injected light propagates similarly to a quantum particle constrained within the comb structure. As shown by Longhi [9], photonic lattices with comb-shaped configurations can simulate anomalous transport phenomena within such systems. Additionally, temporal modulation of the refractive index can be utilized to replicate time-dependent or memory-like potentials. Comb-like optical lattices can also be engineered by interfering laser beams to trap ultra-cold atoms in a backbone-finger arrangement, as demonstrated by the experimental work of Salger et al. [45,47]. We hope that the theoretical results presented here can provide insights into quantum dynamics in backbone-structured media and stimulate further experimental studies involving branched quantum systems that feature memory and spatial heterogeneity. Finally, in future works, we will explore how different forms of nonlocality, i.e., fractional operators, influence the thermal behavior of the wave function.

Author Contributions: Conceptualization, E.C.G., E.K.L., A.S.M.d.C., J.T. and A.M.B.; formal analysis, E.C.G., E.K.L., A.S.M.d.C., J.T. and A.M.B.; investigation, E.C.G., E.K.L., A.S.M.d.C., J.T. and A.M.B.; writing—original draft preparation, E.C.G., E.K.L., A.S.M.d.C., J.T. and A.M.B.; writing—review and editing, E.C.G., E.K.L., A.S.M.d.C., J.T. and A.M.B. All authors have read and agreed to the published version of the manuscript.

Funding: The authors thank the financial support from the Brazilian Federal Agencies: CNPq (Grants: 301715/2022-0); CAPES; Fundação Araucária; São Paulo Research Foundation (Grants: 2024/05700-5 and 2025/02318-5).

Institutional Review Board Statement: Not applicable.

Informed Consent Statement: Not applicable.

Data Availability Statement: The original contributions presented in this study are included in the article. Further inquiries can be directed to the corresponding author.

Acknowledgments: The authors thank 105 Group Science (www.105groupscience.com).

Conflicts of Interest: The authors declare no conflict of interest.

References

1. Sakurai, J.J.; Napolitano, J. *Modern Quantum Mechanics*; Cambridge University Press: Cambridge, UK, 2017. [CrossRef]
2. Schrödinger, E. Quantisierung als Eigenwertproblem. *Ann. Phys.* **1926**, *384*, 489–527. [CrossRef]
3. Schrödinger, E. Quantisierung als Eigenwertproblem. *Ann. Phys.* **1926**, *384*, 361–376. [CrossRef]
4. Gabrick, E.; Sayari, E.; de Castro, A.; Trobia, J.; Batista, A.; Lenzi, E. Fractional Schrödinger equation and time dependent potentials. *Commun. Nonlinear Sci. Numer. Simul.* **2023**, *123*, 107275. [CrossRef]
5. Cohen-Tannoudji, C.; Diu, B.; Laloe, F. *Quantum Mechanics*; Wiley-Interscience: Hoboken, NJ, USA, 2006.
6. Lenzi, E.K.; Gabrick, E.C.; Sayari, E.; de Castro, A.S.M.; Trobia, J.; Batista, A.M. Anomalous Relaxation and Three-Level System: A Fractional Schrödinger Equation Approach. *Quantum Rep.* **2023**, *2023*, 442–458. [CrossRef]
7. Evangelista, L.R.; Lenzi, E.K. *Fractional Diffusion Equations and Anomalous Diffusion*; Cambridge University Press: Cambridge, UK, 2018. [CrossRef]
8. Lenzi, E.K.; Evangelista, L.R.; Ribeiro, H.V.; Magin, R.L. Schrödinger Equation with Geometric Constraints and Position-Dependent Mass: Linked Fractional Calculus Models. *Quantum Rep.* **2022**, *4*, 296–308. [CrossRef]
9. Longhi, S. Fractional Schrödinger equation in optics. *Opt. Lett.* **2015**, *40*, 1117–1120. [CrossRef]
10. Afek, G.; Davidson, N.; Kessler, D.A.; Barkai, E. Colloquium: Anomalous statistics of laser-cooled atoms in dissipative optical lattices. *Rev. Mod. Phys.* **2023**, *95*, 031003. [CrossRef]
11. Laskin, N. *Fractional Quantum Mechanics*; World Scientific Publishing Company: Singapore, 2018.
12. Naber, M. Time fractional Schrödinger equation. *J. Math. Phys.* **2004**, *45*, 3339–3352. [CrossRef]
13. Cius, D.; Menon, L., Jr.; dos Santos, M.A.F.; de Castro, A.S.M.; Andrade, F.M. Unitary evolution for a two-level quantum system in fractional-time scenario. *Phys. Rev. E* **2022**, *106*, 054126. [CrossRef]
14. Cius, D. Unitary description of the Jaynes-Cummings model under fractional-time dynamics. *Phys. Rev. E* **2025**, *111*, 024110. [CrossRef]
15. Plastino, A.R.; Tsallis, C. Nonlinear Schroedinger equation in the presence of uniform acceleration. *J. Math. Phsy.* **2013**, *54*, 041505. [CrossRef]
16. Schwämmle, V.; Nobre, F.D.; Tsallis, C. q-Gaussians in the porous-medium equation: Stability and time evolution. *Eur. Phys. J. B* **2008**, *66*, 537–546. [CrossRef]
17. Serkin, V.N.; Hasegawa, A. Novel Soliton Solutions of the Nonlinear Schrödinger Equation Model. *Phys. Rev. Lett.* **2000**, *85*, 4502. [CrossRef] [PubMed]
18. Rafiq, M.H.; Raza, N.; Jhangeer, A. Nonlinear dynamics of the generalized unstable nonlinear Schrödinger equation: A graphical perspective. *Opt. Quantum Electron.* **2023**, *55*, 628. [CrossRef]
19. Ibrahim, S.; Baleanu, D. Classes of solitary solution for nonlinear Schrödinger equation arising in optical fibers and their stability analysis. *Opt. Quantum Electron.* **2023**, *55*, 1158. [CrossRef]
20. Olavo, L.; Bakuzis, A.; Amilcar, R. Generalized Schrödinger equation using Tsallis entropy. *Phys. A* **1999**, *271*, 303–323. [CrossRef]
21. Iomin, A. Subdiffusion on a fractal comb. *Phys. Rev. E* **2011**, *83*, 052106. [CrossRef]
22. Baskin, E.; Iomin, A. Superdiffusion on a Comb Structure. *Phys. Rev. Lett.* **2004**, *93*, 120603. [CrossRef]
23. Iomin, A.; Méndez, V.; Horsthemke, W. *Fractional Dynamics in Comb-like Structures*; World Scientific: Singapore, 2018. [CrossRef]
24. Hefny, M.M.; Tawfik, A.M. Tempered fractional diffusion in comb-like structures with numerical investigation. *Phys. Scr.* **2023**, *98*, 125258. [CrossRef]
25. Tateishi, A.A.; Ribeiro, H.V.; Sandev, T.; Petreska, I.; Lenzi, E.K. Quenched and annealed disorder mechanisms in comb models with fractional operators. *Phys. Rev. E* **2020**, *101*, 022135. [CrossRef]
26. Sandev, T.; Iomin, A.; Kantz, H. Fractional diffusion on a fractal grid comb. *Phys. Rev. E* **2015**, *91*, 032108. [CrossRef] [PubMed]

27. Masó-Puigdellosas, A.; Sandev, T.; Méndez, V. Random walks on comb-like structures under stochastic resetting. *Entropy* **2023**, *25*, 1529. [CrossRef] [PubMed]
28. Trajanovski, P.; Jolakoski, P.; Kocarev, L.; Sandev, T. Ornstein–uhlenbeck process on three-dimensional comb under stochastic resetting. *Mathematics* **2023**, *11*, 3576. [CrossRef]
29. Méndez, V.; Iomin, A. Comb-like models for transport along spiny dendrites. *Chaos, Solitons Fractals* **2013**, *53*, 46–51. [CrossRef]
30. Iomin, A. Fractional-time Schrödinger equation: Fractional dynamics on a comb. *Chaos Solitons Fractals* **2011**, *44*, 348–352. [CrossRef]
31. Witthaut, D.; Rapedius, K.; Korsch, J. The Nonlinear Schrödinger Equation for the Delta-Comb Potential: Quasi-Classical Chaos and Bifurcations of Periodic Stationary Solutions. *J. Nonlinear Math. Phys.* **2009**, *16*, 207–233. [CrossRef]
32. Zhang, S.; Liu, L.; Ge, Z.; Liu, Y.; Feng, L.; Wang, J. Numerical simulation of the two-dimensional fractional Schrödinger equation for describing the quantum dynamics on a comb with the absorbing boundary conditions. *Commun. Nonlinear Sci. Numer. Simul.* **2025**, *140*, 108407. [CrossRef]
33. Lenzi, E.; Evangelista, L. Space–time fractional diffusion equations in d-dimensions. *J. Math. Phys.* **2021**, *62*, 083304. [CrossRef]
34. Lenzi, E.K.; Evangelista, L.R.; Zola, R.S.; Scarfone, A.M. Fractional Schrödinger equation for heterogeneous media and Lévy like distributions. *Chaos Solitons Fractals* **2022**, *163*, 112564. [CrossRef]
35. Sandev, T.; Petreska, I.; Lenzi, E.K. Time-dependent Schrödinger-like equation with nonlocal term. *J. Math. Phys.* **2014**, *55*. [CrossRef]
36. Petreska, I.; Trajanovski, P.; Sandev, T.; Rocha, J.A.A.; de Castro, A.S.M.; Lenzi, E.K. Solutions to the Schrödinger Equation: Nonlocal Terms and Geometric Constraints. *Mathematics* **2025**, *13*, 137. [CrossRef]
37. Coz, M.; Arnold, L.G.; MacKellar, A.D. Nonlocal potentials and their local equivalents. *Ann. Phys.* **1970**, *59*, 219–247. [CrossRef]
38. Li, C.; Wan, L.; Wei, Y.; Wang, J. Definition of current density in the presence of a non-local potential. *Nanotechnology* **2008**, *19*, 155401. [CrossRef]
39. Chechkin, A.V.; Metzler, R.; Klafter, J.; Gonchar, V.Y. Introduction to the theory of Lévy flights. In *Anomalous Transport: Foundations and Applications*; John Wiley & Sons, Ltd.: Weinheim, Germany, 2008; pp. 129–162. [CrossRef]
40. Allegrini, P.; Grigolini, P.; West, B.J. Dynamical approach to Lévy processes. *Phys. Rev. E* **1996**, *54*, 4760–4767. [CrossRef]
41. Ali, I.; Kalla, S. A generalized Hankel transform and its use for solving certain partial differential equations. *ANZIAM J.* **1999**, *41*, 105–117. [CrossRef]
42. Garg, M.; Rao, A.; Kalla, S.L. On a generalized finite Hankel transform. *Appl. Math. Comput.* **2007**, *190*, 705–711. [CrossRef]
43. Nakhi, Y.B.; Kalla, S.L. Some boundary value problems of temperature fields in oil strata. *Appl. Math. Comput.* **2003**, *146*, 105–119. [CrossRef]
44. Xie, K.; Wang, Y.; Wang, K.; Cai, X. Application of Hankel transforms to boundary value problems of water flow due to a circular source. *Appl. Math. Comput.* **2010**, *216*, 1469–1477. [CrossRef]
45. Einevoll, G.; Hemmer, P.; Thomsen, J. Operator ordering in effective-mass theory for heterostructures. I. Comparison with exact results for superlattices, quantum wells, and localized potentials. *Phys. Rev. B* **1990**, *42*, 3485. [CrossRef]
46. Einevoll, G. Operator ordering in effective-mass theory for heterostructures. II. Strained systems. *Phys. Rev. B* **1990**, *42*, 3497. [CrossRef]
47. El-Nabulsi, R.A. A generalized self-consistent approach to study position-dependent mass in semiconductors organic heterostructures and crystalline impure materials. *Phys. E Low-Dimens. Syst. Nanostruct.* **2020**, *124*, 114295. [CrossRef]
48. Cao, L.q.; Luo, J.l.; Wang, C.y. Multiscale analysis and numerical algorithm for the Schrödinger equations in heterogeneous media. *Appl. Math. Comput.* **2010**, *217*, 3955–3973. [CrossRef]
49. Arvedson, E.; Wilkinson, M.; Mehlig, B.; Nakamura, K. Staggered ladder spectra. *Phys. Rev. Lett.* **2006**, *96*, 030601. [CrossRef] [PubMed]
50. Mota-Furtado, F.; O'Mahony, P.F. Exact propagator for generalized Ornstein-Uhlenbeck processes. *Phys. Rev. E* **2007**, *75*, 041102. [CrossRef]
51. Mota-Furtado, F.; O'Mahony, P. Eigenfunctions and matrix elements for a class of eigenvalue problems with staggered ladder spectra. *Phys. Rev. A* **2006**, *74*, 044102. [CrossRef]

MDPI AG
Grosspeteranlage 5
4052 Basel
Switzerland
Tel.: +41 61 683 77 34

Fractal and Fractional Editorial Office
E-mail: fractalfract@mdpi.com
www.mdpi.com/journal/fractalfract

www.ingramcontent.com/pod-product-compliance
Lightning Source LLC
Chambersburg PA
CBHW040815250926
51850CB00007BA/1174